THE FRIENDSHIP OF THE LORD

To
Del, Rachael and Paul
who share my humanity and our life journey
in a special way

The front cover is illustrated with the impression on clay of a seal
that belonged to 'Berekyahu, son of Neriyahu, the scribe'
(לברכיהו בן נריהו הספר). We can be virtually certain
that this seal belonged to none other than Jeremiah's friend, Baruch,
the scribe, who wrote out the prophet's oracles (Jer 36:4, compare
Jer 32:12ff and 43:1ff). This surviving object belonging to 'Blessed of
Yahweh' (Berekyahu, Baruch) links us visually with a spirituality lived
in a particular time, place and culture remote from ours, yet a
spirituality that speaks to us and whose God offers us his covenant
commitment.

THE FRIENDSHIP OF THE LORD

Deryck Sheriffs

paternoster press

Published by Paternoster Press,
P.O. Box 300, Carlisle, Cumbria
CA3 0QS U.K.

02 01 00 99 98 97 96   7 6 5 4 3 2 1

British Library Cataloguing in Publication Data

Sheriffs, Deryck
    The friendship of the Lord
    1. Bible. O.T.   2. God—Attributes 3. Spiritual life
    I. Title
    221.6

ISBN 0-85364-646-5

Typeset by Photoprint, Torquay, Devon
and printed in Great Britain by
Clays Ltd, St Ives plc

Contents

Abbreviations

JOURNAL TITLE ABBREVIATIONS

AfO	Archiv für Orientforschung
BA	Biblical Archaeology
BSOAS	Bulletin of the School of Oriental Studies
BThB	Biblical Theology Bulletin
CBQ	Catholic Biblical Quarterly
EQ	Evangelical Quarterly
HUCA	Hebrew Union College Annual
IEJ	Israel Exploration Journal
JAOS	Journal of the American Oriental Society
JBL	Journal of Biblical Literature
JCS	Journal of Cuneiform Studies
JNES	Journal of Near Eastern Studies
JSOT	Journal for the Study of the Old Testament
JTS	Journal of Theological Studies
JTSA	Journal of Theology for Southern Africa
OTS	Oudtestamentische Studien
RA	Revue d'Assyriologie et d'archéologie orientale
TB	Tyndale Bulletin
UF	Ugarit-Forschungen
VT	Vetus Testamentum
WThJ	Westminster Theological Journal
ZAW	Zeitschrift fur die alttestamentliche Wissenschaft

SERIES AND REFERENCE WORK ABBREVIATIONS

AB	Anchor Bible
AHw	W von Soden, *Akkadisches Handwörterbuch* (Wiesbaden) 1959–1981.
AfO Bei	*Archiv für Orientforschung Beiheft*
AO/AT	*Alte Orient und Altes Testament*
BDB	Brown, Driver & Briggs, *Hebrew and English Lexicon*, Oxford, 1972.

BZAW	Biblische Zeitschrift für altestamentliche Wissenschaft
CAD	*The Assyrian Dictionary of the Oriental Institute of the University of Chicago* (Chicago-Glükstadt) 1956–.
CAH	*Cambridge Ancient History*, CUP, 1975–1991.
CHALOT	WL Holladay, *A Concise Hebrew and Aramaic Lexcon of the Old Testament*, EJ Brill, 1971.
HSM	Harvard Semitic Monograph series
HSS	Harvard Semitic Studies
ICC	International Critical Commentaries
IDB	*Interpreter's Dictionary of the Bible, Vols 1–5*, GA Buttrick (ed), Abingdon, 1962–1975.
IllBD	*The Illustrated Bible Dictionary*, N Hillyer (ed), IVP, 1980.
JSOTS	Journal for the Study of the Old Testament, Supplement series
LAPO	Littératures anciennes du Proche-Orient
NCB	New Century Bible
NICOT	New International Commentary on the Old Testament
OBT	Overtures to Biblical Theology
OTL	Old Testament Library
OTS	Oudtestamentische Studiën
RAI	Rencontre assyriologique internationale
SAA	State Archives of Assyria, Neo-Assyrian Text Corpus Project
SBLDS	Society of Biblical Literature Dissertation Series
SBT	Studies in Biblical Theology
SVT	Supplement series to *Vetus Testamentum*
TDOT	*Theological Dictionary of the Old Testament*, Botterweck & Ringgren (eds) Eerdmans, 1977–.
TOTC	Tyndale Old Testament Commentaries
WBC	Word Biblical Commentaries
WCC	World Council of Churches
YNER	Yale Near Eastern Researches

PRESS ABBREVIATIONS

CUP	Cambridge University Press
HUP	Harvard University Press
IVP	Intervarsity Press
OUP	Oxford University Press
PIB	Pontificium Institutum Biblicum
SCM	Student Christian Movement
SPCK	Society for the Propagation of Christian Knowledge
UNISA	University of South Africa, Pretoria

YUP   Yale University Press

BIBLE VERSION ABBREVIATIONS

AV   Authorized Version, 1611.
BHS   Biblia Hebraica Stuttgartensia, 1984.
NEB   New English Bible, 1961/1972.
NIV   New International Version, 1978.
NRSV   New Revised Standard Version, 1989.
REB   Revised English Bible, 1989.

BOOK TITLE ABBREVIATIONS

AEL   M Lichtheim, *Ancient Egyptian Literature: Vol 2, the New Kingdom* (Berkeley: Univ of California) 1976.
ANEP   JB Pritchard (ed), *The Ancient Near East in Pictures* (Princeton: Princeton University Press) 1950.
ANET   JB Pritchard (ed), *Ancient Near Eastern Texts relating to the Old Testament* (Princeton: Princeton University Press) 1950; 3rd ed. 1969.
BWL   WG Lambert, *Babylonian Wisdom Literature* (Oxford: Clarendon) 1960.
Conflict   CC Broyles, *The Conflict of Faith and Experience in the Psalms: a form-critical and theological study*, JSOTS 52, (Sheffield: JSOT Press) 1989.
DeutSchool M Weinfeld, *Deuteronomy and the Deuteronomic School* (Oxford: Clarendon) 1972.
Diversity J Goldingay, *Theological Diversity and the Authority of the Old Testament* (Grand Rapids: Eerdmans), 1987.
Hymnes   M-J Seux, *Hymnes et Prières aux dieux de Babylone et d'Assyrie*, LAPO 8 (Paris: du Cerf) 1976.
LAE   WK Simpson, *The Literature of Ancient Egypt* (London: YUP) 1973.
Muses   BR Foster, *Before the Muses: an anthology of Akkadian Literature, Vol. I & II*, (Bethesda: CDL Press) 1993.
OTOT   RWL Moberly, *The Old Testament of the Old Testament: patriarchal narratives and Mosaic Yahwism*, OBT (Minneapolis: Fortress) 1992
SaS   K van der Toorn, *Sin and Sanction in Israel and Mesopotamia: a comparative study*, Studia Semitica Neerlandica 22 (Maastricht: Van Gorcum) 1985.
The Sage   JG Gammie & LG Perdue (eds.), *The Sage in Israel and the Ancient Near East* (Winona Lake: Eisenbrauns) 1990.
Treasures Th. Jacobsen, *The Treasures of Darkness* (London: YUP) 1976.

ABBREVIATIONS AND TEXT CORPUS REFERENCES
IN ASSYRIOLOGY, UGARITIC STUDIES

DN, DNN Divine name, names
GN, GNN Geographical name, names
PN, PNN Personal name, names
RN, RNN Royal name, names

BBR   *Beiträge zur Kenntnis der babylonischen Religion I & II*,
           H Zimmern (Leipzig) 1896, 1901.
BM   British Museum number
CH   Code of Hammurabi
CTA   *Corpus des tablettes en cunéformes alphabétiques découvertes
           à Ras Shamra-Ugarit de 1929 à 1939*, A Herdner (ed),
           Paris, 1963.
EA   El Amarna texts
KTU   *Keilalphabetischen Texte aus Ugarit, Die*, M Dietrich, O
           Loretz, J Sammartin (eds), AOAT 24 (Kevelaer,
           Neukirchen–Vluyn) 1976.
KUB   *Keilschrifturkunden aus Boghazköy* (Berlin)
RS   Ras Shamra text (Ugarit)
PRU   *Palais Royal d'Ugarit, Le*, J Nougayrol *et al*, (Paris)
           1955.
UT   *Ugaritic Textbook*, CH Gordon, Analecta Orientalia 38
           (Rome) 1965.
VTE   Vassal Treaties of Esarhaddon

Author's Preface

I grew up on the Old Testament, and can still picture the illustrations of its bloodthirsty battles and magnificent royal courts in the line drawings and bright colours of my childhood books. The Christian communities that I belonged to did not read the Old Testament for entertainment, or ancient history, or to sharpen their literary critical perceptions, but to deepen their relationship with God. As I passed through undergraduate and post-graduate programmes in Old Testament study, I had to find a way of retaining an authentic devotional reading of the Old Testament alongside my academic study of its language, its surrounding cultures and literatures, and mastering the varying shape of technical Old Testament studies expressed in learned journals, prescribed books and university departments.

I believe that the Old Testament's roots in life guarantee that this goal of holding academic studies and life concerns together can be achieved if there is a will for it, though many of the standard Old Testament theology books grapple so strenuously with the sheer bulk of the Old Testament and with elucidating its many strands that they appear to have little space or energy left to discuss wherein lies its normativeness or its applicability to our very different world, communities and life styles.

It has been a benefit to teach Old Testament theology to groups of highly motivated students from many national backgrounds who want a recognized tertiary qualification but who also want to know if what they are being taught has relevance to the world and varied jobs that they will be going into afterwards. These jobs could range from teaching Religion in schools to pupils without any interest in it, to pastoring churches of various denominations, to working with the socially disadvantaged and marginalized, or working cross-culturally in many countries in a variety of roles, as missionaries, translators or teachers in seminaries. This book is for them and for those who share their questions about the Old Testament and about life.

My teaching role has forced me to think about the recontextualization of the message of the Old Testament over against the reality of its original culture-specific and culture-bound packaging. I do not believe that we can appreciate covenant with Yahweh until we understand the struggle for its existence that Yahwistic faith had amidst attractive alternative cult rituals, worship and world views. So I subject my students to a crash course in Ancient Near Eastern texts. Sometimes the initial effect of this is disconcerting—it seems to rob the Old Testament of its distinctiveness or inspiration. The end result is that they appreciate all the more that theology, including Israel's, is engaged, embedded and embodied, and is not a display of universal, timeless and hygienically bottled truths.

The goal of recontextualizing a normative message from the Old Testament involves hermeneutics, that is, our theory of interpretation which takes account of assumptions and reading strategies. The era is passing when writers pretend that they offer only objective exegesis. Feminism, for one thing, has called that bluff. I have written from a faith commitment. My assumptions, preferences and reading strategies will emerge to view in the ensuing chapters.

I am conscious that in writing a book on spirituality I cannot be all things to all men, and women. Being middle-class, educationally advantaged, white and male is part of my identity, and so are my life experiences. A book on 'biblical spirituality' needs to reckon with the components of our human identity that are rooted in our social background, and readers need to reckon with the biases of perspective of those who write on spirituality. I grew up and did most of my studying and initial teaching in South Africa where I underwent an embarrassingly slow process of conscientization, along with a deepening appreciation for the Old Testament, and a resentment that the Bible could be hijacked by supporters of apartheid. My history and biases are reflected on some pages. I hope consciously so most of the time.

This book was written in a comfortable north-west London suburb, during a time of recession and unemployment in Europe, the falling to pieces of the USSR and Yugoslavia, and the period of Nelson Mandela's release to his inauguration as State President of South Africa. Bombings and shootings occurred in Northern Ireland and London. The sexual abuse of children, including that by clergy, featured prominently in the media. Although I was living in a basically stable part of the world, I could not be immune to the horrors of life that filled our television screens as they reported on mass suffering in civil wars and famines, or personal tragedies afflicting families and children. Nor was our family immune from life's struggle, for my wife has been under treatment by a psychiatrist for major depression, and in addition was operated on for suspected breast-cancer during the two years and more when these chapters were written. In such times, personal or national, faith is severely tested and talk of spirituality seems a luxury when surviving from one end of the day to the other absorbs all available energy.

I have written, then, in acute awareness of our human predicament, its pain and ambiguities, life's paradoxes, and the emotions that flow through us, knowing that for someone to read this book and to be able to take it in, life needs to be 'normal', and money, time and energy need to be available for study.

The chapters were written to make sense as self-contained units, but there are connecting threads between them. The overall sample of topics draws on major blocks of the Old Testament and is roughly representative of what the Old Testament has to offer without attempting to be complete. The title 'The Friendship of the LORD' is lifted from Psa 25 where the motif of 'the fear of the LORD' is introduced. This motif runs through Torah and Wisdom blocks, and appears as a connecting thread in the first six chapters. The understanding of life as a journey walked with God is another connecting thread running through several chapters. The emotions of wonder and delight surface in the chapter on poetry and meditation, to be followed up by the darker emotions of anger, despair and guilt in subsequent chapters. Two chapters in between ponder the relation between down-to-earth secular wisdom and spirituality. Living in time links Qohelet to the last two chapters on the daily rhythm of life and the flow of time and seasons.

I have tried not to use too much academic jargon in the main text. The chapters have an introduction indicating where they are going and a summarizing conclusion, plus sub-headings, to help readers keep their bearings. I would suggest an initial reading through without much attention to the footnotes. The footnotes do several things besides removing distracting technical detail from the flow of the discussion. I am first and foremost writing in interaction with the text of the Old Testament and giving my own re-readings of it, but in doing so I must also substantiate my exegesis or literary perspectives by acknowledging or reacting to other contributions. For those with access to good libraries, the footnotes offer pointers for further reading. They cite places where topics are treated more fully within Old Testament or Near Eastern disciplines. They also refer to books and articles that are not usually on Old Testament reading lists but are relevant to our human situation because they deal with science, or evolutionary biology, or psychotherapy, or physiology, or ageing, or politics, or poetry, and so on. The Old Testament must interact with other shapers of our culture, thinking and experience.

Though I have drawn lines from the Old Testament to the New and to our contemporary world, these comments remain arrows and indicators rather than supplying a detailed application. The real life application of these chapters has to be worked out by each reader for herself or himself in the context of a local community, and in an on-going conversation with God.

Autumn, 1994.

[1]

The Friendship of the Lord

FEELING AT HOME IN THE OLD TESTAMENT

In this chapter we want to do two things—to start tapping into the
spirituality of the Old Testament and in the process become aware
of the nature of the material we are working with, the methods
that we shall need to use, and the assumptions and conditioning
that we bring with us to the task. Where better to start than with a
psalm? Indeed, it is Psalm 25 that supplies the title for this book on
Old Testament spirituality—'the friendship of the LORD'.

At one level, our approach will differ little from a devotional
reading of the Bible. At another level, we need literary sensitivity,
a wide theological background, together with an articulated and
conscious approach to interpretation that helps us to make sense of
what we are reading and also allows other readers to see how to
enter the world of the text, gather its treasure and return to our
contemporary life-context to cash it in. Our hermeneutic needs to
become a conscious technique without burying our quest under a
mound of technicalities. Academics who are professionals in Old
Testament tend to work analytically with the text as an object.
The fruits of their professional analysis are published in the learned
journals and read by fellow academics. No sketch of the professional's social, religious and political allegiances is appended to
the journal abstract. Implicit in this academic convention is an
assumption of objectivity—as though denomination, gender,
race, income and life experience are bracketed out of hermeneutics. Thus the technical tools and the ethos of tertiary education
constitute the hazard of professionalism as well as its resources.

The dichotomy between professional analyst and devout consumer is not confined to theology—one has only to think of the
field of medicine where the patient and the professional practitioner have altogether different experiences and often speak
different languages. 'Myocardial infarction' would not mean
heart-attack to most of its victims. Conversely, many devout

readers of the Bible lack access to the store of information garnered by the Old Testament specialist, information that can illuminate the context from which the narrative, commandment or psalm originates. This lack of access to the information pool is a hazard for amateur enthusiasts. The dichotomy between devotional, subjective reading and analytic objectivist reading of the biblical text is an unhappy one. There are those who travel back into the world of the text's origin and seem to get locked into a time capsule there, never to return. Then there are those who never fully realize or acknowledge that time travel is involved in reading the Bible.

In fact, reflection on this dichotomy between expert and consumer has generated another wave of analysis intent on liberating the Bible from academic captivity.[1] Theological training in seminaries should be a bridge–building operation which equips people to appreciate the text in greater depth while retaining their humanity and open–heartedness. Often that goal remains an ideal rather than a reality.

An analogy may prove helpful here. To walk into the Old Testament and feel at home is rather like a young couple looking for an apartment to rent. If there was a choice, they would like somewhere that could become home rather than feeling like a couple of rooms. Some blocks of flats would be depressing to live in. If our young couple looked round an apartment, they would intuitively feel whether this had the potential to become home. It would take a little imagination. They would need to picture themselves in it with their things spread around. Their pictures on the wall, their breakfast cereal in the kitchen, their bedspread on the bed. This would be all the more important if it were a furnished flat because the colour of the curtains, the pattern on the carpet, the light fixtures, the colour of the walls and the kind of furniture might not be what they would have chosen. Functional, yes, but an expression of their lifestyle, taste or what they were familiar with, maybe not.

So too with the Psalms of Israel. They have been well lived in and they will serve us well in turn, but they may not be exactly to our taste, how we would express ourselves, or what we instantly

---

[1] To cite two examples only from this debate—Walter Wink's *The Bible in Human Transformation* (Philadelphia: Fortress) 1973 expresses disenchantment with the traditional professional programme of academia, and Gerald West, *Biblical Hermeneutics of Liberation*, Cluster monograph series 1 (Pietermaritzburg: Cluster Publications) 1991 continues to struggle with the dilemma of interpretations by the trained reader and the ordinary reader in South Africa where the Bible has played such a prominent role both in oppression and in hope for liberation. West 'calls biblical studies to repentance and conversion' (p. 173).

find familiar. The psalms are designed. They have a décor. A literary analytical approach to the psalms is rather like a walk around an apartment with the architect's drawings and the interior designer's pattern books at hand. More functionally, it is like knowing about the electrical wiring or the plumbing which sooner or later a householder is forced to confront. Analysis of a psalm is simply paying attention to detail. This is a form of homage, a recognition of the author, if one will. But there is something else than noting the detail, something which is more akin to changing the décor, fitting a shower or adding a power point. This something more is the re-reading of the psalm to adapt it within our context. How much latitude is there for re-reading a psalm?

READING AND RE-READING

There is obviously some tension between the original state of an apartment when a couple signs the lease and the degree to which they may alter it. A similar tension exists between reading and re-reading a psalm. When does the re-reading cease to be an enhancement of the original and become a distortion of it? Objectivist readers might adopt a landlord perspective, wanting the apartment to stay as originally designed, and, like landlords, be wary of new tenants and respond very sluggishly to requests for adaptations. Devotional readers might take a tenant perspective and re-decorate on impulse, without reference to fine print in the lease. When it comes to hammering nails into the wall for fixtures, there may be conflicting perspectives!

One thing is certain. The psalms are there to be used, to be lived in. That is why they were collected. The re-reading of the psalm was part of the process leading to its canonization. Some of the headings of the psalms are those nails hammered into the wall for hanging the music or the calendar. Re-reading is not new. Re-reading the Hebrew psalms was an ancient response to them.[2] The Psalms have been repeatedly renovated. In fact, each translation of the Psalms is a renovation, and that includes renditions in Greek,

---

[2] Before Psa 2 with its affirmation 'You are my son, today I have begotten you' was appropriated christologically by the New Testament to explain the sonship and authority of Jesus and his Kingdom (e.g. acts 13:33 and Heb 1:5), it was likely used at coronations of successive Judean kings in Jerusalem, and preserved and canonised, probably motivated by an eschatological hope, after the Davidic dynasty's rule petered out with the Exile to Babylon in 587 BC. The Qumran community drew on Psa 2 to explain their role in the last days in relation to enemies and the Kingdom of God—for the technicalities, see GJ Brooke, *Exegesis at Qumran: 4QFlorilegium in its Jewish context*, JSOTS 29 (Sheffield: JSOT Press) 1985.

Aramaic, Syriac, Latin and, in the last centuries, the numerous English versions.

Yet a Christian re-reading of the psalms has moved on beyond the canonization of the Old Testament and spirituality is not a method of literary analysis but of appropriation. There is more to hermeneutics than acknowledging that as Christians we are moving into an Israelite apartment when we read the Old Testament, but that explicit acknowledgement is important and a starting point.

PSALM 25 AND THE HERMENEUTICS OF APPROPRIATION

Psa 25 opens a door into our study of Old Testament spirituality. In a brief compass it depicts an intimate relationship with the God of Israel and it has phrases, metaphors and concepts which key into Old Testament theology. For the very reason that this psalm, more than many, lends itself to reading in personal devotions, we should start by recognizing its otherness to our culture and Christian framework, recognize that we are re-readers of a literature that belonged to another epoch, another culture, another community, before we find in it a map for our own spiritual journey. The advantages of discerning the gap between the then and the now, between an Israelite and a reader embedded in an English language tradition of the post-imperial era is twofold. The psalm may confront the spirituality of my tradition with perspectives that my tradition or denominational sub-culture has ignored, and I may realize that appropriation of Israel's faith involves more than merely repeating her poets' words in a translation. Acknowledging the gap is the first step forward on the hermeneutical and theological path.

A close reading of the psalm must recognize that we are re-readers in a tradition of re-reading which includes both the unschooled and the schooled. The author-reader gap is accentuated by scholarship because scholarship distracts attention from the I-Thou relationship of the psalm and focuses instead on details of the text. Scholarship may clarify, but often the price for this is a loss of innocence because scholarship adds ambiguity.

For instance, in Psalm 25, we get no further than the rubric $l^e Daw\bar{\imath}d$ = 'to David'. This does not tell us as much as we might want it to. If we first read the psalm as a personal prayer of David either before or after he became king, then this imagined setting may be taken away by scholars questioning the nuance of the Hebrew preposition l^e = 'to', and by their conflicting theories of dating and psalm classification. Does David's name appear as author, literary mentor, originator of a collection of poems later supplemented and adopted for Temple worship, or as one who models an impassioned spirituality?[3] Is the psalm a private literary composition later borrowed for cultic use by individuals or even by the congregation? Does it belong to a covenant renewal festival, or emanate from a royal circle, or from a circle of Wisdom teachers in Jerusalem or in the pious post-exilic community under foreign domination?[4]

Academia often raises questions without arriving at consensus. We cannot unsay the academic questions, but readers may have their own legitimate agendas, their own questions to put to the text. They may not want to wait for academic answers that emerge slowly over decades and in retrospect may seem to be more products of their era and methodology than vital to the relational dimension of God-text-reader. Despite such reservations about the relevance of academic analysis of texts, it would be petulant to dismiss them. Part of ordinary human relationships involves paying close attention to the other person. That is a form of respect, paying regard to another as a person. Paying close regard to the Hebrew text may disclose differences without creating distance. Psa 25 has an acrostic structure. This objective literary observation, that the psalm is written as an alphabetic acrostic, is a simple fact that is not apparent in all printed translations.[5] The acrostic structure forcibly reminds us that even

---

[3] LC Allen 'David as exemplar of Spirituality: The Redactional Function of Psalm 19' *Biblica* 67 (1986) 544–46 finds support in Chronicles for presentation of the David-Solomon era as an exemplary one. He views the juxtapositioning of Psa 19 to Psa 18 as a redactor's effort 'to develop those hints of David as a role model already evident in the royal psalm [Psa 18].' This 'brings him down to the level of the individual believer committed to serving the same God.' The hypothesis that redactors present David as a role model of spirituality is discussed in a technical monograph by GH Wilson, *The Editing of the Hebrew Psalter*, SBL Dissertation Series 76 (Chico: Scholars) 1985, especially pp. 207–228. Psa 25 is not discussed.

[4] PC Craigie considers *Psalm of Lament* and *Psalm of Confidence*, but favours a literary, didactic origin for Psa 25, similar to that of Psa 1: 'Psa 1 is a signpost which directs the wise to the choice of the right road; Psa 25 is a companion for use along the way'—*Psalms 1–50*, WBC 19 (Waco:Word) 1983, p.22. H-J Kraus describes the psalm as 'overloaded with the most varied elements that are closely intertwined in severely limited space' but disapproves Gunkel's devaluation of it as 'more a pious artistic exercise than a personal outpouring'—*Psalms 1–59: a commentary* (Minneapolis:Augsburg) 1988 p.323; ET based on the 1978 German 5th edition.

[5] For instance, NIV, NRSV, Good News Bible. As copied in the Massoretic tradition of printed Hebrew Bibles, Psalm 25 omits the letter 'q' and adds an extra 'p'. Commentators suggest plausible reconstructions of the original wording. There are 9 acrostic psalms in the Psalter: 9–10, 25, 34, 37, 111, 112, 119, 145. For a survey of this literary device in a wider religious setting, see the article by JF Brug 'Biblical Acrostics and their relationship to other Ancient Near Eastern Acrostics', pp. 283–304 in WW Hallo, BW Jones & GL

intimate prayers are shaped by culture and conventions. The acrostic model belongs to Israel's prayers, but not to ours. No matter, perhaps this is a case of alien form but kindred spirit.

Psalm 25
Of David

1 To you, O LORD, I lift up my soul.
2 O, my God, in you I trust;
   do not let me be put to shame;
   do not let my enemies exult over me.
3 Do not let those who wait for you be put to shame;
   let them be ashamed who are wantonly treacherous.

4 Make me to know your ways, O LORD;
   teach me your paths.
5 Lead me in your truth, and teach me,
   for you are the God of my salvation;
   for you I wait all day long.

6 Be mindful of your mercy, O LORD,
   and of your steadfast love,
   for they have been from of old.
7 Do not remember the sins of my youth
   or my transgressions;
   according to your steadfast love remember me,
   for your goodness' sake, O LORD!

8 Good and upright is the LORD;
   therefore he instructs sinner in the way.
9 He leads the humble in what is right,
   and teaches the humble his way.
10 All the paths of the LORD
   are steadfast love and faithfulness,
   for those who keep his covenant and his decrees.

11 For your name's sake, O LORD,
   pardon my guilt, for it is great.
12 Who are they that fear the LORD?
   He will teach them the way that they should choose.

13 They will abide in prosperity,
   and their children shall possess the land.
14 The friendship of the LORD is for those who fear him

Mattingly (eds), *The Bible in the light of Cuneiform Literature: Scripture in Context III*, Ancient Near Eastern Texts and Studies 8 (Lewiston/ Queenstown/Lampeter: The Edwin Mellen Press) 1990. Brug thinks that the extra Hebrew letter 'p' at the end of Psa 25 points to an aleph-lamed-pe ('*lp*) structuring of the beginning, middle and end of the psalm which would encrypt the Hebrew verb '*lp*—'to learn'. This is attractive, but not without some difficulties caused by an irregularity in the *beth* verse.

and he makes his covenant known to them.
15 My eyes are ever toward the LORD,
for he will pluck me feet out of the net.

16 Turn to me and be gracious to me,
for I am lonely and afflicted.
17 Relieve the troubles of my heart,
and bring me out of my distress.
18 Consider my affliction and my trouble,
and forgive all my sins.

19 Consider how many are my foes,
and with what violent hatred they hate me.
20 O Guard my life, and deliver me;
do not let me be put to shame,
for I take refuge in you.

21 May integrity and uprightness preserve me,
for I wait for you.

22 Redeem Israel, O God,
out of all its troubles.

CROSS-CULTURAL FACTORS

There is more to the author–reader gap than poetic conventions. So easy is it to make this psalm's phrases our phrases (unlike expressions in other more bloodthirsty or nationalistic psalms that shock readers' sensibilities) that we might too quickly abandon a 'hermeneutic of suspicion' and simply pass over problematic phrases because they are pious phrases. The cross-cultural factor of verse 22 is easily spotted—'Redeem Israel, O God, out of all its troubles.' This verse stands outside the alphabetic arrangement, after the last Hebrew alphabet letter (Tau) of v.21. Perhaps v.22 was added when a personal prayer became a prayer for regular use at the national shrine, or for use during a national festival. Or the allusion to 'troubles' may point to a historical situation reminiscent of the troubles of Hebrews in the Egyptian delta before the Exodus, only this time under Assyrians, Babylonians or Persians.

We can update the collective term 'Israel' by invoking John Donne's dictum that 'no man is an island'. Even in his or her moments of innermost communion with God, an individual remains embedded in a community of some sort—a family, a seminary, a local district, a local church, a tribe, an ethnic group, a national state, a language group. Verse 22 is not the problem for a Christian re-reading because our cultures do provide dynamic equivalents and our theology reminds us that our spirituality should not isolate us socially. The real theological problem lies in verse 13 and it must have been a problem when the poem was first composed. Speaking of the devout, the psalmist says:

> They will abide in prosperity,
> and their children shall possess the land.

This was certainly not the experience of a Jeremiah or Ezekiel. Even before the 6th century Exile, there must have been exceptions—childless couples and destitute families,[6] while after the Exile and restoration, no autonomous Jewish community 'possessed the land', as Ezra's prayer so poignantly expresses it:

> Here we are, slaves to this day—slaves in the land that you gave to our ancestors to enjoy its fruit and its good gifts. Its rich yield goes to the kings whom you have set over us because of our sins; they have power also over our bodies and over our livestock at their pleasure, and we are in great distress.
>
> (Neh 9:36f)

Qohelet[7] questioned the connection between spirituality and material blessing in the light of the many exceptions he saw, and in the face of death. He did not think that the passing on of an inheritance was a certainty. Nor was prosperity a sufficient consolation for time, fate, chance and oblivion in the grave—all of which he felt himself heir to most keenly. These questions directed at the connection between orientation to God and material circumstances stand in Hebrew Scripture, whether as the questions of a renewal movement (Ezra-Nehemiah), or the questions of an intellectual focused on the individual and his nuclear family (Qohelet). A devout reading of Psa 25 cannot deny the lament of Ezra or the observations of Qohelet. Closing our eyes to empirical reality is never a viable form of spirituality.

---

[6] Deuteronomy 15 recognises the inevitability of poverty at the same time as legislating against it and promising prosperity as a covenant blessing. The distress of childlessness is heightened by the OT's this-worldly perspective in which children also serve the function of perpetuating the name, that is, of keeping the person's memory alive in the community. Israel had no official ancestor cult of prayers and libations for the dead which marked other Semitic cultures. Hannah's infertility prayer (1 Sa:9–16) and the barrenness of patriarchal wives in Genesis, which threatens fulfilment of the Land promise, illustrates the importance of children in Israel's thinking. A Christian re-reading could understand 'children' typologically as spiritual offspring, converts in the Pauline sense of 1 Cor 4:14ff.

[7] Qohelet is the Hebrew word used to refer to the book of Ecclesiastes or its speaking voice. Some English translations offer 'Preacher'. The translation is uncertain.

THEOLOGICAL TRAJECTORIES FROM OLD TO NEW COVENANT PROMISES

This said, Psa 25 can be re-read outside a Deuteronomic prosperity theology and from within a New Covenant commitment. There is a perspective on the problematic v.13 which affirms rather than dismisses it. The Land promise of Deuteronomy connects to the Earth promise of Jesus. Pillars of this flyover include Psalm 25 and Psalm 37. Psalm 37 is affiliated to Psalm 25. It is an acrostic wisdom psalm that urges trust and expectancy despite the buoyancy of the wicked:

 3 Trust in the LORD and do good;
   so you will live in the land, and enjoy security.

 9 those who wait for the LORD will inherit the land

11 But the meek shall inherit the land,
   and delight themselves in abundant prosperity.

22 for those blessed by the LORD shall inherit the land

29 the righteous shall inherit the land,
   and live in it for ever.

34 Wait for the LORD, and keep to his way,
   and he will exalt you to inherit the land.[8]

When Jesus affirms that 'the meek . . . will inherit the earth' (Matt 5:5), he does not discard the land promise of Psa 37 but expands it in three ways. Firstly, Jesus stretches the promise geographically to the world, to planet Earth, taking up the global axis of the Hebrew word *'ereṣ* (= land, earth, country). Secondly, he links it to his Kingdom teaching which stretches the context chronologically in the direction of the eschaton, the Age to come. Thirdly, the promise encompasses Gentiles and all followers of Jesus rather than referring to the national state of Israel promised to Abraham,

---

[8] We have documents from the 2nd millennium onwards in which kings grant land to their loyal executives who were sometimes courtiers or in other instances dependent client-kings, that is, vassals. The vassal documents come from the Hittite chancery records or copies at Alalakh in Syria and at Ugarit. Boundaries and cities may be listed in these treaty documents. First millennium Assyrian documents attest land grants to loyal courtiers. Both treaties and land grants share features with God's bestowal of Canaan, described in Genesis and Joshua. See M Weinfeld, *Deuteronomy and the Deuteronomic School* (Oxford: Clarendon) 1972, pp.74ff and 'The Covenant of Grant in the Old Testament and in the Ancient Near East' *JAOS* 90 (1970), 184–203 supplemented by P Kalluveettil, *Declaration and Covenant*, Analecta Biblica 88, (Rome:Biblical Institute Press) 1982, pp.178ff.

Moses and David and defined by its boundaries.[9] We could say that Jesus returns to the global perspective on *'ereṣ* = 'Earth' of Genesis 1 without putting back the clock.

By demanding that we acknowledge the author-reader gap, hermeneutics has provoked a fruitful theological reflection. It turns out that we may construct a legitimate trajectory arching across time, cultures and covenants and so bridge the author-reader gap without denying it. In doing this, we have changed the referent and the meaning of 'land' in Psa 25 in our re-reading.

There is a further point to highlighting the sixfold mention of Palestine in Psa 37, the quotation of Psa 37:11 in Matt 5:5, and the key confidence about the future of Psa 25:13. It is this: there is no mystical, disembodied, other-worldly spirituality in the psalms. The spirituality of Psa 25 is earthed. Perhaps this is where Psa 25 most successfully confronts its Christian re-readers. The relational quality of the psalm includes the community and its dwelling place. The spirituality cannot be reduced to a timeless, placeless, vertical relationality of psalmist and his God. No more can the spirituality of the Beatitudes or the Sermon on the Mount be lived outside of society, beyond the here and now, freed from the pressures of poverty and persecution. Sociological terms are embedded in the Beatitudes: 'poor', 'hungry', 'rich' (Lk 6:20,21,24).

THE DISSONANCE GAP AND THE TWO-SIDES MODEL

There is a gap of another sort than the author-reader gap, a gap endemic to the psalm itself and in the forefront of the author's consciousness. This gap is signalled by the verb *qwh* = 'to wait' that supports the psalmist's appeal at three points:

3 Do not let those who wait for you be put to shame

5 for you I wait all day long

21 for I wait for you

---

[9] The problem of how to state the continuity/discontinuity between Old and New Testaments is a real one. The Christian church has traditionally seen the Old Testament as part of its Scripture, and hence in some sense authoritative. Specialists have re-examined the typological and canonical approaches as means of connecting Old and New Testaments—see, for example, D Baker, *Two Testaments, One Bible* (Leicester: IVP) 1976 and BS Childs, *Introduction to the Old Testament as Scripture* (London: SCM) 1979 and *Old Testament Theology in a Canonical Context* (London: SCM) 1985. The concept of a trajectory embraces diversity, high points of revelation and continuity of motifs—see J Goldingay, *Theological Diversity and the authority of the Old Testament* (Grand Rapids: Eerdmans), 1987, pp. 40ff, 57f.

The gap is between the now and the not-yet. It does not yawn as wide as its New Covenant counterpart, the already of the Spirit and the not-yet of the Parousia, a gap opened up by an apocalyptic perspective on the future, a perspective that is not articulated by Psa 25. Yet a gap there is, and the psalm reflects a spirituality of the gap, of the dissonance between the way things are and the way the psalmist feels that they should be.

To settle for the present, to come to terms with the way things are, would be a denial of its troubles (vv. 16–18), or a denial of God's desire to take the psalmist's side in them. So the psalmist speaks out. There is no stoicism here. Persistence is expressed in petition not silence. The present moment in its existential immediacy is marked by the psalmist's sense of guilt, of loneliness and of opposition. This sense of *Angst* bridges the gap between author and the modern reader who may live in a culture where basic material needs are cared for but literally millions per annum are spent on anti-depressants, tranquillizers and sleeping-tablets, and informally on alcohol, heroin and other dampers on a reality that has become too painful to face soberly.

The psalmist may lift up his soul to Yahweh (v.1) and affirm that his eyes are continuously focused on God (v.15), but he is motivated, in part at least, by glancing over his shoulder at his 'enemies' who appear at the beginning and end of his thoughts (v.2 and v.19). God is asked to look at this hostile crowd too—'Consider how many are my foes and with what violent hatred they hate me.' This is another reason for asserting the this-worldly and down-to-earth nature of Old Testament spirituality. Israel is pushed towards Yahweh; at times driven, rather than gladly joining in the festal throng to worship. Few psalms ignore the 'enemy' to focus exclusively on God. Psa 23 is typical enough. Even at the banquet, the enemies are within view, though in this instance they seem to look on helplessly. In Psa 25, the foes are far from passive.

In touching on this motif of 'enemy', we are keying into a core metaphor that we may call 'The Two-Sides Model'.[10] Its most

---

[10] The Two-Sides Model of Exod 23:22 ('I will be an enemy to your enemies and a foe to your foes'), which states the friendship and loyalty principle, has a long history back to the 3rd millennium, as attested by the Mesopotamian treaty between King Naram-Sin and Elam, extant in Elamite—'Naram-Sin's friend is my friend and Naram-Sin's enemy is my enemy' (*CAH* 3, Vol 1 Part 2: Early History of the Middle East, pp. 650f) and forwards into the Greek and Roman treaties, as discussed by M Weinfeld 'The Loyalty Oath in the Ancient Near East' *Ugarit-Forschungen* 8 (1976) 379–414, p.390f. The parallels of phrase and form between Ancient Near Eastern treaties and biblical Covenant were studied intensively in the 1970s by scholars such as FC Fensham, KA Kitchen, DJ McCarthy and M Weinfeld. These parallels continue to attract attention

expressive Old Testament demonstration is found in the Exodus story where the cry of Israel under threat and under taskmasters provokes a deliverance that leaves Egyptians drowned and Israelites dry on the far side of the Reed Sea. The Song of the Sea (Exod 15) exemplifies what it means to have Yahweh on your side and what it means to be on the wrong side of Yahweh. Yet after the Reed Sea, it becomes clear that those on the wrong side of Yahweh are not simply the groups listed in the Song, namely, the Egyptians, Philistines, Moabites, Edomites and Canaanites. It is apostate Israelites who die at the very covenant mountain that was their destination from Egypt (Exod 32:26ff).

The 'Two-Sides Model' in Wisdom literature contrasts the wise and the fool, both neighbours. Daniel contrasts the apocalyptically wise with the covenant apostate as well as with the persecuting pagan powers. Exodus, Proverbs and Daniel make it very probable, then, that the enemies of the Psalms are Hebrew neighbours.[11]

THE SOCIO-POLITICAL, SPIRITUAL AND SEMANTIC SPECTRUM

Perhaps modern readers in secular or post-Christian countries experience indifference to their faith more than hostility. Read from this experience, the psalmists may sound as though they are paranoid. Indeed, there is a propensity in certain other-worldly Christian sub-cultures to exaggerate the threat from 'the world' and to foster a persecution mentality. On the other hand, readers who live in countries where human rights and civil liberties are denied may identify with the psalmists. How we read the statements about enemies in the psalms may depend more on whether our names appear in the files of the secret police than on Hebrew exegesis.

The point is that our context may determine how we re-contextualize the spirituality of the psalms. It would be a travesty of the original to de-politicize the psalms in order to make them relevant to the modern world. To turn 'the enemy' into spiritual forces such as demonic powers or our nightmares, fears and

---

—recently KA Kitchen 'The Fall and Rise of Covenant, Law and Treaty' *Tyndale Bulletin* 40 (1989) 118–135.

[11] Except in Royal psalms and Communal laments that explicitly refer to other nations or military situations, though some military events could be internal political upheavals. Absalom's revolt reminds us that palace intrigue, assassination and civil wars marked Israel's history as well as Assyria's and that of surrounding kingdoms. Enemies with swords may be Israelite. For reviews of recent work on 'enemies' in the Psalms, see SJL Croft *The Identity of the Individual in the Psalms* JSOTS 44, (Sheffield:JSOT Press) 1987, Chap.1, pp. 15–48 'The Antagonists in the Psalms'.

temptations may be permissible up to a point—in so far as these forces may open up an existential gap, an *Angst* which alienates us from the love of God. Yet such 'spiritualizing' of 'the enemy' may also be a luxury, and certainly not more Christian than a socio-political reading of the psalms. Liberation Theology should have taught us this much, even if we have read about it rather than lived through a liberation struggle. Besides which, contemporary court records of battered wives, abused children and racial violence provide counterparts for the enemy role within so-called 'civilized', democratic societies. The enemy all too often has a human face.

This said, justification for a full spectrum re-reading of 'enemy', along socio-political, spiritual and psychological lines, could be argued from analogy with the semantic flexibility of the terms for 'poor' throughout the psalms. Yahweh is against the 'enemy' and on the side of the 'poor' in Psa 25, as elsewhere. The 'poor' (*ʿanāwîm*) of v.6 who are helped towards 'justice' (*mišpāṭ*) are in this instance more likely to be the 'poor in spirit' whose humble dependence on the Lord informs their life-decisions and ethical choices. It is less likely that they are poverty-stricken debtors taken to court by rich oppressors.

If the Psalms themselves re-read the vocabulary of poverty or stretch it semantically from literal to metaphorical, then there is a precedent within the living tradition for extension of meaning—provided this extension is a conscious exercise and does not distort and diametrically oppose the original author's orientation. Yet the tailpiece, v.22, linking the nation's troubles to the individual's troubles, reminds us that the inner world and the outer world are connected.[12] Israel's 'troubles' are socio-economic or military, even if the psalmist's are his 'loneliness'(v.16) and sinfulness (v.18).

NUANCES OF TRUE OR FALSE GUILT?

Guilt certainly contributes to the psalmist's distress. The past reaches forward disturbingly into the author's present—'the sins of my youth'(v.7) still press on his mind. From one point of view the 'sins of youth', rash or hot-blooded, might be the least blameworthy and most excusable. Yet the author does not find peace of mind in this thought. The verb 'remember' is reiterated in vv.6–7: 'Be mindful . . .', 'Do not remember . . .', '. . . remember me'. He requests that God forget his past and focus on him in

---

[12] *ṣārāh* is the word used for 'the troubles of my heart' in v.17 and Israel's 'troubles' in v.22.

the present in the light of God's reliable and renowned prior commitment, expressed in covenant-making.

The Christian reader recognizes his own God and his own human nature in Psa 25 at the same moment as recognizing the original reference to the Sinai covenant and its promises in 'from of old'(v.6). Hence the author-reader gap is simultaneously acknowledged and bridged. One human nature, emotionally sensitive, is common to all readers. There is one God committed in covenant relationship.[13]

Our common humanity is important hermeneutically. Spirituality, as well as psychology, recognizes the power of emotions and the damage done in the past which carries forward into the present, whether this involves false guilt or genuine guilt. Time does not heal, though it may paper over cracks. The inner turmoil of the present has roots in the past. Present distress hooks on to memories, pulling them up from the well of experience. This bucketful holds guilt rather than refreshment for the author of Psa 25. The inner world and the author's personal history are thus in clear focus in this psalm. He brings himself, including his past to his prayers. The point is not so much how realistic or imagined is his guilt about the past (had he never mentioned it before in prayer?), or his fear of those who hate him (paranoid or well-founded), but what he does with both, where he takes them.

Furthermore, 'pardon my guilt, for it is great' (v.11) may be an objective assessment of his spiritual state, but it might well be the distorted or exaggerated exclamation of a hypersensitive conscience disclosing his existential anxiety. We cannot always take the words of the psalms at face value because they may function as expressions of feelings rather than as statements of fact.[14] Language has many functions besides factual description. In a realm as nuanced as spiritual awareness, there are several levels of personal response to the same fact. 'My guilt . . . is great' might be an

---

[13] Of course, there are different covenants with different human groups at different times—with Noah-humanity-animals (Gen 9); with Abraham and descendants (Gen 15,17); with Israelites (Exod 24); with Aaronids (Num 25); with David and his dynasty (2 Sam 7). See TE McComiskey, *The Covenants of Promise: a theology of the Old Testament covenants* (Nottingham:IVP) 1985.

[14] A prime example of a real event causing false guilt over a wide time scale is attested by experiences of sexual abuse in childhood. Often the child carries a sense of guilt for what happened—a false guilt—and emotional damage with effects still operative into adulthood and middle age if those experiences are not recalled, verbalised and worked through in therapy. For other examples, see D & M Linn, *Healing Life's Hurts: healing of memories through five stages of forgiveness* (New York:Paulist Press) 1978. See the fuller discussion in the Chapter 'The Experience of Guilt and Confession'.

authentic moment of heightened awareness, awareness of the stark contrast between sinful human nature and the holiness of God.

Peter had such a moment in the presence of Christ when he fell down on his knees exclaiming, 'Go away from me, Lord, for I am a sinful man' (Luke 5:8). We interpret Peter's experience as a moment of authenticity, of deep encounter, of necessary insight, of transforming quality. We arrive at this evaluation by observing the response of Jesus which allays his fear and reinforces his belonging—'Do not be afraid; from now on you will be catching people.' We know about the life-long effect Jesus had on Simon Peter.

When we read a psalm, we have neither a narrative context, nor a biographical trajectory, and seldom a record of God's response.[15] So we will inevitably read our own meaning into 'Pardon my guilt, for it is great' (Psa 25:11b), depending on our own spiritual state at the time of reading and on our perception of the psalmist's use of language.

THE INTIMACY OF THE INNER CIRCLE

If we turn to the positive side of the 'Two-Sides Model', then it is the affirmation of belonging, of being on the safe side of Yahweh and knowing it. The spirit of belonging in Psa 25 reveals its roots in the 'Two-Sides Model' in its opening phrases: 'my soul', 'my God', 'my enemies' (v. 1f). The psalmist wants to be treated as one who belongs to God, not as his enemy, the perfidious, those who 'are wantonly treacherous' (v.3). He argues that to go unanswered, unsupported or undirected would not only leave him in his troubled state but would lead to a public humiliation that would reflect badly on God.

'Shame' is another of the psalm's recurrent motifs (vv. 1,2,20) which contrasts the state of not-as-it-ought-to-be with being guarded and delivered. The antithesis of being shamed is being vindicated. This vindication applies more widely than a court verdict refuting a false accusation or slander. From Old to New

---

[15] For instance, 'My God, my God, why have you forsaken me?' (Psa 22:1) expresses the psalmist's sense of dereliction. The psalm itself, both in its address to God and its outcome, contradicts the fact that God has utterly abandoned the man who prays. The laments express the theological dissonance or gap between expectation and experience. See CC Broyles, *The Conflict of Faith and Experience in the Psalms: a form-critical and theological study*, JSOTS 52, (Sheffield: JSOT Press) 1989, pp.187ff on Psa 22.

Testament there is a vindication trajectory.[16] This link between testaments is epitomized by the Suffering Servant. He is confident of vindication ('He who vindicates me is near', Poem 3, Isa 50:4–9), but passes through injustice and rejection on the road of non-violence and death before his exaltation. The voices of the martyrs under the altar (Rev 6:9ff) echo the 'How long?' of the psalms of Lament.

In Psa 25, 'O my God, in you I trust'(v.2) is spoken from the disturbed side of the dissonance gap, when being publicly shamed seems a strong possibility. Vindication closes the gap. Personal trust must, in the last analysis, be vindicated publicly. Spirituality ceases to be a private matter. If Jesus speaks of an inconspicuous spirituality (Matt 6:1–6,16–18), he also speaks of inheriting the earth. In this sense the spirituality of the Psalms and the spirituality of discipleship and martyrdom from Gospels to Revelation is a public spirituality of belonging to God. Its authenticity will be disclosed 'on that day'. Meanwhile, the experience is—'I wait for you all day long' (v.5).

This belonging is expressed in Psa 25 in terms of an intimacy with God which goes beyond the 'my God' phrase of v.1. The key metaphor is that of belonging to the 'inner circle' (*sōd*).[17] The English translations capture this intimacy quite well in their phrase 'the friendship of the LORD' (v.14). The picture is of an inner circle in contrast to those on the outside. The inner circle are those in the know, those whom God has taken into his confidence, those who keep company with him. In Jeremiah, those on the outside of this circle are the false prophets who eagerly speak in the name of God without first listening and obeying. The result is a delusion, 'a

---

[16]   The word 'trajectory' is a metaphor from archery or ballistics. It pictures the release of a concept as the flight of an arrow or artillery shell. The concept travels a path over time like a projectile, passes through its high point, and comes to rest some distance from where it originated. 'Covenant' is just such a concept that originates hundreds of years before it embeds in Luke 22:20 and 1 Cor 11:25. Concepts, unlike arrows, change shape as they travel. This means that the use of the same word at point of origin and place of embedding does not guarantee identical meaning throughout the trajectory.

[17]   The Hebrew word *sōd* is a secular one. It refers in some places to the company enjoyed in an informal group ('*the gatherings of* young men' Jer 6:11; 'I did not sit *in the company of* merrymakers', Jer 15:17; cf. Psa 55:14). It also refers to what is spoken and heard within the inner circle as 'secret' or 'confidential' (Amos 3:7; Prov 11:13, 20:19, 25:9). Job looked back on the time 'when *the friendship of* God was upon my tent' (Job 29:4) and denied that his comforters were more privy to God's secrets—'Have you listened in *the council of* God?', 15:8).Compare exclusion of the false prophets from the restored company: 'they shall not be in *the council of* my people, nor be enrolled in the register of Israel . . .', Ezek 13:19. The contrast in Proverbs is expressed as 'the perverse are an abomination to the Lord, but the upright are *in his confidence*' (Prov 3:32).

vision of their own hearts' (Jer 23:16). Jeremiah too needed public vindication for his claim to belong to God's inner circle. The optimism of the false prophets, such as Hananiah (chap 28), was based on an orthodox promise theology that was misapplied. This is the false spirituality more deadly than outright wickedness because it masquerades and misleads.

The trajectory of this concept of the inner circle stretches from the psalmist's conflict with his fellow Israelites to Jesus' conflict over who truly belongs to the Father (John 8). It issues in his words defining his inner circle:

> You are my friends if you do what I command you. I do not call you servants any longer, because the servant does not know what the master is doing; but I have called you friends, because I have made known to you everything that I have heard from my Father.
>
> (John 15:15)

The inner circle are marked by inclusion in covenant and by the response of obedience.

THE CIRCUMFERENCE OF COVENANT

In Psa 25, God 'makes his covenant known to them' (v.14b). Here again the psalmist's phrase keys into a central theological concept, probably the central organizing concept of the Old Testament in so far as there is one, namely, covenant.[18] The word itself *bᵉrīt* ('covenant') appears twice in our psalm (v.10,14), but as with so much of the material in the Pentateuch or the Prophets, the centrality of the covenant concept does not rest with the use of the noun *bᵉrīt* alone.[19] In this psalm, the language and assumptions are

---

[18] Nothing since W Eichrodt, *Theologie des alten Testaments* 1933, revised 1957–61 and published as *Theology of the Old Testament* Vol 1 & 2, (London: SCM) 1967 has really displaced Covenant as an organizing concept for Old Testament theology, although Eichrodt's work is pre ancient Near Eastern documents and now very dated. See GF Hasel, *Old Testament Theology: basic issues in the current debate³*, (Grand Rapids:Eerdmans) 1982 Chap.4 'The Centre of the OT and OT Theology' together with J Goldingay's cautions about the plurivocalism of 'covenant' (*Theological Diversity*, p.48 note 67 and pp.178ff).

[19] Semitic *brt*, cognate with the Hebrew *bᵉrīt*= 'covenant' has a long history outside the Bible, of which the most interesting example is probably the 13th century BC Hurrian hymn found at Ugarit. The High God, El, is called 'El of Judgement, El of covenant' ('*El.brt 'El.dn*)—see KA Kitchen, *Tyndále Bulletin* 40 (1989) 121ff. The index to S Parpola & K Watanabe, *Neo-Assyrian Treaties and Loyalty Oaths*, State Archives of Assyria Vol II (Helsinki: Helsinki Univ Press) 1988 conveniently locates key cognate ideas and terms in the 1st millennium Assyrian material, such as *damāqu*—'to be good, nice', *de'iqtu*—'goodness', *kettu*—'truth', *ra'āmu*—'to love', *ṭābtu*—'goodness, favour', *ṭūbtu*—'kindness'.

rooted in the covenant without ever an explicit mention of Sinai, Moses, sacrifice, tabernacle, Ark, Passover or Ten Command-ments. The characteristic recital of Yahweh's mighty acts, of which the Exodus is the epitome, is missing. The spirituality is at first glance that of an individual Israelite asking for protection, moral guidance and forgiveness without reference to Israel's historical and cultic traditions.

Yet 'covenant' is written right across the psalm. It is the basis of its relationality and of its depiction of God. In vv. 5–14, terms are used to characterize God that are disclosed through covenant-making. 'Mercy, steadfast love, goodness, good and upright, faithfulness, integrity and uprightness': *raḥāmīm, ḥesed, ṭōb, ṭōb wayāšar, 'emet, tōm wāyōšer*. They form a rich cluster of covenantal terms, applicable to a God who has pledged himself, who remains loyal and who offers blessings—including, of course, the blessings of 'prosperity' and 'land' of v.13. This is not the Unknown God, but the one who continues to 'make his covenant known'(v.14b).[20]

Many terms of covenant-making are borrowed from political treaties and appear in the documents of the 2nd millennium Hittite and 1st millennium Assyrian empires, though the earliest extant treaty documents stretch back to the 3rd millennium. In these treaties, the Suzerain or 'Great King' bestows a protective rela-tionship on a vassal state, provided that the client state remains loyal and pays regular tribute, or meets the other obligations such as supplying troops for the imperial wars.

In Psa 25, individual belonging rather than national partnership with Yahweh is to the fore. Corporate and individual aspects of covenant membership cannot really be separated, and political treaty-making as well as biblical covenant rituals both use lan-guage which pinpoints the heart of the individual who is taking oath. Political and biblical documents are hypersensitive to a divorce between the heart and the lips, between going through the motions of the ritual and making a wholehearted commitment.[21]

---

[20] Elsewhere in the OT and in the ANE, the verb 'to know' (Heb. *yādaʿ*, Akkadian *idû*) is used of the client acknowledging the reality of the treaty/covenant, as HB Huffmon demonstrated ('The Treaty Background of Hebrew *yādaʿ*' and Huffmon & SB Parker, 'A Further Note on the Treaty Background of Hebrew *yādaʿ*', BASOR 181 & 184, 1966, pp.31–37 & 36–38).

[21] The Akkadian phrases *ina kul libbika* from 2nd and 1st millennium treaties parallel Deuteronomy's 'with all your heart . . .'(*bᵉkol-lᵉbābᵉkā*). See Weinfeld, *Deuteronomy* p.334f.; U-F 8, p.384.

> While you stand on the place of this oath, you shall not swear the oath with your lips only but shall swear it wholeheartedly (*ina gammurti libbakunu*)
> VTE, line 387: Parpola, *State archives*, p.44 para 34.

In our psalm, it is 'the fear of the LORD' (v.12,14), 'preserving the covenant stipulations'(v.10b),[22] and 'integrity and uprightness'(v.21) that are the hallmarks of the true covenanter. In the political documents, 'wholeheartedness' is emphasised. Deuteronomy borrows this phrase and also distinguishes between ritual circumcision and spiritual 'circumcision of heart'.[23] The inner orientation of the participant was essential as well as outward complicity with the stipulations.

THE FEAR OF THE LORD, INTEGRITY AND OBEDIENCE

In our psalm, inner orientation ('fear of the LORD') and outward conduct are interwoven. 'Your paths, your truth, the way, what is right, his way, the way that they should choose' (vv.4,5,8,9,12) all make sense when these terms are related to covenant stipulations.[24] The 'way' is no mystical path, no *via negativa* or dark night of the soul. Nor was the psalmist deliberating over his career path, missionary calling, or prospective marriage partner. If contextualization was in his mind, it was perhaps to do with the application to his circumstances of general principles of the Torah embodied in apodictic commands like 'Love your neighbour as yourself'(Lev 19:18), and 'Love Yahweh your God . . .' (Deut 6:5ff). In Psa 25,

---

22 V.10 'his covenant and his decrees' (*bᵉrîtō wᵉᶜēdōtāyw*) is probably a hendiadys construction with the sense 'covenant stipulations' as PC Craigie suggests (*Psalms 1–50*, p.217).

23 Most of the ANE parallels are discussed by scholars such as M Weinfeld 'The Covenant of Grant in the Old Testament and in the Ancient Near East' JAOS 90 (1970), 184–203; 'Covenant Terminology in the Ancient Near East and its Influence on the West' *JAOS* 93 (1973), 190–199; 'The Loyalty Oath in the Ancient Near East' *Ugarit-Forschungen* 8 (1976) 379–414; *Deuteronomy*, 1972. See too P Kalluveettil, *Declaration and Covenant*, Press) 1982 p.47ff on *ḥesed* and parallels; p.30f on *ᶜēdūt*; p.42ff on *ṭōb*; p.176f on the terms 'good' (*ṭōb*) and 'upright' (*yāšar*) in connection with Deut 12:28 'to do good and right in Yahweh's eyes' and with David's conduct in politicking with Achish, Philistine king of Gath (1 Sam 29). See Gen 17, Josh 5:2ff on circumcision as a rite of Covenant belonging, and compare 'Circumcise, then, the foreskins of your heart . . .' Deut 10:16. cf. Deut 30:6, Jer 4:4, 9:25.

24 Craigie notes the covenant terminology, but concludes that 'a more dominant characteristic of the psalm is the preponderance of language typical of the Wisdom literature' (p.218). In point of fact, 'way', 'fear' and 'good' cannot be claimed for Wisdom exclusively, nor are Wisdom and Covenant without shared concepts, such as 'the fear of the LORD', as scholars such as Hubbard and Weinfeld have noted. The amalgam of covenant vocabulary and didacticism and the similarity with other didactic 'Wisdom' psalms (such as Psa 1 and 37), is not surprising. See DA Hubbard 'The Wisdom Movement and Israel's Covenant Faith' *Tyndale Bulletin* 17 (1966) 3–34 and Weinfeld, *Deuteronomy and the Deuteronomic School* (Clarendon: Oxford) 1972 Part Three, pp. 244ff 'Deuteronomic Literature and Wisdom Literature', noting 3.I.3 'The Fear of God', pp. 274ff, which overlooks Psa 25:12,14.

God is invoked as instructor, a role the teacher fills in Proverbs and Ecclesiastes, and which the Torah fulfils in Psa 119. God himself, the Torah and the teacher are not in competition in Old Testament spirituality. They form a three-fold strand for spirituality to grasp.[25]

'Path'(*orah*) and 'way'(*derek*) language is likewise at home in Wisdom and Covenant settings. In Wisdom, we find the phrase 'the path of life'. This means the chosen moral course which leads to life as opposed to 'the way of death'.[26] The literal path to the prostitute's house is the metaphorical 'path to Sheol' (Prov 5:1–6, 7:1–27, 9:13–18). In covenant context, obedience and disobedience are contrasted as 'life and good, death and evil' (Deut 30:15). Obeying the stipulations is described as 'walking in his ways' (Deut 30:16).[27] Both Covenant and Wisdom contribute to the core metaphor of spiritual pilgrimage—Life's Path, or The Journey. This perception of life as a journey down a road is pervasive. Indeed life journey attracts a cluster of related ideas and could lay claim to being the core metaphor of Western spirituality.[28] Its Old Testament rootage is impressive—nothing less than the Abraham and Exodus traditions which we will examine in subsequent chapters.

Finally, the psalmist hopes, 'May integrity and uprightness preserve me, for I wait for you' (v.21a). The qualities of 'integrity'

---

[25] The psalmist expects God's personal tuition. Both *lmd* and *yrh* mean 'to teach, instruct'(Piel *lmd* v.4,5; Hiphil *yrh*, v.8,12). Compare the intertwining of Yahweh, torah and parent-teachers in Deut 6:4ff.

[26] Kraus, *Psalms 1–59*, p.320f and 323, fastens on *derek* as a leading concept in Psa 25, without invoking the Covenant background of the psalm. It is not necessary to segregate cultic Torah instruction, Wisdom schooling and Deuteronomic Covenant nuances, as though these were exclusive or inimical to one another, especially if the psalm is late and literary and hence draws on a wide spectrum of Israel's theological tradition.

[27] Weinfeld conveniently lists references to the relevant loyalty phrases. For phrases with 'to walk' and its associated 'ways'/'torah'/'before Yhwh', see nos.6,6a,7 and 8 in *Deuteronomy* pp.332ff.

[28] Contemporary writing on Old and New Testament and applied theology are represented by titles such as CE L'Heureux, *Life Journey and the Old Testament: an experiential approach to the Bible and personal transformation* (New York:Paulist Press) 1986, DJ Bosch, *A Spirituality of the Road* (Scottdale:Herald Press) 1979 and Scott Peck, *The Road less Travelled: a new psychology of love, traditional values and spiritual growth* (New York:Simon & Schuster) 1978. Compare R Pooley and P Seddon, *The Lord of the Journey: a reader in Christian Spirituality* (London: Collins) 1986, and the heading 'Some Reading for the Journey' and many titles in the annotated bibliography given in a recent ecumenical publication—S Amirtham & R Pryor (eds), *Invitation to the Feast of Life: resources for spiritual formation in theological education*, WCC Programme on Theological Education, pp.183ff. *Bunyan's Pilgrim's Progress* and its influence on anti-Establishment evangelical piety has probably been profound, as has the Welsh Revival hymn 'Guide me O Thou great Jehovah, pilgrim through

and 'uprightness' (*tōm wāyōšer*) compare with God's character as 'good and upright' (*ṭōb wāyāšār*, v.8).[29] We are hearing the language of covenant belonging.[30] It is set in the context of protection from enemies—his life needs to be 'guarded' and 'delivered' from the 'many foes' (v.19,20).[31] Secondly, absolute loyalty to God as overlord is the first demand of covenant. The whole prayer breathes of this fundamental orientation—the 'lifting of the soul', 'trust' (v.1,2), 'waiting' (v.3,5,21), 'keeping the covenant stipulations' (v.10), 'fear of the LORD' (v. 12,14), 'eyes ever toward the LORD' (v.15).

Verse 21 is not a claim to moral perfection, as though it said 'may my integrity and uprightness stand me in good stead'. No attainment of sanctification, as propounded in certain holiness teachings or 'deeper Christian life' movements, can legitimately be read into it. Nor is it rightly construed as 'justification by works of the law', a doctrine of merit. The sense of sinfulness expressed in the psalm prohibits such conclusions. So does the writer's openness to instruction as a humbly dependent sinner (v.8,9). Rather, the priority and the security of God's commitment—the 'steadfast love'(*ḥesed* v 6,7,10)[32] 'from of old'(*meʿō-lām*,v.6)—undergird the psalmist and form the basis of his appeal.

---

this barren land'. Kosuke Koyama's *Three Miles an Hour God* (London: SCM) 1979 uses the walking metaphor to emphasise its slow, human pace in contrast to the rat-race.

[29] Compare Kidner's comment on v.8: 'God *instructs sinners* not only out of goodness and mercy (cf.7) but as being Himself *good and upright* (8), and therefore concerned to reproduce these qualities in others.'—D Kidner, *Psalms 1–72*, TOTC (London: IVP), 1973, p.116.

[30] Compare the mutuality of commitment (Yahweh's commitment and David's loyalty) in the Dynastic covenant, as summarised in Solomon's prayer:

> You have shown great and steadfast love (*ḥesed*) to your servant my father David, because he walked before you in faithfulness (*beʿemet*), in righteousness, and in uprightness of heart (*beʿyišrat lēbab*) toward you; and you have kept for him this great and steadfast love (*ḥesed*) and given him a son to sit on his throne today. (1 Kgs 3:6)

On *yāšar* = 'to be straight, right', *yāšār* = 'straight, right, just' and *yōšer* = 'straightness, uprightness, honesty, integrity' incorporated into the semantic field of covenant loyalty, see Kalluveettil *Declaration*, p.176ff & 52 with note 147 and Weinfeld, *Deuteronomy*, p.76f, who compares 'walk with integrity'-(*hālak beʿtōm*, Prov 10:9) with the Akkadian phrase *alāku/attalluku šalmiš* in the Assyrian Royal Grant to Baltaya and with the reference to the covenant with Levi (Mal 2:4–6) in which 'he walked with me in integrity and uprightness' (*beʿšālōm ûbeʿmīšōr hālak ʾōtīy*, v.6b).

[31] On military protection and analogies, see FC Fensham 'Clauses of Protection in Hittite Vassal-Treaties and the Old Testament' VT 13 (1963) 133–143.

[32] KD Sakenfeld, *The Meaning of Hesed in the Hebrew Bible: a new inquiry*, HSM 17 (Missoula: Scholars) 1978 is a monograph length treatment of a key term for Covenant concepts. It demonstrates the wide semantic range of *ḥesed* from 'secular' to theological (see Chap.2, 'The Secular Use of *Hesed* in Pre-Exilic

What he is affirming is that he is committed to covenant from his side—he waits for no other: 'because I wait for thee'. It is an I-Thou conclusion.

There is mutuality, there is a correspondence of commitment from the psalmist's side and from the LORD's, even of a like quality of wholeheartedness. Yet the I-Thou relationship is of the suzerain-vassal model, and in the psalm the weaker party is seeking protection from the stronger, the client from the overlord.

SUMMARY

At first glance, Psa 25 can be used by Christians as it stands because it is so much focused on the intimate relationship between the believer and his or her God. After all, an I-Thou relationality lies at the centre of spirituality. 'The friendship of the LORD', we might say, is for all who fear him, anywhere and everywhere.

At this point, hermeneutics intrudes. 'The LORD' in the key phrases 'the friendship of the LORD' and 'the fear of the LORD' is an English word, but spelling it with four capitals is a translator's ploy which both signals the reader-author gap and bridges it. We cannot ignore the fact that the text has 'The friendship of YHWH', conventionally read with vowels as 'Yahweh'. The One addressed was Israel's God before he was our God, as the acrostic on the Hebrew alphabet reminds us.[33] Furthermore, the psalm promises prosperity and land to the devout. We do not hear this psalm as its original readers did, nor do we wish to give it its original meaning. We cannot pray the final verse—or if we do, we have made some assumptions, or executed a complicated hermeneutical manoeuvre. For us, to read the psalm is to re-read it, to re-contextualise the I-Thou relationship into our own situation.

Preferably, we re-contextualise in a way that does most justice to the theology and least disregards the original statement. To deny any continuity with the psalm's socio-political setting cuts its mooring rope to real life. There may be real, violent, threatening hostility, real enemies that impinge on a present reader's consciousness. Denial of human 'enemies' weakens the continuity between author and modern world, excludes God from acting as source of appeal or acting as deliverer and refuge, and implies that spirituality operates outside the domain of disrupted human

---

Prose').. In terms of its associated word clusters, such as *'emet*, see Chap.6, '*Hesed* in Psalms, Proverbs and Related Literature'.

[33] A delightful irony is that our alphabet is borrowed from 2nd millennium Semitic culture in which Israel came to literacy. Replacing cumbersome syllabic scripts, the brilliant simplification of the alphabetic writing from Canaan was exported via Phoenicians to Greece, Rome and to us in the 2nd millennium AD.

relations. Spiritualising the enemy will end up severing the link between God, justice and human rights.

Another level of awareness emerges when we reckon with the complexities of language. This means that we cannot read statements at face value, or the meaning of words from dictionaries.[34] 'Paths', 'mercy', 'steadfast love', 'good and upright', 'his decrees' all have roots in Israel's theological traditions. If we are unaware of the Covenant framework, the Two-Sides model and the Wisdom tradition, then we have lost the conceptual framework that gave these words and phrases meaning to the author. Furthermore, awareness of the Covenant framework immediately results in a re-reading. We have no intention of carrying out the covenant stipulations of circumcision or Sabbath keeping, to mention only two examples.

We know that our fears get exaggerated and that we at times suffer from a hypersensitive conscience, so it is also possible that the psalmist got his enemies and his sins out of proportion too.[35] There is an element of emotion and an element of subjectivity involved in spirituality. This subjectivity is unavoidable, in any case, because it is part of being human and speaking from the heart. The role of exegesis is not to negate the subjectivity and emotions of the psalms, but to see them in context. Neither is it the role of spirituality so to focus on God that the tremulous quality of being human, its fragility and ambiguity, are eliminated. If we start from where our contemporary culture starts, or at least from where its expertise in depth perspectives is located, then the emotions of the psalm will be affirmed, not negated.

To a therapist, the psalmist's statement 'I am lonely and distressed' (v.16)[36] is important as a datum because psychology

---

[34] Even the opening line, 'I lift up *my soul*' (*napšīy 'eśśā'*) is imperilled if dictionary meanings of *nepeš* such as 'throat', neck, appetite, life' were to be inserted mechanically. Neither is 'soul' a safe translation if the 'body as tomb' or 'ghost in the machine' debates of theology and philosophy feed into it. In fact, semantics demands that the translation express the orientation of the whole person to God. The phrase uses spatial metaphor 'up' combined with *nepeš*—'inner being, person' to convey depth and directionality. The language is relational rather than that of component parts.

[35] We put our own frame round Paul's self-description as 'the foremost' of sinners (1 Tim 1:15) rather than taking it at face value. This does not deny the strength of Paul's feelings about his past or the reality of what he did to the followers of Jesus, but neither is it a face-value reading.

[36] The phrase has a brevity and assonance in Hebrew: *kīy-yāḥīd wᵉʿānīy 'ānīy*. Probably 'distressed, miserable, wretched' fits *'ānīy* better than 'afflicted' here. The adjective *yāḥīd* means 'only, solitary, lonely', and its use in Psa 25 is best illustrated from its association with the isolated and vulnerable orphans, widows, homeless and prisoners of Psa 68:5f:

Father of orphans and protector of widows
is God in his holy habitation.

recognizes the power of feelings in human behaviour and in our experience of life.[37] As readers of the psalm rather than acquaintances of the author, we have only the psalmist's expression of how he felt to go on. Our first duty as listeners is to enter his world and view it from his perspective, which is to acknowledge the reality of how he feels. Yet that is not all.

We can say that the psalmist's phrase 'I am lonely' is not simply a sociological statement. He may have had a wife and children, good neighbours, a circle of friends and acquaintances and an extended kin group—as would most Israelites. A therapist listening to this statement, 'I am lonely', would want to point out the potential that all the speaker's relationships hold. A pastor would want to point out that the love of God is mediated through people. They would also point out that the way we experience human relationships and the way we experience a relationship with God have important correlations. If we feel isolated from people close to us, God may seem remote. If we are secure in love relationships and friendships, the love of God becomes more real to us. We cannot simply read the words of Psa 25 and not reflect on that experience and ours. We need to interact with the writer as he expresses his emotions. That too is part of a reader-response hermeneutic. A re-reading is an interactive reading.

CONCLUSION

If we are to use the psalms for our spirituality, then we shall need more than intuition and instant identification with the author as a method. We shall have to work with the psalmist's feelings and our own, put on his clothes and contemplate their fit. At first a loss of immediacy results when the complexity of author-reader-meaning is confronted. Consciousness of hermeneutics intrudes before it helps. Yet after its procedures are made explicit and then become instinctive, the intrusiveness diminishes, the text becomes transparent rather than opaque, and through it we see God. The text is a window, and hermeneutics will enable us in the end to look through the window rather than at it.

In this chapter, we have mostly been working from text to context, from author to re-reader, from Israelite theology towards a re-contextualization within a Christian experience. We could

---

God gives the desolate (*y⁽ᵉ⁾ḥîdîm*) a home to live in;
he leads out the prisoners to prosperity,
but the rebellious will live in a parched land.

[37] An existentialist, philosopher or therapist, would read this as confirmation of a world view in which we are all fundamentally alone and subject to *Angst* by our very being-in-the-world. See existentialist writers or therapists such as Kierkegaard and Yalom.

work the other way round and start from the concerns of our contemporary spirituality and ask if these are reflected in Psa 25. We will work this way round in drawing the chapter to a conclusion.

Western piety will find some of its familiar cultural concerns in the psalm. Psa 25 is an intensely personal poem. Writing private poems may well be one way in which we too express our spirituality. Like Psa 25, our poems may dwell on our intimate relationship with the LORD as well as reflecting our anxieties. We certainly inherit a tradition of writing that is wider than hymn and liturgy.[38] The psalm's mood, being neither triumphalistic nor utterly despairing, may match our average range of emotions more than some other psalms.[39]

Awareness of personal sin and the processing of our personal history may be something we work with in retreats, growth groups, home Bible studies or our personal journal, as well as encountering in the psalms. The dissonance gap between the way things are and the way we long for them to be, whether in our experience of unanswered prayer or unfulfilled hopes may mean that 'for you I wait all day long' has been part of our experience before we read it in Psa 25. The loneliness of the city, or inner loneliness, is certainly an experience of many who are surrounded with the hubbub of life. The quest for guidance and the need for discerning God's will in moral decisions, contingent circumstances and matters of lifestyle is part of the 'burden' of free choice in consumer societies. This may find verbalisation in the psalmist's hope of learning from God what to choose. The two-way communication process pictured in Psa 25 fits our need to be heard and to listen.

'Christ-likeness' as a goal of our spirituality finds its counterpart in Psa 25's correspondence of matching loyalties and personal qualities—'goodness, uprightness, integrity', God's (v.8) and the psalmist's (v.21).

---

[38] Note, for example the publication of poetry in *Theology* or *Christianity Today*. From within an evangelical and charismatic tradition there is the collection of work by a mother-of-five, Luci Shaw, *Polishing the Petoskey Stone* (Wheaton: Harold Shaw) 1989, which spans several decades.

[39] It does not fit neatly into categories such as Lament of the Individual (cf. Psa 88), or Psalm of Confidence (cf. Psa 23), nor into Brueggemann's helpful categories of Orientation (hymns), Disorientation (laments) or Re-orientation (thanksgiving). It is omitted from his recent discussions—*The Message of the Psalms* (Augsburg) 1984 and *Israel's Praise* (Philadelphia:Fortress) 1989. The Psalms of Lament, especially the Communal Laments, may come to life more readily in societies facing national catastrophes such as drought, famine and AIDS, or civil war and the collapse of the economy.

More than ever with today's higher mobility and nuclear family patterns, the need for roots, for identity and to belong will find its realization within the circumference of covenant, within the inner circle gathered around the Lord. For many re-readers of Psa 25, belonging to Yahweh's intimate inner circle will come to a focus at 'the Lord's table', in the sacrament of communion. The specifics of how else Psa 25's spirituality is realized today, the specifics of individual experience and spiritual community, constitute the application of this psalm's dynamics to each reader's real life-setting.

BIBLIOGRAPHY

S Amirtham & R Pryor (eds), *Invitation to the Feast of Life: resources for spiritual formation in theological education*, WCC Programme on Theological Education (Consultation, Indonesia, 1989).

W Brueggemann, *The Message of the Psalms* (Minneapolis: Augsburg) 1984

———,*Israel's Praise* (Philadelphia: Fortress) 1989.

PC Craigie, *Psalms 1–50*, WBC 19 (Waco: Word) 1983.

SJL Croft, *The Identity of the Individual in the Psalms*, JSOTS 44 (Sheffield: JSOT Press) 1987.

J Goldingay, *Theological Diversity and the Authority of the Old Testament* (Grand Rapids: Eerdmans) 1987.

P Kalluveettil, *Declaration and Covenant*, Analecta Biblica 88, (Rome: Biblical Institute Press) 1982.

D Kidner, *Psalms 1–72*, TOTC (London: IVP) 1973.

H-J Kraus, *Psalms 1–59: a commentary* (Minneapolis: Augsburg) 1988; English translation based on the 1978 German 5th edition.

D & M Linn, *Healing Life's Hurts: healing of memories through five stages of forgiveness* (New York: Paulist Press) 1978.

W Wink, *The Bible in Human Transformation* (Philadelphia: Fortress) 1973.

[2]

Walking with God

Three Genesis Prototypes

INTRODUCTION

In this chapter and the next we shall look at the journey metaphor, starting with 'walking with God' and the cluster of ideas associated with it. Simple as 'walking' or the journey metaphor sounds, it exercises a beguiling power over the imagination. As though triggered by an advert for a product that we were not interested in previously but now want immensely, we will suddenly see the metaphor everywhere, in one form or another, shaping our thinking and prompting our behaviour. It may even shape our entire culture and the way we see ourselves and the future. How so?

Consider the way that walking suggests a path or road. That in turn suggests a direction and a destination. Our mind may be set on getting there, or on enjoying the walk. Walking might suggest adventure or survival. The path we imagine might be narrow or broad. It may include twists and turns, hazards and obstacles, uphills and level places. If there are forks in the path, then it implies alternatives and decisions. Some forks may take us to the same destination by alternative routes, but other forks or crossroads may have major consequences in terms of where we end up. The journey may be made alone or in company. It may traverse familiar or uncharted territory. It may be a short distance or exceedingly long and wearisome. There may be significant stages or stops during the journey. Visibility might be good in daylight, or the journey be made at night and require a light. For each of these possibilities there is a cluster of biblical images and English idioms.[1] The links between walking, journeys and stories is

---

[1] For the cluster of biblical words and phrases with Near Eastern cognates and semantic parallels, see Bergman, Haldar-Ringgren, Koch's entry under ' דֶּרֶךְ *derek*', pp. 270–293 in *TDOT*, Vol 3 (1978). From English idiom, compare, for instance, 'the way ahead', 'career path' and wanting or not

strong. Stories were told and still are of epic journeys, solitary journeys on foot, pilgrimages and quests.[2] Poems, songs, and TV documentaries add heroic colour to such journeys and adapt the motifs to our day.[3]

GIANT STEPS FOR MANKIND

Spirituality, or its less religious counterparts, make a profound use of the journey, way and walk cluster of metaphors.[4] Is this proof that Western culture sees itself as the story of progress? Politicians speak of 'the way forward', and protesters march against them, but there are two twentieth century icons that have made a major contribution to the frontier myth and the idea of history-as-progress during this century—space travel and paleoanthropology.

---

wanting 'to go down that road', all using associations of movement with the future and the direction.

[2] In English literature, Bunyan's *Pilgrim's Progress* is a classic example. Notice that progress is built into the idea of pilgrimage in the very title itself; the subtitle defines this as a passage from this world to the celestial destination. Modern allegorical stories such as Tolkien's *Lord of the Rings* or *The Hobbit* and CS Lewis's *Narnia Chronicles* make great use of the journey, quest and destination motifs. In Near Eastern literature, there is the outstanding *Gilgamesh Epic* in which the hero takes to the road in quest of eternal life. Chaucer used a pilgrimage journey to weave together his *Canterbury Tales*.

[3] The exploration journeys of culture heroes like Marco Polo, Columbus and Scott's fated Antarctic expedition have been written about and retraced on camera. Bob Dylan's *Highway 61* Revisited translated journey motifs from the traditions of the Negro spiritual and the Woody Guthrie folksong into the idiom of the Sixties. The Rolling Stones' *Route 66*, and Dire Straits' *Telegraph Road* continued songs of the road within the megaband tradition. The phenomenon of megaband world tours by groups like the rock icons U2 have maintained the myths of heroic endurance or conquest on the road, assisted by truck- loads of electronics, stage props, videos, T-shirts and all the conventions of media hype.

[4] A perusal of the following titles indicates the persistence of the journey imagery: a journal devoted to spirituality entitled *The Way: review of contemporary Christian spirituality* [Philip Sheldrake (gen. ed.), Heythrop College, London]; an exposition of Corinthians by an academic missiologist who recently died in a road accident, DJ Bosch, *A Spirituality of the Road* (Scottdale: Herald Press) 1979; two 'spiritual' guidebooks that are paperback best-sellers, Scott Peck, *The Road less travelled: a new psychology of love, traditional values and spiritual growth* (New York: Simon & Schuster) 1978 and Sheldon Kopp, *If you meet the Buddha on the Road, kill him!* (London: Sheldon) 1974/1991 with chapters on journeys; a political pilgrimage of a contemporary hero Nelson Mandela, *No Easy Walk to Freedom*, Heinemann 1986; two scientific accounts of prehistory by BM Fagan, *The Journey from Eden: the peopling of our world* (London: Thames & Hudson) 1991 and *The Great Journey; the peopling of ancient America* Thames & Hudson, 1987.

The most romantic and mythical images of our time were the footprints on the moon. Neil Armstrong's aphorism 'a small step for man but a giant step for mankind' encapsulates the future via technology. Seeing is believing when planet Earth is a distant sphere in the background and human footprints in Moon dust fill the foreground shot. The second lot of footprints are less well known, but also emotionally charged. They are the footprints left in wet volcanic ash in Laetoli in East Africa made three and a half million years ago by three bipedal hominids, one a youngster, walking in a northerly direction, pausing, and walking on.[5]

In a recent book about human origins, Roger Lewin has drawn attention to the strategy of storytelling in science that draws on the journey motif to describe the evolution of bipedalism. Misia Landau's doctoral research demonstrated that the 'objective' descriptions of bones and skulls by fossil experts consciously and unconsciously incorporated a paradigm of inevitable progress. We may label this storytelling mode in science as 'hermeneutics' because it is a strategy for reading and interpreting the data so as to give them meaning. The more colourful prose belongs to earlier publications. It has patterns that reflect Propp's folktale analyses: 'the hero enters; is challenged by, and overcomes, a series of tests; and finally triumphs.'[6] The story of human evolution is told as a heroic tale using the language of journey. 'Coming to the ground [from the trees] was "a departure", a "decisive step" in human evolution.'[7] 'This notion of an animal committed to a journey with a clearly defined end is frequently expressed overtly in the earlier writings.'[8] A recent example illustrates our walking and travelling motif beautifully:

> In our opinion *Australopithecine afarensis* is very close to a 'missing link.' It possesses a combination of traits entirely appropriate for an animal that had travelled well down the road toward full-time bipedality . . .[9]

There are many other nuances within the storytelling and journey metaphors that Landau uncovered, but her point may be summarised in her own words—'Metaphors cast powerful spells not only

---

[5] Good pictures of the footprints appear in RE Leakey, *The Making of Mankind*, Abacus edition (London: Sphere Books) 1982, pp. 40f.

[6] R Lewin, *Bones of Contention: controversies in the search for human origins*, Penguin, 1989, chap. 2 'The Storytellers', p. 32.

[7] *Bones*, p. 39. Landau citing phrases from anthropologists.

[8] *Bones*, p. 39.

[9] *Bones*, p. 40 quoting from J Stern & R Sussman, 'The Locomotor Behaviour of *Australopithecus afarensis*' *American Journal of Physical Anthropology* 60 (1983) 279–317.

in everyday life but also in science . . . not only do Stern and Sussman speak in metaphor, they also tell a story.'[10]

Genesis tells a story of human origins too. Unlike the scientific disciplines of biology and paleoanthropology in which storytelling and teleological language is out of place, the Genesis story interprets human history on earth in terms of a history that is going somewhere with God. From this Salvation Story, which is not a story of inevitable progress, we shall select three Genesis prototypes. They are not only key figures in the story but crucially for our study of spirituality their lives are described in the metaphor of walking with God.

ENOCH

In 'the book of the generations of Adam', two men stand out—Enoch and Noah. They do so because the editor of Gen 5 breaks into his chronicle of life, paternity and death to give the reader some special information that goes beyond a tally of offspring or years. It interrupts the monotonous conclusion 'and he died'.[11] Noah's birth oracle (5:29) predicts his significant role in the story of mankind, to be continued in chapter 6, but Enoch's life is summed up and concluded within the genealogy itself:

> [21]When Enoch had lived sixty-five years, he became the father of Methuselah. [22]Enoch walked with God after the birth of Methuselah three hundred years, and had other sons and daughters. [23]Thus all the days of Enoch were three hundred and sixty-five years. [24]Enoch walked with God; then he was no more, because God took him.
>
> (Gen 5:22–24)

The words that stand out as a variation from the standard pattern of the genealogical list are '. . . walked with God . . . walked with God; then he was no more, because God took him'. The repetition of 'Enoch walked with God' (*wayyithallēk PN 'et-hā'ĕlōhīm*) is striking. It seems to reflect the editor's intended emphasis—on the

---

[10] *Bones*, p. 40.
[11] If Clines is right to relate the diminishing lifespans and repetitive 'and he died' of the genealogy to von Rad's motif of the spread of sin, then we might extend the element of grace he finds in 'the steady silent expansion of human life' in the genealogies to the extra material on Enoch, where Clines focuses on Noah—DJA Clines, *The Theme of the Pentateuch*, JSOTS 10, (Sheffield: JSOT) 1978, p.67f.

quality of Enoch's life.[12] The first 'walked with God' is a durative action—it lasts three hundred years in v.21. In recurrence in v. 24, the phrase is a summary and summation of Enoch's life before its punctuation point. The punctuation turns out to be a comma, not a full stop. As to the content of that life, we are not informed, though what is missing is significant.[13] Enoch is not a king, a sage, a priest or a discloser of mysteries. There is no mythical ascent to

---

[12] Commentators tend to read Gen 5 in terms of layers of tradition within layers of tradition variously adapted to the canonical context, e.g. P shaping the J-E narrative by utilizing and adapting genealogical lists and supplementary traditions. This source and redactional approach—while quite defensible as a method, especially when dealing with the transmission of discrete genealogical lists within a theological narrative—is liable to an accumulation of fragmenting refinements and speculative hypotheses. Thus Westermann wants to distinguish two distinct layers within v.24b itself, each with its own theological perspective and intention in the two phrases 'then he was no more' and 'because God took him'. He asserts that the latter 'is *certainly* a later statement, an attempt to "rationalize" ' (C Westermann, *Genesis 1–11: a commentary*, 1974 [London: SPCK] 1984, p. 358 italics mine). Of course, this may be Westermann's attempt to rationalize in terms of his own hypotheses. His hermeneutical method in Gen *5:21–24* has as assumptions additional to the documentary hypothesis a theory of repetition as doublets (p. 357) and a theory of concept development—'Only *gradually* did the notion of removal as a state enter into the narrative of removal as an event' (p. 359, italics mine). As expressed, this statement confuses the history of the text and the history of ideas, while both 'histories' are to a large degree speculative reconstructions. Redaction of P material is assumed and the explanation of repetition as subsequent theological glossing is not self-evident. There is no 'certainly' about it. Neither is there much certainty about how much weight to attach to Enoch being the seventh person in the list, or on the correlation between his 365 years and the solar year. See GJ Wenham, *Genesis 1–15*, WBC 1 (Waco: Word) 1987, p. 127.

[13] Rather like the clue in the Sherlock Holmes story where what is absent takes on significance because it runs counter to expectation:

> —Let me draw your attention to the curious incident of the dog in the night-time.
> —The dog did nothing in the night-time.
> —That was the curious incident.

In the normal course of events, the dog should have barked. Given the Mesopotamian background of much of the tradition in Gen 1–11, the Enoch material might have included more exotic details. On these matters, it is silent. This might be a polemic silence.

heaven.[14] Nor does the Enoch of Gen 5 make cosmic journeys to view heaven and hell. He peddles no astronomical theories or eschatological scheme to his contemporaries.[15]

The Enoch verses in Gen 5 are subsumed under a theological heading in narrative form—'When God created humankind . . .'—so their statements are not defined by the genre of genealogy. Gen 5:1bf recapitulates the creation of human beings 'in the likeness of God' from Gen 1:26ff and extends its application to Adam's offspring who are 'in his likeness, according to his image' (5:3b). This means that within Chap. 5 Enoch's intimate association with God is unfolding a dimension of what it means to be created 'in the likeness of God' (5:1), a likeness that is transmitted despite the Fall. Furthermore, the Enoch verses in Gen 5, taken in the context of the canon as a whole, offer a preview of an entire trajectory which culminates in Heb 11:5 and 12:1f, where the pioneers of faith are exalted into the presence of God. What comes through in the descriptions in Hebrews and in Gen 5:24 is the continuity of the relationship with God. Death does not break

---

[14] In the *Sumerian King List*, Etana king of Kish after the Flood is described as 'a shepherd who ascended to heaven' and the *Etana myth* describes his flight on the back of an eagle in quest of 'the plant of giving birth'. The myth goes back the 3rd millennium BC, as we know from its depiction on cylinder seals from the Agade period. See Dalley, *Myths*, pp. 189–202 for an introduction, translation and notes on the *Etana myth*. For the Etana seals, see Collon, *First Impressions*, p. 180 No. 851 & 852; *ANEP*, No. 614f. The *Adapa myth* tells of one of the Seven Sages (*apkallu*) before the Flood, Adapa of the city Eridu, who ascended to heaven but failed to achieve immortality despite being 'holy, pure of hands, the *pašišu*-priest who always tends the rites'. P Steinkeller thinks that an official royal theology from Ur III to the Isin dynasty embraced ascent to heaven by deified kings—'when the divine Shulgi ascended to heaven' (Drehem Ur III tablet). However, the Isin text relates to an issue of pots connected with funeral rites—'(for) the great lamentation, when the king ascended to heaven', which underscores the death of these historical figures from Mesopotamia as well as their deification, both features that are dissimilar to Enoch (*NABU* 1992, No.1, p. 3 No. 4 'Ishbi-Erra's *Himmelfahrt*'). Just as Genesis ascribes walking with God to Enoch and Noah, the Mesopotamian tradition ascribes great sagacity or piety to Adapa and its Flood hero—the same phrase *atra-ḫasīs* 'extra-wise' (or perhaps 'exceedingly pious' in context) is applied both to Adapa and to Atrahasis. See Dalley, *Myths*, p.185 and p. 188 note 2 with AR Millard, 'A New Babylonian "Genesis" Story' *Tyndale Bulletin* 18 (1967) 3–18, p.13f. Millard sees a parallel between the survival of Noah and Atrahasis because of their piety.

[15] Aramaic manuscripts from *1 Enoch* (the apocalyptic book named after its 'author' Enoch, and found among the Dead Sea Scrolls) indicate that some of these esoteric traditions were in written circulation among Jewish sectarian movements in Palestine in the 3rd century BC, though other Enoch material dates well down into the Christian era. See RH Charlesworth (ed), *The Old Testament Pseudepigrapha, Vol. 1 Apocalyptic literature and testaments* (London: Darton, Longman & Todd) 1983, pp. 5ff on *1 Enoch*, and pp. 91ff and 223ff on *2 & 3 Enoch*.

it—neither the death pronounced in the Eden story (Gen 2:17 and 3:19), nor the termination of life in old age.[16]

As to the nuances of 'walked with God', we are left to infer these from the general tenor of the Genesis narrative, or from later occurrences of similar phraseology.[17] If we use as a guideline the intimacy of Eden where God walks (*mithallēk*) in the garden (Gen 3:8f), intending to share the company of the first man and woman, we could see some of this communion surviving or restored in Enoch's walk with God. A similar initiative to God's walking in the garden is displayed in God's 'taking' Enoch. Whereas Eve *took* the fruit to make her godlike and wise (Gen 3:6), and the first human pair were expelled from the garden so that they could not *take* of the tree of life (3:22), God's *taking* Enoch is a divine initiative. It is akin to God's *taking* the man to put him in the garden (2:15) and his *taking* the rib to form woman (2:21)—'takings' that fulfil God's gracious purposes and develop his relationship with humanity.[18]

NOAH

Next we move to Noah who 'found favour in the eyes of the LORD' (Gen 6:8). The information about his lifestyle is packaged under a rubric parallel to that of Gen 5:1a, the generations formula.[19]

---

[16] Because physical death does not ensue instantly after the act of disobedience, as Gen 2:17 appears to say, RWL Moberly argues for a metaphorical understanding of 'death' in Gen 3: 'the true reward of disobedience is personal decay—a kind of dying instantly begins, even though this only becomes apparent in the presence of God' ('Did the Serpent Get it Right?' *JTS* 39.1 [1988] 1–27, p. 17). Wenham sees Gen 3:17–19 in terms of expulsion from Eden, akin to exclusion from the sanctuary and life, and symbolising distance from God (*Genesis 1–15*, p. 83).

[17] For instance, Westermann and Hamilton both incline towards giving weight to the preposition 'with' (*'et*) as indicative of a greater intimacy than walking 'before' (*lip^eney*)—*Genesis 1–11*, p. 358; VP Hamilton, *The Book of Genesis: chapters 1–17*, NICOT (Grand Rapids: Eerdmans) 1990, p.258.

[18] The verb *lāqah*—'to take' is a physical act which implies arms, hands and reaching out. God's acts of taking in Gen 2:15, 21 and 5:24 have this intimate anthropomorphic quality to them. Though the same verb 'take'(*lāqah*) links all these verses mentioned, the comment offered here is a theological one and does not require an intentional connection between these verses in the mind of the writer in Gen 5:24, nor any 'technical' sense for 'take' in 5:24 along the lines of apotheosis (deification), translation or the like.

[19] The *tol^edot* formula appears at Gen 2:4, 5:1, 10:1 and 11:27 marking a new phase in the unfolding story tied in to specific people's lives, except that in Gen 2:4 Heaven and Earth are demythologized and no longer a male and female pair procreating the next generation like Sky god Anu and Earth god Ki in Sumerian myth:

The holy Earth, the pure Earth, beautified herself for holy Heaven,
Heaven, the noble god, inserted his sex into the wide earth,

⁹These are the descendants of Noah. Noah was a righteous man, blameless in his generation; Noah walked with God. ¹⁰And Noah had three sons, Shem, Ham, and Japheth.

(Gen 6:9f)

The same phrase 'walked with God' (*'et-hā'ĕlōhīm hithallēk-PN*) appears here as was used for Enoch. This time it is amplified by the editor's description of Noah as 'a perfectly righteous man'.[20] God offers a similar assessment in direct speech after Noah has fulfilled his divine commission:

²²Noah did this; he did all that God commanded him. ⁷:¹Then the LORD said to Noah, 'Go into the ark, you and all your household, for I have seen that you alone are righteous before me in this generation.'

(Gen 6:22—7:1)[21]

God's assessment—'I have seen'—chimes in with the telling of the story. At key points it refers to God's scrutiny that discerns intentions as well as behaviour:

Let flow the semen of heroes, Trees and Reed into her womb,
The Earthly Orb, the trusty cow, was impregnated with the good semen of Heaven.

(SN Kramer, *From the Poetry of Sumer: creation, glorification, adoration*, London: Univ California Press, 1979, p.30)

20 Commentators attempt to nuance the words *ṣaddiq* 'righteous' and *tāmīm* 'perfect' separately, by relating them to a theological circle such as the priestly one, or to bedouin society and mores, but the syntax itself of 6:9 is ambiguous, as Wenham notes (p. 169), with reference to Cassuto and Job 12:4.

21 According to the documentary hypothesis, Gen 6:9, like 5:24 is the editorial comment of the P strand, as is 6:22, while 7:1 is contributed by the Yahwistic strand (J). Attributing 'blameless' (*tāmīm* 6:9) to P and *ṣaddīq* 'righteous' in 7:1 to J leads Westermann to explain 'righteous' in 6:9 as not original with the Priestly strand—'P appended *tāmīm* to elaborate and clarify'. He locates 'perfect, blameless' within the semantic field of cultic terminology where it describes a perfectly formed and healthy animal suitable for sacrifice. Nevertheless, Westermann can assert that 'both words are in process from a specific to a more general meaning'. In fact, such a sophisticated control over the dating of semantic shifts, when the date of the origins and redactional processes leading to the canonical text before us cannot be accurately determined, seems well beyond such clear cut conclusions. It is not clear how much theological freight from outside the Flood narrative is carried by the words describing Noah's character.

The LORD *saw* that the wickedness of humankind was great in the earth, and that every inclination of the thoughts of their hearts was only evil continually.

(Gen 6:5)

Now the earth was corrupt before God, and the earth was filled with violence. And God *saw* that the earth was corrupt; for all flesh had corrupted its ways upon the earth.

$(6:11)^{22}$

The picture is of a God who watches all that is going on and knows it intimately, even if he is not at any particular moment intervening decisively.[23] As far as the story itself goes, Noah's righteousness is exemplified in his obedience to specific commands from God. At four points Noah carries out what God directed (6:22; 7:5, 9, 16). His sacrifice after the Flood is not specifically commanded but instead stands out as an example of his piety that is well received by God.[24] The 'soothing aroma' is so called

---

[22] 8:21 repeats the assessment of 6:5 forming an inclusio which frames the Flood judgment and highlights God's grace despite the wickedness of the human heart. Henceforth, God will look at the rainbow rather than the wickedness——'When the bow is in the clouds, I will see it and remember the everlasting covenant between God and every living creature of all flesh that is on the earth'(9:16).

[23] Later on the tower and the tower builders' intentions come under close scrutiny from heaven 'and the LORD came down to see the city and the tower which the sons of men had built' (11:5) before God decides to intervene again.

[24] 8:20f contrasts starkly with the theology of sacrifice in the Mesopotamian versions of the Flood story at the very point where the smelling of the sweet odour of the sacrifice draws the Hebrew and extra-biblical versions close together and demands an explanation of their histories and relationship. The Mesopotamian pantheon eat the offering because they are starving and thirsty after being deprived of the regular cult offerings during the Flood. Thus the *Gilgamesh XI* version tells us that

> The gods smelt the fragrance,
> The gods smelt the pleasant fragrance,
> The gods like flies gathered over the sacrifice.
> (Gilg XI, iii, lines 159–161; Dalley, *Myths*, p. 114)

The *Atrahasis* version, source for *Gilgamesh XI*, has the line '[After] they had eaten the offering' (III, v, line 36). The pleasantness of the odour (*eriša ṭāba*) makes more natural sense in the Mesopotamian version because aromatic substances are offered in libation vessels '(essences of ?) reeds, pine and myrtle' (Gilg XI, line 58) and the *Atrahasis* version speaks of 'incense' (*qutrīnu*, III, v, line 41). Noah's sacrifice is a whole burnt offering of birds and animals, with no mention of aromatics or incense, so 'the pleasing odour' (*rēaḥ hanniyhoaḥ*) is pleasant only in a theological sense, that is, fully acceptable to God. 'Pleasing odour'(*rēaḥ niyhōaḥ*) is a phrase used frequently in Leviticus and Numbers. The Genesis version of the Flood also incorporates the distinction of clean and unclean classes of sacrificial bird and animal. The most natural explanation of this feature and the 'pleasing odour' is that the Genesis version of the Flood story has been shaped by the understanding of sacrifice within

because it appeases and pacifies God's anger, leading to God's decision never again to repeat a like judgment. 'soothing' plays on Noah's name, *niyhoah* 'soothing' punning with *nōah* Noah.[25]

To sum up, then, we could say that worship and obedience to God's commands are the way that Noah is characterised in the Flood story. That is his spirituality. He is unlike the colourful characters who are the Flood heroes in the Mesopotamian versions. They also obey their personal deity's directives and so survive the decreed judgment, but they are more humanly appealing. They retch with tension in anticipation of the Flood and weep at the sight of mankind turned back to clay after it. Noah, by contrast, says nothing and feels nothing in the biblical story.[26] The biblical characterisation is completely different, rather flat and lifeless from a literary point of view. Noah has been pared down to the one essential—'Noah did all that the LORD commanded him'. If nothing else, then, 'walking with God', and being a person of complete integrity means obedience to God's directives in this context. We shall have to wait for Job for a literary masterpiece with human emotions.

The Noah story may anticipate a feature of the Abraham cycle, namely the theological concept that one man's complete obedience secures covenant and protection for a wider group, initially in

---

Mosaic Yahwism, and hence dates to the same period as the concepts of acceptable sacrifice in Leviticus. The concepts could be as early as the second half of the 2nd millennium on the basis of analogy with the developed cultic systems known from Hittite, Ugaritic and Syrian (Emar texts) sources from the 14th–12th centuries bc. A common view among Old Testament scholars who do not work with the comparative Near Eastern cultic material is that the Priestly traditions, and their concepts, were composed or compiled as canonical text in Exilic or post-Exilic times, that is the 6th century BC.

[25] Compare the punning in Gen 5:29: 'this person will bring us rest' (*y^enaḥ^amēnū*). See Wenham, *Genesis 1–15*, p. 189f for general comment. The consonants *nh* are basic to the verb and noun variations, a point easier to grasp from the perspective of Semitic roots and Hebrew consonantal text than appears from transliterations into roman alphabet. The verbal root is *nwh*—'to settle, rest'; in the Hiphil 'to provide rest, satisfy, appease'. The noun 'rest, place of rest' (Est 9:17, 2 Chron 6:41) is *nōah* or more frequently with preformative Mem *mānōah*. Mesopotamian prayers regularly hope to calm down the angry heart of the deity so that the god's favour will be restored and express this calming down with the cognate verb in Akkadian—*nâḫu*.

> My ireful god, [tu]rn [your face] to me!
> My goddess full of fury accept my prayer!
> Accept my prayer, let your mind *come to rest*!
> (van der Toorn, *Sin and Sanction*, p. 145, Rev. 9–11)

'Let your mind come to rest' is a smoother English translation of 'let your liver *calm down*' (*linuḫ kabtakki*).

[26] Dalley, *Myths*, p.31 and p. 113, *Atrahasis* III, ii and *Gilgamesh* XI, iii.

Noah's case for those human beings and animals in the ark, but subsequently for all living beings under the sign of the rainbow.[27] With this thought in mind, we pass on to Abraham.

ABRAHAM

In the covenant making of Gen 17 with its sign of circumcision, God addresses Abraham in terms that recall the relationship that Enoch and Noah had with God:

> [1b]'I am El Shadday; walk before me, and be blameless. [2]And I will make my covenant between me and you, and will make you exceedingly numerous.'

'Walk' (*hithallēk*) and 'blameless, perfect' (*tāmīm*) in 17:1b correspond to the same words describing Noah in 6:9.[28] In the light of these correspondences, there is a coherence, as spiritual model, between Enoch, Noah and Abraham. Neither Noah nor Abraham escapes death by being taken by God and hence they do not emulate the outcome of Enoch's spirituality. In this sense Enoch stands alone and others who model spirituality do not match him. In another sense, there is progress. The possibility of walking with God realized only by Enoch among the ancestors broadens out in the book of Genesis with the unfolding of Salvation History. The genealogical chain of the elect line develops through covenant and promise from Noah to Abraham and to Israel.[29] When we reach Deuteronomy, walking before the LORD will have gained specific content in terms of the stipulations of covenant, epitomized by the Ten Commandments, and will be presented to the whole nation Israel as a way of life in the promised land.

---

[27] A Christian re-reading of the Flood story and Abraham stories in terms of obedience, covenant and extension of blessing would naturally run along the trajectory lines that 'one man's act of righteousness leads to justification and life for all . . . by the one man's obedience the many will be made righteous' (Rom 5:18b,19b).

[28] According to source theory, both passages are from the P material and so too the Enoch verses. For some commentators this affords evidence of a flashback technique consciously employed—so S McEvenue, *The Narrative Style of the Priestly Writer*, Analecta Biblica 50 (Rome: Biblical Institute Press) 1971, p.39.

[29] See BT Dahlberg, 'On recognizing the unity of Genesis' *Theology Digest* 24 (1977) 360–367, which influenced Clines, *The Theme of the Pentateuch*. These literary studies of Dahlberg and Clines substantiate the theological conclusions based on the canonical form of Genesis. They confirm the fundamental quality of the promise–fulfilment motif in Genesis, its development between Genesis and Exodus, and its extent in the Pentateuch.

THE INTERPRETATION OF A BLAMELESS LIFE

Before Deuteronomy, our attempts to fill in the meaning or the lifestyle involved in 'walk before me, and be blameless' in Gen 17:1b will involve making some hermeneutical decisions. We might look in Chap. 17 alone, or in the whole book of Genesis, in P material in Genesis, or in the Abraham material that we assume was part of the Abraham cycle before Chap. 17 was added, or in chapters 12–16 that now precede chap. 17, or in Priestly material elsewhere in the Pentateuch. We could range more widely in Hebrew usage throughout the Old Testament regardless of genre with the aid of a Hebrew concordance. A regard for semantics might preserve us from the hazards of word studies. These are the hermeneutical procedures adopted by the commentators whether they are made explicit or not. We cannot diverge from our chosen trajectory to examine each hermeneutical issue involved in handling each text as we go along, but at this point it will be helpful to point out how much our hermeneutical assumptions contribute to our theological reading of a text.

To give one specific example, G von Rad makes a radical distinction between walking '*with* God' in Gen 6:9 and walking '*before* God' in Gen 17:1, ostensibly on the basis of Hebrew semantics, that is, on the difference in prepositions used here. In reality, his comments are based on a theory of epochs or aeons, and a theological interpretation: 'Noah, as the last member of the first aeon and the beginner of a new age, is the last one of whom such a thing can be said theologically. Abraham could only walk *before* God (ch.17.1).'[30] He implies by 'can be said' that his comment expounds the Priestly tradition's viewpoint. This is dubious. von Rad repeats this interpretation in his comment on Gen 17:1 where he excludes 'moral perfection' for *tāmīm* with the following explanation—'not, to be sure, in the sense of moral perfection but rather in relationship to God. It signifies *complete, unqualified surrender*' (italics mine).[31] The latter phrase seems to reflect a Lutheran spirituality rather than a P spirituality.

Commentators on Gen 6:9 often begin their interpretation of *tāmīm* on the basis of source analysis (P in the JEDP paradigm). This means giving *tāmīm* a nuance somehow related to its semantic field in cultic texts—'[*tāmīm*] does not mean "perfect" in an absolute (ie. moral) sense . . . means the condition of a man (or a sacrifice) which *conforms to the cult* and is thereby pleasing to God' (italics mine).[32] So von Rad.

---

[30] G von Rad, *Genesis* (London: SCM) 3rd rev. ed., 1972, p. 126.
[31] *Genesis*, p. 198.
[32] *Genesis*, p. 126.

A double confusion threatens here. A Reformed doctrine of human depravity is obligated to deny that anyone is righteous, let alone absolutely perfect. This truth, central to the Reformed (Lutheran) doctrine of grace and the inadequacy of works, is not demonstrably the concern of the Hebrew narratives at this point, namely at Gen 6:9 and Gen 17:1. Secondly, animals for sacrifice are indeed *tāmīm* by being without physical deformity or disease. This kind of acceptability involves no moral quality. This surely means that *tāmīm* acceptability—priest or animal being free of *physical* deformity—is no help for interpreting *tāmīm* in Gen 6:9 or Gen 17:1. von Rad wants to replace physical perfection in the cultic context with 'pleasing to God', but he also wants to exclude moral faultlessness. It is perplexing to consider how this can be achieved. Instead, we must surely assume that Noah and Abraham are acceptable to God because they live right.

Westermann avoids the nuance of 'cultic piety' in his comment on *tāmīm* in Gen 17:1, but then also excludes a moral nuance—'it has neither moral or religious echo, but is consciously secular'.[33] 'Non-cultic', 'natural', to do with everyday life is what Westermann has in mind for 'walking before God', but why this has no moral resonance is unexplained:

> By the *hithallēk lipney* God orders Abraham (now representing Israel) to live his life before God in such a way that every single step is made with reference to God and every day experiences him close at hand. This is not meant to be some sort of lofty demand; it is something quite natural, as Psa 139 prays in reflection and wonder.

He further interprets *tāmīm* as though he is giving it its meaning in the text. In fact he is recontextualizing the concept into its modern dynamic equivalent: 'P wants to say thereby that "belonging to God is in proper order only when it is without reservation and unconditional" '. 'Without reservation and unconditional' sounds very much like von Rad's 'complete, unqualified surrender'. Westermann, von Rad and others sound as though they are describing a spirituality of the heart which draws its nuances from their own church traditions.

This little excursion into the standard commentaries demonstrates how difficult it is for modern commentators confronted with terse statements in the text to recover original nuances or to separate the author's intended meaning, as deduced using various analytical tools, from their own theologically preferred understandings. Everyone brings things to the text, if not a source theory, then a concept of true spirituality.

---

[33] Westermann, *Genesis 12–36*, p. 259.

One could go outside the text of Gen 6:9 and 17:1 to give content to *tāmīm* in a different way. It seems likely enough that *ṣaddiq* and *tāmīm* conveyed to Hebrew readers the qualities of conduct that God and others recognized as upright, moral, socially responsible and devout. Job is just such a person, for God describes him as 'a man blameless and upright (*'īš tām wᵉyāšar*) who fears God and turns away from evil' (1:8 and 2:3). Job himself echoes this in 12:4, using the words (*ṣaddiq tāmīm*) that appear in Gen 6:9. Job illustrates the content of a life of 'perfect righteousness' in chaps. 29 and 31. These lines paint a portrait of patriarchal integrity before God and community, worked out in social conduct. Job's righteousness certainly included religious practices (sacrifice and intercession—Job 1:5f and 42:8f), but chaps. 29 and 31 concentrate on moral and social conduct. Later on we will suggest an additional background for *tāmīm* and the language of acceptability with God.

COVENANT RELATIONSHIP

We may move our discussion along now in two ways, firstly by noticing the cluster of terminology that connects 'walking before' the LORD with covenant concepts, and secondly by noticing the element of journeying, the physical act of walking, that is introduced into Salvation History with the life of Abraham.

In Gen 17:1 command and promise are bound together: 'walk . . . be blameless' and 'I will . . . I will . . .'. In fact, there are a whole series of commands given to Abraham in the cycle of stories about him, and there are whole clusters of promises—material blessing, an heir, a land, numerous descendants, a royal dynasty, an international status. We would see the core of the promise in the relationship with God. That is true for Gen 17 because immediately following the imperatives is the promise 'I will make my covenant between me and you.' It precedes the promise of being made great through numerous offspring. God's brief speech in Gen 17:1f is programmatic. The rest of chap. 17 expands on it. The expansion is introduced in the words 'As for me, this is my covenant with you . . .' and there follows an elaboration of the promises and the stipulation of circumcision.[34]

---

[34] Circumcision is itself the 'sign of the covenant between me and you' (v. 11) in the same way that the rainbow functioned as a sign. The sign of circumcision —sign being an objective visible symbol in all three covenants—is closer to the sabbath sign of the Sinai covenant in that it must be implemented by the human partner in order to maintain the covenant relationship. Compare Gen 9:9–17 with its a threefold repetition of 'sign' (*'ōt*) and a sevenfold repetition of covenant (*bᵉrīt*) and the Sabbath sign in Exod 31:13,17. The same Hebrew word *'ōt* is used for all three covenant signs, and the language associating

The essence of what is offered is conveyed in the words 'to be God to you'.[35]

> I will establish my covenant between me and you, and your offspring after you throughout their generations, for an everlasting covenant, to be God to you and to your offspring after you.
>
> (Gen 17:7)

God and Abraham are bound together in a relationship involving pledge and commitment.[36] This does not imply equality, for the relationship is at God's initiative and on his terms, but God commits himself to the relationship and to the promises he has made.

'sign' with 'covenant' strongly links the two: 'observing the sabbath throughout their generations, as a perpetual covenant' (Exod 31:16b); 'So shall my covenant be in your flesh an everlasting covenant' (Gen 17:13b). The same phrase 'perpetual covenant' ($b^e r\bar{i}t$ $^{\circ}\bar{o}l\bar{a}m$) is used for all three covenants—Gen 9:16, 17:13 and Exod 31:16.

[35] This formula appears in Lev 26:12 which speaks of God sharing in the life of the Israelites, using a walking metaphor: 'And I will walk among you ($hithallaktiy$ $b^e t\bar{o}k^e kem$), and will be your God, and you shall be my people.' Compare Exod 6:7 and Deut 29:13.

[36] The debate about the etymology of 'covenant' $b^e r\bar{i}t$ and its antiquity can be settled by Near Eastern texts offering cognates and semantic equivalents. The noun brt was used in 2nd millennium Syria and in Egypt (as a loan word) for 'contract'. It was also transposed into religious language in the 2nd millennium to describe a relationship with deity, as we know from the Hurrian hymn at Ugarit describing the high god as 'El/God of covenant, El/God of judgement,' ($^{\circ}l$ brt $^{\circ}l$ dn), a phrase which has Hebrew equivalents in 'El/God of covenant', 'lord of covenant' ($^{\circ}\bar{e}l$ $b^e r\bar{i}t$, $ba^{\circ}al$ $b^e r\bar{i}t$) applied to a Shechem deity in Jdg 9:46, 8:33, 9:4. Its semantic equivalent in Akkadian is $riksu$ which as a physical object is a 'fetter, bond' (AHw, 984f and $rikistu$ $riki\check{s}tu$ $rikiltu$) and is used aptly as a metaphor in treaty texts of the 2nd millennium onwards to describe the bond created between the parties forming the political alliance—'binding the bond' ($riksu$ $rak\bar{a}su$; AHw, 945ff). On Hittite-Ugarit bonds, see LR Fisher(ed), *Ras Shamra Parallels: Vol. 2*, Analecta Biblica 50 (Rome: PIB) 1975, chap. 6 by FB Knutson, 'Literary Genres in PRU IV', pp. 155ff. Of course, the background of a word or phrase does not determine its exact nuance in context, especially if the borrowing is cross-cultural and the idiom develops beyond its starting point. Fetters are imposed, but that is not necessarily the case for treaties and covenants. On the Near Eastern background of $b^e r\bar{i}t$, see KA Kitchen, 'The Fall and Rise of Covenant, Law and Treaty' *Tyndale Bulletin* 40 (1989) 118–135, p. 122f or with fuller detail 'Egypt, Ugarit, Qatna and Covenant' *Ugarit Forschungen* 11 (1979) 453–464. The fundamental and detailed work on semantic parallels between Israel's covenant language and Near Eastern treaty language is available in M Weinfeld's works—'The Loyalty Oath in the Ancient Near East' *Ugarit Forschungen* 8 (1976) 379–414; *Deuteronomy and the Deuteronomic School*, (Oxford: Clarendon) 1972; '$b^e r\bar{i}t$', pp. 253–279 in GJ Botterweck & H Ringgren (eds), *Theological Dictionary of the Old Testament, Vol. 1* (Grand Rapids: Eerdmans) rev.ed. 1977; '$B^e r\bar{i}t$—Covenant vs. Obligation' *Biblica* 56 (1975) 120–128 for a review of E Kutsch.

This commitment from God's side is more dramatically conveyed in the covenant ritual of ch. 15 where the 'smoking firepot and a flaming torch passed between' the dismembered pieces of the animals and birds. The most plausible interpretation of this happening, which the text labels as a covenant-making occasion (v. 18), is that Yahweh, symbolized by the 'smoking firepot and flaming torch' or carrying them, acts out the Near Eastern role of oath-taker and alliance partner.[37]

The oath of alliance was dramatized by self-curses. These would come into effect if the oath were broken in the future. The dramatized self-curse took the form of cutting of a sheep's throat , or the dismemberment of donkeys, goats, puppies or lambs in other cultures, or a symbolic gesture of touching the throat. Touching the throat even has a distant equivalent in the schoolyard gesture and oath 'Cross my heart and hope to die'.[38] The characteristic 'cut a covenant' (*kārat bᵉrīt*) in Hebrew and its widespread semantic equivalents in Aramaic, Phoenician and Greek probably derive from the cutting and dismembering rites of treaty making.[39]

In Gen 17, the particular cutting rite is circumcision. If circumcision in this particular context of covenant-making draws symbolic associations from self-curse rites enacted at treaty-making

---

[37] There are dissenting voices. GF Hasel's 'covenant ratification sacrifice' represents a step away from Near Eastern self-curse oaths ('The Meaning of the Animal Rite in Gen 15' *JSOT* 19 [1981] 61–78) and Wenham moves further away ('A Response to GF Hasel' *JSOT* 22 [1982] 134–137 and *Genesis 1–15*, p.332). Another example of the self-binding oath by God committing himself to what is promised is represented in the words of Gen 22:16: 'By myself I have sworn, says the LORD . . . I will indeed bless you . . .'

[38] Sacrifice is a separate accompaniment to treaty and covenant ratification in Israel and elsewhere, but the widespread use of self-curse formulae and rites from the 2nd millennium onwards is well documented and better explains the rite in Gen 15—see Weinfeld, *UF 11*, p. 400ff 'Dramatization of the Curses' and 'Covenantal Sacrifices'.

[39] See P Kalluveettil, *Declaration and Covenant*, Analecta Biblica 88 (Rome: Biblical Institute Press) 1982, p. 9 note 14 and Weinfeld, *TDOT*, p.259 and *Deut School*, p. 74f note 2. They support this understanding and list the variant phrases involving 'cutting' to establish covenant or alliance. It is clear that 'cut' is applied 'illogically' in the way that the metaphor develops. Thus, to 'cut the *bᵉrīt*', instead of 'severing' the bond, implements it. In Hebrew, Aramaic, Phoenician and Greek you can also 'cut oaths' which is an elliptical way of referring to forming covenant or alliance. 'Cutting oaths' underlines the importance of the verbal element, the oath, in treaty and covenant making . There is, of course, no divorcing of verbal and ritual elements in Near Eastern religion, nor any equivalent to a Western, Protestant, low-church tradition which relegates ritual to a level of secondary importance.

occasions, there is a background for the fate of the covenant breaker. Circumcision then has two sides to it. It is part of covenant-making and a preview of covenant breaking.[40] Cutting off a part, the foreskin, would symbolize a cutting off from the covenant group, as Gen 17:14 states: 'any uncircumcised male who is not circumcised in the flesh of his foreskin shall be cut off from his people; he has broken my covenant.' The physical act of cutting foreshadows the metaphorical 'cutting off'. Because the rite belongs in the context of covenant-making, the circumcision of male children thereafter extends the act of inclusion within the covenant community down the generations. The sign that marks the penis aptly associates the transmission of biological life with the transmission of the covenant relationship.

There is one further dimension to the biblical covenant language and the conceptual analogies with Near Eastern customs that is worth mentioning here because it returns us to our motif of 'walking before God'. The prominence of the promise and blessing elements in the covenant with Abraham, and the gift of land, in particular, points to an analogy not only with Hittite treaty-making where royal guarantees are made but also to broad analogies with another category of document, namely the royal grant. In royal grants a king confers a reward on a loyal servant. This might take the form of a gift of land, or exemption from taxes on land already held.[41] The royal grant uses the language of bestowal, loyalty and faithfulness, and Genesis echoes these terms.

The Assyrian king Ashurbanipal describes his loyal chief of fodder supplies in the following language before granting him tax

---

[40] While this double-sided symbolism is not proven, it is not unlikely since symbols have the ability to combine seemingly contradictory concepts—e.g. looking at the bronze snake, the source of death, produces life (Num 21:9); bread and wine symbolize food and life, as well as death and mutilation; baptism symbolizes death and burial as well as new life.

[41] Sources are listed in Weinfeld, *Deut School*, p. 74. Second millennium treaty texts define boundaries and list cities and other assets in the course of establishing the treaty with a vassal king. Kassite and Babylonian *kudurrus* (boundary stones) define fields awarded to individuals and their heirs. Both treaties and grants are royal edicts and use curse formulae on violators, but in the case of the grants the curses are directed at the recipient's enemies. See Weinfeld 'Covenant of Grant in the Old Testament and in the Ancient Near East' *JAOS* 90 (1970) 184–203 and 'Addenda' *JAOS* 92.3 (1972) p.468f for details. The Neo-Assyrian royal grants confer agricultural assets, or confirm their owners in them with tax exemptions—see JN Postgate, *Neo-Assyrian Royal Grants and Decrees*, Studia Pohl 1 (Rome: BIP) 1961, p. 2ff for a discussion of the Assyrian grant types.

exemptions on land in perpetuity. In a rather literalistic translation this reads:

    16 his heart is totally toward his lord
    17 before me he stood in truthfulness
    18 he walked about with integrity
    19 in the midst of my palace he grew up with a good name
    20 he kept the watch for my kingship[42]

The king speaks of his rewarding 'the one who is reverent, who keeps his royal word' (L. 9). So what we have is a correlation of royal gift and devoted service. This combination of gift and conduct, obedience and reward is reflected in the phrases that describe the patriarch's relationship with God. Line 18, in particular, offers semantic parallels to Gen 17:1b since the cognate Akkadian verb 'walk' is used in a similar metaphorical manner to refer to behaviour before a king or god.[43] The same combination of verb, preposition and description of quality is applied to 'walking about properly before' the deity.[44] The enduring quality of the gift is also common to the treaty, the grant and the 'perpetual covenant'. All of these speak in terms of transmission down the generations:'sons and grandsons', 'to your seed', 'for ever'.[45]

---

[42] Postgate, *Grants*, p. 28, No. 9 translated by him on p. 36 and by Weinfeld, *Deut School*, p. 75. Line 18 reads *ittallaku šalmiš*—'he walked to and fro perfectly', 'acted properly' (CAD S, p. 255 *šalmiš*). The Akkadian verb *alāku*—'to walk, go' is the cognate of Hebrew *hālak*—'to walk, go'.

[43] See *CAD A, alāku*, p. 325, b) 'to live, act' and the noun *alaktu*, p. 297 2. 'behaviour, customary ways, activities, experiences' . A votive gift to a deity is made in the hope of a good career path in the palace—'for his serving the king properly' *šalmeš italluki maḫar šarrišu* (Warka AO.7038 referred to in an article on *kudurru* grants by Thureau-Dangin, RA 16 (1919), p. 123; a Middle Babylonian seal carries the same phrase (*RA* 19 [1922], p. 86 line 10, translated in *CAD A*, p. 326 *alāku* 6b 1').

[44] The Hebrew verb 'walk' *hālak*, preposition 'before' *lipᵉney* and description 'perfectly' *tāmīm* correspond to the Akkadian *alāku, maḫar* and ŠALMIŠ which are used for the presence of king or god—'before your divinity let me walk properly' *ina maḫar ilūtika šalmeš littallak*, a Sumerian-Akkadian bilingual (BA 10/1 69 No.1, rev. 5f; *CAD S*, p. 255). In other contexts *šalmiš* means 'safely, securely, in good condition' (*CAD S*, p. 255), but here in the context of on-going conduct before god or king it takes on a religious or ethical nuance, meaning what is fitting and will be approved. See the references to Psa 101:2 'I will walk with integrity of heart (ʾethallēk bᵉtōm lᵉbābiy) within my house' and Prov 10:9 'Whoever walks in integrity (hōlēk bᵉtōm) walks securely' (Weinfeld, *Deut School*, p. 76 note 2).

[45] Gen 17:7 'and your offspring after you throughout their generations, for an everlasting covenant, to be God to you and your seed' (cf. v. 9 and Gen 13:15). This corresponds to the wording of donation texts from Ugarit in Akkadian and Ugaritic: 'to PN and to his sons for ever', *ana PN ăna mārēšu adi dārīti* and *wlbnh ʿd ʿlm* (PRU III, RS 16.132:27f, RS 16.162: 10 *adi dāriš*, and *PRU* II, RS 16.382). The Babylonian *kudurrus* express perpetuity with various phrases : 'to

The idiom of unswerving loyalty in royal service is an idiom that applies to walking with God. 'Walking before', 'being perfect', 'keeping God's charge' are all aspects of a bonded relationship.[46] Thus in the biblical prospect and retrospect, we find the following language:

'Walk before me and be blameless'

(Gen 17:1b)

'The LORD before whom I walk . . .

(Gen 24:40)

'I will fulfil the oath that I swore to your father Abraham . . . because Abraham obeyed my voice and kept my charge, my commandments, my statutes, and my laws'

(Gen 26:3b & 5)

'The God before who my ancestors Abraham and Isaac walked . . .'

(Gen 48:15)

The idiom of 'walking in righteous or loyalty' is already transferred from a human plane to walking before the gods in righteousness or loyalty by 2nd millennium Hittite texts in Hittite language. The idiom is not confined to the Semitic group or the Assyrian grant texts only, but like all the semantic parallels between treaties, law codes and grants seems to have had a long cross-cultural history, starting early and lasting for centuries.[47] It does seem plausible, then, to invoke this sort of semantic parallel from royal edicts to assist us in catching the nuances of Gen 17:1b.

The Assyrian grant text goes on to specify that when Baltaya dies, 'they shall bury him where he dictates, and he shall lie where it was his wish' (lines 55f). Anyone who disturbs Baltaya's grave is cursed. Abraham, of course, was buried in the cave in Machpelah along with Sarah. They were joined later by Isaac, Rebekah, Leah

---

distant days' (*ana ūmī ṣâṭī* or *ana ṣâṭi*), 'for time eternal' (*ana ūmē dārûti*)—see *CAD S*, 116ff *ṣâṭu*. Treaties are also 'for ever' theoretically—'it is an eternal order, established by the sun god (of Egypt) and the storm god (of Hatti) (*CAD D*, p. 114 *dārītu* 'continuity, lastingness', KBo 1, 7:24); 'the sun god (of Egypt) and the storm god (of Hatti) [remain] in good peace forever', (*CAD D*, p. 113f *dāriš*, KBo 1, 24:12) *dārû*. For references to the Hittite, Aramaic and Assyrian sources, see Weinfeld, *Deut School*, p. 78f and 'The Loyalty Oath' *UF* 11, p. 391f. But note Kalluveettil's evaluation of Weinfeld: 'these texts do not cite his [Abraham's] fidelity as a motive for Yahweh's promise—as the ANE decrees of royal grants invariably do. Rather, promise invites loyalty.' (*Declaration*, pp. 180ff).

[46] The overlap of phraseology between court language (attested in Akkadian documents) and language used about Abraham and David is documented in Weinfeld, *Deut School*, p. 75ff.

[47] References are given to the Hittite treaties in *JAOS* 92.3, p. 468.

and Jacob (Gen 49:29ff). The book of Genesis ends with Jacob's funeral cortège wending its way from Egypt to Machpelah—'thus his sons did for him as he had instructed them' (Gen 50:12). Jacob/Israel and the promise lie in the burial plot awaiting the full terms of the divine land grant to come to their fulfilment.

THE JOURNEY MOTIF

As well as 'walking before' God, Abraham travels. He starts from Haran in Gen 12, but viewed in retrospect the journey began a generation earlier with the migration from Babylonia.[48] In Gen 15, this journey westwards is recounted in a special way. We notice this when Gen 15 and Exod 20 are read in tandem:

> I am the LORD who brought you from Ur of the Chaldeans, to give you this land to possess
>
> (15:7)
>
> I am the LORD your God, who brought you out of the land of Egypt, out of the house of slavery; you shall have no other gods before me
> . . .
>
> (Exod 20:2)

The same verb is used and the same weight rests on God's self identification, 'I am Yhwh'.[49] By themselves these parallel statements might not convey more than the continuity between the God worshipped by the ancestors and the God worshipped by later Israelites. The Exodus narrative states this theological continuity forcefully in telling the story of Moses' encounter at the burning bush (Exod 3:6) and in the re-commissioning of chap 6:2–

---

[48] Gen 11:28, 31.

[49] The Hiphil Participle form of *yāṣa'*—'to go forth, go out'. Variants of the first person pronoun 'I' (*aniy* and *anōkiy*) introduce the clause in each case. There is something of a consensus among commentators on the implicit typology between exodus from Ur and the Exodus from Egypt, despite an impressive disagreement about the JEDP source analysis of Gen 15, its composition and the genre and dating of its component parts. On which, see Westermann's review, 'The History of Exegesis of Gen. 15' (*Gen 12–36*, pp. 214ff.) On the typological parallels, compare the following three statements by Wenham, Westermann and Moberly: 'The parallel with the exodus from Egypt emphasizes once again how the life of Abraham foreshadows the history of Israel, a theme that is explicit in the subsequent dialogue' (Wenham, *Genesis 1–15*, p. 335); '. . .very strikingly recalls Ex 20:2; Deut. 5:6; and Lev 25:38 . . . the bringing of Israel out of Egypt and the grant of land is the background to the formula used here' (Westermann, *Gen 12–36*, p. 22); 'The point of this choice of language is presumably typological . . . Abraham in some sense personifies and embodies Israel's experience' (RWL Moberly, *The Old Testament of the Old Testament: patriarchal narratives and Mosaic Yahwism*, OBT [Minneapolis: Fortress] 1992, p. 143).

8.[50] But there is more to the parallel between the Genesis and Exodus passages than the name Yahweh and his identity with El Shadday. Gen 15 previews the Exodus and the occupation of the Promised Land in two senses. Abraham is told about the years in Egypt and the return to Palestine (vv. 13ff). This is the one sense. The other is the typological preview of Exodus and occupation of Canaan offered by Abraham's own life and travels.

A cluster of motifs contribute to this typological parallel between Abraham's experience and Israel's. For instance, Abraham visits Egypt in a time of famine, the pharaoh and his household are struck with plagues and Abraham leaves Egypt, moving into the arid Negeb, but prospers in livestock, silver and gold (Gen 12:10–13:2).[51] The Israelites did not leave Egypt empty-handed but despoiled the Egyptians, taking jewelry of silver and gold into the desert as well as much livestock (Exod 12:35,38). Abraham is instructed by God to 'possess' Canaan: 'Rise up, walk through the length and the breadth of the land, for I will give it to you' (13:17). This provides a preview of the occupation of the land under Joshua, perhaps even of the north, centre and southern thrusts of the Conquest, if we consider Abraham's altar building as claiming the land for Yahweh.[52]

The journeys of Abraham are very much part of his walk with God. In this case, the metaphor of walking and the life experience match closely. This is more obvious from the use of the Hebrew root *hālak*—'to walk, go'—in significant places than it is in the English translations where 'walk' and 'go' are different verbs.[53] What begins with the command, 'Go from your country and your

---

[50] These two disclosures are often distributed between three sources (JEP), though not with complete agreement, and Exod 6 is often construed as a doublet of Exod 3. We follow the translation and interpretation of 6:3b that takes it to mean that El Shadday was the ancestral name of God and that Yahweh is a new name marking a new phase in Salvation History. This implies that Gen 15:7 is written with hindsight, in the light of the Exodus and is expressing the theological conviction that the covenant God of Sinai was operative in the pre-history of the nation. See GJ Wenham, 'The Religion of the Patriarchs', pp. 157–188 in DJ Wiseman (ed), *Essays on the Patriarchal Narratives* (Leicester: IVP) 1980. On Exod 6 as the narrative sequel rather than the narrative doublet of Exod 3, and on the JEDP paradigm relating to Exod 3 and 6, see the carefully nuanced discussion of Moberly, *OTOT*, chap. 2, pp. 36–67 in particular.

[51] See M Fishbane, *Biblical Interpretation in Ancient Israel* (Oxford: Clarendon) 1985, pp. 375f 'Thus, in all these various forms Abraham came to serve as the prototype of Israel for later generations'.

[52] See Moberly, *OTOT*, pp. 142–146 'The Use of Typology' for an overview of the motifs and implications.

[53] The root *hālak*—'walk, go' is used in places significant to the story and theology of Abraham's life in 12:1, 13:17, 17:1, 22:2, 24:40 and 48:15, for instance.

kindred and your father's house to the land that I will show you'
(Gen 12:1) is completed by the moves around Canaan, and, as we
shall see, by the obedience that is tested to the limit in the
command to sacrifice all the promises and render the whole life
journey meaningless by offering up Isaac (Gen 22).

The obedience motif is highlighted in the retrospective on
Abraham embedded in the Isaac story. It is very clear from the
phrasing that Israel's need to obey the stipulations of the Sinai
covenant shapes the way that Abraham's life journey is summar-
ized:

> . . . Abraham obeyed my voice and kept my charge, my command-
> ments, my statutes, and my laws
>
> (Gen 26:5)

There is no point in trying to distinguish 'commandments,
statutes and laws '(*miṣwot ḥuqqōt tōrōt*) because there are no data
given in the Abraham cycle that correspond to the detailed
stipulations of later covenants, whether one thinks of the Sinai
Covenant Code of Exodus, the Holiness Code of Leviticus, or the
exhortations of Deuteronomy.[54] Rather, Gen 26:5 is inviting
Israelites to see in Abraham a prototypical covenant keeper. In
retrospect, Abraham succeeded. His obedient walk before God
ensured that the promises were transmitted and could come to
fulfilment.

Yet the Abraham narrative still asks the question—was Abraham's obedience effortless, without cost and a foregone conclusion? How we answer that depends on how many deviations, or at
least detours, we read into the Hagar episodes, his policy of
passing Sarah off as his sister and some of the nuances of wording
in the narratives. In one sense, every command that God issued to
Abraham was a test and every choice a next step. On Abraham's
decisions hinged the unfolding of covenant relationship and
promised blessings. Would he linger on in Haran? Would he
traverse Canaan and erect altars to this particular God alone?
Would he believe God and attempt to father a child with Sarah?
Would he assimilate with his Canaanite allies by accepting
marriage-bound alliances, or look elsewhere for a bride for Isaac

---

[54] This pleonasm is found in the covenant renewal context of Deut 11:1,
including the phrase 'keeping the charge' (*šāmar mišmᵉrōt*), a phrase which
belongs to the wider vocabulary of royal service, finding a close semantic
parallel in the Akkadian phrase *naṣāru maṣṣartu* which also occurs in the
Assyrian tax exemption for Baltaya, discussed previously, and commented on
by Weinfeld (*Deut School*, p. 75 and notes 1, 2 & 4). Weinfeld denies that Gen
26:5 is deuteronomic in a source-critical sense. See *CAD M 1*, *maṣṣartu* for
Akkadian references.

and a future for his ethnic group? Would he sub-divide the
Promised Land to accommodate his sons by Hagar and Keturah?

GENESIS 22—A TESTING JOURNEY

If there are decisions and responses that face Abraham as the
narrative unfolds, none surpasses the dramatic climax engineered
by God himself to force on Abraham a choice that still horrifies the
reader.

> 'Take your son, your only son Isaac, whom you love, and go to the
> land of Moriah, and offer him there on one of the mountains that I
> shall show you.'
>
> (Gen 22:2)

Here we shall focus only on the contribution made by the journey
motif to this pivotal moment in Salvation History.[55] This journey
sounds very much like the other journeys, with the command to
leave country, kin and family and go to 'the land that I will show
you' (12:1).[56] But how different. The physical movement contributes to the narrative tension and the spiritual dynamic. Verse 3
begins the saga of Abraham's response—'Abraham got up early in
the morning . . . he arose and he went . . . '. Verse 5 contrasts the
here of the spot where the servants stop and the there of the
destination: 'but I and the lad will go there and worship and return
to you'. Verse 6 focuses on the lonely pair—'and the two of them
went on together' in a silence broken only by Isaac's question.
This is terminated by 'and the two of them went on together',
verse 8. The phrase of verses 6 and 8 on either side of the question
highlights the question, the answered but unanswerable question.

---

[55] There are many full length literary and theological treatments of this
chapter—see conveniently Moberly, 'The Earliest Commentary on the
Akedah' *VT* 38 (1988) 302–323 and JL Crenshaw, *A Whirlpool of Torment:
Israelite traditions of God as an oppressive presence*, OBT 12 (Philadelphia:
Fortress) 1984, pp. 9–29 'A Monstrous Test: Gen 22' for further references.

[56] Westermann concurs with NH Sarna in thinking it probable that the
command 'Get yourself to the land of Moriah' (22:2b) echoes 'get yourself
from your land' in 12:1, since the *lek-lᵉkā* construction is used in both (*Gen 12–
26*, p. 357). Sarna finds several other affinities and concludes that 'The Torah,
then, has used the ancient Akedah tale to encase the account of the spiritual
odyssey of Abraham within a literary framework . . .' (*Understanding Genesis:
the heritage of biblical Israel* [New York: Schocken Books] 1966, p. 161, italics
mine). Compare too R Davidson's comment: 'When Abraham left
Mesopotamia, according to Genesis 12:1, he was sacrificing his past, leaving
country and kinsmen, sustained by a promise; now he is being asked to
sacrifice the future, the God-promised future.'—*The Courage to Doubt:
exploring an Old Testament theme* (London: SCM) 1983, chap 3 'Faith on
Pilgrimage—the patriarchal traditions', p.51.

The repetition also imparts an inexorable forward momentum. Finally, the three–day journey is over. They have reached what Abraham saw 'from a distance' (v.4): 'and they came to the place . . .' (v.9a). The moment of truth can be postponed no longer.

The dénouement is followed by the return journey: 'and Abraham returned to his servants and they arose and they went on together' (v.19). This verse repeats the now sonorous phrase 'they went on together' (vv. 6, 8, 19). This time it is on the other side of the ordeal. 'Returned' signals the fulfilment of the 'we will return to you' of verse 5b. With hindsight, the return to the servants of v.19 adds a dimension of faith to the predicted return. Listeners know that the original statement 'we will return' masks the true nature of the journey, if Abraham was to comply with the test and kill his son. The meaning of the statements 'we will return' and 'God will see to the lamb for sacrifice himself' thus take on another level of meaning in the light of the test passed. They have more truth in them than Abraham originally knew.[57]

There have been two journeys in the story. There is the long journey from Beersheba to Moriah and back (v. 3 and v. 19). Enclosed between this departure and return, is the longer journey still of father and son alone to the top of the mountain.[58] The whole spiritual journey of chap. 22 is described by von Rad with a rather appropriate metaphor:

> . . .it concerns something much more frightful than child sacrifice. It has to do with a road out into Godforsakenness, a road on which Abraham does not know that God is only testing him[59]

We are meant to see this journey as a 'spiritual odyssey', to use Sarna's phrase. The narrative frames it this way with its opening statement 'after these things God tested Abraham' (v.1) and with its divine verdict—'now I know that you fear God, since you have not withheld your son, your only son, from me' (v.12b). From

---

[57] Compare the statement of Caiaphas —'it is expedient that one man should die for the people' (John 11:50f and 18:14)—which in retrospect is identified as an inspired utterance. This moves far beyond the pragmatic sense that Caiaphas and his listeners would have attributed to his utterance.

[58] The narrative slows down with verse 6 by giving attention to the details of the arrangements—wood, fire, knife, silence, question, silence, arrival, altar, wood, binding, knife . . In cinematic terms, one might imagine zoomed–in shots and the use of slow motion for dramatic effect to build tension before the final blow falls. Compare J Licht's comment: 'This is virtual slow motion, used to force the reader's attention to the horror of the fact, while avoiding the slightest, even indirect, word of comment or emotional reaction' (*Storytelling in the Bible*, [Jerusalem: Magnes Press]1978, p. 119).

[59] G von Rad, *Genesis* (London: SCM) 3rd rev. ed., 1972, p. 244.

this test of obedience, passed, flows the renewed pledge of blessing (v. 16 'because you . . . I will . . . ').

We must read Gen 22 in connection with Gen 17:1 because the sacrifice of Isaac puts the command and invitation of Gen 17:1 ('walk before me and be blameless, and I will . . . ') to the most specific test of loyalty and obedience that could be devised.[60] This element of testing and the 'fear of the LORD' resonate with experiences that Israel as a nation underwent in turn. It follows that the spiritual journey of Abraham blazes a trail for Israel. The typological shaping of the Abraham narrative supports this conclusion and so too do the theological demands of the God of Abraham.[61]

PROTOTYPES AS CONTEMPORARY MODELS?

Before we move on in the next chapter to consider how walking with God relates to the journey motif in the experience of Israel , to the 'fear of the LORD' and to testing, we must address the issue of how the Genesis prototypes of walking with God confront the contemporary Christian reader. If anything, the literary analysis of canonical Genesis that we have been following has disclosed a relevance designed for Israel after Sinai. The relevance to Israel's story is more obvious with the Promised Land still ahead and a collection of commandments, statutes and laws written into the covenant document (compare Gen 26:5). On the face of it, nothing could be less relevant to the twenty-first century than these remote figures of antiquity. They belong to Primeval History, or to the Hebrew national archive where the genealogical records that punctuate the stories were stored.

A contemporary might ask, 'What sane person hopes to circumvent physical death, like Enoch?' Enoch certainly offers no

---

[60] TD Alexander translates Gen 17:1 as 'so that I will . . .' and sees the test of Abraham in Gen 22 as a necessary preliminary to the ratification of the eternal covenant offered in Gen 17 ('Genesis 22 and the Covenant of Circumcision' *JSOT* 25 [1983] 17–22). His translation is possible rather than probable. The canonical form of the Abraham narrative and Near Eastern practice suggest rather that covenant and treaty were updated at royal or divine initiative, when guarantees or stipulations were extended or modified. This leaves both Gen 15 and Gen 17 as covenant-making occasions, subsequently confirmed by Gen 22. After all, both Gen 15 and Gen 17 have explicit statements concerning covenant-making, and all three episodes have rituals, of which only the dismemberment of Gen 15 and the circumcision of Gen 17 tie in with covenant-making. The literary links between Gen 22, Gen 17 and the Noah covenant pointed out by Alexander concur with our discussion.

[61] Commentators express this while differing widely among themselves over many points concerning the composition and dating of the narratives. These differences and the theological concerns of the narratives have been reviewed helpfully by Moberly who concludes his comment on Gen 22: 'It is not

encouragement to cryogenics. What sort of model is his walking with God? It has no specific content or application. According to the Noah story itself, there will never be another Flood, and the earth is well enough peopled now, so ark building and the post-diluvian command to 'be fruitful and multiply and fill the earth' (Gen 9:1,7) are superfluous. Abraham's migrations at divine command bear no resemblance either to jet travel or to the lives of displaced refugees, our contemporary world's tent-dwellers.

If Enoch and Noah offer nothing concrete to emulate, then does the lifestyle of Abraham provide a fuller model? In an age of pluralism, some might point to his 'ecumenical bonhomie', the way he lived peacefully among Canaanites and recognized their common worship of 'El Elyon, maker of heaven and earth' (Gen 14:18–22). If so, this ignores the canonical shape of the Pentateuch and the manner in which walking with an undivided loyalty to Yahweh develops.[62] Abraham's sacramental participation in the Salem cult may not prove a reliable guide to Christian spirituality. Nor are Christians heirs to promises of progeny, land, flocks and herds, to Abraham's founding-father status, or to his considerable lifespan and virility. Neither are we commanded to sacrifice our children, or even to circumcise them—though some early Christians apparently thought so (Gal 2 and 5:2ff).[63]

If these items are categorised as cultural artefacts and set aside from the spirituality model, does a nucleus of spiritual experience

---

difficult to see Abraham in Genesis 22 as the typological embodiment of Israel's obedience to Torah' (*OTOT*, p. 145).

[62] 'There is an air of ecumenical bonhomie about the patriarchal religion which contrasts with the sectarian exclusiveness of the Mosaic age and later prophetic demands'— Wenham, 'The Religion of the Patriarchs', p.184 in Millard & Wiseman (eds) *Essays on the Patriarchal Narratives* (Leicester: IVP) 1980. The historical issues of patriarchal religion and Yahwism are discussed by Moberly, who also goes on to raise the theological issues that result from there being two faith communities, Jewish and Christian, both tracing their roots to Abraham and reading these stories as Scripture (*OTOT*, chaps. 3–5).

[63] These comments could indeed be related to contemporary manifestations of fervent Christian groups, albeit regarded as sectarian by mainline denominations. Thus there are groups advocating multi-faith worship, propagating prosperity theology, severing family bonds metaphorically (or by death in the case of Jones's cult, and of Koresh at Waco), practising polygamy or arranged marriages, advocating patriarchal authority, abandoning life with city amenities to found new colonies, and so on. The 'pilgrim and stranger' mentality has generated some bizarre and alienating practices in Christian history. In some of these groups, identification with Abraham and leaving kith and kin and home country may have played a part. One wonders what new forms 'the Pilgrim Fathers' may take in future generations.

remain? This too is problematic. God speaks to Abraham directly
and Abraham dialogues with God and gets a reply—most start-
lingly so in the story of Gen 18. Dialogue with God is not limited
to chapter 18—see Gen 15:2. The Abraham narrative is punctuated
by appearances (12:7f, 18:1) and visions (15:1), as well as by divine
commands and dramatic interventions in Abraham's social milieu
such as the destruction of Sodom and Gomorrah (18:17ff), the
plaguing of the pharaoh (12:17), and the dream message to
Abimelech (20:3). Celestial figures appear, act or speak (16:7, 19:1,
22:11,15).

If it is argued that the supernatural intersects Abraham's life
only infrequently given the one hundred and seventy-five year
lifespan credited to him, then one suspects that some rationaliza-
tion is being offered for the infrequency or absence of such
experiences in our contemporary experience of walking with God.
Historical-critical readings of the Abraham stories that reduce
them to legends, as well as the theological or new literary readings
of them as story or typological model, do not solve the problems
of the supernatural and the question of prototypes for spirituality.
They by-pass them. They by-pass them because these readings are
academic contributions to the history of religion or to Hebrew
narratology. Discussions of the present experience of the supernatural and spirituality 'are beyond the scope of this monograph ',
to use the academic jargon. Those commentators who assume the
historicity of the stories, or who start from a theological affirmation of their truthfulness, seldom seem to have the space left to
offer recontextualizations of their meaning.

If the experience of a prototype is utterly unrepeatable, then it is
not functioning as a model and any typological application to
Christian experience is bogus. No prototype, no model. No
model, no analogy. No analogy, no contemporary application.
The experience of being commanded to sacrifice an only son is by
definition unrepeatable, not only because it is illegal and unthink-
able, but because it could not have the same meaning as it had in
Near Eastern culture and within the framework of the promises
specific to Abraham. This explains why thoughtful typological
applications of Gen 22 draw analogies not between Abraham's
experience and Christian discipleship, but between Abraham's
experience and the experience of Jesus in the crucifixion, whether
that is taken in terms of Christ's 'God-forsakenness', or of
substitutionary atonement, or of the giving of God the Father.

Unlike their colleagues who write books and articles, preachers
and Bible study leaders cannot offer excuses of genre or word-
limits for by-passing the issue of recontextualization. Nor, given
their audience, can they offer theological abstractions with much
credibility. They are addressing the community of faith gathered

around an open book.[64] In fact, therein lies a difference. Enoch, Noah and Abraham did not live by the book. Christians do. This response needs developing, but that must wait until discussing the covenant relationship enshrined in a document that we meet with in Exodus and Deuteronomy. Meanwhile, to catch hold of the transposable spirituality of the Genesis prototypes, we may take a cue from the New Testament.

FAITH AND THE UNFINISHED STORY

Hebrews links Enoch, Noah and Abraham together as prototypes of faith. Abbreviating the argument and the chapter where these prototypes appear, we concentrate on the following verses:

> By faith Enoch was taken so that he did not experience death; and 'he was not found, because God had taken him.' For it was attested before he was taken away that 'he had pleased God.' And without faith it is impossible to please God, for whoever would approach him must believe that he exists and that he rewards those who seek him. By faith Noah, warned by God about events unseen, respected the warning and built an ark . . .
> By faith Abraham obeyed when he was called to set out for a place that he was to receive as an inheritance. By faith Abraham, when put to the test, offered up Isaac. He considered the fact that God is able even to raise someone from the dead—and figuratively speaking, he did receive him back.
>
> (Heb 11:5–6, 7a, 8a, 17a, 19)

The catchword 'faith' leaps out at us, but there is more to it—pleasing God, reward, obedience, judgment, the unseen, and the defeat of death. These all resonate with facets of the Genesis material we have examined. For the recipients of Hebrews, Jesus is now unseen, 'behind the curtain' (Heb 6:19F, 9:11ff). His resurrection is a matter of received tradition rather than appearances experienced. The New Covenant promises of inheritance are not realized. Christians are more like wanderers over the earth (11:38), needing to set out again leaving natural kin–group behind (13:13f), like Abraham, rather than enjoying occupation of the Promised Land. Like the Genesis prototypes, the Christians addressed by

---

[64] Hence the tensions within Latin American Catholicism between the magisterium of the Church exercised downwards and regulated by the Doctrinal Commission in Rome and the grass-roots discussions in the base communities determining the meaning of the Bible from experience, action and reflection. See the hermeneutical review offered by AC Thiselton, *New Horizons in Hermeneutics: the theory and practice of transforming biblical reading* (London: Harper Collins) 1992, chap. 12 and the references to Carlos Mesters and Rowland and Corner's studies.

Hebrews find themselves in the middle of an unfinished saga. Now instead of walking by faith, apparently they must run (12:1).

In like manner, the motifs of the unseen, the unfinished and testing permeate the address of 1 Peter to persecuted Christians: 'although you have not seen him . . . and even though you do not see him now . . . live in reverent fear during the time of your exile' (1 Pet 1:8,17). The 'inheritance . . . is imperishable, undefiled, and unfading, kept in heaven for you . . . a salvation ready to be revealed in the last time' (1:4). Christian discipleship must be worked out between the Now and the Not Yet.[65]

For all the difference between the then of Genesis and the now of Christian discipleship, there is a fundamental and existential orientation that is common to both—faith. This orientation must be maintained within a setting where things have or can go radically wrong. The in-breaking of the supernatural in Genesis should not obscure the violence of the world, as much after the Flood as before it,[66] or the barrenness of the world of promise, and the threats to it. The stories of Genesis are set east of Eden. There was no walking in the garden with God after serpent talk. Contemporary spirituality too is located in territory where 'the imagination of mens' hearts' is the way it was before and after the cataclysm, in a fallen world that has gone wrong in many ways. Contemporary spirituality is forced to place its faith in the unseen because of the inadequacy of the present. The first reason for contemporary faith in the unseen is that the God who appeared in Jesus and said 'Follow me' has disappeared. The second is that the New Covenant and its promises have not come to fruition.

There is a rather close analogy, then, between Abraham setting out from Haran without seeing the land promised (Gen 12:1 'the land that I will show you') and Christian disciples who 'walk by faith not by sight' (2 Cor 5:7), 'because we look not at what can be seen but at what cannot be seen; for what can be seen is

---

[65] The Now and the Not Yet became a key motif in the Biblical Theology movement's engagement with the history, myth and eschatology debate, particularly in Oscar Cullman's, *Salvation in History* (London: SCM) 1967. The following sentences illustrate the point:

> The *new element* in the New Testament is not eschatology, but what I call the *tension* between the decisive 'already fulfilled' and the 'not yet completed', between present and future. The whole theology of the New Testament, including Jesus' preaching, is qualified by this tension. (p. 172)

[66] Gen 8:21 foresees ongoing wickedness. The attack of the coalition which captured Lot, and the wickedness of Sodom and Gomorrah demonstrate this within Genesis.

temporary, but what cannot be seen is eternal . . . (2 Cor 4:18).[67]
In the meanwhile, 'we make it our aim to please him' (2 Cor 5:9b)
in a frame of mind similar to Abraham's when told 'walk before
me and be blameless' (Gen 17:1).

Abraham was given a preview of the promise in vision (Gen
15:12ff) and, to some extent, within visibility:

> 'Raise your eyes now, and look from the place where you are,
> northward and southward and eastward and westward; for all the land
> that you see I will give to you and to your offspring for ever. I will
> make your offspring like the dust of the earth; so that if one can count
> the dust of the earth, your offspring also can be counted. Rise up,
> walk through the length and breadth of the land for I will give it to
> you.'
>
> (Gen 13:14ff)

This walking did and yet did not actualize the promise. The
offspring were at that point not only invisible but non-existent.
Yet the walking that did and yet did not occupy the land was a
step towards the fulfilment of the promise. The literal step was a
spiritual step. This walking towards the promise is the kind of
walking by faith that Paul speaks about. The obedience of pleasing
God does not create the promise or actualize the promise but
precedes arrival at the destination of the promise—'at home with
the Lord'. In Abraham terms, we could say that the fulfilment of
the promise of the whole land populated with prolific offspring
could only come to fulfilment on another plane, not within the
ambit of Abraham's life experience. Actualization of the promises
God made to Abraham was of an order of magnitude so much
greater than the preview of descendants in Isaac and the criss-cross
paths across Canaan where Abraham pitched his tent.

The analogy is closer between Israelites who retold the Abraham stories and Christian disciples who read and rehearse the
Gospel kerygma. Neither Israelites nor Christians receive the
promises face to face from God. For Israelites in the Egyptian
delta, in the desert, in the period of the judges, in a remnant
southern kingdom, in exile in Babylonia, in Palestine as a remnant
under the Persians, in Diaspora within Hellenistic, Seleucid or
Roman cultures, in Auschwitz or Belsen, the gap between what
was promised and life experience is enormous.

For Christians, the centuries since Christ have not seen the
Christianization of the world, nor its transformation. World

---

[67] Paul also speaks of the longing not to die but to be clothed with life so that
'what is mortal may be swallowed up by life' (2 Cor 5:4), a rather Enoch-like
experience, with a destination described as being 'at home with the Lord' (2
Cor 5:8).

population has soared and so have its distresses and its varieties of religion. Two thousand years strains credibility either side of Bethlehem. The faith demanded of Abraham does have some analogy with the faith in an unfinished story that is demanded of disciples today. Both stories could be read as legends. Both could, like life itself, be 'a tale told by an idiot, full of sound and fury, signifying nothing'. Macbeth was deceived by the promises of witches and grasped the kingdom. Disciples must await the Kingdom in the hope that they are not deceived. Disciples, like Abraham, cannot finish the unfinished story. They must live through their portion of it.

THE THEOLOGICAL AUTHORITY OF THE GENESIS PROTOTYPES

Finally, to think of Enoch, Noah and Abraham as prototypes requires assent to the theological authority of the stories. Is the Elohim, El Shadday, and Yahweh of Gen 5, Gen 6–9 and the Abraham cycle the same God as we worship? That was the question that Exodus addressed. Let us assume monotheism. The question then reshapes itself as, 'Do these stories disclose the truth about our God?' If they belong only to the history of religion, they are not theologically authoritative and may best be left behind, if we believe in progress. An Enlightenment stance would demand this. If we persist in declaring them theologically authoritative, then we can take that, in turn, in two ways. Firstly, 'Is God's character the same?' which also affects the way we might relate to him. Secondly, 'Does God act like this today?', which addresses our expectations as well as our theology.

An answer might run along these lines. The future that Enoch enjoyed emerged out of his walk with God. This fellowship was unbroken by death despite the pronouncement of death in Eden and the monotonous fact of death in full evidence around him. Enoch did not engineer the startling disappearance that kept his name off the dead ancestor list but, in retrospect, his life was a preparation for this disappearance, though transcendence of death was not explained to him. Christ is now a better prototype for us than Enoch, and one that substantiates what Enoch symbolized. Christ is a better prototype, not because there is the substantial witness of the New Testament documents to the historicity of his resurrection and ascension, although there is, but because we, unlike Enoch, cannot hope to bypass death. That is an unreasonable expectation. Jesus did not bypass death but offered a model of unbroken fellowship with God and promised it to his followers. Yet, like Enoch, we remain ignorant of what our future identity beyond death entails. This scarcely matters if, like Enoch, walking with God here and now is our lifestyle. Enoch stands as a symbol of life with God for ever. Jesus has become the focus of this Enoch hope, confirming it but also superseding it.

The terrible judgment of the Flood is a preview of an apocalyptic judgment. In ultimate judgment, physical death is no longer the outcome, but the second death. God's present non-intervention despite the violence of the world is implied in the outcome of the Flood. He accepts the fact of the continuing wickedness of humanity and disavows wiping out another complete generation within history (Gen 8:21, compare 6:5). Noah is a prototype of a redeemed remnant for whom walking with God in an obedient righteousness is an ongoing demand.[68] The God of Noah is thus a God of judgment and a God of grace, and there is no human choosing between those qualities of character as though they were alternatives. Rescue from judgment is one of the ways that the New Testament describes what God offers us in Christ, affirming for us a theological continuity with the walk with God and the God Noah walked with.[69]

The God of Abraham commands and promises.[70] The two features cannot be divorced and the initiative lies with God, both in terms of what is offered and what is demanded. Covenant relationship, to be God to us, is the central continuity between the promises to Abraham and to us. 'Walk before me and be

---

[68] GF Hasel offers a study of this concept in its Near Eastern setting to its eschatological development in which the Sumerian, Babylonian and Genesis Flood stories make a contribution—*The Remnant: the history and theology of the remnant idea from Genesis to Isaiah* (Berrien Springs: Andrews Univ Press) 1972.

[69] See, for instance, 1Pet 20ff and 2 Pet 3 for the language of salvation and eschatological judgement.

[70] The whole discussion of covenant, faith and 'works' within Reformed circles has generated some sharp disagreements over covenant of grant versus law covenant (Abraham and Sinai) and uses its own polemic jargon revolving around 'administrations' or 'dispensations'. The problem seems to lie with using theological categories generated in other discourses to exegete the Genesis narratives. OP Robertson, *The Christ of the Covenants* (Phillipsburg: Puritan and Reformed) 1980 and TE McComiskey, *The Covenants of Promise: a theology of the Old Testament covenants* (Nottingham: IVP) 1985 attempt to survey and mediate within this inner-Reformed and Reformed-Dispensational debate.

> it seems that the whole law/grace or law/promise scheme as presented by Kline is a false one. Law simply cannot be set over against grace or promise. The revelation of God's law to his people represents a most gracious provision. The law of God itself embodies the grace of God. (Palmer, 'Current Reformed Thinking on the Nature of the Divine Covenants' *WThJ* 40 [1977] 63–76, p. 74)

> For a recent British review of the Reformed tradition with detailed references, see RT Beckwith, 'The Unity and Diversity of God's Covenants' *Tyndale Bulletin* 38 (1987) 93–118.

blameless' invites and commands this bond. While the demand to sacrifice a child is not the way God operates now, it is the God of Gen 22 we walk before. In the Gospel records, this God incarnate demands loyal obedience to the point of death by martyrdom, and he offers fellowship and a future.[71] The invitation to walk after him embraces both. The demands are not accompanied now by promises of material prosperity, physical protection, long life, sons and heirs, or anything else so characteristic of blessing as it was understood in Abraham's world. Nor can we presently see the outcome of the promises that are made, only a preview of them. Our faith will be tested by this gap between promise and realisation. Our obedience in the face of the death of all we counted on may also be tested. Like Abraham, we may be left to make our own decisions on many matters and some of these decisions may complicate our lives immensely even if they are not necessarily wrong decisions by the norms of our culture or judged by immediate directives from God.

TO SUM UP

Finally, we return to Landau's dictum quoted at the beginning of this chapter: 'Metaphors cast powerful spells not only in everyday life but also in science . . .' We can adapt this to say that the metaphor of 'walking with God' casts a powerful spell for Christian spirituality.

'Walking with God' into old age like the patriarchs certainly carries with it a sense of an Enoch-like destination that is being approached ever more closely step by step. Here we introduce the concept of progress and purpose that is a misfit in the language of science. Indeed, to interpret the individual human lifespan in terms of a progressive journey with God is the only way to rescue old age from being wholly defined by its restricted activity and personal deterioration, a deterioration that is often as distressing to the loved ones as to the person concerned.[72] The destination component of 'walking with God' offers a metaphor of progress for describing a disciple's old age and death. The life of the old person is approaching its 'natural' outcome, an even closer

---

[71] For instance, in the sayings of Jesus such as: 'If any want to become my followers, let them deny themselves and take up their cross and follow me. For those who want to save their life will lose it, and those who lose their life for my sake, and for the sake of the gospel will save it' (Mk 8:34f).

[72] One effect of lengthening lifespans today is the concern within medicine as to whether the final fifteen years will retain quality of life, or simply see a protraction of the period of physical deterioration in terms of loss of hearing, sight, memory, mobility and a prolonging of the pain of osteoarthritis and other non-fatal degenerative diseases. See SJ Olshansky, BA Carnes and CK

relationship with God than has characterised the whole journey. This metaphorical perception of the final stage of the journey with God can and does function to transform self-perception, enhance dignity and offer some comfort for ageing mortals. Without a spirituality and without a spiritual, unseen reality, this perception of progress and destination would, of course, be sheer delusion. One would be left with the often painful or pathetic reality of old age, a reality that cannot be romanticized.

The concept of 'walking with God' in a relationship that demands an obedience such as the one modelled by Noah and Abraham can also function as a critique of the story of human progress imaged by technology and ideologized in politics. The Salvation Story and history co-exist in Genesis.[73] The one cannot be reduced to the other. Nor can the content of biology and evolution be told in Salvation Story language. Life on earth viewed biologically is not teleological, but opportunistic and subject to random effects such as mass extinctions. Yet science, as much as the Genesis genealogies, Creation and Flood stories, affirms the unity of humankind as a single species *homo sapiens*, and scientists are raising questions about the future, and about the inter-relationship on planet Earth of humanity and 'every living creature of all flesh' (Gen 9:12).

Until now, advances in 'civilization', and especially its technology, have been pressed into human warfare—fire, arrows and chariotry in the Ancient Near East. Nuclear power and satellite communication in our day.[74] Abraham's walk with God existed alongside Mesopotamian, Canaanite and Egyptian cultures, all of which were far ahead of Abraham's lifestyle in terms of amenities, not least the amenities of literary texts and education. Genesis does not solve the problems of culture and ecology confronting the twenty-first century, but in its three prototypes of walking with God it invests spirituality with a deep significance of the meaning of being human in the world, if not entirely of it.

BIBLIOGRAPHY

D Alexander, 'Genesis 22 and the Covenant of Circumcision' *JSOT* 25 (1983) 17–22.
Bergman, et al, 'דֶּרֶךְ *derek*', pp. 270–293 in *TDOT, Vol 3*, 1978.
DJ Bosch, *A Spirituality of the Road* (Scottdale: Herald Press) 1979.

Cassel, 'The Aging of the Human Species' *Scientific American* Apr (1993) 18–24.

[73] In Genesis terms, the Table of Nations (Gen 10) points to a wider history than that of the elect line within it that connects it with the Abraham story.

[74] This lends irony to the titles of the widely acclaimed intellectual TV documentaries on cultural history, *The Triumph of the West*, and Bronowski's *The Ascent of Man*.

DJA Clines, *The Theme of the Pentateuch*, JSOTS 10 (Sheffield: JSOT) 1978.

JL Crenshaw, *A Whirlpool of Torment: Israelite traditions of God as an oppressive presence* OBT 12 (Philadelphia: Fortress) 1984.

BT Dahlberg, 'On recognizing the unity of Genesis' *Theology Digest* 24 (1977) 360–367.

R Davidson, *The Courage to Doubt: exploring an Old Testament theme* (London: SCM) 1983.

VP Hamilton, *The Book of Genesis: chapters 1–17* NICOT (Grand Rapids: Eerdmans) 1990.

GF Hasel, 'The Meaning of the Animal Rite in Gen 15' *JSOT* 19 (1981) 61–78.

P Kalluveettil, *Declaration and Covenant*, Analecta Biblica 88 (Rome: Biblical Institute Press) 1982.

KA Kitchen, 'The Fall and Rise of Covenant, Law and Treaty' *TB* 40 (1989) 118–135.

———, 'Egypt, Ugarit, Qatna and Covenant' *UF* 11 (1979) 453–464.

S Kopp, *If you meet the Buddha on the Road, kill him!* (London: Sheldon) 1974/1991.

RWL Moberly, *The Old Testament of the Old Testament: patriarchal narratives and Mosaic Yahwism*, OBT (Minneapolis: Fortress) 1992.

———, 'The Earliest Commentary on the Akedah' *VT* 38 (1988) 302–323.

S Peck, *The Road less travelled: a new psychology of love, traditional values and spiritual growth* (New York: Simon & Schuster) 1978.

NH Sarna, *Understanding Genesis: the heritage of biblical Israel* (New York: Schocken Books) 1966.

M Weinfeld, *'bᵉrît'* בְּרִית, pp. 253–279 in GJ Botterweck & H Ringgren (eds), *Theological Dictionary of the Old Testament, Vol. 1* (Grand Rapids: Eerdmans) rev.ed. 1977.

GJ Wenham, *Genesis 1–15*, WBC 1 (Waco: Word) 1987.

C Westermann, *Genesis 1–11: a commentary*, 1974 (London: SPCK) 1984.

[3]

Life Journey
Stages of Faith: Exodus

INTRODUCTION

In the previous chapter we looked at walking with God in two dimensions. The first was the metaphorical or 'spiritual' dimension of a covenant relationship involving trust and obedience. The second involved physical walking, Abraham's prototypical journey from Ur and Haran to the Promised Land. We turn now from the Genesis preview to the Exodus itself and to the story of a movement which is both a travelogue and a transcript of stages of faith. We shall again need to ask ourselves whether the Exodus experience models aspects of a biblical spirituality still relevant to contemporary faith.[1]

The answer may turn around our working definition of spirituality. It will certainly turn around the legitimacy of a Christian appropriation of the Exodus story. As we shall see, there are two tributaries to this Nile of hermeneutical tradition. There is a stream of devotional re-readings of Israel's Exodus-Conquest stories and a stream of re-readings within Liberation theology. Both sets of re-readings depend upon drawing an analogy between Israel's ancient experience and Christian perception of a personal or communal struggle. While it is beyond our scope and focus to review the whole field, samples of Exodus re-readings will be referred to in our discussion or footnotes.

In the first part of this chapter, we shall follow the Exodus experience in stages from Goshen in Egypt to Sinai and covenant. Then we shall ask what stages of faith were involved. This will lead us to consider the trajectory of the fear of Yahweh and the process of conscientization that developed between slavery and covenant. The beginning of the testing of Israel's faith in the

---

[1] I addressed some of the concerns of this chapter in an article entitled 'Moving on with God: key motifs in Exodus 13–20' *Themelios* 15.2 (1990) 49–60.

wilderness follows departure from Egypt. This motif of Wilderness testing will be more fully explored in Deuteronomy in the next chapter. At the end of the present chapter, we will ask whether the Exodus journey merits a paradigm status within the Old Testament and in contemporary Christian re-readings and what such a paradigm could mean to the second-generation experience that 'knows not Moses'.

MAP AND MODEL OF SPIRITUALITY

In Belden Lane's engaging book *Landscapes of the Sacred* he reproduces a map of Egypt and Palestine which charts Israel's spiritual progress according to Exodus-Numbers under the rubric 'Out of Egypt into Canaan—"Out of Darkness into His marvellous Light"—Where art Thou?'[2] The chart is taken from a devotional work published a hundred years before Lane's book. It is sub-titled 'Lessons in Spiritual Geography'[3]. Egypt is filled in in black with the label 'spiritual night and bondage' in contrast to the Promised Land which is labelled 'Perfect Love' and 'Sunshine Purity and Power'. In between Egypt and Palestine, the route of the Israelites progresses from 'conversion' on exit from Egypt to 'justification' around Sinai, but then 'spiritual twilight' sets in, and 'backsliding' occurs during the wilderness wanderings.

The 19th century author saw a clear typological link between his generation's spiritual life and Israel's. Anyone who has grown up in a holiness church this century could probably identify features of this spiritual map with familiar phrases and sermons. This use of language and analogy drawn from the Exodus-Conquest can shape a congregation's perception of the devotional life. 'The fleshpots of Egypt' are contrasted with the portion of manna, which is spiritual nourishment. Hankering after the 'fleshpots of Egypt' in the context of the devotional map or in holiness churches might be identified with a longing for 'the world' that hinders a growth in spirituality. The specific application may be to pre-conversion addiction to alcohol, tobacco, cards, gambling and associated immorality. It may have been extended to dancing, the theatre and the cinema. There is in all this, whether we look at the devotional book of 1888, or contemporary holiness sermons, a clear link with a 'Puritan' spirituality, both real or caricatured.

Contemporary preachers might update the moral concerns to include comment on the lifestyle accompanying singles clubs, gay

---

2 BC Lane, *Landscapes of the Sacred: geography and narrative in American spirituality* (New York/Mahwah: Paulist Press) 1988, p. 29.

3 MW Knapp, *Out of Egypt* (Cincinnati: Cranston & Stowe) 1888. Under the diagram, the words read: 'This Map is designed to show the routes of Israel

bars, substance abuse, the recreational use of marijuana, ecstasy and crack cocaine, pornographic films, magazines and video nasties. What all these items of 'Puritan' morality have in common is their identification of sin with a-political forms of personal behaviour. Historically the actual Puritans were not so a-political. Yet it will be helpful to bear in mind the contrast between 'Puritan' concern with personal morality and Liberation theology's concern with structural and institutionalised evil. As a reading of Exodus this sort of contrast between personal and communal perspectives is artificial. It is not sustainable on either hermeneutical or theological grounds.[4]

Of course, Christian re-reading of Israel's story began much further back than Liberation theology or holiness teaching. It began in the New Testament with Paul's dictum that these things 'were written down to instruct us, on whom the ends of the ages have come' (1 Cor 10:11). Paul's point is that Christians should not see themselves as superior to the Exodus generation and invulnerable to temptation. Contemporary sermons, either personal or political, may alert us to the hermeneutical issues raised by Christian re-readings of Israel's Salvation History.

EXODUS: FROM GOSHEN TO SINAI

First, we shall look at the role of the physical journey, the literal walk out of bondage which also involves moving on with God spiritually. Before departure from Egypt turns into a spectacular final exit from bondage, the confrontation with Pharaoh revolves around a concession to a three–day journey into the desert to offer sacrifice to the Hebrews' ancestral deity. The ambiguity of this journey seems intended. Pharaoh, Moses and the readers know that more is at stake than three days off for a religious festival. Negotiations, confrontation, plagues and concessions carry the story forward.

> The LORD, the God of the Hebrews, sent me to you to say, 'Let my people go, so that they may worship me in the Wilderness.' But until now you have not listened.
>
> (Exod 7:16, cf. 3:18)

---

and spiritual states illustrated by events occurring in them. It should be carefully studied in connection with the reading of the book.'

[4] For a much broader discussion of spiritual devotion and political action than we have space for here and one that challenges the dichotomising of personal and structural sin as 'the Great Fallacy', see R McAfee Brown, *Spirituality and Liberation: overcoming the Great Fallacy* (Sevenoaks: Spire/Hodder & Stoughton) 1988.

Then Pharaoh summoned Moses and Aaron, and said, 'Go sacrifice to your God within the land.' But Moses said, . . . 'We must go a three days' journey into the Wilderness and sacrifice to the LORD our God as he commands us.'

(Exod 8:25,27)

We have the LORD's festival to celebrate . . . You must also let us have sacrifices and burnt offerings to sacrifice to the LORD our God.

(Exod 10:9, 25)

This focus on the cultic dimension to the Exodus story is maintained by the Passover instructions on the eve of delivery. This resets Israel's calendar so that the year begins with Salvation History—rather than with an agricultural spring ritual. More signs of God's special relationship are added to the story begun by rainbow and circumcision —lamb's blood on doorposts and lintel (12:13), seven days of unleavened bread (13:7ff), the redemption of first-born males and the sacrifice of first-born livestock (13:16).[5]

The final concession is wrung out of Pharaoh by the death of the first-born:

Then he summoned Moses and Aaron in the night, and said, 'Rise up, go away from my people, both you and the Israelites! Go worship the LORD, as you said. Take your flocks and your herds, as you said and be gone. And bring a blessing on me too!'

(Exod 12:31f)

In point of fact, the covenant encounter at Sinai has been the destination of the Exodus from the moment Moses turned aside to look at the burning bush. The return to Sinai was announced as part of his call. The significance of return to Sinai is underlined by describing it as a 'sign' in itself:

I will be with you; and this shall be the sign for you that it is I who sent you; when you have brought the people out of Egypt, you shall worship God on this mountain.

(Exod 3:12)[6]

---

[5] They are all described as 'signs' or functioning like signs, the Hebrew word *'ōt* being used in these three references as well as to describe the rainbow and circumcision.

[6] In the narrative sequence, this is the first 'sign' (*'ōt*). Several commentators point out that this sign does not conform very comfortably to the formal structure of call narratives of God's agents, warriors or prophets, where the supernatural sign confirms the call, reassuring the agent, or authenticates the agent publicly. The form of call narratives was studied by Habel and Zimmerli with slightly differing results. The sign would normally happen before the event envisaged as a guarantee of the future event. Here arrival back at Sinai and encounter with God are, apparently, a sign to reassure Moses of his divine call. BS Childs makes the burning bush itself the supernatural sign because otherwise 'the sign and the fulfilment coalesce'. No doubt the burning bush functions as a supernatural demonstration to Moses. It points beyond

'This mountain' (3:12) is 'Horeb, the mountain of God' in 3:1, which locates the call scene. The locality, the fire, the voice and the call all offer a preview of Israel's Sinai encounter. The narrative is shaped by this typological resonance.[7] The encounter between God and Moses at the burning bush points to the covenant relationship Israel will be offered. Like the sign of Passover blood, the call of Moses is a necessary preliminary to covenant-making with the nation. The burning bush encounter has a presence-address-commitment-relationship pattern similar to the Sinai covenant occasion in a way that invites comparison between Moses' individual experience and the experience of the nation.

The 'mountain of God' as destination offers a reminder that the vertical relationship with God undergirds the political confrontation with Egypt. There is a Sovereign who has a greater claim on Israel than the Pharaoh. Indeed, not simply a claim but an obligation to respond to the 'cry' for suzerain protection: 'God heard their groaning, and God remembered his covenant with Abraham, Isaac and Jacob' (2:24).[8] The story told by Exodus is

---

itself as a symbol in two ways. Firstly, the fire and voice make God real in visual and auditory dimensions. Secondly, the bush burning next to Sinai prefigures the Sinai theophany itself at the covenant-making occasion. The seven branched menorah may well perpetuate this symbolism, combining the fire and light imagery of God's presence with tree symbolism. Thus the menorah historicizes the vegetation–life symbolism from the Near East by displacing it with the burning bush and the Sinai theophany.

[7] BS Childs reviews the form critical analyses of Habel and Zimmerli applied to Moses' call. He offers his own analysis with this conclusion:

> . . . the theophany to Moses was read in the light of the subsequent events at Sinai. Then a typological relation between the burning bush on the holy mountain, and the devouring fire at Sinai was recognized. The sign to Moses was seen as a prefiguration of Israel's experience.
>
> (*Exodus*, OTL [London: SCM] 1974, p. 60)

This conclusion may be accepted as the intention of the theological editor in terms of Hebrew narratology without endorsing the details of Childs's reconstruction of tradition history. See too the discussion of JI Durham who finds a basic 'Presence-response pattern': 'Indeed, the experience of Moses in 3:1–12 is an exact foreshadowing of the experience of Israel, first in Egypt, then in the deprivation of the wilderness, and finally at Sinai' (*Exodus*, WBC 3 (Waco: Word) 1987, p. 30). Moberly's more recent discussion reaffirms the fire and Sinai symbolism of the call narrative and offers advances on the difficulties of reading the text within the JEDP paradigm (*OTOT*, pp. 7ff.).

[8] On the obligation of the overlord to come to his vassal's protection, see FC Fensham, 'Clauses of Protection in Hittite Vassal-Treaties and the Old Testament' *Vetus Testamentum* 13 (1963) 133–143. It is in the Hittite treaties of the 2nd millennium that clauses of guarantee appear, but the Assyrians of the 8th–6th centuries also marched to the defence of vassals without writing military obligations from the suzerain's side into the vassal document. The basis of appeal to the suzerain is the alignment of interests reflected in the phrase, 'I will be an enemy to your enemies and a foe to your foes' (Exod

therefore presented as the continuation of the Abraham story. The bringing out (3:8,10,12) is preliminary to the bringing into covenant and Promised Land (3:8,17).

ARRIVAL AT THE DESTINATION

With chapter 19, the destination is attained—'Israel encamped there in front of the mountain' (19:2). The Promised Land as destination is eclipsed by Mount Sinai in the Exodus narrative, and from the point of view of Exodus, Israel gets no further than Sinai in her journey, either physically or theologically. The final paragraph of the book mentions travelling, but only to focus on the Tabernacle with its powerful visual symbols of God's presence 'before the eyes of all the house of Israel at each stage of their journey' (40:38). Before the Tabernacle is constructed and filled with the glory of Yahweh (40:35), the most holy place in Exodus is 'the mountain of God'. Approaching Sinai is forbidden on pain of death and bounds are set around it for animals and humans (19:12ff). Holiness is expressed spatially, demarcated by an exclusion zone that is penetrated initially by Moses alone, at divine command (19:3,20 20:21). Mount Sinai and surroundings are rather similar, then, to the holy of holies in the Tabernacle which is penetrated once a year by the high-priest alone. We can see that the Tabernacle enshrines and perpetuates the Sinai experience of covenant presence.[9] There is one key passage connected with the journey to covenant which combines retrospect and prospect in a way that gathers up the narrative and its theological message:

You have seen what I did to the Egyptians, and how I bore you on eagles' wings and brought you to myself. Now, therefore, if you obey

---

23:21). This phrasing is already used in 3rd millennium treaties, is characteristic in the 2nd millennium Hittite treaties, and passes down into Greek treaties and loyalty oaths to Roman emperors—see Weinfeld 'The Loyalty Oath' UF 8, 390f.

[9] In chap. 19:10 all the Israelites wash their garments as part of the consecration rites preliminary to being brought 'out of the camp to meet God' (19:17a). In 40:12 Moses brings Aaron and sons 'to the entrance of the tent of meeting' where he 'shall wash them with water' and then anoint them. 'Their anointing shall admit them to a perpetual priesthood throughout all generations to come' (40:15b). Aaron and the priests thus approach the Tabernacle precincts as the Israelites approach the mountain. The descent of cloud and glory on Sinai in 24:15ff are deliberately recalled by the cloud and glory covering the Tabernacle (so, for instance, Childs, p.638 and Durham, p.346 and 550).

my voice and keep my covenant, you shall be my treasured possession out of all the peoples. Indeed the whole earth is mine, but you shall be for me a priestly kingdom and a holy nation.

(Exod 19:4–6)[10]

Here the journey to Sinai is given a profound theological interpretation. The destination is stated, but not in terms of a locality. The destination of the journey is God himself: 'I brought you to myself' (v.4b). The three words in Hebrew have a deep simplicity.[11] God is the focus and spiritual centre to which all the walking is directed. There is a spiritual paradox here because God also accompanied the Israelites all the way.[12] The paradox is resolved by seeing Sinai as the covenant-making occasion. Until the Israelites enter into covenant they have not entered into as full a relationship with God as is possible and intended. The pillar of cloud and fire which guards and leads the Israelites out of Egypt, though a spectacular demonstration of divine presence, is not a substitute for covenant. To enter covenant the Israelites must not only observe the ritual preparations of Passover, and the consecration by washing and abstention (19:14f), but must now proceed to take the oath, be sprinkled with blood and see the covenant ratification sacrifices offered.[13]

---

[10] 'Treasured possession' is a metaphor used in 2nd millennium Near Eastern texts in political and theological contexts. Hebrew *s^egullāh* has Ugaritic and Akkadian cognates —Ugar. *sglth*, Akkadian *sikiltu* with a meaning related to the Akkadian verb *sakālu*—'to set aside'. The vassal is the *sglth* of the Hittite overlord: 'Now you belong to the Sun your master; a servant indeed, his possession (*sglth*) are you'—RS 18.38 [*PRU* 5, No. 69], lines 11f, cf. line 7. See D Pardee, 'A Further Note on *PRU V*, No. 60' *Ugarit Forschungen* 13 (1981) 151–156 for translation and comment on the setting of this complaint by the Hittite suzerain against his vassal 'Ammurapi of Ugarit'. Abban, king of Alalakh in 2nd millennium Syria, is styled as the *sikiltu* of his god on his seal: 'Abban, the mighty king, son of Sharran, servant of the god Adad, beloved of Adad, the *sikiltum* of Adad' (Collon, *First Impressions*, p. 118 No. 511). The *s^egullāh* metaphor applied to Israel as God's 'treasured possession' is well represented in Deuteronomy—7:6, 14:2, 26:18. For a general comment, see Weinfeld, *Deuteronomy*, p. 368.

[11] 'I caused you to come to me' *wā'ābi' et^kem 'ēlay* has a canonical trajectory that issues in the invitation, 'Come to me all you that are weary and carrying heavy burdens, and I will give you rest. Take my yoke upon you and learn from me, for I am gentle and humble in heart and you will find rest for your souls. For my yoke is easy and my burden is light' (Matt 11:28).

[12] G Gutiérrez, *We drink from our own wells: the spiritual journey of a people* (London: SCM) 1984: 'The Jewish people set out in a quest of an encounter with God. But in a way this encounter was already a reality at the beginning of the journey' (p. 77).

[13] It is important to keep the balance of the narrative before us. The threefold repetition of the declaration of loyal obedience underlines that 'they freely and deliberately committed themselves to' Yahweh, so the covenant is not imposed, but at the same time it is a declaration of obedience, of a lesser to a

Willingness to enter covenant and accept its terms are emphasised in the account by threefold repetition of the verbal assent to obedience.[14] The first reaction is spoken here in 19:8 in preparation for covenant, but the culmination comes with the reading aloud of the covenant document, the oath and the sprinkling with blood of the people and God, who is represented by the altar.[15] The representatives of Israel are then invited to the covenant meal on top of Sinai in the immediate presence of God without the threat of death: 'God did not lay his hand on the chief men of the people of Israel; also they beheld God , and they ate and drank' (24:11). This meal on the mountain top is the remote ancestor of the covenant meal in the Upper Room. Both meals speak of an intimate fellowship of *šālōm*, established by blood and offered to human beings at God's initiative.

STAGES OF FAITH

If this free and willing entry into covenant loyalty to Yahweh is the high point of Israel's experience in Exodus, then by what stages of faith was it reached? The editor hands us the key to interpreting the spiritual journey that the community travelled in the Sinai episode itself. We are given a graphic description of the state of mind of the community gathered around the 'mountain of God'. In a nutshell, this state of mind is 'the fear of the LORD'.

When all the people witnessed the thunder and lightning, the sound of the trumpet, and the mountain smoking, they were afraid and

---

greater. See P Kalluveettil, *Declaration and Covenant*, p. 157f. Free will and divine sovereignty are both written into the narrative.

[14] Compare the comment of M Walzer:

But God's service is radically unlike pharaonic slavery (even though the two are named by the same Hebrew word). The difference is this: slavery is begun and sustained by coercion, while service is begun and sustained by covenant.

M Walzer, *Exodus and Revolution* (New York: Basic Books) 1985, p. 73f.

[15] 'Everything that the LORD has spoken we will do' (19:8) is followed up by the announcement of the Ten Commandments and the additional covenant stipulations in chaps. 20–23. In 24:3 'All the words that the LORD has spoken we will do' precede the covenant ratification rituals. Moses reads out the words of the covenant document to which the people respond 'All that the LORD has spoken we will do, and we will be obedient' (24:7) after which they and the altar, which represents God, are sprinkled with blood (24:8). The analogies with treaty-making in the Near East are clear enough, despite Exodus being a theological narrative rather than a covenant document itself. See, for instance, DJ McCarthy, *Treaty and Covenant: a study in form in the Ancient Oriental documents and in the Old Testament*, Analecta Biblica 21a (Rome: Biblical Institute Press), rev. ed. 1978, esp. pp. 266ff. and LR Fisher (ed), *Ras Shamra Parallels, Vol. 2*, Analecta Orientalia 51 (Rome: PIB) 1975, pp. 155ff. by FB Knutson discussing treaty, bond (*rikiltu*), proposal of bond, and letter.

trembled and stood at a distance . . . Moses said to the people, 'Do not
be afraid; for God has come to test you and to put the fear of him upon
you so that you do not sin.'

(Exod 20:20)

There are several points worth commenting on here. First, there is
the paradox of Moses' reply: 'Do not fear . . . so that his fear may
be upon you'. Moses has a long–term objective in mind. The 'fear
of the LORD' should preserve Israel from sin, not on this day only
and not to preserve the boundary around the mountain only, but
into the future and to prevent transgression of commandment
boundaries. Clearly, then, the numinous awe must be converted
from an overpowering emotion with physiological effects ('they
were afraid and trembled') to an attitude that motivates behaviour.
The transition is from affect to effect, from awe to ethics. The
experience is to be internalized and integrated with the covenant
concept. In the light of Exod 20:20 alone, it is apparent that the
phrase 'fear of the LORD' cannot be given a single fixed meaning but
carries a range of nuances determined by context.

Secondly, this charged emotional and theological high point for
the nation resonates with the testing of Abraham in Gen 22. This
emerges from the combination of the 'fear of the LORD', the audible
voice from heaven, and the idea of 'testing' common to both
contexts.[16] If both contexts are occasions of loyal obedience, then
the difference is that Abraham's was the precursor for Israel's. The
covenant with the nation, enunciated with the specific stipulations
of the Covenant Code (Exod 20–23), implies that a wider group
obedience is required for the realisation of the covenant promises.
As we know from the fuller story of Exodus itself with its Golden
Calf incident, and from the narrative sequel in Numbers, the
Exodus generation as a whole fails to live up to the covenant
moment and falls short of the Promised Land. This falling short
includes Moses himself for whom the Promised Land becomes
forbidden territory (Deut 3:23ff).

---

[16] 'In order to test you' (Exod 20:20) corresponds to the chapter heading of Gen
22:1 'God tested Abraham'. The same verb *nsh* in the Piel form 'to put
someone to the test, to exercise, train' is used in both contexts. Likewise,
'now I know that you fear God' (Gen 22:12) shares the root *yr'* with the
double occurrence in Exod 20:20. The Sinai narrative assumes that the
Israelites hear the Ten Words as the direct speech of God (20:19) where Gen
22:11 has the *mal'ak Yhwh* calling out 'from heaven'. Without referring to the
speaking voice, Moberly remarks on Gen 22 that 'especially notable, however, is that the specific juxtaposition of *test* and *fear* occurs in one other
passage in the Old Testament (Exod 20:20)' (*OTOT*, p. 144).

FEAR OF YAHWEH AS A TRAJECTORY
IN EXODUS

If the 'fear of the LORD' links the spirituality of the Abraham cycle with the narrative of Exodus, then the book of Exodus itself chronicles stages along the way to this 'fear of the LORD' which comes to fruition at Sinai. In fact, the motif is introduced in the first chapter of Exodus as soon as the scene has been set of Egypt after Joseph. Here too the 'fear of the LORD' emerges in a test of obedience, not for the nation but for two named individuals, Shiphrah and Puah, the Hebrew midwives. The growth of the Hebrew population (1:7) alerts the reader to the fulfilment of the promise of many descendants to the patriarchs, but it inspires dread in the Egyptians (1:12). Hence Pharaoh's birth-control policy, to be implemented by the Hebrew midwives. Pharaoh prescribes the killing of every male child. Shiphrah and Puah decide on civil disobedience instead and are brought in for interrogation.

> But the midwives feared God; they did not do as the king of Egypt commanded them . . . and because the midwives feared God, he gave them families.
>
> (1:17, 21)

In the Exodus narrative, then, the midwives model what primary loyalty means in this context. From the very beginning of the story, the lines are drawn up. There will be no separation possible between politics and spirituality. The policy of the state has thrust upon these two women the choice as to who is to be feared and obeyed first, in these circumstances a choice between irreconcilable alternatives. The next chapter sees the choice thrust upon Jochebed and Amram, Moses' parents, and with this conscientization of four individuals and their decision to defy the state begins the story that will take all the Israelites out of Egypt and on their way to Sinai years later. We must jump ahead to the scene at the Reed Sea to keep the 'fear of the LORD' motif in its strategic place.

If there is a 'conversion experience' to be found in Exodus, then the narrator has located it at the Reed Sea. There the trapped Israelites look up to see the arm of the state reaching out to enslave them again or wipe them out. Cries, anger, recriminations against Moses and despair ensue:

> In great fear the Israelites cried out to the LORD . . . And Moses said to the people, 'Do not be afraid, stand firm and see the deliverance that the LORD will accomplish for you today; for the Egyptians whom you see today, you shall never see again. The LORD will fight for you, and you have only to keep still.'

Thus the LORD saved Israel that day from the Egyptians; and Israel saw the Egyptians dead on the seashore. Israel saw the great work that the LORD did against the Egyptians. So the people feared the LORD and believed in the LORD and in his servant Moses.

(Exod 14:10f, 30f)

This is a case of 'seeing is believing' for the narrator repeats 'see' three times in v. 13 and twice in vv. 30f in a promise-fulfilment schema. Together with *r̓h*—'to see' is the repeated *yr̓*—'to fear'.[17] The Israelites are converted from a fear of Pharaoh to a fear of Yahweh in an extension of the midwives' faith. The trust of Israel in 14:31b mirrors the trust of Abraham in Gen 15:6—'and Abraham put his trust in Yahweh', 'and they put their trust in Yahweh'.[18] The difference is that Israel believed after the event rather than before it. The nuance of 'fearing the LORD' in the Reed Sea setting will include an emotional component. Previously the chapter gave a graphic description of the Israelites' emotional reactions when trapped. Now 'the Egyptians dead on the seashore' was an awesome demonstration of divine judgment. It was not simply a matter for relief and celebration, though the *Song of the Sea* sounds this jubilant note.

We have seen, then, that the 'fear of the LORD' runs as a leitmotif through the Exodus story from its opening confrontation to its theological climax at Sinai.

OPPRESSION AND CONSCIENTIZATION

Using the language of contemporary ideology to explicate experiences in the world of the ancient Near East risks distorting the ancient text. So too does extrapolating from the canonical text by means of a one-to-one transplant, from the Old Testament to a contemporary situation. Preachers take these risks week by week and may often distort both text and reality in an attempt to tap into the transformative power of the text. Their attempt is legitimate, if not always its results.

Scholars such as Wink, Brueggemann and Bauckham have tried to bridge the gap between academic analysis of biblical texts and

---

[17] Some sound play may be suggested in vv.30b, 31 where 'and Israel saw', 'and Israel saw' is followed by 'and the people feared'—*wayyar̓ Yiśrā̓ēl, wayyar̓ Yiśrā̓ēl, wayyiyr̓ǝû*.

[18] The same Hiphil form of *'mn* with preposition *bǝ* and the divine name is used in both passages. It is, of course, Gen 15:6 which Paul has used as his proof text of saving faith in Rom 4:3.

tapping into their transformative power.[19] 'One does not need to be magical, supernaturalist, or superstitious to argue that this literature proceeds with a discernible power and intentionality that impinges upon and shatters all old descriptions of reality and invites one into a differently described reality.'[20] So Brueggemann, with substantiation.

The question here, then, is whether anything like conscientization, as understood in the tradition of Paulo Freire, is involved in the narrator's presentation of the Egyptian experience and whether a reading of Exodus can conscientize.[21] As a rough definition we may take 'conscientization' to mean both a change of perception and a concerted reaction whereby an oppressed group sees through the oppressive system, decides against its inevitability, and organizes itself to bring about change. Discernment, illumination and consequent shifts of self-perception are cognitive components, but from these develops a further radical transformation, and this involves praxis.

The midwives defy Pharaoh's edict to put to death baby boys because they are motivated by 'fear of God'. As Cheryl Exum remarks—'in the refusal of women to cooperate with oppression, the liberation of Israel from Egyptian bondage has its beginnings.'[22] It does not seem to distort the presentation in Exodus to describe this as an act of 'civil disobedience', anachronistic as this phrase is. Exodus presents us with an example of state law in conflict with moral law so that what is legal by the decree of the

---

19 Brueggemann's essay on Exodus is referred to below. For a study of 'Exodus and Service: Freedom in the Bible' see R Bauckham, *The Bible in Politics: how to read the Bible politically*, Third Way Books (London: SPCK) 1989 Chap. 7, pp. 103–117. Significantly this book is dedicated 'to friends in South Africa and Namibia, with gratitude for a memorable visit in 1987'. Bauckham, like Croatto, discerns a liberative axis running through the Bible in a trajectory from Old to New Testament.

20 W Brueggemann,'The Exodus Narrative as Israel's Articulation of Faith Development', chap. 1 pp. 7–26 in *Hope within History* (Atlanta: John Knox) 1987, p.8.

21 See Paulo Freire, *Pedagogy of the Oppressed* Penguin, 1974. Two interesting offshoots of his experience in Brazil are mirrored in Africa and in India—A Hope and S Timmel, *Training for Transformation: a handbook for community workers*, Vols. 1–3 (Gweru: Mambo Press) 1987, esp. Vol. 1, pp. 6–12 on Paulo Freire; G Matthew, *A Day with Paulo Freire* (Delhi: ISPCK) 1980, esp. pp. 9ff & 67ff on conscientization. For conscientization within Pentecostalism in South America, see Cheryl Johns' analysis of Freire's ideas in *Pentecostal Formation: a pedagogy among the oppressed* (Sheffield: Sheffield Academic Press) 1993.

22 J Cheryl Exum offers a reading sensitive to the literary structuring and the prominence of women in the Exodus liberation in her article ' "You shall let every daughter live": a study of Exodus 1:8–2:10' *Semeia* 28 (1983) The Bible and Feminist Hermeneutics, pp. 63–82, p. 81.

ruler is judged an offence to God. The conscience of the midwives leads them to an act of non-compliance, in this case a disobedience to the state by refusal to act. We could draw analogies with this act of defiance by drawing attention to the role played by women in the struggle against apartheid in South Africa. As well as many personal stories of the heroic suffering by women involved in non-violent resistance to apartheid, there was the mass action march by 20,000 women to the Union Buildings in Pretoria in 1956 in protest against the extension of the pass laws to women. This was organized by the Federation of South African Women and the ANC Women's League.[23]

In Exodus, the defiance of the midwives is not explicit but tacit. Their disobedience is apparently masked by their explanation offered for the failure of state policy (1:19). They act discreetly rather than announcing their policy publicly beforehand. So it could be argued that acts of public civil disobedience, for instance those that were mounted in defiance of apartheid laws in South Africa, go beyond the Exodus narrative in various ways, for instance by being announced publicly in advance, by being enacted collectively as part of a concerted mass action campaign, and by being supported publicly by Christian leaders whose speeches were carefully drafted and released to the international press for circulation.

These distinctions are real, but the civil disobedience of the midwives stands at the head of a record of defiance of the state alongside other Old Testament stories, stories such as those of Daniel and friends in Babylon, or prophets of Yahweh in Israel's northern and southern kingdoms. It has affinities with the defiance of the apostles in Jerusalem when ordered to stop preaching by the Sanhedrin. The Exodus narrative, then, does not stand alone, and it lends itself to re-use by those who would refuse, in the name of God, to comply with state laws, threats or special decrees. It does seem that we can draw authentic analogies between the choice made by the midwives and choices made in other situations by those who 'fear God'. In the case of the midwives, the narrator has inserted a theological comment approving their choice (1:21).

The story of Moses may not be approved in all details by the narrator but we could scarcely read it as anything other than a story in which God is intimately involved. Neither the sparing of Moses by his parents nor the ingenuity or opportunism whereby Miriam successfully offers Jochebed to Pharaoh's daughter as wet nurse receives explicit approval by the narrator, but implicit

---

[23] Eli Weinberg, *Portrait of a People: a personal photographic record of the South African liberation struggle* (London: International Defence and Aid Fund) 1981 pp. 66–77 for a visual window into women's participation in the struggle.

throughout these paragraphs is approval at the baby's concealment from the authorities. The success of the basket episode needs no theological comment from the editor for the reader to see God's hand in it. The rest of the Exodus narrative is the comment.

The next stage is more controversial, but the validity of Moses' inner reaction to what he witnesses as an adult in Egypt is scarcely in question, whatever we make of his act of violence and subsequent flight.[24]

> One day, after Moses had grown up, he went out to his people and saw their forced labour. He saw an Egyptian beating a Hebrew, one of his kinsfolk . . . When he went out the next day, he saw two Hebrews fighting; and he said to the one who was in the wrong, 'Why do you strike your fellow Hebrew?'
>
> (Exod 2:11, 13)

There are identifiable elements of personal growth in this section. Moses has 'grown up' among Egyptians, but identifies with Hebrews. This presupposes self-awareness, feelings of social solidarity and a system of values. We might add as well, a sense of natural justice. In this brief paragraph, Moses takes sides because he cannot remain either Egyptian or a detached bystander. He has committed himself in both examples to the side of the wronged person.

The verb 'to see' is in evidence. 'He saw their forced labour', 'he saw an Egyptian beating a Hebrew', 'he saw two Hebrews fighting'.[25] The word 'saw' that refers to visual imaging does duty for a whole sequence of perception and cognition which the

---

[24] The phrase 'his brothers' (*'eḥāyw*, v. 11 twice, NRSV 'his people', 'his kinsfolk') would be heard positively by an Israelite audience and 'their forced labour' (*siblōtām*) negatively. The narrator has already categorized the workload as designed to oppress in 1:11ff and its end is announced by God himself in 6:6f. These two references use the same term for workload, Hebrew *sibᵉlāh*, as in 2:11, but other passages could be added, such as 2:23 where the word used is Hebrew *ᵃbōdāh*, 'slavery' in NRSV. The narrator does not disclose his perspective on the killing of the Egyptian or on Moses' flight from Egypt. We are probably meant to approve Moses' intervention resisting the shepherds who scattered the flocks of Jethro's daughter at the well (2:17).

[25] Two quotations from Paulo Freire are given a new twist if applied here:

> While no-one liberates themselves by their own efforts alone, neither are they liberated by others. The leaders must realise that their own conviction of the need for struggle was not given to them by anyone else—if it is authentic. . . . Only the leaders' involvement in a real historical situation leads them to criticise it and to wish to change it. . . . At all stages of their liberation, the oppressed must see themselves as people engaged in the vocation of becoming more fully human. Reflection and action become essential. True reflection leads to action but that action will only be a genuine praxis if there is critical reflection on its consequences.
>
> (*The Pedagogy of the Oppressed*, pp. 41f)

narrative style does not directly describe. Despite this trait of Hebrew narrative not to admit readers to the reflective process or stream of consciousness of its main protagonists, we are put into the picture. We do know the way Moses saw it. If readers wondered how Moses handled an awareness of his dual nationality and double identity, this paragraph resolves it. If Moses had not previously questioned social structures in the Delta region, then question and response emerge in action and confrontation. The episode is an epiphany, a moment of destiny which shapes Moses' future. The rest of Exodus will confirm the wrongness of enslavement and of Hebrew-on-Hebrew strife. More significantly, Exodus will unfold a response from God which goes far beyond this response of Moses. Yahweh's killing of Egyptians will be on a far grander scale. On a larger scale too will be the angry rounding on Moses as leader and judge by fellow Israelites for his role in their lives. Brief as this paragraph from Moses' manhood in Egypt is, and restrained as the editorial comment is, it gives us a preview of the events to follow.

If conscientization involves a critical step back from what was previously seen as the normal state of affairs because it exists, is familiar, and has been that way for some time, then Moses took that critical step which threw the whole social and ethnic system into question. Conscientization involves distinguishing human institutions which may be accidental, arbitrary and unjust from structures legitimated by moral values or by God's direct pronouncement.[26]

THE CONSCIENTIZATION OF GOD

The next aspect to conscientization in the Exodus story is more startling in that God himself is conscientized. God is not an active participant in the narrative until the end of the third chapter. On his first appearance, he is conscientized to respond to the oppressive situation by the cries of distress:

---

[26] There are still many societies and cultures today where there is no tradition of questioning tradition. One thinks, for instance, of the role of women in many male-dominated cultures or tribal groups today. When traditional roles are questioned—in relation to womens' legal standing, access to education, contraception or jobs—this questioning of the status quo may be done by only a small minority group and against the background of male resistance and female complicity. The irrationality of male dominance is rather well illustrated by Cambridge University, which resisted awarding degrees to women until decades after the first women had proved their academic ability and after resistance to the political right of women to vote had crumbled away.

The Israelites groaned under their slavery, and cried out. Out of the slavery, their cry for help rose up to God. God heard their groaning, and God remembered his covenant with Abraham, Isaac, and Jacob. God looked upon the Israelites, and God took notice of them.

(Exod 2:23f)

Then the LORD said, 'I have observed the misery of my people who are in Egypt; I have heard their cry on account of their taskmasters. Indeed, I know their sufferings, and I have come down to deliver them from the Egyptians . . .The cry of the Israelites has now come to me; I have also seen how the Egyptians oppress them . . .

(Exod 3:7f,9)

As readers, we are reminded of the time scale before the narrator offers these statements about God's response. The worsening situation began in 1:8 after Joseph's death. Moses has grown up by 2:11, and immediately before God stirs, we are told that it was only 'after a long time' that the pharaoh died from whom Moses fled (2:23). Spectacular as the divine intervention is in Exodus, when it comes, the narrator does not want us to overlook the fact that the bad situation of the Hebrews lasted for a prolonged period, and thereafter only changed for the worse as Pharaoh demanded brick quotas without straw, and state repression increased (5:10ff).

The entry of God into the story as active participant is rather reminiscent of the Genesis Flood and Babel story in its bold anthropomorphisms. God is in heaven. The cries have to 'rise up to God'. God then looks, takes note and comes down to help. The boldness of the spatial metaphor is matched by 'God remembered', as though needing to be prompted by the sound of the distress. There is artistry in the depiction of the distress.[27] The spontaneous groans of 2:23 express pain rather than appeal to God

---

[27] 'Rise up to' is *ʿālāh ʾel*. The use of both the verb meaning 'to ascend, mount, go up' with the preposition 'to, unto' suggests travelling a distance and reaching as far as God. This phrase in 2:23b, and the parallel phrase of 3:9 'has come to me', are complemented by 'going down to deliver' *yārad lᵉ* in 3:8. At Babel, God 'goes down' to have a closer look at the work of the tower builders (*yārad* Gen 11:5, 7). 'God remembered his covenant' (Exod 2:24b) is like the statement 'God remembered Noah' which is set at the hinge of the palistrophe in the Flood narrative (Gen 8:1). Matching these colourful repetitions of cries ('groan' *ʾnḥ*, 'cry out' *zᵉʿq, šwʿ ṣʿq*) and divine perception is the variety of words used to describe the oppressive experience: 'slavery' *ʿᵉbōdāh*, 'misery' *ʿᵒniy*, 'sufferings' *makʾōbāyw*, 'oppression' *laḥaṣ* (2:23 3:7,9). The distribution of these and other terms for oppression in the Old Testament and their significance for constructing a theology of the Old Testament is studied by TD Hanks, *God so loved the Third World: the Bible, the Reformation, and Liberation theologies* (Maryknoll: Orbis) 1983 chaps 1 & 2. For a technical form-critical study, see RN Boyce, *The Cry to God in the Old Testament*, SBLD 103, 1988, pp. 47ff.

for covenant protection. The next phrase speaks of a 'cry for help', but God is not specified as the one addressed. Nevertheless, the cry reaches God and triggers a suzerain response.

We can see the parallels between Moses who 'sees' then acts and God who 'sees' and 'knows' (2:25, 3:7, 9), then acts. If we find conscientization in Exodus, then we will need to admit that it is God who carries out the praxis, who works for radical transformation. The people definitely do not. Though they are brought to a perception of an alternative reality—freedom—they are powerless to work for it. Indeed that very vision is overwhelmed by the misery of their present experience. The initial reaction of the people to the news of rescue delivered by Moses and Aaron is very positive, but when the levels of repression increase distress and anger displace hope.

> The people believed; and when they heard that the LORD had given heed to the Israelites and that he had seen their misery, they bowed down and worshipped.
>
> (Exod 4:31)
>
> Moses told this to the Israelites; but they would not listen to Moses, because of their broken spirit and their cruel slavery.
>
> (Exod 6:9)

There is no smooth journey from one stage of faith to another for either Moses or for the Israelites. In between the two quotations above which describe the state of the people, Moses, bitterly accused by them, himself accuses God, 'O LORD, why have you mistreated this people? . . . you have done nothing at all to deliver your people' (5:23). The Israelites return to trust again only after the 'conversion' experience when they have seen the results of the salvation in the form of the Egyptians lying dead on the seashore (14:31). Without 'seeing', 'believing' is very difficult.

THE TESTING OF RELATIONSHIP

This recurrent pattern of despair and accusation is continued beyond the exodus itself, first in the Marah incident, then after the Elim oasis. After Marah, God issues a conditional promise about physical health dependent on obedience, summed up as a test—'there he put them to the test' (15:25).[28] The incident in the

---

[28] The Piel form of *nsh*—'to test, put on trial' is used in Abraham's test in Gen 22:1, and for Israel's tests in Exod 15:25, 16:4 and 20:20, each time in connection with a command from God which demands obedience as response. The threefold occurrence of 'to test' in Exodus, combined with the typological analogies between Abraham's experience and obedience to torah (Gen 26:5) and Israel's experience substantiates this motif of a spiritual test as a pattern in faith development linking the patriarchal and later national periods.

Wilderness of Sin two months after the exodus is a preview of how Israel will respond to the giving of the Torah.

> I am going to rain bread from heaven for you, and each day the people shall go out and gather enough for that day. In that way I will test them, whether they will follow my instruction or not.
>
> (Exod 16:4)

Once again, as in the Abraham story, a physical journey is the outward and physical accompaniment to the inward and spiritual pilgrimage. Once again, God will test the quality of the response to his instructions. The Hebrew phrase 'I will put them to a trial: will they walk according to my instruction or not?' combines the 'walking' metaphor with the concept of a test.[29] This small instruction (*tōrāh*) on gathering manna is a prelude to the larger *tōrāh* of the covenant stipulations. Some fail, as the maggoty test results demonstrate (16:20).

The two tests of Exod 15 and 16 are benign compared with the command to sacrifice Isaac, and, as we have seen, the walk from Egypt to Sinai was always part of a rescue operation and not a punishment. That this walk through the Wilderness was a 'testing experience' in the colloquial sense is obvious. To borrow Mandela's title, this was *No Easy Walk to Freedom*. There was the unfamiliarity of the environment, the thirst and exhaustion they experienced (15:22, 16:3, 17:1ff), capped by the Amalekite attack (17:8ff). Threading through the journey episodes is the 'murmuring motif' with the verb 'to complain' (*lūn*) first appearing at Exod 15:24 and recurring at key points.[30] Already the reaction of the Israelites to lack of water in chap. 17 has the ironic twist to it of 'putting Yahweh on trial' (*nsh*—'to test' in 17:2b, 7b). The names Massah and Meribah ('Test' and 'Strife') enshrine this episode in their etymologies. This reverberates in Temple liturgy. Psa 95:8 vibrates with the confrontation between the Israelites on one side against Moses and God on the other.

Yet the journey to Sinai is qualitatively different from the forty years of wandering in the wilderness imposed as a discipline because of the Israelites' unwillingness to enter the Promised Land

---

[29] Durham's translation (*Exodus*, p. 215) retains a closer link to the Hebrew than NRSV's.

[30] Following on from the use of 'complain' (*lūn*) 15:24 are 16:2,7,8,9,12 and 17:3. The climax comes in Num 14:2, 27, 29, 36. For a wider discussion, see GW Coats, *Rebellion in the Wilderness* (Nashville: Abingdon) 1968. Behind the name Massah lies the root *nsh*—'to test'; behind Meribah is the root 'to strive, contend, file legal suit' *ryb* and the noun *rīb*—'lawsuit'. On the reverberations of Massah and Meribah, see Num 20:13, Deut 33:8, Psa 106 as well as Psa 95.

after the report of the spies. In Num 14, God complains that the Israelites 'have seen my glory and the signs that I did in Egypt and in the wilderness, and yet have tested me these ten times and have not obeyed my voice' (v. 22). There has been a premonition of this final provocation and desire to 'go back to Egypt' (v. 4) in the Exodus travels.

If there are stages of faith to be found in the Exodus story, then there are also stages of unwillingness and complaint. No neat chart of spiritual formation can be drawn up. If the Exodus story is a chronicle of trial and error learning, then trials were failed and learning did not occur, despite the moments at the Reed Sea and at the foot of Sinai. The Israelite experience simply does not fit into a theory of faith development if we mean by that some sort of process or progress to a stage which once attained becomes a platform for further progress. There is no high plateau of sanctification in Exodus. The Reed Sea and Sinai episodes were 'mountain-top experiences'—to use the language of devotional circles, where Californians might speak of 'peak experiences'. The 'before and after' of these 'conversion' and covenant experiences do not support a growth or development model very happily. We seem to be presented with a series of best moments and worst moments, each emerging out of its own specific set of circumstances.

EXODUS HERMENEUTICS IN RETROSPECT

The Exodus story occupies a privileged position in the hermeneutics of Liberation. Liberation theologians such as Croatto have concentrated on the Exodus as the paradigm of biblical salvation. It unfolds with new meanings as the text is read and re-read in new situations.[31]

---

[31] JS Croatto, *Exodus—a hermeneutic of freedom* (Maryknoll: Orbis) 1981 and 'The Socio-Historical and Hermeneutical Relevance of the Exodus', pp. 125–133 in B van Iersel & A Weiler (eds), *Exodus—a lasting paradigm = Concilium* 189, 1987. For a coherent review of Croatto's hermeneutical method, see G West, *Biblical Hermeneutics of Liberation: modes of reading the Bible in the South African context*, Cluster Monograph series 1 (Pietermaritzburg: Cluster Publications) 1991, pp. 124–139. West categorises Croatto's approach as a reading 'in front of the text' as opposed to readings of the text and behind the text. To simplify, this means taking a committed stance with the poor and viewing the Exodus liberation within the canon conceived as a single text that bears a liberative semantic axis including within it re-readings that cumulatively support God's concern for the liberation of the oppressed.

Indeed, the case for the privileged position of Exodus within the Hebrew canon is a very strong one. Israel's Exodus experience and long walk to the Promised Land have left an indelible mark on the Old Testament. Study of the Exodus used in motive clauses in Torah stipulations, in the language of redemption in the psalms and the use of the New Exodus motif in the prophets, especially in Isaiah 40–55, confirms that the Exodus does occupy a unique position in the Old Testament.[32] Gauged by later allusions within the Old Testament canon, Exodus motifs tend to outweigh other traditions or clusters of imagery from Israel's Salvation History, even the Zion traditions.[33] By comparison, little use is made in the rest of the Hebrew canon of the Abraham narrative or the Eden story.

In Israel's cult too, Exodus-Wilderness associations occupied a prime place, providing a background to the three national festivals which require all males to 'appear before the LORD' (Exod 23:16f), the basis for the Jerusalem festivals referred to in the Gospels and Acts.[34] The reforms of Hezekiah and Josiah (2 Chron 30 and 35)

---

[32] On Exodus motifs in motive clauses, see Exod 22:21ff, Deut 5:12ff, 15:12ff, 24:14ff, Lev 11:45, 19:33ff, Num 15:37ff. On the Exodus as basis for salvation language, see 'save, deliver', 'saviour' (*yšʿ môšîʿa*) Psa 106:8,21 Psa 74:12, Psa 76:9; 'redeem', 'redeemer' (*gʾl gōʾēl*) Psa 77:15, 106:10, 78:35; 'ransom' (*pdh*) Psa 78:42; 'save, pull out' (*ḥlṣ*) Psa 81:7; 'bring out' (*yṣ*) Psa 68:6, 136:11; 'perform justice, do right acts' (*ʿśh ṣᵉdāqōt*) Psa 103:6. On New Exodus imagery in the Prophets, see Isa 11:11ff, Isa 43:14ff, 48:20f, 52:11f, Jer 23:7f, Ezek 20:33ff, Zech 10:8ff. Some have wanted to broaden Liberation theology's Exodus motif—e.g. JH Yoder, 'Exodus and Exile: the two faces of liberation' *Missionalia* 2.1 (1974) 29–41 and J Malan, 'A complement to the Exodus Motif in Theology?' *JTSA* 61 (1987) 3–13. Their theological points may stand, but studies such as M Fishbane's, written outside the circle of Liberation Theology, support Croatto's claims for the privileged position of the Exodus as a typological paradigm within the Old Testament— Fishbane, *Text and Texture* (New York: Schocken) 1979, pp. 121–140 'The "Exodus" Motif/The Paradigm of Historical Renewal' and *Biblical Interpretation in Ancient Israel* (Oxford: Clarendon) 1985, pp. 358ff.

[33] This is especially the case if Exod 15 *The Song of the Sea* is the prime source of the Divine Warrior traditions in the Old Testament. On this, see the seminal discussion of FM Cross, *Canaanite Myth and Hebrew Epic* (Cambridge: HUP) pp. 112ff and the studies of the Divine Warrior in Apocalyptic by PD Hanson—'Jewish Apocalyptic against its Near Eastern Environment' *Revue Biblique* 78 (1971) 31–58; 'Old Testament Apocalyptic Reexamined' *Interpretation* 25 (1971) 454–479; *The Dawn of Apocalyptic* (Philadelphia: Fortress) 1975.

[34] To Passover and Unleavened Bread (Exod 12), one should add the association of the national festival of Pentecost (Exod 23:16) with the giving of the law at Sinai three months after the Exodus, and the feast of Tabernacles' association with living in tents in the wilderness (Lev 23:40ff). See Childs's comments on the three national pilgrim festivals cited in Exod 23:14–17 (*Exodus*, pp.482ff). If the Exodus-Wilderness associations of the Feast of Pentecost and Tabernacles are regarded as secondary, post-exilic developments, this only serves to

give a prominent place to keeping the Passover in particular, while covenant renewals in Deuteronomy, in Joshua, during Asa's reign (2 Chron 15), as a feature of Josiah's reform (2 Kgs 23) and in the post-exilic community of Ezra-Nehemiah all look back to the precedent of the national covenant at Sinai.[35] If elements of the Exodus story are so influential in Israel's literature and self-perception as a nation, this serves only to heighten the hermeneutical debate about Christian re-readings of Israel's national beginnings.[36]

We noted at the beginning of this chapter that there are devotional readings and political readings of the Exodus story. Our study has shown that exodus from Goshen and covenant at Sinai offer a spirituality in which the vertical and the horizontal relationships are held together—as indeed they are in the very content of the Ten Commandments of Exod 20, or in Jesus' summary of the two greatest commandments of the Torah, to love God and neighbour. Yahweh's confrontation with Pharaoh and the Egyptian status quo, leading to liberation in the narrow political sense, is complemented by his demand for the most wholehearted and exclusive devotion possible. Political freedom and a transforming 'fear of the LORD' belong together in Exodus.

As a guiding principle for re-readings of Exodus, we must respect the shape and form of the book as a theological entity and do justice to the ensemble of its key motifs. Thus Exodus is more than the triumphalism of the *Song of the Sea* (Exod 15). It is more than the institution of cultic festivals, cultic paraphernalia and cultic personnel (Exod 12–13, 25–30, 35–40). It is more than a birth legend, a call narrative and a tale of heroic leadership. It is more than the formation of a community with laws regulating its

---

highlight the enduring and influential quality of the Exodus traditions. Compare the prominence the Exodus–Wilderness traditions have in the post-exilic Levitical prayer (Neh 9:9–21)

[35] The post-exilic renewals of Neh 8 and 10 involved reading and re-readings of the Torah. Neh 8 is set within the feast of Tabernacles with Neh 8:17 focusing on the booths as reminders of the Wilderness wanderings. On the process of re-readings involved, see DJA Clines 'Nehemiah 10 as an example of early Jewish Biblical Exegesis' JSOT 21 (1981) 111–117 with HGM Williamson's comments in *Ezra, Nehemiah*, WBC 16 (Waco: Word) 1985, pp. 333ff.

[36] See J Loader 'Exodus, Liberation Theology and Theological Argument' *JTSA* 59 (1987) 3–18 for an attempt to engage with the hermeneutical issues during the intense struggle in South Africa that was sharpened theologically by the formulation of *The Kairos Document: challenge to the Church*, rev. 2nd ed. (Skotaville/Eerdmans) 1986 which itself utilized the Exodus story—see *Kairos* Sections 4.2 and 4.5.

behaviour (Exod 20–23, 34).[37] It is all of this—covenantal, sacramental, supernatural, celebratory, communal—and more. The sum is larger than the parts, and if we are to speak of an Exodus paradigm, it needs to be in terms of the whole, not one selected part.

There is another element to this taking of the whole rather than isolated parts. Beyond Exodus lies the history of Israel and the prophetic denunciations of Israel's own oppressive practices. If Exodus has power to inspire and transform, it is also coldly sobering in itself and in its preview of Israel's history beyond it. In the same way, beyond colonialism and independence in Africa lie the problems of tribalism and new community. Beyond democracy by vote in Europe lie the problems of unemployment and marginalization. Beyond the collapse of communism and its secret police lie the problems of nationalism, crime and poverty. Beyond Pentecost, which celebrated the gift of the Law at Sinai and the gift of the Holy Spirit to the church, lie the records of in-fighting and splits in Christian history, including the sectarian violence in Northern Ireland.

There is a realism within Exodus about covenant relationship and covenant life. Beyond liberation from Egypt lie the laws of covenant that make living together in covenant a possibility. Several of these laws, and especially those dealing with categories of slave and means of dealing with criminality in society, look to us like a contingent adaptation of existing customs and legal codes.[38] Apodictic commands and casuistic case laws and penalties mingle. Ideal and contingent reality are juxtaposed in the Covenant Code of Exod 20–23.[39] No leaving behind of sin is envisaged

---

[37] See now PD Hanson, *The People Called: the growth of Community in the Bible* (London: Harper & Row) 1986 for a major study of the trajectory this motif follows from Old to New Testament with an Appendix on the underlying hermeneutical assumptions involved in such study.

[38] Technical studies of Near Eastern law collections and the drafting of laws in the Pentateuch disclose the contextuality of Israel's laws, especially the case laws. For a recent discussion with references to the previous work of scholars such as JJ Finkelstein, SM Paul, HJ Boecker, BS Jackson and R Westbrook, see GC Chirichigno, *Debt-Slavery in Israel and the Ancient Near East*, JSOTS 141, (Sheffield: JSOT Press) 1993. Of course, there have been devout and intelligent readers of Exodus who have taken its slave laws, together with other canonical material on slaves from Genesis to Paul, as a biblical endorsement of slavery—most notably the Reformed theologians Charles Hodge of Princeton and John Murray of Westminster Theological Seminary in the 19th and 20th centuries. See the informative article by K Giles, 'The Biblical Argument for Slavery: can the Bible mislead? a case study in Hermeneutics' *EQ* 66:1 (1994) 3–17.

[39] For instance, the ideal of equal justice for all without bribery or bias (Exod 23:3, 6–8) and the prohibition of oppression of aliens, orphans and widows (Exod 22:21ff) alongside the contingent 'When a man sells his daughter as a

for this redeemed community. This emerges from a holistic reading of Exodus. There is a lot of pain and failure in the Exodus story, including Hebrew fighting Hebrew at the beginning, followed by bitter regrets and complaints beyond Egypt. If there is the pillar of cloud and fire, there is also the Golden Calf in Exodus. If there is covenant at Sinai, there are also the broken tablets. The stages of faith are convoluted and jerky.

Further clues to guide our reading of Exodus and our reading of the world may lie within Exodus itself and within the Old Testament. We found that Exodus follows on from Genesis, linked by Joseph (Exod 1:5,6,8 and Exod 13:19). There is continuity of story, continuity of promise and continuity of covenant relationship (Exod 2:24). Within Exodus there is typology which is itself a form of continuity. We noted the burning bush and the Sinai theophany, the consecration of the people at Sinai and the consecration of the priests for Tabernacle service. Typology needs continuity if it is to avoid arbitrariness of comparison. If there is continuity, there may be analogy. One context may mirror another, at least in some respects. As we noted, both holiness and liberationist readings assume a continuity, an analogy of struggle and passage to freedom. The fundamental continuity informing our Christian re-reading of Exodus is the continuity of God and of covenant renewal. The New Covenant meal in the Upper Room at Passover is in continuity with the covenant meal on top of Sinai (Exod 24:9–11).

There is another kind of continuity in Exodus. Experience of liberation from Egyptian oppression is extended to commandment not to oppress (Exod 22:21 and 23:9). The motive clause 'for you were strangers in the land of Egypt' commits liberated Israelites to an imaginative reading of life from the underside. The white American readings of Exodus as endorsing slavery discussed by Giles under the provocative title 'The Biblical Argument for Slavery: can the Bible mislead? a case study in Hermeneutics' are not readings from the underside, readings by the oppressed. No more were the readings of the Bible by white Dutch Reformed theologians in South Africa that justified or tinkered with apartheid. The hermeneutical stance of both these American and Afrikaner readings of text and context was not that demanded by the Exodus rubric, 'you know the heart of a stranger, for you were strangers in the land of Egypt' (Exod 23:9). Ironically, those whites who opposed the abolition of slavery in

---

slave . . .' (Exod 21:7ff), which is probably an Israelite adaptation of the slave-daughter adoption contract known in the Near East that offers some protection and rights to the departing daughter—see Chirichigno, *Debt-Slavery*, p. 244ff.

America and of apartheid in South Africa were also those whose forebears had emerged from British colonial rule. In theory they should have identified with an underside reading of their contemporary contexts all the more readily. This illustrates the truth of Nürnberger's observation:

> All of us are located somewhere in the social system and . . . this location has profound effect on how we see reality, how we feel and what we think. Normally theologians underestimate this effect of structural situation on mentality and concentrate on convictions . . .[40]

A holistic approach to salvation does more justice to the Exodus story as a paradigm.[41] One such approach is found in Brueggemann's essay 'The Exodus Narrative as Israel's Articulation of Faith Development'. This essay emphasizes the communal and personal polarities in spiritual transformation, the liturgical and the political, the theological and covenantal, arriving at this conclusion:

> In choosing this new God who is dangerously jealous and radically compassionate, the peasant community always found it had also chosen *a new mode of social existence* along with the *new God*. This God may not be chosen apart from a particular social existence.[42]

This summary statement neglects neither the socio-political nor the transcendent dimensions of Exodus. It also implies that commitment to this new God, who is not so new now, will just as likely involve us in a commitment to a social existence that runs cross-grain to contemporary states, cultures and communities in our world. Dislocating ourselves from the inertia of compliance with these cultural patterns will involve some wrenching experiences. That this will involve an identification with the experience of the oppressed and marginalized within these societies is the persuasive argument of liberationist re-readings.

Our concern has been more specific here than to offer an in-depth review of the hermeneutics of liberation theology or of

---

[40] C Nürnberger 'How does the Church address the Structure-related Convictions of its Members?' *Journal of Theology for Southern Africa* 53 (1985) 22–53, p. 27.

[41] See the summaries of group interaction on the Exodus in ML Branson & CR Padilla, *Conflict and Context: hermeneutics in the Americas* (Grand Rapids: Eerdmans) 1986, section 2.1.1 S Reid 'The Book of Exodus: a laboratory for hermeneutics' pp. 155–164, section 2.1.2 E Sánchez-Centina 'Hermeneutics and Context: the Exodus', pp. 165–170, section 2.1.3 'Report by Thomas McAlpine' pp. 171f, and section 2.1.4 J Stam 'Final Report from the Exodus Group' pp. 173–177.

[42] *Hope within History*, p. 26 italics Brueggemann's.

holiness church piety. Instead, we have focused on human and divine responses to the situation of Egyptian oppression, Hebrew slavery and what Brueggemann called the 'wrenching transitions' involved in spiritual growth. The Exodus-Wilderness story is as profoundly supernatural as it is religious, political and sociological. The events of Passion Week are likewise profoundly religious, sociological, political —and supernatural. They involve the Sanhedrin, the Roman Empire, Jesus and his circle of disciples. There is experience of conflict, crying out, death—and resurrection. The Exodus-Wilderness story is profoundly relevant to the kind of God who calls human beings into covenant with himself. So too is the meal in the Upper Room, the walk to Emmaus and the breakfast on the shore of Lake Galilee. The fear of the Lord, new covenant commitment and meals, characterize both narratives, the Exodus story and the Passion narratives.

SECOND-GENERATION RE-READING

As Christian re-readers of the Exodus-Wilderness stories and as readers of the Gospels, we are not participants in those original transforming experiences. Yet history and experience show that those narratives hold an inspiring power of transformation and offer it to a responsive faith. Second-generation Israelites who lived within the boundaries of the Promised Land did not experience God in the same way as the Exodus generation. Manna gave way to ploughing, sowing, weeding, reaping, threshing and grinding.[43] No more is our experience of Christian discipleship the same as the apostolic generation's experience. The original circle of Christian disciples met God incarnate face to face before and after the crucifixion. That is not an option today.

For Liberation Theology, the problem created by focusing on the Exodus story is the secular, non-interventionist, 'second generation' experience of contemporary history. Why does God not respond to the cry of the oppressed today in the way that he responded to the Hebrews in Egypt—if that story is a paradigm? This is a burning question. One response would be to decide that the Exodus is legendary as event and illusory as paradigm. Indeed, this has the powerful attraction of confirming our worst moments

---

[43] Josh 5:10–12 links the celebration of Passover with the cessation of the manna and eating the produce of Canaan. Westermann subdivides a study of salvation in Old Testament theology into the two complementary components of deliverance and blessing. Exodus represents the deliverance and crops the blessing. Sometimes these polarities are presented as Salvation History and Creation theologies. For a discussion of this dialectic, see J Goldingay, *Theological Diversity and the Authority of the Old Testament* (Grand Rapids: Eerdmans) 1987 Chap. 7 'A Unifying Approach to "Creation" and "Salvation" in the Old Testament', p. 200ff.

of cynicism and world-weariness. There is abundant evidence to cite in support of the thesis that nothing much has changed about the world since the Exodus—and since the Christ event. Alternatively, we might, with regret but less despair, conclude that God no longer operates in the world through supernatural intervention on such a public and national scale as the Exodus story attests. This seems to be a somewhat obvious truth. This might leave the Exodus as anomaly rather than paradigm, depending on what expectations are raised in a reader response.

Within the Old Testament there is a hermeneutic that points the way to a 'second-generation' use of the Exodus experience and one that is not supernatural and interventionist in the manner of the Exodus story itself. Within the Old Testament, the re-use of Exodus imagery contributed to the interpretation of the Babylonian bondage. Yet the Exile came to an end through Persian politics—not through miracles and a journey home through a desert that blossomed. The return to the Promised Land was sanctioned and supported by the Persian authorities. Because the exodus from Exile was without miracle, it is, like contemporary history, open to a secular re-reading, in this case revolving around a change of Persian policy that was not confined to Jewish subjects. Furthermore, the freedom produced by this Persian policy switch was relative. This is clearly enunciated in Nehemiah:

> Here we are, slaves to this day—slaves in the land that you gave to our ancestors to enjoy its fruit and its good gifts. Its rich yield goes to the kings whom you have set over us because of our sins; they have power also over our bodies and over our livestock at their pleasure, and we are in great distress.
>
> (Neh 9:36f)

The sentiments expressed here are the post-exilic expression of 'the critique of ideology', 'the embrace of pain' and the 'practice of social imagination'—phrases that are part of Brueggemann's analysis of Exodus. Neh 9:36f serves to remind us that our Christian experience, like that of the refugees from Babylonia, is one of relative freedom only, whether we are speaking in terms of freedom from oppressive structures, or personal freedom from sinful attitudes, habits and behaviour.[44] Liberationist and Holiness stances must surely both recognize this relativity and the 'not yet'

---

[44] We can illustrate both the continuity of the freedom trajectory within the canon and its incomplete realization by reference to the communal struggle in Galatians ('for freedom Christ has set us free' [Gal 5:1], and the lapses of Peter and the Galatians [Gal 2:11ff and 3:1ff]), as well as by reference to its complement, the internal struggle within the believer between 'the flesh' and the Spirit (Gal 5:16ff).

component of human experience, whether communal or individual.

The theological and social insight of Ezra's prayer is accurate. There is a realism about it. It is also true that a vision of a greater freedom and a deeper realization of covenant promises surfaces as a longing within this very lament. This said, we shall have to conclude that insight and transformation are not one and the same, though they may be related. This applies to the vision for transformation of socio-political contexts and just as much to the transformation of an individual's inner being. The paradigm is filled with unfulfilled possibilities whether that paradigm is the Exodus story or the Easter story. 'Today you will be with me in Paradise' (Lk 23:43) is one such paradigm promise which, if appropriated as a promise by Christian re-readings of the Passion narrative, remains for us unfulfilled in the here and now. The world is no paradise and to read our times as proof of a linear progress would be naively optimistic, whether we are looking at the environment, world peace, health, poverty or evangelism.

When we read the Exodus-Wilderness story of liberation and covenant in its canonical trajectory, this trajectory opens new windows on God's involvement, and yet it also postpones the ultimate 'Promised Land' even further. Isa 40-55's re-reading of the Exodus paradigm includes the mysterious figure of the Suffering Servant whose mission embraces world justice, covenant renewal and suffering pain.[45] If we take our hermeneutical cue from the Old Testament's own re-reading of the Exodus-Wilderness in Deutero-Isaiah, a Christian spirituality will hear the 'Fear not . . .' oracles and the invitation to come into covenant, to 'seek the Lord while he may be found' (Isa 55:6). It will reflect this call in its evangelistic preaching and respond to it in personal devotion. A Christian re-reading will also respond to the model of Servanthood that Israel was called to, with its promise that one who 'fears the Lord and obeys the voice of his servant' will not 'walk in darkness'(Isa 50:10). And a Christian spirituality will be confronted with the pain from which covenant servanthood is not exempt.

SUMMARY AND CONCLUSION

Exodus occupies a privileged place in the Old Testament analogous to the Easter story in the Gospels and offering a continuity of

---

[45] For an expansion of this point, see J Goldingay 'The Man of War and the Suffering Servant: the Old Testament and the Theology of Liberation' Tyndale Bulletin 27 (1976) 79–113 together with TD Hanks, *God So Loved the Third World*, Chap. 5 'The Oppressed Servant: a *relectura* of Isaiah 52:13–53:12', pp. 73–96 and FE Deist, 'Reflections on Reinterpretation in and of

trajectory from Sinai covenant to New Covenant, from Passover to Upper Room. Each Christian re-reading of Exodus has an implicit typology bridging ancient and contemporary contexts. Delineating the continuities and discontinuities between the ancient context and ours is facilitated by the re-use of the Exodus within the Old Testament itself by 'second-generation' Israelites. But our hermeneutics is affected by becoming aware of our location in the social system and how it biases our reading of the Bible. The false polarities of individual piety and public politics are challenged by Exodus.

The Israelites go through various stages of pain, faith, fear and despair during their stay in Egypt and along their journey through the Wilderness. We cannot speak about these stages of faith as though there is a progress in spiritual maturity that matches the number of kilometres travelled from Egypt. Despite this lack of spiritual development in a linear sense, there are moments of conscientization and moments of faith in Exodus in which Israel, or some individuals within it, grasp with lucidity what it means to truly respond to Yahweh.

The Exodus story has transformative power when read as a whole. Its unmasking of oppression in structural and ideological guises is mingled with its invitation into covenant and community and 'fear of the LORD'. There is testing of faith and failure. There is covenant, covenant breaking and covenant renewal. There are ideals for new community and contingent, contextualized social codes in juxtaposition. Exodus keeps alive a vision of freedom and divine presence alongside a realism about the present as transitional, partial and contingent. Exodus offers us a story centred around a journey. Its primary destination is God himself: 'I bore you on eagles' wings and brought you to myself' (Exod 19:4).

BIBLIOGRAPHY

R Bauckham, *The Bible in Politics: how to read the Bible politically*, Third Way Books (London: SPCK) 1989.

ML Branson & CR Padilla, *Conflict and Context: hermeneutics in the Americas* (Grand Rapids: Eerdmans) 1986.

R M Brown, *Spirituality and Liberation: overcoming the Great Fallacy*, (Sevenoaks: Spire/Hodder & Stoughton) 1988.

W Brueggemann, 'The Exodus Narrative as Israel's Articulation of Faith Development', chap. 1 pp. 7–26 in *Hope within History* (Atlanta: John Knox) 1987.

BS Childs, *Exodus*, OTL (London: SCM) 1974.

Isaiah 53' pp. 1–11 in *Old Testament Essays Vol 3*, Dept of OT UNISA, Pretoria, 1985 with application to surrender of white power in South Africa.

RL Cohn, 'Liminality in the Wilderness', pp. 7–23 in *The Shape of Sacred Space*, (Chico: Scholars Press) 1981.

JS Croatto, *Exodus—a hermeneutic of freedom* (Maryknoll: Orbis) 1981

——, 'The Socio-Historical and Hermeneutical Relevance of the Exodus', pp. 125–133 in B van Iersel & A Weiler (eds), *Exodus—a lasting paradigm*, = *Concilium* 189, 1987.

JI Durham, *Exodus*, WBC 3 (Waco: Word) 1987.

JC Exum, ' "You shall let every daughter live": a study of Exodus 1:8–2:10', *Semeia* 28 (1983) The Bible and Feminist Hermeneutics, pp. 63–82.

M Fishbane, 'The "Exodus" Motif/The Paradigm of Historical Renewal', pp. 121–140 in *Text and Texture* (NewYork: Schocken) 1979.

——, *Biblical Interpretation in Ancient Israel* (Oxford: Clarendon) 1985, pp. 358ff.

Paulo Freire, *Pedagogy of the Oppressed* Penguin, 1974.

K Giles, 'The Biblical Argument for Slavery: can the Bible mislead? a case study in Hermeneutics', *EQ* 66:1 (1994) 3–17.

TD Hanks, *God so loved the Third World: the Bible, the Reformation, and Liberation theologies*, (Maryknoll: Orbis) 1983.

PD Hanson, *The People Called: the growth of Community in the Bible* (London: Harper & Row) 1986.

A Hope & S Timmel, *Training for Transformation: a handbook for community workers*, Vols. 1–3 (Gweru: Mambo Press) 1987.

C Johns, *Pentecostal Formation: a pedagogy among the oppressed*, (Sheffield: Sheffield Academic Press) 1993.

G Gutiérrez, *We drink from our own wells: the spiritual journey of a people* (London: SCM) 1984.

BC Lane, *Landscapes of the Sacred: geography and narrative in American spirituality*, (NewYork/Mahwah: Paulist Press) 1988.

J Malan, 'A complement to the Exodus Motif in Theology?' *JTSA* 61 (1987) 3–13.

TW Mann, *Divine Presence and Guidance in Israelite Traditions: the typology of exaltation*, (London: Johns Hopkins) 1977.

S Parpola & K Watanabe, *Neo-Assyrian Treaties and Loyalty Oaths*, SAA 2 (Helsinki: Helsinki Univ Press) 1988.

DCT Sheriffs, 'Moving on with God: key motifs in Exodus 13–20' *Themelios* 15.2 (1990) 49–60.

M Walzer, *Exodus and Revolution* (New York: Basic Books) 1985.

JH Yoder, 'Exodus and Exile: the two faces of liberation' *Missionalia* 2.1 (1974) 29–41.

[4]

Integrated Faith
A Walk Through Deuteronomy

INTRODUCTION

Following the trajectory of the 'fear of the LORD', of 'walking in his ways' and of God's testing of faith beyond the Exodus story, we arrive at Deuteronomy. We shall explore what Deuteronomy means by walking in God's ways, and draw on extra-biblical sources to elucidate the covenant vocabulary that Deuteronomy employs.[1] Though we shall nowhere discover parallels for the exclusive allegiance to Yahweh that Deuteronomy demands, we will find extra-biblical support for its vision of spirituality as a combination of devotion to God with harmony in communal relations.

Deuteronomy offers a retrospective on the entire wilderness experience as a test, preliminary to its record of the renewal of covenant, the transfer of leadership and entry into the Promised Land. Balancing the challenge to renewed allegiance, the book is pervaded with a spirit of rejoicing in the presence of Yahweh, and receiving the Promised Land as gift.[2]

---

[1] This treaty and covenant vocabulary is studied in great detail by Weinfeld and the Deuteronomic phrases are conveniently collected in Appendices (*Deut School*, pp. 320ff). His earlier study was 'Traces of Assyrian Treaty Formulae in Deuteronomy' *Biblica* 46 (1965) 417–427. This work is reflected in his volumes on Deuteronomy for the Anchor Bible series—*Deuteronomy 1–11*, AB 5 (London: Doubleday) 1991.

[2] JG McConville notes that there are some 131 occurrences in Deuteronomy of the verb *nātan*—'to give' with Yahweh as subject. The majority of these refer to the giving of the Promised Land (*Law and Theology in Deuteronomy*, JSOTS 33 [Sheffield: JSOT Press] 1984, p.12). On rejoicing before Yahweh in cultic ritual, see too Deut 12:11f referring to the occasions of burnt offerings and sacrifices, tithes, donations, and votive gifts; the national 'feast of weeks' at grain harvest, Deut 16:11; the first-fruits ceremony, Deut 26:11; the land occupation ceremony, Deut 27:7.

The laws on the tithe capture this tone and illustrate the inseparable link between gift and response, blessing and obedience, fear of the LORD and rejoicing:

> Set apart a tithe of all the yield of your seed that is brought in yearly from the field. In the presence of the LORD your God . . . you shall eat the tithe of your grain, your wine, and your oil, as well as the firstlings of your herd and flock, so that you may learn to fear the LORD your God always . . . and you shall eat there in the presence of the LORD your God, you and your household rejoicing together.
>
> (Deut 14:22f,26b)

The 'fear of the LORD' in this quotation is a learned behaviour that spans a lifetime, not an emotional moment. In fact, the recurrent 'fear of the LORD' in Deuteronomy, a phrase which is one of the hallmarks of its spirituality, carries a range of meanings determined by immediate context. At one edge of the range is the broad concept of moral awareness.[3] The centre of this semantic cluster of 'fearing Yahweh' is covenant-keeping. We know this from the dominance of covenant in Deuteronomy, but more specifically from the way that the 'fear of the LORD' is clustered with parallel phrases in verses such as the following:

> [12]So now, O Israel, what does the LORD your God require of you?
> Only to fear the LORD your God,
> to walk in all his ways,
> to love him,
> to serve the LORD your God
> with all your heart and with all your soul,
> [13]and to keep the commandments of the LORD your God
> and his decrees that I am commanding you today,
> for your own well-being.
>
> [20]You shall fear the LORD your God;
> him alone you shall worship;
> to him you shall hold fast,
> and by his name you shall swear.
>
> (Deut 10:12f, 20)

In this excerpt from chap. 10, the 'fear of Yahweh' is clustered with 'walking in all his ways', loving, serving, keeping the

---

[3] The Amalekite raiders who attacked Israel in the desert (Exod 17) 'did not fear God' (Deut 25:18), that is, they attacked without threat or provocation 'when you were faint and weary, and struck down all who lagged behind you'. Deuteronomy apparently judged this a breach of inter-group relations and norms of war. On 'The Fear of God' in Deuteronomy, see Weinfeld's discussion (*Deut School*, pp. 274–281).

commandments, worship and exclusive loyalty.[4] This is a spirituality of heart and behaviour. Chapter 10:16 speaks of circumcising 'the foreskin of the heart'. Decoded, the metaphor means internalizing the sign of the covenant so that the covenant relationship works out in attitude and behaviour towards God and fellow Israelites. It would be mistaken to describe the dictum of Deut 10:16 as a 'spiritualizing' of ritual, as though Deuteronomy were advocating that metaphorical 'circumcision' were to replace the physical rite. Clearly, Deuteronomy sees no inherent contradiction between inward spirituality and communal ritual. Deuteronomy is pressing home the idea of spiritual integrity within covenant, that is, the alignment of outward profession and inward disposition.[5] Hence Deut 10:17–19 applies covenant allegiance to social behaviour, the practice of justice and care for the alien, orphan and widow.

SOME LIGHT ON LAW AND WAY OF LIFE
FROM HAMMURABI

At this point, it will be helpful to draw some comparisons between law and piety in Mesopotamia and the biblical 'fear of the LORD' with its observance of covenant stipulations. The extra-biblical sources can be seen as alternatives to and as rivals of Yahwism, but they also confirm that there is a fundamental human need for a spirituality that embraces justice and harmonious social relations. The fact that our contemporary societies cannot function without developing laws on the same topics that are treated in the Mesopotamian collections supports our argument for a spirituality that embraces ethics, community and inward orientation.

Babylonian kings saw the observance of just laws as a way of life, and they made use of 'walking a path' imagery to describe the living out of these social codes. They held the vertical and horizontal of their piety together. The Akkadian phrase 'truth and

---

[4] Other passages where the 'fear of the LORD' appears are Deut 4:10f, 5:29, 6:2ff, 6:24, 8:6–10, 13:3f, 14:22f, 17:18ff, 28:58f, 31:12f.

[5] The same point about the need for integrity of outward sign and inner reality is made by Paul, though his argument supports the replacement of physical circumcision as unnecessary in a covenant relationship with God through Christ on the grounds that the inner reality of the covenant sign was present: 'For a person is not a Jew who is one outwardly, nor is true circumcision something external and physical. Rather, a person is a Jew who is one inwardly, and real circumcision is a matter of the heart—it is spiritual and not literal.' (Rom 2:28f)

equity' (*kittu u mīšaru*) from Mesopotamian edicts is in several
ways parallel to the Hebrew hendiadys 'justice and righteousness'
(*mišpāṭ wᵉṣᵉdāqāh*).[6] According to Psa 72, this 'justice' and 'righteousness' should be characteristic of a Judean king, and it should
epitomize the laws that his people live by. Moses depicts the Sinai
laws as the epitome of justice: 'And what other great nation has
statutes and ordinances as just as this entire law that I am setting
before you today?' (Deut 4:8). Hammurabi likewise describes his
rulings as 'just laws' (*dīnāt mīšarim*),[7] while 2nd millennium
Mesopotamian kings claimed 'truth and equity' in promulgating
their reform edicts. To be 'king of justice' (*šar mīšarim*) meant to
shepherd their people aright.

In promulgating his laws, Hammurabi links his concern for
social justice with his reverent fear of the gods: '(the gods) named
me, Hammurabi, the devout, god-fearing prince, to cause justice
(*mīšaram*) to appear in the land . . . I established truth and equity
(*kittu u mīšaru*)'.[8] Hammurabi is piously attentive to the gods'
shrines and festivals, as the rest of his Prologue goes on to describe
in some detail. These cultic details give substance to his phrase 'the
devout, god-fearing prince'.[9] 'Justice' and 'truth and justice' are
given concrete expression in the inscribed laws.

---

[6] See M Weinfeld, ' "Justice and Righteousness"—*mišpāṭ wᵉṣᵉdāqāh*—the
expression and its meaning' pp. 228–246 in HG Reventlow and Y Hoffman
(eds), *Justice and Righteousness: biblical themes and their influence*, JSOTS 137
(Sheffield: JSOT Press) 1992. Covering similar ground but with more detailed
reference to Yahweh's promulgation of law, see Weinfeld's ' "Justice and
Righteousness" in Ancient Israel against the background of "Social Reforms"
in the Ancient Near East' pp. 491–519 in H-J Nissen and J Renger (eds),
Mesopotamien und seine Nachbarn Teil II, Berliner Beitrage um Vorderen
Orient Band 1 (Berlin: Dietrich Reimer Verlag) 1982.

[7] Where NRSV has 'just', the Hebrew has *saddīq* 'righteous', an adjective that is
normally used of persons—Weinfeld, Deut, p. 195. Weinfeld suggests that 'by
using the exceptional expression, "just laws (*mišpaṭim ṣaddiqim*)", the author of
Deuteronomy employs a polemical note against the Hammurabi Code
because the Code of Hammurabi was copied for a thousand years in the
'canon' of Mesopotamia and so perhaps was known as an exemplar of laws
outside the Mesopotamian scribal circle (p. 202). Such a nuanced and allusive
reference to Hammurabi's Code by the Hebrew author, or direct knowledge
of it, seems a rather remote possibility.

[8] CH Prologue ia:28ff and va:20ff; *ANET*, 164f. The hendiadys 'truth and
equity' (*kittu u mīšaru*) appears at the end of the Prologue, leading into 'At that
time (I decreed) . . .'. Then follows the listing of the laws.

[9] '. . .the devout prince, the one who fears the gods' *rūbam na'dam paliḥ ilī*.
The adjective *na'du, nādu* 'attentive, devout' (verb *na'ādu* 'to watch, be
concerned with') expresses the pious vigilance that Hammurabi maintains
towards the gods. He is fond of this adjective 'devout' and uses it repeatedly in
the Prologue —1a: 30,61, iiia: 13, iva: 33, 64.

Out of Hammurabi's close relationship with the gods comes the revelation of 'truth' from Shamash, the Sun god: 'I am Hammurabi, the king of justice, to whom Shamash granted truth'[10]. In context, the 'truth' referred to here must refer to the list of laws on the stele. Hammurabi presents himself as modelling a bipolar spirituality—cultic piety and just rule. We moderns might be inclined to divide that spirituality into the sacred and the secular—shrine building, prayers, festivals and heeding divine oracles as the sacred on the one hand; political and judicial activity as the secular on the other. Yet Hammurabi presents his civil laws about lost property, loans, deposits, land use, theft, damages, marriage contracts and slave purchases as a revelation from Shamash, the god of justice and oracular inquiry. He depicts himself at the top of the stele standing in the immediate and unmediated presence of the Sun god in reverent audience.

No doubt we should read Hammurabi's claims in his Prologue and Epilogue with a hermeneutic of suspicion. He praises himself. His collection of laws is probably not that original, but owes much to Mesopotamian precedents and predecessors. His stele is religious propaganda, self-legitimation. Nevertheless, Hammurabi's worldview has this much validity—it illustrates the cohesion of cultic worship with civic, judicial and communal life. Though we discount god Shamash as a source of revelation, we can affirm the concept of God as source and scrutineer of social ethics before whom we must stand. Deuteronomy's code was likewise based on the coherence of cultic worship and covenant stipulations governing civil, social and family life. It shares a unified vision for spirituality and community.

In his Epilogue, immediately after the last law, Hammurabi sums up the relationship between the rulings carved on his stele and a way of life:

> The laws of justice (*dīnāt mīšarim*) that Hammurabi, the renowned king, set up,
> so that he caused the land to hold to the way of truth (*ūsam kīnam*) and good conduct.[11]

---

[10] CH Epilogue xxvb:95–98. The noun is *kinātim* from *kittu* 'truth'. Meek's translation 'committed law' (*ANET*, 178) paraphrases.

[11] Driver's translation obscures the idiom, as does *ANET*'s, but compare *CAD* 'who directed the country on the proper course (*ūsam kīnam*) and toward the correct way of life' (*CAD S*, p.34 under *ussu*). See *AHw*, 1438 *ūsu ussu*, „(rechte) Bahn, Ordnung" and *AHw*, 981 *rīdu, riddu* „(gute) Führung; Verfolgung", from the verbal root *redû* which conveys motion in a direction, 'to flow, go, lead'. The *CAD*'s 'correct way of life' seems preferable as a translation for the second phrase here (*rīdam damqam*) rather than Driver and *ANET*'s 'good governance, government', and Weinfeld's 'the road of kindness'.

He is confident that this stele inscribed with his rulings will show his successors 'the path and (good) conduct'.[12] The noun *kibsu* meaning 'path', from the verbal root *kabāsu*—'to tread', continues the metaphor of good conduct as a walk along a path which the ruler sets out straight before his people. Justice and 'walking a straight path' are linked concepts both in Akkadian and Hebrew, while 'a crooked path' describes moral deviousness.[13] These Semitic idioms depict the life journey as a course of conduct, an ordering of life by observance of justice and righteousness.

In both Hammurabi's Code and Deuteronomy, the ideal of social justice is made practical and context-specific through particular pronouncements, mainly in the form of case law, designed to create a community in which the widow, orphan and poor are protected from oppression and the wicked and the evil are rooted out of the society.[14]

Of course, there was a gap between the ideal of social protection and justice in the land and life as it was actually lived in those societies. Indeed, the Mesopotamian *mīšarum* edicts were billed as reforms of a system that had deteriorated. SN Kramer reminds us of the tension that ever existed between the ideal, reflected in the self-laudatory royal hymns from Sumer, and the actual state of affairs that we read between their lines.

> The ideal society envisaged and longed for by the temples and court poets who composed these hymns was one characterised by harmony, unanimity, truth, justice, kindliness, compassion for the weak and powerless, family concord, honesty, proper performance of one's duties, purity, cleanliness. But indirectly and unintentionally these hymns tell us no little about the actual, concrete specific, day-to-day

---

[12] CH xxvib:80 *kibsam rīdam*; *ANET*, 178; Driver, 99.

[13] Weinfeld draws attention to Prov 8:20, Isa 26:7, Isa 588f and to Psa 23:3 'He leads me in the paths of righteousness.' In Akkadian the noun for 'justice' *mīšaru* derives from the verb *ešēru* 'to be straight', in the causative S-theme 'to make straight, to direct, guide'. In Hebrew, we may compare *yāšar* 'to be straight' and the adjective *yāšar* 'straight, right' and the noun *yōšer* 'uprightness, honesty, integrity'. For a full discussion of these idioms of the 'way of life', see *TDOT* III (1978) pp. 270ff under דֶּרֶךְ *derek*. This article includes a review of the parallel Egyptian and Akkadian idioms involving walking along a path.

[14] CH Prologue a: 32–39 (Driver, p.6f; *ANET*, 164 'to cause justice to prevail in the land, to destroy the wicked and the evil, that the strong might not oppress the weak') and CH Epilogue xxivb: 59–62 (Driver, p. 96; *ANET*, 178 'in order that the strong might not oppress the weak, that justice might be dealt the orphan and the widow'). Hammurabi inherited these statements of principle and purpose from previous Mesopotamian law collections such as those of Ur-Nammu. Compare Exod 22:21ff and FC Fensham's discussion, 'Widow, Orphan and the Poor in Ancient Near Eastern Legal and Wisdom Literature' *JNES* 21 (1962) 129–139.

social practices and behaviour of the people, and these reveal a society marred by discord, injustice, deception, family dissidence, cruelty, oppression of the weak and powerless, of the widow and orphan, arrogance, dishonesty, neglect of one's duties, impurity—in brief a society quite the opposite of the desired and desirable ideal.[15]

Deuteronomy is full of foreboding, warnings and exhortations against a decline into idolatry and social disorder, a decline from the covenant ideal of a worshipping community. Debt and poverty are an important part of this social disorder according to Deut 15. Moses describes the degeneration as 'turning aside from the way':

> For I know how rebellious and stubborn you are. If you already have been so rebellious toward the LORD while I am alive among you, how much more after my death! . . . For I know that after my death, you will act corruptly, turning aside from the way that I have commanded you.
>
> (Deut 31:27,29)

This metaphor of 'turning aside from the way' (*wᵉsartem min-hadderek*, 31:29) contrasts with 'walking after' Yahweh. It is used in Deuteronomy as a living metaphor of spatial direction, sometimes with the phrase 'to the left or to the right' added.[16] The literal and the metaphorical uses of the idiom are well illustrated by the following passages:

> If you let me pass through your land, I will travel (*hālak*) only along the road (*derek*); I will turn aside (*swr*) neither to the right nor to the left.
>
> (Deut 2:27)

> You must therefore be careful to do as the LORD your God has commanded you; you shall not turn (*swr*) to the right or to the left. You must follow (*hālak*) exactly the path (*derek*) that the LORD your God has commanded you, so that you may live, and that it may go well with you, and that you may live long in the land that you are to possess.
>
> (Deut 5:32)

> and if you do not turn aside (*swr*) from any of the words that I am commanding you today, either to the right or to the left, following (*hālak aḥᵃrey*) other gods to serve them.
>
> (Deut 28:14)[17]

---

[15] SN Kramer, 'Law and Justice: gleanings from Sumerian literature' pp. 77–82 in M Lebean and P Talon (eds) *Reflets des Deux Fleuves: mélanges offerts à André Finet*, Akkadica (Leuven: Peeters) 1989, p. 81f.
[16] The literal use of the verb *swr*—'to turn aside', *hālak* 'to walk' and *derek* 'road' is illustrated by Deut 2:27

Here is the choice that Deuteronomy presents. To walk along the road of life following Yahweh or to turn off the road of life and follow other gods along a path headed towards curse, death and exile. The laws of Deuteronomy are like a straight road. To follow Yahweh is to follow these righteous laws.

INTEGRITY AND WHOLEHEARTEDNESS

A dominant concern in the Near Eastern treaties is that the vassal's conduct and profession would match up, but the reality was often different. The principle enunciated was one of integrity. The vassal should not go through the motions of swearing loyalty but simultaneously harbour inward reservations and subsequently fail in behaviour. That is why the phrase 'with all your heart and with all your soul', which sounds so Deuteronomic, is nevertheless a phrase at home in the idiom of treaty-making.[18] There the vassal is commanded: 'you shall not swear the oath with your lips only but shall swear it wholeheartedly.'[19] In like vein, the vassal must offer

---

[17] Compare 'turning from the way' (*swr+derek*) in the Golden Calf incident (Deut 9:12,16), and 'turning away' to other gods in Deut 11:16, 'turning from the way' in Deut 11:28, 'turning aside to the right or to the left' from the interpretation of the law by levitical priest and judges (Deut 17:11), and a future king's heart 'turning away' from Yahweh (Deut 17:17).

[18] The treaty phrases which militate against outward complicity and urge unreserved and unswerving loyalty use the language of the 'inner being' to do this: 'wholeheartedly', 'with all your heart' (*ina gummurti libbi, ina kul libbi*), 'in the truth of your heart' (*ina kitti ša libbikunu*) in Akkadian. The phrases occur in Aramaic and Assyrian treaties and loyalty oaths of the 8th and 7th centuries. Note the Aramaic of the Sefire treaty 2 'if you say in your soul and think in your mind' *hn t'mr bnbšk wt'št blbb[k]* (Sefire 2, Face B, line 5; JA Fitzmyer, *The Aramaic Inscriptions of Sefire* Biblica et Orientalia 19 [Rome: BIP] 1967, p.80f). These concepts and phrases originate in the 2nd millennium with examples in the treaties from the Hittite empire— Suppiluliumash (E Weidner, *PDK*, No. 3, p. 60 line 19 & p. 62 line 23; No. 4, p.72 lines 13,20) and Mursilis II's treaty with Ugarit (RS 17.353, lines 20,21,24). See R Frankena, 'The Vassal Treaties of Esarhaddon' *OTS* 14 (1965) 122–154, p. 140ff for a list of phrases with line references and a discussion. The Assyrian texts are available in Reiner's translation, *ANET*[3], pp. 532f &534ff; for the Akkadian of the Ashurnerari V treaty and the *VTE* with English translation see S Parpola & K Watanabe, *Neo-Assyrian Treaties and Loyalty Oaths*, SAA 2 (Helsinki: Helsinki Univ Press) 1988, p. 8ff & 28ff. The match between covenant and treaty-making, and the commonality of the idiom 'with your whole heart' does not of course exclude use of the 'whole heart' phrase from contexts other than treaties where sincerity is the point at issue. Note, for example, Hammurabi's injunction to a subsequent ruler to honour his laws, his memory and 'let him pray with his whole heart for me' (*ANET*, 178; CH Epilogue xxvb: 45f *ina libbišu gamrim*).

[19] Parpola & Watanabe, p. 44, *VTE* line 386f 'wholeheartedly' *ina gummurti libbikunu*; *ANET*[3], p. 538, §34.

military support 'with full heart', love the suzerain 'as you love yourself' and be prepared to fight and die for him.[20] This is wholehearted devotion which starts with an attitude but ends in military action and self-sacrifice. Nothing less is asked of the Israelites by their covenant Overlord.

Two more passages of direct relevance to 'fear of the LORD', 'walking in his ways' and 'testing' are worth adding to the core statement of Deut 10:12ff. The first concerns the lure of the supernatural away from exclusive allegiance to Yahweh. A false prophet might emerge appearing to have a hot line to God through dream interpretation and offering omen signs to confirm his or her oracular utterances.[21] Yahwists should resist this incentive to syncretism:

> and they say, 'Let us follow other gods' (whom you have not known) 'and let us serve them,' you must not heed the words of those prophets or those who divine by dreams; for the LORD your God is testing you, to know whether you indeed love the LORD your God with all your heart and soul. The LORD your God you shall follow, him alone you shall fear, his commandments you shall keep, his voice you shall obey, him you shall serve, and to him you shall hold fast.
>
> (Deut 13:2b–4)

'Hold fast' is another Deuteronomic covenant idiom. This verb *dābaq*—'cling, cleave to, hold fast to' is familiar to us from Gen 2:24 where it describes the marriage relationship in terms of a man quitting the child–parent relationship to enter marriage. Treaties drew on kinship terms such as 'father', 'son', 'brother', 'brother-hood' and 'love' to describe political relationships between suzerain and vassal or between equal partners, so it is likely that

---

[20] The 1st millennium Assyrian texts have 2nd millennium antecedents and Greek and Roman descendants. From the antecedents, see the Sausgamuwa treaty (Hittite language) and Niqmepa treaty (Akkadian) cited by Weinfeld, *UF* 8, p. 384f 'Devotion':

> And if you . . . Sausgamuwa do not come to aid with full heart (*šakuuaššarit ZI-it* = Akkadian *ina kul libbi*) . . . with your army and your chariots and will not be prepared to die with your wives and your sons (for the King)

> If you Niqmepa do not guard with your army and your chariots and with all your heart (*ina kul libbika*) and if you do not fight with all your heart

[21] Hebrew *nābî'* 'prophet' has the Akkadian cognate *nābi'ūtum*, reported from 3rd millennium Ebla (Pettinato, BA 39.2 [1976] p. 49). Prophetic oracles, including dream revelations, are well known from 2nd millennium Mari texts in which the oracle is often delivered in the name of Dagan—see A Malamat's publications and the references given there—'A Forerunner of Biblical Prophecy: the Mari documents', pp. 33–52 in PD Miller et al, *Ancient Israelite Religion* (Philadelphia: Fortress) 1987; *Mari and the Early Israelite Experience*, The Schweich Lectures 1984, OUP, 1989, 'Intuitive Prophecy', pp. 79ff.

Deuteronomy exploits this relational nuance of *dābaq* for covenant fidelity.[22] Here 'hold fast' and 'love with all your heart and soul' are combined with 'serve', 'obey', 'fear' and 'follow'.

The translation 'follow' rather obscures the 'walk' metaphor which runs through Deuteronomy. A number of variants are used with the verb 'walk' (*hālak*):

to walk after Yahweh (ie. to follow)[23]
to walk in the way or ways of Yahweh
to walk in all his ways
to walk in the *tōrāh* of Yahweh
to walk before Yahweh with wholeheartedness and integrity
to walk before Yahweh with all the heart
to walk before Yahweh in truth and righteousness

It seems likely that these 'walking' metaphors originate in the political sphere where allegiance to a king meant 'walking after him' in the sense of joining in the advance of his army. 'Walking after' then becomes a term for 'making, or being in, alliance with'. In 2nd millennium letters we read of the shifting pattern of alliances in terms of 'walking after' first one alliance partner then another. The Akkadian *alāku arki* 'walk after' is the equivalent of the Hebrew phrase *hālak aḥᵃrey*. The Assyrian king Shamshi-Adad complained about a devious ally in terms of his 'walking after':

> Surely you have heard about the hostility of PN . . . Prior to this he walked after the leader of the PNN1, deserted the leader of the PNN1 and walked after the leader of the PNN2. He deserted the leader of the PNN2 and walked after the PNN3. He deserted the PNN3 and

---

[22] To 'cleave to Yahweh' (*dābaq*) appears five times, in Deut 4:4, 10:20, 11:22, 13:5 and 30:20. That *dābaq* can carry non-relational nuances in Deuteronomy as well is evident from 13:17 where forbidden booty must not 'stick to' the Israelites' hands. On 'love' (*'hb*) as a relational term borrowed by treaty discourse with the nuance of fidelity, loyalty note 'If you do not love RN . . . your lord, as you love your own lives . . .' (*VTE* §24, line 268 *ANET*³, p. 537: Akkadian *râmu, ra'āmu*—'to love' used with *napištu*—'throat', 'life' cognate with Hebrew *nepeš* 'soul' in older translations). Compare Deut 6:5, 10:12, 11:1, 13 & 22, 13:14, 19:9 and 30:6, 16,20. See W Moran, 'The Ancient Near Eastern Background of the Love of God in Deuteronomy' *CBQ* 25 (1963) 77–87. For references to 'love' in the 2nd millennium treaties, see McCarthy, *Treaty and Covenant*, p. 43 and p. 81 note 88. The Mari letters of the 17th century and the Amarna Letters of the 14th century exhibit this kinship vocabulary of 'father', son' and 'brother' in diplomatic contexts. See the references to treaties and letters in *CAD A*, p. 188 *aḫḫūtu* —'brotherhood') between rulers.

[23] These idioms are conveniently collected with verse references by Weinfeld, *Deut School*, Appendix A, pp.332–334, Nos. 1, 6, 7, 8. Compare p.320, No.1 'to walk after foreign gods'.

walked after me. Even me he deserted and has been walking after the leader of PN4. Moreover, to all these kings he has sworn an oath. It is scarcely three years since he became an ally and an enemy of these kings . . .[24]

In the Amarna Letters from 14th century Canaan, the idiom 'walking after' is used for making alliances. Temptations to disloyalty were spurned in this letter:

> May the king, my lord, heed the words of his servant. Men of Gubla, my own household, and my wife, kept saying to me, 'Ally yourself (*alikmi arki* 'walk after') with the son of PN so we can make peace between us.' But I refused. I did not listen to them.[25]

If you were allied to another power group, marching into battle with them was, after all, the supreme test for an ally, whether the alliance was between equals or involved a vassal supplying troops to his suzerain. The story of David turning out in support of his Philistine overlord Achish illustrates this testing situation (1 Sam 29).[26]

In addition to these idioms of 'walking after Yahweh', disloyalty to Yahweh is expressed in Deuteronomy by 'walking after foreign gods', and by expressions for deviating from the true path—'to turn aside from the way', 'to turn to the right or to the left', 'to be led astray from the way of Yahweh'.[27] We should

---

[24] *ANET*[3], p. 628 Shemshara letter. cf. the words from the Mari letter: 'There is no king who is strong just by himself. Ten to fifteen kings are walking after Hammurapi the leader of Babylon . . . and twenty kings are walking after Yarim-Lim the leader of Yamhad.' (p. 628 letter **b**).

[25] EA 136:6–15 in Moran, Amarna Letters, pp. 216f. The idiom *alāku arki*—'to walk, go, follow after' is also used to refer to forming an alliance in EA 280:16–24 (Moran, *Amarna Letters*, pp. 321f; cf. EA 149:40–54, pp. 236f).

[26] See the study of the Achish-David alliance and the treaty terms involved in Kalluveettil, *Declaration and Covenant*, 172ff.

[27] *Deut School*, Appendix A, p. 339 No. 2a, 2c, p. 341 No. 10a, and probably p. 339 Nos. 2 'turn away' and 2b 'to turn away from Yahweh' with the concept of 'way, path' or 'following after' assumed to complete the image. Of course, it is characteristic of metaphor that the original setting drops into the background, that the associations of the imagery are no longer evoked and that the phrase remains in use as a stock phrase or dead metaphor. This happens in the English phrase 'way of life' which evokes no image of 'way, road, path'. 'Going or walking after foreign gods' likely became a dead metaphor for worshipping other gods. The dominance of treaty vocabulary in Deuteronomy does suggest, however, that the many phrases drawn from treaty language had not passed into the realm of dead metaphor. Indeed, those scholars such as Frankena and Weinfeld who are most impressed by the range of treaty vocabulary with an Assyrian background see Deuteronomy as an interaction with and a reaction to this experience of Assyrian political domination in the 7th century BC.

probably see the apostasy of 'walking after foreign gods' in terms of a military alliance metaphor. Military standards decorated with symbols of the gods were carried on campaign and the gods were believed to participate in the battles. We know this both from descriptions in the royal campaign reports and in artistic portrayals of the battles.[28]

Germane to allegiance and running through Scripture, there is what we may call the 'Two Sides' metaphor. There is God's side and the side of his enemies. This is a fundamental way of interpreting life for Israelite theology. The setting could be Israelites dancing opposite Egyptians dead on the seashore, or Yahwistic prophets confronting the monarchy over political alliances, or a psalmist appealing to God against his enemies within the Israelite community itself. In Deuteronomy, the enemy is represented by historical groups such as the Egyptians, Amalek and the Canaanites, but even more by the gods of the Canaanites (Deut 12:2ff, 29:17ff) and their spiritual representatives, the divination experts, spiritists and prophets (Deut 13, 18:9ff), as well as any Hebrews who conspire with them.[29] This 'Two Sides' metaphor drawn from battle has a biblical trajectory that culminates with apocalyptic war in the book of Revelation.

In the light of this military model of apostasy, we can draw the following points together. The Exodus tradition plays a dominant role in Israel's faith. Worship of Yahweh as a warrior God (Exod 15:3) plays a dominant role in the Exodus story. Rejection of Mosaic Yahwism is reflected in the phrase 'make gods for us who shall go before us (^{a}šer yēl^{e}kū l^{e}pāneynū, Exod 32:1). This 'going before' language is best read against the background of the 'vanguard motif' in the Near East which describes divine presence in the battle column. War was the main field of operation that tested loyalty. The Near Eastern treaties and loyalty oaths reflect this. Hence, it is quite plausible to see Deuteronomy's theological

---

[28] See TW Mann, *Divine Presence and Guidance in Israelite Traditions: the typology of exaltation* (London: Johns Hopkins) 1977, especially pp. 131ff and illustrations pp. 265ff. There are analogies with Israel following the pillar of cloud and fire in the Exodus journey. Mann (p. 253) notes the use of 'go before' *hālak lip^{e}ney* with Yahweh as vanguard in Exod 13:21, 14:19, 23:23, 32:1,23,34 Num 14:14, Deut 1:30,33 20:4, 31:6,8 with echoes in New Exodus use of the 'vanguard motif' in Isa 45:2, 52:12, 58:8. The Ark was probably carried in procession on cultic occasions. The images of the gods in Mesopotamia certainly were, as we know from art and ritual texts (e.g. the Babylonian New Year ceremonies). So it is possible that a cultic setting for 'walking after foreign gods' contributes to the idiom. Yet cult and battle cannot be rigidly separated in the Near East in any case.

[29] Conspiracy and revolt are major concerns in the Assyrian loyalty oaths to the crown prince and there are strong injunctions to report every rumour of a conspiracy. See *VTE* §26–29 *ANET*[3], p. 537.

vocabulary as shaped by a combination of Near Eastern idiom juxtaposed with Israel's Exodus experience.

TESTING BY GOD IN A TRAJECTORY FROM DEUTERONOMY ONWARDS

Finally, we return to the concept of the wilderness journey as a test, as it is described in the retrospective of Deuteronomy. The key passage runs as follows:

> [2]Remember the long way that the LORD your God has led you these forty years in the wilderness, in order to humble you, testing you to know what was in your heart, whether or not you would keep his commandments.[3]He humbled you by letting you hunger, then by feeding you with manna . . . in order to make you understand that one does not live by bread alone, but by every word that comes from the mouth of the LORD.
>
> (Deut 8:2f)

This presents the wilderness experience as a trial by ordeal. In particular, the ordeal of hunger is related to humbling, which in the context envisaged suggests coming to the end of all inner resources as well as natural resources and human independence. The anthropomorphic 'to know what was in your heart' suggests that Yahweh was running a field test, an experiment to discover a result which could not be predicted in advance.

Indeed, RL Cohn has offered an interpretation of the Wilderness experience that draws on field anthropology, in particular the initiation ordeals involved in rites of passage which play a part in the formation of community.[30] The wilderness is the margin which provides a threshold experience at the brink of death. Passing through the ordeal opens the way for incorporation into *communitas*, a bonded social relationship. The Exodus represents separation, the Wilderness liminality (being at the margin), and reincorporation is represented by crossing the Jordan and entering the land. The Torah displaces the lore of the tribe in this model, and instead of a young generation of adolescent initiates being instructed in tribal lore by tribal elders during a segregated period away from the village, the nation Israel as a whole is instructed in torah by God's representative Moses in the desert. Like all analogies, this model should not be pressed too hard, but the concept of test by ordeal, and of 'growing up' into responsible

---

[30] RL Cohn 'Liminality in the Wilderness', pp. 7–23 in *The Shape of Sacred Space* (Chico: Scholars Press) 1981. Cohn draws from the work of the anthropologist Victor Turner in Zambia and his general theory of social process arising from his studies of rites of passage, millenarian movements and pilgrimages.

conformity to a social norm under exhortation by the tribal leader do find points of affinity with Israel's Exodus–Wilderness experience.

Central to Deut 8, however, is the concept of the Father provider as well as the Father as discipliner. In Deut 8:3 there is already the statement that God 'fed' as well as 'made hunger'. We saw that the testing referred to in Exod 16 concerning the manna was in the setting of manna being provided and instructions being given about gathering it. Deut 8:4 similarly emphasizes God's provision—clothes that did not wear out. Nor was the long walk physically injurious—'your feet did not swell these forty years'. This leads on to the enunciation of a general spiritual principle:

> Know then in your heart that as a parent disciplines a child so the LORD your God disciplines you. Therefore keep the commandments of the LORD your God, by walking in his ways and by fearing him.
>
> (Deut 8:5f)

In this paragraph of exhortation, the motifs of 'fearing the LORD', 'walking in his ways', 'to test' and obedience to the commandments are strongly linked to what God promises. Deut 8:7 goes on to describe the delights and resources of the Promised Land, concluding 'you shall eat your fill and bless the LORD for the good land that he has given you' (v. 10). Israel as Yahweh's 'son' has been a key motif in the confrontation with Pharaoh: 'Israel is my firstborn son. I said to you, "Let my son go that he may worship me" '(Exod 4:22f, cf. Hos 11:1). Deuteronomy extends the Father–son motif to the wilderness setting.

TESTING EXPERIENCES

The analysis of the Abraham cycle first alerted us to the journey motif, and his travels turned out to foreshadow the Exodus. Likewise, the testing of his faith found a continuity in the testing of the Israelites' obedience during the wilderness period. In Deuteronomy, this led to a retrospective summary of the whole wilderness experience as a testing of devotion to Yahweh. Does this way of understanding God's ways continue? Is there a case to be made for a wider biblical teaching on spiritual growth through test, through ordeal or through commandment?

The answer to this question must be affirmative because the statements of Genesis, Exodus and Deuteronomy do not stand alone in the Old Testament, or in the Bible as a whole. We can see an extension of the testing of Abraham in the drama of Job, 'a blameless and upright man who fears God and turns away from evil' (Job 1:8, 2:3). The mechanism is very different—the adversarial stance of the Satan, instead of a direct command by God.

This indicates that the terrestrial realm is becoming the scene for a wider conflictual model than the Exodus story overtly presents.[31] The conflict will eventually embrace the celestial realm in apocalyptic literature (Isa 24:21, Dan 10:13ff, Rev 12:7ff).

Human onslaught has been present in the story since the system of state bondage in Egypt and the Amalekite attack in the desert, but in apocalyptic literature human persecution mirrors supernatural onslaught. Peter describes persecution as 'trial by fire' and names the adversary as the devil who is prowling around like a roaring lion looking for someone to devour (1 Pet 1:6f, 5:8). Jesus encounters testing when he recapitulates the wilderness experience of Israel. Luke speaks of Jesus being 'led by the Spirit in the wilderness where for forty days he was tempted by the devil' (Lk 4:1f). Mark uses stronger language—'And the Spirit immediately drove him out into the wilderness' (Mk 1:12). Both Luke and Matthew strengthen the analogy with Israel's wilderness experience by incorporating the quotation from Deut 8:3b. Obedience to God's commands and not bread alone is seen as the basis for life.[32] This is the testing of vocation, not an obedience of a single moment.

Returning to the statement of Deut 8:5 that 'as a parent disciplines a child, so the LORD your God disciplines you', we might look for a setting that turns this historical retrospective into an ongoing truth. Indeed, this aphorism has a parallel in Proverbs:

> [5]Trust in the LORD with all your heart,
> and do not rely on your own insight.
> [6]In all your ways acknowledge him,
> and he will make straight your paths.
> [7]Do not be wise in your own eyes;
> fear the LORD, and turn away from evil.
> [8]It will be a healing for your flesh
> and a refreshment for your body.
> [9]Honour the LORD with your substance
> and with the first fruits of all your produce;

---

[31] Exod 12:12 does include the gods of Egypt as Yahweh's opponents: 'on all the gods of Egypt I will execute judgements.' The plagues which involved polluting the Nile and darkening the sun may carry this implication since the Nile and the Sun were deified, as indeed was the pharaoh himself. Certainly the New Testament, and possibly the Old Testament at places, saw the demonic behind idolatry (1 Cor 10:20f; cf. Deut 32:17, Psa 106:34ff, Isa 65:3ff).

[32] For a fuller discussion of the typology, see the studies from the Biblical Theology period: B Gerhardsson, *The Testing of God's Son* (Lund: CWK Gleerup) 1966 and UW Mauser, *Christ in the Wilderness* (London: SCM) 1963. An updated bibliography is given in WD Davies and DC Allison, *Matthew*, ICC (Edinburgh: T&T Clark) 1988.

¹⁰then your barns will be filled with plenty,
and your vats will be bursting with wine.
¹¹My child, do not despise the LORD's discipline (*mūsar Yhwh*)
or be weary of his reproof,
¹²for the LORD reproves the one he loves,
as a father the son in whom he delights.

(Prov 2:5–12)

Theological convergence rather than a literary relationship explains the overlap of motifs between Prov 3 and Deut 8. This convergence includes the promise of material prosperity (vv.9f; Deut 8:7–10), reference to bodily health (v.8; Deut 8:4b), the role of the heart (v.5 'with all your heart'; Deut 8:2b), fearing the LORD (v. 7b; Deut 8:6b) and the concept of fatherly discipline (v. 12; Deut 8:5).³³ Prov 3 is an impressive example of a covenant theology re-expressed in a different instructional setting.

There is another trajectory for the proverb of fatherly discipline. The writer of Hebrews borrows this concept of disciplinary treatment from Proverbs, following up his direct quotation with an application: 'endure trials for the sake of discipline' (Heb 12:7). The context is 'your struggle against sin', but from the phrase 'to the point of shedding your blood' and the rest of the letter, the context is not some individual and internal struggle with fallen nature or even an inclination to apostasy in and of itself, but a trial in the form of religious persecution. This had resulted in deaths in the early church, such as Stephen's martyrdom, and might progress in that direction again for the readers.

The New Testament instances of the trial and testing motif militate against a trivializing of the biblical concept of testing.³⁴

---

³³ A shared vocabulary would suggest interdependence, but Prov 3:12 speaks of the love of the father, which Deut 8 does not, and the verbs for 'disciplining' are different—Piel of *ysr* twice in Deut 8: 5, but Hif. of *ykḥ* in Prov 3:12; the noun *mūsar* based on the root *ysr* is used in Prov 3:11a, but this is a standard Wisdom word quite explicable in this discourse without reference to *yissēr* in Deut 8:5. Proverbs does refer to the human discipline of children using *yissēr* in Prov 19:18 and 29:17, while Psa 94:12 uses *yissēr* of God's discipline and instruction from torah, which shows that concepts analogous to Deut 8:5 were current. In general, Proverbs works with a theology of reward akin to Deuteronomy's obedience–blessing, and contacts between Deuteronomic theology and Wisdom theology in Proverbs in particular have been pointed out by Weinfeld, *Deut School*, Part 3 'Deuteronomic Literature and Wisdom Literature', pp. 244ff and by others, such as DA Hubbard, 'The Wisdom Movement and Israel's Covenant Faith' *Tyndale Bulletin* 17 (1966) 3–33.

³⁴ The specific circumstances of what James 1 refers to by 'trials of any kind' (1:2 compare 1:12) is not immediately obvious but might include the pressures of poverty and disadvantaged circumstances (1:27) and oppression by the rich (5:10f) rather than any lesser temptation to wavering doubt or sinful inclination.

Neither persecution and martyrdom, nor the testing of Jesus' obedience to vocation, allows us to lightly take this language of testing on our lips. Referring to difficulties as a 'cross to bear' or as 'testing experiences' in colloquial parlance trivializes the biblical concept of testing. Biblical testing stares death in the face. Life is difficult in many ways, even when the pressures are chosen pressures, as students often realise during examination periods. But the demands of life, whether for achievement or for survival in the face of poverty, illness and accident are not the exact dynamic equivalents of a testing of faith directed by God himself with Abraham, Israel and Job, or involving physical onslaught by enemies that threatens to take life.

THE PATH OF WISDOM AND DISCIPLESHIP

If we were to follow through what Proverbs understands by 'the fear of the LORD' and God's discipline ('the discipline of Yahweh' *mūsar Yhwh*, Prov 3:11), it would point to the shaping of moral decision-making, and the avoidance of the behaviour that characterizes the fool. We see this substantiated by the recurrent 'fear of the LORD' motif in Proverbs.

The 'fear of the LORD' becomes a key motif in Wisdom literature, the more impressive when one considers how 'secular' are many of the proverbial sayings and observations of life. Within the empirical and phenomenological approach of Wisdom, the undergirding theological perception is encapsulated in the saying: 'The fear of Yahweh is the first principle of knowledge; fools despise wisdom and instruction' (Prov 1:7).[35] The 'fear of Yahweh' is associated in parallel lines with 'the knowledge of God' (Prov 2:5b), or 'knowledge of the Holy One', 'insight' (Prov 9:10b) and 'instruction in wisdom' (Prov 15:33). It has a strong ethical nuance, being linked to moral choice. This is stated tersely in Prov 8:13: 'The fear of the LORD is hatred of evil', or 'by the fear of the LORD one avoids evil' (Prov 16:6), or, as stated positively: 'Those who walk uprightly fear the LORD but one who is devious in conduct despises him' (Prov 14:2). The same reflection on theology, ethics and wisdom is offered in Job—'And God said to mankind, "Truly, the fear of the Lord, that is wisdom; and to depart from evil is understanding" ' (Job 20:28). This element of moral choice is, of course, forcefully presented in Deuteronomy as the choice between life and death, which is coterminous with being in covenant with Yahweh or choosing other gods: 'See, I

---

[35] For a basic study of the translation and meaning of this proverb, see H Blocher 'The Fear of the Lord as the "Principle" of Wisdom' *Tyndale Bulletin* 28 (1977) 3–28.

have set before you today life and prosperity, death and adversity'
(Deut 30:15).[36]

It is no surprise, then, when Proverbs states that 'The fear of the
LORD prolongs life, but the years of the wicked will be short' (Prov
10:27), or that 'The fear of the LORD is a fountain of life so that one
may avoid the snares of death' (Prov 14:27). Finally, Qohelet's
editor-in-chief reminds students of that provocative work that at
the end of the day when all has been said, they should 'Fear God,
and keep his commandments; for that is the whole duty of
everyone' (Ecc 12:13).[37]

We can see, then, that so far as 'the fear of the LORD' and 'testing'
go, Exodus extends Genesis, and Deuteronomy elaborates on
Exodus. Beyond this, these motifs have a canonical trajectory that
leads through Wisdom literature and on into the New Testament.

'Walking before Yahweh' offers a similar scenario. The
question of Deuteronomy, 'So now, Israel, what does the LORD
your God require of you?' (Deut 10:12), was answered there by
the statement of wholehearted covenant commitment. This
question of God's requirements is asked again in the prophets and
answered using the same motif of 'walking before Yahweh':

> He has told you, O man, what is good;
> and what does the LORD require of you
> but to act justly,
> and to love loyally,
> and to be careful to walk with your God?
>
> (Mic 6:8)

This is a repetition of the covenant call of Deuteronomy uniting
horizontal and vertical components, attitudinal and behavioural,
theological and ethical.[38]

---

[36] With Deuteronomy's association of 'fear of the LORD' and covenant faithfulness, we may compare the association of 'fear of the LORD' in Leviticus with
loving your neighbour as yourself: 'you shall not cheat one another, but you
shall fear your God' (Lev 25:17 and 25:36, 43).

[37] Other references to fearing God in Qohelet are found in the body of the work
and should be taken as the author's, rather than as editorial insertions. These
statements form one aspect of Qohelet's ambiguous relationship with the
Wisdom tradition—Ecc 5:7, 7:18, 8:12f.

[38] 'Good' (Hebrew *ṭōb*) is a concept linked with the benefits of a covenant
relationship. The suzerain offers blessings for obedience. What is it that
Yahweh will categorize as 'good'? What is it that is in the interests of the
questioning Israelites that is 'good'? The answer is covenant loyalty and
becoming conduct. On Hebrew *ṭōb* and the related Akkadian *ṭūbtu, ṭābūtu* and
Aramaic *ṭwbh* and Akkadian *damiqtu, damqātu*—'good, favourable' see the
studies of Weinfeld, 'Covenant Terminology in the Ancient Near East and its
Influence on the West' *JAOS* 93.2 (1973) 190–199 plus the previous work of
Moran and Hillers cited there. When covenant relationship with Yahweh is

Deuteronomic literature offers the same perspective. Samuel as priest, prophet and covenant mediator in a parallel role to that of Moses in Deuteronomy renews covenant and gives valedictory instruction. He sketches his role and Israel's response: 'I will instruct you in the good and right way. Only fear the LORD, and serve him faithfully with all your heart; for consider what great things he has done for you' (1 Sam 12:23b–24). [39]'The good and right way' is Samuel's equivalent to Micah's way of 'justice' and 'loyalty'.[40] This way should be apparent 'to one who walks uprightly' (Mic 2:7) in contrast to those who 'walk haughtily' (Mic 2:3). What is just, right and straight is conduct that respects the commandments governing relationships within the community. We may sum these up as 'Love your neighbour as yourself.'[41]

The New Testament develops this connection between covenant relationship and ethical behaviour in its own way. Ephesians 5:15 seems to echo Mic 6:8 and the Wisdom tradition in the exhortation to 'look carefully then how you walk, not as unwise men but as wise' (RSV). This introduces a section on ethical conduct.[42] Indeed, 'walk', *peripatein* in the Greek, is probably a Hebraism derived from the Septuagint translation of Hebrew *hālak*. Ephesians favours this idiom for describing the believer's life style in contrast to the moral conduct of pre–conversion days: 'the trespasses and sins in which you once walked . . . the good works, which God prepared beforehand, that we should walk in them (2:1,10); 'walk worthily of the calling to which you have been called . . . you must no longer walk as the Gentiles do' (4:1,17); 'walk in love . . . walk as children of light' (5:2,10). The

---

refused, this can be summed up in the words 'Israel has rejected the good' (Hos 8:3).

[39] See McCarthy, *Treaty and Covenant*, pp. 206ff.

[40] 'Loyalty' *hesed* is another term at home in covenant making. It can refer either to God's 'steadfast love', that is his loyal commitment to the relationship, or it can refer to Israel's need for loyalty, or to both, or to the horizontal outworking of loyal dealing between Israelites made into neighbours and brothers through the covenant. Compare 'But as for you, return to your God, hold fast to loyalty (*hesed*) and justice, and wait continually for your God' (Hos 12:6). On the interconnections between Micah and covenant concepts, see the comments of LC Allen, *The Books of Joel, Obadiah, Jonah and Micah*, NICOT (Grand Rapids: Eerdmans) 1976, pp. 371ff.

[41] Compare Jesus' analysis with Paul's (Matt 22:39//Mk 12:31; cf. Lk 10:27; Rom 13:9). This basic tenet appears in the Holiness Code of Leviticus 18–20 (19:17) under the section heading 'You shall be holy; for I Yahweh your God am holy' (19:2). No collection of Near Eastern laws combines distilled statements of general ethical principle with specific instances of application of the kind that we meet with in Lev 18:9–18.

[42] According to AT Lincoln, 5:15 'walk wisely' may cover the whole section, including the 'household code' to 6:9 (*Ephesians*, Word 42 [Dallas: Word] 1990, p. 338 with the citations of *peripatein* as characteristic Pauline usage).

peripatein Hebraism is characteristic of Paul's descriptions of discipleship, whether expressing this in theological terms ('walk by the Spirit', Gal 5:16; cf. Rom 6:4, 8:4), or in ethical terms (Rom 13:13, Col 1:10, 3:7).[43]

The Johannine corpus uses 'walking in the light', and not 'walking in darkness'. 'Walking in the light' goes together with 'having fellowship' with God and with one another, a description of a covenant bond in all but name (1 John 1:6f). As for the dynamic equivalent of 'to walk after' in Near Eastern alliance and Hebrew covenant, there is the invitation to Christian discipleship —'Follow me . . .' , which in John 8:12 is associated with 'walking': 'he who follows me will not walk in darkness, but will have the light of life' (cf. Isa 51:10 and Jn 12:35). In other paradigm examples, the physical act of walking is combined with its spiritual and metaphorical nuances. Jesus, passing along, sees Levi son of Alphaeus sitting at the tax booth and gives the command which is an invitation: ' "Follow me." And he got up and followed him' (Mk 2:14).[44] Like the Near Eastern loyalty oaths, this allegiance of 'following', of 'walking after' requires loyalty to the point of death: 'If any want to be my followers, let them deny themselves and take up their cross and follow me. For those who want to save their life will lose it, and those who lose their life for my sake, and for the sake of the gospel, will save it' (Mk 8:34f//Lk 9:23).

SUMMARY AND CONCLUSION

Deuteronomy teaches that a response to Yahweh involves an unreserved and wholehearted commitment made from the inner being. This expresses itself in the individual and national choice to obey the commandments and live as a covenant community. This steady choice is described as 'fearing the Lord' and 'walking in the ways of Yahweh.' Deuteronomy reviews the wilderness journey to the bank of the Jordan as God testing the inner disposition of the Israelites in a discipline that goes with the privileged status of 'sonship'. Deviation from 'walking in the ways of Yahweh' involved 'turning aside' to 'walk after foreign gods' or disobeying commandments regulating community relationships. For Deuteronomy, the treatment of the poor and those in debt-slavery in the

---

[43] English translations often do not reflect the use of *peripatein* 'walk' but opt for a non-metaphorical 'live', 'conduct yourself'. This conveys the sense but not the underlying idiom.

[44] Mk 2:14//Matt 9:9, Lk 5:27 all with *'akoloutheo*—'to follow' as a disciple. Compare the call of Simon and Andrew in Mk 1:17 *opiso moi*—'after me'. Compare Lk 9:59, 18:22, John 1:43, 12:26, 21:19, 22.

community is a practical test of loyalty to Yahweh (Deut 15).[45] Both Deuteronomy and Mesopotamia harbour an ideal of social justice and devout worship. The 'sacred' and the 'secular' are integrated in the 'fear of' the deity. Both Mesopotamia and Deuteronomy record and anticipate degeneration from this twofold ideal.

Only an inseparable loyalty to the One who walks before matches the call of Deuteronomy to choose life and the call of Jesus to follow him. To follow is to take sides. The New Covenant takes Deuteronomy's invitation into a covenant relationship another step forward with Jesus' call to follow him. This loyalty risks death. Allegiance to Jesus may be tested to the limit by the pressures of persecution. The teaching of Jesus and the letters of the New Testament develop an understanding of discipleship in terms of lifestyle and community, using phrases such as 'walking in the light' to describe the ethics of personal integrity before God that this discipleship calls for.

The context of this life journey is, like Israel's, social and political as well as individual and inward. Both these dimensions will colour the experience of life and of God's involvement in it. For Christians, 'walking with God' cannot be turned into an individualistic and apolitical activity divorced from communal and context-specific ways of choosing what is just and right, not if a continuity with Deuteronomy's concept of covenant and Proverbs' concept of instruction are affirmed. The fact that walking after Jesus in the 1st century AD might mean being crucified by the Roman state ensured that there was a public and political dimension to the 'fear of the LORD' in the New Covenant era.

The use of the 'follow' and 'walk' metaphor cluster in the Gospels and Paul continues the trajectory that originated in the Old Testament. The widespread distribution and adaptability of the 'walking' metaphor within the Bible and outside it suggests that the whole complex of associated metaphors of life journey, path and body-movement is a basic human way of interpreting our passage through time.[46] The application of this 'walk with a

---

[45] For detailed studies of debt-slavery in Deuteronomy and Near Eastern sources, see now GC Chirichigno, *Debt-Slavery in Israel and the Ancient Near East*, JSOTS 141 (Sheffield: JSOT Press) 1993, in particular Chap. 7, pp. 255ff.

[46] Compare the way that this life-journey metaphor surfaces in Existential psychotherapy. From a chapter on 'Clarification of Worldview':

Instead of using a diagnostic framework which categorizes and labels personal characteristics, the existential approach proposes a framework which describes the basic dimensions of human existence instead. The idea is to provide a map of the different areas through which people travel so as to facilitate their journey through life and encourage expansion into new territory rather than restricting and limiting them by assigning them certain qualities and characteristics.

Emmy van Deurzen-Smith, *Existential Counselling in Practice* (London: Sage Publications) 1988, p. 69.

whole heart' to vertical and horizontal planes is demonstrated by Deuteronomic covenant stipulations. The metaphor also lends itself to reflective psalms of individual experience, for instance 'the paths of righteousness' and the walk through 'the valley of the shadow of death' of the best loved psalm in the Bible.[47]

In the next chapter, we shall use the path-walking metaphor to cross over into Psa 119 where we will meet with the concept of 'the whole heart' once again, this time in connection with the guiding role of Torah and the Old Testament concept of meditation.

BIBLIOGRAPHY

H Blocher, 'The Fear of the Lord as the "Principle" of Wisdom' *TB* 28 (1977) 3–28.

GC Chirichigno, *Debt-Slavery in Israel and the Ancient Near East*, JSOTS 141 (Sheffield: JSOT Press) 1993.

WD Davies & DC Allison, *Matthew*, ICC (Edinburgh: T&T Clark) 1988.

FC Fensham, 'Widow, Orphan and the Poor in Ancient Near Eastern Legal and Wisdom Literature', *JNES* 21 (1962) 129–139.

B Gerhardsson, *The Testing of God's Son* (Lund: CWK Gleerup) 1966.

DA Hubbard, 'The Wisdom Movement and Israel's Covenant Faith' *TB* 17 (1966) 3–33.

P Kalluveettil, *Declaration and Covenant*, Analecta Biblica 88 (Rome: BIP) 1982.

JA Fitzmyer, *The Aramaic Inscriptions of Sefire* Biblica et Orientalia 19 (Rome: BIP) 1967.

R Frankena, 'The Vassal Treaties of Esarhaddon' *OTS* 14 (1965) 122–154.

SN Kramer, 'Law and Justice: gleanings from Sumerian literature', pp. 77–82 in M Lebean and P Talon (eds) *Reflets des Deux Fleuves: mélanges offerts à André Finet*, Akkadica (Leuven: Peeters) 1989.

TW Mann, *Divine Presence and Guidance in Israelite Traditions: the typology of exaltation*, (London: Johns Hopkins) 1977.

UW Mauser, *Christ in the Wilderness* (London: SCM) 1963.

DJ McCarthy, *Treaty and Covenant*, Analecta Biblica 21a (Rome: BIP) 1978 rev.ed.

---

[47] Psa 23:3 *yanḥēniy bᵉmaʿgᵉley-ṣedeq* 'he leads me in right paths', or 'paths of righteousness'(NRSV, text and footnote). The noun 'paths' *maʿgāl* is a strongly visual image, namely, the rut or track of a wagon. The second word in the construct with it is *ṣedeq* which could be given either its ethical nuance of 'righteous' or its geometric nuance of 'straight'. In v. 4, the traditional translation 'valley of the shadow of death' is defensible. The word *ṣalmāwet* is a compound of *selem* 'shadow' and *māwet* 'death'. NRSV follows D Winton-Thomas in seeing 'deathly' as an intensifier, yielding a superlative—'the darkest valley', where REB offers a compromise 'valley dark as death'. In any case, death is arguably the darkest shadow to fall over an individual's

JG McConville, *Law and Theology in Deuteronomy*, JSOTS 33 (Sheffield: JSOT Press) 1984.

W Moran, 'The Ancient Near Eastern Background of the Love of God in Deuteronomy', *CBQ* 25 (1963) 77–87.

———, *The Amarna Letters* (Baltimore/London: Johns Hopkins) 1992.

S Parpola & K Watanabe, *Neo-Assyrian Treaties and Loyalty Oaths* SAA 2 (Helsinki: Helsinki Univ Press) 1988.

M Weinfeld, 'Traces of Assyrian Treaty Formulae in Deuteronomy' *Biblica* 46 (1965) 417–427.

———, *Deuteronomy and the Deuteronomic School* (Oxford: Clarendon) 1972.

———, 'Covenant Terminology in the Ancient Near East and its Influence on the West', *JAOS* 93.2 (1973) 190–199.

———, 'The Loyalty Oath in the Ancient Near East' *UF* 8 (1976) 379–414.

———, *TDOT III* (1978) pp. 270ff under; דֶּרֶךְ *derek* 'way, path'

———, ' "Justice and Righteousness" in Ancient Israel against the background of "Social, Reforms" in the Ancient Near East' pp. 491–519 in H-J Nissen and J Renger (eds), *Mesopotamien und seine Nachbarn Teil II*, Berliner Beitrage um Vorderen Orient Band 1, (Berlin: Dietrich Reimer Verlag) 1982.

———, *Deuteronomy 1–11*, AB 5 (London: Doubleday) 1991.

———, ' "Justice and Righteousness"—*mišpāṭ weṣedāqāh*—the expression and its meaning', pp. 228–246 in HG Reventlow and Y Hoffman (eds), *Justice and Righteousness: biblical, themes and their influence*, JSOTS 137 (Sheffield: JSOT Press) 1992.

existence. See DJA Clines's comment on the translation of Job 10:21b where ṣalmāwet appears (*Job*, WBC 17 [Dallas: Word] 1989, p. 223).

[5]

The Way Of Reflection
Poems and Meditation

INTRODUCTION

Before stepping out of the Pentateuch and into another topic, we need to recap and indicate the kind of continuity that exists between Torah, commandment and reflection. In the chapters on 'Walking with God' and 'Life journey', we looked at an understanding of life in terms of directional movement. The life of Abraham and of the Exodus generation was typified by walking towards a destination that was defined by God's promise. The linear passage of time towards the realization of the promise was marked out by births and generations. The journey itself was characterized by stopping points and stages. Punctuating the days and the distance travelled were visual experiences of God's appearance and presence. In both Genesis and Exodus, mundane experience is interwoven with the extraordinary—for instance, the three visitors to Abraham's tent (Gen 18) and the burning bush in desert grazing grounds (Exod 3). Conversely, what is originally extraordinary may settle into being the everyday—for instance, Isaac growing up, the diet of manna and the pillar of cloud.

The very human reactions of the participants are woven into this life journey down Salvation History. Abraham trusts and questions, Sarah laughs in disbelief, Moses strikes out and runs away, Israelites dance and despair. If there are peak moments of worship and awe, then there is also the price the participants pay for the disruption of their life by divine promises, divine demands and divine testing.

We followed the concept of walking with a whole heart and the discipline of the testing of faith into the book of Deuteronomy. There the fear of the LORD is worked out in terms of a covenant community confronted with the choice of life and death, of right and wrong defined by the stipulations of covenant. Justice and righteousness, together with the corollary of protection for the disadvantaged, corresponded with ideals for society expressed by Mesopotamian kings when promulgating law reforms and claiming the title 'king of justice'.

We shall now cross the bridge of 'walking before the LORD' in 'the fear of the LORD' from Genesis, Exodus and Deuteronomy into Hebrew poetry, using torah as the walkway that links the covenant loyalty of the community with the spirituality of the individual.[1] We will look at four dimensions to meditation that appear in the Old Testament—internalizing torah, pondering creation, being still in the presence of Yahweh and contemplating God.

WALKING IN THE FEAR OF THE LORD: PSALM 119

Moses posed the question:

> For what other great nation has a god so near to it as as Yahweh our God is whenever we call to him? And what other great nation has statutes and ordinances as just as this entire law that I am setting out before you today?
>
> (Deut 4:7f)

Psalm 119 is a reflective response to being in possession of torah. It is our starting point, for in this the longest poem in the psalter, the focus is on a spirituality of the Word.

In the Old Testament canon, reflection on torah becomes an act of devotion characteristic of one strand of spirituality, torah piety. This is commonly linked with the Wisdom school because of its instructional tone. Psalm 119 with its twenty-two acrostic sections and sheer length is the epitome of this reflective tradition. It draws on literature already understood as canonical Scripture. Deuteronomy is the most probable exemplar because of the phrases Psalm 119 shares with it and Deuteronomy's status enshrining covenant commandments.[2]

---

[1] We shall use 'torah' in this chapter because 'law' is an inadequate and misleading translation of the word. 'Torah' with a capital is generally equated with the Pentateuch as we know it. Using 'torah' in lower case transcribes the Hebrew in the passages that we shall be studying and reminds us of the need to determine both its referent and its nuance in English translation.

[2] Studies have suggested that Psa 119 draws on Isaiah, Jeremiah and Proverbs as well as Deuteronomy. The psalm has often been dated to the Exilic or post-exilic period because it interacts with accumulated sources of divine revelation. Some suggest it was written to conclude the collection of Psalms as a pair with Psa 1 which introduces the collection. For details, see the more recent commentaries such as LC Allen, *Psalms 101–150*, Word (Waco: Word) 1983, pp. 125–145.

In Psalm 119, 'fear of Yahweh' is piety. It characterizes the devout: 'I am a companion of all who fear you, of those who keep your precepts' (v. 63). In a psalm as individual as this, verse 63 is a recognition of the community of faith, but so brief that we cannot characterize it. The 'companions' could even refer to characters in the sacred writings that the poet studied—though elsewhere they are indeed his contemporaries.[3] This circle keeps God's 'precepts'. The word translated 'precepts' (*piqqūdim*) is used more than twenty times in Psalm 119 and is virtually exclusive to it. Because of the associated cluster of vocabulary, and the probable late date of the psalm, there is little doubt that 'precepts' refers to the covenant stipulations accumulated in the various Pentateuchal books, though it could embrace a wider syllabus.[4]

Before pursuing the connection between 'fear of the LORD' and torah piety, we should note that once in Psalm 119 the 'fear of Yahweh' has a numinous quality to it: 'My flesh shudders with the terror of you, and I am afraid in the face of your verdicts' (v. 120).[5] Verse 120 is closer to the Reed Sea and Sinai experience of Yahweh than to torah piety. This mention of the physiological reaction together with 'fear' in the parallel line clearly goes beyond the idea of torah piety, which is an obedience or a devout attitude. This reminds us to avoid semantic shoehorning of the 'fear of the LORD', but it does not alter the fact that torah piety is the focus of Psalm 119.

Prominent as a recurrent motif here is the cluster of imagery that relates wholehearted devotion and obedience to sticking to God's path. The opening of the poem sets this tone:

---

[3] Compare 'Those who fear you shall see me and rejoice' (v. 74) and 'Let those who fear you turn to me' (v.79).

[4] In Psa 103:18 *piqqūdim* is used in parallel with *bᵉrit* 'covenant'; in Psa 19:8 it appears as a synonym in a list that relates 'the fear of the LORD' to reflection on and keeping his torah. Besides 'precepts', the covenant stipulations are referred to in the opening verses of Psa 119 by the synonyms 'laws', 'testimonies', 'statutes', 'ordinances', 'commandments' (*tōrāh, ʿēdūt, ḥuqqim, mišpāṭim, miṣwōt*). It is possible that 'precepts' embraces Wisdom teachings in proverb, dialogue or autobiographical genre such as are reflected in Proverbs, Job and Ecclesiastes. See JD Levenson 'The Sources of Torah: Psa 119 and the Modes of Revelation in Second Temple Judaism' pp. 559–574 in PD Miller, *Ancient Israelite Religion*, 1987.

[5] The phrase in v.120a combines *smr*—'to shudder', with 'fear of you' *paḥdᵉkā* from *pāḥad* 'trembling, terror' both strongly physiological and emotional. The more usual verb 'to fear'(*yrʾ* in phrases about the 'fear of Yahweh') appears in v.120b, as well as in the other verses in this cluster, namely, vv. 38, 63, 74.

¹Happy are those whose way is blameless,
who walk in the torah of Yahweh.
²Happy are those who keep his decrees,
who seek him with their whole heart,
³who also do no wrong,
but walk in his ways.

The vocabulary is very reminiscent of the covenant concerns of Deuteronomy—'wholeheartedly' (*b*ᵉ*kol-lēb*), 'walking in the torah of Yahweh' and 'walking in his ways'—and the reference to 'decrees'(ᶜ*ēdōtayw*), which one might translate as 'covenant stipulations'.⁶ The 'walking' phrases might be considered as stereotyped and dead metaphors were it not that a cluster of 'path' and 'foot' imagery pervades the poem, animating it with a pilgrim piety. Perhaps the best known lines from Psalm 119 picture walking along at night with a lamp, associating Yahweh's word with a source of light that makes it possible for the devout to find their way in the dark. The Scripture Union organisation based its logo on this verse, spreading the imagery as well as the spirituality of devotional reading of the Old Testament around the world. In fact, verse 115 is not an isolated couplet, but more like one bead on a string of beads, as the following 'walking' excerpts demonstrate:

¹⁰⁵Your word is a lamp to my feet
and a light to my path.

¹⁰With my whole heart I seek you,
do not let me stray from your commandments.

³²I run the way of your commandments,
for you enlarge my understanding.

³⁵Lead me in the path of your commandments,
for I delight in it.

⁴⁵I shall walk at liberty,
for I have sought your precepts.

⁵⁹When I think of your ways,
I turn my feet to your decrees;

---

⁶ The Hebrew ᶜ*ēdūt* certainly seems to do duty for 'covenant, pact' in 2 Kgs 11:12. It has etymological and semantic parallels in Akkadian *adē* and Aramaic '*dy*', both of which refer to the 'oaths' of treaty and by metonymy come to mean 'treaty'. For Hebrew ᶜ*ēdūt* in Deuteronomic passages where it is paired with other words for 'covenant stipulations', see Weinfeld, *Deut School*, p. 338 Nos. 21d, 21e, 21i, 21j. It seems to be one of a number of synonyms for the 'covenant stipulations' used interchangeably in Psa 119. Following LC Allen, we may compare Psa 132:12 'If your sons keep my *covenant* and my *decrees* that I shall teach them . . .', where *b*ᵉ*rītiy* and ᶜ*ēdotiy* are in parallel (*Psalms 101–150*, p. 134 note 2a).

[60]I hurry and do not delay
to keep your commandments.

[101]I hold back my feet from every evil way,
in order to keep your word.
[102]I do not turn away from your ordinances

[128]Truly I direct my steps by all your precepts;
I hate every false way.

[133]Keep my steps steady according to your promise,

[176]I have gone astray like a lost sheep;
seek out your servant

When the various verbs ('stray', 'run', 'walk', 'turn', 'hurry', 'hold back', 'turn away', 'go astray') are added to the nouns 'feet', 'steps', 'path' and 'way', the imagery of spirituality as a life journey involving choices, direction and consistency emerges clearly. In a psalm about the studying of torah, living the torah is the goal in mind. Torah is map, living is locomotion.

We now move from the journey-of-life aspect of Psalm 119 to consider the psalm as a sample of Hebrew meditation.

MEDITATION IN AN OLD TESTAMENT FRAMEWORK

As we explore Hebrew poems we need to ask a few more questions about 'meditation' within an Old Testament context. The problem with using a word like 'meditation' is that it conjures up associations that may be alien to the primary texts of the Old Testament that are the starting point for discussion. Current nuances of 'meditation' may suggest New Age philosophies and Californian versions of Eastern religions. Transcendental Meditation (TM), Yoga, EST, Zen and other consciousness-raising or consciousness-altering practices spring to mind.[7] Alternatively, 'meditation' might suggest to some a Catholic mystical tradition, with associations from the Desert Fathers to Thomas Merton. To

---

[7] A discussion of whether or how body positions, breathing techniques, centering down and the like may be incorporated into Christian meditative spirituality belongs to another conversation for which there is not space here. Such topics are included in handbook guides like R Foster, *Celebration of Discipline: the path to spiritual growth* (London: Hodder & Stoughton) 1980 Chap. 2 'The Discipline of Meditation', or Una Kroll, *The Spiritual Exercise Book* (London: Firethorn Press) 1985.

others a Sufi strand of Islam might come to mind.[8] Thus conceptual and cultural context is vital for determining what process is involved in 'meditation'.

1. MEDITATION AS INTERNALIZING TORAH

Eight times in Psalm 119, the verb 'meditate' characterizes the poet's interaction with God's commandments (vv. 15, 23, 27, 48, 78, 97, 99, 148). The Hebrew verb translated 'meditate' is *síaḥ*, meaning 'to be concerned with, occupy one's attention with'. The activity is cognitive. It is concentrating on, thinking about, reflecting on the torah as a body of revealed truth. Three verses underline the metaphor of a cognitive focus:

> [6]Then I shall not be put to shame
> having my eyes fixed on all your commandments.
>
> [15]I will meditate on your precepts,
> and fix my eyes on your ways.
>
> [18]Open my eyes, so that I may behold
> wondrous things out of your law.

'Fix the eyes on' starts from the literal aligning of scroll and eyeball in the process of reading and moves on to the figurative sense of aligning the mind, that is, concentrating on. The 'ways, paths' of v.15 could include God's acts of Salvation History such as the Exodus events. The uncovering of the eyes, 'open my eyes' in v.18, is a metaphor for the unveiling of the mind, that is, for spiritual enlightenment through the study process.

Psalm 119 sets the internalizing of torah at the centre stage of meditation. The psalmist practising this spirituality is at first glance not humanly endearing, certainly not in his claims and boasts. He claims to fill his mind with God and torah continuously around the clock: 'at all times', 'continually, for ever and ever', 'in the night', 'at midnight', 'all day long', 'for ever', 'for ever, to the end', 'before dawn', 'before the watches of the night', 'seven times a day' (vv. 20, 44, 55, 62, 97, 111, 112, 147, 148, 164). This

---

[8] This is more likely since recognised specialists in Old and New Testament studies such as John Eaton and John Robinson have written books that open a dialogue with Eastern traditions. See J Eaton, *The Contemplative Face of Old Testament Wisdom in the context of world religions* (London: SCM/Philadelphia: Trinity Press International) 1989 and JAT Robinson, *Truth is Two-eyed* (London: SCM) 1979. Sometimes the Hebraic and Christian strand is represented as 'prophetic' while Eastern religions are seen as the expression of the contemplative and mystical. Robinson wants to recognize the 'Two Eyes on Reality'. His opening chapter is sub-titled 'Journeying into life'—another example of this irresistible metaphor of the life journey.

saturation is not simply one of duration but of intensity—'with open mouth I pant, because I long for your commandments' (v. 131). The phrase 'with my whole heart' appears repeatedly (vv. 10, 34, 58, 69, 145). He will never 'forget your commandments' and the result is apparent—'I have more understanding than all my teachers', 'I understand more than the aged' (v. 99, 100). Does he exaggerate? Is this too good to be true?

For all this immersion in study and orientation to God, his meditation does not bring him tranquillity of mind. The wicked intrude. He feels persecuted. His emotions break through his piety. Far from being secure and self-satisfied, he cries aloud for help and the vigil of the early hours in particular seems to relate to the 'trouble and anguish' that have come upon him (v. 143).

> [145]With my whole heart I cry:
> answer me , O LORD.
> I will keep your statutes.
> [146]I cry to you; save me,
> that I may observe your decrees.
> [147]I rise before dawn and cry for help;
> I put my hope in your words.
> [148]My eyes are awake before each watch of the night,
> that I may meditate on your promise.

The language of lament intersperses the poem, signalled not only by words such as 'call out', 'cry' (vv.145, 146, 147) and 'sorrow', 'distress', 'trouble and anguish', 'misery'(vv. 28, 50, 92, 143, 153), but by lament phrases such as 'my soul clings to the dust', 'my soul melts away for sorrow', 'my soul languishes for your salvation', 'my eyes fail with watching', 'I ask, "When will you comfort me?" ', 'How long must your servant endure?' (vv. 25, 28, 81, 82, 84).

His internalizing of torah turns out to be a survival technique against the external and internal pressures of persecution and sin. He is a more troubled man than we might have allowed at first glance, and the psalm as a whole, despite his assertions and claims, reads rather more like a confession than a post-graduate certificate in torah piety. The question posed at the beginning, 'How can a young man keep his way pure?' and that gained the response 'by guarding it according to your word' (v. 9) and his statement of intent 'I treasure your word in my heart, so that I may not sin against you' (v. 11) leads to a final admission that he has wandered off the path of life—'I have gone astray like a lost sheep; seek out your servant, for I do not forget your commandments' (v. 176).

The spirituality involved in 'meditation' in Psa 119 is far from an emptying of the mind, seeking detachment, or generating alpha rhythms. Torah is no mantra or mandela. Yet we see in the juxtaposition of lament language and precept language a context for the kind of meditation that Psa 119 promulgates. Peace of mind is involved and study of torah is a method of paving the way forward in life with what the psalmist can rely upon. The content of torah is something solid, a basis for living. It contains an ethic. It consists of 'righteous ordinances' (vv. 7, 62, 160, 164; cf. 137f, 142, 144).

Psalm 119 does not stand alone in interpreting meditation as internalizing torah. Psalm 1, aptly set as the canonical introduction to Israel's collection of hymns and prayers, speaks of meditation in the context of two contrasted ways of life.

> [1]Happy are those who do not follow
> the advice of the wicked,
> or take the path that sinners tread,
> or sit in the seat of scoffers;
> [2]but their delight is in the law of the LORD,
> and on his law they meditate day and night..
>
> (Psa 1:1f)

Here again we find the pervasive 'walk' and 'way', journey-of-life metaphors. The righteous do not 'walk in' (*hālak b^e*) or 'stand on the path of' (*'āmad b^{e}derek*) the wicked. The life style of the righteous arises from within, from the inner wellsprings of motivation fed by torah. Translation of v.2 by 'law of the LORD' (NRSV) for the Hebrew *tōrat Yhwh* risks importing into this poem echoes of Pauline debates about the Law and Christian reactions against salvation by works. A translation of *tōrāh* as 'teaching, revealed truth' avoids these negative nuances and couples better with the 'delight' involved. The meditate verb, (*hāgāh*—'to murmur, ponder') is best understood in the context clusters of Pss 19:15, 63:6, 77:12 and 143:5.[9] It may have the nuance range of 'murmuring, muttering, reading aloud or reciting to oneself', but the meditation verbs in this cluster are not concerned to detail a technique.

> Let the words of my mouth and the meditation of my heart
> be acceptable to you,
> O LORD, my rock and my redeemer.
>
> (Psa 19:15)

---

[9] The verbs associated with *hāgāh* in these references are: *zākar*—'to remember', and *śiah*—'to occupy one's attention with'. The poet of Psa 77:2f is an insomniac who combines his reflections with emotions:

> I think of God, and I moan,
> I meditate, and my spirit faints.

when I think of you on my bed,
and meditate on you in the watches of the night;

(Psa 63:6)

I will meditate on all your work,
and muse on your mighty deeds

(Psa 77:12)

I remember the days of old,
I think about all your deeds,
I meditate on the works of your hands.

(Psa 143:5)

In the lines above, 'meditate' renders *hāgāh* while the cluster covers various conscious reflective processes that we might describe as 'recalling, turning over in the mind, focusing upon, thinking about, memorizing, reciting aloud, pondering, concentrating on, studying, wondering about' and the like. In Psa 1, the torah is likely to be revealed truth in the form of canonical Scripture, as it is in Psa 119, but we can see in the quotations from Pss 63, 77 and 143 above that God himself, the deeds of Salvation History and the acts of creation may form the subject for reflection.[10]

2. MEDITATION AS PONDERING CREATION

Nature is sometimes said to be God's "other book", but what you see depends on what you are looking at. Is it mass extinctions, predator and prey populations, or the replication of bacteria, parasites and viruses?[11] Or is it the power of nature released in floods, eruptions, earthquakes, asteroid impacts and supernovae? In this amoral world of nature there is design and disaster, population boom and bust, nuclear fusion and black holes. From pulsars to microbes, volcanoes to cancer cells, nothing breaks the laws of physics or genetics. There is no 'disorder'. Intellectually we are better equipped than ever to appreciate this order and the

---

[10] It is not always possible to specify whether phrases such as 'mighty deeds', 'wonders' and 'days of old' refer back to Exodus events, miracles from other occasions, interventions in battles, or include primeval events of creation.

[11] Note Stephen Jay Gould's three cheers for bacteria: "The most salient feature of life has been the stability of its bacterial mode from the beginning of the fossil record until today and, with little doubt, into all future time so long as the earth endures. This is truly the 'age of bacteria'—as it was in the beginning, is now and ever shall be . . . The number of *Eschericia coli* cells in the gut of each human being exceeds the number of humans that has ever lived on this planet." ('The Evolution of Life on the Earth', pp. 62–69 in *Scientific American* Oct 1994, special issue *Life in the Universe*).

complexity in cosmos and planet, ecologies and brain functioning. Science assumes and uncovers order from sub-atomic particles to food chains of Antarctic krill and whales. And yet . . . For all our appreciation of the physics and biology involved, the natural world is hugely ambiguous in its emotional impact on us. Popular Christian poetry has tended to look at 'all things bright and beautiful' where Blake looked at the tiger in the forests of the night. What of the Old Testament? What aspects of nature did poets and sages contemplate?

Psalm 19 is our best starting point. It links this section of the chapter on pondering creation with the previous section on internalizing torah because the poet's perspective on creation in Psalm 19 was that it is a reflection of the one recognised through torah. A second reason for starting here is that what you see is what you get in the sense that the composing of the psalm is itself an outstanding example of Old Testament meditation. The final verse, already quoted above, offers God 'the words of my mouth and the meditation of my heart.'[12] Though this could be a perennial prayer for acceptability extending to all the poet's life and worship, in its immediacy this wish applies to the poem itself, for this is the product of his mind and lips. To compose a psalm is to 'meditate'.

The parts of the psalm form an integral whole, vv. 1–6 about creation and vv. 7–10 about torah, with a personalised application and concluding prayer in vv. 11–13.[13] Clines has made a good case for understanding the psalm as a meditation on Gen 1–3. The first six verses correspond to the Creation account of Gen 1. The 'law, decrees, precepts, commandment, ordinances' (19:7–9) find a contact point in the apodictic command—'of the tree of the knowledge of good and evil you shall not eat' (Gen 2:17, 3:3,11). The hidden sin and proud thoughts the poet fears may lurk within him (19:11–13) point back to the initial disobedience and hubris in the garden of Eden. The torah of Yahweh now 'makes wise' (19:7b) and 'enlightens the eyes' (19:8b) in the way that the forbidden fruit failed to do (Gen 3:5f). The tree of the knowledge

---

[12] The spoken and the thought are in parallel. 'Meditation of my heart' (*hegyōn libbiy*) is probably a little misleading in nuance for English speakers since 'thoughts of my mind' would be a more straightforward translation.

[13] Recent commentators such as Anderson, Clines and Craigie explain the coherence of the psalm in a way that overcomes the strictures of earlier writers such as A Weiser who found 'two independent songs' and was at a loss to establish 'why these dissimilar poems were united in one single psalm'—The *Psalms*, OTL (London: SCM) 1962, p.197. See AA Anderson, *Psalms Vol. 1*, NCB (London: Oliphants, MM&S) 1972, pp. 167ff; DJA Clines, 'The Tree of Knowledge and the Law of Yahweh (Ps XIX)' *Vetus Testamentum* 24 (1974) 8–14 and PC Craigie, *Psalms 1–50*, WBC 19 (Waco: Word) 1983, pp. 177ff.

of good and evil was 'good for food', 'a delight to the eyes' and 'desired to make one wise' (Gen 3:6). Now torah is 'sweeter also than honey, and the drippings of the honeycomb' (19:10b). Instead of a sentence of 'Guilty!', the poet asks for God's help so that he may be 'blameless and innocent of great transgression' (19:13). The fear and guilt of Paradise lost—man and woman being afraid of God and hiding themselves and their nakedness——may be replaced by 'the fear of the LORD' that 'is pure, enduring for ever' (19:9a). In Gen 1, Day 4 corresponds with Day 1 (Light with sun, moon, stars) and receives extra space. The sun receives special mention in Psalm 19 and there is an implied typology between the sun (vv. 4b–6) that shines brightly illuminating the whole world and the torah that 'enlightens the eyes' (v. 8b).[14]

If Gen 1–3 is a source of inspiration for the poet of Psalm 19, then we have an example of double reflection on canonical truth within the psalm—on the Genesis material and on Israel's covenant stipulations. Three strands of meditation emerge—the poet's reflections on nature, his reflections on scripture and the artistic process itself that led to the psalm in its finished form.

Turning to the pondering of creation itself in vv. 1–4, we find that it is the sky that the poet looks at—'the heavens' and 'the firmament'. Day and night are both mentioned but only the sun is singled out for fuller comment (vv. 4b–6). Perhaps the 'glory of God' ($k^e b\bar{o}d$-$^{\prime}\bar{e}l$, v.1) comes to a focus in the sun in that its dazzling brightness and the felt presence of its heat on earth ('nothing is hid from its heat', v.6b) combine as imagery that makes graphic the transcendence and immanence of God. There is certainly a long tradition in the Near East of associating the sun, majesty, radiance as a cloak or nimbus halo surrounding deities and kings, and light that dispels darkness.[15] Kings and gods are called *šamši*—'majesty', based on *šamšu* 'sun', and they are clothed in dazzling brightness, as the following lines describing the warrior champion Marduk illustrate, followed by lines from Psa 104:

---

[14] CS Lewis, Craigie and others extend the sun~torah typology to compare 'nothing is hid from its heat' (19:6b)—'so too the *Torah* can be both life-imparting, but also scorching, testing, and purifying' (Craigie, *Psalms 1–50*, p.184). Clines uses the sun~torah typology as an argument for the coherence of the psalm, quoting S Mowinckel ('The Tree of Knowledge' *VT* 24, p.12 note 4). The association of the sun god Shamash with justice is cited in support.

[15] See AL Oppenheim's study 'Akkadian *pul(u)ḫ(t)u* and *melammu*' *JAOS* 63 (1943) 31–34 and *CAD M*, p.10ff *melammu*; *CAD N*, p.237ff *namrirrū, namru, namurratu*; S Dalley, 'The God Salmu and the Winged Disk' *Iraq* 48 (1986) 85–101.

Son, majesty, majesty of the gods!
Clothed in the radiant mantle of ten gods, worn high above his head
Five fearsome rays were clustered above him.

Clothed in a cloak of awesome armour,
His head was crowned with a terrible radiance.

Let the Son, Majesty of the gods be his name!
In his bright light may they walk forever more:
The people whom he created, the form of life that breathes.

O Yahweh, my God, you are very great.
You are clothed with honour and majesty,
wrapped in light as with a garment.[16]

The 'glory of God' of Psa 19:1 is linked with majesty, transcendence, the heavens and splendour. The sun is like a 'bridegroom' and a 'strong man' (*gibbōr*) as it 'runs its course with joy'. The Mesopotamian god Shamash is likewise heralded in heroic terms as he rises and traverses the heavens and underworld.[17] Like Shamash, Yahweh as warrior-king and suzerain over Israel is also depicted with strongly masculine, warrior-hero imagery (Exod 15:3,18). Underlying the parts of Psalm 19, therefore, we find a three element association: God-in-his-glory/the heavens and sun/torah. The two books of divine disclosure are the heavens and torah. Of course, the poet composes in a period when the traditions, if the not the final redaction of Pentateuchal materials themselves, were before him, and so he looks at the heavens through the lens of Israel's history and theology. It is to the mind that already knows God as Yahweh of covenant that the heavens

---

[16] Psa 104:1f with *hōd wᵉhādār* 'majesty and splendour'. Compare Psa 96:1–8 where the association cluster describing Yahweh embraces 'glory', 'honour and majesty', 'strength', 'beauty' (*kābōd, hōd-wᵉhādār, ʿōz, tipʾeret*). For *Enuma elish*, see Dalley, *Myths*, pp. 236, 251, 265 Ee 1:101ff, 4: 58, 6: 127f where *šamši* 'majesty', *melammu* 'radiance, awe-inspiring sheen, mantle of radiance', *namru* 'radiant, brilliant' and *puluḫtu* 'fearsomeness, terror' form an association cluster. Compare the translation of BR Foster, *Before the Muses*, pp. 357, 374, 389.

[17] Besides god Sun's dazzling image, his heroism emerges as traveller of regions unknown:

Your splendour envelops the distant mountains,
your glare has filled all the lands. (line 19f)
You cross time and again the vast expanse of the seas,
[Whose] depths not even the Igigi-gods know. (line 35f)
Among all the Igigi-gods there is none who does such wearisome toil but you,
Nor among the sum total of the gods one who does so much as you. (lines 45ff)
(Foster, *Before the Muses*, p. 537f; *ANET*, 387ff)

speak loudly and in a monotheistic dialect about the glory of their Creator.[18]

The glory of the sky catches hold of the poet's imagination in Psalm 8 as well:

> [1b]You have set your glory (*hōd*) above the heavens.
>
> [3]When I look at your heavens, the work of your fingers,
> the moon and the stars that you have established;
> [4]what are human beings that you are mindful of them,
> mortals that you care for them?

The question 'What are human beings?' hangs in air that hisses with the background radiation from the Big Bang. The vast scale of the universe was barely glimpsed in the poet's day, so the question is vastly intensified by the billions of galaxies too dim for him to see, receding at unimaginable velocities and distances computed in light years. That he star-gazed without wearing mythological spectacles is a clue as to how he answered his own rhetorical question. Without the opening words *Yhwh 'ᵃdōneynū* 'Yahweh our lord', the vision of humanity's executive role on earth would be wishful thinking. Today there are those who find it a natural step to move from the vast size of the universe to the conclusion that individual human beings, or even humanity as a whole, are totally insignificant.

We take note of Thorkild Jacobsen's comments on the Mesopotamian wish that cosmic deities would pay attention to the human individual. This is a hurdle at which in his judgment Mesopotamian religion falls. In his chapter on 'Second Millennium Metaphors. The Gods as Parents: Rise of Personal Religion', he comments:

> the penitent and his personal affairs are not only thought to matter, but matter supremely. They swell to fill the whole picture. The penitent becomes so centrally important in the universe that he can monopolize God's attention . . . before this onslaught of unlimited ego, the figure of God appears to shrink: no longer the awesome creator and ruler of the All, he dwindles to 'the God of *my* salvation.'
>
> . . . the paradoxical character of personal religion, with its conspicuous humility curiously based on an almost limitless presumption of self-importance, its drawing the greatest cosmic powers into the little personal world of the individual . . .

---

[18] Commentators point out that *'ēl* 'God' is used in the opening part whereas the personal name Yahweh appears in vv. 7ff with *tōrat Yhwh* 'the torah of the LORD'. Use of *'ēl* is no warrant for Morgenstern's hypothesis that vv. 1–6 were originally an early and non-Israelite hymn to Canaanite El as creator deity.

Jacobsen does not usually allow value judgments to intrude into his descriptions of Mesopotamian religion, but here he seems to pillory the personal laments in a manner that applies equally to Israel's Laments of the Individual. Paradoxically, he ends his chapter with approving remarks for Israel's national sense of 'moral responsibility' and its 'concept of history as purposive'.[19] Perhaps this ancient issue of individual suffering resonates with our existential vision of human fragility, of *Homo sapiens* as a species but recently emerged on a planet that is a speck of dust in a vast and violent universe. When we wave goodbye to mythological Shamash and Marduk, the sky is left empty. When the sky is the sky is the sky, it is not absurd to think that we are left alone in the universe. A Darwinian perception of the emergence and extinction of species, combined with a modern cosmology, in and of themselves offer us the anthropic principle at most—that we would not be here to view the universe and reflect upon it were the universe not as finely tuned to being the particular universe that it is and that allows for carbon-based life like ourselves to arise on planet earth. The anthropic principle can scarcely be transubstantiated into an argument for a God of covenant blood and commitment to intimacy.

Accordingly, Psalm 8 starts with 'Yahweh, our lord' (known in covenant) and not from 'the heavens, the moon and the stars.' What we also notice is that it begins with 'Yahweh our lord' on the lips of an Israelite in a worshipping community, but extends its compass to humanity—'human beings', 'mortals' (v. 4).[20] The reflection of an individual, the worship of a community, the vision for humanity, and an imagination sparked by the visual are combined in the meditation that is Psalm 8.

There is another related mode of reflecting on nature. It has roots in the Wisdom tradition. Here there is observation, curiosity, delight and wonder.

[18]Three things are too wonderful for me;
four I do not understand:

---

[19] *Treasures*, p. 164. He speaks of the righteous sufferer, including Job: "The contradictions are indeed insoluble as long as the attitude of personal religion is allowed to reduce existence, the infinite universe, to the narrow compass of a personal world, andexpect it to centre in an individual and his personal needs. With this understanding of national life and fortunes as lived under ultimate moral responsibility, Israel created a concept of history as purposive—one which in basic essentials still governs conceptions of meaningful historical existence." (p. 163) His final sentence seems to grant permanent ethical approval to Israel's national theology but to equate Mesopotamian personal religion and Israelite prayer of the individual as 'in all essentials the same' and in need of adjustment to the way things are in the universe.

[20] See JL Mays 'What is a Human Being? Reflections on Psalm 8' *Theology Today* 50.4 (1994) 511–520 for a reflection on a reflection.

¹⁹the way of an eagle in the sky,
the way of a snake on a rock
the way of a ship on the high seas,
and the way of a man with a girl.

(Prov 30:18f)

Eagle, snake and ship are marked by the strong visual appeal of effortless movement, while the fourth seems to delight the poet by the interplay of masculine and feminine, human beings acting in their natural element of social and biological attraction. No moral is sought or drawn. There is a delight at the ways things behave when they are being themselves. Verses 29–31, like vv.18–19, enjoy looking at four good movers—the lion, rooster, he-goat and king. A different level of observation accompanied by reflection applies to the statements about ants, hyraxes, locusts and lizards (vv. 24–28). Here the natural world is a see-through mirror for human society. The small, weak or insignificant can compensate for their disadvantage by prudence, shrewdness and strategy.[21]

From these observations of nature, we turn to Psalm 104. Like Psa 19, it has been compared with Near Eastern praise poems.[22] It is sometimes classified as an individual hymn, and certainly speaks of 'singing to Yahweh' in v.33, but it has not acquired a rubric for the Temple musicians. Whether sung in communal worship when collected in the canon or not, the poem began life as a reflection offered to God: 'may my meditation (*śīḥiy*) be pleasing to him, for I rejoice in the LORD' (v. 34). The flow of the psalm well illustrates the principle enunciated above that the Hebrew poet starts his observation of nature with a knowledge of God drawn from Israel's theological traditions. In this instance, the poem opens with lines descriptive of God in his glory as Creator before passing on to details of nature known to the poet from his environment.[23]

---

[21] Children's talks based on animal tales and object lessons are heirs of this sort of Wisdom reflection. The *Jungle Doctor* series of books by Paul White with animal cartoon illustrations offers parables, proverbs and Christian doctrine in a way that demonstrates prime concern with the message, using observation, humour and story-telling as the art of the genre: *Jungle Doctor's Fables, Hippo Happenings, Monkey Tales, Tug-of-War* published originally by Paternoster Press. See FW Golka, *The Leopard's Spots: biblical and African Wisdom in Proverbs* (Edinburgh: T&T Clark) 1993 for a technical study of the proverb genre in the Old Testament and Africa.

[22] See, for instance, PC Craigie, 'The Comparison of Hebrew Poetry: Psa 104 in the Light of the Egyptian and Ugaritic Poetry' *Semitics* 4 (1974) 10–21 and the interaction with this in LC Allen, *Psalms 101–150*, WBC 21 (Waco: Word) 1983, pp. 23ff.

[23] His source may well be the monotheistic Creation theology of Gen 1 or similar material. See Allen's review of Humbert, van der Voort, Gunkel, Anderson and Craigie for a representative discussion on the links between

In this poem, the threatening elements of nature are acknowledged but viewed as put in their place by Yahweh. The waters that topped the mountains fled at Yahweh's rebuke (v. 7) and are now confined within boundaries.[24] The denizen of the deep, Leviathan, 'you formed to sport in it' (v. 26).[25] This leaves the benevolent springs, streams and rains with grass, plants and 'abundantly watered trees' where birds nest (vv. 10–17). Darkness is made by God and the nocturnal animals complement the daytime ones. The most fearsome of predators, the lions, emerge and 'roar for their prey, seeking their food from God' (v. 21). Death appears when God 'takes away their breath' and they 'return to their dust' (v. 29).

The poem begins and ends with images of theophany, and in between celebrates the diurnal rhythm of day and night, sunrise, work and sunset. The poet has not excluded predators and death—nature red in tooth and claw—from his picture of the natural order. Whether the poet would or could have written the kind of poem he did in a region not watered by rain and streams but, like Bangladesh, subject to catastrophic flooding or typhoons is a moot point.[26] This said, Psalm 104 is not an 'all things bright and beautiful' poem. Its most dramatic insight is that the violent and powerful side of nature is overwhelmed by the frightening side of God himself who issues forth with 'wind, fire and flame' as his messengers and 'who looks on the earth and it trembles, who touches the mountains and they smoke' (vv. 3–4, 32).

The poet uses mythological imagery freely because he is not its prisoner. The elements of nature are not personified as deities. If the mountains smoke, it is because God has touched them not because a belching volcano is a manifestation of a deity Vulcan in the way that Mesopotamians and the mythologers of Ugarit

---

material in Gen 1 and in Psa 104. He approves a theological connection along the lines of Craigie's 'relatively independent expressions of the same part of Israelite theology.'

[24] For the Babylonian concept of 'the bolt, the bar of the sea' *šigaru naḫbalu tiʾāmtim* in *Atrahasis*, see OB Tablet 1:15, and BE 39099 lines 6,10 and following (Lambert & Millard, *Atrahasis*, pp. 119 & 166; Dalley, *Myths*, p. 37 note 26). Compare with Job 38:8–11.

[25] On Leviathan compared with Lotan at Ugarit, see the commentaries on Job 41 and L Fisher, *Ras Shamra Parallels, Vol. 3*, Analecta Orientalia 51 (Rome: PIB) 1981, pp. 388ff. Here in Psa 104: 26, in association with 'ships', *liwyātān* seems to be demythologized and be a reference to a known animal, not a mythological one. It may refer to the whale (Allen, p. 27 note 26b).

[26] We can compare Psa 104 with the hymn of praise, Psa 65, in which vv. 9–13 offer thanksgiving for 'the river of God' 'full of water' that produces abundance in crops and flocks.

experienced thunder storms as manifestations of Ninurta or Baal.[27]

The same is true of Psalm 29. This psalm has sometimes been regarded as a Canaanite original with 'Yhwh' substituted for 'Baal'.[28] 'Yahweh sits enthroned over the flood' while 'in his temple all say, "Glory!" ' (Psa 29:9f). In fact, this poem demythologizes the power of the thunderstorm rolling across the Mediterranean and breaking over the mountains of Lebanon that 'skip like a calf'. For the Yahwistic poet, the thunder is symbolically or metaphorically God's voice, and not literally so—any more than Sirion and Lebanon are mountain deities that get up and dance (vv. 5f).[29] The poet can hear the thunder as God's majestic voice

---

[27] T. Jacobsen has offered many penetrating studies of Sumerian myths in which the powers of nature are personified as deities who were worshipped in the cult. Farmers and fishermen, agriculturalists and herdsmen worshipped the forms of the deities making up the Sumerian pantheon of Nippur that were most relevant to their livelihood. 'Ninurta, god of the thunderstorm and spring flood . . . is predominantly a god of the farmer'; 'Ishkur seems to belong specifically to the herdsmen' (*Treasures*, pp. 127ff). Amalgamation of economic interests led to gods like Dumuzi combining various associations——with date-palm, sheep and milk, barley and beer, and orchards. On the Dumuzi texts and the agricultural cycle, see Jacobsen's *Harps*, Part One.

[28] So FM Cross, *Canaanite Myth and Hebrew Epic: essays in the history of the religion of Israel* (Cambridge: Harvard University Press) 1973, pp. 151ff. The comparisons Cross and others make with Ugaritic material are convincing, but allowance must be made for a Yahwistic hermeneutic within an Israelite context. See BC Ollenburger, *Zion, City of the Great King: a theological symbol of the Jerusalem cult*, JSOTS 41 (Sheffield: JSOT Press) 1987 for an exposition of the Yahwistic hermeneutic applied to the New Year festival and the kingship of Yahweh; on Psa 29 in this setting, see pp. 32f and 51f. Comparisons demonstrate a common pool of poetic language and imagery, such as that which depicts the Divine Council and Divine Warrior. Orthodox and monotheistic Yahwists could freely exploit this language and indeed turn it to polemic effect, just as Yahweh is portrayed as the dragon-slayer in Psa 74:13f or the slayer of Leviathan in Isa 27:1ff. That many Israelites were syncretistic or polytheistic much of the time and absorbed such language and imagery uncritically is overwhelmingly probable in the light of Judges, Solomon's reign, what happened in the Jerusalem temple itself, particularly in Manasseh's reign, the cakes offered to 'the queen of heaven' in Jeremiah's time subsequent to Josiah's reforms, not to mention religion in the northern kingdom. We should distinguish orthodox Yahwistic theology from Israelite religion as it was actually practised. Canonical books like Kings inveigh against Israelite religion. See Craigie, *Psalms 1–50*, pp. 241ff for a careful review of the Ginsberg-Cross hypothesis for Psa 29. With Craigie, we would read Psa 29 as Yahwistic polemic against Baal, but would feel caution towards Craigie's chronological hypothesis about the poem as a development of the Victory Hymn celebrating the Divine Warrior in historical battles. For an overview of the Baal myth, Victory hymn, and Divine Warrior complex, see *Ras Shamra Parallels, Vol. 3*, III.1, pp. 233ff.

[29] Significant mountains and rivers (the Nile and Euphrates) are deified in the Ancient Near East. There are specifically named deified mountains such as the

and pass imaginatively from the phenomena of the electrical storm to the glory of God.

We can distinguish Psalm 29 and its inspiration from the altered state of consciousness that Ezekiel labels as 'visions of God' when he encountered the rumbling and flashing chariot-throne of Yahweh developing out of 'the stormy wind out of the north' (Ezek 1). Neither Ezekiel nor the poet of Psalm 29 worships Yahweh as god Storm in the way that Mesopotamians hymned Enlil as Lord Windstorm or thought of Adad as 'bellowing from the clouds' in the Flood.[30]

Psalm 29 ends with the thoroughly Israelite prayer, 'May Yahweh bless his people with *šālōm*' (v. 11b). In the 'his people', 'bless' and *šālōm* we glimpse the worshipping community gathered in his earthly temple. Behind the words 'his people' and 'bless with peace' stands covenant and priestly blessing, as depicted in the Aaronic blessing of Num 6. It is probably fair to say, then, that this poem which opens with an address to the celestial beings and borrows freely from mythological warrior imagery nevertheless takes its starting point from covenant relationship with Yahweh and celebration of his kingship, a kingship that was as much historical and political as a sovereignty over the seas, storms and seasons.

Finally, we should note the references to nature in Job. The forces of nature in their destructive power make an early appearance in the book—'the fire of God' that 'fell from heaven and burned up the sheep and the servants' (Job 1:16), and the 'great wind' that 'came across the desert, struck the four corners of the house' (1:19) so that its collapse killed Job's children. When Yahweh puts in his appearance, he 'answered Job out of the whirlwind' (Job 38:1). The poet presents a world that is ordered yet awesome. The barring of the sea symbolizes the primeval ordering of the cosmos:

Hurrian 'divine (mountain) Haman', the Hittite divinized Namni and Hazzi, and the Ugaritic *'il ṣapān* 'the divine mountain Zaphon', as well as the mountains listed as deities along with other natural elements who witness Hittite treaties—mountains, rivers, wells, the great abyss, heaven and earth, winds and clouds. See RJ Clifford, *The Cosmic Mountain in Canaan and the Old Testament*, HSM 4 (Cambridge, Mass; HUP) 1972, pp. 58ff on the material from Ugarit in which Baal's deified mountain Zaphon appears in myth, pantheon list and offering lists. Compare M Weinfeld 'The Loyalty Oath in the Ancient Near East' *Ugarit-Forschungen* 8 (1976) section M. Witnesses to the Covenant, pp. 394–397.

30 Sumerian Enlil, based at Nippur, and Semitic Adad are both powerful deities in the *Atrahasis* myth. On Enlil, see Jacobsen, *Treasures*, pp. 98ff and *Harps*, 101ff. On Adad in *Atrahasis*, see Tablet 2 on the Adad cult, and Tablet 3 on his role in the Flood (Dalley, *Myths*, p.21 and 31; Foster, *Before the Muses*, p.171f and 179).

⁸Or who shut in the sea with doors
when it burst out from the womb?—
⁹when I made the cloud its garment,
and thick darkness its swaddling band,
¹⁰and prescribed bounds for it,
and set bars and doors,
¹¹and said, 'Thus far shall you come, and no farther,
and here shall your proud waves be stopped'?

(Job 38:8–11)

The war horse symbolizes the harnessing of nature to human purpose. Yet this harnessed power remains frightening:

¹⁹Do you give the horse its might?
Do you clothe its neck with mane?
²⁰Do you make it leap like the locust?
Its majestic snorting is terrible.
²¹It paws violently, exults mightily;
it goes out to meet the weapons.
²²It laughs at fear, and is not dismayed;
it does not turn back from the sword.
²³Upon it rattle the quiver,
the flashing spear, and the javelin.
²⁴With fierceness and rage it swallows the ground;
it cannot stand still at the sound of the trumpet.
²⁵When the trumpet sounds, it says 'Aha!'
From a distance it smells the battle,
the thunder of the captains and the shouting.

(Job 39:19–25)

In a subtle way, the terror of human armies lurks behind the prancing stallion in the foreground. This reminds readers that the world of humanity as well as that of nature is dangerous and violent.

The poem moves on to describe Behemoth and Leviathan. Leviathan is impervious to the worst that human beings can do:

¹⁸Its sneezes flash forth light,
and its eyes are like the eyelids of the dawn.
¹⁹From its mouth go flaming torches;
and sparks of fire leap out.
²⁰Out of its nostrils comes smoke,
as from a boiling pot and burning rushes.
²¹Its breath kindles coals,
and a flame comes out of its mouth.
²⁶Though the sword reaches it, it does not avail,
nor does the spear, the dart or the javelin.
²⁷It counts iron as straw,
and bronze as rotten wood.

²⁸The arrow cannot make it flee;
slingstones, for it, are turned to chaff.
²⁹Clubs are counted as chaff;
it laughs at the rattle of javelins.

(Job 41:18–21 & 26–29)

The natural world of these divine speeches is complex, mysterious and filled with powers that are not there to benefit human beings. Nevertheless, this is God's world. It pleases him. Perhaps it reflects its Maker in being mysterious, surprising, awesome and not transparent to human questions. The best answer that the book offers Job, when God himself appears and speaks, is no answer, but a series of rhetorical questions and does not even supply Job with the information given to the readers in the opening scenes.³¹

For our purposes, we may take note of the way that the observations and artistry of these poems in Job presuppose a tradition of reflection and craftsmanship. The natural world is there and the human mind explores it far beyond any utilitarian benefits that such observation and imagination may bring. There may be an analogy with a tradition of exploration in this century's climbing of Everest and landing on the moon. They reflect an engagement with the world and a flight of the human spirit that, like the poetry of Job, offers a paradox. Conquering Everest and the moon symbolize what human beings can achieve when they collectively set their minds to it, yet these very achievements paradoxically highlight the mess that human beings make of living in community and peace on a mundane plane. Job's paradox lies in the tension of its being a literary masterpiece that stands out still in world literature, and yet one that highlights the issues of suffering, disorder, justice and theodicy that remain unanswered in the timespan of Job from birth to old age and death.

There is no greater pondering of creation in the Bible than we find in these speeches in Job, yet in so far as there is a clue to God within the natural world, in our view it lies in the existence of the human artist who composed Job rather than in the created world that captures his imagination. It is not what the lines say but that a human being exists composing this quality of poetry. It is not

---

³¹ Interpretation of the divine speeches in terms of a response or non-response to Job's questions has a chequered history among commentators. While some find them educative, others are scandalized by their evasiveness or bullying tone. See L Alonso-Schökel's helpful article 'God's Answer to Job' pp. 45–51 in *Job and the Silence of God = Concilium* 169, 1983. In Job, the divine speeches are not the last word and 'it must be admitted that the ending of the book undercuts to some extent the divine speeches of chaps. 38–41'(DJA Clines, *Job 1–20*, WBC 17 [Dallas: Word] 1989, p. xlvii).

Leviathan, Behemoth, the war horse, the ostrich, hawk or gazelle but the human being who is writing the poetry that furnishes the best clue to God and the meaning of creation. This is the statement of Gen 1:26ff. It will come to full fruition in the Incarnation. Accordingly, the best place from which to view creation is not the whirlwind tour of the divine speeches in Job but the Upper Room discourse where bread, wine and Jesus of Nazareth offer more illuminating clues to being in the world than any other aspect of life on the planet.

3. MEDITATION AS BEING STILL IN THE PRESENCE OF YAHWEH

From meditation as pondering creation, we turn to 'being still' as the inward side of reflection. It is only one mode of being in the presence of God, and there is no value scale that we can detect in the canonical collection of the Psalms that elevates being still before God as superior to singing, dancing, fasting or lament in his presence. Indeed, one might argue that 'being still', or even reflection itself, is a matter of culture or temperament rather than the epitome of spirituality.[32] Perhaps an analogy between stillness and reading offers a helpful perspective. Human beings have the potential for learning to read but many millions live human lives, work, love, marry, raise children, communicate, without being able to read. Most people set a value on reading. Many have the basic skill but do not read much for information or pleasure. Some cannot live without a book. Some write books but do not excel in face to face communication. Perhaps, then, 'being still' is a skill or capacity like reading that is not as natural as learning to talk but can be developed and fitted into ordinary life to varying degrees depending on culture, situation and temperament.

It is rather unfortunate that the proof-text phrase from the Old Testament, now sung as a worship chorus, may not say what it seems to in its customary translation of 'Be still and know that I am God' (Psa 46:10). The worship song does indeed evoke the mood of a quiet waiting on God, but the Hebrew psalm is more likely a rebuke from God to a restive and warring world—'Stop!'[33] In fact, as a proof-text for meditators the familiar

---

[32] Jung's observations on people's preferred modes of operation (sensation, intuition, thinking, feeling) are a starting point for a clinical psychologist's article on the devotional life—DE Bunker, 'Spirituality and the Four Jungian Personality Functions' *Journal of Psychology and Theology* 19.1 (1991) 26–34.

[33] The imperatives 'be quiet and know' might be addressed to Israel (so Craigie, *Psalms 1–50*, p.345 'relax'). It is more likely that they are spoken by God as a tough command directed towards the warring nations and cautioning them to stop fighting and recognize his sovereignty (so, for instance, Kidner, *Psalms 1– 72*, p.176 ' "Quiet!, leave off!" . . . a rebuke to a restless and turbulent

Psalm 23 offers a better starting point with its 'green pastures', 'waters of rest', 'lying down' and its spirit of trustful confidence. The psalm is not entirely tranquil or motionless for there is the walk through the valley of v.4, yet the opening and closing lines form an inclusio by reflecting a similar idea of peaceful, secure enjoyment of God's presence. The poet is fed, led and restored in vv. 1–3, while in vv. 5–6 he is fed, blessed and settled. 'Lying down in green pastures' matches 'dwelling in the house of the LORD'. Sheep and guest metaphors ring the changes on the peaceful scene. A relational intimacy through covenant pervades both the shepherd and host imagery.[34]

If Psalm 23 points to and conveys a sense of peaceful intimacy within a life where enemies exist (v. 5) that make protection by 'rod, club' a necessity, then it is a little ironical that it has come to be read in Christian funeral services when life is over. The 'green pastures', 'waters of rest' and restoration of life are a here and now experience in the psalm, whereas a funeral re-reading relocates 'I shall dwell in the house of the LORD' to heaven by associating it implicitly with John 14:2f.

Quietness of spirit is recommended in Psalm 37, this time in the face of the fretting, discontent, anxiety and anger provoked by the flourishing of the wicked:

> [7]Be still before the LORD,
> and wait patiently for him;
> do not fret over those who prosper in their way,
> over those who carry out evil devices.
> [8]Refrain from anger, and forsake wrath.
> Do not fret—it leads only to evil.
> [9]For the wicked shall be cut off,
> but those who wait for the LORD shall inherit the land.
>
> (Psa 37:7–9)

---

world'). Hebrew *yāda'* means 'to acknowledge, recognize as suzerain' in political contexts. The verb *rāpāh* behind Craigie's translation 'relax' and Kidner's 'Quiet!, leave off!' often means 'desist, leave off' and when it is used in the sense of 'go slack', then 'slack' carries the connotation of 'being idle, sinking down, losing courage, being discouraged', which is not the same thing at all as 'being still' in a meditative, composed and trusting manner.

[34] The phrase 'goodness and mercy' (*ṭōb wāḥesed*) resonates with covenant associations, and the psalm might have been used on any occasion of thanksgiving by an individual for a blessing that produces such a sense of covenant well-being, of *šālōm*. Studies such as DN Freedman's and P Milne's (discussed by Craigie, *Psalms 1–50*, p. 205ff) find a number of allusions to the Exodus-Wilderness experience behind the language of the psalm, which if credited, strengthen the connection with Israel's experience of covenant and being led through the wilderness.

The imperative *dōm* 'be still' from the root *dāmāh* carries the nuance of quietness (sometimes 'being dumb') as well as 'come to rest, come to an end'. We could translate 'be silent to Yahweh' (*dōm laYhwh*), provided the idea is 'while you are orientated towards Yahweh in expectation' rather than implying 'Be silent and say nothing to Yahweh about these matters.' From the context, the waiting is done patiently in active expectation rather than passively emptied of all emotion.[35] The anger and fretting refers to the inner state of mind, and probably implies that this tension is expressed as angry thoughts that go round and round in the person's head rather than being expressed to God in prayer. Ultimately this anger may be anger at the way the world is, and that perspective may lead to an anger with God and a confrontation with him about personal circumstances of the kind found in the God-laments.[36] We will leave confrontation with God to explore in the later chapter on anger.

Psalm 37 is often classified as a Wisdom psalm because of its instructional tone, the autobiographical snippets from an older man (vv. 25, 35f), inclusion of maxims such as 'Better is . . . ' (v. 16) and its grappling with theodicy. It is optimistic that the reward-retribution pattern will be vindicated in this life. Though the advice to 'Be still before the LORD, and wait patiently for him' is as helpful a form of stress management as most, the thought of the psalm is problematic, measured against the realities of poverty or wickedness that are not 'cut off' but continue unchecked in the world.

Jesus offers an implicit re-reading of Psalm 37 in one of the Beatitudes. 'Blessed are the meek for they shall inherit the earth' (Matt 5:5) replaces 'the meek shall inherit the land, and delight themselves in abundant prosperity' (Psa 37:11). In the psalm, *'ereṣ* is 'land', meaning Palestine, the Promised Land and not 'earth' —compare vv. 3, 9, 18, 19, 22, 29, 34. Jesus picks up the affirmation that applies to the meek, those who wait quietly for righteousness and wickedness to be rewarded appropriately. He loosens it from its Israel / Land setting in Psa 37 and locates its

---

[35] In v.7, the verb is *hithōlēl lᵉ*. The context and the parallel lines support the translation of NRSV and REB 'wait patiently', 'be patient til' with a nuance of expectation rather than of anguish. There is difference of opinion among Hebraists about the verbal root (*ḥūl* or *yāḥal*: BDB, p. 297, 403). The 'wait' of v.9 and v. 34 is a different verb *qāwāh* 'to wait for' with implied eagerness.

[36] Compare this assessment with Craigie's comment: 'the type of "anger" against which this warning is issued is almost certainly "anger against God" ' (*Psalms 1–50*, p. 297). On the God-lament psalms, see C Broyles, *The Conflict of Faith and Experience in the Psalms*. See Psa 39:1–3 for a psalmist who holds his tongue publicly but subsequently bursts out into emotional words before God with tears (v. 12).

hope within an eschatological Kingdom. The negation of fretting will need to be extended to the eschaton.

This psalm, therefore, is a witness to a Hebrew mode of Wisdom reflection, being itself a reflection and advocating quiet reflection. Within its this-worldly Wisdom and Land setting it creates problems for contemporary readers. Even re-read within a framework of Christian eschatology, the being 'still before the Lord' of Psalm 37 bears at best a tangential relationship to the practice of solitude and silence within a tradition of Christian meditation.

Waiting in quiet hope for God to act is different from the practice of silence in Christian spirituality. More light is shed on the Hebraic waiting in silence on God by Psalm 62 and Lamentations 3:

> [1]For God alone my soul waits in silence;
> from him comes my salvation.
> [5]He alone is my rock and my salvation,
> my fortress; I shall never be shaken.
>
> (Psa 62:1,5)

> [25]The LORD is good to those who wait for him,
> to the soul that seeks him.
> [26]It is good that one should wait quietly
> for the salvation of the LORD.
> [27]It is good for one to bear
> the yoke in youth,
> [28]to sit alone in silence
> when the LORD has imposed it,
> [29]to put one's mouth to the dust
> (there may yet be hope),
> [30]to give one's cheek to the smiter,
> and be filled with insults.
>
> (Lam 3:25f)

The setting and date of Psalm 62 are elusive, but the spirit of trust in God is obvious and complements a distrust of human deviousness. This reflection fills the interlude before God acts on the poet's behalf. By way of contrast, the setting of Lamentations after the fall of Jerusalem clearly locates this sitting in silence 'when Yahweh has imposed it'. It breathes repentance and a hope for restoration on the other side of judgement. Reflection is involved. It is the contemplation of the destruction of Judah, Jerusalem, monarchy, Temple and populace with all its horrors. In such circumstances, the numbness or dumbness is natural.[37]

---

[37] The Hebrew verbs *dāmāh II, dāmam, dûm* pose problems for translators. Baumann notes that contexts such as Lam 3 link *dāmāh* with mourning, and with the hope for restoration by its association with verbs such as *yāḥal*—'to wait' and *qāwāh*—'to hope'(' דָּמָה dāmāh II' pp. 260–265 in *TDOT* 2, p.

Once again, what Hebraic reflection means in practice is best illustrated from the composition of Lamentations itself. Lamentations is the product of reflection and combines a theological evaluation of Jerusalem's sinfulness with an intense emotional reaction to the horrors of the siege and deportation. We might describe it as a theological processing of experience turned into a dialogue with God and probably taken up and used in congregational lament. We now know a good deal about post-traumatic stress disorder, though seldom needing to relate it to the horror of cannibalism (Lam 2:20 & 4:10). The therapeutic value of talking out the emotions and reactions that are touched off by traumatic stress is recognized. This applies to those who are victims and to rescuers who witness horrific scenes.

Lamentations is a carefully crafted acrostic poem, suggesting that its author turned to a medium of expression that was already a natural one for him to use, much as an artist might paint the scenes of war, imprisonment and torture, or a film director make a filmed reconstruction. Yet the tension of Lamentations is rather different from the stress of victims caught up in modern disasters and wars. Its author believed that God himself was the Enemy that destroyed Jerusalem (2:1–8, 3:43–45, 4:11,16). The Babylonians are never mentioned by name. This theological dimension and the tension it creates in the poet's spirit between assent (1:5,8,18, 2:17, 3:40–42) and horror means that this particular Hebrew sample of reflection must be read in context. 'To sit alone in silence' (3:28) bears no relation to reflection as tranquillity and an emptying of the mind. This is a post-traumatic and penitent silence in the hope of restoration.

There is, however, in the Psalms one picture of tranquillity and contentment that is as delightful as it is brief.

¹O LORD, my heart is not lifted up,
my eyes are not raised too high;
I do not occupy myself
with things too great and too marvellous for me.
²But I have calmed and quieted my soul,
like a weaned child with its mother;
my soul is like the weaned child that is with me.

(Psa 131:1–2)

The psalmist pictures himself as a breast-fed baby cradled in its mother's arms. It is a place of security, contentment and calming

---

263f.) . Compare the differing translations of Lam 3: 26 *wᵉdūmām* 'that one should wait quietly' NRSV, 'to wait in patience' REB; v. 28 *yēšeb bādad wᵉyiddōm* 'to sit alone in silence' NRSV, 'to sit alone and sigh' REB.

down. This is a deliberately chosen state of mind because its childlikeness is contrasted with arrogance—the heart and eyes are not elevated in praise in v. 1 but 'lifted up' in an idiom akin to acting sinfully 'with a high hand'.[38] What exactly he is referring to as matters that are beyond him eludes us—though some might enjoy reading it as a description of academic theology. The tenor of the poem is plain enough. The psalmist has deliberately come to rest in a trusting relationship with God: 'Indeed, I have composed and quieted my soul.'[39]

4. MEDITATION AS 'CONTEMPLATING GOD'

There is a fourth component to Old Testament meditation. It arises out of an intimate relationship with God and expresses orientation towards him. It is God rather than the created world that the poet is looking at in the psalms that we shall discuss (Pss 63, 42, 27). The language of 'seeing God' will alert us to the difficulty of exegesis. This 'seeing' is more difficult to interpret than the human activity of waiting, or listening, or being quiet. Even our heading 'contemplating God' might prove misleading.

In English idiom we have a pathway from the physical to the 'spiritual' via metaphor. We use terms metaphorically without noticing it or thinking about the physical process that the words sign. Consider the kind of 'seeing' that is referred to in the following phrases: 'try to see it my way', 'I don't see that as a problem', 'he has no insight into the problems he causes', 'she is a very perceptive child', 'I didn't foresee those consequences', 'she sees right through me', 'I must look into that', 'that's your point of view, not mine', 'they see it as a black and white issue', 'that was an eye-opener', 'I can't see the point of that.' In these phrases, the seeing is done with the mind, not the retina. The physical act of looking, perceiving and seeing becomes a metaphor for the forming of concepts, a mental process.

---

[38] See Num 15:30 'whoever acts high-handedly' (*b^{e}yād rāmāh*) . . . shall be cut off from among the people'; compare 'the Israelites went out boldly in the sight of all the Egyptians' (Num 33:3 and Exod 14:8 'with a high hand' *b^{e}yād rāmāh*, where 'proudly' in a positive sense would be an apt translation; REB, 'defiantly'). Compare 'high eyes' (*^{e}ynayim rāmōt*, Prov 6:17) meaning 'arrogance' as the first of a list of seven things that the LORD hates (compare Prov 30:13, Psa 18:27). See Allen, *Psalms 101–150*, pp. 197ff for comment on the translation of v.2b along the lines adopted by NRSV.

[39] Allen's translation probably does more justice to the Hebrew *šiwwiytiy w^{e}dōmamtiy napšiy* than REB 'No; I submit myself, I account myself lowly.' The NEB underlines the contrast with the arrogance, where NRSV and Allen link the lines with the image of the contented and secure baby. The Piel of *šāwāh* is attested only a couple of times in the OT but 'soothed, quieted, smoothed' fit here. This form of *dāmam* appears only once, but probably with the nuance of stillness of movement, silence, or both here.

In the psalms that we shall discuss now, excerpting just the key verses, the physical senses and the verbs depicting their operation describe a spiritual and inward orientation towards God.

[1]O God, you are my God, I seek you,
my soul thirsts for you;
my flesh faints for you,
as in a dry and weary land
where there is no water.
[2]So I have looked upon you in the sanctuary,
beholding your power and glory.

(Psa 63:1f)

The first thing that we notice is the intensity of the longing for God. The poet turns to metaphors based on thirst, hunger and the survival instinct. He craves God. In other verses, he searches and grasps for God ('My soul clings to you',v. 8a).[40] He has a level of desperation like a traveller stranded in a desert and staring death in the face. Invoking these basic drives—thirst, hunger, self-preservation— associates the relationship with God with life itself. In fact, the poet goes one step beyond biological survival in his exclamation—'your covenant-love is better than life' (v. 3).[41]

When we look at the heading to Psalm 63—'when he was in the Judean wilderness,'—we glimpse the way that the early editors' minds worked. The metaphors of hunger and thirst suggested the wilderness. David was on the run from Saul in the wilderness (1 Sam 23, 24), and Saul was seeking to destroy his life (Psa 63:9). David trusted God to protect him and secure his kingship. Whatever we make of this early understanding of the original setting for the psalm, the metaphors of dehydration and faintness make more sense on the lips of someone who has experienced 'a dry and weary land where there is no water'. Whether it was David or not, the wilderness environment mirrored the author's spirit.

In 63:2, Temple worship is the locality for an equally intense experience of God. We have a range of options for decoding 'looked upon you' and 'seeing your power and glory'. The Hebrew verbs and nouns really give no better clue as to what the

---

[40]   The word 'cling, cleave to' *dābaq* is used in Gen 2:24 for the bonding between husband and wife. In Deuteronomy, it is used to describe the covenant relationship of wholehearted devotion to God. The metaphor of clinging is as intense and powerful an image as the thirst and hunger metaphors.

[41]   The phrase reads *kiy-ṭōb ḥasdᵉkā mēḥayyim* where *ḥesed* is the loyalty from God's side to the covenant relationship. NRSV 'steadfast love' captures this better than REB 'true love' which might unhappily import nuances from pop lyrics.

psalmist meant than their English translations. We will need to weigh various options: (a) a 'seeing' in vision through altered state of consciousness, (b) a dramatic metaphor for reflection based on profound theological realization, that is, a grasping of revealed truth in a fresh manner, or (c) some physical starting point to a spiritual experience within cultic worship. The physical sanctuary and the worship located there seem to be undisputed referents in v. 2—*baqqōdeš* 'in the holy place', yet what the psalmist imagined himself to be looking at, if it was a physical object at all, is not clear. In the Near East, the answer would have been the statue of the deity or its symbolic cult object paraded on a festival day, or perhaps accessible to view on a podium or in a niche in the wall of the shrine. In Israel, the Ark may have been carried in festival on occasion, but normally was inaccessible and not visible behind the curtain in the Tabernacle or Temple. Nothing in Psalm 63 specifically locates the author or his poem in a cultic ceremony that had powerful visual components.[42]

Lacking detailed data on Jerusalem cult rituals, commentators are left to exercise their imaginations when confronted with expressions like 'beholding your power and glory' (63:2). Hypotheses about cult-dramas and covenant festivals, Zion festivals, or New Year Enthronement ceremonies have linked cloud and fire of theophany with incense and torches, or trumpets, cymbals and congregational shout with Sinai thunder, and so on. Recently, one scholar has linked the language of 'seeing God' to a kind of epiphany at sunrise after a night vigil in the Temple.[43] The invisibility of Yahweh weakens analogies with polytheistic cult-dramas involving deities like the Sun or Marduk.

---

[42] For a review of the suggestions and lack of consensus about the psalm's setting, and the translation of v. 2, see the recent commentaries such as ME Tate, *Psalms 51–100*, WBC 20 (Dallas: Word) 1990, pp. 123ff.

[43] MS Smith, *Psalms: the divine journey* (Mahwah: Paulist) 1987 Chap. 4, section 'b. God and the Sun', pp. 52–57; 'Seeing God in the Psalms: the background to the beatific vision in the Hebrew Bible' *CBQ* 50 (1988) 171–183; 'The Near Eastern Background of Solar Language for Yahweh', *JBL* 109/1 (1990) 29–39; *The Early History of God: Yahweh and the other deities in ancient Israel* (London: Harper & Row) 1990, Chap. 4 'Yahweh and the Sun', pp. 115–124. Speaking of Pss 17, 27 and 63 he uses phrases such as "an experience of Divine presence which the sun perhaps helped to evoke . . . (*Psalms*, p. 57f)" "As psalms of vigil, Psalms 17, 27, and 63 do not reduce the experience of God's presence to a solar theophany; but it is possible that the experience of the dawn after the night vigil helped to provoke the perception of the luminescent dimension of the divine presence." (*CBQ* 50, p. 181)

Whereas the hypothesis of a solarized Yahwism fits plausibly with syncretistic data on the Jerusalem cult, the dawn epiphany hypothesis seems to push the language of normative Yahwism into a realm of implausible speculation. Arguments for psalm settings within temple vigils are not all that strong, let alone for morning-after experiences of the sunrise.

An alternative to cult-dramatic representation of 'your power and glory' is a personal visionary experience, perhaps similar to the Temple vision of Isaiah 6, which may be understood as an altered consciousness somehow triggered off by participation in cultic worship, a worship that involved coals, tongs, smoke, chanting and sanctuary decorations portraying celestial beings such as the cherubim in the Jerusalem Temple. Finally, one could argue for a purely metaphorical perception of the 'power and glory' of God on the grounds that the phrase 'your right hand upholds me' (63:8b) is certainly metaphorical, as are the wings in 'and in the shadow of your wings I sing for joy' (v. 7b).

Two reasons suggest that we should reach tentative conclusions only about the 'seeing'. Firstly, the language of the psalms draws on reservoirs of figures of speech, sometimes called poetic stereotypes. This makes decoding lament language difficult so that commentators cannot be sure whether the psalmist is suffering from a physical illness, guilt, social alienation, legal proceedings or a combination of several factors. Secondly, commentators differ in cultural and denominational experiences of communal ritual and worship, as well as in personal devotional experiences. These factors exercise their influence on how this language of the psalms is decoded.

What we should not devalue in the decoding is the intensity of this spirituality in Psalm 63. On the basis of common human experience (or a review of David's life as offered us by his Old Testament biographers) we could say that such intense longing represents a peak moment.[44] Our minds are normally full of many things during a day, and many things during a worship service. It will only be at moments of peak intensity that last in that intensity for a short span that our bodily thirst, hunger and instinct for survival are supplanted by such an intense longing for God himself. Thus the language of this psalm is dangerous language to take on our lips without risk of perjuring ourselves. To say it without an intense longing is to decode the phrases into a debased language.

When we read v. 6 ('meditate on you in the watches of the night' and 'think of you on my bed'), and ask Psalm 63 as a whole what it means to 'meditate', we could reply that meditation means to reflect on life itself, our deepest needs and orientation, to write a poem, to find culturally contextualized imagery for expressing spirituality (ie. for us not 'with fat and fatness' as the Hebrew of

---

[44] David is portrayed as as passionate a man as any, motivated by intense desire for Yahweh's honour, for self-preservation, for Bathsheba, for Bethlehem well-water, for revenge, for food from the tabernacle, for victory in battle, for Absalom's safety and for cultic dancing, to mention a few instances.

v. 5a reads), to see symbols such as the landscape or surroundings as a mirror of the soul (v. 1), to recollect, visualise and imagine, to talk in I-Thou 'my God' terms, to adopt a body position that expresses the spirit (v. 4b) and to capture the moments of intensity as a precious truth among the other pressing realities of living.

Like Psalm 63, Psalm 42–3 looks to experiences in temple worship from a position of longing expressed with similes and metaphors of craving:

> ¹As a deer longs for flowing streams,
> so my soul longs for you, O God.
> ²My soul thirsts for the living God.
> When shall I come and behold the face of God?
>
> (Psa 42:1f)

> ³O send out your light and your truth;
> let them lead me;
> let them bring me to your holy hill and to your dwelling.
> ⁴Then will I go to the altar of God,
> to God my exceeding joy;
> and I will praise you with the harp,
> O God, my God.
>
> (Psa 43:3f)

Even without the wishes of 43:3–4 being re-attached to Psa 42, we could still locate 42:2b in a sanctuary setting because of the recollection of the 'procession to the house of God' and the 'festival' of 42:4. Yet relating 42:2b to the Temple only sharpens the problem of decoding what it means. 'When shall I come and see the face of God' is very likely what the poet wrote, as the NRSV translators have decided, though Massoretic copies have the vowels for 'be seen' with God doing the looking. 'Come and see the face of God' is a way of expressing being in the presence of God, no doubt, but is it simply an alternative way of saying 'come and stand before God', or even an idiom for 'enter the sanctuary', an idiom established in Semitic polytheism when the actual face of the deity's effigy was visible?[45]

---

[45] The alternative translation would be 'When shall I come and appear before the face of God?' Yet the MT is awkward grammatically and lacks a preposition '(before)'. MT Niphal form, 'be seen' or 'appear', may well be explained by a theological embarrassment that developed in later Judaism with the concept of seeing God's face. For comment, see AA Anderson, *Psalms Vol. 1*, p. 330 and Tate, *Psalms 50–100*, p. 354 note 8b on Psa 84:7[MT, v.8]. Compare WL Holladay, *CHALOT*, p.328 under nifal *rāʾāh* = 'appear' –'but perhaps originally Qal, "see the face of Yahweh," text then changed for theological reasons.'

Imagination will need to bridge the gap between our cultural experience of worship and the shrine-centred and festival-spirit of Israelite communal worship. We cannot relive the Israelite experience, only observe it from a distance, so to speak. This is where pilgrim psalms such as Psa 84 must supplement Psalm 42–43 and its language of being led templewards by God's 'light and truth'(43:3). In Psa 84, we find the same intensity of longing expressed in a psychosomatic and physiological idiom:

> ²My soul longs, indeed it faints
> for the courts of the LORD;
> my heart and my flesh sing for joy
> to the living God.
>
> ¹⁰For a day in your courts is better
> than a thousand elsewhere.
>
> (Psa 84:2,10)

This is employing a vocabulary of the whole person. The Hebrew 'soul', 'heart' and 'flesh' (*nepeš lēb bāśar*) need a dynamic equivalent translation that says in English 'with my whole being'. A triple non-technical string such as 'body, mind and spirit' comes close.[46]

Psalm 27 is similar to Pss 63, 42–3 and 84 in expressing an intense desire for the presence of God in a cultic setting:

> One thing I asked of the LORD,
> that will I seek after:
> to live in the house of the LORD
> all the days of my life,
> to behold the beauty of the LORD,
> and to inquire in his temple.
>
> (Psa 27:4)

If we decode 'to live my whole life in Yahweh's temple' as 'to participate in the cultic worship at the Jerusalem Temple every day of my life' it seems to lose something that the figure of speech encodes. Nobody lived inside the Jerusalem Temple, though there were rooms in its adjacent precincts, but that is not the point. The

---

[46] For all our scientific sophistication, we still grope towards an integrated understanding of personality and biochemistry and a holistic language for expressing our self-understanding. Words such as 'psychosomatic' have passed into current usage, but descriptions and understanding of consciousness are still evolving away from the brain-mind dichotomy. It would be a mistake to canonize either the Hebrew terminology of the Old Testament as though it were not culture-bound or, equally so, the terminology in current research and debate. See HW Wolff, *Anthropology of the Old Testament* (London: SCM) 1974, Part 1, 'The Being of Man', for a standard discussion of the Hebrew terminology.

hyperbole is a metaphor along the lines of a servant being in daily attendance on his master in his master's home. This role is, in metaphorical terms, what the poet craves in Yahweh's household. The word *bayit* 'house' facilitates the household metaphor because it does duty in Hebrew for 'house', 'household, family, dynasty' and for 'temple, shrine'.

The phrase 'to behold the beauty of Yahweh' likewise suffers if we try to decode it into actualities. What was there to see? The Hebrew *laḥªzōt bᵉnōʿam-Yhwh* offers us no definite clue. Translators waver between a visual quality ('beauty') and a quality of God's character ('kindness, graciousness, favour'; compare Psa 90:17).[47] If an actual cultic sight is in the poet's mind, then we may assume that what he is looking at in this cultic setting opens a kind of sacramental, symbolic door of spiritual perception in his mind. If it is a metaphor without a specific, visible cultic referent, then the door of spiritual 'seeing' is opened in the poet's psyche by the general ambience of worship. What the poet 'sees', that is, perceives, would take the form of a deep theological appreciation of Yahweh.

It is perhaps fortunate that our exegetical and hermeneutical path peters out at this point, confronted by the cultural gap, the ambiguities of language and the fact that metaphor does not translate into prosaic description without loss. There is a surplus to metaphorical language. We lack detailed phenomenological description in our Hebrew sources of what exactly the psalmist's experiences entail and reading experiences back into the psalms is

---

[47] *CHALOT,* p.240 *nōʿam* 'kindness (of God)'; *BDB,* p. 653 'delightfulness'. The verb *nāʿam* means 'to be pleasant, agreeable, taste good, be dear to'. In Psa 135:3 the adjective *nāʿim* and its referent are just as difficult to determine. The verb, noun and adjective point to the quality of something to be enjoyed. NRSV and REB opt for 'beauty' in their translations of Psa 27:4, but this translation still leaves open the task of interpreting the meaning. Where Anderson reviews possibilities, Craigie, in the tradition of Mowinckel, comes down decisively on the visual physical referent, specifically the Ark as mediating the beauty of God himself: " 'to gaze upon the beauty of the Lord', not to be interpreted literally, but as implying the extraordinary experience of God's beauty and glory as symbolized in the temple, specifically the Ark." (*Psalms 1–50,* p. 232) "such terms ['behold the face of the god', 'see the god in his beauty' or 'grace'] were also adopted in Israelite religion (cf. Ps 27:4), but there they were taken in a spiritualized sense about the way *faith* 'beholds'. But even in Israel this 'beholding' was attached to a visible symbol, namely, to the holy ark of Yahweh, which to all appearance was a focal point in the festal procession at the enthronement" (Ps. 132; cf. 2 Sam 6). (Mowinckel, *The Psalms in Israel's Worship, Vol. 1,* p. 142; cf. Anderson, *Psalms Vol. 1,* p. 222)

all too easy.[48] In Pss 63, 42–43 and 27, we are confronted with profound longings, longings that are themselves peak experiences of intensity. These longings are expressed in poetic language, and, being distinctively Israelite, would not necessarily transpose neatly into our cultural, theological and experiential terms even if we could be quite sure of the exact nuances originally intended. If we opted for describing these Hebrew poets as 'mystical' this would only import into exegesis a term with all sorts of nuances drawn from very different cultural settings and end up as a distorting factor in our perception of their experience.[49]

We simply note that 'contemplating God'—for want of a better term—is part of Hebrew 'meditation'. In Pss 63, 42–43 and 27, this 'contemplation' is linked to a cultic experience of Presence, expressed with verbs of 'seeing' in certain passages. For all its intensely personal dimension, this is a contemplation envisaged as coming to fulfilment within communal worship.

SUMMARY AND CONCLUSION

We found that Psalm 119 sets out a spirituality that makes the covenant and communal fear of the LORD of Deuteronomy into a

---

[48] Despite lack of phenomenological data, some writers in the Kabbalah tradition attribute to the ancient Hebrew poets the various altered states of consciousness that are cultivated within Kabbalah meditation. See A Kaplan, *Meditation and the Bible* (York Beach: Samuel Weiser) 1978, paperback edition 1988. For examples of a philological method that disregards semantics, see 'Part III: Verbal Archaeology'. For example, Kaplan first associates the root *śîaḥ* with various other roots *śwḥ, nśḥ, mśḥ, śḥḥ, śḥ, śˀ,nśˀ* in diverse contexts and then concludes: 'So the word Siyach also has the connotation of floating or rising to the top of a lower level. Through Siyach-meditation, the individual rises spiritually, floating through the supernal Universes. Just as a swimmer floats to the top of the water, so one engaged in Siyach-meditation floats above the mundane world, entering the realm of the transcendental. . . . the word Siyach therefore also indicates a process whereby the individual enters into his own spiritual essence, climbing the spiritual ladder of his own soul.' (p. 105 & p. 107) Contrast our discussion of *śîaḥ* in Psa 119:15, 23, 27, 48, 78, 97, 99, 148 under the heading '1. Meditation as internalizing torah.'

[49] S Terrien's Old Testament theology raises problems of terminology in the chapter 'The Psalmody of Presence' under the sub-heading 'Mystical Quest' (*The Elusive Presence: toward a new Biblical Theology*, Religious Perspectives 26 (London: Harper & Row) 1978, pp. 304ff. In his discussion of Psa 27 he uses the phrase 'engaging in a mystical quest' and imports 'in a trance', arguing quite speculatively that 'to inquire in his temple' (Psa 27:4c) means 'to have a vision in the sanctuary', adding the comment 'sacramental presence is a means for ecstasy' (p. 308f). However, he rightly notes that the poet expresses his longing as a wish rather than a continuous experience, and rightly states with reference to 27:11f 'teach me your way, O LORD and lead me on a level path' that 'Hebraic spirituality is never divorced from ethics' (p. 312). Whether Psa 27 can be read under the rubric 'the theology of the name has overcome the theology of the glory' is very dubious. Terrien sees the psalmist abandoning

personal project of walking life's journey in the light of torah. This study and internalizing of torah is characteristically a content–filled, object–orientated form of meditation. It is cognitive without excluding emotion. In Psa 119, the internalizing of torah counteracts the pressures on the poet's life that come from temptation and social hostility. These pressures threaten to knock the writer off course and they stir his emotions to the point of crying out. In Psa 1, reflection on torah issues in a lifestyle that contrasts in spirit and direction with alternatives and one that is sustained by and rooted in this spirituality.

In Psa 19, the poet sees the glory of God in the splendour of the skies and in the torah. His poem discloses that he has reflected on torah and creation in the light of Genesis 1–3, while the poem itself is the best demonstration of what it meant to him to meditate. Psa 8 and clusters of proverbs illustrate Hebrew reflection as an interaction with features of the natural world, features that catch the eye or impress the spirit. Psa 104 observes the familiar aspects of vegetation, landscape, animal and bird life and concludes that this ecology manifest a dependence on a Creator God who is painted in numinous colours. Psa 29 worships Yahweh, who rules in the celestial realm and whose electrifying power and thundering voice are mirrored by the storm.

The most extensive poetry on the natural world is found in Job and is placed on the lips of Yahweh, who appears in theophany. The author has composed a reflection that provokes different reader responses, from admiration of its artistry to queries as to how well its tone and tenor match the issues raised in the dialogues. As Pss 29, 104 and 8 affirm in their own way, the poems that comprise the divine speeches in Job focus on a world that is larger, more awesome and less domesticated than the family life that occupies much of Wisdom or torah's concerns.

An alternative strand of Hebrew meditation, related to worship and an intimate relationship with God, deals with an enjoyment of the Presence of God. There is a quiet waiting before God for him to act and a processing of traumatic or disturbing experience, such as we find in Lamentations or in Psa 37's perspectives on the wicked. This solitude and silence is intercessory and not directly comparable with the practise of solitude and silence in Christian meditation. The epitome of restful trust and quiet assurance is displayed in Pss 23 and 131. The quietness of spirit there contrasts with the disorientation of lament. This quiet confidence and sense of Presence contrasts with an intense longing for God that overwhelms the poet and displaces natural craving for water, food

---

his longings for trance experience in v.4 and settling for ethical instruction in v.11. This reading is not convincing.

and human company. The poets of Pss 63, 42–43 and 27 desire to encounter God and feast their eyes on him. They look to the temple as the locus for this intense experience of Presence.

The way of reflection in the Old Testament is, of course, in its broadest terms much larger than this overview allows for. There is all the reflection on earlier traditions—for instance, the way that Exodus imagery appears in the poetry of Isa 40–55. But an extended discussion of this would blur the boundaries of the topic and defocus our concern with the practice of spirituality. What we have reviewed is Hebrew poetry that refers to 'meditation' and that in and of itself demonstrates by its very composition what this meditation consists of. In the poems referred to, every form of thought, the interaction with the visual, the clustering of associations, the choice of imagery and metaphor, the tapping into theological traditions, are part of Hebrew reflection. What this poetry expresses arises out of a knowledge of God rather than offering us a technique for knowing God. Exegesis does not disclose a list of Israelite meditative techniques and altered states of consciousness of the kind described in books on meditation in local libraries.

The church is heir to this Hebrew poetry. It has stimulated Christian hymns that continue the Hebrew reflective process. Composing poems and songs, or reciting poetry and singing do not require formal literacy, yet use of the written medium for meditation is what allowed for this Hebrew cultural and theological gift to the world. The Hebrew canon played its role then and has again and again. There is a special relationship, then, between Hebrew reflection as a thought process and as a literary exercise. To write, to compose, to express thoughts within a familiar genre is to articulate for others. Hebrew meditation is personal yet communal in orientation. Hebrew meditation is a sample of Israel's spirituality, one that is culturally contextualized and responsive rather than prescriptive. Worship in the Jerusalem Temple, accompanied by its music, liturgies and cultic rites is not possible or normative for Christians. No more is writing a poem in an acrostic form such as we have in Pss 119, 37 and Lamentations. Christian spirituality will necessarily involve an appropriation of Hebrew meditation based on a re-reading and a re-voicing of the Hebrew exemplars. Christian meditators have every reason to delight in their ancestral roots in Israel's thought, worship and poetry, but to be true to what Hebrew reflection was in its time Christian meditation will be different. Real descendants of Israelite spirituality will be marked by using their own language, imagery and tone as well as literary genres. These meditations will be as culturally contextualized as the psalms were in their day.

For some, Bunyan's *Pilgrim's Progress* or Milton's *Paradise Lost* might be heirs to the life-journey image and to reflection on Genesis. For others, the poetry of Gerard Manley Hopkins, his poems expressing delight in nature or his Lamentations-like agonizing over 'The Wreck of the Deutschland' might be embraced as the offspring of canonical ancestors.[50] Others again would feel more at home with poets and songwriters who borrow phrases from the psalms, or who respond to God through a sensuous reflection on nature.[51] The radical re-reading that all these Christian derivatives of Hebrew poems and songs exhibit lies in their christology. For these offspring, the Jerusalem Temple and the Promised Land are no longer the focus of Presence. The Shepherd of Psa 23 is 'the Good Shepherd' of John 10:11. The creation and God have come to a focus in Jesus, God Incarnate. Christ is the torah of covenant and the teacher.

Thus the 'seeing' that is Christian contemplation is re-expressed by Paul in a trinitarian theology:

> And all of us, with unveiled faces, seeing the glory of the Lord as though reflected in a mirror, are being transformed into the same image from one degree of glory to another; for this comes from the Lord, the Spirit. (2 Cor 3:18)

No less than the Hebrew psalms, this Pauline statement relies on metaphor and allusion to convey what it means to contemplate God, and in doing so it also draws on the Old Testament.

In closing this chapter, we want to draw attention to a single feature of contemplation. The process of reflection that is attested by Paul and the Old Testament poetry we have reviewed is not a focus of consciousness in a search for information, but for transformation. And that focus on transformation expresses the core of spirituality.

---

[50] In 'The Wreck of the Deutschland', written after a disaster when five Franciscan nuns and many others drowned, Hopkins wrestles with human suffering and God. Poems delighting in the grandeur of God in creation include 'God's Grandeur', 'The Starlight Night', 'Spring', 'The Windhover', 'Pied Beauty'—GM Hopkins, *Poems and Prose*, Penguin Classics, 1985.

[51] Examples quite widely known in worship circles would be the music of Taizé, of John Michael Talbot, and of Graham Kendrick. The nature poems by Luci Shaw 'New Birth', 'Heartspring', Small Song', 'Of Elms and God', 'The Groundhog', 'Spring Pond', 'May 20: very early Morning', 'Equilibrium', and 'The Omnipresence' appear in her anthology volume *Polishing the Petoskey Stone* (Wheaton: Harold Shaw) 1990.

BIBLIOGRAPHY

LC Allen, *Psalms 101–150*, WBC 21 (Waco: Word) 1983.
L Alonso-Schökel, 'God's Answer to Job' pp. 45–51 in *Job and the Silence of God = Concilium* 169, 1983.
AA Anderson, *Psalms Vol. 1*, NCB (London: Oliphants, MM&S) 1972.
DE Bunker, 'Spirituality and the Four Jungian Personality Functions', *Journal of Psychology and Theology* 19.1 (1991) 26–34.
DJA Clines, *Job 1–20*, WBC 17 (Dallas: Word) 1989.
———, 'The Tree of Knowledge and the Law of Yahweh (Ps XIX)', *VT* 24 (1974) 8–14.
PC Craigie, 'The Comparison of Hebrew Poetry: Psa 104 in the Light of the Egyptian and Ugaritic, Poetry' *Semitics* 4 (1974) 10–21.
———, *Psalms 1–50*, WBC 19 (Waco: Word) 1983.
J Eaton, *The Contemplative Face of Old Testament Wisdom in the context of world religions*, (London: SCM/Philadelphia: Trinity Press International) 1989.
L Fisher, *Ras Shamra Parallels, Vol. 3*, Analecta Orientalia 51 (Rome: PIB) 1981.
BR Foster, *Before the Muses: an anthology of Akkadian literature* (Bethesda: CDL Press) 1993.
R Foster, *Celebration of Discipline: the path to spiritual growth*, (London: Hodder & Stoughton) 1980.
GM Hopkins, *Poems and Prose*, Penguin Classics, 1985.
U Kroll, *The Spiritual Exercise Book* (London: Firethorn Press) 1985.
A Kaplan, *Meditation and the Bible* (York Beach: Samuel Weiser) 1978, paperback edition 1988.
JD Levenson, 'The Sources of Torah: Psa 119 and the Modes of Revelation in Second Temple Judaism', pp. 559–574 in PD Miller *et al*, *Ancient Israelite Religion* (Philadelphia: Fortress) 1987.
JL Mays, 'What is a Human Being? Reflections on Psalm 8' *Theology Today* 50.4 (1994) 511–520.
JAT Robinson, *Truth is Two-eyed* (London: SCM) 1979.
L Shaw, *Polishing the Petoskey Stone* (Wheaton: Harold Shaw) 1990.
MS Smith, *Psalms: the divine journey* (Mahwah: Paulist) 1987.
ME Tate, *Psalms 51–100*, WBC 20 (Dallas: Word) 1990.
S Terrien, *The Elusive Presence: toward a new Biblical Theology*, Religious Perspectives 26 (London: Harper & Row) 1978.

[6]

Wisdom for Life
A slice of Proverbs

INTRODUCTION

The fear of the Lord is fundamental for wisdom

(Prov 1:7)

As this verse suggests, there is a real continuity of spirituality between the 'fear of the LORD' in the Pentateuch, in Psalm 119 and in the Wisdom literature of the Old Testament. For one thing, it is reverence for Yahweh and not blandly the 'fear of God' that constitutes the foundation, first principle and framework of biblical Wisdom. We shall explore Job and Ecclesiastes in other chapters, but in this present one the slice of wisdom for life comes from Proverbs.

We cannot avoid the implications of a Christian re-reading of this material. How transposable is this wisdom and its educational packaging? People have strong views on education. Some opt into the state schooling system and others prefer denominational foundations and so-called Christian universities. Theological colleges and seminaries are prime examples of the institutional divorce of 'spiritual' education from secular, though the teaching methods, skills, modes of assessment and awards may be identical. The issue of secularity, spirituality and frame of reference is a lively one, and one that relates directly to Proverbs. Common to Proverbs, contemporary education and Christian discipleship is the role of the mentor, and we shall find that role written large both in our slice of biblical Instruction and in its Near Eastern counterparts.

Since Proverbs as a whole is too large a book to study in a chapter, we shall select a sub-section of Proverbs, namely 22:17–24:22, as a basis for probing its spirituality. This handful of maxims is representative enough of Proverbs, but it will be as well to remember that the field of Wisdom is a wider one and includes those adjacent acres, cultivated by Mesopotamians and Egyptians. An acre adjoining Prov 22:17–24:22 is *The Instruction of Amenemope* and we shall find ourselves looking over the fence into that field from time to time. The fence separates the field of Yahwistic monotheism from the fields of Near Eastern polytheism. Ancient boundaries are important, as Prov 22:17–24:22 twice reminds us, and yet similar things grow on each side of this fence in the earth of Wisdom.

The image of a cultivated field suits Proverbs. Its furrows of couplets are man-made and well worked. It is like a vegetable garden contributing staple diet foods, not a hothouse for orchids, an exotic herb garden or a colourful jungle—imagery we might choose for other kinds of Old Testament poetry, for instance for eschatology or apocalyptic. Wisdom's admonitions are more often like a bunch of carrots or a sack of potatoes—earthy, unromantic, even rather plain and uninteresting. When we go shopping for vegetables, we expect to find them sorted on market stalls or displayed in their own shelf compartments. In Proverbs, the maxims seem to come unsorted—a potato, a carrot, a tomato, a cucumber, a cabbage, a carrot, a green pepper.[1] The lack of order is disconcerting. So too is their brevity, since many maxims in Proverbs are simple two-liners. We need to process them using an appropriate hermeneutic.[2]

THE LIFE-SETTING OF PROVERBS 22:17–24:22

To start with, we need to ask about the setting of these admonitions, the field in which they grew. More important still is the kitchen where these earthy vegetables were processed and served. There are two lines of evidence to consider—analogy with Egyptian Instruction texts and the internal data within this clearly defined subsection of Proverbs. The internal data point unequivocally to a male audience—'my son' (23:15,19,26 24:13,21), and sins characteristic of males such as consorting with immoral women (23:27), crimes of violence (24:1,15) and drunkenness (23:20f, 22:29ff). This particular male has a career path ahead of him involving dining with dignitaries (23:1ff) and the possibility of

---

[1] For our purposes, the broad terms maxim, admonition, instruction, precept and exhortation will be used interchangeably, but there are technical discussions of the Instruction genre such as JG Gammie, 'Paraenetic Literature: toward the Morphology of a Secondary Genre', which offers a sophisticated taxonomy (*Semeia* 50, 1990 *Paraenesis: Act and Form*, pp. 41–77).

[2] The nearest cultural equivalents of two-line maxims are probably sound bites—those short, memorable wrap-up lines given to politicians by their speech writers. Compare advertising slogans such as the Road Safety poster 'Children should be seen and not hurt', or the Blood Donor poster: 'Doctors

promotion to high office (22:29). He may also find himself chasing riches (23:4) and partying (23:20f). He will have opportunity to exploit the law (22:22) and alter boundaries (23:10). In age, he might be anywhere in adolescence or early adulthood—his parents still alive (23:22), his sexual instinct awakened (23:27) and becoming a parent a possibility (23:13). How far ahead the career possibilities lie we cannot tell.[3]

Egyptian and Mesopotamian Instruction texts may originate in real father–son relationships, but their re-use is more pertinent.[4] In the late second millennium, Amenemope writes for his son Hor-em-maakher.[5] The father is an Egyptian official responsible for land registration and his son will follow in his footsteps, so biological succession is paralleled by continuity of profession. The Egyptian Instruction texts were re-copied, sometimes over a period of a thousand years, and thus became 'canonical'. In Egypt, this meant that they were revered and became part of the syllabus in scribal schools. The question mark over Israel's canonical Instruction texts is—'In what educational setting were they used?' Was it at home, or in schools?[6] In re-use at least, the 'my son' of

---

saved his leg, donors saved his life' that exhibits a contrastive poetic parallelism. A suitable hermeneutic is needed to interpret modern maxims.

[3] The social dynamics surrounding Instruction is reviewed in a stimulating way by LG Perdue—'The Social Character of Paraenesis and Paraenetic Literature', *Semeia* 50 (1990) 5–39 with an extensive bibliography.

[4] The data are gathered by KA Kitchen 'Proverbs and Wisdom Books of the Ancient Near East' *Tyndale Bulletin* 28 (1977) 69–114. See pp.76ff for details on titles and personal address formulae. RJ Williams notes that the scribe Khety is credited with the composition of 'The Teaching of Amenemhet I', which makes this a pseudepigraph —'The Sage in Egyptian Literature', pp.19–30 in JG Gammie & LG Perdue (eds), *The Sage in Israel and the Ancient Near East* (Winona Lake: Eisenbrauns) 1990, p.21.

[5] The main copy is the hieratic papyrus BM.10474, dated 950–650BC (22nd–26th Dynasties). A Cairo ostracon dated as early as the 21st Dynasty indicates the copying process was well under way, and the date of composition for *Amenemope* agreed by Egyptologists is the late 2nd millennium, about 1100BC (Williams—'twelfth century B.C.E. or even slightly earlier', but certainly prior to Solomon). See the excellent colour photos, p.427 & p.1291 in N Hillyer(ed), *The Illustrated Bible Dictionary*, (IVP 1980). Compare the hieratic ostracon, pictured on p.1143. This depicts the 'Educational Instruction of the scribe Amennakhte to his apprentice, Hormin', dated to the New Kingdom, c.1250BC. It is referred to as text E.19 in Kitchen's article, *TB* 28, p.112.

[6] On the debate about schools, see the summary articles of JPJ Olivier, 'Schools and Wisdom Literature' *JNSL* 4 (1975) 49–60 and JL Crenshaw 'Education in Ancient Israel' *JBL* 104 (1985) 601–615. The implications of epigraphy, especially *abcedaries*, for schooling is disputed. A Lemaire recently reviewed it with a comprehensive bibliography 'The Sage in School and Temple', pp.165–181 in *The Sage*. The strongest opponent of schools sees instruction given by father to son in hereditary professions—see FW Golka 'The Israelite Wisdom School or "The Emperor's New Clothes" ' Chap.1 pp. 4–15 in *The*

Prov 22:17–24:22 in particular would most likely refer to an apprentice official, if a career path behind Prov 22:17–24:22 can be identified.

A clue to the career path may be given by Prov 22:19, especially if a general parallel with *Amenemope's* concluding remark is allowed:

> Do you see those who are skilful in their work?
> they will serve kings;
> they will not serve common people.

> (Prov 22:19)

> Look to these thirty chapters,
> They inform, they educate;
> They are the foremost of all books,
> They make the ignorant wise.
> If they are read to the ignorant,
> He is cleansed through them.
> Be filled with them, put them in your heart,
> And become a man who expounds them,
> One who expounds as a teacher.
> The scribe who is skilled in his office,
> He is found worthy to be a courtier.

> (*Amenemope*, Chap. 30)[7]

The maxim in Prov 22:29, like that of the last two lines of *Amenemope* above, is optimistic—it does not reckon with nepotism, mass unemployment and other disruptions to stable and fair employment, such as foreign invasion. By itself, the maxim might make no more than the general point 'that there is no limit to what a man can achieve who does his work efficiently and skilfully', though Whybray concedes it is 'possible or even probable that the author had the scribal profession in mind'.[8] When taken as a whole, Prov 22:17–24:22 offers a job profile which matches the role of an official. The young man is not destined for kingship, but may serve the king as a high official, perhaps an officer of court, be that as scribe, diplomat or public administrator.

Leopard's Spots: biblical and African Wisdom in Proverbs (Edinburgh: T&T Clark) 1993.

[7] Quotations are from M Lichtheim, *Ancient Egyptian Literature, Vol.II The New Kingdom*, (Berkeley: Univ. California Press) 1976, p. 162. Compare the translations of WK Simpson, *The Literature of Ancient Egypt* (London:Yale) 1973, p.247ff and JA Wilson, *ANET*³, p.422 which show that although some lines from this section are difficult, the main points are absolutely clear.

[8] RN Whybray, *Wealth and Poverty in the Book of Proverbs*, JSOTS 99 (Sheffield: JSOT Press) 1990, p.91.

The argument for schooling in Israel is largely based on inference, especially when we are speaking about 'higher education' beyond basic reading and writing skills. No state with a centralized bureaucracy could have managed its financial and diplomatic business without a trained elite, nor is literature of the quality of the Old Testament produced without exposure to and practice in a wide tradition of literature. Maxims, as such, may be coined in village and farm by all kinds of speaker, including the illiterate, but their collection in Israel was explicitly a court activity, credited to Solomon and 'the men of Hezekiah' (Prov 25:1).

This information combines to make a plausible case for Prov 22:17–24:22 being used to instruct privileged young males, probably the offspring of officials of various kinds who might be expected to follow in their father's footsteps. The instructor would be a father figure, not the parent. The admonitions to honour father and mother given in 23:22–25 fit comfortably into this school setting.[9]

CHARACTERIZING THE SPIRITUALITY OF PROVERBS
22:17–24:22

At first glance there is no 'spirituality' in these maxims—no mention of prayer or fasting, of meditation, of the study of Torah, of worship.[10] There is nothing about the transforming quality of suffering, about waiting patiently for the Lord, about an intimate belonging in covenant. Instead there are cameos satirizing drunkenness (23:29–35) and going to lunch with a dignitary (23:1ff), and reminders that you might land with a bump on the floor if you become a guarantor for someone's debts (22:27). Only 7 verses out of 70 make reference to God, with Yahweh's name contributing only 5 of the 552 Hebrew words.[11] This means that sixty-three of the seventy verses read as 'secular' wisdom. If we hesitate to classify the material as 'theological', what is its syllabus status

---

[9] Despite the truth of Crenshaw's statement: 'As a matter of fact, every single use of father and son within Proverbs can be understood as precisely that, a father instructing his son, rather than technical language for teacher and student', (*JBL* 104, p.614). We are speaking about the re-use of this material, just as *Amenemope* was copied and re-used.

[10] *Amenemope* specifically recommends morning prayer:

> You shall pray to the Aten when he rises,
> Saying: 'Grant me well-being and health';
> He will give you your needs for this life,
> And you will be safe from fear.
>
> (Chap. 7, 11:12–15; *AEL2*,153)

[11] Yahweh in 22:19,23; 23:17; 24:18,21. To these add 23:11, 24:12 as references to God.

compared with what might appear in a unit of today's theological education?

There are too few statements of fundamental principle for this Instruction to rank as Ethics by our criteria and too little detail for it to rank as a handbook or owner's manual on a specific topic such as money, career or child rearing. Nor can its list of bad types—angry hotheads, the stingy, fools, gluttons, drunkards, prostitutes, adulterers, the wicked, schemers, scoffers, the criminally violent—be called analysis, or used to reconstruct a sociology of Jerusalem. The maxims deal with attitudes, behaviour and motivation, but scarcely qualify as Psychology. The instructor admonishes, but this is not a sermon or a model for homiletics. Could we utilize this material in a contemporary syllabus on Spirituality?

Firstly, we must address the issue of 'secularity' and 'spirituality'. Is there a spirituality of the 'secular', and is this what we meet with in Proverbs? Surveying Proverbs as a whole, Kidner remarks:

> the explicitly religious material has to be hand-picked from a large mass of sayings in which religion is only implicit. And we should do Proverbs a poor service if we contrived to vest it in a priestly ephod or prophet's mantle, for it is a book which seldom takes you to church . . . Its function in Scripture is to put godliness into working clothes . . .[12]

The statistics on 'secular' and theological material are not in dispute. Rather it is the significance of the ratios. We noted that only 10% of Prov 22:17–24:22 is theologically explicit material, but von Rad cautions us against false dichotomising and imposing our theological constructs on the text.

> The modern exegete is always tempted to read into the old texts the tensions with which he is all too familiar between faith and thought, between reason and revelation.[13]

That Israel's Wisdom is to do with 'godliness', and was from its inception, is now affirmed strongly against the view of some scholars that an originally 'secular' clan wisdom or international

---

[12] D Kidner, *Proverbs*, TOTC (London: Tyndale Press) 1964, p.35.
[13] G von Rad, *Wisdom in Israel* (London: SCM) 1972 p.61.

common stream wisdom was spiritualised by an injection of Yahwistic concepts in later stages of editing.[14]

The analogies with Egyptian and Mesopotamian Instruction texts—from earliest 3rd millennium examples down through 2nd millennium to 1st millennium material—supports the viewpoint that 'profane' and 'sacred' maxims were collected together from earliest times and continued like this over centuries and across cultures. Once collected in writing, the presumed oral original and its setting falls into the back- ground. The written collection now assumes the features of a distinct literary genre.[15]

Israel's collections of sayings and admonitions juxtapose empirical observation and theological convictions. The 'secular' and the 'theological' were amalgamated in an effort to distil a wisdom to live by. The Near Eastern worldview, polytheistic or monotheistic, did not allow for a 'secular'/'theological' dichotomy. Likewise, this Wisdom material does not allow for a separation of theory and practice. In Instruction texts, the body of accumulated knowledge derives from experience *and* faith. This knowledge is fed back into experience in the form of behaviour. We can test the hypothesis of an integrated spirituality by looking at the 'theological' and the 'secular' material in Prov 22:17–24:22.

FIVE INTEGRAL PERSPECTIVES IN PROVERBS 22:17–24:22

In our chosen excerpt from Proverbs, we could take the five passages which speak about God as pointers to the spirituality of the whole. From the first two, the name of God is missing, yet the passages are important clues. Prov 24:11f indicates that God oversees all of life.

---

[14] Recently, FM Wilson, 'Sacred and Profane? The Yahwistic Redaction of Proverbs Reconsidered', pp.313–334 in KG Hoglund et al (eds), *The Listening Heart: essays in Wisdom and the Psalms in honor of RE Murphy*, JSOTS 58 (Sheffield: JSOT Press) 1987 with support of G von Rad and RE Murphy. They are writing against a Yahwistic redaction position, epitomized by W McKane, *Proverbs* (London: SCM) 1970.

[15] KA Kitchen reviews the varieties and affinities of the Instruction material within the Wisdom genre in an article 'Proverbs and Wisdom Books of the Ancient Near East', *Tyndale Bulletin* 28 (1977) 69–114. He characterises Proverbs 1–24 as Solomon I, a Type B form, whose formal affinities include *Ptahotep* and *Shuruppak* from the 3rd millennium, down to *Ankh–Sheshonqy* and *Ahiqar* in the 1st millennium, with the well preserved 2nd millennium Egyptian Instruction texts of *Aniy* and *Amenemope* providing interesting comparisons in terms of content.

if you hold back from rescuing those taken away to death,
   those who go staggering to the slaughter;
If you say, 'Look, we did not know this'—
   does not he who weighs the heart perceive it?
Does not he who keeps watch over your soul know it?
   And will he not repay all according to their deeds?

                                         (Prov 24:11f)[16]

The One who 'weighs the heart' and 'keeps watch over your soul' notes sins of omission, feeble excuses and wilful ignorance. This maxim is in the spirit of Psa 139's acknowledgment of Yahweh's searching gaze. It accords with other proverbs—

For human ways are under the eyes of the LORD,
   and he examines all their paths.

                                         (Prov 5:21)

The eyes of the LORD are in every place,
   keeping watch on the evil and the good.

                                         (Prov 15:3)

Sheol and Abaddon lie open before the LORD,
   how much more human hearts!

                                       (Prov 15:11)

All one's ways may be pure in one's own eyes,
   but the LORD weighs the spirit.

                                       (Prov 16:2)

The admonition of Prov 24:11f keys into mainstream Old Testament concepts, namely, the presence of God, God's evaluation of human motivation, and God's concern for the oppressed. The Instruction material affirms the presence of the all-seeing God, not dramatically in theophany and apocalyptic, nor culticly at festival and sacrifice, but in the course of mundane commercial and social life. Mundane life is open to Yahweh who discerns the thoughts and intents of the heart, the hearts of neighbours, friends, traders, husbands, wives, children, servants, kings and counsellors. This is a genuine spirituality of the secular because the 'secular' is not profane for being mundane. Rather, the mundane is incorporated within Yahweh's domain. This sense of the presence of God within the mundane anticipates a classic of Christian spirituality,

---

[16] This might refer to miscarriage of justice, as implied by the prohibition against 'crushing the afflicted at the gate (ie. lawcourt)', 22:22. Alternatively, RN Whybray suggests criminal violence which is mentioned in 24:1f and 15 (*Wealth and Poverty*, p.96ff).

Brother Lawrence's reflections on practising the presence of God during his kitchen work.[17]

The second verse from our section of Proverbs which refers to God, but not by name, likewise speaks of him as the unseen watcher who intervenes on behalf of the vulnerable against the wickedness of those with opportunity and apparent impunity:

> Do not remove an ancient landmark
> > or encroach on the fields of orphans,
> for their redeemer is strong;
> > he will plead their cause against you.

(Prov 23:10f)

'Their redeemer' must refer to Yahweh here, though in other contexts the *goʾēl* was the human guardian, the kinsman acting as advocate.[18] The vulnerable were vulnerable because they must often have lacked a powerful or willing kinsman. A maxim similar to 23:10f names Yahweh as the widow's champion:

> The LORD tears down the house of the proud,
> > but maintains the widow's boundaries.

(Prov 15:25)

Within Prov 22:17–24:22, this thought is paralleled by Yahweh's intervention on behalf of the poor: 'for the LORD pleads their cause and despoils of life those who despoil them'(22:23). This uses the same legal terminology as 23:11 (Hebrew *yārīb rībām*—'represents them in their case'). The role of the deity as intervening champion appears in like context in *Amenemope*. Divine retribution protects widow's boundaries. The oppressor 'will be caught by the might

---

[17] Brother Lawrence, the 17th century Carmelite, was a cook who brought spirituality to his kitchen work— *The Practice of the Presence of God* (London: Hodder & Stoughton) 1985 ET by EM Blaiklock. S Terrien, *The Elusive Presence—toward a new biblical theology*, Religious Perspectives 26 (London: Harper & Row) 1978, used Presence as its organising centre, including a section on Wisdom, pp.350ff, but drew little on the Instruction material in Proverbs.

[18] Hebrew *goʾēl*—'redeemer' (NRSV, 1989), was interpreted as 'Redeemer' with a capital letter meaning God himself in the RSV 1952 edition. J Ruffle seems to take 23:11 to mean the literal kinsman initiating legal action—'the perpetrator will be disagreeably surprised to find that the defenceless orphan in fact has a powerful ally who will take him to court' . He then decides that 'the threat [in *Amenemope*] that a dread thing will carry you off is hardly comparable' ('The Teaching of Amenemope and its Connection with the Book of Proverbs' *Tyndale Bulletin* 28 (1977) 29–68, p.62). Contrast McKane, *Proverbs*, p.379; L. Boström, *The God of the Sages: the portrayal of God in the book of Proverbs*, Coniectanea Biblica OT Series 29, (Stockholm: Almqvist & Wiksell) 1990, p.106, 198ff; and Whybray, *Wealth and Poverty*, p.993.

of the Moon' (Chap 6, vii:19).[19] An official should 'Beware of the Lord of All' (Chap 6, viii:14).

A striking difference between Ancient Near Eastern and Western cultures is the latter's separation of legality and spirituality when it comes to land. Land in Genesis, Deuteronomy and Psa 25 or 37 is not real estate but a place with Yahweh. Land grants and boundary stones from Mesopotamia bore the names and icons of the gods as legal witnesses.[20] Of course, this did not guarantee justice and it lent itself to turning theology into a legitimating ideology where land was at royal disposal. Liberation Theology offers a programme for questioning political ideologies and reinstating land as God's concern. Contemporary theological questions about land acquisition give the admonitions of Proverbs a new lease of life and a genuine re-contextualisation into contemporary politics, and this is at the level of physical land, not to mention dynamic equivalents which embrace economic resources such as jobs, money and marketable skills.[21]

So far then, we have seen that Yahweh's personal intervention is referred to in motive clauses as a deterrent to oppressive behaviour (24:12, 23:11 and 22:23). To these we should add 24:21f. This too speaks of retribution:

---

[19]   *AEL*, p.151f. Besides the 'Moon' and 'Lord of All' in the lines cited, 'god' appears in three more of the 36 lines of Chap 6, which demonstrates how religious this section of the Instruction text is.

[20]   See JN Postgate, *Neo-Assyrian Royal Grants and Decrees*, Studia Pohl 1, (Rome:Biblical Institute Press) 1961; WJ Hinke, *A New Boundary Stone of Nebuchadnezzar*, Philadelphia, 1907; LW King, *Babylonian Boundary Stones*, London, 1912 and photos in JB Pritchard (ed), *The Ancient Near East in Pictures*[2](New Jersey: Princeton) 1969 Nos. 519–522; J Oates, *Babylon*[rev] [ed](London: Thames & Hudson) 1986, pls. 70,72,73,78. New examples turn up, such as those published by Khalid Al-Admi, 'A New Kudurru of Marodul-nadin-ahhe: IM.90585', *Sumer* 38 1/2 (1982) 121–133 and by MY Taha, 'A Boundary Stone from Khan Beni Sa'ad', *Sumer* 38 1/2 (1982) 134–136.

[21]   An example is The National Conference of Churches in South Africa, Nov 1990, which issued the *Rustenburg Declaration*. This reflects on the subversion of theology by the Apartheid ideology and in section 4.1.2. affirms:

> After decades of oppression, the removal of discriminatory laws will have to be accompanied by affirmative acts of restitution in the fields of health care, psychological healing, education, employment, economic infrastructure, and especially land ownership. For many years, greed has led to the taking of land from the poor and weak. Both church and state must address the issue of restoring land to dispossessed people. (*JTSA* 74 March (1991), p. 67)

The West Bank represents another high profile land debate—see NS Ateek, *Justice and Only Justice: a Palestinian Theology of Liberation* (Maryknoll: Orbis) 1989. Compare L Weber, BF Evans, GD Cusack (eds), *Theology of the Land, papers presented at the First Theology of Land Conference*, St.John's University, Collegeville, Minnesota (Liturgical Press), 1987.

My child fear the LORD and the king,
   and do not disobey either of them;
for disaster comes from them suddenly,
   and who knows the ruin that both can bring?

Despite textual difficulties, the gist is clear—it is best to avoid disaster and ruin by due awareness that Yahweh and the king are forces to be reckoned with in life. 'Suddenly' underlines the swift and dramatic reversal of fortune resulting from their intervention. The maxim is not expounding a theory of monarchy or a theology of state. Its reciter might have assumed, as does much of the literature from the Monarchy period, that the kingdom of David and the Kingdom of God are concentric, but the maxim does not spell this out or rule out of court a prophetic denunciation of apostate kings. What it does do is to add the political domain to the sayings referring to the judicial and administrative spheres reviewed above. All these spheres which we distinguish for practical purposes, Proverbs has convened for instruction.

In 24:17f, the scrutiny of Yahweh is made explicit by the use of the verb 'to see':

Do not rejoice when your enemies fall
   and do not let your heart be glad when they stumble,
or else the LORD will see it and be displeased,
   and turn his anger away from them.[22]

Yahweh sees into the person's spirit and reacts to its attitudes and emotions before they have come to expression in behaviour. Of course, the prohibition against coveting in the Ten Commandments likewise intercepts what is passing through the mind before it results in theft. The maxim here adds the sphere of the human spirit to the political, judicial and administrative spheres as the realm of Yahweh's jurisdiction.

THE 'FEAR OF THE LORD' AS THIS-WORLDLY WISDOM

Two Yahweh sayings remain for mention. Both are fundamental to the Wisdom ethos. The first, 24:17f, needs to be read in

---

[22] McKane chooses to be scandalized—'The absence of every trace of human feeling for the enemy who is down and out is uncanny and unpleasant', p.404—but needlessly so. The admonition is likely denouncing malicious glee and implying that it will incur Yahweh's action—. . . .'and turn his anger onto you', which is ironical. See Boström, *The God of the Sages*, p.109 citing Toy, p.448; cf. Kidner, *Proverbs*, p.155, minus the reference in footnote 2.

conjunction with 24:14 and 24:19f to do justice to the thought of these admonitions.

> Do not let your heart envy sinners,
>   but always continue in the fear of the LORD.
> Surely there is a future,
>   and your hope will not be cut off.
>
> (Prov 23:17f)[23]

> Know that wisdom is such to your soul;
>   if you find it, you will find a future,
> and your hope will not be cut off.
>
> (Prov 24:14)

> Do not fret because of evildoers.
>   Do not envy the wicked;
> for the evil have no future;
>   the lamp of the wicked will go out.
>
> (Prov 24:19f)

By juxtaposing the first two maxims, we see that 'wisdom' and 'the fear of the LORD' lead to a bright future. There is no suggestion in Proverbs that this future involves life after death. Rather, these maxims place enormous value on this life, and are concerned with the results or outcome of behaviour.

The pupil's actual future, be that soon realised in his career path, or realised in long-term in a life to ripe old age and grandchildren, depends on his 'zeal'. Appetite for honey (24:13a) should be matched in its intensity and pleasure by hunger for 'wisdom'; the strength of jealousy at the success of sinners (23:17a) surpassed by zeal for Yahweh.[24]

The 'fear of Yahweh' is this-worldly and therein lies the 'secularity' of Proverbs. The 'fear of Yahweh', as the phrase itself

---

[23] The parallelism between 'hope' (*tiqwāh*) and 'outcome' (*'aḥᵃrīt*) converges towards our English expression 'a bright future'. The word for 'future' (*'aḥᵃrīt*), the 'afterwards, result, outcome, outworking' of the present action or attitude forms a connecting thread on which proverbial beads are hung throughout Proverbs—5:11, 14:12, 14:13, 16:25, 19:20, 20:21, 23:18, 23:32, 24:14, 24:20, 25:8, 29:21. Wisdom is foreseeing the end result of a line of action and acting in the light of it. G von Rad highlights this aspect of Wisdom in the title and sub-title of Chap. 7 'The Essentials for Coping with Reality', 2. Cause and Effect. The Act-Consequence Relationship (pp. 124–137).

[24] The verb *qn'*—'to envy, be jealous' used in 23:17a is probably implied in the verbless line of v.17b (there is no verb 'continue' in the Hebrew). If *qn'* is read into v.17b, a word play is created which exploits the semantic range of *qn'* for aroused passion. This semantic range of *qn'* is quite well expressed by 'jealous-zealous' in English. See Boström, *The God of the Sages*, p.107 and McKane's comment: 'There is a right and a wrong aspiration or jealousy; the one is a disease and the other a valuable spiritual exercise' (*Proverbs*, p.387).

conveys, is also 'spiritual' and Wisdom's first principle. This is a leit-motif of Proverbs:

> The fear of the LORD is the first principle of knowledge;
> fools despise wisdom and instruction.
>
> (Prov 1:7)[25]
>
> The beginning of wisdom is the fear of the LORD
> and knowledge of the Holy One is understanding.
>
> (Prov 9:10)

In Prov 23:17 above, 'fear of the Lord' is contrasted with envy of sinners. By implication, both are inward orientations, a tug that is felt Godward or manward. Between inward orientation and its outworking in behaviour there is a small step only. The envy of sinners slides into behaving like them, while the fear of Yahweh strengthens right conduct because 'those who walk uprightly fear the Lord, but one who is devious in conduct despises him' (Prov 14:2). This accords with Prov 3:7-

> Do not be wise in your own eyes;
> fear the Lord and turn away from evil.
> It will be a healing for your flesh
> and a refreshment for your body.

This speaks of a moral choice, as does 23:17, and it could claim the support of modern medicine in the sense that a range of diseases in affluent societies are self-induced by lifestyle, or are psychosomatic manifestations of disrupted relationships and unfaced reality. 'The fear of the Lord is hatred of evil' (8:13), and the evil concerned is not demonic or cosmic, but the down-to-earth evil of human 'pride', 'arrogance' and 'perverted speech'(v.13b). It is in this sense of moral choice that 'the fear of the Lord is a fountain of life, so that one may avoid the snares of death'(14:27). 'Flesh', 'body', 'death' remind one how this-worldly is the spirituality of the 'fear of the Lord'—'the fear of the Lord prolongs life'(10:27). This is why Proverbs is unabashed to link its spirituality of the fear of the Lord with the reward of 'riches and honour and life'(22:4).

---

[25] There are several suggestions for the nuance of Hebrew *rē'šīt* in Prov 1:7 and Psa 111:10. NRSV offers 'beginning' ; other scholars 'culmination', 'essence', 'fruit', 'choicest part' . H Blocher makes a good case for 'first principle' in the sense of 'the fear of the LORD' being foundational to wisdom— 'The Fear of the Lord as the "Principle" of Wisdom', *Tyndale Bulletin* 28 (1977) 3–28, p.14f. Certainly the 'fear of the LORD' is the first step towards wisdom, the point of departure, as *tᵉhillāh* 'beginning' in Prov 9:10 says. Yet it is also what one arrives at and what one rests in, as Prov 23:17 indicates.

These are covenant blessings for obedience to covenant stipulations, as Deut 28 so plainly states, speaking at national level.

The spirituality of 'fear of the Lord' is both the deep inward orientation and its practical outcome in behaviour. These are integrated. The sages will need to say more about the exceptions to prospering in the fear of the Lord and the inappropriateness of linking adversity with disobedience. It falls to Qohelet to integrate the fear of the Lord with a resolutely this-worldly realism.[26]

THE 'SPIRITUAL' AND 'SECULAR' SIDES OF PERSONAL DEVELOPMENT

We can now appreciate the 'sacred' admonition that introduces these 'words of the Wise' (22:17a) and epitomises the spirituality of the 63 + 7 verses. The instructor describes his teaching objective as follows:

> So that your trust may be in the LORD,
> I have made them known to you today—yes, to you.
>   Have I not written for you thirty sayings of admonition and
>   knowledge,
>   to show you what is right and true,
> so that you may give a true answer to those who sent you.
>   (Prov 22:19–21)

In this introduction, the 'secular' and 'sacred' are combined in several ways. Firstly, the instructor unabashedly steps forward as an authority, recommending himself and promoting his latest book. Culturally, this jars. It seems immodest, pompous and authoritarian. Yet he combines this self-confident tone with a pointer beyond himself—'that your trust may be in the LORD'. There are evidently two teachers; behind the 'secular' teacher, there stands the 'sacred' Teacher who is to be revered above all, certainly above the king. The 'fear of the LORD' has first motivated the instructor. It was this experience that enabled him to become

---

[26] After Proverbs, Wisdom literature will have to wrestle with the exceptions to the rule of obedience-blessing and resist linking adversity to disobedience. It does this in Job, though the Epilogue all but reverts to a piety prosperity, constrained as the poet is by the this-worldly horizon for his drama, and perhaps by the traditional story handed to him. Qohelet faces the affluence of the wicked and the adversities of the righteous in his own inimical way, completing the contribution of Wisdom literature. See Ecc 3:14, 5:7, 7:15–18, 8:12f. A helpful overview of 'The Religious Dimensions of Israelite Wisdom', majoring on the 'fear of the Lord', is given by RE Murphy, taking it through to Ben Sirach—Chap. 23, pp. 449–458 in PD Miller, PD Hanson, SD McBride (eds), *Ancient Israelite Religion: essays in honor of FM Cross* (Philadelphia: Fortress) 1987.

the mediator of wisdom. Secondly, the 'spiritual' orientation of 'trust', that dependence and commitment which honour God, is complemented by the utilitarian goal—knowing what to say as a response to those who have sent the pupil.[27] Thus our section of Proverbs interweaves pleasing the instructor (23:15f), honouring other authorities such as parents (23:22,24,25 and 22:21) and trusting God (22:19).

McKane explains this interwoven texture of wisdom as a 'theological reorientation'. He says 'instruction is subsumed under Yahwism, education, rigorously conceived, capitulates to piety and the educator is replaced by a religious teacher'.[28] This reads into Israel's literature a dichotomy from post-Enlightenment Europe where the direction higher education has taken has been from a religious foundation to secularity. The oldest Universities exemplify this developing polarity. To read such a polarity into Instruction texts does an injustice to the spirituality of Egyptian sages, such as *Amenemope*, who offer very practical instruction alongside admonitions which invoke deities. *Amenemope* invokes by name Re the Sun-god, Aten the solar disc, Khons the Moon god, Thot the divine scribe (Ibis & Ape), and Khnum the Potter, not to mention the many references to 'God' scattered throughout the 30 chapters and to other deities named respectfully in the Prologue. What McKane's statement does draw to our attention is the *integration* of 'theological' and utilitarian in Instruction texts. In other words, whether we are reading the papyrus in Egyptian or Hebrew, we encounter a spirituality of the secular.

INTEGRATION OF EXPERIENCE

The integrated perspective on life found in Proverbs is expressed in a modern maxim on spirituality:

What is natural should become thoroughly spiritual
and what is spiritual should become perfectly natural.

The admonitions in Prov 22:17–24:22 combine the 'theological' or 'sacred' with the 'secular' by the spectrum of motivations offered for keeping the admonitions. The admonitions are not a straight

---

[27] In 22:21, 'those who sent you' (*šōlᵉheykā*—the plural Participle of *šlḥ*—'to send') might be identified as the pupil's parents (parents are referred to in 23:22) or his superiors (e.g. the 'ruler' of 23:1). This depends on how we construe the age of the pupil, the school setting and the parallels with Egyptian Instruction texts in which the pupil is being groomed for the scribal profession, diplomatic corp or royal court.

[28] McKane, *Proverbs*, p.376.

list of *Dos* and *Don'ts*. Many are reinforced with positive fulfilment or warnings. The latter are based on God's direct judgment
(22:23, 23:11, 24:12,18,22) or natural consequences such as debt,
poverty and derangement (22:27, 23:21,32ff).[29] The positive gains
include a secure relationship with God, successful parenting, a
good future, your parents' pride and a social standing (22:19,
23:14,18,24f 24:3–7).

These positive and negative reinforcements retain value, but a
contemporary re-reading of the text could begin from an awareness of the many factors that actually shape our attitudes and
behaviour. This exercise will uncover the fact that there are a
surprisingly high number of shaping factors recognised by the
human sciences (Education, Sociology and Psychology) that are
reflected in the Wisdom Instruction of Prov 22:17–24:22. The
difference is that the contemporary source of the shaping factor is
not so likely to be parental admonition or school education.
Another difference is that 'Instruction texts' nowadays come in the
form of magazines and paperback books written by adults for
adults, though versions of these are distilled for school-going
ages.

Our contemporary 'Instruction texts' are the popular sources of
wisdom on parenting, marriage, childbirth, the effects of childhood experience, depression, retirement, patterns of addiction,
social skills, self-understanding, job-seeking, self presentation in
curriculum vitae and interview, the overcoming of serious dis-
abilities, advice on nutrition and the investment of money,
information on the transmission of hereditary defects, and the
avoidance or management of diseases such as cancer, coronary
thrombosis and AIDS. The authors may often have a tertiary
education and professional experience in medicine, counselling,
social work or journalism. In works composed for a wide
readership, they share their own life experiences, experiences
culled from their circle of friends, or experience gained through
participation in small groups and specialised seminars, supported
by formal or informal research. It may be that some of this
information is disseminated through schools or by government
agencies, rather than through paperbacks and magazines, but if so
it is more likely to be the medical information than the relational
or spiritual. In practical terms, then, our 'wisdom to live by' is
drawn from many secular experiences and sources, including the

---

[29] The motive clauses are often signalled grammatically by the Hebrew particle
kīy—'for', 'because', 'so that' which occurs 12 times, introducing both
positive   reward   and   things   to   avoid—22:18,23   23:5,7,11,13,21
24:2,6,16,20,22; *pen*—'lest' appears in 22:25 and 24:18. Other constructions
supply motives as well as these.

soaps on television. In all this range of subject matter and packaging, seldom, if ever, is wisdom for life integrated with faith perspectives.[30]

The Wisdom Instruction of Proverbs or texts from Egypt prepare no one adequately for managing home finances, marriage, parenthood, old age, terminal illness or career choice. In its practicalities, the ancient wisdom has been com- pletely eclipsed by contemporary productions. Yet Proverbs exhibits an awareness of shaping factors that are still operative on the individual in today's society. These include social standing, social conscience, circle of friends, other people's expectations, parental example, crime, competition, ambition, greed, indolence, tenacity, goal-setting, evaluation of consequences, lifestyle, speech, observation, avoidance, addiction, gratification deferment, time investment, money and faith. These shaping factors are all present, explicitly or implicitly, in the maxims of Prov 22:17–24:22.[31] It follows that any Christian effort that claims Proverbs as its inspiration should work at an integration of 'spiritual' and social science perspectives, rather than ignoring the immense power of the factors studied by social science, or pretending that our location in our social structure is automatically over-ridden by our Christian conversion.

The seeds of disciplines such as Sociology and Psychology are evident in the approach of the ancient Instruction material because its generalisations are based on observation of human behaviour.

---

[30] There is no telling how influential are the non-fiction paperbacks in bookshop chains and airport bookstalls but they seem to represent a whole sector of informal education. While some best-sellers could be satirised as pop-psychology or part of a Californian cult of self-actualisation, many are written by professionals, such as those which popularised Transactional Analysis therapy in the 1970s—Eric Berne, *Games People Play, What do You Say after You Say Hello?*; Thomas Harris, *I'm OK, You're OK*; Muriel James, *Born to Win.* Paperbacks written on Feminist and Environmental issues may inform and influence the 1980s and 1990s the way that A Tofler's *Future Shock* and V Packard's *The Waste Makers* influenced the 1970s. Recently Stephen Hawking's *A Brief History of Time* has put Cosmology without God on the best-selling list, while Richard Dawkins's *The Selfish Gene* and *The Blind Watchmaker* have done the same for Biology. Taken together, the range of paperback sellers from Cosmology to Biology to Human Behaviour is fairly comprehensive. It has roots in human curiosity and observation and is reflected in Wisdom texts. Of course, global village culture is different and today's media, particularly advertising, television, newspapers and the music industry, are immensely influential and without parallel in ancient times.

[31] Tribalism, nationalism and racialism were powerful factors shaping the Near East's cultures and are powerfully operative today, for instance in the former Soviet bloc and Eastern Europe, as well as in Africa and in urban injustice and violence in the USA and UK. Wisdom literature seems to largely ignore these socially divisive forces in its rather humanistic internationalism.

Academic textbooks disclose that conflicting viewpoints characterise Sociology and Psychology. It is scarcely surprising, then,
that Old Testament scholars find tensions within the Wisdom
material and between Wisdom formulae and life. The contingency
and ambiguity of life explain many of these tensions. Human
behaviour does not yield hard data for observation in the way that
allows particle physicists with their supercolliders and under-
ground lairs to describe the behaviour of quarks and neutrinos
with mathematical formulae. We should expect tensions in
proverbs that reflect the complexity or ambiguity of human
behaviour and social arrangements. One tension that we will
certainly encounter in Proverbs is the conflict between an
acknowledged ideal and the way people do or do not respond to it.

THE IDEAL AND THE REALITY

Within Prov 22:17–24:22, a dissonance gap materialises when the
maxims admit that the present situation contradicts the ideal or the
theological frame of reference. For instance, sinners may well be
enviable (23:17, 24:1f) and the wicked continue to be impervious
(24:19). The righteous unfortunately may 'fall seven times'
(24:16). Affluence may be delectable (23:3,6). Admonitions *not* to
participate in exploitation, injustice and violent crime imply that
bad things happen to good people and may be perpetrated by the
educated. Maxims are not prophetic denunciations of social evil,
and Proverbs tends to cope with the disparity between what is and
what ought to be by taking the long-term view or by placing faith
in divine reward. The same is true for our Christian spirituality. It
may likewise lengthen the time-scale for sanctification or invoke
the afterlife to cope with the dissonance between expectation and
experience, and be- tween our self-directed admonitions and our
actual behaviour and attitudes.

Proverbs holds onto its ideals while it offers 'neutral' observations. It speaks of the way things are and the way they could be,
of what is and what ought to be. In combining report and
admonition, observation and ideal, motivation based on avoidance and motivation based on fulfilment, the Instruction material
has a degree of realism about it that marks it as a down-to-earth
form of spirituality.

The truth ideal advocated in 23:22 even has an ironical down-
to-earthness about it when re-contextualised into theological
education today.

> Buy truth, and do not sell it;
> buy wisdom, instruction, and understanding.
>
> (Prov 23:23)

Here are four words, in this context as good as synonyms: 'truth', 'wisdom', 'instruction', 'understanding'. When we ask what the content of this 'truth' might be, the answer is not a metaphysics. The 'truth' on offer is Prov 22:17–24:22. The truth is encapsulated in the maxims. This is an example of self-reference, the self-conscious recommendation of its teachings so characteristic of the Instruction genre.

The maxim is not concerned with 'How much?', but with 'How much valued?' 'Buy . . . and do not sell': acquire it and never part with it. 'Buy' and 'sell' are metaphors. But there is another level to this which we might express with a modern maxim—'there is no such thing as a free lunch'. There was probably no free lunch in Jerusalem either. The argument for setting this material in a school for professionals is a strong one. Granted this setting, someone paid the teacher. In our day, someone still pays the teacher. Theological education is not free. Whether we think in terms of Hebrew youths memorising and reciting from a papyrus manuscript by rote, or of a library with shelves of resource material, in the form of clay tablets, leather scrolls or hard-back books, the spirituality of attaining truth has a literal price tag. Genuine education demands a profound invest-ment of money, time and energy.

Wisdom Instruction is realistic enough to remind us of this cost factor to spirituality. Books, music and retreat centres cost money. Theological lecturers, or spiritual directors, have invested thousands of pounds in the accumulation of their degrees and expertise,[32] and if they have a role as mentors in spirituality they will recognise its dependence on all sorts of down-to-earth needs being met in order that we may the better read and write and reflect.[33] Where Instruction acknowledges that 'the drippings of the honeycomb are sweet to your taste' (Prov 24:13), we might recognize the secular benefits of other energy sources, such as electricity and aerobics. Prov 24:14 immediately moves from honeycomb to wisdom. 'Honey' and 'the honeycomb' function as an analogy, a typology for wisdom. Yet the enjoyment of honey

---

[32] Paul, the theological lecturer and spiritual director, was well schooled—at the feet of Gamaliel (Acts 22:3)—and well travelled. He also valued his 'books and above all the parchments' (2 Tim 4:13).

[33] We can affirm this without endorsing the whole of Maslow's approach to the hierarchy of needs culminating in self-actualization. (See note 80 to Chapter 11.) Yet there is truth in the African proverb 'An empty belly has no ears', which applies just as much to receiving education as to receiving the Gospel. The proverb was quoted in *Evangelism and Social Responsibility: an evangelical commitment*, The Grand Rapids Report, Lausanne Committee for World Evangelization/World Evangelical Fellowship, (Exeter:Paternoster) 1982, p.20.

itself is not devalued for all that. There is 'secular' delight and 'spiritual' delight; each enhances the other. Acquiring wisdom through education may be a delight, but there are tuition fees to pay.

A SPIRITUALITY OF THE MENTOR ROLE

Spirituality is not the property of intellectuals any more than wisdom was the property of court scribes. If court scribes collected Instruction literature and ran schools using this material, the re-application of their spirituality would be this—that academics, theological educators and any in teaching roles in local churches, para-church organisations and the like should reproduce what the Instruction writers modelled in themselves. To subscribe to what they were, and not simply to what they recorded, means that we consider their privileged education. This advantagedness challenges academics to place a value, as does Prov 22:17–24:22, on an integrated life in which theory and practice, faith and facts, observation and reflection, experience and formulation, learning and teaching are integrated. It may be that academia is the field where the hazards are greatest for a divorce between conceptualising and living, between dealing with facts and integrating a faith orientation, of retaining the seven theological verses as foundational amidst the seventy without an explicit acknowledgement of God.

The spirituality modelled by Prov 22:17–24:22 is a spirituality applicable to the academic discipline of theology. One of the plethora of nouns used to describe the process or end-product of Wisdom education is *mūsar*—'discipline, correction, training'. In our Instruction text, *mūsar* appears three times (23:12,13,23), twice translated 'instruction' and once 'discipline'. The context of 'Do not withhold discipline from your children'(v.13) is physical punishment. Hence, 'beat them with a rod'. But the semantic field of *mūsar* is transparently wider than corporal punishment, because the previous verse ('Apply your mind to instruction') refers to cognition, and *mūsar* is bundled with 'knowledge', 'truth', 'wisdom' and 'understanding' (*daʿat, ʾemet, ḥokmāh, bīynāh,* vv.12,23), referring to the learning process itself.

The study of theology as an academic discipline must include a growth in 'wisdom' and *mūsar* in the practitioner —if it is to rise to the level of Old Testament Wisdom Instruction. The material itself should operate on the theological teacher in 'correction, training, discipline'. This is strikingly similar to the effect of Scripture according to 2 Tim 3:16—'for teaching, for reproof, for correction, and for training in righteousness'. It is no coincidence that Paul pointed to his own example as a visual aid, urging his disciples to imitate his way of life, and in Paul's relationship with Timothy we see the outworking of the mentor role.[34]

The *medium* of Instruction texts is useless as a learning model in the family, in school education or in seminaries in the *form* in which it is packaged. To read it aloud would make it sound too much like an authoritarian list of Dos and Don'ts—the Don'ts dominate in Prov 22:17–24:22—for it to communicate with independently minded people. Its apparently random order of topics makes for a jumbled impression. Its implicit memorisation learning method—'it will be pleasant if you keep them within you, if all of them are ready on your lips'(22:18) is unaided by rhyme. Besides which Western culture perceives rote learning as counterproductive to the whole ethos and aim of education.[35] Admonition without group interaction, fact sheets, debates, humour, role-plays, simulation games, drama sketches, puppet theatre, stories, cartoons, overhead projectors, videos and the like has been abandoned with good reason by Sunday Schools and Christian organisations working with children, young people and adults. The canonical *form* of Prov 22:17–24:22, as opposed to its actual life-setting in Israelite culture, is an obstacle to its usefulness today.

But there is more to the model of Instruction text spirituality than the mode and medium of learning. There is a concept of discipling built into the relational dynamic which infuses life into the admonitions, repetitions, motivation clauses and exhortations.[36]

---

[34] See Phil 3:17, 1 Thess 1:6, 2 Thess 3ff, 1 Cor 4:16, 11:1, 1 Tim 4:12. Compare other references to imitation of example in Jam 5:10, 1 Pet 2:21, Heb 6:12, 13:7.

[35] Ruffle points out that the Turin writing board (No.6237) text of *Amenemope* has marginal signs indicating Day 4, Day 8, Day 10, Day 12 and Day 18 'irregularly spaced but possibly indicating set portions for a pupil's study' (*TB* 28, p.33). *The Instruction for Merikare* cautions against executing a former fellow-pupil with whom the king had recited texts in class—'with whom you once sang the writings' (Williams, *Scribal Training*, p.216; *LAE*, pp.180–192, line 50f p.183). Memorisation and sing-song recitation in class might well be a method of education used with Instruction material in Israel too. It is not a Western method of adult canonical re-reading!

[36] We could think of these formal characteristics as the surface structure. In Prov 22:17–24:22 the discourse has grammatical features such as imperatives ('Incline your ear', 'Listen to your father'), prohibitions with *'al*—('Do not rob the poor'), motive clauses with *kiy* and *pen* ('for the LORD pleads their cause', 'lest you learn their ways'), personal address (*beniy*—'my son'), repetition of topic (boundaries, alcohol abuse, envy of wicked), repeated exhortations to learn (22:17–21; 23:12,15F,19,26; 24:13f). The deep structure is the relationship (father-son, instructor-pupil, professional-apprentice) which centres on the educator as role model. Because it is the deep structure, it may not be found stated in so many words.

The father, instructor or professional responsible for inculcating the maxims belonged to a tradition and acknowledged this. He had also made the material his own. Hence Prov 22:17–24:22 is both 'the words of the wise'—acknowledging his predecessors —and 'my teaching', introduced with a flourish—'have I not written for you thirty sayings?'. He sees himself as disciple and then discipler.

In Egypt and perhaps in Israel too, the discipling model may have originated in biological and professional kinship, but the mentor role extends beyond this immediate relationship through the canonical status of the text and the dynamics of its re-use. In its conclusion *Amenemope* gives a striking statement of the discipling model.

> If they are read to the ignorant,
> He is cleansed through them.
> Be filled with them, put them in your heart,
> And become a man who expounds them,
> One who expounds as a teacher.
> The scribe who is skilled in his office,
> He is found worthy to be a courtier.
>
> (Amenemope, Chap. 30)[37]

The Egyptian text compiled by 'the overseer of fields, experienced in his office, the offspring of a scribe of Egypt' (Prologue, 1.13f) urges his son to 'become a man who expounds . . . who expounds as a teacher'(Chap 30, 27:14f). The model is Listen–Learn–Live–Teach, a process which Amenemope had been through as 'offspring of a scribe' and 'son of Kanakht' (Prologue 2:11) and which he now prescribes for 'his son, the youngest of his children, the smallest of his family'(Prologue 2:13f), Horem-maakher.

A MODEL OF INTEGRITY WITHOUT CLASS CONSCIOUSNESS?

The problem with the professional base to the Egyptian Instruction material is that it generates and perpetuates a class consciousness that glorifies scribal professionalism.[38] The biblical text has affinities with the discipling model enunciated by Egyptian

---

[37] *AEL*, p.162; *LAE*, p.265; *ANET*³, p.424.
[38] The works from Mesopotamia and Egypt which praise the scribal profession originate in the teaching setting and were copied and recopied as part of the education syllabus. See RJ Williams, 'Scribal Training in Ancient Egypt', *JAOS* 92.2 (1972) 214–221. 'May you be a scribe and attend the House of Life!', exhorts Amennakhte (late 2nd millennium). The 'House-of-Life' is the school, scriptorium and library. See the texts translated in Simpson, *LAE* Part 5. *The Scribal Tradition and Several Incomplete Instructions*, pp. 329–347.

Instruction texts but with this difference—it lacks any overt glorification of a professional elite.[39] Our text, Prov 22:17–24:22, casts no aspersions on promotion (22:29), but also, like *Amenemope*, warns against 'wearing yourself out to get rich'(23:4). The discipling goal is then expressed as follows:

> My son, if your heart is wise,
>   my heart too will be glad.
> My soul will rejoice
>   when your lips speak what is right.
>
> Hear, my son, and be wise,
>   and direct your mind in the way.
>
> The father of the righteous will greatly rejoice;
>   he who begets a wise son will be glad in him.
>
> My son, give me your heart,
>   and let your eyes observe my ways.[40]

(Prov 23:15f,19,24,26)

The Israelite instructor refers to father–son reduplication (wise father, 'wise son', v.24) and points to his ways, as well as his sayings, as a model(v.26).[41] The integrity of the teacher was integral to the Instruction genre. The wise could not tolerate disparity between tongue and deed, between what was said and

---

[39] See the Middle Kingdom, early 2nd millennium *Satire on the Trades* (Khety for son Pepy)—*LAE*, pp.329–336 and the New Kingdom text offering the decidedly unspiritual incentive: 'Be a scribe, that your limbs may be smooth and your hands languid, that you may go out dressed in white, being exalted so that courtiers salute you' (Papyrus Chester Beatty IV, vo.4/3–6: cited by Williams, 'Scribal Training', p.218).

[40] Read 'Let your eyes observe (*tiṣornāh* from *nṣr*—'to keep, observe') my ways' with the ancient versions and suggested Massoretic reading, the Qere; the Kethib reading, has 'delight' (*rṣh*) but lacks the usual preposition— 'delight *in*'. Either verb fits our point. The instructor's 'ways' (*dᵉrākay*—'my ways') are held up as a model. Compare McKane's 'Take my life as a paradigm' (*Proverbs*, 390). NRSV ties the exhortation to the next lines, making it specific to the sexual immorality, which the instructor has shunned. But *kīy* (in NRSV 'for, because') is more likely the emphatic particle ('Yes, indeed, surely') introducing a separate exclamation: 'Indeed, a prostitute is a deep pit'. This would leave v.26 as a self-contained exhortation of general application, as REB suggests.

[41] Compare with this Prov 31 in its canonical form. The mother of Lemuel taught him about 'a woman who fears the LORD' (v.30), portraying her in a vivid vignette. To speak in such terms, Lemuel's mother had to identify with the good wife's values, including her lifestyle and fear of the LORD. Presumably, then, she modelled these values as well as teaching her son these poetic lines. Kitchen argues for the compositional unity of vv.1–9 with vv.10–31, as analogous to Type A sectioned Instruction texts, such as *Merikare* (*TB* 28, p.100f). Even if the juxtaposing of vv.10–31 with vv.1–9 is redactional rather than original, the canonical thrust of their present ordering supports the point being made.

what was thought, between what was taught and what was modelled.[42]

It is all the more ironical, then, that a truly momentous dissonance characterises Israel's Wisdom enterprise. It is the breakdown of the discipling model in the dissonance between Solomon, the founder model of the wise man in Israel, and Solomon the apostate. In two chapters (1 Kgs 10 and 11), Solomon moves from impressing the queen of Sheba as no other had to building idolatrous temples in Jerusalem. In the editor's eyes, Solomon progresses from renown to ignominy. In Wisdom terms, this is a massive loss of credibility. Whether Solomon's folly was the subject of discussion by Wisdom educators as well as by the editors of Kings, we can only guess. It certainly deserved to appear on the syllabus.[43]

The positive trajectory of discipling in the Wisdom tradition stretches from the book of Proverbs to the Epilogue of Qohelet.

> Besides being wise, the Teacher (Qohelet) also taught the people knowledge, weighing and studying and arranging many proverbs. The Teacher sought to find pleasing words, and he wrote words of truth plainly.
>
> (Ecc 12:9f)

This eulogy could be spoken only by someone who had imbibed deeply and appreciatively. If his pen continues in vv. 11–14, then he both sounds the familiar note of the Instruction spirituality and underlines its foundational quality:

---

[42] Compare the dissonance of heart and lips highlighted by Prov 26:24–26, and the lines of *Amenemope*:

> Do not speak falsely to a man,
> The god abhors it;
> Do not sever your heart from your tongue,
> That all your strivings may succeed.
> You will be weighty before the others,
> And secure in the hand of the god.
> God hates the falsifier of words,
> He greatly abhors the dissembler.
>
> (Chap. 10, 13:15–14:3; *AEL*, 154; *LAE*, 252f; *ANET*³, 423)

or the disparity of the act of careful weighing with the use of false weights (Prov 11:1, 20:10,23) and Chaps. 16 & 17 of Amenemope, invoking Thot, patron god of the scribe, as witness of false measurement (*AEL*, 156f; *LAE*, 256f; *ANET*³,423).

[43] It is ironical that the author of Qohelet seems to use Solomon in his opening autobiographical section as a persona for expressing his reflections on life's absurdity. We might see this as Solomon deconstructed.

The end of the matter; all has been heard. Fear God and keep his commandments; for this is the whole duty of Man.

(Ecc 12:13)

Beyond the Hebrew canon in the Wisdom tradition stands the figure of Jesus ben Sirach whose 51 chapters were translated by his grandson in the late 2nd century BC. Many topics reappear which were subject matter centuries earlier. Sirach expands the Instruction genre beyond admonitions and maxims with additional formal units and thematic blocks. There is the historical review of Israel's leaders, and there are prayers and hymnic pieces, reflections on creation, sin and death—unfortunately marred by appalling male gender bias against women. There are many references to 'the fear of the Lord', clustered together in Chaps 1 and 2, as well as scattered throughout the book. In some, but by no means all, of these 'fear of the Lord' sayings there is a strong association of wisdom, fear of the Lord and the Torah (developed further in Sirach 24).

All wisdom is the fear of the Lord,
    and in all wisdom there is the fulfilment of the law.

(Sir 19:20)

Whoever keeps the law controls his thoughts,
    and wisdom is the fulfilment of the fear of the Lord.

(Sir 21:11)[44]

Like his Egyptian predecessors, Sirach held out 'the council of the people', 'the public assembly' and 'the judge's seat' as reward for 'the wisdom of the scribe' (Sir 38:24, 33f). He gives a value to 'secularity' by commending the skill of artisans who 'keep stable the fabric of the world' and whose 'prayer is their trade'. Yet he reserves the study of Torah for the educated. It is preferable to secular spirituality, and thereby Sirach sounds a patronising note.

The attempt to link Wisdom Instruction with the professional classes, especially the court circle, the literati and the intelligentsia, has initiated vigorous debate. If the Instruction material in Proverbs was disseminated by the educationally elite, the urban well-to-do, professional scribes operating in the Jerusalem capital, associated with the court and machinery of state, including eminent figures like Shaphan, the secretary of state in Josiah's

---

[44] As we observed, the link of covenant, commandments and 'fear of the Lord' is already present in Deuteronomy and Psa 25. See Weinfeld, *Deuteronomy*, pp. 274–281 section 3. 'The Fear of the Lord' in particular, and more generally all of Part Three, pp. 244ff.

cabinet, then does this Wisdom material reflect an ideological bias and serve a self-legitimating purpose?[45]

JESUS AND WISDOM INSTRUCTION

If the charge of ideological bias in favour of hierarchy, of professionalism, of upward social mobility can be proven against Wisdom Instruction—as opposed to the educated professionals acting as its transmitters, and the proof of this charge is disputed, then Jesus reverses any class ethic attached to education in his clashes with the scribes, lawyers, Sadducees and Pharisees. The quality of his teaching remains an enigma to those who see him as 'Joseph's son' from Galilee (Lk 4:22).[46]

Recently, New Testament scholarship has examined the content and teaching style of Jesus in the light of Wisdom instruction. The technical field of Synoptic studies falls outside our interest here, but we note that Jesus' instruction of his disciples makes use of maxims and touches on motifs such as the fear of God, avoidance of hypocrisy, moral principles expressed in behaviour, as well as on poverty and riches, and the tongue, all characteristic of Wisdom Instruction.[47]

How consciously Jesus was modelling his teaching role as 'one greater than Solomon' on canonical Wisdom, we can only

---

[45] The issues of education, social status and power are inter-related, yet distinct. Academics today, especially theological teachers, would see themselves as financially and politically impoverished compared with top business men, particularly those at the top of multinational corporations. Social standing in the community and in state machinery do not correlate today. BW Kovacs, *'Is there a Class-Ethic in Proverbs?'* addresses the Testament Ethics (New York: Ktav) 1974, but his study excludes Prov 22:17–24:22. JD Pleins makes a good case for Wisdom literature's limited concerns compared to the poverty-exploitation link denounced by the Prophets, but he exaggerates the class distinction of Proverbs—'Poverty in the Social World of the Wise' *JSOT* 37 (1987) 61–78. The ideological questions need to be asked and Solomon's association with Wisdom makes this pressing—see W Brueggemann, 'The Social Significance of Solomon as a Patron of Wisdom', pp.117–132 in JG Gammie & LG Perdue (eds.), *The Sage in Israel and the Ancient Near East* (Winona Lake: Eisenbrauns) 1990. See too RN Whybray, 'The Sage in the Israelite Royal Court', pp.133–139.

[46] Likewise, his eloquent disciples, Peter and John, are puzzlingly 'uneducated and ordinary men' who have been 'companions of Jesus' (Acts 4:13).

[47] The strongly eschatological dimension to the Kingdom of God, especially the parables, so characteristic of Jesus' teaching, cautions against overemphasising parallels between Jesus and the Near Eastern teachers, besides any Christological consideration of his person. See RA Piper, *Wisdom in the Q—Tradition: the aphoristic teaching of Jesus*, SNTS 61 (Cambridge: CUP) 1989; the review in Chap. 1, pp.1–11 shows that the existence of schools as transmitters of maxims is debated for this period. BB Scott, 'Jesus as Sage: an innovating voice in common wisdom' adds another dimension by stressing that Jesus

speculate. A point that is worth making, though, is this: the process of discipling and reproducing himself in his followers, especially the inner circle of leadership, brings to a climax the Discipler role glimpsed through the Instruction texts. Whether in his attitude to money, children, and the poor, or in the footwashing expressing his style of leadership, Jesus modelled what he taught in all manner of ways.[48]

The spirituality of Wisdom culminates in a spirituality fulfilled and lived out by Jesus.

SUMMARY AND CONCLUSION

The collection of admonitions in Prov 22:17–24:22 seems ill suited to the syllabus of spirituality, at first glance. As a medium, it is culture-bound to a style of education long passed, and has been replaced by other modes of learning. On closer inspection, first impressions of obsolescence may prove misleading. This material presents an integrated spirituality that recognizes the many factors that shape us as individuals in our society. It offers a theological and ethical framework for its secular observations.

The dichotomies that plague Christian denominations and books on personal sanctification are not found in these maxims in Proverbs. Thus injustice, exploitation and oppression are as forcefully dealt with as drunkenness and sexual immorality. This contrasts with the division into other-worldly, and apolitical segments of the Christian church, on the one hand, and the politically conscientized on the other. In the twentieth century, these blocs were often openly hostile to each other.

Wisdom Instruction holds together 'fear of the Lord' at the core of one's being with the way in which one carries out one's job, the inward orientation with the outward behaviour. In its overlaps with Egyptian teachings, without surrendering Yahwism to an alternative religion, Hebrew Wisdom discloses a base in a common humanity and a sense of ethics that is vital to our pluralistic societies. By advocating moral discipline and eschewing upward social mobility for its own sake, canonical Instruction avoids promoting insidious class distinctions. The Wisdom instructor of Prov 22:17–24:22 works with the learner person to person, and works as mentor and confidential adviser on life more than as doctoral expert. The end goal is maturity and holistic wisdom, not information transfer. The spirituality comes through

---

subverts received wisdom—JG Gammie & LG Perdue (eds.), *The Sage in Israel and the Ancient Near East* (Winona Lake: Eisenbrauns) 1990, pp.399–415.

[48] See for instance, M Griffiths, *The Example of Jesus* (London: Hodder & Stoughton) 1985 and PT Chandapilla, *The Master Trainer*, 2nd ed. (Bombay:

integration of faith and life. Wisdom must be lived out as a down-to-earth spirituality within the detail of the mundane.

BIBLIOGRAPHY

H Blocher, 'The Fear of the Lord as the "Principle" of Wisdom' *TB* 28 (1977) 3–28.

L. Boström, *The God of the Sages: the portrayal of God in the book of Proverbs*, Coniectanea Biblica OT Series 29, (Stockholm:Almqvist & Wiksell) 1990.

W Brueggemann, 'The Social Significance of Solomon as a Patron of Wisdom', pp.117–132 in JG Gammie & LG Perdue (eds.), *The Sage in Israel and the Ancient Near East* (Winona Lake: Eisenbrauns) 1990.

PT Chandapilla, *The Master Trainer*, 2nd ed. (Bombay: Gospel Literature Service) 1982.

JG Gammie & LG Perdue (eds), *The Sage in Israel and the Ancient Near East* (Winona Lake: Eisenbrauns) 1990.

D Kidner, *Proverbs*, TOTC (London: Tyndale Press) 1964.

KA Kitchen, 'Proverbs and Wisdom Books of the Ancient Near East' *TB* 28 (1977) 69–114.

BW Kovacs , 'Is there a Class-Ethic in Proverbs?' pp.173–189 in JL Crenshaw & JT Willis (eds), *Essays in Old Testament Ethics* (New York: Ktav) 1974.

M Lichtheim, *Ancient Egyptian Literature, Vol.II The New Kingdom*, (Berkeley: Univ. California Press) 1976.

RE Murphy, 'The Religious Dimensions of Israelite Wisdom', , pp. 449–458 in PD Miller, PD Hanson, SD McBride (eds), *Ancient Israelite Religion: essays in honor of FM Cross* (Philadelphia: Fortress) 1987.

LG Perdue, 'The Social Character of Paraenesis and Paraenetic Literature', *Semeia* 50 (1990) 5–39.

JD Pleins, 'Poverty in the Social World of the Wise' *JSOT* 37 (1987) 61–78.

J Ruffle, 'The Teaching of Amenemope and its Connection with the Book of Proverbs', *TB* 28 (1977) 29–68.

WK Simpson, *The Literature of Ancient Egypt* (London:YUP) 1973.

G von Rad, *Wisdom in Israel* (London: SCM) 1972.

RN Whybray, *Wealth and Poverty in the Book of Proverbs*, JSOTS 99 (Sheffield: JSOT Press) 1990. 'The Sage in the Israelite Royal Court', pp.133–139 in JG Gammie & LG Perdue (eds.),

——, *The Sage in Israel and the Ancient Near East* (Winona Lake: Eisenbrauns) 1990.

RJ Williams, 'Scribal Training in Ancient Egypt', *JAOS* 92.2 (1972) 214–221.

FM Wilson, 'Sacred and Profane? The Yahwistic Redaction of Proverbs Reconsidered', pp.313–334 in KG Hoglund et al (eds), *The Listening Heart: essays in Wisdom and the Psalms in honor of RE Murphy*, JSOTS 58 (Sheffield: JSOT Press) 1987.

Gospel Literature Service) 1982, especially Chap. 8, pp.39–45, 'The Quality of Practicality'.

[7]

Facing Mundane Reality
Qohelet's Spirituality

BACKGROUND, ASSUMPTIONS AND FOCUS

In this chapter, we shall move on from listening to the reassuring tones of the mentor in Proverbs to listen to another Wisdom teacher's voice. Where the Instruction material of Proverbs 22:17–24:22 was situation-specific in addressing the future of a young man with prospects, the book of Ecclesiastes ranges over the whole of life. If the importance of the mentor role emerges from Proverbs in a fatherly manner, then the tone of this teacher is anything but reassuring. Mentor he may be, and young men may be the target of some of his admonition, yet he is tormentor as much as mentor, tormentor of those with a comfortably assured handle on life. His role turns out to be more like that of a provocative seminar leader probing and prodding participants to examine their assumptions, forcing them to think by confronting them with ambiguities, reversed statements, uncorrelated facts and unanswerable questions. Though he admonishes like Proverbs—'Remember your Creator in the days of your youth . . .' (12:1)—and enforces this by spelling out what lies ahead, he also throws in epistemology: 'Who knows whether the human spirit goes upward . . . ?' (3:21).

By choice, Qohelet omits much from his discussion, including nearly all the distinctives of Israel's covenant experience. Yet, like Proverbs, he includes many observations of life. He conflicts with the Wisdom tradition of Proverbs, yet is commended by an editor from the Wisdom school for 'weighing and studying and arranging many proverbs', for being wise and teaching the people knowledge (12:9). Qohelet is disturbing. Is he an orthodox Yahwist or a heretic? Is he Solomon or himself? He is intuitively identifiable as our contemporary, and yet he is pre-Christian. Qohelet seems full of contradictions. He finds life absurd, yet he holds onto the reality of God.

Qohelet has a sense of the presence of God, of a kind. 'God is in heaven and you upon earth; therefore let your words be few' (5:2b). He says, 'Never be rash with your mouth, nor let your heart be quick to utter a word before God' (5:2a), but after reading his book we might wonder whether his reflections on life comply with his own dictum. His are certainly not hasty words, but what of his conclusion that everything is 'totally absurd'? This conclusion could lead us straight to atheism, or, if we draw back from the brink, to an attenuated deism.

Qohelet is not ready to withdraw from traditional cultic rituals and stop attending the Temple (5:1,4), though he is cautious about worship, preferring 'to draw near to listen' than to present 'the sacrifice offered by fools'(5:1).[1] God seems to operate at a distance ('in heaven'), yet also to observe life 'under the sun' acutely—God takes note of the vows individuals make and holds them accountable for their words (5:4–7).

Qohelet did not take the route of absurdity to atheism. In fact, he does not always follow his own logic. Against his dictum that 'everything is absurd', and without evidence from life, Qohelet hangs onto an undefined conviction that God will judge: 'I said in my heart, God will judge the righteous and the wicked, for he has appointed a time for every matter, and for every work' (3:17). His belief in God's judgment clashes with his observations of how well the wicked are getting on in this life. Instead of postulating a judgment after death, he confines his theology of the moral order and the judgement of God to a this-worldly and observable existence.[2] Long before the 'hippy' era of the 1960s, Qohelet tells young men to 'do their own thing': 'follow the inclination of your heart and the desire of your eyes' (11:9). Yet he follows this up with, 'Know that for all these things God will bring you into judgment.' When and how, this mentor does not explain. In full

---

[1] He is aware that 'the wicked . . . used to go in and out of the holy place, and were praised in the city . . . '(8:10), so he does not measure spirituality by participation in cultic activity, any more than the prophets did.

[2] That this judgment means premature death is clear both from Qohelet's questioning that anything follows death and from his statements in 8:13—'but it will not be well with the wicked, neither will they prolong their days like a shadow, because they do not stand in fear before God'. Compare 7:17—'why should you die before your time?', admonishing against folly and wickedness. JL Crenshaw's statement that 'it was Qohelet's special burden to be unable to believe in divine justice' eliminates a tension in the book, a tension that we must retain as a characteristic of this work (Crenshaw, *A Whirlpool of Torment: Israelite traditions of God as an oppressive presence*, OBT 13, Philadelphia: Fortress, 1984, p.91).

accord with mainline Yahwism, he admonishes his reader with a central tenet of canonical spirituality—'fear God'(5:7b).[3]

That life is 'utterly absurd' is Qohelet's considered viewpoint more than a passing mood. Qohelet looks at the evidence ('I saw . . .', 'I said in my heart . . .') before coming to conclusions. Yet he omits the evidence Israelites found most vital to discerning God's overall purposes, namely, the stories of Abraham and David, the Exodus and the Promised Land. In Qohelet's work there are no miracles, no Passover, no covenants, no promises, no angel of the Lord, no prophecy, no apocalyptic and no messianic hope.[4] In one sense, this is no surprise since Wisdom literature is a distinct genre and has its own starting point and focus. Qohelet belongs to this Wisdom tradition, and yet places far more weight on his personal observations and experience than on received wisdom.[5]

Because of this personal empiricism, we might choose to discard certain of his conclusions because they are based on an experience that is too narrow, or that does not match our own.[6]

---

[3] See 3:14, 5:7, 7:18, 8:12f for phrases including 'fear' of God. The attitude of reverent respectfulness is even more pervasive. The 'fear God' of the epilogue (12:13) accords with Qohelet's orientation, but was written by a disciple of his. Crenshaw, who has written extensively on Old Testament Wisdom traditions, thinks that for Qohelet fear of God 'takes on a wholly new meaning . . . dread, that is, terror before the divine' (*Whirlpool*, p.83). This is unconvincing on two counts—'a wholly new meaning' is inherently improbable within a tradition and Qohelet is certainly more considered than emotional. The nuance of a guarded, prudent recognition of God's reality and the reality of judgment fits the tenor of the book far better. Neither is Qohelet's deity 'wholly indifferent to what transpires under· the sun' (p.83)—he is not indifferent to foolish and unfulfilled vows, for instance (5:4–6).

[4] Jerusalem, the Temple and the Davidic monarchy appear—but these are stage-props. The covenant with David is not referred to, nor David's story and his passionate relationship with God.

[5] There is a helpful discussion of the Wisdom tradition in J Goldingay, *Theological Diversity and the Authority of the Old Testament* (Grand Rapids: Eerdmans) 1987, pp.206ff in which he speaks in terms of the polarity, interplay and dialogue within Wisdom, between Wisdom and Salvation History, and between Genesis Creation and 'life east of Eden'(p.225).

> Ecclesiastes is Job without the theophany. The author is both more rigorous in (and earns more admiration for) his unremitting insistence on a verifiable worldview, and in the end more wrong (if taken as the whole truth). (p.209)

[6] When Qohelet records his experience of human unreliability in 7:23ff, we may discard it by contrasting it with our own experience of dependable friends. Yet we will not discard his general conclusion—'God made human beings straightforward, but they have devised many schemes' (7:29)—unless we also wish to discard Creation and Fall doctrines, or by some other means exculpate human deceitfulness. However, the autobiographical summary—'One man among a thousand I found, but a woman among all these I have not found'

Qohelet offers global statements based on personal observation, a curious meld of subjective and objective elements, of assured results and lingering tensions. For some readers the tension in Qohelet will be the tension of utter inconsistency, for others the tension of faith. As a Hebrew monotheist, Qohelet is not ready to contemplate atheism or agnosticism. His theology of life turns out to be a theology of the mundane pushed to its Hebrew limits.

His focus on the mundane has corollaries. The mundane excludes the occult, the paranormal and the charismatic. An immediate plus factor for us is Qohelet's scientific modernity. Some subjects fall outside his chosen field of operation. If he has not met a Hebrew prophet or visionary to interpret the world of his experience, neither is he looking to the alternative Near Eastern pseudo-science of divination as a clue to destiny, fate and the doings of the deity.[7] Given today's resurgence of astrology, a technique that began life as part of the repertoire of Mesopotamian divination and a subordinate one to liver divination at that, Qohelet's ideas about fate and destiny are refreshingly straightforward: 'time and chance happen to them all' (9:11b). Near Eastern divination, by contrast, represents an impressive, but entirely false, correlation of empirical data. Divination correlated liver colorations or planetary positions with political events.[8]

(7:28b)—registers with us as disparaging to women. Probably the author speaks through the mask of Solomon and there is irony in the passage. See M Fox, *Qohelet and His Contradictions*, JSOTS 71, Bible and Literature 18, (Sheffield: Almond Press) 1989, pp.236–238, 241–243 and Excursus III, Author and Speaker; the Epilogue, pp.311ff. RE Murphy seeks to exonerate Qohelet from misogyny, but only to concede to the obscurity of the passage (*Ecclesiastes*, Word, 1992, pp. 74ff). If the misogyny is more probable, coming from 'Solomon', it lies in typical tension with Qohelet's advocating enjoying life 'with the wife whom you love' (9:9) and seeking the companionship which applies to a marriage partner—'if two lie together, they keep warm; but how can one keep warm alone?' (4:11).

[7] The Babylonians produced both astronomical and astrological texts, the latter contributing the signs of the zodiac and personal horoscopes to Greek astrology and modern variants. The Astronomical texts are the precursors of exact science, involving observations and mathematics—see A. Aaboe, 'Babylonian Mathematics, Astrology, and Astronomy', Chap.28b in J. Boardman et al(eds), *The Cambridge Ancient History, III. Part 2*, CUP, 1991. On Divination and omens, see HWF Saggs, *The Encounter with the Divine in Mesopotamia and Israel* (London: Athlone) 1978, Chap.5, pp.125–152 'Communication with the Divine'. On the place of omen texts within the scribal curriculum, see Erica Reiner, 'First-Millennium Babylonian Literature', Chap. 28c in *CAH III.2*.

[8] Oracular consultations yielding Yes! and No! answers are a little different. In this category of divination, Israel had its Urim and Thummim, and Proverbs allows an interplay between human efforts to obtain divine guidance and Yahweh's activity in the process—'The lot is cast into the lap, but the decision is the LORD's alone' (Prov 16:33). Yet the Urim and Thummim disappear from

By contrast with divination, Qohelet found correlations between events and the divine will impossible to discern. Indeed, he saw no consistent pattern to life, apart from ageing and death. He reports this perspective as a matter of fact. His refrain 'absurd', 'utterly absurd', 'chasing after wind' constitutes a conclusion more than an emotion-laden outburst in a psalm of Lament. Elements of his outlook may happen to mirror our mood when we feel depressed, cynical and alienated, but we should not dismiss Qohelet's thought as merely the product of a mood, a low ebb in his life.

Qohelet lived with the ambiguity of a received faith and his personal observations. Certainly he left tensions in his writing that reflect tensions in his mind.[9] Certainly his writing evokes our uncertainties. But the main question for our discussion now is this—'Is there a spirituality to be found in this experience of tension?'

The short answer as to wherein lies Qohelet's spirituality is his realism. Despite attempts to read Qohelet as despairing, or as an embittered sceptic, or as a hedonist, a reading that retains Qohelet's tensions points towards a spirituality achieved by grappling with mundane experience with realism.[10] It is Qohelet's realism that calls into question the validity of certain of the received Wisdom's truths, and this is our starting point, the testing of received truths.

Israelite religion whereas astrology develops and spreads from the Assyrian empire of the 7th century BC onwards.

[9] Many modern commentators resist the attempt to resolve contradictions by excising verses, nor do they minimise tensions in the interests of logical coherence or a more consistent radicalism. Fox admits that 'there is a tremendous interpretive pressure to raise the valleys and lower the hills' rather than 'describe the territory with all its bumps and clefts' (*Qohelet and His Contradictions*, p.28). For all this, approaches to the contradiction element differ. Compare Fox's review of Loader's polarity theory (JA Loader, *Polar Structures in the Book of Qohelet*, BZAW 152, Berlin: Walter de Gruyter, 1979) and J Ellul's approach in *Reason for Being* (Grand Rapids: Eerdmans) 1990.

[10] Overall assessment depends on identifying core and peripheral statements, whether key motif or secondary motif, and in the way that the tensions between motifs are handled. In a 1982 article, RN Whybray focused on the seven passages which advocate enjoyment of mundane pleasures—food, drink, work and wife (2:24a, 3:12, 3:22a, 5:17, 8:15a, 9:7–9a, 11:7—12:1a: 'Qohelet,Preacher of Joy' *JSOT* 23 (1982) 87–98. In commentaries written seven years later, he does not minimize these 'enjoy life' passages but sets them in an overview of Qohelet's thought which allows for 'the unsystematic and sometimes contradictory character of his thought'—*Ecclesiastes*, OT Guides (Sheffield: JSOT Press) 1989, Chap. 5, pp.63–83 'Qohelet's Characteristic Ideas' and *Ecclesiastes*, New Century Bible, (Grand Rapids: Eerdmans/London: Marshall,Morgan & Scott) 1989, 'E. Thought', p.22ff.

TESTING THE REALITY OF RECEIVED TRUTHS

First we need to go back to Prov 22:17–24:22 and select a couple of maxims so as to examine their validity, before considering Qohelet's own assertions. This will give us a feel for how far a maxim can be stretched to fit life and whether Qohelet is questioning the applicability of a maxim, or rejecting the maxim's validity altogether.

In the view of the Wisdom instructor of Prov 22:17–24:22, self-induced poverty and premature death were two evils that wisdom can avert. Drunkards and gluttons squander their money, incapacitate themselves, and end up in rags (Prov 23:19–21). The truth of this maxim contributes to the Prodigal Son parable told by Jesus. Excess leads to want. The maxim makes no claim to explain all poverty as self-induced poverty. Now the dissolute do not always come to grief in a spectacular manner, but the act-consequence sequence of this maxim is confirmed often enough by stories in today's tabloids.

Yet a scrutiny of other maxims calls into question not so much the field of their applicability as their fundamental reality. This question mark hangs over those maxims which speak of God's active involvement in social life. Just when Liberation Theology has put the issues of justice and oppression on to the theological agenda and proclaimed a God who sides with the poor, the question of empirical evidence for this version of 'The God who Acts' thrusts itself forward with renewed insistence.[11]

If Wisdom instruction in Proverbs proclaimed a God who acts in society, then it must face the follow-up in Qohelet, where substantiation for this belief is called for. As we saw, Proverbs, like the Prophets, does speak of a God who actively intervenes against oppressors:

> Do not rob the poor because they are poor,
>   or crush the afflicted at the gate;
> for the LORD pleads their cause
>   and despoils of life those who despoil them.
>
> (Prov 22:22f)

> Do not remove an ancient landmark
>   or encroach on the field of orphans,

---

[11] GE Wright, *God who Acts: biblical theology as recital*, SBT8 (SCM), 1952. The title reflects the polemic of the biblical theology movement on behalf of Old Testament faith, a polemic for genuine revelation in history against spurious claims of Near Eastern mythological religions and against revelation being equated with the propositional formulations of systematic theology. Liberation Theology likewise champions the Exodus paradigm and looks to a new phase of Salvation History to be worked out in today's world.

for their redeemer is strong;
  he will plead their cause against you.

(Prov 23:10f)

Qohelet finds no evidence for this.

Again I saw all the oppressions that are practised under the sun. Look, the tears of the oppressed—with no one to comfort them! On the side of the oppressors there was power—with no one to comfort them. And I thought the dead who have already died more fortunate than the living, who are still alive; but better than both is the one who has not yet been, and has not seen the evil deeds that are done under the sun.

(Ecc 4:1–3)

In my *hebel* life I have seen everything; there are righteous people who perish in their righteousness, and there are wicked people who prolong their life in their evil-doing.

(Ecc 7:15)

There is a *hebel* that takes place on earth, that there are righteous people who are treated according to the conduct of the wicked, and there are wicked people who are treated according to the conduct of the righteous. I said that this also is *hebel*.

(Ecc 8:14)

There are now two issues to discuss relating to these quotations from Qohelet; firstly, how to understand *hebel*, because it is a key to his thought, and secondly, whether to agree with his conclusion.

The NRSV translation 'vain, vanity' (replaced in our quotations by the Hebrew *hebel*) is quaint English, misleading and quite inadequate to convey the protest that Qohelet is making. The whole book is framed by 'Vanity of vanities! All is vanity' in 1:2 and 12:8.[12] A viable hermeneutic looks for a coherent translation of this opening and closing phrase, one that eliminates as many extraneous nuances of the Hebrew word *hebel* as possible in favour of a centred semantic field or core of meaning that embraces most

---

[12] In Hebrew *hᵉbēl hᵉbālim hakkōl hābel*. The first phrase in Hebrew ('vanity of vanities' in the AV) is a way of expressing the superlative. Just as 'king of kings' means 'the supreme king, the king par excellence', so the Construct chain of singular and plural noun means the superlative and absolute instance of this phenomenon. If we choose to translate the noun *hebel* as 'absurdity' then the Construct phrase would come out as 'utter absurdity'. In English, an adjectival phrase yields a more idiomatic translation, hence 'utterly absurd'. The meaning of *hebel*, and especially this Construct phrase which Qohelet seems to have coined himself, must, of course, be determined by the way Qohelet uses it in the book. It would be no translation at all to render the phrase 'vapour of vapours'. This is a clear example of the process of translation itself as a hermeneutical exercise.

or all of the occurrences in Qohelet. Translations such as 'transient, ephemeral', 'futile, pointless', 'meaningless', 'incomprehensible' and the like fit some individual verses well but fail to frame them inside Qohelet's scheme.[13] 'Absurd, absurdity' seems as close a fit to the overall spirit of the book as possible.

In the three quotations given above, it is 'absurd', that is, it is deeply incongruous and twisted, that evil-doers flourish and the righteous perish. In Qohelet's terms, things that are 'absurd' may also be 'a great evil'.[14] They are out of kilter, they offend a sense of rightness. 'Utterly absurd, everything is absurd' captures the thrust of Qohelet. It is an instinctive protest against the way things are.

Secondly, we have to agree with Qohelet's observations in the three passages cited (4:1ff, 7:15, 8:14). It appears to be as true in our times as in his. The evidence, as we look around, is that no act of God rescues the oppressed. Indeed, 'act of God' is a phrase that has taken an ironical twist. It now does duty for earthquakes and droughts that kill thousands. We have no wish to label these disasters as God's intervention. They do, however, underline the non-intervention of God, but reverting to oppression, poverty and the intervention of God, what do we observe? Outside the theatres of war and revolution, death comes to the poor and oppressed before their time without divine intervention. Reporting this today, we might speak more about causality, about connecting links, than Wisdom literature does, adding more layers of cause-effect, act-consequence to the characterisation of life than

---

[13] REB 'empty, emptiness' misses it; NIV 'meaningless' is much better. See M Fox 'The Meaning of Hebel for Qohelet' *JBL* 105/3 (1986) 409–427 and *Qohelet and His Contradictions*, Chap 1. Fox allows that 'ephemeral' fits some passages well (3:19, 11:10, 6:12, 7:15, 9:9) and that context-sensitive approaches are usually correct, but this is overridden by the thematic declaration and formulaic character of the *hebel* sayings. 'The *hebel leitmotif* disintegrates if the word is assigned several different meanings ' when 'there is a single quality that is an attribute of the world . . . manifest in the particular *hᵃbalim*' (p.36). RE Murphy sticks to 'Vanity of vanities' in his translation for a paradoxical reason: ' "vanity" is certainly not the best rendering, but I am using it as a code word in the translation in order to call attention to *hebel* as it occurs in the book' (*Ecclesiastes*, WBC 23, Dallas: Word, 1992, p.lix).

[14] Other phrases support the badness of *hebel* and are used in conjunction with it. There are phrases with *rāʿ* and *rāʿāh*, something bad, a misfortune, an evil: 'an unhappy business' (*ʿinyan rāʿ*, 1:13), 'a great evil' (*rāʿāh rabbāh*, 2:21), 'an unhappy business' (*ʿinyan rāʿ*, 4:8), 'grievous ill' (*ʿinyan rāʿ*, 5:13), 'an evil' (*rāʿāh*, 6:1), 'a grievous ill' (*hᵒliy rā*, 6:2), 'an evil' (*rāʿ*, 9:3) in NRSV. There is *rᵉʿūt rūaḥ* and *raʿyōn rūaḥ*, 'a chasing after wind' (1:14, 2:11,17,26 4:4,6 6:9 and 1:17, 4:16). This may be 'futile' or 'pointless' as an activity, but the full impact of 'chasing after wind' includes the frustration or vexation to the spirit which this futile exercise produces (see Fox, p. 48f).

do the brief Wisdom maxims. For instance, we would instinctively want to spell out the way that premature death is linked to oppression, poverty and disease.

Poverty is inevitably linked to disease—by malnutrition, lack of clean water and inadequate health care, including the inoculation of children. Poverty means high infant mortality rates and low adult life expectancy. Death from poverty is premature and avoidable death when deaths result from neglect, injustice, exploitation and oppression, in other words when the poverty is exacerbated by or directly results from ideologies, corruption or mismanagement by those in power. Landlessness, low wages, inadequate housing, disadvantaged education, racial, tribal and gender discrimination, and minimal legal rights, including lack of a meaningful vote, may be some of the mechanisms by which poverty is perpetuated. God's intervention to halt this perpetuation of poverty and bring its perpetrators to book is not discernible in our world.

Wisdom instruction indicts corrupt practices by officials who rob the vulnerable of their land and use the law to oppress (Prov 22:22f, 23:10f). Qohelet would not disagree with this indictment in Proverbs, he would not contest the oppression-impoverishment nexus, but Qohelet cannot see Yahweh as the kinsman protector (the *gōʾēl*) intervening to redress matters. We too see the oppression of the poor, but do we see God 'despoiling of life those who despoil them' (22:23b)? Proverbs and Qohelet share a realism about corrupt practices going on in Israelite society. Proverbs expects a divine response. Qohelet wishes for it as well, but does not observe it.

Qohelet's quest for realism devolves on to us. What do we accept as evidence for God's involvement? Is the statement that 'Yahweh . . . will despoil of life' those who despoil the oppressed an empirical statement? Can it be falsified? What constitutes evidence for divine intervention, for retributive justice, in our world today? No deaths of the first-born of Egypt, no plagues or pillars of fire mark God's intervention today. Indeed it is hard to adduce anything in support of the statements quoted from Proverbs, if we wish to speak of God's personal intervention against oppressors. Perhaps there are stories that oppressed individuals could tell, but these are outweighed by the scale of oppression.

Whether we look at the slave trade of previous centuries, or look at the twentieth century, reigns of terror have decimated whole populations, and atrocities on a national scale continue unabated. Victims of the oppressive policies of Hitler, Stalin and Mao run into millions, whether they died by violence or by starvation or in gas chambers. Amnesty International is hard pressed to keep track of the thousands of 'the disappeared', the tortured and the detained of this generation. More information through the media only means less evidence for preventative or retributive divine intervention in today's world.

Christians escape from the horrors of a non-interventionist theology only by abandoning hope for a this-worldly moral order superintended by an intervening God in favour of a judgment after death. The *sheol* of Proverbs is replaced by Heaven and Hell. Premature death is compensated for by the hope of eternal life. If Yahweh no longer acts against oppressors in the here and now (and in Qohelet's perspective he does not), he will hereafter. Justice and judgment are deferred. God's intervention, though not necessarily all his involvement in the world, is for Christians focused in the *parousia*.

Of course, this way of looking at divine judgment must be evaluated within the context of the whole of New Testament theology. According to the New Testament, the focus for God's involvement after the Ascension is the Spirit and the church. Where the Old Testament looks to politics, history and the nations, interpreted by the prophets, as the arena of God's activity, the New Testament looks to the Kingdom of God, a domain that lacks territorial and national boundaries. Prior to the *parousia*, individual conviction of sin and conversion are emphasized as the positive on-going evidence for God's intervention in human lives, along with healings and exorcisms, rather than judgments on oppressors.

It is true that Yahweh's concern for the oppressed can be mediated through human agency. Indeed, this is a perspective that is found in Prov 24:11 where it speaks to the young men of 'rescuing those taken away to death, those who go staggering to the slaughter.' As well as this perspective on responsibility, Wisdom instruction conscientizes by its very admonitions against oppression. Yet in Old Testament theology, the judgment of God is not entirely reducible to social action by the courts, the king and administrators, though Torah, prophets and sages do indeed expect the machinery of the state to defend the vulnerable and to bring justice.[15] Fire and brimstone from heaven, the outbreak of plagues, angelic visitations to rescue victims or strike down

---

[15] Psa 72 is a particularly strong statement of the royal ideal.

> May he defend the cause of the poor of the people,
> give deliverance to the needy,
> and crush the oppressor.
> For he delivers the needy when they call,
> the poor and those who have no helper.
> He has pity on the weak and the needy,

oppressors do not happen in Qohelet's world. Nor do they appear to in ours.

All this means that Qohelet has spoken with an undeniable realism about the way things are in our experience. We cannot see God intervening in history to redress moral wrongs or to avert premature death. Oppression and corruption continue in politics as ever, but without Jeremiah to announce an invasion and exile as punishment. The poor are pawns of those wielding power, without a Rescuer. This brings a spirituality of realism to bear on life. We call it realism because it is not cynicism or indifference. Qohelet has not abandoned his wish that things should be otherwise. Against the flow of his own observations, he has held on to a hope of this-worldly judgment. He has held on to his moral categories of 'wicked' and 'righteous'. He has registered the tears and the absence of comfort as scandalous. To record oppression without redress, to characterize the situation as *hebel*, as 'absurd', as 'a grievous evil', is to assume and believe that the world *should* be otherwise.

Behind Qohelet's realism about the way things are lies the ought-to-be of moral evaluation. This is a transposable perspective. Not only theologians, but our contemporary societies have to deal with the *is*, the *is not* and the *ought to be* factors. Think only of racism. We read the pronouncements of social workers, psychologists, educators, criminologists, lawyers, politicians, international aid agencies and the United Nations Security Council against it. They are grappling with the seemingly intractable feature of racial and social animosity. Without a moral norm or ideal for the way that multi-ethnic, national or urban society should function, they would be unable to comment. Racism and ethnic discrimination are 'absurd', yet characteristic of our world. A spirituality will work with this reality in ourselves, in our Christian communities and in the world without expecting God to change it by direct intervention.

Qohelet is not an atheistic existentialist who decides that life is meaningless and that the only meaning it has is the meaning that we arbitrarily assign to it. On the other hand, it will not be easy for triumphalistic Christians to accept Qohelet's findings, to accept that the world is as bad as it is, that human wickedness is not restrained, and that 'there are righteous people who perish in their righteousness' (Ecc 7:15) without explanation. Were we to repress Qohelet's report of the way things are, we would be

---

and saves the lives of the needy.
From oppression and violence he redeems their life;
and precious is their blood in his sight.

(Psa 72:4, 12–14)

duplicating the suppression of independent journalism by tyrannical regimes. The spirituality of realism involves facing the fact of life's lack of moral justice without surrendering the fear of the LORD. If we care, this will create real tensions within us, as it did for Qohelet.

THE REALITY OF LIMITED KNOWLEDGE

The next great realism of Qohelet is his perception of the limits of human knowledge. These limits take several forms. One is the limit of predictability. Can the future be predicted? Of course, this question is of practical, not theoretical, concern because it has a bearing on how things turn out, on human plans. Agriculture exhibits an interplay between predictability and unpredictability that is still with us. We know the mathematical predictability of solar cycles and can measure the spin of the earth by seconds. Tide tables and navigation are two practical results of this predictability being understood and put to work. Yet weather forecasting that impinges on living in a practical way is not and cannot be based on mathematical formulae that yield assured results. Weather systems are subject to the perturbability that marks fundamentally unpredictable, random events, even though some statistical patterns may be discerned. Qohelet comments on one form of unpredictability as follows:

> In the morning sow your seed, and at evening do not let your hands be idle; for you do not know which will prosper, this or that, or whether both alike will be good.
>
> (Ecc 11:6)

This kind of unpredictability is not disconcerting for Qohelet because there is a practical approach—'go ahead'. The directive to stop dithering and act follows on from the wry remark that 'Whoever observes the wind will not sow; and whoever regards the clouds will not reap' (11:4). But between v.4 and v.6, there is a different level of limited knowledge:

> Just as you do not know how the breath comes to the bones in the mother's womb, so you do not know the work of God, who makes everything.
>
> (11:5)

Advances in embryology scarcely refute this observation because Qohelet selects it as one sample of 'the work of God'. The embryo was not directly observable in Qohelet's day, so this example serves his purpose well. There are still many things that cannot be observed or measured or quantified or rendered explicable, though these days they are not so likely to fall within the field of microbiology in particular or science in general. There remain imponderables. The degree to which the future is determined by the present is a case in point.

Qohelet takes his reflections further than the natural occurrences of fetal development and the weather. He posits a limit to human knowledge that is built into life by God himself and one that we will never succeed in bypassing. Events will happen as God sees appropriate, but we will never comprehend God's activity:

> He has made everything suitable for its time; moreover he has put a sense of past and future into their minds, yet they cannot find out what God has done from the beginning to the end.
>
> (Ecc 3:11)[16]

> When I applied my mind to know wisdom, and to see the business that is done on earth, how one's eyes see sleep neither day nor night, then I saw all the work of God, that no one can find out what is happening under the sun. However much they may toil in seeking, they will not find it out; even though those who are wise claim to know, they cannot find it out.
>
> (Ecc 8:16f)

When we inquire what it is exactly that Qohelet wants to pin down, the answer seems to be the connection between present action and future results. Qohelet sees no pattern, that is, no moral order.[17] 'What happens afterwards' in an individual's life cannot be predicted.[18] The outcome seems random.

---

[16] The best translation of Hebrew ʿōlām—'all time, for ever' in this context is difficult. RSV 'eternity' is replaced by 'a sense of past and future' by NRSV to retain the this-worldly horizon of Qohelet; REB offers the same solution—'a sense of time past and future'; Murphy opts for 'duration' in contrast to ʿēt 'time'. Fox emends ʿōlām to ʿāmal—'toil, distress', supposing a shift of consonant in the copying process (*Qohelet*, p.194), but this is speculative and not wholly persuasive.

[17] See Fox, *Qohelet and his Contradictions*, chap 4 'Justice and Theodicy' for a good discussion of the tensions involved in holding onto a sense of moral order.

> Underlying Qohelet's hebel-judgments is an assumption that actions should invariably produce appropriate consequences . . . Qohelet believes in the rule of divine justice. That is why he does not merely resign himself to injustice. He is shocked by it: it clashes with his belief that the world must work equitably . . .'Everything is absurd' is finally a complaint against God . . . (p.47)

[18] The Hebrew word ʾaḥᵃrāyw—'his afterwards' is used in 3:22, 6:12, 7:14,10:14. It speaks of the future as the outcome or 'afterwards' of the present.

> Again I saw that under the sun the race is not to the swift, nor the battle to the strong, nor bread to the wise, nor riches to the intelligent, nor favour to the skilful; but time and chance happen to them all.
>
> (Ecc 9:11)

However often the prize may go to the deserving, disconcerting exceptions prove that there is no rule. Things do not work out as expected, but appear to be random. What happens happens. 'Time' and 'chance' are not so much forces operating contrary to the will of God as 'happenstance', simply the way things are.

Now this observation appears to hold true when we test it against modern life. Even though data can yield up some pattern of probability when statistical methods are applied, the individual instance is unpredictable. Deaths by road accident per annum are predictable statistically, yet each particular accident is exactly that, an accident, unplanned and unpredictable. Medical statistics and epidemiology disclose patterns of disease with quite a high degree of predictability for a population, but cannot predict a person's death by cancer or the course of an HIV infection, even for an individual in a high risk group. 'No man knows when his hour will come' (Ecc 9:12a REB). The unexpected disaster happens, catching us out like animals that do not notice the hidden net or snare awaiting them (9:12b).

Whether we emphasize the sovereignty of God with Calvin or emphasize human choice with Arminius, we all experience life's contingencies as unpredictable. When close friends have been killed or maimed in meaningless accidents, this sad fact of life's unforeseen tragedy shifts from a peripheral awareness to a theological problem. We struggle to find meaningful words to utter face to face, or to God, when the unpredictable touch of disease or accident fingers a fellow-member in our fellowship. 'Time and chance' operate now, as then.

THE REALITY OF DEATH

Death itself is the most certain outcome of a person's life, and it comes to all regardless. Regardless, that is, of the way they have lived, regardless of distinctions between good and bad.

> the same fate comes to all, to the righteous and the wicked, to the good and the evil, to the clean and the unclean, to those who sacrifice and those who do not sacrifice. As are the good, so are the sinners; those who swear are like those who shun an oath. This is an evil in all that happens under the sun, that the same fate comes to everyone.
>
> (Ecc 9:2f)

The absurdity is palpable and exasperates Qohelet, for in his view this kind of levelling by death makes a mockery of righteousness.

The meaning of being devout, of spirituality itself, is called into question by this result. Qohelet is not a neutral observer of death as a universal event. He protests against this 'single event' that happens to all; it is, in his language, 'an evil'.[19]

Death is our undoing in a factual way—'the dust returns to the earth as it was, and the breath returns to God who gave it' (Ecc 12:7). This is Qohelet's last statement before his concluding summary that everything is utterly absurd (v.8). There is no warrant for interpreting the return of the 'breath' or 'spirit' to God as a belief in afterlife, a survival in disembodied form. Qohelet believes in creation from dust and divine breath, as the Genesis stories tell it, and he lives in the awareness of the divine pronouncement 'dust you are, and to dust you shall return' (Gen 3:19, cf. 2:7). He also shares the perspective of the Flood story which describes the death of humans and animals as one event.[20] Yet this orthodox understanding of human and animal life in its origin and in its transience oppresses him.

> I said in my heart with regard to human beings that God is testing them to show that they are but animals. For the fate of humans and the fate of animals is the same; as one dies, so dies the other. They all have the same breath, and humans have no advantage over the animals; for all is *hebel*. All go to one place; all are from the dust, and all turn to dust again. Who knows whether the human spirit goes upward and the spirit of animals goes downward to the earth?
>
> (Ecc 3:18–21)

He comes down on the side of 'one breath', one death. Biology reigns. As far as human death goes, it is a case of one race, 'one

---

[19] The word translated as 'fate' (NRSV, REB) or 'destiny' (NIV) can too readily accrue transcendent powers in the way that Death did in polytheistic religions. In 2nd millennium Ugarit, death was personified as the god Mot with gaping jaws. In Ecclesiastes, death is not personified, nor is 'fate'. The noun *miqreh*, derived from the verb *qārāh*—'to happen, come', refers to what happens. Death is an event, an occurrence, a happening—rather than a mythological power. See Ecc 3:18–21 for *miqreh* applied to animals and humans alike. Death is *miqreh 'eḥād*—'one event, the same occurrence' (3:19).

[20] 'All flesh died . . . everything on dry land in whose nostrils was the breath of life died' (Gen 7:21,22). The Hebrew *nišmat-rūaḥ ḥayyīm bᵉʾappāyw* ('in whose nostrils was the breath of life', v.22) is factual physical language, based on the connection of breathing through the nostrils with being alive. The Genesis author presents the mass expiry in the Flood as the reversal of creation. The rainbow covenant likewise embraces humanity and animals—'between God and every living creature of all flesh that is on earth' (Gen 9:16). Qohelet asserts that humans and animals share 'one spirit', better translated, 'one breath' (*rūaḥ 'eḥād*) to reflect the Hebrew connection with physical life and eliminate the misleading nuances of immortality which 'spirit' has acquired in English.

place'.[21] He answers his own rhetorical question about what comes next (6:12 and 3:21). In a word—'Sheol': 'for there is no work or thought or knowledge or wisdom in Sheol, to which you are going' (9:10). The 'afterwards' is not an afterlife: 'and after that they go to the dead' (9:3b). So whether he speaks of those with evil and madness in their hearts (9:3), or to the reader who is exhorted to enjoy life while he can, in his beloved's affection (9:9a), the end result is the same. All end up in Sheol, dead. 'And the dead know nothing'(9:5).[22]

AGEING IN REALISTIC PERSPECTIVE

We must now stand back and survey this. Where is the realism that contributes to a spirituality for our times? It is not in Qohelet's conclusion about the finality of death, for more compelling evidence has since come to hand that Qohelet was not able to invoke. Death is not final. The dead are raised.[23] Realism does not demand that we abandon the Christian hope and cease to celebrate Easter. The enduring realism that Qohelet offers us lies in his insistence that we face our mortality and work out the meaning of our life in the light of our ageing and death. What was true then is true now—'No one has power over the wind to restrain the wind, or power over the day of death' (8:8).[24] What is not so true now, as it was for Qohelet, is an engagement in open discussion of the process of ageing and death in Christian fellowships. This discussion will force itself on to the Christian agenda eventually because of demographic changes in population

---

[21] 'One place' (*māqōm 'eḥād*—3:20a, 6:6b) joins 'one event' (*miqreh 'eḥād*) and 'one breath' (*rūaḥ 'eḥād*) as witness both to Qohelet's style and to his universal perspective and striving for a unified, coherent viewpoint.
[22] Qohelet has not shifted his viewpoint in 12:7. This verse speaks of the withdrawal of life in terms of life as God's gift and prerogative. The words 'and the *rūaḥ* returns to God who gave it' describe expiry, the surrender of life-breath, not the transmigration of the soul. The background is once again Gen 3 and the 'dust to dust' formula. See, for instance, RE Murphy —'This is a picture of dissolution, not of immortality, as if there were a *reditus animae ad Deum* "the return of the soul to God" ' (*Ecclesiastes*, p. 120). For a wider perspective on Israel's beliefs about death in Near Eastern context, see LR Bailey, *Biblical Perspectives on Death*, OBT 5, (Philadelphia: Fortress) 1979. A more recent work at a technical and exegetical level is K Spronk, *Beatific Afterlife in Ancient Israel and in the Ancient Near East*, AO/AT 219 (Neukirchen–Vluyn: Neukirchener Verlag/Kevelaer: Verlag Butzon & Bercker) 1986.
[23] To affirm that the dead are raised is not the same as saying that humans are immortal or have immortal souls. See J Murray Harris, *Raised Immortal* (London: Marshall,Morgan & Scott) 1983 and *From Grave to Glory* (Grand Rapids: Zondervan) 1990 for discussion of New Testament concepts.
[24] NRSV, REB and NIV admit the ambiguity of Hebrew *rūaḥ* by offering 'wind' in the text and 'breath' or 'spirit' in the footnotes. RSV and Fox opt for

biology. As an article in *Scientific American* opens dramatically —'For the first time, humanity as a whole is growing older.'[25]

Qohelet is somewhat ambiguous about a long life. He admits that 'light is sweet, and it is pleasant to see the sun' (Ecc 11:7), yet the Israelite ideal of a long life and fullness of days is clouded for Qohelet by the finale.

> Even those who live many years should rejoice in them all; yet let them remember that the days of darkness will be many. All that comes is *hebel*.
>
> (Ecc 11:8)

Living to a hundred, or having as many children, is no blessing in itself 'if he does not enjoy life's good things, or has no burial' (Ecc 6:3). This sounds very much like modern discussions about the 'quality of life', some of which end in advocating euthanasia. Yet suicide, by any name, is not on Qohelet's mind. He does offer alternative comment on growing old. Deuteronomic theology saw old age as a blessing for covenant fidelity, noting the vigorous longevity of Moses himself (Deut 34:7), and Proverbs concurs:

> Gray hair is a crown of glory;
> it is gained in a righteous life.
>
> (Prov 16:31)

Adopting a stance closer to Qohelet's, McKane commented on this maxim:

> It is remarkable that old age is viewed so exclusively in its aspect of fulfilment—it is a crown of glory—and that nothing of the sadness and despair of old age is allowed to emerge, the failing of strength and the withering away of powers.[26]

Qohelet does not reaffirm the connection between age and righteousness that Proverbs makes here and in Prov 10:27: 'The fear of the LORD prolongs life, but the years of the wicked will be

---

'spirit', 'life-spirit'. Qohelet may play on the ambiguity of *rūaḥ* because both 'wind' and 'life–spirit' meanings of *rūaḥ* are found in his book.

[25] SJ Olshansky, BA Carnes and CK Cassel, 'The Aging of the Human Species' *Scientific American* April (1993) 18–24.

[26] W McKane, *Proverbs*, SCM, 1970, p.501. Human fertility (Deut 28:4,11) includes living to see your children's children and the blessing of 'growing old in the land' (Deut 4:25,40)—'that you may fear the LORD your God, you and your son and your son's son . . . all the days of your life; and that your days may be prolonged' (Deut 6:2). See A Malamat 'Longevity: biblical concepts and some Ancient Near Eastern Parallels' *AfO* 19 (1982) 215–224 for a review with citations of many texts.

short.' He points out that old age and wisdom may not cohere. Using a traditional maxim form, he says—'Better is a poor but wise youth than an old but foolish king, who will no longer take advice' (Ecc 4:13). The combination of royal status and age should guarantee wisdom, but in fact may not. Qohelet underlines this,[27] but his main comment on ageing is reserved for his concluding remarks.

Against the generally positive Israelite evaluation of age as maturity, Qohelet's closing reflection on old age is sombre indeed. Old age is characterized in contrast to youth as pleasureless 'days of adversity'(*yēmay hārāʿāh*) (Ecc 12:1).[28] There is no mention of any rewarding quality of advanced years. Proximity to death is the major characteristic of old age in Qohelet's presentation.

An analogy is helpful here. The link between large families and divine blessing does not transplant into New Covenant theology or urbanized culture. It remains rooted in Near Eastern concepts of divine blessing. The value set on large numbers of children, especially boys, is a product of a patriarchal and tribal culture rather than a revealed truth. The Near Eastern link between old age and wisdom is likewise a cultural product. The elderly in a rapidly changing society may not be a repository of wisdom. At the individual level, old age is more likely to accentuate the characteristics of middle age, good and bad. We would judge biblical wisdom to be more a product of emotional and spiritual maturity than of chronological accumulation. The processing of experience is of greater value than stockpiling it. We can say that

---

[27] The tribal chieftain, Jethro, father-in-law to Moses, not only lives to see his children's children but wisely advises his son-in-law on how to organise the judicial administration of tribal Israel (Exod 18). In this setting, experience counts. For scepticism about wisdom residing in the aged, compare Job's comment: 'Is wisdom with the aged, and understanding in length of days?'(Job 12:12). In like vein, Elihu is scathing about the responses of his elders (Job 32:6–10).

[28] Hebrew *seybah*—'gray-headedness, old age'—is used in parallel with *zaqen*— 'old'—in the Holiness Code exhortation: 'You shall rise before the aged(*śeybāh*) and defer to the old; and you shall fear your God: I am the LORD your God' (Lev 19:32). The Ancient of days in Daniel's vision '(Dan 7:9) is whitehaired. Canaanite El, the head of the pantheon, 'the king, father of years', 'the eternal king' is addressed by his chief Lady Asherah: 'Thou art great O El, verily thou art wise/ Thy hoary beard indeed instructs thee' (CTA 4,5:66). The goddess Anat is the violent iconoclast when she threatens El—'I shall make your grey hair flow with blood,/ Your grey beard [run] with gore.' (CTA 3, 5:32f). Cognate words (Heb.*śeybāh* = Ugar. *sebati*) and cognate concepts of patriarchality link old age, wisdom, decisions and governing in Canaan and Israel. On Canaan, see FM Cross, *Canaanite Myth and Hebrew Epic* (Cambridge: HUP) 1973 p. 15ff and ET Mullen, *The Divine Council in Canaanite and Early Hebrew Literature*, HSM 24, (Chico: Scholars) 1980, p.62f & 145f.

both Proverbs and Qohelet stand witness to the value set on the processing of experience, yet Qohelet is more burdened by the encroachment of death on life.

If Qohelet leaves a question mark hanging over links between loyalty to God and attainment of old age, or between wisdom and years, we can only agree. There is no necessary connection between old age and wisdom. The concept of royalty or literal 'elders'($z^eq\bar{e}nim$) as repositories of wisdom for the community does not survive transplant from traditional cultures well. Tribal and village life may represent a pattern of doing things that can persist for centuries in the absence of new technologies or political systems. In these communities, accumulation of experience transmitted orally and an accumulation of years may contribute to a wisdom resource invested in the senior members of the clan, village or tribe.

As modern a science as biochemistry gives a nod in this direction—botanists are working with traditional herbalists in several parts of the world to garner their experience before this accumulated knowledge dies out. This is an example of practical wisdom accumulated in senior practitioners in village cultures. Nomadic, tribal and village forms of social stability do not survive urbanization and rapid technological developments unaltered. In urban cultures, people perceive innovation and problem solving, rather than traditional lore, as beneficial. The need to create employment, feed the world and dispose of waste products demands both innovation and problem solving skills on a scale that matches the multiplicity of mouths and the by-products of urbanization. Within the Christian domain, growing churches do not limit 'eldership' to those over sixty years old, and few churches of any sort have 'elders' who continue in office indefinitely without retirement. Despite the hangover of patriarchality in church life, spirituality is not convincingly equated with being male and growing old. If there is a spirituality about ageing itself, Qohelet cannot see it.[29] We may concur.

MEANINGFUL LIFE IN THE LIGHT OF DEATH

But what of death in Qohelet and contemporary cultures? The avoidance and denial of death takes many forms in cultures where life expectancy is long and funeral parlours do not advertise their

---

[29] Commentators divide over the exact decoding of the language and imagery of vv.2–7. For Fox, it does not yield an allegory of decrepitude so much as of isolation, mourning and death. See the discussion of literal, figurative and allegorical imagery in Fox, *Qohelet and His Contradictions*, 'Excursus II Aging and Death in Qohelet 12', pp.281–298 and sympathetic review of this and other interpretations by RE Murphy, *Ecclesiastes*, pp. 115ff.

trade.[30] In the southern hemisphere many populations have a preponderance of under 25s, but an ageing leadership, like China's, that hangs onto power, apparently defying death but certainly frustrating political development. Northern hemisphere countries with ageing populations paradoxically show no inclination to abandon media images of youthfulness, real or apparent, in favour of promoting the pleasures of being over sixty-five. Average life expectancy in affluent countries such as the UK, America, Japan and Scandinavia has increased. Some may offset the effects of ageing and of death artificially with cosmetic surgery, or less expensively with a healthy diet and exercise.[31]

Qohelet cannot be invoked to criticize the enjoyment of a healthier, longer life. He could be, however, if this quest for greater life expectancy entails avoiding the topic of death. In the UK and the USA, it has taken the work of Kübler-Ross *On Death and Dying*, the hospice movement and AIDS to put the subject of death and how to face it back on the agenda.[32]

In his facing of death and the absurdity of life, Qohelet could be seen as an existentialist ahead of his time. Yet he was not the first to wrestle with mortality and meaningfulness. The second millennium *Epic of Gilgamesh* could lay claim to being the earliest and greatest reflection on coming to terms with mortality. Spurred by the death of Enkidu, his companion in heroic exploits, Gilgamesh faces the horror of his own mortality and embarks on a quest to avoid it and find eternal life. The most sobering advice is offered

---

[30] E Becker, *The Denial of Death* (London: Collier Macmillan), 1973 argues that the repression of death gives rise to neuroses rather than Freud's central concepts—the repression of sexuality and aggression. The paradox is that the book was awarded the Pulitzer prize and sold many copies. RG Dumont & DC Foss, *The American View of Death: acceptance or denial?* (Cambridge, Mass.: Schenkman) 1972, reviewed the debate over American culture. That billions is spent on 'gadgets, cosmetics and techniques to prevent us from looking old', but comparatively little on the aged, receives comment in H Nouwen & WJ Gaffney, *Aging: the fulfilment of life* (London, New York: Doubleday) Image editions 1974, 1990, p.26.

[31] In the USA in 1900, those over 65 constituted 4.1% of the population. By 2000, this percentage is expected to rise to 13.1% and by 2030 to 21.1%. Countries in Europe show equivalent increases. The average lifespan of an American today is 26 years more than one born in 1900. These figures are given by JG Harris, *Biblical Perspectives on Aging: God and the elderly*, OBT 22 (Philadelphia: Fortress) 1987 p.1f and notes p.117.

[32] E Kübler-Ross, *On Death and Dying* (London: Tavistock) 1969 and repeatedly reprinted in paperback. She observed a possible five stages in the process of facing death—denial and isolation, anger, bargaining, depression and hope. The fact that this book and others are prescribed reading in theological education does not necessarily mean that death is being faced. Cerebralising about death can itself be a means of avoiding its emotional and existential dimensions.

him by a barmaid, Siduri, at her tavern on the sea-shore beyond
the sunrise:

'Gilgamesh, whither are you roaming?
Life, which you look for you shall never find.
(For) when the gods created man, they set
death as share for man, and life
grabbed away in their own hands.
You, Gilgamesh, fill your belly,
day and night make merry,
daily hold a festival,
dance and make music day and night.
And wear fresh clothes,
and wash your head and bathe.
Look at the child that is holding your hand,
and let your wife delight in your embrace.
These things alone are the concern of man.'[33]

This advice has often been compared with Ecc 9, and indeed
Qohelet recommends the enjoyment of meals, conviviality and
wife as a 'gift of God' (9:19), while they last. The irony is that in
Mesopotamian tradition, though Gilgamesh failed to live for ever
under the sun, he was bequeathed a judgment throne in the
underworld in connection with the cult of dead kings.

Qohelet is thus more radical than *Gilgamesh*. His this-worldly
focus and his perspective on the finality of death aligns him with
those European existentialists who talk of death in terms of
nothingness and non-being.[34] The philosophical writings of Sartre
and Heidegger and the literary works of Camus and Kafka are
often referred to in academic discussions, though not popularly

---

[33] See S Dalley, *Myths from Mesopotamia*, World's Classics (Oxford: OUP) 1991,
pp.39–153; *ANET*, pp.72–99 and 503–507. The perceptive studies of Thorkild
Jacobsen have highlighted both the literary structure of Gilgamesh and the
concept of maturity by heroic failure, the coming to terms with death—
'Second Millennium Metaphors: "And Death the Journey's End": The
Gilgamesh Epic', pp.193–219 in *Treasures of Darkness* (Yale: YUP) 1976 and
'The Gilgamesh Epic: Romantic and Tragic Vision', pp.231–249 in T Abusch
et al, *Lingering over Words* (Festschrift WL Moran), HSS 37, (Atlanta: Scholars
Press) 1990. To these add BW Jones who argues for Qohelet's borrowing
from Siduri's speech in 'From Gilgamesh to Qoheleth' pp. 349–379 in WW
Hallo et al (eds), *The Bible in the Light of Cuneiform Literature: Scripture in
Context III*, ANE Texts and Studies 8, (Lampeter: Edwin Mellen) 1990. In
more popular form, Gilgamesh is discussed by the existential therapist
Sheldon Kopp, *If You Meet the Buddha on the Road, Kill Him!* (London:
Sheldon) 1974, 14th impression, 1991, pp.23–39.

[34] Recent commentators on Qohelet cite European existentialists—e.g. M Fox
makes frequent references to the French existentialist Albert Camus' work
The Myth of Sisyphus and J Ellul refers to the writings of the Danish Christian
existentialist Soren Kierkegaard.

read. Yet popularized existential concepts have influenced
Western culture. In the UK or the USA, we can point to
psychotherapy as one field concerned with making sense of life.
Viktor Frankl's influential book *Man's Search for Meaning* was
first published under the title *From Death Camp to Existentialism*,
based as it was on his experience of the Nazi extermination centre
at Auschwitz. Realistic confrontation with mortality has remained
central to existential psychotherapy. Core beliefs invoked by the
existential school of psychotherapy are: that we are essentially
alone in life, that the meaning of life is self-determined, that we
must make choices, that death is final, that authenticity is achieved
by living in awareness of these truths.[35] It is no surprise, then, that
chapters of a book by a leading proponent of the existential school
of psychotherapy sound as though they might be based on
Qohelet. These chapters are headed 'Life, Death and Anxiety',
'Death and Psychotherapy', 'Meaninglessness', 'Meaninglessness
and Psychotherapy'.[36] In exploring the client's physical world
(*Umwelt*), social world (*Mitwelt*), personal world (*Eigenwelt*) and
value-beliefs (*Überwelt*),

> progress, from an existential perspective, is seen as the ability to live in
> time. Living in time is that mode of existence where a person is aware
> of their own inevitable progression from birth to death. . . . While a
> belief in after-life and God may have a pacifying influence, it can never
> fully replace the need to come to terms with the apparent absurdity
> and relentlessness of earthly existence.[37]

A Christian spirituality must likewise come to terms with 'living
in time', 'earthly existence', 'inevitable progression from birth to
death' and 'apparent absurdity', with life's mundaneness.

---

[35] Psychotherapy is relevant to spirituality, even having a credible claim to be a
secular spirituality because it parallels many of the concerns and techniques of
spirituality. The therapist is 'spiritual director'. Deep listening, reflecting
back, questions, dialogue and exercises are used for clarification. Profound
reflection and commitment of the person to the process are essential for
progress. Processing of the past, of anger, anxiety and deceits are used as steps
towards maturity. Metaphors of journey and discovery abound in each.
Revelation comes as insights which need to be incorporated and translated
into behaviour. For therapists drawing on existentialism, see ID Yalom,
Existential Psychotherapy (New York: Basic Books) 1982 from the USA, and
Emmy van Deurzen-Smith, *Existential Counselling in Practice* (London: Sage)
1988 as a proponent in the UK.
[36] ID Yalom, *Existential Psychotherapy*.
[37] van Deurzen-Smith, *Existential Counselling* from Chap. 3 'Clarification of
Personal Worldview' p. 69, and from Chap. 6 'Coming to Terms with Life',
p. 222.

There are points at which Christians find their faith has gone dead on them, when faith does not offer a meaningful solution to ordinary living. Redundancy, long-term unemployment, retirement, being incapacitated by a progressive disease or a bereavement may highlight the difficulty of living in time. Immersion in time and repetitiveness produces boredom, despair, directionlessness, apathy and depression. In such contexts, to achieve meaningful existence, even as a believer, is a struggle, part of the 'toil' or 'trouble' of being human that Qohelet is so aware of.[38] Many Christians have found that an exploration of their life, assisted by a trained counsellor, is helpful or necessary for processing their experience and finding a new courage to be. Adherence to theological doctrines does not suffice. Qohelet sets a precedent for this exploration of experience, for examining what it means to be living in time.

If Qohelet and the existential school of therapy agree that facing death has a bearing on meaningfulness and living in time, then the difference between the existential school in its most secular form, particularly its atheistic versions, is also apparent. Christians would prefer to affirm that we are essentially not alone, though recognizing the loneliness, personal pain and the barriers to intimate relationships that all psychotherapy addresses. Spirituality would affirm that we must make choices and commitments, would affirm continuity of the I–Thou relationship with God through death, and would find primary meaning in being loved and loving. Nevertheless, an openness to God as Father and Friend, to moral values grounded in God's character, to the existence of a supernatural dimension to life, to life after death, all this does not guarantee authenticity in living. This authenticity, which is so valued in existentialism, may be controverted by an escapist Christian spirituality that substitutes dubious coping mechanisms and spiritual-speak for facing what is painful.

History, and the advantage of cultural distance, disclose that there are spurious Christian spiritualities. For instance, there is an asceticism that negates what is good in sleep, food, leisure, company and love-making, and in so doing clashes with Qohelet. There is a spirituality that expects health, wealth and prosperity, that explains persistent symptoms of ill health as due to lack of faith, that disapproves of expressing grief in bereavement, that passes off responsibility for choices and their consequences by talking about them as divine guidance, that escapes the pain in others with clichés, and so on. The hyper-spiritual approach is

---

[38] The Hebrew word *'āmāl* has a semantic range that embraces 'toil, effort, distress, trouble, misfortune, disaster'. In Ecclesiastes, it is used 33 times and describes human existence as a wearisome struggle.

often marked by a triumphalism that ignores the real state of the church and the world, denies the fact of a common humanity in favour of a false separateness, or offers a formula for spiritual arrival that glosses over the reality of abiding human sinfulness.

This unauthentic pietism can maintain an oblivion to structural evil and remain unaware of our participation in oppressive or polluting systems, be they social, economic, political or ecological. Along with a reality-denying other-worldliness, there may go a certitude expressed as moral majority dogmatism, or a denial of the ambiguity of many facets of life—for instance, ambiguities of motive, of experiences, or of what constitutes an answer to prayer.[39] Against such forms of unauthentic spirituality, Qohelet's down-to-earth realism exercises a critique.

REALISM VERSUS REDUCTIONISM

Some of Qohelet's conclusions emerge as artefacts of his mode of observation. For instance, he concludes that there is 'nothing new under the sun'. This dictum holds true in so far as life is a treadmill trod by generation after generation.[40] It holds true in that human nature does not change. Birth, toil and mortality are invariables. The dictum that 'there is nothing new under the sun' does not, of course, hold true in a different framework, for instance the framework of biological life on earth. The emergence of modern humans after a million or more years of *Homo erectus* was something qualitatively without precedent. In the framework of innovative human technologies, agriculture was revolutionary, as was the use of metals, and the generation of electricity. 'Nothing new under the sun' is even less true in the light of Jesus'

---

[39] There is ambiguity, for instance, about phenomena such as speaking in tongues, the kind of collapse known as being 'slain in the Spirit', the laughing, barking and crying of what has been called 'the Toronto blessing', visions, prophecies and healings. Such phenomena, and depending on their context, could be attributed to the Spirit, to the demonic, or to mechanisms of human consciousness. Likewise, there are issues of human behaviour which appear ambiguous in that they straddle ethical boundaries, depending on how they are interpreted and by whom—for instance, whether something is described as the exercise of legitimate force, or as violence. Where some would see ethical decisions in terms of black and white, others would see the available options in terms of shades of grey.

[40] RE Murphy offers a good review of the way that commentators have produced divergent interpretations of the book's opening poem in which 'the constant repetition of an action in nature'—sun, air and sea—'serve as an analogue to aimless and futile human experience' (*Ecclesiastes*, p. 8f.).

incarnation and resurrection. So we need to make allowance for Qohelet's chosen standpoint, or historical situation.

By excluding the paranormal, the occult and the supernatural, Qohelet restricted his observation of reality. He risked constructing a model that did not encompass and integrate all the available facts of human experience, or all of the evidence. Current scientific paradigms based on observation and experiment emerge from restricting their field to what can be investigated by methods that yield verifiable results.[41] Methodological reductionism is quite acceptable as a simplifying procedure. It has a modesty about it. Yet scientists can lapse into triumphalism when so-called Theories of Everything cease to be popularizing tags and instead become beguiling misnomers.[42]

---

[41] The writings of Paul Davies, the mathematical physicist, over the last decade chronicle developments in physics which appear to herald a new synthesis or new model—*The Accidental Universe* (1982), *Superforce* (1984), *The Cosmic Blueprint* (1987) *God and the New Physics* (1983), *The Mind of God* (1991). In *The Matter Myth: towards 21st-century science* (London: Viking) 1991, written with John Gribbin, the authors speak of the end of the mechanistic paradigm and 'a growing awareness of the need for a new paradigm of wholeness within the physical sciences' (p.304). This paradigm shift must take the model beyond Einstein by incorporating irreversibility and non-linear dynamics more effectively than the time reversible equations have done so far—P Coveney & R Highfield, *The Arrow of Time* (London: WH Allen) 1990. Yet there is no sign so far that authentic paranormal events can be accommodated within a scientific paradigm. Undoubted success at debunking folk-lore, superstitions, frauds and fantasies has obscured the inadequacy of the scientific model to incorporate many supra-normal phenomena. For a recent and sober evaluation of poltergeist and occult phenomena in a Western setting, see M Perry (ed), *Deliverance: psychic disturbances and occult involvement*, [Anglican] Christian Exorcism Study Group (London: SPCK) 1987.

[42] Ellul inveighs against the triumphalism of the scientist Jacques Monod who said 'we now know that humanity is alone in the world' (*Chance and Necessity: an essay of the natural philosophy of biology*, p.180 cited in Ellul, *Reason for Being*, p.297). Compare the recent triumphalist statements on the irrelevance of God by Stephen Hawking. They relate to his hypothesis that 'The boundary condition of the universe is that it has no boundary': 'My paper was rather mathematical, however, so its implications for the role of God in the creation of the universe were not generally recognized at the time (just as well for me). However, if we do discover a complete theory . . . we shall all . . . be able to take part in the discussion of the question of why it is that we and the universe exist. If we find the answer to that, it would be the ultimate triumph of human reason—for then we would know the mind of God,—*A Brief History of Time* (New York: Bantam) 1988, p.136 and 175. As reviewers pointed out, this sort of statement is neither good physics nor good theology. God is neither invoked nor excluded by the statement 2+2=4, nor by the mathematics of quantum gravity. If there is an ultimate equation, it could scarcely empower us in the way that Hawking seems to suggest. If Hawking is merely saying that God does not exist and that mathematics is the sole explanation of existence, that is a faith commitment he is quite entitled to. His brilliance in physics in undisputed; whether that qualifies him to pronounce on all facets of

Qohelet's reduction of reality to his chosen empirical field leaves the usefulness of observation and verification intact, if not all of his conclusions. His overall verdict on making moral sense of life between birth and physical death is difficult to contest. If this is all that there is, and life is as he describes it, then within this framework human life is indeed absurd. Furthermore, the act-consequence sequence does not run smoothly along moral lines, nor can we fathom God's mode of operation in events, or predict future outcomes of the present. Qohelet's method yields results that we can verify without canonizing his paradigm.

As for the 'day of prosperity' and the 'day of adversity' —'God has made the one as well as the other.'[43] That leaves 'enjoy' and 'reflect' (7:14a). But it also leaves us confused and perplexed and without an assured interpretation of many events in life. Such happenings, and the confusion they induce, are *hebel*. Qohelet comments on the jumble of experiences. He urges readers to 'consider', that is, to 'reflect on' the jumble of fortunate and adverse events (rᵉʾēh—'see, consider, take note of', Ecc 7:14a).

As a sequel to Qohelet's perspective, we can cite a saying of Jesus. Jesus cautions against a misreading of the deaths of the eighteen people killed by the collapse of the tower of Siloam (Luke 13:4f). They may not have been 'righteous people who perish in their righteousness' (Ecc 7:15), but they were not the wicked either. It was not 'an act of God' in the theological sense. It seems to fall into Qohelet's category of unpredictable event, of time and chance without moral sense, of *hebel*. Jesus does not interpret the event itself. In this case, Qohelet's 'consider' is amplified by Jesus' prophetic 'do you think that they were worse offenders than all the others living in Jerusalem? No I tell you; but unless you repent, you will all perish just as they did.' The fact of mortality, the fact that death may come unpredictably, should lead to a life-revision exercise. 'Perish just as they did' does not, of course, mean that all Jesus' audience would be killed by falling masonry, or die in meaningless accidents. In Jesus' perspective, to 'perish just as they did' means to be caught out living lives that were

---

reality, especially those that cannot be expressed in equations, is another matter. The astronomer John Barrow is not convinced that physicists who do not stray into philosophy or theology but work mathematically can encompass 'Everything' in their field. In Barrow's terms, 'prospective properties' lie beyond computable and listable categories, and 'Theories of Everything can make no impression on predicting these prospective attributes of reality', *Theories of Everything* (Oxford: OUP) 1991, p.210.

[43] 'so that mortals may not find out anything that will come after them' is the usual translation of 7:14b, though Murphy offers 'so that no one can find fault with him'. Whichever translation fits best, the opaqueness of events, either in their sequence or in their meaning, remains a truth that we must concur with.

unprepared for death. 'To perish' means not to live in the light of human mortality and the fear of God. Jesus underlines a state of being and a way of life to positively avoid, rather than predicting a premature death for all his audience.

ICONOCLASM

Qohelet wrote as an iconoclast. His this-worldly down-to-earthness effectively demythologizes the icons of his times, kings, sages and the rich. By using Solomon as a mouthpiece in his initial chapters, this founder of Israel's Wisdom movement is demythologized and deflated.[44] Neither his riches, his 'wisdom' nor his power prevent 'Solomon' from reaching the conclusion that it all adds up to nothing, or worse to absurdity, 'a grievous evil' and a troubled mind (1:12, 1:14, 1:17, 1:18, 2:11, 2:17, 2:21, 2:23).

Western culture— journalism in particular—is iconoclastic, yet in this secular century in Europe new icons, idols and mythologies have kept emerging, based on image rather than on reality.[45] We need Qohelet's iconoclasm. We cannot afford to beatify our contemporary spiritual gurus and heroines if this means obscuring their limitations and the reality of their fallen humanity.[46] Christians are no less prone than their neighbours to romanticize, be it

---

[44] Compare Ellul's remarks:

> Qohelet appears as even more of an iconoclast than we thought. He questions not only traditions, theologies, ideas, and sermons, but a man: Israel's hero and model . . . Solomon himself is reduced to nothing . . . (*Reason for Being*, p.202)

Compare other vignettes that are more in the Wisdom tradition. Being poor, young but wise is better than being an old and foolish king who no longer listens to advice (7:13). This suggests that old and foolish kings were not unknown. A poor wise man, though overlooked socially and soon forgotten, offered a scheme that delivered a city from a powerful besieging king (9:13ff). Qohelet values the enjoyment of material blessings as a gift of God (5:18–20), but notes that 'the surfeit of the rich will not let him sleep' (5:12b).

[45] Besides the heroes who profess to explain the world such as Nietzsche, Karl Marx or Keynes and the crash of systems based on their theories, there have been individuals whose heroic image has crumbled. Recent examples that have been deflated in the media or in biographies include political figures (John F Kennedy), pop idols (Elvis Presley, Michael Jackson), business tycoons (Robert Maxwell), tele-evangelists (Jimmy Swaggart) and theologians (Paul Tillich, Alan Boesak).

[46] Martin Luther King's advocacy of non–violence, his leadership in the civil rights movement, his inspirational oratory in speeches such as "I have a dream . . .", and his assassination elevate him into a tragic hero. His infidelities to Coretta King are also truths of his life. After courageous resistance to apartheid and being called 'Mother of the Nation', Winnie Mandela was implicated in events leading to the murder of a black 13-year-old, Stompie, and misappropriation of ANC funds. Marital issues lead to Nelson Mandela's separation from her. The heroic accomplishments of Martin Luther King and Winnie Mandela are not in question, but the full reality of their lives needs to

their missionaries, musicians, communicators or authors. Where these, like Solomon, are founding fathers of an institution, an organization, a movement, a community, or a school of thought, the dangers of idolizing them are apparent. They need their Qohelets or our spirituality will suffer in the long run.

Spirituality has suffered its own dissolution of the monasteries—literally some centuries ago, presently in redefinitions of personal and ecclesial vocation.[47] The church still faces critical reflection on spirituality in relation to some of its cherished institutions, be they seminaries or missionary societies, ecclesiastical hierarchies, charismatic renewal movements, or denominations. This is not a phenomenon of Western Christendom only, for indigenous and contextualized African spirituality, which absorbs millions of adherents today, also raises questions about its traditions, leaders and splintering separatist groups.[48] Qohelet reminds us that the individual must confront his or her tradition without necessarily abandoning it. Qohelet challenges each person to find meaning in the midst of their social milieu and in the mundane of life's eventualities, if they can, rather than submerging themselves in an unquestioning allegiance to a group or a tradition, even as respectable a one as the Wisdom tradition was in Israel. A realism within the faith and a questioning of the tradition remain on the agenda of spirituality.

SUMMARY AND CONCLUSION

Qohelet faces life, ageing and death with realism. He works with what he can observe in a this-worldly horizon. Our horizons have been expanded by the suffering and resurrection of Christ. We have these new facts, and an in-breaking of the supernatural in Jesus' demonstrations of the Kingdom in the form of miracles, healings and exorcisms. However, it remains true that our everyday life as Christians is more mundane than supra-normal. This is typified by the process of ageing and dying that we face

---

be retained. Scriptural heroes of spirituality such as Moses and David are not beatified.

[47] Celibate orders are dwindling and the vocation to poverty is under redefinition in Latin America. On the latter see Enrique Dussel, 'Exodus as a Paradigm in Liberation Theology', in B van Iersel & A Weiler(eds), *Exodus—a lasting Paradigm* = *Concilium* 189 (1987) 83–92 and G Gutiérrez, *We Drink from our Own Wells: the spiritual journey of a people* (London: SCM) 1984.

[48] A sympathetic study by GC Oosthuizen entitled *The Healer-Prophet in Afro-Christian Churches* (Leiden: Brill) 1992 offers the following statistics. In 1913, there were 32 denominations, by 1948, 800. In 1960, there were 2,000 denominations and by 1980 3,270 denominations with nearly 6 million adherents. By 1990, it is estimated that 4,000 denominations grouped together

without a supernatural bypass.[49] For all the benefits of living beyond Qohelet's era, we must also admit to our limited knowledge, our inability to discern divine intervention in sociopolitical events, and the remaining ambiguity or absurdity of much of what happens. Belief in divine judgment remains unsupported by tangible evidence. Despite surveying all available data, there remain too many unforeseen events and outcomes for us to feel certain of life. We, like Qohelet's original readers, cannot foresee the future, or even know the time of our own death.

Qohelet consciously works within the Wisdom tradition, and yet calls it into question. Spiritual maturity demands that we, like Qohelet, live with the contradictions thrown up by our theistic perception of life, and with the tensions created within our own Christian traditions and institutions. Like the Wisdom tradition, none of our Christian traditions appears to hold the answers or offer a mastery of life's enigmas. New spiritual solutions to living seem to generate new problems as each wave of Christian enthusiasm or success gathers momentum and then fragments —from monasticism to the Holy Roman Empire to Pentecostalism, and beyond. Inevitably we, like Qohelet, will place great weight on our personal experience and observation, as well as on received tradition. Yet if we follow Qohelet, living with the tensions of *hebel* will not allow our realism or iconoclasm as detached observers to degenerate into cynicism, or corrode into a negation of what may be legitimately enjoyed in life as a gift of God. Detachment, cynicism and negation are coping mechanisms that dissolve the tension between the fear of God and life's absurdity.

Authentic spirituality in the Qohelet mode offers no escape from living in time, and living in time means being caught up in

---

about 35% of the African population with about 8 million adherents. 'This is the fastest growing church movement in Southern Africa' (p.1).

[49] Ageing is less easy to romanticize than youth, or even to accommodate. In Western culture, churches that hold special childrens' services and youth services with adapted worship and music do not seem to hold over sixty-five services. Does this negate the pain and potential of ageing? Writing in existential vein, H Nouwen and WJ Gaffney describe the choices: 'Is aging a way to the darkness or a way to the light? . . . No one can decide for anyone else how his or her aging shall or should be. It belongs to the greatness of men and women that the meaning of their existence escapes the power of calculations and predictions. Ultimately, it can be affirmed only in the freedom of heart. There we are able to decide between segregation and unity, between desolation and hope, between loss of self and a new, recreating vision. Everyone will age and die, but this knowledge has no inherent direction. It can be destructive as well as creative, oppressive as well as liberating.' (*Ageing*, p.86)

the randomness and repetition of life. To be humanly wise is to
observe, consider and finding meaning in the mundane, in the
'toil' that is part of being human, a meaning that is informed and
enhanced by the fact of our mortality. Qohelet reminds us that
fearing God and being existentially comfortable about life are not
compatible. There is too much truth in the 'utterly absurd' for
that. Nevertheless, with Qohelet, we may affirm that realism
within our limited wisdom and fearing God do belong together.
This is the mundane spirituality that we inherit from Qohelet.

BIBLIOGRAPHY

LR Bailey, *Biblical Perspectives on Death*, OBT 5, (Philadelphia: Fortress)
1979.
E Becker, *The Denial of Death* (London: Collier Macmillan) 1973.
JL Crenshaw, *A Whirlpool of Torment: Israelite traditions of God as an
oppressive presence* OBT 13, (Philadelphia: Fortress) 1984.
RG Dumont & DC Foss, *The American View of Death: acceptance or denial?*
(Cambridge, Mass.: Schenkman) 1972.
J Ellul, *Reason for Being* (Grand Rapids: Eerdmans) 1990.
M Fox, 'The Meaning of Hebel for Qohelet' *JBL* 105/3 (1986) 409–427.
———, *Qohelet and His Contradictions* JSOTS 71, Bible and Literature 18,
(Sheffield: Almond Press) 1989.
J Goldingay, *Theological Diversity and the Authority of the Old Testament*,
(Grand Rapids: Eerdmans) 1987.
JG Harris, *Biblical Perspectives on Aging: God and the elderly*, OBT 22,
(Philadelphia: Fortress) 1987.
T Jacobsen, 'Second Millenium Metaphors: "And Death the Journey's
End": The Gilgamesh Epic', pp.193–219 in *Treasures of Darkness* (Yale:
YUP) 1976.
———, 'The Gilgamesh Epic: Romantic and Tragic Vision', pp.231–249
in T Abusch *et al, Lingering over Words* (Festschrift WL Moran), HSS
37, (Atlanta: Scholars Press) 1990.
BW Jones, 'From Gilgamesh to Qoheleth' pp. 349–379 in WW Hallo et al
(eds), *The Bible in the Light of Cuneiform Literature: Scripture in Context
III*, ANE Texts and Studies 8, (Lampeter: Edwin Mellen) 1990.
S Kopp, *If You Meet the Buddha on the Road, Kill Him!* (London: Sheldon)
1974, 1991.
E Kübler-Ross, *On Death and Dying* (London: Tavistock) 1969.
JA Loader, *Polar Structures in the Book of Qohelet*, BZAW 152, (Berlin:
Walter de Gruyter) 1979.
RE Murphy, *Ecclesiastes*, WBC 23 (Dallas: Word) 1992.
H Nouwen & WJ Gaffney, *Aging: the fulfilment of life* (London,New
York: Doubleday) Image editions 1974, 1990.
SJ Olshansky, BA Carnes &, CK Cassel, 'The Aging of the Human
Species' Scientific American April (1993) 18–24.
K Spronk, *Beatific Afterlife in Ancient Israel and in the Ancient Near East*,
AO/AT 219, (Neukirchen-Vluyn: Neukirchener Verlag/Kevelaer:
Verlag Butzon & Bercker) 1986.

E van Deurzen-Smith, *Existential Counselling in Practice* (London: Sage) 1988.
RN Whybray, 'Qohelet,Preacher of Joy' *JSOT* 23 (1982) 87–98.
——, *Ecclesiastes*, OT Guides (Sheffield: JSOT Press) 1989.
——, *Ecclesiastes*, NCB (Eerdmans/ Marshall,Morgan & Scott) 1989.
ID Yalom, *Existential Psychotherapy* (New York: Basic Books) 1982.

[8]

Confronting God
The Language of Anger and Despair
in Job and Jeremiah

In the previous chapter, we found Qohelet advocating the fear of God, despite an inability to make sense of life. In this chapter, we move from the more philosophical assessment of the human condition to intensely personal and emotional responses, not so much to life, as to God himself. It is a transition from the cognitive to the emotional. From Qohelet's mode of observing, documenting and drawing the conclusion that 'everything is absurd', we move to expressions of angry protest.

A point worth noting from the outset is that confrontation is a part of intimacy, albeit a hazardous one. Married couples, friends and families know this only too well. Intimacy and confrontation with God are very evidently a part of Old Testament spirituality. In dialogues with God, a whole spectrum of emotions comes into play—anger, hurt, despair and bitterness—expressed in accusation, plea and questioning.

We will track the turbulent language of lament to where it sounds a crescendo in Jeremiah and Job. Insecurity and tears surfaced intermittently in the reflective Psalm 119, but Jeremiah and Job go beyond lament to confront God with the full force of their feelings. We will use Job and Jeremiah as specific examples, with a glance at God-lament psalms, in particular Psalm 22. Our study will stumble over imprecatory prayer. When human beings surround the poet with a wall of hostility as he tries to get through to God, they come in for strong language too.

THEOLOGY, EMOTION AND SPIRITUALITY

First, we should pause to clarify the relationship between emotion and theology, and ask what hermeneutical issues are raised when we attempt a transfer from the ancient text to contemporary spirituality. Emotions are not theology. Nor, for that matter, are the writings of the Old Testament. Theology—in the western academic tradition—works towards conceptual lucidity by trying to avoid contradictions and the contamination of ideas by unhelpful associations. This is a cognitive exercise and one that deals in propositional truth.[1] Theology, like philosophy, strives for objectivity in argument and end-product. Someone else who reads the material should follow the argument. A position is set out and defended against objections past, present or anticipated. The medium for theology is prose in print, read by one person silently to themselves, often in a library. The form is an essay, treatise or book that is studied by underlining, highlighting and note-taking.

Spirituality involves the response of the person to God. It works towards coherence of spirit, our own within ourselves and with God, rather than towards a conceptual coherence. The degree of subjectivity is greater. The words of spirituality might be written or memorized, prose or poetry, thought, spoken aloud or read silently, recited liturgically or sung communally. On the other hand, there might not be words, but silence. Or words formed in spontaneous prayer, instead of lifted from a text. For all these differences of genre and setting, spirituality is not devoid of theology. Nor is our theology uncoloured by our emotions.

Emotions are rather like colours. The spectrum arranges them in adjacent gradations but they also come in odd mixtures. Emotions are first felt before they can be named. They present themselves with a startling immediacy ahead of our ability to describe them in words. Indeed, feelings can exist without words, whereas theology cannot. Psychologists consider our emotions as already interpretations of reality before the stage when we can name them. Our cerebral cortex attaches a meaning to the physiological sensations passed to it through neural pathways in the brain.[2] Words are attached to this perception of sensation and

---

[1] Compare the remarks of Goldingay contrasting Western theology and biblical material, and then theology and symbolism: 'In what sense does the term theology apply to the OT? While the term can be applied loosely to refer to any talk of God, more strictly it denotes a particularly analytic, conceptualizing, reflective, systematic way of speaking about God . . . Biblical writers tell stories, declare judgment, expound hope, write letters, lay down laws, offer advice, lament affliction, and celebrate blessings, but they do not do theology as such.

Symbolism, imagery and metaphor characteristically work at a more intuitive level . . . They involve the whole person's feelings, memories, experiences, and attitudes, as well as conscious thought-processes.' (Goldingay, *Diversity*, p.173 and 175)

[2] Psychology confronts the brain-mind issues when attempts are made to define and explain emotions. The autonomic nervous system, blood-borne hormones, neurotransmitter chemicals, 'the animal brain', ie. the limbic system, especially the hypothalamus and amygdala, and neural pathways in the brain

meaning-analysis in order to express the emotion more fully to ourselves or to others. Christian spirituality contributes a distinct cognitive framework for processing the emotions we experience. That framework is both cultural and theological.

At this point a visual image of emotion will be helpful. We can think of emotions as ripples on the surface of a pool. The edge of the pool is not the ripple, but it contains and contributes to the pattern of the ripple. If a stone is dropped into a pool near to the edge, ripples will run back from the edge and intersect with others as they radiate across the surface, more if the edge is steep, less if it is flat. The shape and height of the edge will contribute to the shape of the ripple in a dynamic way. In this way, our perceptual framework—the edge—contributes shape to the ripple of emotion without being the emotion. Our personality, upbringing, culture and theology form the conceptual and interpretive edge to our pool of emotions. To appreciate this, one has only to consider the various ways in which Christians worldwide feel and give expression, or do not give expression, to grief.

Strong emotions such as anger, fear and guilt are feelings that we have towards fellow human beings and towards God. It is an added complication that two planes of expression are involved—the horizontal and the vertical. These axes can be readily distinguished, but they are related, as biblical psalms of lament demonstrate. They mix imprecations against enemies with their protests to God. These two planes of emotional expression characterize the confrontational experiences of Job and of Jeremiah.

CROSS-CULTURAL TRANSFERENCE?

To study the expression of anger, fear or guilt in the Old Testament means starting from the texts that reflect experiences of these emotions in a personal way. Obviously, as readers our own experiences of anger, fear and guilt are brought into play. We identify with the emotions in the text and so enter into the world of the text. How do we make this cross-cultural and theological

---

are all involved in generating emotions. The frontal cortex, that is, the cognitive department of the brain, imparts a meaning-analysis to data from the limbic system. For instance, so-called fight-flight arousal depends on physiological changes governed by the Sympathetic nervous system, but cognition decides what to feel and do in the circumstances. The emotions accompanying fight-flight arousal could be fear, exhilaration or anger. This meaning-analysis function of the cortex allows for complexity of emotions. It also allows for feelings of anger, fear or sadness to be generated by reading words on a page—the way that a good novel draws us into its world and makes us laugh, cry or feel fear. See FE Bloom and A Lazerson, *Brain, Mind*

transfer to and fro, from our experience to the world of the text and back again? After all, it is our temperament, our contemporary culture and our Christian theology, not those of the writer, that habitually give meaning to our emotions of anger, fear and guilt. Secondly, if we can get hold of the emotions in the ancient text and describe them coherently enough, should we use these expressions of emotion as a model for our own spirituality? Thirdly, should our prayers include expression of our strongly confrontational or negative emotions towards other human beings? In using the language of the Old Testament as a model, can we distinguish between cultural difficulties involved in using that model, difficulties that we could overcome, and theological difficulties with the model that we should not try to overcome?

One example will illustrate the dilemma of Old Testament model and Christian recontextualization—the curse formula. In Deut 27, a rubric for a covenant ceremony is set out. Six tribes stand on Mount Gerizim and six tribes stand on Mount Ebal, representing the blessing and curse of covenant. The Levites take the lead in pronouncing a series of curses to which the people must respond with 'Amen!'. The Christian church has appropriated the Hebrew 'Amen!' (*'āmēn*), literally, into its pattern of spiritual expression, but it has not appropriated tribal structures or the curse formulae. These are perceived as culture-bound elements, belonging to the Sinai covenant and not to the Upper Room covenant.

The actual content of the Levites' curse utterances have a mixed status in a Christian context. We retain the incest ethic of Deut 27:20,22,23 in Christian morality enforced through church discipline, and even incorporated into state law via Act of Parliament. However, neither church communities nor state authorities enforce the penalties prescribed for breach of the Sinai covenant laws, for instance the death penalty for incest and bestiality.[3] The

and Behaviour, (New York: WH Freeman) 2nd ed 1988 Chap.7, pp.207–237 'Emotions: the highs and lows of the brain.'

[3] Sex with animals, cursed in Deut 27:1, incurs a death penalty in Exod 22:19 and Lev 20:15. For the death penalty and incest, compare Deut 27:20 and 22f with the references in the Holiness Code (Lev 18:6–18,23 and 20:11f,14–17, the latter chapter detailing the death penalty; in one instance death by burning, v.14). The death penalty for fifteen crimes, based on pentateuchal laws, has been advocated in Reconstructionist writing in the USA, exemplified by GL Bahnsen. This has led to vigorous hermeneutical debate about transposability from Israel's covenant to contemporary contexts. See, for instance, DA Oss, 'The Influence of Hermeneutical Frameworks in the Theonomy Debate' *WThJ* 51 (1989) 227–258 and the articles in *Transformation* 5.2 (1988), 5.3(1988) and 6.1 (1989) by Bahnsen, GJ Spykman and NL Geisler.

Christian community reproduces Old Testament forms of expression and behaviour selectively. Ritual as such is retained, but New Covenant rites do not involve circumcision, animal sacrifice and blood sprinkling. Denominational debate rages about the legitimacy of reproducing a 'levitical class' structure that divides the Christian community into lay and ordained strata, of male or mixed gender. Denominations dispute the transposing of various rites involving the use of incense, oil and water.

If contentious issues of cross-cultural and theological transference emerge in matters of ritual and morals, then we can expect that the expression of anger, fear and guilt will be controversial too. Indeed, the expression of anger with human enemies and the pronouncing of curses on them in the so-called imprecatory psalms does trouble devout readers of the Bible. As robust and unsqueamish a man of letters as CS Lewis could not rescue these prayers from his own censure. He staged a strategic retreat from 'the spirit of hatred which strikes us in the face . . . like heat from a furnace mouth'. He even detects crudity in Psa 23. In a quintessentially English manner, he remarks:

> This [Psa 23:5] may not be so diabolical as the passages I have quoted above; but the pettiness and vulgarity of it, especially in such surroundings, are hard to endure.[4]

He uses stronger adjectives—'contemptible', 'vindictive', 'ferocious', 'self-pitying', 'barbaric', 'devilish'—in the course of his discussion, but as a prelude to his reflections, he says:

> We must not either try to explain them away or to yield for one moment to the idea that, because it comes in the Bible, all this vindictive hatred must somehow be good and pious. We must face both facts squarely. The hatred is there—festering, gloating, undisguised—and also we should be wicked if we in any way condoned or approved it, or (worse still) used it to justify similar passions in ourselves. Only after these two admissions have been made can we safely proceed.[5]

He does proceed, cautiously, to identify with the psalmists by admitting to feelings of 'resentment', but he immediately denies that we 'dream of quite such appalling revenges'. Considering that

---

[4] CS Lewis, *Reflections on the Psalms*, 1958 (Fontana, London: Collins) 1961, p.24. Words like 'petty' and 'vulgar' signal the class consciousness and social snobbery so prevalent in the Oxbridge culture of Lewis' day. Male chauvinism and a 'stiff-upper-lip' approach to emotions ruled. See the biography of Lewis by AN Wilson, *CS Lewis* (London: Collins) 1990.
[5] *Reflections*, p.24f.

he went through the experiences of a British boarding school and the trenches of the First World War, one can only applaud his restraint. Yet Lewis aside, what we see illustrated in his remarks is that the personal, cultural and theological framework of the interpreter is not neutral, objective or disengaged during the process of interpreting and appropriating the text of the Old Testament. There is a cultural gap to bridge even to understand the material in its own context, let alone to recontextualize aspects of it within a contemporary Christian spirituality.

With this acknowledgement of hermeneutical operations involved in reading and reacting to the expression of emotion in the Old Testament, we turn now to the emotions in the book of Job, and to the story of Job's orientation, disorientation and re-orientation.[6]

A. CONFRONTATION IN THE BOOK OF JOB

JOB: THE MAN WE MEET

Job is introduced as a man who was 'blameless and upright, one who feared God and turned away from evil' (1:1). He expressed his piety as patriarchal head of house through sacrifice (1:5), and, as we learn later, in just and caring relations in his community (Chap. 30).

He is presented as a model of spirituality. God says so to Satan, echoing the narrator's words (1:8, cf. 1:1), and Job proves to be such after the initial round of disasters. He prostrates himself in worship before God and utters a blessing (1:20), persisting in his integrity (2:3).

After the second round of Satan's attentions, Job's wife urges him to curse God and die. Cursing God was what Job feared his children might have done and a motive for his offering sacrifice on their behalf (1:5b). He roundly rejects his wife's suggestion, remaining guiltless 'with his lips' (2:10b). The three friends hear of his sorry state, travel to meet him and sit with him on the ground in silence seven days and seven nights.

---

[6] W Brueggemann wrote a seminal article entitled 'Psalms and the Life of Faith: a suggested typology of function' *JSOT* 17 (1978) 3–32 in which he reviewed hymns, laments and thanksgivings in terms of the worshipper's orientation, disorientation and reorientation. J Goldingay offered a response in 'The Dynamic Cycle of Praise and Prayer in the Psalms' *JSOT* 20 (1981) 85–90. The point is that spirituality does not produce a plateau of equilibrium. Spirituality involves a dynamic reaction to life events that is reflected in dialogue with God. Job as a literary piece ends with equilibrium restored, but life does not allow for that reorientation to continue untroubled. Another cycle of disequilibrium and the need for reorientation is bound to follow.

Nothing prepares us for what happens next after this interlude of silence—'after this Job opened his mouth and cursed the day of his birth' (3:1). Job carries no guilt, but he does admit to fear: 'Truly the thing that I fear comes upon me, and what I dread befalls me' (3:25). This fear is a counterpoint to his fear of the Lord. Cursing the day he was born comes perilously close to cursing his Creator. Is this displaced anger? Certainly, with this soliloquy we leave patient Job behind—compare his forceful statement later on: 'As for me, is my complaint addressed to mortals? Why should I not be impatient?'(21:4).[7] The previous spirituality has cracked open. It cannot contain what he is feeling any longer. The wisdom aphorisms that summed up his reaction to the first and second trials are now seen as a shell of piety that must break open, if new life is to be released:

> Naked I came from my mother's womb, and naked shall I return there; the LORD gave and the LORD has taken away; blessed be the name of the LORD.
>
> (1:21)
>
> Shall we receive the good at the hand of God, and not receive the bad?
>
> (2:10)

Initially, Job had found these aphorisms adequate expressions. In retrospect, they were the last vestiges of his previous piety, the last trace of orientation before disorientation displaces it. He will need a new spirituality and one that embraces emotions other than resignation to replace the old. But before any new equilibrium develops, emotional disequilibrium must be given its due.

Eliphaz is the first friend to speak after Job's soliloquy. He recalls Job's fear of God and integrity politely (4:6), but passes a more critical comment on Job's impatience and dismay (4:4f). He follows through with a theological exposition and some recommendations towards a renewed spirituality—'as for me, I would seek God' (5:8). And so begins the debate which will mount in emotional intensity over the next chapters.

GENRE, THEOLOGY, IMAGERY AND EMOTIONS

We could follow the theology of this debate. Indeed a case can be made that 'the book aims at *speaking correctly* about God'.[8]

---

[7] 'Be impatient'—Hebrew *tiqṣar ruḥīy*. Root *qṣr*—'to be short' is used referring to God in Micah 2:7 *hᵃqāṣar rūah Yhwh*—'Has the spirit of Yhwh become short?', meaning 'Has Yahweh lost his temper?', LC Allen, *Joel,Obadiah, Jonah & Micah*, NICOT (Grand Rapids: Eerdmans) 1976, p.292.

[8] LG Perdue, *Wisdom in Revolt: metaphorical theology in the book of Job*, Bible & Literature 29 (Sheffield: The Almond Press) 1991, p.75. He continues: 'The entire movement of the book is theological, that is, the articulation of language about and to God.'

Certainly there are theological propositions and postulates bandied to and fro. Yet there is another level to the interaction in Job than theological truths. There are the emotions expressed. Some scholars speak of Job as a Wisdom debate, others see in it more of a lawsuit or lament, and there is truth in these characterizations in terms of the language forms employed. For our purposes, to debate the literary genre of Job would be a sterile exercise.[9] It is clear from recent discussions that interpreters bring their own agendas to this book more than to many, and that the book has a richness that supports several approaches without being defined by them.[10]

In relational terms, the book is a series of personal confrontations—between Satan and God, Job and his wife, Job and his friends, Elihu and the four others, God and Job, God and Job's friends. The reader is drawn into taking sides. But who is the hero? Job or God? If these two come into confrontation, with whom do we side?

In lawsuit terms, Job asserts his innocence and demands a hearing at which God should appear. In lament terms, Job details his suffering. This detailing of suffering as well as more explicitly confrontation language functions as the complaint or accusation directed to and at God. As his friends fail to deter him from this, and fail to coerce him into admitting guilt, the interchanges become more and more heated. This drama of confrontation is stagelit with emotions. Job's anger with God first surfaces as anger

---

[9] The literary form of the canonical Job is more than its parts and their literary history. There is nothing really comparable with Job in Near Eastern literature because of Job's scale, artistry and monotheism. For helpful reviews of Job's literary form, see RE Murphy, *Wisdom Literature*, FOTL 13 (Grand Rapids: Eerdmans) 1981, pp.16ff and JE Hartley, *Job*, NICOT, (Grand Rapids: Eerdmans) 1988, pp.35–43. Approaches along lines of the New Criticism are represented in *Semeia* 7 (1977) *Studies in the Book of Job*, edited by R Polzin and D Robertson. DJA Clines's contribution to the Word Biblical Commentary series offers the fullest recent review of literature and hermeneutics—*Job 1–20*, WBC 17 (Dallas: Word) 1989.

[10] Job shows us a way with his vigorous protest, his discovery of concrete commitment to the poor and all who suffer unjustly, his facing up to God, and his acknowledgement of the gratuitousness that characterises God's plan for human history. It is for us to find our own route amid the present sufferings and hopes of the poor of Latin America . . . *On Job: God-talk and the suffering of the innocent* (Maryknoll: Orbis) 1987, p.102.

Gutiérrez brings his concerns with praxis, contextuality and the suffering of the poor to bear on Job. He agrees with Perdue that talking about God, that is, theology, is the issue. Yet Perdue and Gutírrez could hardly have produced more different books. For Gutírrez, the language of prophetic solidarity with the poor and the language of contemplation of the gratuitous love of God are combined in Job.

with his friends who are defending God. Sarcasm is the first indicator of Job's deep anger.

> No doubt you are the people,
>   and wisdom will die with you.
> But I have understanding as well as you;
>   I am not inferior to you.
> Who does not know such things as these?
>
> (12:1)

> What you know, I also know;
>   I am not inferior to you.
> But I would speak to the Almighty,
>   and I desire to argue my case with God.
> As for you, you whitewash with lies;
>   all of you are worthless physicians.
> If you would only keep silent,
>   that would be your wisdom!
>
> (13:2–5)

> I will defend my ways to his face.
>
> (13:15)

Eliphaz cannot see this attitude of confrontation with God as an advance in spirituality. Far from it. Eliphaz sees it as undermining spirituality:

> But you are doing away with the fear of God,
>   and hindering meditation before God.
> For your iniquity teaches your mouth,
>   and you choose the tongue of the crafty.
>
> (15:4f)[11]

Job's feelings have got the better of him, Eliphaz says:

> Why does your heart carry you away,
>   and why do your eyes flash,
> so that you turn your spirit against God,
>   and let such words go out of your mouth?
>
> (15:12f)

---

[11] The key words about spirituality are *yir'āh*—'fear' ('of God' is supplied by NRSV, correctly; alternatively with NIV, 'piety'), and *śīḥāh*—'occupation of mind, concern, focus', which is used in Psa 119:

> [97]Oh, how I love your law!
> it is my meditation all day long.
> [99b]for your decrees are my *meditation*.

See Psa 119:15,23,48,78,148 for further uses of the verbal root *śyḥ* or noun.

MOUNTING ANGER, MOUNTING ACCUSATION

By the time we reach Chap. 16, Job has spoken four times—the soliloquy of Chap. 3, and three responses in the first debate cycle (chaps. 6–7, 9–10, 12–14).[12] In terms of anger with God, Chap. 16 is the climax. The violence of the imagery reflects the power of Job's emotions. On the surface, the emotion of Job at this point is brokenness of spirit. He weeps tears of despair that he will ever be vindicated.

> My face is red with weeping,
>   and deep darkness is on my eyelids,
> though there is no violence in my hands,
>   and my prayer is pure.
>
> My friends scorn me;
>   my eye pours out tears to God,
> that he would maintain the right of a mortal with God
>
> (16:16,20f)

He is worn out and exhausted (16:6, 17:1). Yet alongside the despair and frustration which exhausts him, there is an energetic accusation of God in the most violent of terms. Job likens God's attack on him to that of a wild beast or warrior.

> He has torn me in his wrath, and hated me;
>   he has gnashed his teeth at me;
> my adversary sharpens his eyes against me.[13]

---

[12] Job's soliloquy (chap.3) is followed by alternating speeches: Eliphaz-Job, Bildad-Job and Zophar-Job on this scheme. Eliphaz begins the second cycle (chap.15) and the pattern Eliphaz-Job, Bildad-Job and Zophar-Job is duplicated. Cycle 3 breaks this symmetry because Zophar has no speech assigned to him. The cycle begins with Chap.22 and runs Eliphaz-Job, Bildad-Job and continues with Job from chap.26–31 where the debate with the three friends ends. Scholars often re-assign speeches here, and explain Chap.28 and the Elihu speeches of Chaps.32–37 as secondary additions to the book.

[13] FI Andersen strengthens the carnivore metaphor of v.9 on the grounds that 'wrath' (NRSV) can be given the physical connotation of the Hebrew word *'ap*—'nose, wrath', and 'hated'(*śṭm*) a proposed meaning 'hunt'. Animal 'teeth' are rendered 'fangs' in more dynamic English.

> [9]With his snout he ripped me and chased me,
> He slashed me with his fangs.
>
> *Job*, TCOT (Leicester:IVP) 1976, p.181.

While this translation can be defended linguistically, it loses something of the play on ideas by over-animalizing the imagery. For instance, 'gnashes his teeth at me','grinds his teeth at me' (NIV; REB) combines the physical threat with the emotional connotation of grinding the teeth in anger, rather than 'slashed me with his fangs' (*ḥāraq 'ālay b'šinnāyw*). As LG Perdue points out, *ḥrq* 'expresses deep feelings of intense anger against an enemy, resulting in the gnashing or grinding of teeth (Pss. 12:10, 35:16, 37:12, Lam 2:16)'—*Wisdom in*

I was at ease, and he broke me in two;
　he seized me by the neck and dashed me to pieces;
he has set me up as his target;
　his archers surround me.
He slashes open my kidneys, and shows no mercy;
　he pours out my gall on the ground.
He bursts upon me again and again;
　he rushes at me like a warrior.

(16:9, 12–14)

The readers know that this ferocity of God is imagined, not real, because we have the information of the narrative prologue, denied to Job and his friends. The violence of Job's language about God signals a violence of emotion within himself, his own anger projected on to God.

After Job's speech of Chap. 16–17, Bildad characterizes Job as angry—'you who tear yourself in your anger'(*tōrēp napšō bᵉᵃappō*, 18:4). These words of Bildad pick up the wording of 16:9—'he has torn me in his wrath' (*'appō ṭārap*). To paraphrase Bildad—'Your anger will destroy you.' The fact that Job's speech in chaps. 16–17 reflects other emotions such as scorn, grief, despair, weariness and even a ray of hope (16:2,16,20 17:7 and 16:19) simply confirms the phenomenon that emotions come in complex bundles. The particular emotions may seem contradictory and mutually exclusive, but are not so since emotions are feelings, not reason, and disclose ambivalence. The author has mirrored life skilfully.

In Chap.19, Job is still oscillating between aggressive protest and self-pitying reactions both to his friends and to God, while in Chap. 30 the summary of his abject state includes both his social ostracism and God's violence and indifference.

Even when I cry out, 'Violence!' I am not answered;
　I call aloud, but there is no justice.

Have pity on me, have pity on me, O you my friends,
　for the hand of God has touched me!
Why do you, like God, pursue me,
　never satisfied with my flesh?

(19:7,21f)

With violence he seizes my garment;
　he grasps me by the collar of my tunic.

Revolt, p.171 note 3. Metaphor preserves the tension between the animal and the personal qualities —which enhances the effect.

He has cast me into the mire,
  and I have become like dust and ashes.[14]

You have turned cruel to me;
  with the might of your hand you persecute me.

(30:18f,21)

Unable to shift Job from his insistence on his innocence, Job's three friends fall silent (32:1). We are back to the beginning. As then, so now, the silence is a pregnant one, for Job has dared to confront God himself, the Friend who has not turned up to commiserate with him.[15]
Before God does appear, Elihu breaks this angry silence.

Then Elihu son of Barachel the Buzite, of the family of Ram, became angry. He was angry at Job because he justified himself rather than God; he was angry also at Job's three friends because they had found no answer, though they had declared Job to be in the wrong.

(32:2f)

The temperature of the encounter rises, if not the quality of the debate. Elihu is furious with pent–up feeling. The fourfold repetition of the phrase 'his anger burned' emphasizes this.[16] 'No fear of me need terrify you' (33:7), he assures Job, but he concludes by recommending that Job fear before God who is awesome in theophany—'Therefore mortals fear him' (37:24).
The debate between Job, Eliphaz, Bildad, Zophar and Elihu has ranged over many theological truths, but in one sense it can be co–ordinated with reference to the three emotions of anger, fear and guilt. Everyone has become angry, but Job has refused to feel guilty. The four representatives of conventional wisdom stick to the fear of the LORD as their first and last principle, whereas Job's wife advocates defiance of God. Job neither sticks to the fear of the LORD in a conventional sense, nor curses God in defiance. He expresses anger with God. Emboldened by his innocence, Job moves beyond a traditional fear of the Lord. His anger is scarcely

---

[14] The Massoretic text seems less reliable than the Septuagint, with some support from 11QtgJob. Commentators wrestle with exact details. God is the subject of these verbs of violent action and is addressed directly in vv.20ff.

[15] In Chap.29, Job recalls his previous intimacy with God in terms of belonging to his inner circle, using a vocabulary found in Jeremiah: 'when the friendship of God (*sôd ᵉlôāh*) was upon my tent' (29:4). On *sôd*—'intimate circle, friendship', see the discussion of Psa 25:14 in Chapter 1.

[16] In Hebrew idiom, his nostrils burn. *ḥārāh* + *'ap* is used 4 times in vv.2,3,5 to emphasize how angry this young man Elihu has become. Commentators are divided over these speeches in terms both of authorship and contribution to the flow of thought. We can see that their author has woven them into the mood of the confrontations.

confined to cursing his birth or refuting his friends. Job's anger leads him into head-on confrontation of his God.

CONFRONTATION AND THEOPHANY

Into this charged atmosphere bursts Yahweh and speaks out of the whirlwind.[17] His confrontational tone and his use of creation as leading motif seem to re-establish the position of traditional Wisdom. Surely this God of earth, water, wind and fire demands awe? He refuses to answer Job's questions hurled at him in anger, grief and despair. Instead, God depicts Behemoth and Leviathan using violent imagery.[18] The fierceness of the anger generated in the debate is counterpointed by the ferocity of Leviathan.

> Its sneezes flash forth light
>   and its eyes are like the eyelids of the dawn.
> From its mouth go flaming torches;
>   sparks of fire leap out.
> Out of its nostrils comes smoke,
>   as from a boiling pot and burning rushes.
> Its breath kindles coals,
>   and a flame comes out of its mouth.
>
> (41:18-21)

---

[17] Commentators evaluate God's speeches differently. G von Rad notes that 'all commentators find the divine speech highly scandalous, in so far as it bypasses completely Job's particular concerns and because Yahweh in no way condescends to any kind of self-interpretation . . . God makes creation bear witness to himself' (*Wisdom in Israel*, SCM 1972, p.225). On the contrary, Luis Alonso-Schökel points out that Job achieves his goals. He reaches and meets God. God speaks no word that affirms the retribution on Job threatened by the friends, and the whole guilt/acquittal axis of the debate is sidelined. Neither Job nor God is guilty. The audience is not forced to side with God against Job, and God's control over his universe is reaffirmed ('God's Answer to Job' *Concilium* 169 (1983) *Job and the Silence of God*, pp. 45–51).

[18] Perdue, *Wisdom in Revolt* interprets the whole book in terms of intersecting conflict—a) the conflict of God as Warrior versus chaos, and b) the conflict engendered by the revolt of man as slave against God. This mythic patterning is exemplified in *Enūma eliš* and *Atraḫāsis* respectively. It supplies root metaphors burgeoning in the language of Job, according to Perdue. The cosmic creation and warrior language certainly contributes to Job, as the appearance of Rahab and Leviathan attest (26:12 and 41). Perdue sees Job's revolt as a bid to be the Primal Man, picked up by Eliphaz' accusation ('Are you the first-born of the human race?' *hᵃrî'šôn 'ādām tiwwālēd*, 15:7) and Job's assertions of his innocence in Chap.29 and 31. This leads Perdue to describe the tale of Job as 'a redescription of the mythic drama of the fall. Job is the man who would be God' (p.193). This reading is not convincing because it exaggerates the mythic warrior imagery to global proportions in the book. Moreover, the Primal Man interpretation misrepresents Job's anger with God and his eagerness to prove his innocence.

God has stolen Job's thunder—'can you thunder with a voice like his?'(40:9). The theophany has reduced Job to silence—'I lay my hand on my mouth' (40:4). Job returns to a fear of the Lord after seeing God (42:5f). This is based on personal experience rather than tradition ('I had heard of you by the hearing of the ear', v. 5a).

Yet the irony is that Job's expression of guilt-free anger with God is upheld by God's own last word in the book. The last vestige of anger in the book is expressed by God against the three friends:

> my wrath is kindled against you (Eliphaz) and your two friends; for you have not spoken of me what is right, as Job my servant has . . . my servant Job shall pray for you, for I will accept his prayer not to deal with you according to your folly; for you have not spoken of me what is right, as my servant Job has done.
>
> (42:7f)

Spirituality has come full circle.[19] Job comes back to sacrifice and prayer, but his journey of faith has taken him through the fire of anger with God. From a fear of God which avoided confrontation, Job moved through anger to a fear of God that risked everything. Then Job the confronter was himself confronted in theophany. On the other side of anger, Job has a fear of the Lord that is more than a theology of transcendence and immanence. Experience and emotion have enriched Job's spirituality. But at what cost!

If there is a model of spirituality in Job's experience, in his confrontation with God, in his anger and in his humility, then it may need other experiences of lament and protest to confirm this. Otherwise Job's unique circumstances, the God—Satan interaction and the personal theophany might distance Job from common experience. The psalms of Lament provide this data, for here other voices of complaint and accusation, disappointment and despair are raised against God. Instead of turning to the samples in the psalter at this point, we shall focus on Jeremiah and ask whether

---

[19] W Vogels detects seven types of language in Job and five stages of growth ('The Spiritual Growth of Job' *BThB* 11.3 July [1981] 77–80). The language types are: popular faith, doubt, theological, prayer, prophetic, veneration, mystical. The stages of growth correspond with Kübler-Ross's characterization of terminal patients: denial, anger, bargaining, depression, acceptance. This approach is stimulating, but the correlations of language type and emotions, and progress through the stages, are a little forced. Bundles of emotion rather than stages 2 to 4 occur after Job's denial (his patience and inadequate aphorisms) and before his humble acceptance. Vogels's assertion that Job 'has become a much 'richer' person . . . is what the final conclusion tells us in a very simple way' may be too neat a way of rescuing the epilogue's material rewards from their this-worldly and Near Eastern culture-boundness.

his confrontation with God provoked by his vocation as a prophet opens a window on to the expression of powerful emotions.

B. JEREMIAH CONFRONTS GOD

When we turn from Job to Jeremiah, we move from the context of Wisdom to the context of prophecy, from the land of Uz to the land of Israel. If there were private and public aspects to Job's life, polarities of family and community, of friends and inner being, then Jeremiah brings public and private life into a more heightened tension still. Jeremiah models a vocation, where Job acted as head of family. This means that God's word and its reliability is bound up with Jeremiah. Will God leave Jeremiah exposed to the plots and rejection of his people as he left Job exposed to Satan's attentions?

In this case, it is not God's word spoken to the accuser behind the scenes in the realm of the heavenly court that is at stake but rather God's word preached to the court of Judah and proclaimed publicly in the streets of Jerusalem. What happens between Jeremiah and God will have direct repercussions on what happens between God and Israel. If Job displays the emotions of a righteous man in conflict with God, then Jeremiah embodies the reactions of a righteous Israelite living in a doomed community. What emotions is a prophet allowed?

CONFRONTATION I: ANGER, NOT THEODICY (JER 11:18–12:6)

If Job begins with a statement from God that Job is righteous, then Jeremiah's Confessions begin with a statement that God is righteous. God's statement in Job and Jeremiah's statement both stand, yet each turns out to be the prelude, not the conclusion. What happens after these declarations of righteousness is head–on conflict.

> ¹You will be in the right, O LORD,
>   when I lay charges against you;
>   but let me put my case to you.
> Why does the way of the guilty prosper?
>   Why do all who are treacherous thrive?
> ²You plant them, and they take root;
>   they grow and bring forth fruit;
> you are near in their mouths
>   yet far from their hearts.
> ³But you, O LORD, know me;
>   You see me and test me—
>   my heart is with you.
>
>   (Jer 12:1–3)

Just as Job wished to bring God to the bar for an independent adjudication, and pointed out the anomaly of the wicked living untroubled, so Jeremiah has questions to put to Yahweh.[20] Verse 1 uses the language of the lawsuit.[21] Though Jeremiah knows God will win an acquittal, and even believes that God is righteous (*ṣaddīq*)—the statements carry both disapproval and recognition—he feels a compulsion to question him. The questions of v. 1b have the form of questions but actually serve as accusations against God who is given responsibility for planting and prospering the wicked. The tree metaphor parodies the piety of Psa 1:3 where it is the righteous who flourish as God's planted tree. Verse 3 sounds the note of spirituality—all things are open to Yahweh, as Psa 139 affirms, especially the depths of the human heart. Jeremiah has nothing to hide. He is wholeheartedly on Yahweh's side, whereas the rebels are duplicitous. Their lips say one thing, their intentions are quite different.

The questions of v. 1 sound like general questions about the rule of God, yet this is no wisdom debate about theodicy. Jeremiah is frightened and angry, not in philosophical mood. We know this from the context, for this first of the so-called Confessions of Jeremiah turns around Jeremiah's discovery that people from his hometown of Anathoth are plotting his assassination and intimidating him against preaching his message of judgment.[22] Using language and forms similar to psalms of Lament, Jeremiah both accuses God and appeals to him for protection.[23] The prophet is

---

[20] For Job's accusations against God about the prosperity of the wicked, see 9:22,24 10:3, 21:7–33.

[21] NRSV brings out the basic metaphor well with coherent connotations 'in the right', 'lay charges' and 'my case' for the Hebrew words *ṣaddīq*, *rīb* and *mišpāṭīm*.

[22] The First Confession begins at 11:18 and runs to 12:6. It is sometimes divided into two pericopes 11:18–23 and 12:1–6. The two parts are linked by key metaphors—the tree metaphor (11:19b and 12:2), by confession of Yahweh as righteous judge (11:20 and 12:1) who tests hearts (11:20 and 12:3a), by sheep slaughter imagery (11:19 and 12:3b) and by reference to Jeremiah's kinsfolk (11:21,23 and 12:6). The links may be editorial. See the discussion in KM O'Connor, *The Confessions of Jeremiah: their interpretation and role in Chapters 1–25*, SBLDS 94 (Atlanta: Scholars) 1988, pp. 7–26. She argues for literary unity in the form of a two strophe poem (11:18–20 and 12:1–3) with redactional prose additions (vv.21–23 and 12:6). AR Diamond goes further and argues for 12:1–6 as coherent, with v.6 as poetry—*The Confessions of Jeremiah in Context: scenes of prophetic drama*, JSOTS 45 (Sheffield: JSOT Press) 1987, pp.21–51.

[23] O'Connor notes that the statement of trust and the expression of praise are missing elements from the Lament form here. They are elements 4 and 7 from the conventional scheme of Laments: 1. Direct address to Yahweh, 2. Complaint or description of speaker's predicament, 3. Plea of innocence, 4. Statement of trust that Yahweh will intervene, 5. Petition for God's intervention, 6. Divine oracle of assurance, 7. Vow or expression of praise

trapped in his vocation between God who commissioned him and his people who wish to eradicate him.

He feels himself to be an innocent and he reacts with fear and anger both manward and Godward.

> [19]But I was like a gentle lamb
>   led to the slaughter.

> [20]Pull them out like sheep for the slaughter,
>   and set them apart for the day of slaughter.

The imagery has shock value. It mirrors Jeremiah's shock when he discovers the plot by his own family. It also affirms divine retribution in the form of dramatic reversal of fortunes. The persecutors should become the victims. Of course, we cannot add 'and the victim, the persecutor' because this would be untrue to the dynamics. Jeremiah had no counterplot other than prayer. Hence his appeal to the righteous Judge.[24] Jeremiah wishes to hold Yahweh to who he is, but God's tough response holds Jeremiah to his vocation. In place of a reassuring oracle of deliverance, Jeremiah is told the going will get tougher, horses to race against instead of men, thickets to traverse instead of open field (12:5). This double-sided conflict with God and with countrymen will develop beyond the First Confession.

CONFRONTATION 2: ANGER AT BETRAYAL (JER 15:10–21)

The Second Confession begins with Jeremiah's bitter lament that he was born to such trouble.

> v.10 Woe is me, my mother, that you ever bore me, a man of strife and contention to the whole land! I have not lent, nor have I borrowed, yet all of them curse me.

The curse in the Near East was a solemn thing, somewhat akin to a spell in that the words were believed to produce effects in the public realm of politics or the private world of bewitchment. In Egypt, for instance, the names of enemies and curse formulae were inscribed in ink on plaster figurines or pottery bowls that

---

(p.24). Diamond describes the language of accusation in 12:1 as 'near-blasphemous' (p.45).

[24] Yahweh is the *šōpēṭ ṣedeq* (11:20). Echoing *šōpēṭ* is *mišpāṭīm* in 12:1c with *ṣaddiq* repeated in v.1a.

were smashed to inflict the curse on those named.[25] When Jeremiah pronounced judgment on Judah, accompanied by the symbolic smashing of an earthenware jar, the public who were involved in Baal worship would very likely have read this dramatic act as more than a visual aid to his message (Jer 19). It is probable, then, that when they cursed Jeremiah (15:10), they were not simply expressing political anger but fear, and were counteracting his pronouncements of judgment with maledictions of their own.

Jeremiah suffered a reaction to this antagonism. In this Confession, he characterizes himself as 'a man of strife and contention'—not by temperament, but by prophetic vocation. In the Call Narrative, God told the reluctant Jeremiah that he had been selected and consecrated from the womb for his vocation (1:5), so the reference here to his mother and his birth is really a reference to his prophetic calling. He laments his calling because it landed him in perpetual conflict. The woe on his birth, then, amounts to distress with God's call.

Yet Jeremiah experiences ambiguity. Along with the insults 'on your account' (15:15b), he experiences a deep belonging to God and a delight in God's word.

> [16]Your words were found, and I ate them,
>   and your words became to me a joy
>   and the delight of my heart;
> for I am called by your name,
>   O LORD, God of hosts.

The emotions of 'joy' and 'delight' jostle with despair and anger. Verse 16 might allude to his call or to the discovery of the covenant document in the Temple during Josiah's reform. On the other hand, it may simply be referring to psalms or Torah learned

---

[25] The Egyptian Execration Texts from Middle Kingdom Thebes and Saqqara around 1800 BC are evidence of curse rituals. Names of enemies and lands were written in hieratic script on clay figurines or pottery bowls which were then smashed. See *ANEP*, 196 No. 593 and *ANET*, 328f. Curses to be implemented by the gods were appended to international treaties for breach of oath, or to inscribed stele, such as Hammurabi's Code, to protect against defacement. The rites and covenant curses of Deut 27 and 28 show how Ancient Near Eastern curses were adapted into monotheistic and non-magical Yahwism. See DJ McCarthy, Treaty and Covenant[rev.ed]., Analecta Biblica 21a (Rome: Biblical Institute Press) 1978, pp. 172ff and the studies by scholars such as Blank, Brichto, Hillers, Fensham, Frankena and Weinfeld referred to by McCarthy.

in a lifetime of spirituality.[26] Certainly, v.16 fits the spirituality of
the Psalms, for instance the expressions of delight in God's word
in Psa 119.

The irony is that the Confession models a spirituality of
struggle with God, not a praise mode of communing. Jeremiah
sets his delight in and internalizing of God's words and his deep
sense of belonging in the starkest contrast with his life of conflict.

> [17]I did not sit in the company of merrymakers,
>   nor did I rejoice;
> under the weight of your hand I sat alone,
>   for you had filled me with indignation.
> [18]Why is my pain unceasing,
>   my wound incurable,
>   refusing to be healed?
> Truly, you are to me like a deceitful brook,
>   like waters that fail.

Belonging to Yahweh meant that he did not belong to other
intimate circles.[27] He was an outsider in his own community. The
next chapter tells the story of Jeremiah's singleness. He is
commanded by God not to marry and have children because the
country is coming under judgment and mothers and fathers, sons
and daughters, will perish (16:1–4). His solitariness is a sign to the
community.

Here in the Confession, Jeremiah blames his isolation on
God—'under the weight of your hand I sat alone' (v.17b).[28]
Elsewhere, the metaphor of God's hand touching or resting on
someone can convey that God is communicating with them in a
special and personal manner. Jeremiah's contemporary, Ezekiel,
describes his altered states of consciousness in which he saw
visions and received God's word as 'the hand of the LORD being
strong upon me' (Ezek 3:14).[29] For Jeremiah, the hand singling

---

[26] Ezekiel ate the scroll with honey flavour at his call, but Jeremiah did not
savour his vocation, so the parallel between Ezek 3:3 and Jer 15:16 may be
misleading. Diamond (p.75f) inclines towards the Josiah scroll as source of
delight.

[27] An instance of Hebrew *sôd*, here 'company of merrymakers' (*sôd m^e saḥ^a qîm*).
See the remarks on the *sôd Yhwh* of Psa 25:14 in Chap. 1. 'Merrymakers' has
no in-built moral negative, as though it meant drunken revelry. Merrymaking
could, for instance, characterise wedding celebrations.

[28] NRSV supplies 'weight of' to convey the uncomfortable aspect of God's
hand. The Hebrew is *mipp^e nêy yād^e kā*—'because of your hand'.

[29] Compare also Ezek 1:3, 3:22, 8:1, 33:22, 37:1, 40:1.

him out meant separation and being filled up with anger.[30]
Jeremiah himself was made to feel God's angry reaction to Judean
sin. It is as though Jeremiah was a vessel first filled to the brim
with divine anger and then used to pour the anger out on its
proper object.

This experience of being a prophet left Jeremiah wounded in
spirit and feeling betrayed by God in his isolation.

> [18]Why is my pain unceasing,
>   my wound incurable,
>   refusing to be healed?
> Truly, you are to me like a deceitful brook,
>   like waters that fail.

Here Jeremiah moves from laying responsibility on God (v. 17) to
outright accusation. Even within the verse, there is a shift in
intensity from the rhetorical question 'Why . . .?' to the assertive
'Truly . . .'.[31] From focusing on his human antagonists, Jeremiah
has moved to open confrontation with his God. The image of a
dried–up wadi is striking, given that water is so often a symbol of
life in Hebrew poetry. Jeremiah himself had presented God as 'the
fountain of living water' (2:13).[32] Verse 18 is meant to shock, and
the graphic imagery ensures that this is achieved. It presents us
with a Jeremiah who is in his spiritual death throes. His condition
is excruciating and terminal. His last energy, his anger overriding
his despair, is used up, as it were, in confronting and accusing
God.

Insofar as Jeremiah has modelled his Confession on a psalm of
Lament, we should expect an oracle of reassurance to be
included.[33] In one sense, there is, because vv. 20–21 constitute an

---

[30] The Hebrew *zaʿam* is a strong word, rendered 'indignation' by NRSV, NIV,
REB and *BDB*, but 'curse' by WL Holladay, *CHALOT*, p. 91. Here is an
example of anthropomorphism but in a special context. Jeremiah feels
emotion, but his emotion is actually God's own emotion transferred and
mediated through the prophet.

[31] The Hebrew *lāmmāh*—'why?' introduces a self-addressed question, Jeremiah
speaking aloud, lamenting his sorry state. But because he is in dialogue with
God the question is also addressed to God and takes on the function of an
accusation. The last two English lines of v. 17 begin with the Infinitive
Absolute construction in Hebrew. This is the way Hebrew expresses something to be strongly the case: 'you have certainly become to me . . .'

[32] See for instance, WH Propp, *Water in the Wilderness: a biblical motif and its
mythological background*, HSS 40 (Atlanta: Scholars) 1987 for a technical study.
Jesus adopts the water–life symbolism to describe his gift of eternal life and of
the Spirit in John 4 and 7:37–39. The association of water imagery, God's
spirit and covenant renewal is already made in Isa 44:3.

[33] See Diamond, pp. 66–78, for a detailed discussion of the form-critical issues
and the coherence of Jer 15:15–21.

oracle of salvation without the 'Fear not . .' formulary. But v.19 is the immediate response to the accusation and is as tough and abrasive a response from God as was Jeremiah's accusation. Jeremiah is confronted with his need for repentance, and God's acceptance is conditional upon this turn-around.

> [19]Therefore thus says the LORD:
> If you turn back, I will take you back,
>   and you shall stand before me.
> If you utter what is precious,
>   and not what is worthless,
>   you shall serve as my mouth.
> It is they who will turn to you,
>   not you who will turn to them.

God's language to Jeremiah echoes the prophet's own preaching against the Judeans, summoning them to repentance.[34]

BEYOND LAMENT

If we were to draw conclusions for spirituality about the expression of anger, fear and guilt in the Confession of Jer 15:10–21, then they might go as follows. The two in confrontation, God and Jeremiah, have an intimate relationship. This means that distance is not the issue here. God is not remote to Jeremiah, an absent God, a silent God. So Jeremiah does not speak his words into the void. Just as the intimacy of marriage brings with it a greater potential for destructiveness than other relationships carry, so Jeremiah experiences his intimacy with God as inducing deep damage. At this point in the intimate relationship, there is so much pain that divorce is the prospect.

Jeremiah is an Israelite but not an ordinary Israelite. His approach to God reflects a psalm of Lament, yet goes beyond them. He is a prophet and that kind of intimate relationship dictates the kind of divorce. It is a divorce from his vocation. Yet his vocation and his being are inseparable because he was called

---

[34] See Jer 3:21–4:4, noting the conditional 'If you return, O Israel . . . if you return to me' (4:1). The Hebrew root *šûb* does duty for physically turning around and for spiritually turning around, *šûb*—'to turn, return, repent'. In v.19, *šûb* is used 4 times. Diamond (*Confessions in Context*, p.75) notes that 'the lack of formal elements expressing confidence already sets the complaint on the borders of normal Psalm laments and intensifies the negative tone of the lament. The negative slant is enhanced further by biting ironic plays upon divine epithets . . . Though accusations in the Psalms come close, they never go so far as to depict Yahweh explicitly as a liar (cf. Pss 44:10ff, 88:7ff, 89:39ff). In effect, the accusation reduces Yahweh to the status of Israel's idols.'

from the womb. He cannot separate his prophetic role from his life style and relations with his community. Already divorced from his community, he now faces divorce from God who has betrayed him.

These pressures on Jeremiah squeeze out the juices of despair, hurt and anger. Not guilt. Jeremiah feels and expresses no guilt. Yet God's reply commands him to repent. The resolution of this paradox of the absence of guilt and the command to repent lies in the issue of vocation. Jeremiah has not broken the covenant, but is breaking off his vocation. The Judeans have broken the covenant but were not called with Jeremiah's calling. God has no rebuke for the expression of despair and anger. The rebuke targets the renunciation of vocation.

CONFRONTATION 3: RETRIBUTION AND RESPITE (JER 17:14–18)

The Third Confession arises from delay in the fulfilment of Jeremiah's preaching and the resulting scorn with which he and his message is treated.[35] Jeremiah is the recipient of the derisive question 'Where is the word of the LORD?'(v.15). Yet God is the source of this message—'You know what came from my lips; it was before your face' (v.16). Jeremiah is trapped as the man in the middle. He is frightened by his human enemies, expresses his fear of being left without vindication by God, and adds in a complaint addressed to God: 'Do not become a terror to me' (v.17a).[36] Fear and anxiety lead into the anger expressed against his opponents. On them he wishes a retribution which contrasts with his vindication: shame, dismay and 'double destruction' on 'my persecutors'(v.18). For himself, he asks God directly—'heal me'[37] and 'save me'(v.14), expressing his need for rescue from the hostility and recuperation from the impact it had had on his inner being.

---

[35] Some scholars include vv.12–13 as an opening hymn of praise which links with v.14b 'you are my praise'. On this and for the fullest discussion of the Third Confession, see T Polk, *The Prophetic Persona: Jeremiah and the language of the self*, JSOTS 32 (Sheffield: JSOT Press) 1984, Chap. 5 'The Confessions', especially pp.131–152.

[36] To judge by the use of *mᵉḥittāh* in Jer 48:39 and Isa 54:14, the emotions evoked by a 'terror'(*mᵉḥittāh*, v.17a) would be strong ones.

[37] The Hebrew *rāpā'*— 'to heal' is the usual word for physical healing, but here is being used metaphorically. Perhaps it alludes to his incurable emotional wound of the previous Confession: 'my pain unceasing, my wound incurable, refusing to be healed (*hērāpē'*)' (15:18). Compare the comment: 'The appearance of these two words [*rāpā'*—'to heal', *yāša'*—'to save, rescue'] in parallel provides a stronger picture image than either word alone . . . The petition of v.14 is for wholeness within and liberation from external troubles—'PC Craigie, PH Kelley, JF Drinkard, *Jeremiah 1–25*, WBC 26, (Dallas: Word) 1991, p.234f.

The difference between this Confession and the previous one is that it lacks any reassuring oracle from God. Silence is always difficult to interpret, but we can rule out the idea, as culturally biased, that God is affronted by Jeremiah's anger or disapproves of his imprecations.[38] That explanation does not account for the canonizing of imprecatory psalms. The next Confession has more elaborate imprecations still. At this point, we will refer to Polk's comment and then return to the topic of model and imitation later:

> As the psalmic parallels attest, a curse on one's enemies, who are understood as God's enemies, was hardly an aberrant feature of ancient Israelite piety and could even be taken as an expression of one's commitment to Yhwh's cause. The problem would seem to be a modern one, therefore, and a hermeneutical (rather than exegetical) issue.[39]

CONFRONTATION 4: IMPRECATION (JER 18:18–23)

The Fourth Confession is marked by less conflict with God himself and more extensive imprecations against human opposition. The formal elements of psalms of Lament are used: lament, complaint, profession of innocence, confession of trust and petition.[40] It is necessary to emphasise this formal affinity between Jeremiah's poems and Israel's canonical material to appreciate the way in which the culture allowed for personal expression within formalized genres. Jeremiah's poems are marked with his own vocabulary and style. They clearly emerge from his real historical

---

[38] Note, for instance, 'the following:Here no assurance is given. Indeed, there is no response from God at all, only silence. God's silence to Jeremiah's prayer matches his silence to his people. We hear Jeremiah's complaint and his pain and then . . . nothing'—PC Craigie *et al, Jeremiah 1–25*, p.237.

'God's silence to the poet corresponds to the absence of God announced to the whole people . . . The poet experiences the very absence that is the destiny of Israel'—W Brueggemann, *Jeremiah 1–25*, ITC (Grand Rapids: Eerdmans) 1988, p.158.

Both comments reflect the helpful interpretative approach which sees Jeremiah as the paradigm or model in his vocation of what Israel should have been. On paradigm, see Polk, *Persona*, pp.170ff 'The Portrait of a Paradigm: Jeremiah and the Reader'. If we follow Polk and Diamond in using the redactional setting of the Confessions as part of the presentation of a vocational paradigm and part of the message itself, then the record of these personal outpourings of the prophet has a didactic purpose.

[39] Polk, *Persona*, p.151.

[40] Slightly different form-critical analyses of the Lament structure are represented in the commentaries, but these are in very minor details from our perspective. The consensus is that Jeremiah has modelled his poem closely on the conventions of Lament psalms. See, for example, Craigie, p.252f; Diamond, p.89f; O'Connor, pp.55–59.

conflict, yet Jeremiah participates in an approach to God which is a well-trodden path in Zion. To lose sight of Jeremiah's individuality or of his cultural solidarity would be to arrive at a distorted perception of his spirituality.

This Confession reflects a transition from prophetic intercession to imprecation.

> [22b]Remember how I stood before you
> to speak good for them,
> to turn away your wrath from them.
> Therefore give their children over to famine;
>
> [22b]For they have dug a pit to catch me,
> and laid snares for my feet.
> [23]Yet you, O LORD, know
> all their plotting to kill me.
> Do not forgive their iniquity,
> do not blot out their sin from your sight.
> Let them be tripped up before you;
> deal with them while you are angry.

The vigour of the language itself witnesses to the feelings of the prophet, and yet, without diminishing this level of emotion, there is more to the prayer language than a strong emotional reaction to the assassination plot. There is a judicial-theological dimension to this poem. The curses of famine, sword and pestilence are standard in Near Eastern documents. They are characteristic maledictions for breach of covenant both in Deuteronomy and Jeremiah's preaching of divine judgment. By ceasing to intercede for the nation or its leadership, Jeremiah steps aside, leaving them wide open to God's judgment. Jeremiah's personal outrage at the plot is something less than Yahweh's wrath with Judah. The 'wrath' is primarily 'your wrath' (v.20b), that is, Yahweh's. The imprecations depend on this—'deal with them while you are angry' (v.23b).[41] The prophet has no power to implement his imprecations. Forgiveness of sin (v.23) is God's prerogative alone.

In the case of Jeremiah, at least, imprecatory prayer is more than the expression of vindictive feelings. This is obvious because the whole context is one in which Jeremiah is Yahweh's representative on earth, pronouncing Yahweh's judgments at Yahweh's command. He is not a freelance individual, nor merely an outraged citizen. What we see here is the dramatic embodiment of God's

---

[41] The Hebrew words for anger carry the 2nd masc. sing. suffix referring to God ($h^{a}am\bar{a}t^{e}k\bar{a}$ and $'app^{e}k\bar{a}$, vv.20,23). Likewise, 'when you bring' ($t\bar{a}b\hat{i}'$, v.22) is 2nd masc. sing. with God as active subject. The whole sequence is to happen 'before you' ($mill^{e}p\bar{a}neyk\bar{a}$ and $l^{e}p\bar{a}neyk\bar{a}$, v.23b), that is, before God.

anger in Jeremiah. Up to this point, the prophet has pleaded with God against judgment. Now he sides with God and concurs actively in visualizing the results of divine judgment on his fellow countrymen. This shift within Jeremiah, and his anger with those who oppose him, mirrors Yahweh's shift from covenant partner to executor of its curses. The man Jeremiah is the message.

We may think of the Confrontations as a sequence, either reflecting the order in which they were experienced by Jeremiah, or presented to us by the editors as a sequence related to their setting in the book and a means of portraying the persona of Jeremiah and his fulfilment of his vocation. We might be forgiven for thinking that the sequence would end with the alignment of the prophet and his God detected in this Fourth Confession discussed above. Yet the reality is that a Fifth Confession follows, and this leaves the relationship between the prophet and his God and the prophet and his task in a dreadful tension.

CONFRONTATION 5: ACCUSATION AND PRAISE (JER 20:7–18)

The Fifth Confession opens with outright confrontation, Jeremiah accusing God of manipulating him into an impossible position.

> ⁷You persuaded me, O LORD, and I was persuaded;
>   You overpowered me, and you overcame.
> I have become (an object of) derision all the time,
>   everyone mocking me.[42]

The conflict was not external and political only, but went deeper. It tore Jeremiah in two. He felt the conflict of bearing 'the word of the LORD'(v. 8b) that acutely.

> ⁹I have said, 'I refuse to mention him,
>   I refuse to speak in his name';
> but it is in my heart like a burning fire
>   being shut up in my bones,
> I am exhausted from holding it in,
>   I cannot overcome.
> ¹⁰Indeed I have heard many slanders:

---

[42] See the commentators for discussions of how well the Lament (v. 7–12), the Praise (v. 13) and the Curse (v. 13–18) hang together as a single literary piece and to what degree this material reflects the prophet's emotions, what its setting in the book implies and whether the setting in history can be pinpointed. What the answers to these questions contribute to interpretation is reviewed in the articles by DJA Clines and DM Gunn, 'Form, Occasion and Redaction in Jeremiah 20' *ZAW* 88 (1976) 390–409 and ' "You Tried to Persuade Me" and "Violence! Outrage!" in Jeremiah 7–8' *VT* 28 (1978) 20–27 which proved seminal to this discussion. See Polk, *Persona*, p. 152ff.

' "Terror on every side!"
Inform! Let us inform on him!'
  Everyone who wishes me well
  is watching for my stumbling.
'Perhaps he can be persuaded and we can overcome him,
  then let us take our vengeance on him.'

In these two verses, the external and internal pressures on the prophet are vividly depicted, the conflict with God and the conflict with his countrymen. The language and repetition of verbal roots accentuates the parallels. Both God and the enemies want to 'persuade' (*pth*, v.7, 10) Jeremiah in order to control him. In v.7, God 'persuaded', 'overpowered' and 'overcame' him (*pth, ḥāzaq, yōkal*). In v.10, his opponents hope he can be 'persuaded' and 'overcome'.[43] The power struggle is really between God and the rebel Judeans, but it is worked out through Jeremiah who feels manipulated and intimidated by these strong-arm tactics from both sides.

How then does the prophet move from protest against God to praise in v.13? The irony is that Jeremiah has experienced Yahweh's overwhelming pressure on him, and, building on this experience, he realizes that his human opponents will fare no better against God than he has.

[11]But the LORD is with me
  like an awe-inspiring hero.
Therefore the ones pursuing me will stumble,
  they will not overcome.
[12]O LORD of armies, the one testing the righteous,
  the one seeing inner parts and heart,
let me see your vengeance on them
  for unto you I have revealed my case/complaint.

---

[43] The translation is from Craigie *et al*, p.269. See too their form-critical discussion on the coherence of v.7–13 as lament, and the interaction with Clines and Gunn. The NRSV translation ('entice') hints at a sexual seduction and rape metaphor. Some commentators see this as the connotation of the key verbs (e.g. Bright, Berridge, Thompson). NRSV 'entice': *pth*—Piel. 'to deceive, seduce, persuade'. Clines and Gunn (*VT* 28, p.20ff), as well as Craigie *et al*, discount the sexual innuendo on grounds of context. RP Carroll reacts most strongly against the sexual interpretation, the rape of a celibate, as 'too grotesque and modern', *Jeremiah*, OTL (London: SCM) 1988, p.398. All this illustrates the hazards to hermeneutics of dictionaries on the one hand and of cultural intuitions on the other.

His opponents 'will not overcome' (*yōkal*), they will lose the power struggle.[44] Given this dramatic setting in Jeremiah's prophetic ministry, we can appreciate that his anger—'let me see your vengeance on them' (v. 12)—though no doubt spoken with feeling, is more than anger. In the poem itself, 'vengeance' in v. 12 matches 'vengeance' in v. 10b. What his opponents wished upon him (v. 10b), the prophet prays that Yahweh will deflect and turn against them. Jeremiah can wish this divine retribution upon his enemies with a clear conscience. He addresses Yahweh as the one who 'tests' for righteousness and discerns the inner being with its motives.[45]

While we have no wish to downplay the anger of the poem, it does have this judicial aspect to it. Yahweh is Divine Warrior and Covenant Partner, who is obligated to come to the military defence of a vassal attacked. Jeremiah, as God's covenant partner, appeals to Yahweh. He expects vindication here, just as he appealed to 'Yahweh of hosts, the righteous judge' in 11:20.[46] The English translation 'vengeance' sounds the wrong note. If Jer 20:11 is construed as 'revenge' or 'retaliation', the nuance of vindication is suppressed. Given the covenant roots, the verb *nāqam* used in v. 12 carries connotations of legitimate force and judicial retribution. They lead to personal vindication.[47] The

---

[44] Clines and Gunn point out that *yākōl*—'to be able to, have power to, to prevail' is a pivotal term in the poem. Together with *pth* 'persuade' the repetitions underline 'this fundamental parallelism between Yahweh and the persecutors' (*ZAW* 88, p. 396f).

[45] The echo in 20:12 of 11:20 and of 12:3 is striking. The verb 'test'(*bāḥan*) and the concept of the 'heart' or 'inner being' (*kᵉlayōt wālēb*—'kidneys and heart') is a key concept in Jeremiah. See Polk, *Persona*, Chap. 2:25–34 'The Metaphor of the Heart and the Language of the Self' and Chap. 3: 35–57 'The Heart in Context: Jeremiah 4 and the Enactment of Identity.'

[46] Like 'hero, warrior–hero'(*gibbōr*) in Jer 20:11, 'hosts' in the phrase 'Yahweh of hosts' (*Yhwh ṣᵉbāʾōt*, Jer 11:20) is a military term, probably referring to the heavenly armies of Yahweh as Warrior King. The wigged and gowned association of 'Judge' in English culture does not reflect Jeremiah's appeal. This evokes the role of ancient kings in arbitration, law-drafting and military leadership (e.g. Saul). Then there is the wider application of *šāpaṭ šōpēṭ* to the freedom fighters who delivered Israel in the book of Judges, supported by the use of cognate Semitic forms in Akkadian and Ugaritic. All this suggests that Jeremiah thinks of 'Yahweh of hosts, righteous judge' in terms of warrior-kingship and covenant suzerainty, rather than as a magistrate figure.

[47] GE Mendenhall's study of *nāqam* focused on the nuances of rescue and 'punitive vindication'—*The Tenth Generation* (Baltimore: Johns Hopkins) 1973, pp. 69–104 'The "Vengeance" of Yahweh', p. 97f. See too Brueggemann, *Jer 1–25*, p. 111 on Jer 11:20 and p. 175.

lament of the Fifth Confession ends at v.13 on a high note of praise, anticipating this vindication.[48]

THE ARROW OF ANGER

Unlike the arrow of time which points in one direction only, the arrows of anger can fly off in any direction, including the archer's. It comes as a surprise to readers to discover that the editors of the book of Jeremiah have not chosen to make this a story with a happy ending. Verses 14–18 launch into a self-curse like Job's at his most wretched.[49]

> [14]Cursed be the day
> on which I was born!
> The day when my mother bore me,
> let it not be blessed!

> [18]Why did I come forth from the womb
> to see toil and sorrow,
> and spend my days in shame?

The 'shame' could be specific to Jeremiah's humiliating arrest and restraint in the stocks at the hands of Pashur, described just prior to the Fifth Confession. On the other hand, it might relate to his whole prophetic ministry, his lack of public credibility and the delay in fulfilment of his predictions of doom.[50] The 'shame' is in any case not guilt-related. Jeremiah never confesses to guilt in his Confrontations, which is one reason that their conventional title 'Jeremiah's Confessions' is most unfortunate.

To wish yourself never born is to wish yourself dead. It is splitting hairs when commentators say that Jeremiah curses 'the

---

[48] Clines and Gunn argue for the coherence of v.7–13 on the basis of many parallels of phrase and concept with the canonical psalms of lament, including the note of praise (*ZAW* 88, p.392f, 398ff). Note the Liberation Theology implied in 20:13—'for he has delivered the poor (*'ebyōn*) from the power of evildoers'.

[49] Craigie *et al*, p.277ff interact with Clines and Gunn as well as listing the formal parallels with Job 3. We agree with Polk (*Persona*, p.158ff) and Craigie that however formulaic the language may be, it remains an expression of Jeremiah's personal distress about his ministry and not just a formal reaction to bad news, solemnizing his message of judgment. 'The immediate juxtaposition of the two units of first-person speech, without any hint of lapse of time or altered situation, impels that they be read as the words of a single persona torn by radically conflicting emotions.' (*Persona*, 159)

[50] There are three passages referring to Jeremiah's birth—1:5, 15:10 and 20:14ff. The latter two lament it. The self-curse of 20:14ff echoes the woe and curses of 15:10. The Call is from birth and it is his vocation that landed Jeremiah in the 'toil and sorrow' of 20:18. For discussion of editorial blocs and literary-critical issues, see Craigie *et al*, interacting with O'Connor, and Clines and Gunn.

day' of his birth and the 'messenger', not his mother or himself or his Maker. The fact is that however formulaic the phrasing, Jeremiah is saying that his present experience of 'shame', 'toil and sorrow' negates his life. Verse 14 speaks of his birth, but the final verse speaks of his present. To negate his present life and his birth is to negate his election by Yahweh and so, albeit indirectly, to negate God.

The mood of 20:14–18 is anger and despair. Whereas the anger of the lament (v.7–13) was focused on God and then on the opponents, the anger of v.14–18 is focused on himself in his situation. We cannot really separate the man and his vocation. His identity is too bound up with his ministry. Role and experiences contribute to identity. To say, then, that Jeremiah bitterly laments his role as prophet is to discern the conflict he carries within him. At times this conflict generates anger with God who pushed him into this role and keeps pushing him to an ever more radical obedience. At times his anger is directed at those humans who scorn, demean and intimidate him. At times he loathes his life, combining anger with despair.

MODEL PROPHET? MODEL OF PRAYER?

Is this spiritual struggle set out for us as a model? There are two related parts to this question—the one wrapped up with literary critical analysis, and the other to do with imitation and spirituality. Academics seldom achieve consensus, but the three recent monographs cited in the footnotes do make a major contribution. As Polk observes, commentators who wrote about 'the religious susceptibility of the individual soul' and the emergence of 'the perfect religion . . . sprung from the bosom of a national faith' were projecting their own humanistic sentiments on to Jeremiah, oblivious of their own culture-boundness. Jeremiah does not mark the 'discovery of individual fellowship with God'. His poetry is embedded in the literary forms and national identity of his Judean soil.[51]

Conversely, historical agnosticism and form-critical rigidity have stifled Jeremiah in mid–soliloquy, pushing him back behind

---

[51] The words quoted are from J Skinner, *Prophecy and Religion* (Cambridge: CUP) 1930, p.30 cited in Polk, *The Prophetic Persona*, p.12f. Polk reviews Rudolf Kittel, Fleming James and John Skinner with the advantage of an historical and cultural distance that discloses how much the interpreters' cultural embeddenness determine their hermeneutics. In Skinner's case, it is the evolution of religion to higher forms of individual sensitivity, a concern of the *religionsgeschichtliche* school. Awareness of reader contribution leads to Polk's reader-response hermeneutic. This is 'to acknowledge that reader subjectivity is fundamental to meaning-making' but it can allow the text to

the stage scenery. All we see is the liturgical stage set. The actor has disappeared. We are left with a few psalms of Lament and conventional reactions to bad news.[52] There is no Jeremiah the individual in emotional dialogue with God, only fixed forms and redactors. Event, person and emotions have disappeared into language samples. While it is necessary to avoid creating Jeremiah in our own image, and necessary to avoid hailing him as without precedent in Israel's spirituality, there is no need (on academic grounds) for minimalizing the Confrontations as a contribution to spirituality. This, we could claim, was the redactor's spirituality rather than the man of Anathoth's. But there is no need to put it that way.

The most recent monographs have, with due caution, resuscitated Jeremiah the person. The actor speaks through the persona of psalm forms and phrases. We may not be able to reconstruct the 'day in the life'. The Confrontations are after all only snippets or freeze-frames from a lifetime of ministry. The setting of the Confrontations in the book may be editorial. Their intention may not be to create a chronological or autobiographical record, but to illuminate the message for the benefit of a generation in exile. Nevertheless, the very process of editorial imagination, inserting the Confrontations in the places they occupy and in their order of appearance, must support, not negate, the paradigmatic quality of the prophet.

We can have it both ways without sleight of hand. We may choose to credit more to Jeremiah than to his editors. The prophet Jeremiah made use of Lament psalm language from Israelite tradition to express himself in his uniquely precarious situation. There is a self-authenticating quality to the Confrontations. Individually and collectively they reflect an emotional complexity that mirrors life. As Polk puts it,

> his anguish consists of grief, fear and anger compounded. Moreover, these smaller elements proved complex also: Jeremiah grieves, for example, for himself over against both God and the people; he grieves for and with his people over against God; and he grieves with God over his people. Similarly, he fears for himself and for and with the people—and this while sharing God's anger toward the people, or even while being angry at God. Such emotional complexity is of course profoundly realistic, and typically human. And by being

---

regulate the subjective in the reading process. See *The Prophetic Persona*, Chap. 6 'Summary and Concluding Hermeneutical Reflections', pp.163–174.

[52] *The Prophetic Persona*, p. 170.

oriented at every point to God his action can be theologically paradigmatic.[53]

A MODEL FOR CONFRONTATION?

When Job, Jeremiah and Lament psalms confront God in similar ways, we can speak about a shared tradition. When Job is finally commended, when Jeremiah ends his life as a prophet as well as living it as a prophet, and when Lament psalms are canonised, this must mean that the type of language used to speak to God face to face, the language of confrontation, becomes part of the model of an intimate relationship which God provokes and responds to.

One might argue that Job and Jeremiah are special cases, yet their God-talk links them with a wider fellowship that made use of the Lament language. If we follow the recent form-critical work on Lament psalms, then we could point to a substantial group of psalms that confront God. In the words of Broyles, 'of the approximately 65 lament psalms in the Psalter, there are roughly 21 that contain a "God-lament" that connotes complaint.'[54] The distinction between Lament as plea and Lament as complaint is drawn on the basis of who is held responsible for the situation. If God is held responsible more than human enemies, then blame or rebuke is implicit in the address to God. Often it is explicit.

The rebuke may be theologically motivated. If there is a disparity perceived between the way God acted in the past and his apparent indifference, non-intervention or hostility in the present, then we have a theological argument against God presented to God. The charge is inconsistency. These psalms of confrontation are the most foundational form of protest literature. They should certainly strike a chord in cultures where protest songs, marches and demonstrations have characterised political life. It is a pity, then, if church leadership so identifies God-talk with praise and intercession and 'safe' forms of prayer that psalms of confrontation are ignored or suppressed. In fact, a cursory glance through

---

[53] Clines and Gunn build on DR Hillers, 'A Convention in Hebrew Literature: the Reaction to Bad News' *ZAW* 77 (1965) 86–90, p.407, in which Hillers says: 'The poet's use of traditional literary formulae prevents us from drawing any conclusions as to his individual psychology'. Clines and Gunn then argue that 20:14–18 'did not originally express the prophet's private emotions of despair at some personal calamity (such as disappointment in his prophetic ministry)'. This supposes much in terms of culture and convention as well as redactional judgments as to the origin of 20:14–18 prior to its appearance here in the book. Elsewhere Clines and Gunn affirm that a public orientation as opposed to a private diary setting 'does not remove the element of "spiritual struggle" (*Seelenkämpfe*'), p.402.

[54] CC Broyles, *The Conflict of Faith and Experience in the Psalms: a form-critical and theological study*, JSOTS 52, (Sheffield: JSOT Press) 1989, p.40. He lists these

contemporary song books and books of prayer reveals how little these productions mirror the struggle with God that marks Jeremiah's obedience.

One problem with making confrontation language part of our prayer language may be our veneer of 'niceness' instead of reality. This is a social hazard whereby 'politeness' and manners which are drawn from social conventions dictate how we talk to God in personal and public prayer. No one who has listened to the prayers of recent converts could doubt that churches wittingly or unwittingly brainwash members out of their natural speech forms and into a particular language of piety. The psalms suggest that Israel's natural speech patterns were far closer to her prayer language. The very imprecations which appalled CS Lewis bear out this conclusion.

Another problem with adopting the language of confrontation psalms may be that we inwardly oscillate between blaming God for situations and realizing that there are other causes or responsible agents involved. If we feel anger with the devastation wrecked by drought, earthquake and hurricanes and hold God responsible because humans cannot control the weather systems or seismic events, this anger may be muted by the realization that science brings knowledge which brings responsibility. Areas subject to devastation are identifiable. Volcanoes, earthquakes and hurricanes can be monitored. Food can be distributed where crops have failed. The human genome is currently being mapped so even genetic disorders might become more predictable and possibly better treated. There may be procedures for combating viruses in addition to inoculation. An eye to causality would confirm that many diseases are human-induced through pollution, addiction, obesity, laziness and neglect. If we accept the neutrality of nature instead of a Near Eastern polytheistic mythologizing of it, then we will tend to focus on physical and biological causality as something in the domain of science rather than of religion. We will also realize that political will, cooperation and economics carry much responsibility for the human condition rather than God.

Nevertheless, we are human. There will always be the need to cry out. If we accepted the world the way that it is, there would be something wrong with us. Protest is endemic. Besides which, emotions are feelings that are colourful rather than rational. Who is there to blame for a cot death? Why does God not intervene more evidently if he can? In pastoral terms, the Christian fellowship will always include those who are living with a deep anger directed at God. We will never move beyond the tides of emotion

---

as Pss 6, 9–10, 13, 22, 35, 42–43, 44, 60, 74, 77, 79, 80, 85, 88, 89, 90, 102, 108—which includes both Individual and Communal samples.

to some island paradise without spiritual weather. There will be tidal waves of human emotion that sweep over us, including anger. Whether this anger is directed at God or at others, our spirituality will be affected. We cannot excise the 'Oh, God!', the 'Why?' and the 'How long, O Lord?' from our speech, though we might mutter them under our breath lest we appear to be 'unspiritual'.

The CS Lewis who philosophized about *The Problem of Pain* also penned *A Grief Observed* when his wife died of cancer. He found himself thinking of God as Cosmic Sadist, torturer, and door-slammer to those who knock thinking it will be opened. In another journal entry, he wrote:

> All that stuff about the Cosmic Sadist was not so much the expression of thought as of hatred. I was getting from it the only pleasure a man in anguish can get; the pleasure of hitting back. It was really just Billingsgate—mere abuse; 'telling God what I thought of him.'[55]

The anger which this quotation alludes to was confrontational God-talk and part of a healing of grief. The point is not so much whether God is to be blamed for cancer. The point is that all the human emotions are taken up in God-talk, rather than censored out. What happens after that is part of a process over which we have no absolute control but in which we are partners and participants in a dialogue.

IMPRECATORY PRAYER REVISITED

When we looked at the curse ceremony in Deut 27 earlier in this chapter, we found elements that transferred and elements which did not transfer into a New Covenant setting. What of the curses embodied in the psalms in prayer? They are certainly in evidence in Jeremiah's Confrontations, but are they a transferable part of that model?

The first response will have to be 'No'. Jeremiah is more than an individual who is finally so outraged by his enemies and their assassination plots that he curses them dead. He is a prophet who never ceases to love his Judean people. In the end he stops praying for God's mercy on them because he is forced by their reaction to his message to concur with God's implementation of the covenant curses. As individuals, our anger with human beings does not often fit so neatly into a covenant framework. Our anger may not be God's anger. Our anger may run ahead of God's patience,

---

[55] CS Lewis, *A Grief Observed* (London: Faber & Faber) 1961, p.33.

mercy or grace.[56] Jeremiah had to catch up with God's intention of implementing judgment on Judah. In our exclamations of 'Damn you!', we run ahead of spiritual reality. In sober moments, rather than wishing Hell upon human enemies, we may feel horrified by the prospect of hell that the Gospel holds in store for those who are finally counted as God's enemies.

But there is more to be said. A second response is that there is a prophetic role for the church in which the language of confrontation is at home, both in anger expressed to God in prayer and in anger expressed to human authorities face to face. This prophetic role sets the church, rather than the individual, in confrontation with systems, institutions and power blocs. The state is a collective entity, but it comes to focus in a president, a minister of justice, a police chief, a general. There may come a time when the church prays for the removal of the system which means the replacement of the government. This comes down to the removal of individual people from office. This is 'praying against' rather than 'praying for'

In recent times, this moment came in South Africa's history when many denominations joined in *Prayer for the End to Unjust Rule* and denounced the minority white government as morally and politically illegitimate.[57] This step was taken only after forty years of fruitless protest and increased and brutal repression. In its prayers and in its pronouncements, the language of prophetic denunciation has marked the church's resistance of evil, particularly of injustice on a national or international scale.[58] We should not assume that spirituality has no language of confrontation. The language of John the Baptist continued the speech of the prophets. The language of Jesus towards his enemies within Judaism was

---

[56] Jesus offered no encouragement to the sons of thunder in calling down divine judgment on a Samaritan village, though he himself pronounced Woes on cities in the day of judgment to come—see Lk 9:54f and Lk 10:13ff.

[57] The South African Council of Churches adopted a statement called 'A Theological Rationale and a Call to Prayer for the End to Unjust Rule' in 1985 as a guideline for the 16th June Soweto Uprising commemorations. There was a furore in the press and strong government reaction. Some churches disassociated themselves from the position adopted. See 'Southern Africa Today: Prayers for the End to Unjust Rule' *Journal of Theology for Southern Africa* 52 (1985) 56–71. These responses and the original document were reprinted with supporting essays in AA Boesak and C Villa-Vicencio, *A Call for an End to Unjust Rule* (Edinburgh: St Andrew's Press) 1986.

[58] Pronouncements may take various forms and there is a notable history of such church statements this century—many in opposition to apartheid in South Africa alone. Public speech is one form, but press releases from conferences, or declarations adopted, or pastoral letters from bishops to be read in all member churches are other genres. Note, for instance, the Catholic Bishops' letter released in Malawi in 1992.

abrasive and confrontational.[59] So there is place for a horizontal expression of anger within the prophetic speech of the church. Here consensus and collective responsibility rule out personal vindictiveness.[60]

A third response to imprecatory prayer in the Old Testament, this time at the level of the individual, would be to ask what Christian spirituality does with the feelings of fear and anger towards fellow human beings. While it is clear that the New Testament requires prayer for enemies and persecutors and discourages destructive anger, it is also self-evident that the New Testament offers no treatise on anger and conflict resolution. It says nothing about any therapeutic procedure or technique for dealing constructively with anger. The same is true, of course, of other strong emotions such as fear. Nor would we expect to find in the Bible any therapeutic guidance on post-traumatic stress disorders, phobias or obsessive-compulsive behaviour.

This means that common sense, experience and professional resources must teach us how to deal with overwhelming emotions constructively. Certain approaches to emotions are liberating. When it comes to anger, recent studies emphasize the importance of verbalisation and letting go of it.[61] There is an irony in this. Prayer is above all verbalization in the belief that there is a Listener who understands the whole situation and all that is going on within the heart. The biblical prayers of imprecation have this

---

[59] The 'brood of vipers' language of John (Matt 3, Luke 3) and Jesus' denunciation of hypocrisy in Matt 23 and of assassination plots in John 8. There is also one incident in which Paul's imprecation on the magician Bar-Jesus was answered instantly. Since Luke describes Paul as 'filled with the Holy Spirit' as he confronts Elymas, this stands out as a divinely inspired utterance and rather a special case (Acts 13:6ff).

[60] Additionally, a distinction of utmost importance in this discussion is the difference between words and deeds. Prayer is words, not conspiracy, insurrection or the armed overthrow of the state, though in oppressive régimes arrests, imprisonment and torture have been a regular response to the church's words. A fuller discussion would need also to consider action, the spirituality of civil disobedience and the issue of force and violence. This is beyond our scope here.

[61] M McKay, PD Rogers and J McKay quote research which shows that ventilating anger verbally is not in itself enough to avoid solidifying the anger into a permanent attitude which has negative effect on the angry person —*When Anger Hurts: quieting the storm within* (Oakland: New Harbinger) 1989. Anger is seen as a stage to traverse in recovery from bereavement or depression. Anger that is unrecognized or denied, that is, anger in pre-verbalized forms, is destructive to its carrier. See M Chave-Jones, *Living with Anger* (London: Triangle, SPCK) 1992 and HG Lerner, *The Dance of Anger: a woman's guide to changing the patterns of intimate relationships* (New York: Harper & Row, 1989/London: Thorsons, Harper Collins, 1990).

merit, then, of therapeutic verbalization and delivering the situation to God. They create a space for God to act. That space may be inside the person praying. To express the violence, fear or jealousy within to God is different from denying such 'unspiritual' feelings, and different from plotting and wrecking vengeance.

Critics who take an imprecatory utterance in a psalm as the last word rather than one step in a spiritual process are overlooking the narrative quality of lament psalms. We do not know what happened next, after the prayer. What we do know, from our own experience of life, is that when we have said things aloud, forcefully, we often think about them for a long time and sometimes come to a quite different perception of ourselves and the whole situation. We can allow that this might also have happened to Israelites who expressed their fear of enemies and their anger at them to the Lord.

C. PSALM 22 RE-CONTEXTUALIZED

To round off this study of God-confrontation and the expression of emotions in prayer, we will use Psalm 22 as a bridge between the language of the Old Testament and the model of the New.

There is pause for thought in this confrontation psalm. It opens with a rhetorical question:

> [1]My God, my God, why have you forsaken me?
>   Why are you so far from helping me,
>   from the words of my groaning?
> [2]O my God, I cry by day but you do not answer;
>   and by night but find no rest.

Even without the insistent 'Why?' (*lāmmāh*), verse 2 is more than narrative description. With the repeated 'Why?' of verse 1, the psalmist expresses more than distress. This is the language of confrontation.[62] There may well be a bundle of emotions accompanying this utterance. Indeed, volume and tone of voice could bring one or other to the fore—anger, misery, despair, exhaustion, bewilderment. But there is no doubt about who is being confronted and held responsible. It is God. This holds true even when we learn later in the psalm that 'a company of evildoers',

---

[62] The same holds true for the use of the rhetorical question 'How long?', which, as Broyles points out, is not asking for information on the duration of the distress but is confronting God with what he will do to end it. Broyles notes that '*lāmmāh* is the most frequent interrogative, occurring 11 times in 7 psalms . . . "How long?" appears 8 times in 7 psalms' (*Conflict*, p.80f, section D.'The Complaint in a Question Form'.

'strong bulls of Bashan', 'the sword', 'the dog', 'the lion' encircle the speaker.[63] It is God who is addressed and confronted.

Yet it is not God—and herein lies the spirituality—but 'my God' (*'ēlīy 'ēlīy*, v.1 and *'elōḥāy*, v.2). The language of confrontation is the language of belonging. There is a tension, the tension of intimacy and the stress of deep expectations. The tension would not exist to feed energy into the confrontation if there were no experience of intimacy and no expectations of this relationship. This is why the language of confrontation belongs to spirituality and not to religiosity. Religiosity does not permit rocking the boat. Only so much of a person can enter the temple of nominal religion. The rest of the person must stand outside. This is not the way of the psalms of confrontation. They bring their anger, despair and affronted sense of justice into the sanctuary, and once there they do not whisper.

Is it a coincidence, then, that Jesus does not whisper these words beneath his breath but shouts them in the darkness of the crucifixion?

> When it was noon, darkness came over the whole land until three in the afternoon. At three o'clock Jesus cried out with a loud voice, 'Eloi, Eloi, lema sabachtani?' which means, 'My God, my God, why have you forsaken me?'
>
> (Mark 15:33f; cf. Matt 27:45f)

The words were misunderstood, but the misunderstanding of them as a call for Elijah is nothing. The risk was that to say such words as these aloud, so publicly, would signal the surrender of an intimate relationship and the end of any claim to a special sonship. No re-reading or tradition of spirituality can duplicate the shock of hearing these words from the lips of Jesus. In Mark's narrative and in Matthew, there is another loud cry before Jesus breathes his last, but the last actual words spoken in his life-time that they record are the confrontational words from Psa 22.[64]

This stark narrative may be modified by the reflection that Psa 22 does not end in despair or confrontation but in a thanksgiving banquet and testimony. We may assume that the whole psalm was running through the mind of Jesus, and we may believe that he clung to its outcome as applicable to his context. The words from Luke and John would support this. Yet this wider context does not detract from the cry of dereliction. The unique context of the

---

[63] Verses 12, 16, 20 and those who 'mock', 'make mouths' and 'shake their heads' perhaps as a wider group who express a slightly more passive antagonism.

[64] Neither Mark nor Matthew records the words of different tone— 'Father, into your hands I commit my spirit' (Luke 23:46) or, 'It is finished!' (John 20:30).

crucifixion and the belief that the Scriptures found their fulfilment in Jesus does not negate the use of psalm prayer by his disciples.

EXPRESSIONS AS PART OF THE STORY

Something happens in prayer. The prayer becomes a part of the story.[65] To speak to God from the heart is a transforming process. Experience supports this. Talking to a friend adds an illuminating analogy. Form-criticism concurs with this. Psalms of Lament, including psalms of confrontation, quite often include a dynamic shift between the opening statements of accusation or distress and the concluding reflections. Mixed in with confrontation, there may be expression of trust and assurance of being heard.[66] If confrontation with God achieves nothing else, the sense of being heard is a key to an ongoing relationship. In Jeremiah, there are responses and silences. In both, there is enough sense of being heard, so it seems, to hold Jeremiah steady in his vocation, though his ministry was not marked by greater success.

Job and Jeremiah in one sense got more than they bargained for when they confronted God. If they talked straight to God, yet when he did break the silence, it was with matching straight talk.

> Gird up your loins like a man,
>   I will question you, and you shall declare to me.
> 'Where were you when I laid the foundation of the earth?'
>
> (Job 38:3–4a)

> If you turn back, I will take you back,
>   and you shall stand before me.
> If you utter what is precious, and not what is worthless,
>   you shall serve as my mouth.
>
> (Jer 15:19)

The energy of the human anger was matched by the vigour of the divine come-back. Yet here is the point. There is reciprocity. What a compliment and an irony in the phrase 'like a man'! There

---

[65] Compare Broyles' introductory statement: 'A lament psalm relates an experience, so it conveys a narrative. It presents this within a metrical structure, so it is poetry. It asks for something from God, so it is prayer. It pleads a case, so it is argument. It expresses a faith, so it is theology' *Conflict*, p.13.

[66] Broyles reviews the function of hymnic and praise phrases, expressions of trust and assurance of being heard in Lament psalms. .As one might expect, these 'positive' elements are more frequent in the plea and distress laments than in the confrontational 'God-laments', where they may heighten the thrust of the complaint. He notes that the assurance of being heard motif appears four times in the God-lament psalms—in Pss 6, 9–10, 22, 85 (*Conflict*, p.48 and the wider discussion in Chap. 2 'Psalms of Plea and Psalms of Complaint', p.35ff.)

is a healthy congruence in what each side judges that his antagonist can take. There is a dealing in reality, and the relationship survives it, strengthened. \

In the end this is not surprising because three intimate human relationships, which in the Bible serve as metaphors for the relationship with God, can also accommodate the expression of strong emotions such as anger, fear and guilt. These three intimate relationships are those between friends, between wife and husband, and between parent and child. In each, when the bonds are strong, there is room for an expression of anger that is not destructive. The more security, the greater the level of intimacy and communication, the greater the spectrum of emotions that may flow. There is risk, but the enhanced reality is rewarding.

On the other hand, where the relationship lacks reality, has little history, or is blighted with insecurity, strong emotions are hazardous. The chances that expressing anger will be destructive rather than constructive are great. Conflicts may accumulate rather than being resolved. Distancing, rather than engagement, may characterize these interactions.[67]

In these human relationships, there is often little or no training. Formal education offers no school-leaving certificate in friendship, no award for skills in conflict resolution. No marriage preparation. In the psalms and in Israel's use of them, there were models of emotional expression. Perhaps their availability as part of the indigenous culture facilitated their use when personal circumstances made their language of plea or confrontation timely. Jeremiah's poems suggest that this was so. Whoever wrote Job had learned his poetry and his God-talk before putting pen to papyrus.

The situation has changed. The Christian spirituality on offer in many churches today provides very little in the way of a model for a God-talk that includes turbulent and dangerous emotions. To imagine that we inhabit a less fallen, pressurized or damaged humanity than the psalmists did is a delusion and a vain hope. To deny or exclude strong feelings from our communion with God is, in the last analysis and in the light of Job and Jeremiah, an insult to our Maker.

SUMMARY AND CONCLUSION

Job and Jeremiah are outstanding models of an Old Testament spirituality that has room for confrontation with God. The

---

[67] The better books on marriage deal with the expression of 'negative' emotions and with conflict resolution. One such provides a paradoxical phrase in its title that could be applied to God in the confrontation psalms—'the intimate Enemy' (R Bach, *The Intimate Enemy*, New York: Corgi, 1978).

strength of their relationship with God allows for the use of the strongest language, language that both questions God, demands his response, argues and expresses anger. Detailed study of Israel's psalms of Lament has disclosed that the poetry of Job and Jeremiah draws heavily on this tradition. This means that we can extrapolate more widely from Job and Jeremiah. They may be particularly graphic products of the Wisdom tradition and the prophetic vocation but they speak an Israelite language of lament. As well as this, the redactional processes involved in arranging the components of Job and the Confrontations of Jeremiah serve only to underline their didactic role. The words of Job and Jeremiah make available a means of expressing confrontation with God.

Any shock that we register at the intensity of emotion expressed in Job's speeches, Jeremiah's Confrontations and the dramatic opening of Psa 22 reminds us of two aspects of reader-response that are not primarily theological. The first is our own cultural conventionality, and the second is our own human make-up. Scripture has no intention of canonizing a polite and restrainedly modulated tone for communicating with God, nor a restrained and emotionally inhibited temperament. If our public worship and private prayer censors out expression of anger, pain and accusation, then our spirituality is less than human. It passes judgment on Old Testament spirituality without offering an alternative.

In fact, there is more hope for developing a Christian spirituality that matches our humanity when the emotions of anger, despair and hurt are given expression in dialogue with God and in dialogue with skilled human listeners. Our theology, our cognitive apparatus brought to bear on the subject, should support this perception because it has reason to, if our analysis of Job, Jeremiah and psalms of Lament has hermeneutical credibility. Neither our theology nor our literary analysis will supply us with the exact vocabulary, genres and settings for our contemporary God-speech because we must still recontextualize what we learn from this psycho-dynamic aspect of Old Testament spirituality in order to take it into our cultures and communities

Jesus 'cried out with a loud voice' in his tortured state, using words from Psalm 22. He spoke as an Israelite and as a human being, and he cried out at his moment of most intense public exposure. Our spirituality may never be so tortured, nor so much on public display. Yet if we follow Jesus in taking the 'My God, my God . . .' of belonging onto our lips, and the relationship that it implies, we may, like Jeremiah, find that an authentic spirituality will force out of us cries of anger, pain and despair raised in protest to God. These may be private moments, but the strength of the Old Testament is that these emotional moments came to expression through a shared vocabulary and were treasured in the community and passed on to us. Our communities would do well to treasure the expression of confrontation with God, not suppress it.

BIBLIOGRAPHY

LC Allen, *Psalms 101–150*, WBC 21 (Waco: Word) 1983.

L Alonso-Schökel, 'God's Answer to Job', pp. 45–51 in *Concilium* 169 (1983) *Job and the Silence of God*.

FI Andersen, *Job*, TCOT (Leicester: IVP) 1976.

FE Bloom & A Lazerson, *Brain, Mind and Behaviour*, (New York: WH Freeman) 2nd ed 1988.

AA Boesak & C Villa-Vicencio, *A Call for an End to Unjust Rule* (Edinburgh: St Andrew's Press) 1986.

CC Broyles, *The Conflict of Faith and Experience in the Psalms: a form-critical and theological study*, JSOTS 52, (Sheffield: JSOT Press) 1989.

W Brueggemann, 'Psalms and the Life of Faith: a suggested typology of function' *JSOT* 17 (1978) 3–32.

——, *Jeremiah 1–25*, ITC (Grand Rapids: Eerdmans) 1988.

RP Carroll, *Jeremiah*, OTL (London: SCM) 1988.

M Chave-Jones, *Living with Anger* (London: Triangle, SPCK) 1992.

DJA Clines, *Job 1–20*, WBC 17 (Dallas: Word) 1989.

PC Craigie, PH Kelley & JF Drinkard, *Jeremiah 1–25*, WBC 26, (Dallas: Word) 1991.

AR Diamond, *The Confessions of Jeremiah in Context: scenes of prophetic drama*, JSOTS 45 (Sheffield: JSOT Press) 1987.

G Gutiérrez, *On Job: God-talk and the suffering of the innocent* (Maryknoll: Orbis) 1987.

JE Hartley, *Job*, NICOT, (Grand Rapids: Eerdmans) 1988.

HG Lerner, *The Dance of Anger: a woman's guide to changing the patterns of intimate relationships*, (New York: Harper & Row) 1989; (London: Thorsons, HarperCollins,) 1990.

CS Lewis, *Reflections on the Psalms*, 1958 (Fontana books, London: Collins) 1961.

——, *A Grief Observed* (London: Faber & Faber) 1961.

M McKay, PD Rogers & J McKay, *When Anger Hurts: quieting the storm within* (Oakland: New Harbinger) 1989.

KM O'Connor, *The Confessions of Jeremiah: their interpretation and role in Chapters 1–25*, SBL DS 94 (Atlanta: Scholars) 1988.

LG Perdue, *Wisdom in Revolt: metaphorical theology in the book of Job*, Bible & Literature 29 (Sheffield: The Almond Press) 1991.

T Polk, *The Prophetic Persona: Jeremiah and the language of the self*, JSOTS 32 (Sheffield: JSOT Press) 1984.

R Polzin & D Robertson (eds), *Semeia 7* (1977) *Studies in the Book of Job*.

W Vogels, 'The Spiritual Growth of Job' *BThB* 11.3 July (1981) 77–80.

[9]

Guilt and Restoration
Psalms 51, 32, 38

AN INTRODUCTION TO GUILT

If you, O lord, should mark iniquities,
Lord, who could stand?
But there is forgiveness with you,
so that you may be revered.

(Psa 130:3)

In the previous chapter, we looked at confrontation with God in which the expression of anger, despair and bitterness played a major part. In this chapter, we look at another kind of confrontation involving another powerful human emotion that is relevant to Christian spirituality, namely, guilt. Interacting with guilt are the processes of repentance, confession and forgiveness, leading to the feelings of relief, release and the sense of restoration to God and the community. The issue of guilt and restoration has a personal and a communal dynamic to it in Old Testament spirituality. Looking at guilt and restoration will also entail exploring our model of human personality and the interface between medical, psychological and theological perspectives. The question of our flawed human nature and 'perfectionism' also emerges from a study of guilt and restoration. Then there are the issues of private and public confession, and the role of ritual and of experts in the process of mediating forgiveness and renewal. This may awaken our denominational and cultural sensitivies, and readers will need to work out the detail of the recontextualization of the Old Testament material within their own contexts.

We shall draw on two main text sources, the biblical and the Mesopotamian. We need the latter to fully appreciate the former. Besides which, there are many places in the world today where rituals, somewhat akin to Mesopotamian procedures, are practised by experts for the relief of guilt, anxiety and demonic oppression.

We will not be able to document and explore these contemporary contexts within the space of this chapter, but they appear fairly frequently in television documentaries and are discussed in anthropological and missiological literature.[1] There are other contemporary contexts such as the courts and counselling services that deal with guilt. They may provide metaphors or perspectives to integrate with Christian practice.

Before proceeding any further, we need to draw a distinction between the feeling of guilt and the reality of guilt. Guilt is a bundle of feelings that may include shame, anxiety, self-loathing, a sense of doom, a sense of failure and the fear of rejection, among other things. 'Guilty!' is a verdict reached after a careful examination of the facts of a case and the cross-examination of witnesses. Guilt as a theological term is a state of being involving feelings towards God and fellow human beings based on the conviction that wrong has been done or thought. Feelings of guilt may not be a reliable guide to the reality of guilt. Likewise the absence of feelings of guilt.

False guilt is a common experience in trivial as well as tragic form. In tragic form, it is, for example, the guilt of a child that feels responsible for its parents' divorce, for the death of a sibling, or for the sexual abuse perpetrated by an adult. False guilt involves all the feelings that accompany real guilt but lacks the substantiation. It is a state of self-accusation. There is no acquittal from false guilt because there is no trial that scrutinises evidence objectively and offers an independent verdict. False guilt is often a

---

[1] See, for instance, GC Oosthuizen, *The Healer-Prophet in Afro-Christian Churches*, Studies in Christian Mission 3 (Leiden: Brill) 1992, which documents and discusses the explanation and treatment of diseases, anxieties and beliefs about ancestors, witchcraft and the need for purification, using rituals of prayer, chicken sacrifice, exorcism, washing in the sea, and restoration to community. Anthropological studies such as those by Mary Douglas on dietary taboos and Leviticus, or of Victor Turner on separation, transition (liminality) and re-incorporation (communitas) may alert one to ritual dimensions relevant to guilt and restoration in the Old Testament and Ancient Near East, but they require competence beyond Old Testament studies to evaluate. For reflection on hermeneutics in anthropology, see most recently Edith Turner, *Experiencing Ritual: a new interpretation of African Healing* (Philadelphia: Univ Pennsylvania Press) 1992, a sequel to Victor Turner's *The Drums of Affliction: a study of the religious processes among the Ndembu of Zambia*, OUP, 1968. Edith Turner's book is reviewed along with Oosthuizen's work in *Journal of Religion in Africa* 24.2 (1994), pp. 182ff. See too the comments in the article by B Jules-Rosette, 'Decentering Ethnography: Victor Turner's vision of anthropology', pp. 160–181.

conditioned reaction.[2] Real guilt, on the other hand, is a condition of humanity, though in the context of our discussion of Christian spirituality, real guilt begins with a specific sin at a point in linear time in the life of a Christian believer. Guilt feelings may linger after confession of sin because forgiveness and absolution, though accepted as real in the mind, do not always extinguish the feelings of guilt that form a halo around the event in memory. There is thus a psychological dimension to guilt that operates in parallel with the theological evaluation of guilt and reconciliation with God.

Spirituality must reckon with both forms of guilt, the true and the false, because both distort minds, depress spirits and disrupt relationships. Likewise spirituality must reckon with the lingering of guilt feelings after confession of sin. This is one reason why Christian spirituality cannot afford to be a privatized practice. Without the objectivity of a discerning other, and the restorative effect of a communal fellowship, the subjectivity of an endless guiltiness threatens to subvert and overwhelm the spirituality of a sensitive or emotionally damaged person.

TWO VIGNETTES OF GUILT

When we turn to the Old Testament, we would expect to find many examples of the experience of guilt and confession. Surprisingly, there are not. At least, there are not many descriptions of the experience of guilt from the inside. In narrative, there are many incidents which record real guilt, but few that also tell of real confession. In one rare incident of guilt experienced and acknowledged, the moment of insight is obliterated by a return to

---

[2] The analogy with cats conditioned to feel anxiety at sharpening claws on chairs and 'stealing' food off tabletops is helpful. When humans punish them, an activity natural to cats becomes fearful for them. Conversely, Pavlov's dogs wagged their tails and salivated when given electric shocks because food was presented after the pain. Parents condition children to respond by various forms of reward and punishment, some of which enforce moral issues, while others reflect parental preferences. This means that conscience is partly a cultural artefact. The insights of therapists about guilt are helpful. Paul Tournier reviews guilt according to Freud, Adler, Jung and Buber in 'True and False Guilt', Chap. 7:63–71 in *Guilt and Grace* (London: Hodder & Stoughton) 1962. The secular and existential therapist Yalom speaks of the guilt induced by the failure of individuals to be themselves, that is, to live up to their potential. This 'sin' is sin against the self by omission or refusal, a concept that links self-actualisation with Angst and guilt. He traces this guilt concept through Kierkegaard, Heidegger, Buber and Tillich (*Existential Psychotherapy*, 1980, p.276–285). This guilt is different from disobedience to

the deed not a return to the deity. The incident involves Saul, confronted with his conduct by David.

> When David had finished speaking, Saul lifted up his voice and wept. He said to David, 'You are more righteous than I; for you have repaid me good, whereas I have repaid you evil. . . . Now I know that you shall surely be king . . .'
>
> (1 Sam 24:16ff)

The moment of reality passes. After the subsequent round of hot pursuit, Saul is moved once again to a public confession. In the memorable words of the King James Version: ' "I have played the fool, and have erred exceedingly . . ." ' (1 Sam 26:21).

These two episodes combine a sense of God's reality with human interaction.[3] Guilt towards David is guilt before God. We also see the struggle of conflicting motivations and moods within the framework of faith in Yahweh, and the difference that there is between words and deeds.

The story of primal guilt is not a story of confession. Perhaps this explains why guilt, confession and repentance are seldom found linked together in the Old Testament. The Eden story paints a vivid picture of guilt in a few brush strokes. 'Hid . . . afraid . . . naked'. No words of confession were spoken in Eden.

> But the LORD God called to the man, and said to him, 'Where are you?' He said, 'I heard the sound of you in the garden, and I was afraid, because I was naked; and I hid myself.'
>
> (Gen 3:9f)

This is an explanation, not a confession. It leads nowhere. What follows is not forgiveness, but cross-examination by the further questions: 'Who told you that you were naked? Have you eaten from the tree of which I commanded you not to eat?' (v. 11). And as the Man speaks again, we know that his first statement was not a confession. Immediately, he senses that the full facts of his

---

revealed divine commandments, transgression of the Torah. As an individualised and Westernised version of vocation-failure Yalom's concept of existential guilt has some affinities with Israel's failure to be itself as witness among the nations.

[3] Note how David invokes Yahweh as Judge and Vindicator (1 Sam 24:15), and note how Saul's speech accepts Yahweh's involvement in the events and requests an oath by the LORD (v. 21). Saul's blessing in 26:25 implicitly invokes Yahweh: "Blessed are you [by Yahweh], O my son, David!" '. The protagonists both acknowledge that there is more to their relationship than rivalry. The narrator weaves theology into the speeches. There is more to politics than politics, as Ellul's book title reminds us—*The Politics of God and the Politics of Man* (Grand Rapids: Eerdmans, 1972).

nakedness, temporarily concealed by the foliage and the fig leaves, will emerge. His next words attempt to transfer guilt rather than confess to it.

To the next Old Testament question on whereabouts—'Where is your brother Abel?' , there is a reply innocent of all guilty tones—'I do not know; am I my brother's keeper?' (4:9). Where Adam's reply was some of the truth, Cain's is none of it. Progress has been made to the blatant lie and flat denial—of responsibility in general, or of guilt in particular. This is true guilt without acknowledgment of guilt, a deeper state of guilt yet.

A. GUILT CONFESSED: AN ANALYSIS OF PSALM 51

Passing from these vignettes of guilt exquisitely narrated, we move on to the first–person voice of the psalms speaking to God. Arriving at the threshold of Israel's best-known confession of guilt before God, Psalm 51, we might enter into it by the front or the back door. Both are marked 'Public'. The front door carries the rubric 'To the leader', 'for the director of music' or the like. The exit turns out to be via the Temple doors and gates of Zion (v.18,19). What we might take for the intensely personal and private, Israel has labelled for public use. The canonical form of this psalm presents us with a piece of liturgy, not a private poem secreted in the pages of a personal journal. Western spirituality might advocate the confidentiality of the confessional or of a conversation with a counsellor for the resolving of guilt. These may indeed be helpful cultural recontextualizations, but it is thought-provoking that Israel provides for a public recitation.

There are other dimensions of this psalm to consider besides place or forum. Time for instance. There is real time, emotional time and liturgical time. Psalm 51 is a form of words recited aloud in a little under three minutes. Those three minutes are the epitome of the liturgical time. Not the totality, for if the psalm was to be sung at the Temple, then the worshipper would have left home and walked there in real time and waited for the service to begin.[4] If the canonical form of the psalm points to a Temple service, then this cultic event would scarcely have been over in three minutes. It likely included other items.

This underlines the fact that the where and when and how long of the singing is not identical with the transforming process,

---

[4] ME Tate, *Psalms 51–100*, WBC 20 (Dallas:Word) 1990, p.11f thinks that a priest might have visited a sick person at home for a recital of the psalm in a ritual of repentance and confession. Compare James 5:14ff and the visit for confession made by the church elders. Tate is following the suggestions of

though we can assume that it was intended to facilitate the process. When did the emotional movement take place? During the time of recital? After recital? Before singing the psalm? Does the psalm capture the movement of repentance and renewal, or bear witness to its prior occurrence? When is forgiveness experienced? Is punctiliar thinking relevant or misleading? How are assurance and transformation realized? Once we ask these questions that are directly related to spirituality, we are confronted by more than a literary analysis of Psalm 51 can disclose. It is as well to be aware of these dimensions to the dissolving of guilt, lest we constrict spirituality within theological concepts, liturgical events or tides of emotion. Spirituality may include and depend on all of these things but is fundamentally relational. Relationality has its own dimensions. Scholars attempt to pinpoint a cultic *Sitz im Leben* (life-setting) for the psalm, but setting is only half the story.

We noticed that this psalm is public liturgy.[5] This presupposes participation in a community of faith. Unresolved guilt introduces a negating factor that disrupts community and public worship. Without confession and repentance, sacrifice and public worship are positively displeasing to God (v.16). The corollary of v.16 is that public liturgy may be maintained outwardly while vitiated inwardly—a perspective familiar from prophetic indictments of the Temple rituals.[6] The contrast between the lips and the heart is not unique to confession but is familiar from covenant and treaty-making ceremonies where the verbal oath and the inner intention must be fully congruent to avoid the curses coming into operation. Confession of guilt and covenant oaths joined heart with lips, individual with community.

Psalm 51 is not introducing a new and improved spirituality that discards sacrifice, liturgy and song in favour of some advanced ingredient. Far from it. No such evolution of spirituality was contemplated within Yahwism.[7] The psalmist does want to open his lips and praise God publicly (v.15). He uses imagery drawn from purification rituals to picture his transformation from

---

Seybold and Gerstenberger. This practice would have analogies in Babylonian religion, for which refer to the discussion in the latter half of this chapter.

[5] The closing verses, vv.18–19, as well as the rubric 'for the leader' show that it was being used in public prayer at the time when it was made part of the canon.

[6] Passages from prophetic preaching include Amos 5:21ff, Hos 6:6, Mic 6:6ff, Isa 1:11ff, Jer 7:21ff, Isa 58:1ff. With these compare the statements in Prov 21:3, Pss 40:7, 50:13f, 69:31f and the review given in Tate, *Psalms 51–100*, p.27ff.

[7] The last two verses of the psalm, possibly added during the Exile, look forward to the restoration of Temple worship and sacrifice and for the community to 'rebuild the walls of Jerusalem', v.18.

the exclusion zone to re-acceptance with God ('purge me with hyssop and I shall be clean', v.7).[8] He could scarcely use the imagery from ritual to express himself, if he despised ritual as such. Israelite spirituality from Moses to Jesus never did dispense with communal rituals, whether sacrificial, festal or liturgical.[9] Indeed the very introduction of New Covenant in the Upper Room is built on Jesus' earnest desire to keep the Passover ritual with his disciples. Forgiveness of sins is emphatically linked with a communal meal and blood ritual in Christian spirituality from its beginnings.[10] Neither Old or New Covenant spirituality can be characterized as anti ritual. Both covenants affirm that there is more to spirituality than liturgy or ritual. The inner-being of the person, the 'me' and the 'I' of Psa 51:7 is fundamental.

The movement in the psalm is from the personal to the communal—from 'Have mercy on me' (v.1) to 'Do good to Zion' (v.18). Signs of restoration before the end of the poem occur at v.13 onwards where the psalmist imagines himself modelling a restored lifestyle that overflows in praise. This influences other sinners to return to God. The movement from preoccupation with personal state to embracing a social perspective seems true to experience. Like pain, illness and anxiety, the misery of guilt expands to fill up available inner space, contracts awareness of others, and squeezes the rest of the world out to the periphery.

---

[8] Sacrifice and confession to adultery or murder were not options the Law offered. These carried a mandatory death sentence. David's adultery with Bathsheba and his planning of the death of Uriah placed him beyond restoration or sacrifice, except for the grace of God over-ruling the Law. In Josh 7, Achan makes a public confession of sin and is executed. This indicates that confession and remission of sentence are separate entities. The Achan text makes no comment about divine forgiveness given or withheld.

[9] As late as 1959, in the German 5th edition of Artur Weiser's *Psalms*, subdued echoes of Wellhausen's and Gunkel's views of Israel's spiritual evolution are sounded. Protestant, post-Enlightenment, romantic, individual pietism glorified the Prophets against Law and Cult and drew lines straight to Jesus. Weiser slides towards this evolutionary approach when he writes: 'The unflinching candour with which the worshipper carries his thoughts and emotions before God enables us to gain most valuable insights into the struggles of a human heart as it strives upwards until it has reached the heights of prophetic experience and thus prepares the way for a piety which brings us right up to the New Testament.' *Psalms*, OTL (London: SCM) 1962, p.401. It is, of course, easier to detect cultural biasing from outside the culture and when its era and style of writing has passed.

[10] 'When the hour came, he took his place at the table, and the apostles with him. He said to them, "I have eagerly desired to eat this Passover with you before I suffer" ' (Lk 21:14f). Jesus pronounced forgiveness of sins during his ministry before this communion rite. Nevertheless, it is the New Covenant relationality which mediates forgiveness of sin and response to Jesus involves response to his atoning death, symbolized by participation in the bread and wine (cf. John 6:53ff).

Forgiveness restores a wider perspective and allows horizontal relationships their place after the relationship with God is healed. The process involves the movement from self-absorption in guilt to Godward orientation in confession This leads to social re-orientation in renewal.

Some graphic imagery depicts the state the psalmist is in before restoration. He feels dirty, condemned and broken. In v.8, he says 'let the bones that you have crushed rejoice', which is a paradox.[11] Broken bones can do nothing but generate agonizing pain. Here they spring to life like the man healed at the Beautiful Gate who entered the temple, 'walking and leaping and praising God' (Acts 3:8). Crushed bones rejoicing is a powerful metaphor for restoration of the person. The bones represent the person's inner strength and dynamic which had been brought to a crunching halt before God. Verse 8 recognizes God as the active agent in a characteristically direct way. We might feel crushed with guilt. The psalmist felt crushed by God. In v.17, he recognizes that this broken state is a starting point not a terminal state—'a heart shattered and crushed, O God, you will not despise.' Animals that were lame or physically defective were unacceptable as cultic offerings; likewise males with crushed testicles. Priests with this and other forms of physical damage or defect were debarred from approaching God in the sanctuary.[12] It is thus paradoxical that the one who brings a 'shattered spirit' and a heart that is 'crushed' is precisely the kind of person who is acceptable. The same verb 'crushed' is used of the heart in v.17 as is used of the bones in v.8.[13]

---

[11] The Hebrew of v.8b *tāgēlnāh ʿaṣāmōt dikkiytā* is a three-word phrase more concise and punchy than the English eight-word translation. On the 'bones' idiom, see Prov 15:30 and 17:22 where 'good news refreshes the bones' but 'a downcast spirit dries up the bones', referring to strength of inner being renewed and sapped. For variations on the idiom, see Psa 6:2, 31:10, 32:3 'body', 38:3. Western culture might express things in a more psychological vein—'I did what I knew was wrong, suffered from terrible feelings of guilt, accompanied by psychosomatic symptoms, and in remorse turned to God.'

[12] See Deut 23:1 (*dakka'* a verb similar to *dkh*) applying to males in general and Lev 21:18ff discussing officiating priests. Mal 1:8,13f condemns the offering of lame, sick or mutilated animals.

[13] The Hebrew phrases in v.17 are *ruaḥ nišbārāh*—'a shattered spirit' and *lēb nišbār wᵉnidkeh*—'a shattered heart and crushed'. Both verbs (*šbr* and *dkh*) are used of vigorous physical blows that smash things. This produces a dynamic metaphor here. Unfortunately, the translation in NRSV and NIV 'contrite heart' eliminates the metaphor. On *ruaḥ* and *lēb* and parts of the body used to express what we would call emotions, reactions or thoughts, see HW Wolff, *Anthropology of the Old Testament* (London: SCM) 1974 Part One, pp.7–78, Chap. 4 on *ruaḥ* and Chap. 5 on *lēb*.

The state of the psalmist when approaching God is further indicated by v.4 where he admits he is under sentence of condemnation and that the verdict of 'Guilty!' is a just one. The graphic court-room metaphor fulfils various functions. Theologically, it ascribes righteousness and justice to God. Psychologically, it makes objective and theological the pangs of conscience that produce this state of awareness. The poet has given a theological interpretation to his sense of guilt. He assents to God's perspective. In English, the word 'conviction' corresponds rather well with what is going on in v.4 because 'conviction' is judicial language but is used outside a court setting for expressing a deep certainty, thus distinguishing it from an impression, notion or theory.[14] This realignment with what is right is part of the process that transforms the poet from a guilty state to a state of grace. Again, it is paradoxical because v.4 apparently deepens the doom by focusing on the sentence hanging over his head ('you are justified in your sentence and blameless when you pass judgment').

In vv. 2, 7 and 10, the metaphor for the state of sin is being dirty. There are several associated nuances to being unclean and clean. 'Whiter than snow' (v.7) speaks for itself and uses the visual contrast of dirty and dazzling. The washing metaphor is a vigorous one because washing clothes involved treading, kneading and beating, and the writer requests a thorough treatment (v.2).[15] The implication is that he feels filthy.

'Purify me with hyssop' (v.7) has cultic associations. The verbal root behind 'purify' means 'to sin' in its basic Qal form. Used in its intensive Piel form in a cultic context, it refers to ritual procedures that purify, hence meaning to dispel sin, that is, 'to de-

---

[14] In the holiness church sub-culture, to speak of being 'under conviction' is a slightly archaic colloquialism which can be used seriously or jokingly. Used seriously, it is a way of attributing a persuasive power to God that is impinging on an individual, forcing a change of mind or a recognition of sin. Behind it probably lies an allusion to John 16:8 and the work of the Spirit—'he will convict the world of sin, and righteousness and judgment' (NRSV footnote translation).

[15] The verb 'wash' in v.2 and 7 is Piel *kibbēs* which is used for washing dirty clothes, not for washing face or body. 'Thoroughly' (*harbēh*) is added in v.2 for increased effect. The futility of a self-administered washing process is denounced by Jeremiah:

> Though you wash with natron,
>   and use much alkali,
> the stain of your guilt is still before me,
>   says the Lord GOD.

(Jer 2:2)

sin, purify, expurgate, decontaminate'.[16] Contamination, that is, cultic pollution, excludes a worshipper from the sanctuary. Exclusion is certainly in our psalmist's mind as one of the consequences of guilt, and exclusion from approaching God in the sanctuary makes real an exclusion expressed in relational terms in v.11: 'Do not cast me away from your presence.'[17]

In Israel's theology, dead bodies, adjacent objects, menstrual blood, skin diseases and other physical phenomena could spread cultic uncleanness in the community and even threaten to contaminate the shrine. This being so, we can see that Israelites could commit unwitting 'sin' involving ritual cleanness. Quite clearly Psalm 51 is not concerned with contamination uncleanness. Its language simply transfers imagery of cultic exclusion to depict moral defilement produced by deliberate sin. To enter into the distress of Psalm 51, we need to take a cross-cultural step into the possibilities of purification for moral sin in Israel's system. The psalmist is aware that a priest cannot help him. For his deliberate sin, there is no purification ritual of washing in water or being sprinkled with blood. Only God could purify him and pronounce him 'Clean!'. For deliberate and serious moral sin, the rubrics of the Holiness Code do not offer a path back into restored relationship via a cultic ceremony —in fact, the laws of the

---

[16] The verb is *ḥāṭāʾ* in its Qal form. Using the intensive Piel form, Lev 14:49,52 speaks of decontaminating a house using a hyssop sprig (NRSV 'cleansing, cleanse', *leḥaṭṭēʾ weḥiṭṭēʾ*). See J Milgrom, *Leviticus 1–16*, AB 3 (New York: Doubleday) 1991, p.827ff for discussion of the purificatory rites using hyssop in Lev 14. Hyssop and the verb *ḥiṭṭēʾ* feature in Num 19:11ff. This deals with decontamination rituals after contact with dead bodies. See ER Dalglish, *Psalm Fifty-One in the light of Near Eastern Patternism* (Leiden: Brill) 1962, p.134ff. For detailed technical discussion of the complexities of purification rituals, see DP Wright, *The Disposal of Impurity*, SBLDS 101 (Atlanta: Scholars) 1987 and N. Kiuchi, *The Purification Offering in the Priestly Literature: its meaning and function*, JSOTS 56 (Sheffield: JSOTP) 1987.

[17] The Hebrew *milepāneykā*—'from before you' could quite naturally refer to the sanctuary presence of God, but does not necessarily do so. Though the Ark and Temple gave focus to God's presence amidst the community, Israelites were not so naive as to confine God to the sanctuary locality. Spatial metaphor is an essential part of theological language but is more difficult to decode in cross-cultural contexts. The exclusion or expulsion motif, which depends on the spatial metaphor of presence, pervades not only Israel's cultic language about the camp in the wilderness and rites such as the driving out of the scapegoat, but also Genesis 1–11 with expulsion from the Garden of Eden, the expulsion of Cain from God's presence and the scattering after Babel. Compare David chased 'from the presence of the LORD' by Saul (*mineged peney Yhwh*, 1 Sam 26:20), probably with both territorial and cultic reference.

Pentateuch speak about being 'cut off', or paying criminal damages, or being executed.[18]

This thought of no way forward apart from God is developed in v. 10: 'create in me a clean heart, O God.' The plea is addressed to God himself directly. The verb 'create' (*bārā'*) seems to be reserved for God's creative activity in Old Testament usage.[19] A 'pure heart' (*lēb ṭāhōr*) requires more than a ritual procedure. It requires a creative act by God.[20] That God himself is addressed and asked to perform the purifying and renewing work flows from the perception expressed in v.4 that it is 'against you, you alone, that I have sinned.' This statement does not deny injury caused to others by sinful behaviour. Rather, it is an intense recognition of guilt before God, a guilt that continuously confronts the poet—'my sin is ever before me', v.3.

This guilt is recognised as endemic as well as specific.

> [5]Indeed, I was born guilty,
> a sinner when my mother conceived me.

The psalmist is working backwards from his present to his birth, and then further still to his conception. No more comprehensive a perspective on himself could he offer. His present experience of his sinfulness is one of a piece with his previous life experience and, by hyperbole, with his pre-birth existence. The interpretive NRSV translation steers us away from reading v.5 as laying the blame elsewhere, that is, on his mother, or on humanity, or on

---

[18] This can be tested against the law collections known as the Covenant Code (Exod 20–23) and the Holiness Code (Lev 18–21). The 'if . . . then' or 'whoever . . . ' laws prescribe punishments. The laws expressed in apodictic form ('Thou shalt . . . ' or 'thou shalt not . . . ') do not prescribe penalties, but penalties such as the death sentence are attached to the crime when it is mentioned elsewhere. 'Thou shalt not commit adultery' (Exod 20:14) without a penalty attached must be matched with the casuistically formulated laws of Lev 20:10 and Deut 22:22 which prescribe death for adultery. The rubric attaching Psa 51 to David's adultery with Bathsheba reads this confession as dramatically as possible, for by law restoration was impossible and sacrifice was never a means of atonement for the double sin of adultery and the 'murder' of Uriah.

[19] Other verbs expressing God's activity, such as *'āśāh*—'to make' are used with human subjects or God interchangeably.

[20] The adjective 'pure' *ṭāhōr* of v.10 (*lēb ṭāhōr*—'pure heart') echoes the verbal form used in v.2,7 (NRSV 'cleanse','be clean'). Both verb and adjective are at home in cultic contexts and frequent in Leviticus. If Tate is right, then being renewed with a steadfast spirit in the parallel line, v.10b, refers to a divine transplant—'it is quite probable that the spirit in v.12 is God's steadfast and firmly reliable spirit, which is given to those who serve him' (*Psalms 51–100*, p.23). This would emphasize the renewal as God's work more than human response.

Adam.[21] The psalmist's statement is not an excuse. It functions as an admission that the sinful act is in character rather than out of character.[22] It may also express solidarity with sinful humanity, a social dimension that would match the social awareness expressed in v.13 concerning restoration: 'then I will teach transgressors your ways, and sinners will return to you.'

If verse 5 looks back as far as possible into the psalmist's past, much of the psalm carries a time future orientation, anticipating the mercy of God begged for in the opening words of the poem. If the record of his sin is deleted (v.1,9), this deals with the sinful event, but much more must follow for a relational future: 'purified heart', 'steadfast spirit' (v.10), 'spirit of your holiness' (v.11), 'joy of your salvation', 'a willing spirit' (v.12).[23] This speaks of a radical renewal, of transformation.

It finds a parallel in Ezekiel's eschatology describing spiritual renewal after the Exile:

> I will sprinkle clean water upon you, and you shall be clean from all your uncleannesses, and from all your idols I will cleanse you. A new heart I will give you, and a new spirit I will put within you; and I will remove from your body the heart of stone and give you a heart of flesh. I will put my spirit within you, and make you follow my

---

[21] Hebrew *'āwōn* does duty for the act and the effect of the act, i.e. the state that results, hence v.5a *be'āwōn* = 'in iniquity' or 'in guilt'. Verse 5 could theoretically refer to the act of conception and to the mother's state at that time, rather than being a poetic way of expressing the psalmist's state stretching back to his earliest moments. NRSV opts for an interpretive translation that affirms it is the poet's nature that is the focus. Tate summarizes the discussions of sex and childbirth as (culticly) impure (*Psalms 51–100*, p.18ff). With Tate, we must dismiss non-moral, cultic uncleanness associated with intercourse or childbirth (Lev 12:2,5 and 15:18) as an explanation for this verse. Such an exegesis would diminish or excuse what the rest of the psalm amplifies, namely, the psalmist's personal moral responsibility.

[22] Compare Kidner's comments: 'This crime, David sees, was no freak event: it was in character; an extreme expression of the warped creature he had always been, and of the faulty stock he sprang from . . . David is, of course, not speaking against his mother in particular, nor against the process of conception. Nor is he excusing himself.' (*Psalms 1–72*, p.190f.)

[23] The exact nuance of *ruah*—'spirit' in 'right spirit', 'your holy spirit', 'a willing spirit' (the construct Hebrew phrases *ruah nākōn, ruah qodšekā, ruah nedībāh*) is difficult to determine, especially whether it refers to God's vitality or the human psyche. The repetition of *ruah* in the b-lines of three consecutive verses is striking. Tate concludes that 'it is probable that *ruah* in vv. 12,13 and 14 refers to the spirit of God in each case' (*Psalms 51–100*, p.25). NIV 'your Holy Spirit' is a Christian reading, not so much wrong as idiomatically a little previous.

statutes and be careful to observe my ordinances. Then you shall live in the land . . .

(Ezek 36:25ff)[24]

Ezekiel combines individual renewal with communal. The heart and spirit comes down to the heart and spirit of each individual, yet the renewal involves a group living in the land. Similarly, our psalmist looks to personal renewal of heart and spirit which works out in the community. The way that it works outwards from the psalmist to others is through the power of speech.

The psalm gives a special place to words. After all, a confession involves words. To articulate these words, to address them to God, gives expression to a spiritual reality that has taken place before the words were formed. The very opening words 'Have mercy . . .' express an inward orientation. Repentance has already occurred, and yet these words of the psalm actualize the movement from repentance to renewal by articulating it. There is a difference between words thought and words spoken aloud. This is the experience of anyone who sits with a counsellor expressing aloud what they must often have said in their minds. Yet to hear the words spoken aloud, and to say the words aloud in someone's hearing marks a new moment and creates new possibilities. The psalmist expresses the value of words in his own way, making it graphic by referring to the organs of speech, the 'tongue', 'lips' and 'mouth':

[13]Then I will teach transgressors your ways,
 and sinners will return to you.
[14]Deliver me from bloodshed, O God,
 O God of my salvation,
and my tongue will sing aloud of your deliverance.
[15]O Lord, open my lips,
 and my mouth will declare your praise.

At one level, these promises are an inducement to God to respond with forgiveness. If God does so, then this will redound to his glory and the psalmist will publicize it. Psalms of Lament regularly motivate God to respond favourably and in doing so they resort to accusations, charges of inconsistency and vows of thanksgiving to get God to act.

Yet this is only one level of what is going on. Another is epitomized by the words of v.15: 'O Lord, open my lips.' Here a spiritual reality is acknowledged. It is akin to the aphorism 'Unless the Lord build the house, they labour in vain who build it' (Psa

---

[24] There are links in vocabulary such as 'new'(*ḥādāš*), 'clean','cleanse' (*ṭāhōr, thr*), 'heart'(*lēb*), 'spirit' (*ruah*) and conceptual links, e.g. of covenant relationality —'you shall be my people and I will be your God' (v.28), of presence—'in the land', and of communal collectivity—'O house of Israel'(v. 22).

127:1). There is a synergism involved. Verse 15 distinguishes words spilling out at human instigation from words uttered in response to what God has done. Without renewal the psalmist is as good as dumb. If he is turned away, he must depart from God's presence into silence. If he is restored, this will release him into praise. He cannot truly open his lips unless God opens his lips. He recognizes that the initiative lies with God if the outcome is to glorify God. What God does for him is primary. This articulation of spirituality is fundamental.

B. GUILT AND *ANGST* IN MESOPOTAMIA

We cannot really appreciate Psalm 51 without looking at those Near Eastern approaches to the deity that express guilt, or, to put it better, existential *Angst*. In them, we see many features of our common humanity. Yet they also express concepts quite alien to orthodox Yahwism. We can follow the link between a penitential attitude and appeasement of divine anger from 3rd millennium Sumerian roots. It develops into lament and penitential prayers of various genres by the 2nd millennium, and a very brief outline of this literary and conceptual development follows.

Sumerian lasted as a vehicle of prayer and literary composition for centuries after it disappeared as a spoken language —rather like Latin in Christendom. The first Sumerian text we shall mention is composed by Enheduanna, daughter of Sargon the Great, founder of the first Semitic empire stretching from Iraq to Lebanon. She appeases the angry heart of Inanna, the goddess of love and war: 'Your holy heart is lofty, may it be assuaged on my behalf!'[25] This phrase referring to the angry heart of the god being assuaged becomes characteristic of Mesopotamian penitential prayers.

---

[25] Sargon of Akkad united Sumerians and Semites under his rule c.2300 BC and installed his daughter Enheduanna as high priestess of the Moon god of Ur and the Sky god of Uruk. *The Exaltation of Inanna* is dedicated to the Sumerian goddess of love and war, Inanna, known in Semitic as Ishtar. In it there are lines referring to soothing the heart of Inanna:

> 110 Your holy heart is lofty, may it be assuaged on my behalf!
> 121 O my queen, beloved of An, may your heart take pity on me!
> 143 The first lady, the reliance of the throne room,
> 144 Has accepted her offerings
> 145 Inanna's heart has been restored.

WW Hallo & JJA van Dijk, *The Exaltation of Inanna*, YNER 3 (London: YUP) 1968, pp. 29,31,35. Another translation is SN Kramer's, *ANET*³, p. 579ff.

Laments over cult-shrines and their alienated gods constitute a distinct Mesopotamian genre, but there is continuity of phraseology and concept with prayers to angered personal gods who might also be the main cult deities of a city or region.[26]

We should probably think of two parallel streams of lament tradition from the end of the 3rd millennium onwards. These are the laments of the individual and laments for city-shrine and country. The latter are represented by the great Sumerian laments over cities, the best known examples being *The Lament for Ur*, and *Lamentation over the destruction of Sumer and Ur*. They were probably composed after the Ur III Empire had disappeared and rebuilding work had begun at the turn of the 2nd millennium.[27]

The *Lament over Ur* ascribes the city's fate to the implacable decree of the senior gods, An the Sky god and Enlil, Lord Windstorm. The human grief and *Angst* generated by the military invasion and sacking of the Ur empire is projected onto goddess Ningal, the spouse of the Moon god of Ur. She laments that she was powerless to overturn the fateful verdict and now weeps bitterly outside the desecrated city. The poem ends with an appeal to Nanna the Moon god to return to his temple and city. His 'penetrating gaze searches the bowels' of the human lamenter. The reciter asks god Moon to absolve his sins and that he may 'appear

---

[26] RW Klein points out that 'the formula *sà ki-bě gi₄* [heart being assuaged: *libbu ana ašrišu tāru* in Akkadian], which is a key term in cultic penitential psalms, marks the very beginning of Enheduanna's "prayer of complaint", as well as the beginning of the episode of her restoration'—' "Personal God" and Individual Prayer in Sumerian Religion' pp. 295–306 in *AfO* Beih. 19 (1982) *Rencontre assyriologique Internationale in Wien*, p. 301. Hallo and van Dijk had noted that the assuagement phrase 'is a standard conclusion of prayers, both the earlier letter-prayers and the later *ir-ša-hun-gǎ* prayers which replaced them' (*Exaltation*, p. 81 *ki-bě. . .gi₄*). Klein goes on to remark that: 'The most interesting fact about these early "individual complaints" is, that basic elements or topoi of these passed through the OB penitential psalms to the Biblical psalms of "individual complaint", as well as to the Biblical didactic psalms of thanksgiving.' (p. 302)

We would want to point out that there is a fundamental theological discontinuity between lament in Mesopotamia and lament in the Jerusalem Temple. This does not deny common metaphor, phraseology or motifs but does distinguish Yahweh's anger from Mesopotamian polytheistic caprice.

[27] See Th.Jacobsen, *The Harps that once . . .: Sumerian poetry in translation* (London: Yale) 1987, pp.447ff. 'Lament for Ur'. *The Lament for Ur*, and Kramer's translation of this and *Lamentation over the destruction of Sumer and Ur* are available in *ANET*, 455ff and *ANET³*, pp.611ff. These Sumerian texts are known from copies in the Old Babylonian period of the early 2nd millennium.

pure'. We might conclude that if goddesses like Ningal were unable to avert the wrath of executive deities like Enlil, then how much more should human beings fear the caprice of these cosmic deities and try to keep on the right side of the powers that be.[28]

The *City laments* are closely related to the Sumerian *balag*-compositions. The *balags* are known from copies of Old Babylonian date (the earlier 2nd millennium) and copies of late date. The great libraries of Assyria and Babylonia in the 7th and 6th centuries have catalogues of the *balag* liturgies which disclose that over 50 compositions were current, and scribes continued to copy them down into the Seleucid period of the 3rd century BC. The *balag* liturgies were not confined to the occasion of the razing and rebuilding of a cult-shrine but passed into the monthly cultic repertoire and were the responsibility of cultic personnel known by the Sumerian/Akkadian title of *gala* or *kalû* priests who recited them in a wailing tone. Some of these laments run to 500 lines, and their length, the persistence of their transmission over hundreds of years and the frequency of their cultic recital, underline the fundamental *Angst* that characterized Mesopotamian polytheism.[29] As their modern editor com- ments,

> Serving not only to placate divine anger over specific activities, the *balag*-lamentation was one vehicle by which the priests maintained an ever-constant vigil against the capriciousness of the gods. The regular recitation of lamentations on fixed days of each month and on festivals hopefully insured tranquillity for a nation ever afraid it might unknowingly commit an offence against the divine powers.[30]

---

[28] SN Kramer reviews texts in which a goddess experiences grief and laments a destruction or the death of a beloved male deity that she was powerless to prevent in 'The Weeping Goddess: Sumerian Prototypes of the "Mater Dolorosa" ' *BA* 46.2 (1983) 69–80.

[29] An Uruk calendar specifies six days of each month for recital of balag liturgies—days 1,2,7,14,15 and 20. Day 7 required five liturgies—three for god Sky (An), one for god Moon (Nanna), and one for goddess Venus-star (Inanna/Ishtar). Two months required special recitals. See ME Cohen, *balag-compositions: Sumerian lamentation liturgies of the second and first millennium bc*, Sources and monographs from the Ancient Near East Vol. 1 fascicle 2 (Malibu: Undena) 1974, p.15. Now available is Cohen, *The Canonical Lamentations of Ancient Mesopotamia* Vol. I & II (Potomac: Capital Decisions) 1988 with a comprehensive treatment of these texts.

[30] Cohen, *balag-compositions*, p.15 and compare his quotation from EA Speiser, p.5, who remarks on 'the anxiety and the insecurity of the mortals who must forever be intent on propitiating the gods in order to obtain a favorable decision'.

MINISTRY TO THE DISTRESSED: EXPERT DIAGNOSIS

All this means that the cultic laments and the personal penitential prayers from Mesopotamia belong in a milieu in which gods are conceived of as irascible.[31] Individual Mesopotamians usually took some omen or distress in their lives as a starting point and inferred from it that their distressing circumstances were the result of divine displeasure. The distress often falls into categories such as illness, insomnia, nightmares, fevers and pains. The Mesopotamians went beyond a biological model of disease and beyond a psychosomatic level of explanation. Their world view included gods, demons and sorcery as causes of disease or untoward circumstances.[32] Sin extended beyond the breach of ethical norms to infringement of cultic taboos and, characteristically, to angering the gods in some unavoidable and unwitting way.

When symptoms were understood as 'the hand of god', first recourse may have been to divination to ascertain whether the client had done anything to incur divine anger. An Old Babylonian letter reports this procedure, but in this case the divination exonerates the young man from all guilt. The consultant divination expert examined the innards of the slaughtered animal (extispicy divination) in an inquiry based on the hair and fringe of the ill man that served as identity tags:

> Concerning the hair and fringe of the young man which you sent me, I have performed an extispicy to obtain an omen about the hair and fringe and the omens are favourable. The young man who is afflicted with the 'hand of the god' is very . . .; there is no question of guilt

---

[31] The early development of the Sumerian prayer tradition has been described by WW Hallo in 'Individual Prayer in Sumerian: the continuity of a tradition' *JAOS* 88 (1968) 71–89. R Klein modifies this by tracing penitential prayer in the form of 'a lament of supplication to a man's (personal) god' to Sumerian times independently of *Letter-prayers*, rather than as a development from *Letter-prayers*. For the later developments into personal prayers to relieve guilt, see the section M-J Seux devotes to 'Prières Pénitentielles' in *Hymnes et Prières aux dieux de Babylone et d'Assyrie*, LAPO 8 (Paris: du Cerf) 1976, pp.139–211 which collects most of the material scattered in Assyriological publications since 1900. For comparisons with Psa 51, Dalglish remains useful—ER Dalglish, *Psalm Fifty-One in the light of Near Eastern Patternism* (Leiden: Brill) 1962.

[32] Some representative Sumerian and Babylonian texts documenting these beliefs are discussed by T Nash 'Devils, Demons, and Disease: Folklore in Ancient Near Eastern Rites of Atonement', pp.57–88 in WW Hallo, BW Jones & GL Mattingly (eds), *The Bible in the light of Cuneiform Literature: Scripture in Context III*, Ancient Near Eastern Texts and Studies 8 (Lewiston/Queenston/Lampeter: The Edward Mellen Press) 1990.

(*ḫīṭum*). And there was here also one young man afflicted with the 'hand of god'; there was no question of guilt with him either.[33]

'The hand of god being upon him' means some nasty symptoms were in evidence, an illness in all probability. 'There is not guilt upon him', given as the verdict of innocence, parallels 'the hand of a god upon him'.[34] In this case, the omens indicated that the young man was in the clear as regards guilt before the gods, even if he was not well physically.[35]

In the poem *Ludlul Bēl Nēmeqi* ('I will praise the Lord of wisdom'), the sufferer is not so fortunate. He relates that 'His hand was heavy upon me, I could not bear it.'[36] Marduk's hostility

---

[33] S Dalley, CBF Walker, JD Hawkins, *The Old Babylonian Tablets from Tell al Rimah*, British School of Archaeology in Iraq, 1976, p. 64, No. 65, lines 4–16.

[34] The Akkadian reads: *qāt ili elišu ibašši* and *mimma ḫīṭum elišu ibašši* (lines 14–16). The wording 'there is . . . upon him' (the preposition *eli-* 'upon' and the verb *bašû*—'to be') is used in both phrases.

[35] Collections of *Tamītu* texts (oracular inquiries put to the Sun and the Weather gods Shamash and Adad) in the late Assyrian library suggest that this kind of questioning was in use over the centuries. An inquiry on behalf of a sick man serves as an illustration.

> Shamash, lord of judgment, Adad, lord of divination, to what I am going to ask you, give me a reliable answer!
> So and so, the owner of this hair and hem, who ails and lies on his death bed—through a positive answer from Shamash, lord of judgment, (and) Adad, lord of divination, (let me learn): If so and so will live as long as one hundred days, (if) he will take food and water with the living, (if) he will walk in good health in the streets of his city.
> Let those who can see, see (the sign), (let) those who can hear, hear (the sign).
> (By means of) *scraps* of white facial hair, (and) *scraps* of red wool, together with these waters, which I have placed before your great divinity, let me understand and let me see your true decision.
> Disregard the fact that he died in a dream!
> Disregard the fact that he recovered in a dream!

> Earl Leichty, 'A *Tamītu* from Nippur', pp. 301–304 in T Abusch (*et al*), *Lingering over Words: studies in Ancient Near Eastern Literature in honor of WL Moran*, HSS 37 (Atlanta: Scholars) 1990.

This is not a parallel to Hezekiah's illness. Hezekiah prayed but made no oracular inquiry. Isaiah's oracle of recovery was unsolicited. There is oracular inquiry in Israel through *Urim* and *Thummim*, though we do not hear much about it after the time of David. If we were to speculate, then, it seems more likely that questions were put to the prophets and answers received intuitively rather than through ritual procedures. Support for this would come from the stories of consulting Samuel and Elisha in the instances of Saul's lost donkeys and Benhadad's illness (1 Sam 9ff and 2 Kgs 8:7ff).

[36] WG Lambert, *Babylonian Wisdom Literature* (Oxford: Clarendon) 1960, p. 48f, Tablet III:1. The poem is translated in *ANET*, 434–437 and most recently in B Foster, *Muses*, pp. 308ff. Its English title is *The Poem of the Righteous Sufferer*, but as the editors point out the author, Shubshi-meshre-Shakkan, does not protest his innocence with energy and anger like Job. The piece is a praise poem to Marduk and so the Akkadian title, abbreviated to *Ludlul* ('I will praise') is apt and is used by Assyriologists. It was probably composed in the

to him was inexplicable, and in lines that are classic, the sufferer
expresses his sense of alienation:

34 What is proper to oneself is an offence (*gullultu*) to one's god,
35 What in one's own heart seems despicable is proper to one's god.
36 Who knows the will of the gods in heaven?
37 Who understands the plans of the underworld gods?
38 Where have mortals learnt the way of a god?[37]

He goes on to describe gruesome symptoms of body, mind and
spirit produced by demonic attack from the underworld. In this
instance, the divination experts were no use at all in diagnosing the
cause of his terrible symptoms, nor did they offer a consoling
message from Marduk:

4 I called to my god, but he did not show his face
5 I prayed to my goddess, but she did not raise her head.
6 The diviner with his inspection has not got to the root of the
   matter,
7 Nor has the dream priest with his libation elucidated my case.
8 I sought the favour of the *zāqīqu*-spirit, but he did not enlighten
   me;
9 And the incantation priest with his ritual did not appease the divine
   wrath against me.[38]

---

later 2nd millennium, the Kassite period. Marduk's 'wisdom' (*nēmequ*) is his
knowledge of the appropriate ritual incantations. The suffering is resolved in
the end by Marduk's dispatch of a *mašmaššu* incantation priest (Tablet
III:41f—*BWL* p.50f.; *Muses*, p. 318) with a 'sign' of renewed favour and with
rituals to perform. This is heralded by a dream. p.50f.

[37] *BWL*, p. 40f. (*Muses*, p.314f). Tablet II:34–38 is translated in the discussion by
K van der Toorn, *Sin and Sanction in Israel and Mesopotamia: a comparative study*,
Studia Semitica Neerlandica 22 (Maastricht: Van Gorcum) 1985, p. 96. See too
his Chap 4 'The Wrath of the Gods. Religious Interpretations of Adversity and
Misfortune', pp.56–93.

[38] Tablet II:4–9 (*BWL*, p. 38f) with which compare Tablet I:49–54 (*BWL*, p. 32f;
Muses, p. 311f) and his return to this topic at the end of Tablet II (*BWL*,44f):

    The omen organs are confused and inflamed for me every day
    The omen of the diviner and dream priest does not explain my condition

    (I:51–52)

    My complaints have exposed the incantation priest,
    And my omens have confounded the diviner.
    The exorcist has not diagnosed the nature of my complaint,
    Not has the diviner put a time limit on my illness.

    (II:108–111)

The range of experts involved are the *mašmaššu, bārû, āšipu, šāʾilu*—'incantation priest', 'diviner', 'exorcist' and 'dream priest' A useful overview
which reflects the ethos of Babylonian concern with the supernatural is given
in HWF Saggs, *The Greatness that was Babylon*, 2nd rev.ed. (London: Sidgwick
& Jackson) 1988 Chap.11 'Magic and Religion', especially pp.254–281.

In this religious milieu, where for no apparent reason the deity could abandon his protegé to demonically induced illness, there develops a range of ministries to the anxiety-ridden individual, including divination questions put to the deity, exorcisms, incantations to counter witchcraft, apotropaic rituals, release rituals and prescribed prayers officiated by the appropriate experts to deal with sin, curse or other expressions of supernatural hostility.

MAKING A GOOD CONFESSION

Mesopotamian *Penitential prayers* are not confined to confession of a specific sin. Indeed there is a desperation expressed that leads on one and the same occasion to the assertion of ignorance of any sin, to denial of specific sins and to confession of lists of sins.[39] A *Prayer to Every God* captures this phenomenon well because the distressed person does not know which god to address, who it is he or she has offended. So the penitent matches the inclusive confession with inclusive address to deities 'known and unknown'. After several lines with a refrain 'my transgressions are many, great are my sins'(lines 21–25),[40] the supplicant pleads complete ignorance of any variety of offence: 'I do not know' (lines 26–29). This phrase 'I do not know' crosses centuries, languages and genre boundaries from Neo-Sumerian *Letter-prayers* to tablets used centuries later in Assyria and Babylon.[41] This *Prayer to Every God* also has a statement on human solidarity that excuses angering the gods on the grounds of crass ignorance:

51 Humanity is stupid, it knows nothing.
52 Whoever exists, what do they know?

---

[39] These perspectives are well documented by K van der Toorn in Chap. 5 'In Search of Secret Sin. Confessions of Ignorance and Pleas for Illumination', pp. 94–99 in *SaS*. See too *Muses*, III.49 a-d, pp. 640–645 for translations of relevant material.

[40] The Akkadian words used for the sins are *annu/arnu epēšu*—'to commit an offence', *ḫīṭû ḫāṭu*—'to sin a sin', *ikkibu akālu*—'to infringe a taboo' and *anzillu kubbušu*—'to trample on a prohibited thing'. See van der Toorn, p.42ff for discussion of these terms, and *CAD A, H, I, K* for references and translations. *Hymnes*, lines 26–29 = Langdon, lines 42–47.

[41] Van der Toorn cites detailed references to the occurrence of phrases expressing complete ignorance of the offence in *eršaḫunga, dingiršadibba, šigû* and *šu'ila* prayers. Some have a slightly comical touch for us: 'I cannot remember the transgression I did' and 'I do not know my sins which are numerous' (p.208 n 2).

53 Whether one does evil, whether one does good, one does not know.[42]

From the early 2nd millennium comes a Babylonian *Literary Prayer to Marduk* that was being copied over a thousand years later for Ashurbanipal's library in Nineveh. It achieved a 'canonical' status in Mesopotamian religion somewhat comparable to Psa 51. A few excerpted lines will indicate the tone of the prayer. They were apparently spoken by the officiant on the penitent's behalf.

> 1 O furious lord, let [your heart] be c[almed],
> 15 O Marduk, you know how to pardon the flagrant crime,
> 16 To waive the punishment in even grievous cases.
> 57 O lord, look upon your exhausted servant,
> 58 Let your breeze waft, release him quickly,
> 59 Let your heavy punishment be eased,
> 60 Loosen his bonds, let him breathe right away![43]

The priest appeals on the basis of a creation theology—'Do not destroy the slave that your own hands fashioned'(line 66). He demands what use the man would be to the god if dead—'The one who has been changed into clay, what profit is there in him?'(line 67). He asks who it is that does not sin (lines 104–106), asserts that only the gods know and can disclose what is good and what is bad (line 107f), moves on to list his maladies of headache, insomnia, terrors and weeping (line 125ff), and then quotes the penitent's own confession:

> 138 "My lord, I have indeed transgressed, let me escape from distress,
> 139 "Many are my guilty deeds, I have sinned in every way!
> 140 "O Marduk, I have transgressed, let me escape from distress!"

It is with intentional exaggeration that he says 'many are my misdeeds, I have committed every sin' (lines 137,139).[44] He

---

[42] *ANET*[3], p. 391f; *Muses*, III.54, p. 685ff; *Hymnes*, pp. 51–53. 'Stupid' is a semantic fit for the D-form stative of *sakāku*—'to be stopped up, deaf' (cf. 'dumb' in American slang). The word for 'humanity' is *amēlūtu/awīlūtu*. It is used with universal reference to humanity in the Flood story, e.g. speaking of Mami as the 'creatress of mankind' and of the 'noise of mankind' which provoked the Flood (*Atrahasis* I:194,358 & II:i,7; Dalley, *Myths*, pp. 15, 18, 20 and *Muses*, II.39, pp. 165, 169,171).

[43] *Muses*, III.29, p. 520ff. For the original, see WG Lambert *AfO* 19 (1960) 47ff 'Three Literary Prayers of the Babylonians', *Prayer to Marduk No.1*. A French translation appears in *Hymnes*, p. 172ff., *À Marduk*, 2.

[44] The quotation of lines 137 & 139 is in the translation given in *CAD H*, p. 157 *ḥatû* 2: *ma'dūma annūa aḫtati kalama*. Lambert translates 'I have committed many trespasses indeed.' This is too weak. Better is *CAD A2*, p. 296 *arnu* 6 'my misdeeds are numerous, I have transgressed in every respect' with which Foster's translation concurs. Compare *Hymnes*, p. 178 'nombreuses sont mes fautes, j'ai manqué en tout.' The statement excusing sin as universal is clear if slightly broken: 'Who is he that [. . .], not s[inned]?, Who is he so watchful

promises that, restored, he will offer lavish offerings and bear living testimony by provoking the response ' "Marduk causes the dead to live" '(lines 181ff).[45]

Some examples from a collection *Incantation for Appeasing an Angry God* illustrate Mesopotamian theology of guilt and restoration in its characteristic setting. These prayers are usually addressed to the personal god for release from the supposed curse that embodies divine anger. Bad omens conveyed in dreams or discerned in the entrails of divination animals, or circumstances described in the diagnostic texts of ritual experts might precipitate these penitential prayers and rituals. The rituals for individual penitents were more effective if performed on the eleventh day of the tenth month, a concept based on astrology—'the pacification of an angry god was thought to be favourably influenced by the Pleiades.'[46] There is a telling rubric for such occasions:

> He shall recite, "*Ea, Shamash and Marduk, what are my iniquities?*"
> He shall stand facing the ritual paraphernalia of a man's god and goddess and
> He shall recite, "*My god, I did not know*" and "*My god, my lord*".[47]

Anxiety seems more fundamental than actual guilt to judge from rubrics such as the following:

---

that has incurred no sin? Which is he so circumspect that has committed no wrong-doing?' (*Muses*, p. 522, lines 104–106; line 105f *ḫiṭītu*—'sin', and *gillatu wabālu*—'to bear, carry sin').

[45] Lines 181–84 are not a statement about personal bodily resurrection, nor would Lambert's translation intend that:

> 181 May he who sees him in the street mark your divinity
> 182 Let them say to one another, 'The Lord is [able to raise] the dead'.
> 183 May he who sees him in the street mark your divinity,
> 184 Let them say to one another, 'Marduk is able to raise the dead'.

Marduk mītu bulluṭ—'Marduk causes the dead to live' is highly metaphorical. It means he, the sufferer, is as good as dead in his present sorry state ('turned to clay', lines 54,56,67), but if absolved and restored to favour will undergo an amazing recovery from his maladies. The verb *balāṭu*—'to live' is used in the D-form 'to cause to live, be alive'.

[46] *SaS*, p.124.

[47] WG Lambert 'Dingir.ša.dib.ba Incantations' *JNES* 33.3 (1974) 267–322, p. 268, BBR 26, v:78–81 from the *Bīt Rimki* washing rituals. "*Ea, Shamash and Marduk what are my iniquities?*" is the opening line of the *Dingiršadibba* prayer presented by Lambert, p.274ff (*Muses*, III.37, p. 554). The stereotyped Akkadian phrases denying consciousness of sin go back to Sumerian prototypes in *Letter-prayers* addressed to 'my god' or 'my king'—where the king is either the god addressed as king or a deceased and deified monarch, or perhaps occasionally a living one (see Hallo, 'Individual Prayer', p.79).

Text (to be recited) in case a man is constantly worried, in order to pacify the angry heart of the god.

his god will have a friendly disposition towards him (and) he will have no worry

[When a man] contemplates f[oolish]ness and [he] repeats [his] sayings, now he is asleep, now he is awake, and he cannot control his thoughts: the wrath of his god is upon him . . .[48]

RELEASE FROM CURSE

The sin for which the person is suffering could be the sin of a previous generation. Its baleful effect can be combated with magical rituals. Brief excerpts from a *Dingiršadibba* incantation and a related genre, the *Sigû prayer* are given below:

109 My god, great one, who grants life,
110 Who gives judgments, whose command is not altered,
111 . . . you, my god, I have stood before you, I have sought you my god, [I have bowed] beneath you.
112 Accept my prayers, release my bond
113 Relax my banes, tear out the . . . of my evil, drive away my trouble.
114 Drive out from my body illness from known and unknown iniquity,
115 The iniquity of my father, my grandfather, my mother, [my] grandmother,
116 The iniquity of my elder brother, and elder sister,
117 The iniquity of clan, kith and kin,
118 Which has come upon me because of the raging of the wrath of my god and goddess.
119 Now I burn their images before your great divinity.
120 Release my bond, grant me reconciliation.[49]

★★★

[48] *SaS*, p.122f. Van der Toorn also provides a text and translation of KUB 4,47 from the Hittite capital, Boghazkoy. The text has three Akkadian *šigû* prayers but diagnostic and ritual sections in Hittite. It deals with anxiety and insomnia, prescribing rituals for set dates. The rituals involve nail clippings, armpit hairs, coloured wools, and various offerings along with the rubric 'He shall cry for mercy for his sin' (p.125ff). The word *šigû* was originally an exclamation, appears in the phrase *šasû šigû*—'to cry *šigû*, ie. to cry for mercy, and becomes the name of a genre of individual penitential prayer (*SaS*, 117ff).

[49] Lambert, '*Dingir.ša.dib.ba* Incantations', p.280f., lines 109–120. The text also appears in Akkadian and in French translation in M-J Seux '*Siggayôn = šigû?*', pp.419–438 in A Caquot & M Delcor (eds), *Mélanges bibliques et orientaux en l'honneur de M.Henri Cazelles*, AOAT 212 (Kevelaer: Neukirchen-Vluyn) 1981, Text G, p.435ff and in *Hymnes*, p.206ff in French translation.

47 Thus you shall speak: O Shamash, my sins, (brought upon me) by my forefathers,

48 (the consequences of) my careless acts, the curse, the oath (uttered by) the lips, may it not reach me!

49 May the body absorb the sin and the curse;

50 Shamash, what(ever) you know and I do not know

51 may it cross the river Hubur, together with the figurine of my father;

52 may a happy future be decided![50]

'Iniquity' in English does not have the semantic range of *arnu* in Akkadian—sin, guilt and the penalty involved.[51] The person praying interprets his sufferings as the penalty for the sin and guilt of his kinsfolk. The 'banes', 'evil', 'trouble' and 'bond' (lines 113,120) are various ways of referring to the curse that binds the sufferer, producing the bodily symptoms referred to in line 114.[52] The recited words are accompanied by the ritual burning of the effigies. Destroying the effigies eradicates the iniquity and nullifies the ill effects that it exercises on the sufferer.

ANTIDOTE OR REPENTANCE?

Orthodox Christian theology has a place for the demonic, for the reality of divine anger, for links between physical symptoms and spiritual causes, for corporate guilt, for consequences of sin that have effects across generations, but not in the same way as

---

[50] *SaS*, p.134 a hemerological text (ie. a listing of lucky days), KAR 178 rev. vi:34–52.

[51] See *CAD A2*, 294 *arnu* '1. guilt, wrongdoing, misdeed, offense, 2. punishment, fine'; *AHw.*, p. 70 'Schuld, Unrecht, Sünde'. Just as there are clusters of associated terms for the binding curse, so too there are clusters of terms for sin. They may not be synonyms, but it is not always possible to catch distinguishing nuances. With *arnu*, compare *gillatu gullultu, ḫiṭītû, ḫīṭu, šērtu, šettu, šētu* as translated in *CAD G*, 72,131 and *CAD H*, 210 and the verb *ḫaṭû*, 156ff and *AHw.*, 288, 297, 337, 350, 1218, 1221.

[52] 'Banes' line 113 is quaint English for Akkadian *māmītu*. In a treaty-making context, the *māmītu* is the binding oath. When the oath is broken, the curse is inflicted and *māmītu* takes on the nuance of 'curse'. See *CAD M*, 189ff '1. oath, sworn agreement, 2. curse (consequences of a broken oath attacking a person who took it, also as demonic power)'; *AHw.*, 599f 'Eid;Bann. *māmītu* 6. als Dämon'. Just as we speak of a 'binding oath' in English, the Mesopotamians thought of a 'binding curse'. The metaphor of 'release' applies. The semantic range of *māmītu* from reference to the utterance of human words to a semi-autonomous divine penalty to a demonic power illustrates the world of Mesopotamian concepts which moves beyond metaphor to magic and occultism.

Mesopotamia believed them to operate.[53] Mesopotamian theological understanding moves instinctively away from ethical norms towards rituals, incantations and magic.

By way of contrast, the prayer of Dan 9 interprets the Exile in terms of the norms of Torah, while recognising corporate guilt and the reality of 'the curse and the oath':

> All Israel transgressed your law and turned aside, refusing to obey your voice. So the curse and the oath written in the law of Moses, the servant of God, have been poured out upon us because we have sinned against you.
>
> (Dan 9:11)[54]

This biblical confession of sin has no magical antidote attached to it. It is accompanied by 'prayer and supplication with fasting and sackcloth and ashes' (Dan 9:3). The dramatic maximum accompanying words of intercession is summed up in the reactions of Ezra:

> When I heard this, I tore my garment and my mantle, and pulled hair from my head and beard, and sat appalled. Then all who trembled at the words of the God of Israel, because of the faithlessness of the returned exiles, gathered around me while I sat appalled until the evening sacrifice. At the evening sacrifice I got up from my fasting, with my garments and my mantle torn, and fell on my knees, spread out my hands to the LORD my God and said, 'O my God, I am too embarrassed to lift my face to you, my God, for our iniquities have risen higher than our heads and our guilt has mounted up to the heavens . . .
>
> (Ezra 9:3–6)

This way of reacting is culturally alien to contemporary spirituality. Wearing sackcloth, daubing oneself with ashes, tearing one's clothes and pulling out body-hair are symbolic gestures at home in a different culture. Yet, though culture-bound, these gestures are not alien theologically. They express repentance, deep grief and sincerity. The expression of guilt in the prayers of Daniel and Ezra is first person plural confession: 'from the days of our ancestors to

---

[53] There was a popular proverb in exilic times which ran—'The fathers have eaten sour grapes and the children's teeth are set on edge' (Jer 31:29, Ezek 18:2), but the prophets engage with this perception of solidarity and speak both of a new thing God is doing, terminating the judgement (Isa 40–55) or of God's dealing with the individual as individual (Ezekiel 18).

[54] The Hebrew used for 'the curse and the oath' is *hāʾālāh wᵉhašᵉbūʿāh* which is a paired phrase, better translated 'the covenant oath' or the like. It has a 2nd millennium antecedent in the Akkadian phrase *riksu u māmītu*—'bond and oath-curse, binding oath' referring to political treaties.

this day *we* have been deep in guilt . . .' (Ezra 9:7); '*we* have sinned
and done wrong, acted wickedly and rebelled, turning aside from
your commandments and ordinances. *We* have not listened to
your servants the prophets . . .' (Dan 9:5f). There is therefore a
discontinuity of theology between Yahwism and Mesopotamia,
and a discontinuity of cultural expression between Yahwism and
today. There is, however, a theological trajectory in the understanding of guilt and restoration from the Old Testament to the
New Covenant.

SOLIDARITY IN SINFULNESS

Where Israel's theology admits sinful solidarity, Mesopotamia
tends to refer to the universality of sin and to mitigate it. In an
early *Letter-prayer* concerning the infringement of a cultic taboo,
the writer reminds the goddess of the universality of sin before
asking for exoneration:

> To my Lady who loves life speak: Thus (says) Ur-Utu, your servant.
> 'As my Lady knows, there does not exist the servant with respect to
> his master, the servant-girl with respect to her mistress, who does not
> bear sin and guilt.'[55]

Because 'Lord' and 'Lady' (*bēl* and *bēltu*) can apply to humans or
gods, and 'servant' likewise to the household slave or the temple
devotee, the writer draws a forceful analogy. He says, in effect,
that the most devoted servants will inevitably carry sin and guilt,
flaws in their record.[56] He thus merges himself into the general
background of human reality in order to diminish his personal
guilt toward the deity.

The same idea can be put across with rhetorical questions.

132 Who is there who has not sinned against his god?
133 Who that has kept the commandment for ever?

---

[55] Tablet Di 525 from Ammisaduqa's reign around 1700 BC is published by L de
Meyer 'Une Lettre d'Ur-Utu GALAMAH á une Divinité', pp. 41–43 in M
Lebeau & P Talon (eds), *Mélanges André Finet*, Akkadica 6 (Leuven: Peeters)
1989. The *Letter prayer* is from a lamentation priest to his goddess Inanna-
Ishtar and mentions a 'taboo of Adad'. The type of cultic infringement
referred to *asakkam akālu*—'to eat the *asakkam*', ie. to infringe the taboo, is
familiar from the Mari texts. See A Malamat, *Mari and the Early Israelite
Experience* (Oxford: OUP) 1989, pp. 70–77 who relates it to the ban inflicted
on Achan in Joshua 7. Van der Toorn associates *asakkam* with food connected
with oath-taking and oath-breaking and which works like a curse (*SaS*,
p.26,42).
[56] L de Meyer opts for a nuanced translation of *ḫīṭu*, and *gillatu* 'de faute (par
négligence) ou de faute (consciente)' as the brackets indicate, but whether sins
of omission as well as commission are really in mind here is dubious.

134 All of mankind who exist are sinful
135 I, your slave, have committed every sin

137 I spoke lies, I pardoned my own sins
138 I spoke improper things, you know them all.
139 I committed offence against the god who created me
140 I did abomination, ever doing evil.[57]

There follows a list of sins majoring on cultic taboos, but the sequence of thought in lines 132–135 expresses it all. By confessing to everything, the sufferer is simply covering himself against every eventuality, all witting or unwitting sin. The same is true for *Release liturgies* to undo the effect of sin and curse (*arnu* and *māmītu*). In one of these, the speaker is bothered by whether he has unwittingly stepped in someone's dirty washwater, touched their nail-pairings, shavings from their armpit, shoes with holes in them, a tattered belt, a leather bag with paraphernalia for black magic or similar unlucky objects associated with spell-making. He implores the Sun god, Shamash, to release and absolve him, adding philosophically:

50 (Through) all my sins, all my errors, all my crimes
51 may the unbeliever learn from my example,
52 who was neglectful, who committed grievous sins against his god and his goddess,

55 I am . . . , I am dazed, I am . . . , I do not know where I am going,
56 The sins and crimes of mankind are more numerous than the hair of its head;[58]

Finally, the absolution of sin offered in such texts as the *Release litanies* involves language that goes far beyond simile and metaphor in depicting the removal of sin from the person of the afflicted penitent. In the *Release Litanies*, for example, concatenations of similes picture the removal of the sin/guilt/penalty. A few lines from the Type I, 1 Litany will convey this. The whole Assembly of gods is invoked:

71 wipe out his sins, remove (his) oath, drive out his curse,
72 remove, keep far, drive out from his body
73 the weariness that is in the body of NN, son of NN!
74 May the tamarisk purify him, may the *maštakal*-plant absolve him,
75 may the palm-cabbage release his sin, may Nisaba, the queen, Anu's daughter, take his sin off him,

---

[57] Lambert, '*Dingir.ša.dib.ba* Incantations', p.282f.
[58] E Reiner, 'The *Lipšur* Litanies' *JNES* 15 (1956) 129–149, p.143 Type II.1 line 50 ff.

76 may the incantation-formula of Ea and Asalluhi keep away his sin,
77 may his sins be absolved, his offences wiped out,
78 his crimes washed off, his curses absolved,
79 his pains driven out—may they be peeled off like an onion,
80 stripped off like dates, unravelled like a matting![59]

It is evident that the removal of sin, of the curse, and of the divine anger behind the curse relies not simply on penitential prayers in Mesopotamia but on ritual action and on words of incantation undertaken by a divination expert or other specialised cultic officiant.

This is epitomized by the collection of incantations known as *Shurpū*, which compiles lists of sins and effects of the curse.[60] These are dealt with by ritually attaching the effects of the sin or sorcery to objects and then burning these items with accompanying incantations. This purifies and absolves the sufferer by annihilating the binding curse. Thus onions are peeled, dates stripped off, matting unravelled, wool and goat's hair plucked apart and thrown into the fire with the words,

67. (so) invocation, oath, retaliation, questioning,
68. the pain of my hardship, sin, transgression, crime, error,
69. the sickness that is in my body, my flesh, my veins,
70. may be stripped off like these dates,
71. may the fire consume it entirely today,
72. may the oath leave so that I may see the light!

(*Shurpû*, Tablet V–VI)[61]

---

[59] 'The *Lipšur* Litanies', p.137. The usual cluster of words describing the problem occurs in this text. A listing by line is as follows: line 71 *ḫiṭātu nīšu māmītu*—sin, oath, curse; line 75 *arnu šērtu*—sin, sin; line 76 *ennettu*—sin; line 77 *arnu ḫiṭātu*—sin, offence; line 78 *gillatu māmītu*—crime, curse; line 79 *murṣu*—pain. From this list, one can see that Erica Reiner has translated four separate Akkadian words as 'sin' in these lines (*ḫiṭātu arnu šērtu ennettu*). This illustrates how difficult it is to give the right nuances to this semantic cluster, if indeed distinctions are intended. The 'weariness' of 'body' (*tānēḫu, zumru* line 73) and 'pains'(line 79) are physical symptoms which suggest that sickness or severe psychosomatic malaise prompt the visit to the ritual expert. In line 73, the text envisages the insertion of the name of the sick person to be treated.

[60] E Reiner, *Shurpû a collection of Sumerian and Akkadian Incantations*, AfO Beih. 11, Graz 1958, Tablet V–VI, pp.32ff. Excerpts from *Shurpû* are given in W Beyerlin, *Near Eastern Texts relating to the Old Testament* (London: SCM) 1978, p.131ff. and *Muses*, IV.42, p. 877. See the index under *Shurpû* in *SaS*, p. 237 for van der Toorn's discussion of this material.

[61] Tablet V–VI, p.31 lines 67–72 which are repeated with each incantation substance. Whereas lines 35–59 immediately before the onion incantation give a resumé mentioning onion, dates and matting, the focus there is on curses by family members or unknown murder. The next incantations specify the individual's sins (*tānēḫu, arnu, šērtu, gillatu, ḫiṭātu*) and sicknesses as the cause of his problems. The word 'oath' (*māmītu*) in line 72 is the curse adjuration, from whose effects the sufferer seeks release. If the adjuration was pronounced against him, we would translate *māmītu* as 'curse'. If he swore an oath which

Likewise, the washing rituals using Euphrates water or sea water remove effects of sins where the client is the responsible, if unwitting, agent, as well as the effects of sorcery where the client is the one sinned against.

78. Today may the great gods who dwell in the heaven of Anu release [you], absolve you in their assembly
79. Taboo, interdict, sin, transgression, crime, error, retaliation, que[stioning],
80. bad luck may move away, be far off; the invocation, oath, sin e[rror],
81. blasphemy against god and goddess, the evil (effect) of sorcery, spittle, dirt, evil machinations
82. may they be released for you, absolved for you, wiped off [you] today.
83. He is purified, cleansed, bathed, washed, cleaned (var.: with flowing river-water),
84. with water of the pure Tigris and Euphrates, the water of the sea (and) [vast] ocean . . .

(Tablet VII)[62]

Though some Levitical rituals have been compared with the washings or removals of guilt in *Shurpû* and related texts, there are fundamental differences of theology.[63] For one thing, the *Shurpû* texts use the same ritual and incantation routine for dissolving the ill effects of demonic oppression, family curses, sicknesses and

---

he then broke, it is a self-curse. Treaty-oaths are, in effect, self-curses in the breach.

[62] *Shurpû*, p.43f
[63] Nash wants to use the term 'magic' because 'that probably remains the best way to describe a series of Israelite rituals that imitate Sumerian and Babylonian atonement rites' ('Devils, Demons and Disease', p.59), and he refers to the expiation ritual for an unsolved murder in Deut 21:1–9, particularly the act of handwashing. He assumes that they are 'symbolically offering the "blood" of atonement not by smoke and flame into the sky, but down into the depths of an untilled ravine, an earthly *Sheol*' (p. 81). The text itself does not mention the heifer's blood, only a broken neck, though blood running away in a flowing stream is a symbolism possibly implied with magical overtones. The text does not make a connection with banishing underworld spirits or disembodied ghosts. Nash admits that the parallels with Hittite and Assyrian rites are at best partial and singularly lacking in 'the repetitive incantation phrases of Mesopotamian magic' (p.82) as well as its developed demonology. Comparisons of ritual acts across cultures need to take seriously (a) the total cultural context, and (b) the shift of meaning inevitably involved in cross-cultural transference, and (c) the probability of polemic alternative when monotheistic Yahwism adopts and adapts Canaanite or Near Eastern symbolism. On Deut 21:1–9 see too the comments of DP Wright, *The Disposal of Impurity*, SBLDS 101 (Atlanta: Scholars) 1987, pp. 272ff and his article 'Deuteronomy 21:1–9 as a rite of Elimination' *CBQ* 49 (1987) 387–403.

personal sins.[64] We are really in a different theological world from the Psalms—and the difference does not consist solely in the polytheism:

76. May the god and goddess of him with whom they are angry, be reconciled with him today;
77. may the anger of the heart of the god and goddess of NN, son of NN, be averted from him,
78. may his sin be shed today, may it be wiped off him, averted from him.
79. May the record of his sins, errors, crimes, oaths,
80. (all) that is sworn, be thrown into the water,
81. may his errors be wiped out, his crimes removed,
82. his oaths undone,
83. his diseases driven away;
84. his headache, his restlessness, his gloom, his bad health,
85. woe and lament, sleeplessness, his worry, his gloom, his weariness,
86. drive them out today from the body of NN, son of NN.
87. Through the invocation of your pure name may be removed, driven away, expelled
88. the sin and oath which are there to torment men.

(Tablet IV, lines 76–88)[65]

The water here is real and we are in the world of magic and incantation rather than the world of metaphor and Yahwistic prayer which we meet with in the psalms.

Mesopotamian spirituality, to our minds, involves compound category confusions. The supplicants themselves are confused as to what, if anything, they have done wrong and how their misfortunes relate to this. Their physical or psychological symptoms are multiplex and intertwined with taboo infringement and occult powers, and little or no sense of ethical orientation enters this picture of the disturbed state.

It is true that recent studies have demonstrated many parallels of conceptual category between Israel's sense of cultic uncleanness

---

[64] For example, *Shurpû*, p.26, Tablet IV, lines 45–54 lists seven types of demon and ends with the named ones *Lamaštu, Labaṣu* and *Aḫḫazu,* then line 55 uses the four words common for the effects of sin (*arnu, māmītu, ḫiṭītu, gillatu*), and line 58 specifies curses by father and mother, elder brother and elder sister from which release is secured. For a review of cursing in a context of biblical theology, emphasising the distinctives and relationality, see MJ Evans, ' "A Plague on both your houses": cursing and blessing reviewed', *Vox Evangelica* 24 (1994) 77–89.
[65] *Shurpû*, p.27f.

and Near Eastern concepts.[66] Despite living with a consciousness of ritual uncleanness which augments moral and ethical guilt, Israel's prayers used at the sanctuary focus on God himself rather than on cultic regulations. This is a point made by Psa 51 when it relegates sacrifice to a secondary role. We will not fully appreciate the absence of contamination *Angst* in Israelite spirituality until we have stepped into the world of taboos, incantations, exorcisms, hemerologies (lucky and unlucky days—see Section D1 in Chap 11 below) and ritual release procedures in Mesopotamia.

Though cultic uncleanness must have been a pervasive and everyday experience for Israelites, there are no psalms asking for forgiveness for witting or unwitting infringements of the purity laws. The Torah regulations governing diagnosis of skin diseases, the exclusion time and the reincorporation of the sufferer into living area and sanctuary were handled by the priests, yet they have left no undisputed trace in the Psalms.[67] While ritual impurities could have increased an Israelite's spiritual *Angst* immensely, they are not reflected in those prayers of Israel that are protests of innocence or pleas for mercy. Nor do we learn about divination rituals to ascertain whether an Israelite had infringed a taboo of his or her God. In this respect Israelite prayer, as preserved for us, appears radically different from prayer in Mesopotamia that relied upon divination experts. Nor are there biblical psalms that list and confess to all conceivable means of offending the deity in the hope of covering all unknown eventualities.

By contrast, the biblical Psalms articulate all the distress that Mesopotamians experienced, but mediate an authentic forgiveness and a restoration into covenant relationship because that relationship is governed by covenant stipulations that are fundamentally moral and ethical. Sin is recognizably sin. This we can illustrate from Psalms 32 and 38.

---

[66] For recent technical work on cultic holiness, see the monographs by DP Wright, *The Disposal of Impurity: elimination rites in the Bible and in Hittite and Mesopotamian Literature*, SBLDS 101 (Atlanta: Scholars) 1987; PR Jenson, *Graded Holiness: a key to the Priestly conception of the world*, JSOTS 106 (Sheffield: JSOTP) 1992 and W Houston, *Purity and Monotheism: clean and unclean animals in biblical law*, JSOTS 140 (Sheffield: JSOTP) 1993.

[67] The Hebrew ṣāraʿat, no longer translated 'leprosy', covers a range of skin conditions. It occurs nowhere in the psalms. See *SaS*, p. 24ff for a comparison of attitudes and experiences to approaching the deity in states of purity and impurity, and p.72ff Section 5. *Leprosy* on šaḫaršubbû as 'the great curse', linked to the Moon god in Mesopotamia.

GUILT AND ITS PSYCHOSOMATIC SYMPTONS

In Psalm 32, very like the Marduk texts of *Ludlul* and the *Literary Prayer to Marduk*, we hear of 'the hand of God' being heavy on the supplicant with the result that he experienced psychosomatic symptoms of guilt.

> ³When I kept silence, my bones wasted away.
> through my groaning all day long.
> ⁴For day and night your hand was heavy upon me;
> my strength was dried up as by the heat of summer.
> ⁵Then I acknowledged my sin to you,
> and I did not hide my iniquity;
> I said, "I will confess my transgressions to the LORD,"
> and you forgave the guilt of my sin.

We cannot be specific about the physical symptoms in the sense of giving a medical name to 'my bones wasted away' (v. 3a) or to the sapping of strength (v. 4b) because the language is partly metaphorical—'bones' and 'strength' do duty for inner being and vitality. We can follow the psalmist in the causality he delineates. The cause of his distress is specific and undeclared guilt (v. 5). He drops his pretence of innocence and opts for open confession. The positive result, his sense of forgiveness, followed. The change is from sin that is covered up by the sinner to sin that is covered by God—'whose sin is covered . . . and in whose spirit there is no deceit' (vv. 1b & 2b).[68] The same verb *ksh* is used in v. 1a 'Happy are those . . . whose sin is covered' as is used in v. 5 'and I did not hide(cover) my iniquity.' This draws together and contrasts the destructive covering of sin by the sinner and the reconstructive covering of it by God. This psalm is thus the diametrical opposite of those Mesopotamian pieces that express ignorance of what offended the deity and assume unwitting guilt.

Unlike Psalm 32, which expresses the joy of forgiveness, Psalm 38 emerges out of the distress of spirit prior to restoration. The language is highly metaphorical, yet we would be justified in speaking of the psychosomatic symptoms of guilt without treating the metaphors as medical diagnostics. The psalmist identifies the root cause of his distress unequivocally as his own sin, which he now confesses:

---

[68] Four Hebrew words are clustered together in Psa 32:1–2: *pešaʿ, ḥᵃṭāʾāh, ʿāwōn, rᵉmiyyāh*. The first three are general words for sin, while the last, 'deceit' *rᵉmiyyāh*, seems to refer to the inclination to cover over the sin and matches the 'hide' of v. 5a and the 'kept silent' of v. 3a. The same verb *ksh* is used in v. 1a 'whose sin is covered' (*kᵉsūy ḥᵃṭāʾāh*) as is used in v. 5 'and I did not hide (cover) my iniquity.'

¹⁷For I am ready to fall,
and my pain is ever with me.
¹⁸I confess my iniquity;
I am sorry for my sin.

If sin is the underlying cause, then God's reaction to it, Yahweh's personal anger, is the cause of his profound symptoms:

¹O LORD, do not rebuke me in your anger,
or discipline me in your wrath.
²For your arrows have sunk into me,
and your hand has come down on me.
³There is no soundness in my flesh
because of your indignation;
there is no health in my bones
because of my sin.
⁴For my iniquities have gone over my head;
they weigh like a burden too heavy for me.
⁵My wounds grow foul and fester
because of my foolishness;
⁶I am utterly bowed down and prostrate;
all day long I go around mourning.
⁷For my loins are filled with burning,
there is no soundness in my flesh.
⁸I am utterly spent and crushed;
I groan because of the tumult of my heart.

We immediately notice the Near Eastern 'your hand has come down upon me' (v. 2b), a metaphor that expresses relationality and effects. Verse 2b is, of course, a theological interpretation of the psalmist's condition. In this poem, the personal attitude of God is conveyed by the cluster 'anger', 'wrath', 'arrows', 'hand', 'indignation' (vv. 1–3). The effects are felt in the psalmist's 'flesh', 'bones', 'head', 'wounds', 'loins', 'heart', 'strength' and 'eyes', and he speaks of being 'weighed down', 'bowed down', 'prostrate', 'spent' and 'crushed' (vv. 3–10). He mentions 'mourning', 'groans', 'sighing', a pounding heart and exhaustion. He is like a deaf or dumb person (v. 13). He suffers social ostracism and isolation as a result of his condition—'my friends and companions stand aloof from my affliction, and my neighbours stand far off' (v. 11). The word 'affliction' (*nega'*) encompasses the entire symptomology because of its associations with plague, skin disease and a divinely struck blow.

It would be a mistake to attempt a modern medical diagnosis of the psalmist on the basis of the poetry of lament with its colourful metaphors. How, for example, would one decode 'for your arrows have sunk into me' (v.2)? Even to decode the 'arrows' as physical pain obscures the writer's primary point, namely, God's expressed anger. Nor could we reinterpret the author's condition as disease superstitiously attributed by him to God's hostility. This would negate the theology of sin in the psalm. This said, and accepting both the fact of colourful metaphor and the correctness of the theological perception, we may find an aptitude in the metaphors of physical ailments.

Our justification for this lies in the reinstatement of the complex systemic functioning of the person in modern medicine, psychology and psychiatry. These explain that conditions of stress and depression impair the efficient functioning of the immune system, allowing viral and bacterial infections a freer course. Furthermore, bodily symptoms such as joint pain, without viral infection, commonly accompany clinical depression, as does exhaustion. Anxiety attacks produce pounding of the heart. All this makes it overwhelmingly probable that in a condition of deep spiritual distress resulting from real guilt there would be depression, insomnia or other presenting symptoms that could be actual biological illnesses or psychosomatically produced effects. Theological guilt can produce physical symptoms. So the metaphors of Psalm 38, without being literal, may point beyond themselves to both physical as well as spiritual distress.

It is evident that this psychosomatic interplay, emphasized in modern medicine, was observed and is captured in the following Israelite proverbs:

A tranquil mind gives life to the flesh
but passion makes the bones rot.

(Prov 14:30)

Anxiety weighs down the human heart,
but a good word cheers it up.

(Prov 12:25)

A cheerful heart is a good medicine,
but a downcast spirit dries up the bones.

(Prov 17:22)

Pleasant words are like a honeycomb,
sweetness to the soul and healing to the bones.

(Prov 16:24)

The human spirit will endure sickness;
but a broken spirit—who can bear?

(Prov 18:14)

A gentle tongue is a tree of life,
but perverseness in it breaks the spirit.

(Prov 15:4)

The recognition in these proverbs of the power of words and of the effect of the mind on the body without recourse to theology or to demonology underlines the need for a careful diagnosis of emotional distress, especially where feelings of guilt are a component.

We come back, then, to the statement of Psa 38:3b, 'there is no *šālōm* in my bones because of my sin.' We could paraphrase this as 'my whole inner being and vitality is disrupted by my sin.' The word *šālōm* with its network of associations fits beautifully here. As part of a physical metaphor with 'bones', *šālōm* could be read as 'health' —'there is no health in my bones' (NRSV). Yet *šālōm* in many Old Testament contexts extends to a 'well-being' that includes 'peace' with God in harmonious covenant relationship, an association relevant to Psalm 38 as a whole. As the language of Deuteronomy with its blessings and curses shows, the well-being of covenant, its *šālōm*, ranged over a spectrum from health, fertility and long life to an intimate relationship with God. Sin and guilt disrupted all of this and the result for the individual was understood to be an experience such as Psa 38 expresses.

Christian spirituality retains much, but not all, of this dynamic. Health, wealth and prosperity are not promised in the New Covenant, except through bodily resurrection beyond biological death. Yet the nexus of sin, guilt and malaise may be a dynamic that operates within a Christian spirituality, and one that needs careful distinguishing from false guilt and its symptoms, as well as from organic disease without sin. The fact that the Psalms, unlike their Mesopotamian equivalents, offer no publicity to the demonic in their symptomology underlines the theological distinctiveness of the Hebrew material. It also gives pause for thought in relation to some of today's cultural or sub-cultural perceptions and hasty recourse to exorcism.

RELATIVE AND CORPORATE GUILT

Mesopotamia and Israel agree that humanity finds itself in a predicament. Worshippers wish to approach their deity in the sanctuary, but are their hands clean?[69] Psalm 24 stresses that this pure state is a prerequisite for approaching God:

---

[69] Cleanness should be taken metaphorically here. Washing of body and clothes for ritual purity were important in Mesopotamia and in Israel. See *SaS*, p.31ff for a discussion. Explanations of washing rites that stop at hygiene fail to make the cross-cultural step into a whole world of religious thinking alien to western Christianity because of its new conceptual framework in New Covenant and medical science. Jesus' washing of Peter's feet is a more familiar biblical washing with a symbolic interpretation given (John 13:4ff). The value of washing of hands remained a disputed element in 1st century Jewish spirituality—see Mark 7:1ff.

Who shall ascend the hill of the LORD?
    And who shall stand in his holy place?
Those who have clean hands and pure hearts

(Psa 24:3f)

Cleanness of hand and purity of heart covers deeds and thoughts, outward conduct and the internal conversation with oneself that discloses preoccupations and motives. Yet on this score and taken strictly, no Israelite could have gone up to the Temple conscience-free.[70] Purity is relative not absolute.[71] This perspective of a relative purity perhaps comes easier in a culture where all values and public figures are regarded with a degree of cynicism. 'Saints' are passé. Nothing and no one is sacrosanct or holy, and the tabloid press or the new genre of biography leave few paragons of virtue intact. In this cultural ethos, it is not the prophetic denunciations of the priesthood or Jesus' denunciation of the hypocrisy of religious leaders that seem striking, but the idea that anyone should be revered as 'holy' at all, regardless of their role in worship or spiritual practice.

Indeed, the reality of a fallen humanity necessitates our acceptance of relative righteousness and real guilt, as well as our solidarity with and complicity in collective guilt.[72] The alternative

---

[70] At the other extreme to relative innocence, contrast Lady Macbeth's troubled conscience as she sleepwalks and washes her hands—'Here's the smell of the blood still: not all the perfumes of Arabia could sweeten this little hand. Oh, oh, oh!' This Shakespearean scene dramatizes guilt very powerfully.

[71] Christian theology works with a concept of imputed or conferred holiness linked to the Atonement, but still commands that a person examine themselves before participation in eating the bread and drinking the cup of the new covenant rite (1 Cor 11:28).

[72] Collective guilt is a subject in itself, and difficult to deal with. Some specific examples of collective guilt with lingering aftermath might include the slave trade, exploitative colonialism, occupation of the land of indigenous peoples, white benefit from apartheid, male and female complicity in the oppression of women, war crimes on a large or official scale, Hutu massacres of Tutsi in Rwanda, and so on. Each of these may have been publicly and ideologically justified at the time by Christians, but have left scars and caused pangs of conscience for many since, including those who were not themselves the active perpetrators or participants. There is also a need for practicality in working out a Christian response to issues that involve corporate guilt on a diffused scale, or guilty feelings about such contemporary conditions as racism, gender discrimination, poverty and famine. Response to such issues is very much a part of a Christian spirituality that needs to be worked out at each level—e.g. the response of the individual, of the local church, of the denomination, and at the ecumenical and the national level. The alternative is a confused morass of real and false guilt stimulated by each day's newspaper, television or charity appeal. This is a corollary for a spirituality that is linked to the global village of our era where the disasters of the world are beamed into homes creating awareness, but also raising feelings of guilt amidst circumstances of peace and social stability.

would be the pursuit of an unreal perfectionism. Perfectionist teachings have circulated in Christian sub-cultures this century.[73] However, sinless perfection and absence of specific guilt are not options available in an authentic spirituality. Spirituality will always wrestle with the paradox of proximity—that the closer we come to God, the more we sense the gap between our flawed human nature and God's character. This returns us to the psalm quoted at the head of the chapter: 'If you, O LORD, should mark iniquities, Lord, who could stand?' (Psa 130:3).

The psalm that most acutely expresses the burden of sinfulness begins 'Have mercy on me, O God, according to your steadfast love' (Psa 51:1). Taking this as fundamental, we can say that neither absolute purity nor perfect repentance is held out as the prerequisite for an approach to God. Rather what is foremost is God's mercy, the complement to his holiness and justice. 'Have mercy on me' precedes 'clean hands and pure hearts'. Yahweh's 'steadfast love' (*ḥesed*), his commitment to relationship, has the first and the last word.

This applies as much to the nation as to the individual. Solomon, voicing the covenant theology of Deuteronomy, anticipates on a national scale the wilful sinfulness of disloyalty to Yahweh when he says at the Temple dedication:

> If they sin against you—for there is no one who does not sin—and you are angry with them, and give them to an enemy, so that they are carried away captive . . . yet if they come to their senses . . . and plead with you . . . saying, 'We have sinned, and have done wrong; we have acted wickedly'; if they repent with all their heart and soul in the land of their enemies . . . and pray to you toward their land . . . , then

---

[73] Aside from what Wesley meant or was taken to mean by 'perfect love', there have been various spiritual renewal and revival movements with a tendency towards offering another plane of spirituality that we could picture as a 'higher ground', plateau spirituality. The 'second blessing' experience was one such that held out a life, free from conscious sin, entered by a post-conversion second experience. These 'higher ground' spiritualities could be loosely clustered as sanctification teachings, whereas Pentecostal renewal has generally focused on empowerment and the release of charismatic gifts. The East African revival emphasized 'walking in the light' on the basis of 1 John 1:7ff, which is different in that the Scripture passage emphasises the reality of continuous sinfulness and confession. For a helpful discussion of Atlantic movements, see RF Lovelace, *Dynamics of Spiritual Life* (USA: IVP/Exeter: Paternoster) 1979 dealing with revival and renewal movements and using social concern as a key criterion in evaluation. See also RL Timpe's article 'Perfectionism: positive possibility or personal pathology', pp. 23–34 in *Journal of Psychology and Christianity* 8.2 (1989) for a brief orientation to Wesley, Oberlin, Finney, Keswick and other strands of sanctification teaching as compared with theorizing within the humanistic psychology of the Adler, Maslow and Erikson schools.

hear in heaven your dwelling place their prayer and their plea . . .
forgive your people who have sinned against you, and all their
transgressions that they have committed against you . . .

(1 Kgs 8:46ff)[74]

Israel, then, is measured by the norms of covenant stipulation.
This was affirmed after the broken relationship resulting in exile
by the prayers of Daniel 9 and Ezra 9. Before the Exile, Psa 24
excludes from worship those who 'lift up their souls to what is
false' and who 'swear deceitfully'. This makes relationship and
loyalty, epitomized by exclusive allegiance to Yahweh and the
relinquishing of all other gods, the heart of the matter.[75] Yahweh
alone is to be the focus of trust, loyalty and obedience.

SUMMARY AND CONCLUSION

We have compared and contrasted Mesopotamian guilt and
restoration with expressions of guilt and prayer for restoration in
Israel, taking samples from the 'canonical' literature of both
cultures. Both cultures use a rich vocabulary for sin, interpret
certain distressing personal circumstances as the consequences of
the anger of the deity, and plead for restoration of relationship.
Both cultures reflect a fundamental human *Angst*. Yet theologically Yahwism is distinctive in many ways and offers a trajectory
into Christian spirituality via a realism about sin, about our
psycho-biological functioning and about approaching a God who
is holy but not capricious.

'Mesopotamian spirituality' alerts us to contemporary pastoral
issues, particularly false guilt. Our only hope of progressing
beyond a 'Mesopotamian spirituality' when confronted with guilt
in Christian believers is to work with real guilt, not false guilt, to
distinguish as far as is possible psychosomatic symptoms which
may accompany both real and false guilt from straightforward
disease symptomology, and to distinguish psychological and
psychiatric states from demonization.

---

[74] There is not space to discuss repentance and restoration in Deuteronomy and
the so-called deuteronomic literature here, but reference can be made to Deut
30:1–11, its affinities with Jeremiah's 'Book of Consolation' (chaps. 30–32)
and Isaiah 55:6f, all of which speak about restoration to covenant and land on
the basis of grace and repentance, a message to a Judean community consigned
under guilt to Exile. For the G von Rad and HW Wolff line on repentance as
the thrust of deuteronomic literature, see RW Klein, *Israel in Exile: a theological
interpretation*, OBT (Philadelphia: Fortress) 1979.

[75] The most natural interpretation of *šāw*—'what is false', and *mirmāh*—'deceit',
in context, would be the forming of idolatrous relations with other deities
instead of recognizing the Divine Warrior supreme. This idolatrous orientation and oathing is the supreme example of misplaced trust and duplicity.

In contemporary church life, taboo may creep back into spirituality. There is a need to assess whether Christian spirituality is in danger of being subverted into a 'Mesopotamian spirituality' regulated by experts with sanctuary regulations, rituals, physical objects and fixed formulae deemed efficacious. Likewise, when 'holiness' and freedom from guilt is interpreted in terms of conformity in avoidance of foods, art forms, music, hair or dress styles, long after these items have lost any anti-Christian symbolism in the wider culture or could be considered taboo.[76]

There is also the problem of false guilt generated in connection with illness and absence of healing. The ancient social stigma of leprosy can be replaced by the stigma of medical symptoms that persist after participation in a healing campaign or rite. If the healer promises mass healings and implies that lack of faith is the problem when they fail to materialize, there is a strong message given to the sufferer that induces false guilt or angry cynicism. Likewise, damage is done when exorcism is attempted on sincere believers when no demonization is involved in the presenting symptoms.

If the penitential prayers of Israel are taken as sign-posts on the spiritual journey, then they point us to Person-centredness, to God himself and away from words that become magical incantations. In Israel there is personal and corporate prayer, not divination and the utterance of formulae by experts. The penitential psalms' main concern is confession of specific sin, heart-renewal and restoration of relationship with God and with the community. This preserves the supplicant from false guilt and moves him or her into a relationship with God based on confession of known sin and forgiveness secured on the basis of God's own commitment to an intimate communion.

BIBLIOGRAPHY

ME Cohen, *The Canonical Lamentations of Ancient Mesopotamia* Vol. I & II, (Potomac: Capital Decisions) 1988.

ER Dalglish, *Psalm Fifty-One in the light of Near Eastern Patternism* (Leiden: Brill) 1962.

MJ Evans, ' "A Plague on both your houses": cursing and blessing reviewed', *Vox Evangelica* 24 (1994) 77–89.

WW Hallo, 'Individual Prayer in Sumerian: the continuity of a tradition' *JAOS* 88 (1968) 71–89.

---

[76] There is an irony in the fact that legalism can flourish in holiness style denominations that apply a strict sub-cultural conformism in dress, body-decoration, gender roles, the drinking of alcohol, tea and coffee, and so on. Cross-cultural experience of Christian fellowship can serve to unmask the sub-cultural basis of legalism and confront each sub-culture with its spiritual blind spots.

RW Klein, ' "Personal God" and Individual Prayer in Sumerian Religion', pp. 295–306 in *AfO Beih.* 19 (1982) *Rencontre assyriologique Internationale in Wien.*

WG Lambert, *Babylonian Wisdom Literature* (Oxford: Clarendon) 1960.

——, 'Three Literary Prayers of the Babylonians', *AfO* 19 (1960) 47ff.

——, '*Dingir.ša.dib.ba* Incantations' *JNES* 33.3 (1974) 267–322.

——, & AR Millard, *Atra-ḫasīs, the Babylonian story of the Flood,* Oxford: Clarendon, 1969.

Earl Leichty, '*A Tamītu* from Nippur', pp. 301–304 in T Abusch (*et al),* *Lingering over Words: studies in Ancient Near Eastern Literature in honor of WL Moran,* HSS 37 (Atlanta: Scholars) 1990.

RF Lovelace, *Dynamics of Spiritual Life* (USA: IVP/Exeter: Paternoster) 1979.

J Milgrom, *Leviticus 1–16,* AB 3 (New York: Doubleday) 1991.

T Nash, 'Devils, Demons, and Disease: Folklore in Ancient Near Eastern Rites of Atonement', pp. 57–88 in WW Hallo, BW Jones & GL Mattingly (eds), *The Bible in the light of Cuneiform Literature: Scripture in Context III,* Ancient Near Eastern Texts and Studies 8, (Lewiston/ Queenston/Lampeter: The Edward Mellen Press) 1990.

GC Oosthuizen, *The Healer-Prophet in Afro-Christian Churches,* Studies in Christian Mission 3 (Leiden: Brill) 1992.

E Reiner, *Shurpû a collection of Sumerian and Akkadian Incantations,* AfO Beih. 11, Graz 1958.

——, 'The *Lipšur* Litanies' *JNES* 15 (1956) 129–149.

HWF Saggs, *The Greatness that was Babylon,* 2nd rev.ed. (London: Sidgwick & Jackson) 1988.

M-J Seux, *Hymnes et Prières aux dieux de Babylone et d'Assyrie,* LAPO 8 (Paris: du Cerf) 1976.

ME Tate, *Psalms 51–100,* WBC 20 (Dallas:Word) 1990.

RL Timpe, 'Perfectionism: positive possibility or personal pathology', *Journal of Psychology and Christianity* 8.2 (1989) 23–34.

P Tournier, *Guilt and Grace* (London: Hodder & Stoughton) 1962.

E Turner, *Experiencing Ritual: a new interpretation of African Healing,* (Philadelphia: Univ Pennsylvania Press) 1992.

V Turner, *The Drums of Affliction: a study of the religious processes among the Ndembu of Zambia,* OUP, 1968.

K van der Toorn, *Sin and Sanction in Israel and Mesopotamia: a comparative study,* Studia Semitica Neerlandica 22 (Maastricht: Van Gorcum) 1985.

HW Wolff, *Anthropology of the Old Testament* (London: SCM) 1974.

DP Wright, *The Disposal of Impurity,* SBLDS 101 (Atlanta: Scholars) 1987.

I Yalom, *Existential Psychotherapy* (New York: Basic Books) 1980.

[10]

The Daily Rhythm of Life

INTRODUCTION

In the previous two chapters, we looked at emotional and relational fluctuations in the rhythm of life. We explored Job's orientation to God, initially displaying an equilibrium that gave way to disorientation marked by the turbulence of anger and confrontation. Jeremiah and Lament psalms bore their testimony to spiritual upheaval and tides of emotion. Then we traversed the dark tunnel of guilt before mercy, confession and forgiveness bring daylight to communion with God. We found that we can identify with these spiritual fluctuations in a relationship with God that flow through our psyche and affect our emotions, attitudes, behaviour and how we relate to our community.

In this chapter, we turn to another rhythm of life that has its own distinctive patterns. In its simplest and external form it is about the passage of time and the accompanying activities that fit into a twenty-four hour period between waking up and going to sleep. It is the day-in-the-life, not a sabbath or festival day, but an ordinary day in the working week. We shall look at it in terms of its beginning and the first things that come into our minds on regaining consciousness, in terms of the world of work and promotion, in terms of crossing thresholds, of opening and closing doors, of going out and coming back home. Spirituality must somehow fit into this rhythm of daily life in a way that allows for all the human activities, tasks and responsibilities to be fulfilled, without these activities on the human plane excluding who we are spiritually.

From the Old Testament, we shall draw on the rubrics of Deuteronomy, on the psalms and on Qohelet's evaluation of work and pleasure. From the Near East, we shall cite lines of Sun poems that picture all of life enacted before the deity. Other texts disclose that looking to the king for favour ranked as highly as striving for promotion in the company does today.

BIORHYTHM AND TEMPO OF LIFE

The daily rhythm of life and the patterns of work and leisure often express a culture's distinctive attitudes towards time and social values. In this century, the spread of industrial and commercial technology across the continents has resulted in the development of cities and megacities. People have been drawn away from rural poverty and towards conurbations by the need for employment.[1] A certain cultural variety has survived urbanization, but worldwide the main contrast in way of life lies in the contrasting diurnal patterns of the city and the areas which supply its food. Life in rural areas, life in the tribal village, or life on the vast outbacks, wheat belts, beef ranches and ocean fishing grounds runs to a different rhythm. Remote areas may wake up to the radio and retain a link with the cities this way, but life without industry and even more life without electricity was and is more likely to co-ordinate a population's times of sleep and work. Without electricity, the earth's daily rhythm of light and darkness plays a larger role in setting body-clocks and co-ordinating social activities. In industrialized societies, power stations run, lights burn and night shifts keep airports, hospitals, mines and factories functioning around the clock. News gathering, news bulletins and newspaper production go on day and night. In big cities, the traffic never stops. Nor does crime. Urban populations do have a daily rhythm, but it relates to work shifts and not to daylight hours. This is especially true for northern cities in winter where people go to work in the dark and darkness returns by mid-afternoon.

Against this background of the world's millions living in the cities and moving to an industrial tempo we might wonder what relevance there is, if any, in the way that Israelites integrated body-clock and Yahwistic faith. The body-clock still regulates our biology, but where does spirituality fit into our biorhythms?[2] First

---

[1] There has been a stream of theological reflection on urbanization and inner city malaise from the sixties onwards. One thinks of the trajectory from Jacques Ellul's books such as *The Technological Society* (1964), *The Meaning of the City* (1970) and Harvey Cox, *The Secular City* (1967) to The Report of the Archbishop of Canterbury's Commission on Urban Priority Areas, *Faith in the City: a call for action by Church and Nation* in the mid 1980s.

[2] While sleep and waking are the most obvious human biorhythms, there are many biological clocks which regulate physiology in a twenty–four hour pattern from the fluctuation of temperature, urine production and brain cycles to the differentiation of sleep itself into five phases detectable by EEG. See FE Bloom & A Lazerson, *Brain, Mind and Behaviour*, 2nd edition (New York: Freeman & Co) 1988, Chap. 6 'Rhythms of the Brain'. An associate professor of physiology at Harvard, M Moore-Ede, has recently published a study of the cost of human errors when shift work ignores the demands of the body-clock and accidents result, such as the Exxon Valdez oil spill off Alaska (*The*

we must examine the pattern of daily life reflected in the Old Testament before canonizing or dismissing it from the discussion of spirituality.

A. I FROM THE RISING OF THE SUN . . .

Tent-dwelling patriarchs, tribal Israelites, agricultural village communities and Jerusalem Temple worship are indeed remote from life in the modern metropolis. At the beginning of the day, pips and alarm clocks have displaced cock–crow in rousing the human body for the day's activity. It is from agricultural settings without street lights and night shifts that Israel's perspectives on daily life emerged. What, then, did Israelites make of sunup, sundown and in between in their Yahwistic faith?

Not every Israelite was an early riser, as the wry proverb reminds us:

> Whoever blesses a neighbour with a loud voice,
> rising early in the morning,
> will be counted as cursing.
>
> (Prov 27:14)

The cheerful at dawn are not rated as super-spiritual in this little vignette. But metaphorically or in real time, the psalmist can leap out of bed singing when his prayer has been heard and he wakes up safely after 'lying down with lions':

> Awake, my soul!
> Awake, O harp and lyre!
> I will awake the dawn.
> I will give thanks to you, O Lord,
> among the peoples;
> I will sing praises to you among the nations.
>
> (Psa 57:8f)[3]

The dawn chorus was a little different in surrounding cultures. We know, for instance, that Dawn and Dusk were deified in the

---

24 Hour Society, Piatkus, 1993) and has set up a consultancy called Circadian Technologies.

[3] The heading sets this safe awakening in the cave where David slept when he was on the run from Saul. The words also appear in Psa 108, perhaps for use before a dawn attack.

Canaanite religion of the Ugaritic texts.[4] Instead, our psalmist is intent on praising God, not worshipping the sky at dawn.

This leads us on to ask whether jumping up to praise God at dawn was the result of a special deliverance from deadly peril overnight or whether daybreak carries an association with regular Yahwistic worship. Is first light a symbolic and psychological moment? Psalm 46, confessing Yahweh as 'refuge and strength', expects early help for Jerusalem: 'God will help it when the morning dawns'.[5] Likewise the individual Israelite looks for support at daybreak: 'let me hear of your steadfast love in the morning' (Psa 143:8), words that are echoed in the plea of Psa 90:14 'Satisfy us in the morning with your steadfast love.' These passages probably speak of a new start after a metaphorically dark period, as does Psa 30:5.

> For his anger is but for a moment;
> his favour is for a lifetime.
> Weeping may linger for the night,
> but joy comes with the morning.

The same reaching out to God after the horrific descriptions of the siege of Jerusalem and God's wrath is expressed in the moving words of Lamentations:

> The steadfast love of the LORD never ceases,
> his mercies never come to an end;
> they are new every morning;
> great is thy faithfulness.
> "The LORD is my portion," says my soul,
> "therefore I will hope in him."

> (Lam 3:22f)

---

[4] The Ugaritic text CTA 23 (= UT 52) describes the birth of Dawn (*šaḥaru*) and Dusk (*šālimu*), sired by El the head of the pantheon (see Cross, *Canaanite Myth*, pp. 22f). Isa 14:12 seems to draw satirical imagery from a myth about the demotion of a god, Helel, 'son of Dawn', thus exhibiting knowledge of a Canaanite myth not yet documented in clay tablets recovered to date. The Hebrew name *šᵉḥaryāh* Shehariah, meaning 'Yahweh is (my) dawn' (1 Chron 8:26), probably embodies a metaphor of daybreak, the idea being that Yahweh, like dawn, brings light and hope after the darkness of night. Compare *ᵃḥīšaḥar*—'[God] My (divine) Brother is dawn', assuming a theophoric reference. Other Israelite names with similar associations include 'Urīyāhū—'Yahweh is my light' and 'Urī'ēl-'God is my light'. See JD Fowler, *Theophoric Names in Ancient Hebrew*, JSOTS 49, (Sheffield: Sheffield Academic Press) 1988.

[5] Psa 46:.5b *lipnōt bōqer*—'in the presence of morning', or in the quainter wording of the KJV—'and that right early'.

This hope of a new dawn contrasts with the lament language of 3:1ff which speaks of 'the rod of his wrath' driving the poet 'into darkness without any light'.

The urgency and demand for attention inspire the reference to the first thought and action of the day in Psalm 5. Verse 3 refers to the morning, hard on the heels of the opening imperatives—'Give ear . . . give heed . . . listen to . . .' (vv. 1–2) :

> O LORD, in the morning you hear my voice;
> in the morning, I plead my case to you, and watch.
>
> (Psa 5:3)

Psalm 59 too opens with a string of imperatives. The speaker implores God for deliverance from enemies. In contrast with and despite the wicked who return in the evening like a pack of howling dogs prowling the streets, the rescued psalmist would 'sing aloud of your steadfast love in the morning' (Psa 59:16). A different and assured opening, breathing thankfulness, inspires Psalm 92's approach to God-consciousness: 'It is good . . . to declare your steadfast love in the morning, and your faithfulness by night' (Psa 92:1f). This contrasts with the depths of darkest despair suffered despite a life of regular devotion. Psalm 88, paradoxically writes off daily prayer as futile in its effect, and yet is itself a prayer:

> when, at night, I cry out in your presence,
> let my prayer come before you.
>
> But I, O LORD, cry out to you;
> in the morning my prayer comes before you.
> O LORD, why do you cast me off?
> Why do you hide your face from me?
>
> (Psa 88:1b–2a & 13f)

Reviewing the references to morning prayer in the psalms just quoted, we see that the emphasis falls in two places, on a life of continuous prayer morning, noon and night, as Psa 55:17 states, or on the priority, urgency and new scope for an answer to be given.[6] In Psalm 88, nothing lightens the darkness. Morning prayer brings no dawn, but opening of the eyes and opening of the heart synchronize. For a devout Yahwist, thankful or despairing,

---

[6] The narrative describing Daniel's habit of thrice daily prayer (Dan 6:10) shows that fixed times spread throughout the day might have been observed as part of a Yahwistic spirituality, and so 'evening and morning and at noon' (Psa 55:17) may reflect this, rather than simply being a figure of speech for 'morning, noon and night', meaning 'all the time, continuously, non-stop'.

this spirituality is instinctive. Intensity of experience means that the mind fills with phrases from Israel's repertoire of prayer on waking up in the morning, whether the mood on awakening is one of desperation or delight.

There is a counterpart to the psalmist's mind filling with phrases of praise or petition. In the third of the so-called Servant poems of Isaiah 40–55, we read of an input from God which is couched in the imagery of waking and obedience:

> Morning by morning he wakens—
> wakens my ear
> to listen as those who are taught.
> The Lord GOD has opened my ear,
> and I was not rebellious,
> I did not turn backward.
>
> (Isa 50:4bf)

A prompting from God floods the prophet's mind daily and directs his behaviour towards fulfilling his vocation despite deterrence and abuse. He receives these instructions from God as a model pupil and himself becomes a model of spirituality. 'Morning by morning' by itself might suggest 'daily, day by day', but coupled with the verb 'to rouse, wake up', 'morning by morning' attracts the nuance of priority, of 'first things first'.

In English the phrase 'first thing' can imply the time or the priority allocated. If one promises to do something 'first thing', it could be both. In Hebrew, there is a verb for getting up early in order to do something, the verb *šākam*. Some activities, such as a long journey or urgent business, demand an early start and Hebrew narrative offers examples from Salvation History.[7] There are also the early starts to prepare for covenant rituals at Sinai when Moses 'rose early in the morning, and built an altar at the foot of the mountain, and set up twelve pillars . . . ' (Exod 24:4), or when he carried out the instructions for renewing the covenant after the Golden Calf incident:

> Be ready in the morning, and come up in the morning to Mount Sinai and present yourself there to me, on top of the mountain . . . So Moses cut two tablets of stone like the former ones; and he rose early in the morning and went up Mount Sinai . . . '
>
> (Exod 34:2,4 and 34:4).[8]

---

[7] A journey and the urgency of the business in hand underlies the early starts referred to in Genesis narratives such as Gen 19:2,27, Gen 20:8, Gen 21:14, Gen 22:3. Moses confronts Pharaoh first thing in Exod 8:20, and 9:13. Further references to early starts in narrative may be found under root *šākam*—'to rise early' (Lisowsky, *Konkordanz*, p. 1432f.; *BDB*, p.1014).

These references are specific to their narrative settings and there is no evidence that Israel's normal cultic worship commenced at dawn.[9] The Pentateuch does not specify the hour of the regular morning sacrifice (Num 28:4), so there is no reason to associate it symbolically with first light or sunrise.[10]

A.2 SUNRISE AND CULT IN MESOPOTAMIA

If there is no cult at sunrise in Israel, the same is not true for Mesopotamia. The ritual expert rose early 'at dawn, before sunrise' to perform his task.[11] The link between early prayer and sunrise is a natural one in Mesopotamia because Shamash, the Sungod, was consulted in divination inquiries and invoked in apotropaic rituals. In one of the major incantation collections known as *Maqlû*, the Firegod Gibil is invoked at night and the Sungod at dawn:

> Incantation. Dawn has broken; doors are (now) opened;
> The traveller has passed through the gate;
> [The messenger] has taken to the road.
> Aa! w[i]tch: you labored in vain to bewitch me!
> Aa! [enchantress]: you tried for nought to enchant me!
> For I am now cleansed by the light of e (rising) sun;
> [And whatever] witchcraft [you d]id or had done (against me during the night)
> May they ([?] the traveller, messenger) turn back (against you)
> so that it seizes you, yes you!
>
> (*Maqlû* VII:153–160)[12]

---

[8] The oaths of alliance between Isaac and Abimelech are taken early before the return journey—'In the morning they rose early and exchanged oaths; and Isaac set them on their way, and they departed from him in peace' (Gen 26:31).

[9] In different parts of the world, Christian worship has developed a tradition of sunrise services to celebrate the resurrection on Easter Sunday, but the correlation between recapitulation of the dawn visit to the tomb in the Gospels and the symbolism of sunrise make this Easter service particularly apt and an exception to the regular pattern of worship in many Christian denominations.

[10] Mishna Tamid 3.2 indicates that there was some discussion by rabbis of the Second Temple period as to how light it should get before it was time for the burnt offering. The observer reports, " 'It is daylight'. Mattithiah b. Samuel used to say: [He that perceives it says,] 'The whole east is alight.' 'As far as Hebron?' and he answered, 'Yea!' " (H Danby, *The Mishnah*, London: OUP, 1933, p. 584).

[11] Compare the sentence "May your servant make his offering at dawn", relating to the work of the divination expert, noted by I Starr, *Queries to the Sungod: divination and politics in Sargonid Assyria*, SAA 4, (Helsinki: Helsinki Univ Press) 1990, p. xxvi.

Darkness and dawn contribute a symbolism. Night is the time of darkness when dark powers operate. Daylight dispels darkness and the Sungod dissipates binding curses.[13]

The apotropaic rituals of *Shurpû*, which are akin to *Maqlû*, link the rising of the Sungod with release from the *māmītu* curse:

> he has asked for a sign at sunrise and sunset
> he has asked for a sign leaving the city and entering the city,
> he has asked for a sign leaving the city-gate and entering the city-gate,
> he has asked for a sign leaving the house and entering the house
> Be it released, O Shamash, you jud[ge],
> release it Shamash, lord of above and below [. . . .]
>
> Shamash, when he rises, may extirpate its darkness,
> may the Oath (*māmītu*) not stay in the house
> > (*Shurpû* II:120, 123–125, 129–130; Appendix 28–29)[14]

The rising of the Sungod over the eastern mountains is one of the earliest motifs of Mesopotamian cylinder seals with beautifully executed 3rd millennium examples from the Semitic empire of Sargon of Akkad.[15] The scene represented pictorially on the seals is later translated into the poetry of the *Shamash Hymn*. The

---

[12] T Abusch, 'Mesopotamian Anti-Witchcraft Literature: Texts and Studies, Part I: the nature of *Maqlû*: its character, divisions, and calendrical setting', *JNES* 33 (1974) 257–262, p.257f. Besides 'dawn has broken' *ittamra šēru* of VII:153 above, variants are *tebi šēru* 'dawn has approached' (VII:147) and *šērumma šēru* 'Dawn, dawn!' (VII:161), each marking the beginning of an incantation. Abusch demonstrates that *Maqlû* tablets I–V and VI–VII 57 were performed at night and tablets VII 58–VIII on the morning of the following day, beginning at dawn. He also argues persuasively for the performance of this extensive ritual in the month of Abu with its associations with the Netherworld and the expulsion of ghosts and other troublesome spirits.

[13] A Phoenician amulet hung in the doorway of the house makes the same connection between darkness and the demonic realm when it invokes sunrise against one of the dangerous occult powers: "Rise, O sun, for Sasam!". This line of the Arslan Tash plaque is inscribed on Sasam, the threatening male figure wielding an axe. See JC de Moor, 'Demons in Canaan', *Ex Oriente Lux* 27 (1981–82) 106–119; *ANEP*, p. 216 No. 662.

[14] E Reiner, *Shurpû*, *AfO* Bei. 11, Graz 1958, pp.16, 52.

[15] See the depiction of the Sungod on Seals *102, 103, 105, 761, 766, 767, 769* in D Collon, *First Impressions; cylinder seals in the Ancient Near East*, London: British Museum Publications, 1987, p. 34f. & 166f. (*ANEP*, Nos. *683, 684, 685*). As she notes, the Sungod 'remained the most popular deity in Mesopotamia from Akkadian times onwards' (p. 167). Old Babylonian seals from the 2nd millennium show Shamash with one foot resting on the mountain top, an image derived from the earlier sunrise scenes.

literary design of this 200–line composition follows the movements of the Sungod from his rising to his setting, and his passage
through the Underworld back to the point of sunrise.[16] The first
52 lines deal with the awaited dawning of the day from which the
following lines capture Shamash's welcome role as dispeller of
darkness:

> O Sun, illuminator of the entirety of the heavens,
> Brightener of darkness for mankind far and wide
>
> Of the remotest mountains you lighten the shadows
>
> O Sun, as you rise, men are on their knees
>
> On their knees before you are all men,
> O Sun, the universe longs for your light.[17]

The instinctive association between light and life is captured in
Qohelet's aphorism 'Light is sweet, and it is pleasant for the eyes
to see the sun' (Ecc 11:7). For an alternative monotheism of life
and light, we need to turn to the Amarna period in Egypt, when
the Hebrews lived in the Delta region. This Amarna spirituality
focused on the solar disc, celebrating the sunrise and life in its
cultic poetry.[18]

---

[16] GR Castellino and Erica Reiner have offered independent appreciations of the
poem which concur in detecting this patterning of the material according to
the journey of the sun—Castellino, 'The Shamash Hymn: a note on its
structure', pp. 71–74 in the SN Kramer *Festschrift*, ed. BL Eichler, *AOAT* 25
(1976); Reiner, *Your thwarts in pieces, Your mooring rope cut: poetry from
Babylonia and Assyria*, Michigan Studies in the Humanities 5, Univ of
Michigan, 1985, Chap. IV, pp. 68–84 'A Hymn to the Sun'. The poem was
edited by WG Lambert, *Babylonian Wisdom Literature*, Oxford: Clarendon,
1960, pp. 121ff., but gaps in extant copies still remain to be filled by further
discoveries. Reiner 's translation is an improvement on *ANET*, 387ff.; the
most recent translation is by Foster, *Muses*, III.32, pp. 536ff.

[17] Lines 3–4, which parallel lines 1–2, line 6, line 15 and lines 51f.—*Thwarts*, p.
69f & 72. These lines are echoed later in the section dealing with the summer
zenith and the calendar:

> Lightener of darkness, illuminator of obscurity,
> Dispeller of shadows, illuminator of the broad earth,
> Brightener of the day, . . .

(lines 176ff;, *Thwarts*, p. 81f.)

[18] Pharaoh Akhenaten reigned from 1350–1334 BC (on a probable low chrono-
logy and depending on co-regency reckonings). See WL Moran, *The Amarna
Letters*, London: Johns Hopkins, 1992, pp. xxxiv–xxxix for references. The
late dating of the Exodus at around 1280 BC would place the birth of Moses
within the Amarna period, an interesting point but not one that can be used
for drawing conclusions about Yahwism.

A.3 SUNRISE IN EGYPT

In Egypt, solar worship was even more prominent than in Mesopotamia and indeed it became the exclusive official religion of Akhenaten to the extent that he commanded not only that the names of other deities were to be excised from the monuments but also the plural form 'gods'.[19] This monotheism, centred on the solar disc, the Aten, and on the Aten's son, Pharaoh Akhenaten, has left a handful of surviving hymns which celebrate the rising of the sun. It is a spirituality which begins the day with worship and thankfulness. The following lines capture the spirit of these sun poems.

Splendid you rise in heaven's lightland,
O living Aten, creator of life!
When you have dawned in eastern lightland,
You fill every land with your beauty.

Earth brightens when you dawn in lightland,
When you shine as Aten of daytime;
As you dispel the dark,
As you cast your rays,
The Two Lands are in festivity.
Awake they stand on their feet,
You have roused them;
Bodies cleansed, clothed,
Their arms adore your appearance.
The entire land sets out to work,
All beasts browse on their herbs;
Trees, herbs are sprouting,
Birds fly from their nests,
Their wings greeting your *ka*.
All flocks frisk on their feet,

---

[19] The years of 'the heretic pharaoh' have intrigued Egyptologists and religionists alike. Two full scale treatments of the period are DB Redford, *Akhenaten the heretic king* (New Jersey: Princeton Univ Press) 1984 and CH Aldred, *Akhenaten: king of Egypt* (London: Thames & Hudson) 1988. Akhenaten was followed by Smenkhare and then Tutankhamun, whose name is familiar to the general public from Carter's sensational discovery of his unplundered tomb. Fewer people would realize that Tutankhamun's name at death represents a religious upheaval, a rejection of Atenism and a reversion to traditional Egyptian polytheism. God Amun has replaced god Aten in the compound name. During Akhenaten's reign, Tut-ankh-Amun was Tut-ankh-Aten. Smenkhare and Tutankhamun were probably Akhenaten's brothers.

All that fly up and alight,
They live when you dawn for them.
Ships fare north, fare south as well,
Roads lie open when you rise;
The fish in the river dart before you,
Your rays are in the midst of the sea.[20]

Aten monotheism excluded a struggle with deified powers of darkness and other graphic ways of picturing the sun's transition from sunset to sunrise involving an underworld journey through regions populated with other deities. Despite this, there is a restrained symbolism of darkness and light in the *Great Hymn*. Besides the line 'you dispel the dark', in the excerpt above, the preceding section speaks of the earth in darkness 'as if in death', the dark providing an opportunity for undetected robbery and for dangerous animals such as the lion emerging from its den and serpents that bite. 'Darkness hovers, earth is silent' while the Creator Sungod rests. The silence provides a contrast to the joyful response of nature and humanity at sunup. But there is more to it than stopping work at the end of the day.

All eyes are on <your> beauty until you set,
All labour ceases when you rest in the west.[21]

The spirituality consists in the unceasing consciousness of majestic divine presence throughout the day and in the modelling of human work and rest on the rhythm of the Aten's own untiring work for humanity and creation. The rhythm of life expressed in terms of activity and rest is taken beyond the diurnal pattern and into a life–death dimension in the lines immediately preceding the couplet just quoted:

<Those on> earth come from your hand as you made them,
When you have dawned they live,
When you set they die;
You yourself are lifetime, one lives by you.

---

[20] M Lichtheim, *Ancient Egyptian Literature: Vol 2, the New Kingdom* (Berkeley: Univ of California) 1976, p.97 from 'The Great Hymn to the Aten'. Other translations are available in Aldred, Redford, *LAE* and *ANET*.
[21] *AEL* 2, p. 99 from *The Great Hymn's* closing section.

This is a version of the spirituality found inside and outside the New Testament, expressive of human dependence on God. In his address to the Areopagus, Paul uses the aphorism 'In him we live and move and have our being.' He develops a theology of creation and creaturely dependence—'as even some of your own poets have said, "For we too are his offspring" '. 'The God who made the world and everything in it, he who is lord of heaven and earth . . . gives to all mortals life and breath and all things' (Acts 17). All these words could have been lifted out of *The Great Hymn to the Aten* a millennium and a half earlier. Apparently, it is a deep human instinct to believe that life is given and sustained by more than natural parents and biology.[22] The recognition of this is woven into the Yahwistic and Egyptian beginning and end of each day. After all, each day is a lifetime with a beginning and an end. Waking up recapitulates birth, and sleep mirrors death. In between, there is the phenomenon of consciousness and this may be punctuated with an awareness of God.[23]In the *Short Hymn to the Aten*, humans lying down, heads covered and breathing suspended, contrast with the vociferous festivity of singers, musicians and worshippers in the daytime cult.

Splendid you rise, O living Aten, eternal lord!

---

[22] By way of contrast, we might note that modern atheism is sometimes based in a biological perspective that regards concepts of a creator deity as an artefact of pre-scientific explanations of the natural world. The Oxford biologist Richard Dawkins is a most lucid and evangelistic proponent of a creator-free interpretation of life on earth in his best-selling paperbacks *The Selfish Gene* (OUP, 1989) and *The Blind Watchmaker* (Penguin, 1989) and in his understanding of *Homo sapiens* ('Meet my cousin, the chimpanzee', *New Scientist* 5 June 1993, 36–38). Similarly, Richard Leakey, *Origins Reconsidered: in search of what makes us human* (London: Little, Brown & Co) 1992. There is, of course, much truth in what they say about the continuity between pre-human, hominid, *Homo* and 'biblically human' forms of life. The debate about consciousness, which is the mechanism for relationship with God and for spirituality, is likewise a lively one in the field of psychology and artificial intelligence.

[23] In English the word 'consciousness' embraces both reflective consciousness and sensory awareness. The fact that the word 'perception' slides between visual processing such as distinguishing shape and colour and thought processes such as the formation of attitude or evaluation indicates that the field of consciousness raises all the brain/mind issues. For an accessible overview of the concept of consciousness in contemporary discussion see Chap. 4 'Consciousness', pp. 34–53 in ER Valentine, *Conceptual Issues in Psychology*, 2nd ed (London/New York: Routledge) 1992, DC Dennett, 'Consciousness' in RL Gregory (ed), *The Oxford Companion to the Mind* (Oxford: OUP) 1987 and *Consciousness Explained*, Penguin 1993 and GM Edelman, *Bright Air, Brilliant Fire: on the matter of the mind*, Penguin, 1992. The field is developing rapidly with debate between philosophers, neurologists, psychologists, computer scientists and quantum theorists such as the mathematician Roger Penrose. For the flavour of the debate and its contributors, see J. Horgan's

You are radiant, beauteous, mighty,
Your love is great, immense.
Your rays light up all faces,
Your bright hue gives life to hearts,
When you fill the Two Lands with your love.
August God who fashioned himself,
Who made every land, created what is in it,
All peoples, herds and flocks,
All trees that grow from soil;
They live when you dawn for them,
You are mother and father of all that you made.[24]

The sun as image of divine splendour, transcendence, immanence, source of life and universal domain can scarcely be bettered, nor can the intimate delight in the creation of life which mixes theological language with the observation of nature.[25] In Atenism, sun imagery includes anthropomorphic language. Thus the *Short Hymn to the Aten* mentions 'love' and offers inclusive language with its 'father and mother' image, adding an emotional tone to its depiction of majesty in much the same way as the Amarna art humanizes the pharaoh by depicting him in family scenes with children on his lap.[26] For all this, Akhenaten's monotheism contrasts with Yahwism. Lyrical as the Amarna poetry is in its celebration of sunrise, creation and life, Akhenaten's is also a political poetry which explicitly serves to legitimate the king, and,

---

review of trends in neuroscience in 'Can Science Explain Consciousness?' *Scientific American* July 1994, pp. 72–78.

[24] *AEL* 2, p. 91.

[25] Particularly winsome is the description of the chick hatching out of his shell in *The Great Hymn to the Aten*;

When the chick in the egg speaks in the shell,
You give him breath within to sustain him;

When you have made him complete,
To break out from the egg,
He comes out from the egg,
To announce his completion,
Walking on his legs he comes from it.

(*AEL* 2, p. 98)

[26] Atenism is sometimes characterized as impersonal, yet the *Short Hymn to the Aten* uses these emotionally toned anthropomorphisms and the disc iconography is humanized by the hands at the ends of the solar rays. The hands hold the *ankh* sign for blessing or are cupped in blessing over the king and queen. There is thus a continuity of a kind with the blessing scene of Genesis where the patriarch Jacob transmits the blessing by the laying on of his hands—Gen 48:14.

in the case of the *Great Hymn*, his wife too, the beautiful Nefertiti.[27]

A form of solar worship found its way into the Jerusalem temple.[28] In the canonical perspective of Kings and Ezekiel this solar cult is clearly regarded as deviant.[29] Worship of the visible heavenly body has moved beyond an orthodox use of light metaphors and symbolism.[30] This was not the spirituality of orthodox Yahwism celebrating the experience of life at the beginning of each day in poetic terms. Nor was it the celebration of the Creator's glory displayed in creation of the kind that we encounter in Psalm 19:

> The heavens are telling the glory of God;
> and the firmament proclaims his handiwork.

> In the heavens he has set a tent for the sun,
> which comes out like a bridegroom from his wedding canopy,

---

[27] The final stanza of the *Great Hymn* opens with the lines

> You are in my heart,
> There is no other who knows you,
> Only your son, Neferkheprure, Sole-one-of-Re,
> Whom you have taught your ways and your might.

> (*AEL* 2, p. 99)

This claim to be the exclusive source of authoritative teaching, to be the mediator of revelation and probably more, certainly appears to diminish the role of cult officiants of the Aten, let alone the role of the priests of outlawed Egyptian deities such as Amun of Thebes, and no doubt contributes to the resentment with which Akhenaten was remembered as 'that heretic'. The other Amarna hymns and prayers translated by Lichtheim reflect Akhenaten's personal royal ideology. The pharaonic ideology and the solar language both have antecedents in Egyptian religion prior to Akhenaten, but nothing matches his exclusive Atenism and his apparently exclusive mediatorship.

[28] Smith (*JBL 109/1, 1990*) has argued that the evidence of 2 Kgs 23 and Ezek 8 can be construed as 'a form of solarized Yahwism', indigenous rather than imposed and somewhat akin to the Canaanized Yahwism which gave Yahweh a consort, Asherah, the mother of the gods and chief wife of El at Ugarit. See Smith's article for references to the Near Eastern sources and the older and more recent scholarly discussion.

[29] Kings commends Josiah for removing 'the horses that the kings of Judah had dedicated to the sun, at the entrance to the house of the LORD . . . then he burned the chariots of the sun with fire' (2 Kgs 23:11). Ezekiel sees twenty five men in the temple precincts 'their faces towards the east, prostrating themselves to the sun toward the east' (Ezek 8:16).

[30] Interpretation of polytheistic sun worship must allow for a worship of the Sungod manifested in, through and behind the various representations of the solar deity. Thus in Mesopotamia, to judge by the stone Sippar cult relief (BM 91000), the anthropomorphic cult statue of Shamash and a large solar disc cult object both do duty as representations for the Sungod or, to put it differently, for the sun in the sky. The relief depicts the male idol, the solar disc emblem and a geometric Shamash symbol. These three levels of representation or symbolization of the Sungod in the Sippar relief are discussed by Th Jacobsen,

and like a strong man runs its course with joy.
Its rising is from the end of the heavens,
and its circuit to the end of them;
and nothing is hid from its heat.

(Psa 19:1, 4b–6)

In this poem, the sun is an object distinguishable from Yahweh himself and hence safely personified in verse 5. The poet draws analogies between the glory of the sun, the glory of a male in full vigour and regalia, the glory of creation and the glory of Yahweh. There is also an analogy implied between the lights in the sky and the light of torah 'enlightening the eyes' (v.8b). Both are sources of revelation disclosing the character and power of Yahweh. Psalm 19 is not a sun hymn and there is no reason to think that it was recited at sunrise.[31]

B. I THE WORLD OF WORK

In the language of Psa 104, nocturnal animals return to their lairs at daybreak, giving place to human beings going about their daily work.

When the sun rises, they withdraw
and lie down in their dens.
People go out to their work
and to their labour until the evening.

(Psa 104:22f)

Getting up in the morning is naturally associated with leaving the house and going to work. The question is whether this crossing of the threshold is marked in any particular way.

If we turn to Deuteronomy, the answer given will surely be a positive one. There Israelites are instructed to continually keep the commandments in mind. In the first place, this means internalizing them, keeping them 'in your heart'.[32] Secondly, it is imparting

---

'The Graven Image', pp. 20–23 in PD Miller *et al*, *Ancient Israelite Religion* (Philadelphia: Fortress) 1987. Photos of the Sippar relief: *ANEP*, No. 529; A Parrot, *Nineveh and Babylon* (London: Thames & Hudson) 1961, pp. 213 & 215.

[31] On Psa 19 as a sample of Hebrew meditation, see the discussion in Chap. 5 'The Way of Reflection'.

[32] Hebrew *lēb*—'heart' is often best translated into English 'mind', and Deut 6:5 speaks of loving God using three terms, including *lēb*. Any attempt to translate one culture's metaphors into another's referents will not manage exact equivalence and Hebrew culture's physiological metaphors and modern psychology's preferred delineations of human personality are essentially functional models of a complex unity. A study of consciousness, cognition, emotion, motivation and other categories in psychology textbooks will confirm the current diversity of theory and model. Essentially Deut 6 is

them by recital for the children to memorize. Thirdly and fourthly,

> talk about them when you are at home and when you are away, when you lie down and when you rise. Bind them as a sign on your hand, fix them as an emblem on your forehead, and write them on the doorposts of your house and on your gates.
>
> (Deut 6:7–9; cf. 11:18–20)

This means more than 'obey them all the time', or 'let them guide your every thought', though it certainly includes these ideas. What we have here is a very effective use of spatial language. The command is earthed. Generality is replaced by specific points of reference—'at home', 'away'; 'lie down', 'rise'; 'hand', 'forehead'; 'doorposts', 'gates'. The language certainly carries the temporal message 'all the time', but it roots it in physical reality, the where as well as the when. Domestic life and public life are specified, parent roles and social roles. People get up, leave the house and pass through the city gates to go about their business.[33] There are two thresholds—the doorpost of the private dwelling and the gate of the communal town. In crossing these daily thresholds to and fro, the devout Israelite is to interweave his or her daily pattern with obedience to the Lord's commandments. This is a spirituality of daily living. It is the mundane, the routine, the so-called 'secular' life that is specified, rather than sabbath, festival and cult.

Between the threshold crossed in the morning and re-crossed in the evening, *The Shamash Hymn* , as well as Psalm 104, focuses on daily occupations. In the *Shamash Hymn*, worship at sunrise is supplemented by the access each person has in prayer to the Sungod who moves overhead and acts as their spiritual mentor.

> You shepherd all those endowed with breath,
> you alone are their pastor above and below
>
> Of all countries, diversified as their tongues may be,
> You detect the plans, you observe their ways,

---

speaking about an unreserved, loyal attachment to God which involves the whole person.

[33] The Hebrew *beˡlektˡkā badderek* 'in your walking on the road' is the antithesis paired with 'in your house'. It could mean away from home on a journey or simply when you are out and about. The pairing of 'hand' and 'forehead' hold activity and reflection together.

On their knees before you are all men.[34]

Shamash is god of justice and liberation for the imprisoned and the poor. A number of professions are mentioned, either because they involve justice or because the daily life of their practitioners takes them to remote places that are nevertheless not remote from the Sungod. So we have mention of the traveller, seafarer, hunter, merchant, the deported and imprisoned in lines 65–74, and the judge and the moneylender in lines 100–120. Shamash is praised as a listening god:

> You listen to men, discern them, you discern (the merit of) the case of
>   the wronged.
> Each and every person is entrusted to your hands,
> You make liver omens concerning them come out right, you undo
>   what is tied fast.
> You hear, O Sun, prayer, supplication, and homage,
> Prostration, kneeling, whispered prayer, and adoration.
> With constricted throat the feeble calls to you,
> The simple-minded, the weak, the wronged, the poor,
> Daily, regularly, constantly prays to you.
> Whosoever's family is far away, whosoever's city is distant,
> The shepherd amidst the terror of the steppe prays to you.
> The shepherd boy in distress, the herder among the enemy,
> The caravan passing through a terrifying terrain prays to you, O Sun.
> The itinerant merchant, the apprentice who carries the weight pouch
> The net-casting fisherman prays to you, O Sun.
> The hunter, the beater who rounds up the game,
> Behind the screen the fowler prays to you.
> He who slinks stealthily is also a petitioner of the Sun,
> On the tracks of the steppe the vagabond turns to you.
> The roving dead, the lost soul
> Have prayed to you, Sun, you heard all.[35]

This prayer is a spirituality of everyday life. With the exception of omen divination, in which Shamash played a traditional role as addressee of questions by petitioners, religious experts are not involved. The prayers described here are anywhere and everywhere by all sorts, from professionals to the marginalized in society. This communion with the deity is not tied to temple and cultic events but issues from individuals in the midst of their daily

---

[34] Reiner, *Thwarts*, p. 71f lines 25f & 49–51 from her Part II of which she says,

> The world that the sun is slowly illuminating as it climbs higher and higher has just intruded into the poet's consciousness, which has thus far been directed toward the contemplation and adoration of the sun itself; now we are ready to look at the world beneath the sun. (p. 74)

[35] *Thwarts*, p. 78 lines 127–146 from Reiner's Part IV.

pursuits. The lonely, isolated or endangered may pray with assurance of being noticed. So too may those involved in the regular activities of food gathering in the marshes of Iraq. All can count on the Sungod's vigilance and personal care. This is midday religion in its individual form.

We might identify its Yahwistic counterpart in prayers of the individual, such as Psalm 121:

> I will lift up my eyes to the hills—
> from where will my help come?
> My help comes from the LORD,
> who made heaven and earth.
>
> The LORD will keep your going out and your coming in
> from this time on and forevermore.
> (Psa 121:1–2, 8)

There is the same sense of God's accessibility when help is needed and the concept of the high God 'who made heaven and earth' being the God of daily life. This is made specific by the mention of 'your going out and your coming in', an inclusio for the beginning and end of the day, and, more generally, for the whole of your life as you live it in waking hours.[36]

The mention in Psalm 104 of 'people going out to their work and to their labour until evening' repesents human work as part of the daily cycle, part of the natural rhythm of life, like the alternation of daylight and darkness, or the activities of birds and wild animals in their natural habitats (vv. 11–21). Human work is placed within the context of God's providence so that food production flows naturally from the gift of water (vv. 10–13). The link between work and the diurnal rhythm of nature is strong because the particular kind of work the psalmist has in mind is not done in an office block, factory or down a mine. When introduced, it is explicitly agricultural work, to do with 'plants' and 'food from the earth' (v.14).[37] Wine, oil and bread 'gladden the human heart', 'make the face shine' and 'strengthen the human heart' (v. 15). God opens his hand and gives food to all at the appropriate time (v. 27f). The genre is a hymn. Celebration of the

---

[36] The strong ethical tone of *The Shamash Hymn* is missing from Psa 121, but is of course well represented in Torah and the crossing of the threshold in Deut 6.

[37] There may be conscious links between v.14 and Genesis signalled by the overlap of vocabulary—*'ēśeb* 'plant', the root *'bd* 'to work', *hā'ādām* 'Man', *hā'āreṣ* 'the earth'; compare Gen 2:5. Verse 23 of the Psalm may broaden the scope of the work envisaged to include other skills, crafts and occupations of the time.

Provider is furthered by a fundamentally optimistic description of how the natural world operates.[38]

Also optimistic and thoroughly positive in tone is the description of the competent wife in Prov 31. She works non-stop for the good of her household and husband. Her activities embrace several spheres, from domestic management to business transactions. The rhythm of her daily life is captured in these excerpted lines:

> [15]She rises while it is still night
> and provides food for her household
> and tasks for her servant girls.
> [16]She considers a field and buys it;
> with the fruit of her hands she plants a vineyard.
> [17]She girds herself with strength,
> and makes her arms strong.
> [18]She perceives that her merchandise is profitable.
> Her lamp does not go out at night.
>
> (Prov 31:15–18)

This acrostic vignette carries a Wisdom spirituality, culminating as it does in its focus on 'a woman who fears the LORD is to be praised' (v. 30b). The poem values spirituality rather than 'charm' and 'beauty' in v. 30. It credits the woman with business acumen, creative skills and forward planning (vv. 13, 16, 18, 19, 21, 22, 24, 27), and with compassion and generosity—'she opens her hand to the poor, and reaches out her hands to the needy' (v. 20).

Yet for all this, we probably feel a little uneasy with this piece now, rather than responding with wholehearted admiration. The woman is a wife, mother and employer rather than an individual person. She has gifts, a social role and a level of affluence that are open to few. In other words, the portrait is culture-specific, gender-specific, role-specific and income-specific. The positive evaluation of the woman is enunciated from a male and husbandly perspective—'A capable wife who can find?' (v. 10). She is an asset and credit to her husband who enjoys a public life in leadership: 'Her husband is known in the city gates, taking his seat among the elders of the land' (v. 23). What we can say with some truth is that in many cultures to the present day, male dominated as they are,

---

[38] Carnivores do not trouble the lyricist, but the wicked do and he wishes that they were eliminated from the world. The Hebrew word *'ereṣ* does duty for both 'land' and 'planet earth, the world'. Psa 104, like *The Great Hymn to the Aten* and *The Shamash Hymn*, has a universal setting and refers to the setting of the earth 'on its foundations', so the wider sense of *'ereṣ* fits v. 35 as well as v. 5. See Chap. 5 'The Way of Reflection' for a discussion of Psa 104 as an example of Israel's reflection the world of nature.

wives and mothers have not been allowed such scope as this woman has. What we should not say is that this vignette portrays 'the ideal wife' or woman. Nevertheless, in terms of this chapter's focus on the daily rhythm of life and the integration of work and spirituality, the vignette of Prov 31 makes a contribution. One might even say that re-read with humour, it portrays men as sitting around talking and being 'important', while women put in the long hours of hard work: 'she rises while it is still night . . . her lamp does not go out at night' (vv. 15 & 18).

For our purposes, we also need to remind ourselves that our theology is not one of deuteronomic prosperity. A grimmer perspective on what happens between breakfast and supper is demanded by the information fed into homes along with the morning weather forecast and the evening newscast. There can be no ignorance of rural areas devastated by famine when water from heaven has failed, nor ignorance of industrial areas hit by mass unemployment where there is no work to go out to or return from in the evening. For millions of the world's population, whether in Third or First World, the sufficiency and joy of Psa 104 or Prov 31 does not reflect their life experience, through no fault of their own. For millions more, there is no creativity in work, only production and soul–destroying, mindlessly repetitive tasks with no room for individual initiative. Nor is a romantic view of work sustainable when work conditions are hazardous, confined, polluted, isolated, inimical to human dignity or outrightly oppressive, as they are in so many situations today. We shall need more than the hymnic mood of Psa 104, or the admiration of Prov 31, if the spirituality of pre-industrial Yahwism is to be transposed into a spirituality for factory workers and commuters.

B.2 WORK AND PLEASURE

The Old Testament writers are aware of brick quotas without straw and toil that is unrewarding but, of course, the Old Testament is not addressing the contemporary issues of mass unemployment or life below the bread line. We are asking too much of the Old Testament if we demand an off-the-shelf spirituality for every situation. Nevertheless, the Old Testament contains a book which reflects on work and pleasure and which does offer transposable perceptions— Ecclesiastes.

There is a framework for Qohelet's reflections. Life is no paradise. It is life beyond Eden. Qohelet's perception of human experience is one of painful effort terminated by a return to dust.[39]

---

[39] On the echoes of Gen 1–3 in Qohelet's thought, see particularly the passages about God as Creator, human sinfulness, toil and death. These motifs are discussed by HC Shank, 'Qohelet's World and Life View as seen in his

Yet is this all, or does Qohelet offer a spirituality of work? Firstly, Quohelet's vocabulary is not that of Psa 104:23. Qohelet speaks of 'toil' not 'work'.[40] He poses the question of the fruit of human toil,[41] and he answers it as follows:

> What accrues to human beings from all the stress and strain with which they labour under the sun? For their day to day experience is one of pain and frustration. Even at night their minds do not relax. This also is absurd.
>
> (2:22f)

In this section Qohelet is describing the highly motivated worker who brings all his or her inner resources into play to achieve goals. The anomaly of effort versus result is highlighted by the profits of this effort falling into the lap of someone who has not laboured like that, or by the restless, stressful effects of this lifestyle on the executives themselves. The disparity between drive and benefit prompts Qohelet's summary comment, "Absurd!"[42] Qohelet condemns the motivation behind this sort of executive drive, observing that it is fuelled by envy and the desire to outdo the peer group and accumulate possessions in a way that can never be satisfied. Affluence does not buy peace of mind, indeed the rich will lie awake worrying over their assets, whereas the menial labourer is more likely to sleep peacefully however much or little he has had to eat. The irony is that the person who loves money and its advantages will never be satisfied.[43] Nor has this kind of

---

Recurrent Phrases' *WThJ* 37 (1974) 57–73, while the background for Ecc 3:20 in Gen 3:19 is noted by commentators, most recently RE Murphy, *Ecclesiastes*, WBC 23a (Dallas: Word) 1992, p.37.

[40] Psa 104:23 uses nouns based on 'doing' and 'serving' (*p'l* and *'bd*: NRSV 'work' and 'labour') whereas Qohelet uses the root *'ml* which turns 'work' into stress and strain. In general, the verb *'āmal* means 'to exert yourself, to labour' and the semantic field of the noun *'āmal* embraces both 'toil, effort' and 'distress, trouble, misfortune, disaster'. Gen 3:17 & 19 use the phrases 'in toil' (*'iṣṣābōn*—'hardship, pain, distress', as in Gen 3:16) and 'by the sweat (*zēʿāh*) of your face' to describe the effort involved in living off the cursed ground. On *'ml* in Ecclesiastes, see MV Fox, *Contradictions*, Chap. 2, §2.11 'Toil and its products', p.54ff. Murphy, citing Loretz, notes that *'ml* is used 33 times in Qohelet, making it one of Qohelet's most dominant concepts.

[41] Compare 3:9 'What gain has the worker from his toil?' The concept of *yitrōn* meaning 'gain, pay-off, advantage' or 'pleasing result' is one of Qohelet's favourite yard-sticks for evaluating effects. It appears 15 times in the book.

[42] Fox has argued persuasively for a coherent concept uniting the various contexts in which Qohelet offers his recurrent comment of *hebel*, and 'absurd' fits this requirement because it underlines the disparity between the way things ought to be and the way they actually are. The results do not match, the act–consequence nexus is broken, the outcome is an affront to reason or morality or justice or expectations or endeavour .

[43] See 4:4,6–8 and 5:10–17.

person anything to show for it in the long run because he arrived in this world empty-handed and will certainly not take anything with him when he exits from it. Indeed, in this light all his drive to accumulate riches is viewed as damaging.

> What is more, all his days are overshadowed; gnawing anxiety and great vexation are his lot, sickness and resentment.
>
> (5:17 REB)

All this may be readily recontextualized into the mega-city context, the stockmarket, the ethos of sudden redundancy layoffs, executive burn-out, the investigations of insider dealing and serious fraud, bankcruptcies and financial scandals, stress disorders and the diseases of A-type personalities such as heart-attack and ulcers. Indeed, the insidious effects of riches on the mind, motivation and morality of those with career prospects is a traditional topic in Near Eastern wisdom literature.[44] But this said, does Qohelet offer an alternative approach?

The fact that Qohelet has been accused of recommending hedonism suggests that there is more to Qohelet's perspective on work than condemning laziness, indifference and obsessional drive.[45] Indeed, some commentators regard Qohelet's positive recommendations on how life is to be lived as coming to focus in his sayings about work and the enjoyment of life.[46]

> There is nothing better for mortals than to eat and drink, and find enjoyment *in their toil*. This also, I saw, is from the hand of God; for apart from him who can eat or who can have enjoyment?
>
> (2:24f)

---

[44] For instance, compare Prov 23:4f with *Amenemope* 10: 7ff (*AEL* 2, p. 152), both of which speak of riches taking wings and flying away.

[45] That Qohelet echoes traditional Wisdom sentiments regarding folly and contentment seems clear enough. There is some debate as to whether he cites the proverbial sayings quoted below as contrastive and complementary to one another or whether both are regarded as inadequate, but in any case they need to be taken with the rest of what Qohelet says about work and obsession with riches.

> Fools fold their hands
> and consume their own flesh.
> Better is a handful with quiet
> than two handfuls with toil,
> and a chasing after wind.
>
> (4:5f)

[46] Most recently and assertively RN Whybray, 'Qohelet, Preacher of Joy' *JSOT* 23 (1982) 87–98 and *Ecclesiastes*, NCB, Eerdmans/Marshall, Morgan & Scott, 1989; with qualification, D Kidner, *A Time to Mourn and a Time to Dance* (Leicester: IVP) 1976 and MA Eaton, *Ecclesiastes*, TOTC, Leicester: IVP, 1983.

I know that there is nothing better for them than to be happy and enjoy themselves as long as they live; moreover it is God's gift that all should eat and drink and take pleasure *in their toil.*

(3:12)

This is what I have seen to be good: it is fitting to eat and drink and find enjoyment *in all the toil with which one toils* under the sun the few days of life which God gives us; for this is our lot. Likewise all to whom God gives wealth and possessions and whom he enables to enjoy them, and to accept their lot and find enjoyment *in their toil*—this is the gift of God. For they will scarcely brood over the days of their lives, because God keeps them occupied with the joy of their hearts.

(5:18–20)

So I recommend enjoyment, for there is nothing better for people under the sun than to eat, and drink, and enjoy themselves, for this will go with them *in their toil* through the days of life that God gives them under the sun.

(8:15)

Go, eat your bread with enjoyment, and drink your wine with a merry heart; for God has long ago approved what you do. Let your garments always be white; do not let oil be lacking on your head. Enjoy life with the wife whom you love, all the days of your vain life that are given you under the sun, because that is your portion in life and in *your toil in which you toil* under the sun. Whatever your hand finds to do, do with your might; for there is no work or thought or knowledge or wisdom in Sheol, to which you are going.

(9:7–10)

In each of these quotations, the concept of *'āmal*—'toil' appears. This guarantees that Qohelet is not speaking about a life of idleness or of hedonism. For Qohelet, life has about it that quality of uphill, of struggle, of toil. Work is an effort. But neither does Qohelet offer a secular and cynical understanding of work. He moves within the framework of the given, in the awareness that life does not deal everyone an even hand. The cumulative effect of reflection on the lot and limits of human expectation points towards an enjoyment of what is enjoyable as a blessing from God. If it is possible to gain satisfaction from your work or its results, then do so. Make the most of your opportunities or what lies to hand while life lasts. If these pleasures that he lists fall to your lot, enjoy them. It is noteworthy that 'God' appears in each of these passages as well as 'toil'. Qohelet connects the two.

There is a natural link between working and eating and Qohelet makes his comment on it—'All human toil is for the mouth, yet the appetite is not satisfied' (6:7). Yet this treadmill of work-hunger-food is not Qohelet's definitive observation. There is more to eating and drinking than energy balance in Qohelet's perspective. Indeed, the specific acts of eating and drinking probably imply a trans-biological perspective. They would carry a social dimension in Israel's culture diametrically different from the nuance that eating and drinking in the fast-food chains or anonymous bars of today's mega–cities might have. Enjoyment of eating and drinking implies enjoyment of company, a thought congruent with the aphorism that 'two are better than one' argued in 4:9–12. Even if there is an undertone of irony in the recommendation of gaiety and enthusiasm in 9:7–10, because of the inevitability and the finality of death, this does not devalue in themselves job satisfaction or the other enjoyments. Qohelet simply recognizes that you cannot hold on to these rewarding features of life, nor can satisfaction be guaranteed.[47] Nothing is guaranteed.

In the end, Qohelet is speaking about an attitude rather than laying down a work ethic. His whole comment on 'toil' applies to the realities of life after Eden. The universal scope of his observations on human work make his statements sound remarkably modern. They are certainly not propounding the American dream, a Protestant work ethic, Victorian virtues, a patrician perspective, the utopia of the classless society, or the cult of leisure. Qohelet is too aware that the world is not what it should be to propound an economic policy or even a personal investment plan.[48]

More could be said about finding meaning in work and about the kind of job satisfaction that is not related to salary. But Qohelet has said enough to indicate that what happens between sunup and coming home at night is part of Israel's life before God. How that reflection and its spirituality is transposed into contemporary contexts of longterm unemployment or of mindless and exhausting production is a theology of praxis. It cannot be composed by those with the education to write or read these words, neither the ancient literati like Qohelet, nor the products of

---

[47] R Johnston makes the distinction between the mastery of life and the art of steering through life, applying this to Qohelet's verdict on work and pleasure. The verdict goes against 'an obsessive work-orientation' and in favour of enjoying life's 'gifts from God as they unfold'—' "Confessions of a Work-aholic": a reappraisal of Qoheleth' *CBQ* 38 (1976) 14–28.

[48] The discussion by Fox in his chapter on 'Toil and Pleasure' (*Contradictions*, pp. 53–77) makes a strenuous effort to do justice to the linking of the fields of 'work', 'toil', 'gain', 'lot', 'pleasure', 'joy', what is 'good' and the tension between their limitations and the experiencing of them. Certainly Qohelet's view of them is an unromantic one.

modern university departments of theology.[49] The degreed and employed are not qualified to delineate that spirituality.

B.3 OPPORTUNITY AND PROMOTION

In the centres of dense population represented by such places as Hong Kong, Buenos Aires, Delhi, Tokyo, New York, London, Cairo and Mexico city, riches and poverty coexist in close proximity, separated by an enormous social gulf. City life unites and divides the population. Money circulates in handfuls of coins, or in computer transactions shifting vast quantities of capital electronically at the press of a button. The disparity between working hours and daily wage can never have been so great as when a commercially valued person today earns enormous surpluses per hour over living requirements. In London, the phrase to 'work in the city' ironically does not include all the varied jobs from news vendor, to traffic warden, to bar-tender to MP, but means to work in the square mile of high finance and astronomical earnings.

The Ancient Near East equivalent of today's banks, stockmarkets and multinationals were the temples and royal courts. These were centres of enormous affluence and monopoly in their time. In Egypt, Assyria and Babylon conquest, trade and prosperity created an international flow of population. Cities attracted migrants as well as conquerors. The walls of civilization built against the pressures of mountain and desert tribes in Mesopotamia did not prevent the overrunning of the prosperous Ur III Empire by the mountain Guti at the end of the 3rd millennium, nor the intrusion of the Amorites from the western steppe a century or two later. The pressure of the uncivilized have-nots on Mesopotamia's urban centres overwhelmed them. Yet the social and commercial disruption caused by Amorite and Kassite settlement in the early second millennium was quickly forgotten as city life absorbed the newcomers into its style. Babylonia prospered under these alien rulers. It was the Amorite, Hammurapi, who put Babylon on the map in the 19th century, paving the way for the rise of its city-god Marduk to a world-creating rank under Nebuchadnezzar I in the 12th century. This prominence was emulated and excelled in the western empire of his namesake, the

---

[49] One might hope that the Christian church may prove to be one forum where the disadvantaged may give voice to their experience and their wisdom and it be transcribed into the book form of the educationally advantaged with relatively little ideological distortion. Compare the efforts of the Institute for Contextual Theology in South Africa and their publications such as JR Cochrane & GO West (eds), *The Three-Fold Cord: theology, work & labour*

biblical Nebuchadnezzar II in the 6th century. So it was that the royal armies, building projects and bureaucracy came to pattern the rhythm of daily life beyond Israel's borders for hundreds of years before and after Israel's own moment of empire and trade in the days of Solomon.

Long before Louis XIV of France called himself 'Le Roi Soleil', there were Sun kings in the Near East. To secure their blessing was to achieve promotion and opportunity of the kind craved by today's yuppies and executives. A court language developed addressing the king with a profusion of titles and flatteries as useful to vassals and courtiers then as they seem ridiculous today. Near Eastern kings were addressed as 'my Sun'.[50] 'I am the dirt under the sandals of the k[ing, my lord,] and the king is the Etern[al] Sun', writes Abi-Milku of Tyre.[51] In another letter, he compares the Pharaoh to two deities: 'O king, my lord, you are like the Sun, like Baal, in the sky.'[52]

Moran has labelled one of Abi-Milku's letters 'A Hymn to the Pharaoh' and a few lines of its sun language show why:

> To the king, my lord, my god, my Sun . . . my lord is the Sun who comes forth over all lands day by day . . . who gives life by his sweet breath and returns with his north wind . . . Whoever gives heed to the king, his lord, and serves him in his place, the Sun comes forth over him, and the sweet breath comes back from the mouth of his lord. If he does not heed the word of the king, his lord, his city is destroyed, his house is destroyed, never (again) does his name exist in all the land. (But) look at the servant who gives heed to his lord. His city prospers, his house prospers, his name exists for ever. You are the Sun who comes forth over me . . . [53]

(Pietermaritzburg: Cluster Publications) 1993 which alludes to Qohelet 4:9–12 in its title.

[50] MS Smith, 'The Near Eastern Background of Solar Language for Yahweh' *JBL* 109/1 (1990) 29–39 suggests that this common metaphorical language for monarchy and the international diplomatic correspondence in Akkadian which is exemplified by the Amarna Letters contributed to the use of sun and light metaphors for royalty and for Yahweh in Israel. This is not really demonstrable. There is more agreement that the solar disc icon, but not the Amarna version, spread from Egypt across the Near East and came to be used to represent a range of deities in Assyrian, Aramaic and Arabian areas. See S Dalley, 'The God Salmu and the Winged Disk' *Iraq* 48 (1986) 85–101.

[51] Moran, *The Amarna Letters*, p. 241, EA 155.

[52] EA 149, *The Amarna Letters*, p. 236 cf. 'who is like Baal and Shamash in the sky' (EA 108, p. 181). The stock epithets 'the king, my lord, my god, my Sun, the Sun from the sky' are sometimes lengthened with the addition of 'son of the Sun' (EA 319, p. 350). Compare 'I looked this way, and I looked that way, and there was no light. Then I looked towards the king, my lord, and there was light' (EA 296, p.338 & 266, p. 314).

[53] EA 147, *The Amarna Letters*, p. 233; *ANET*, p. 484.

Babylonian and Assyrian kings were not deified like the pharaohs but they also generate a similar self-legitimating language. Hammurapi calls himself 'the ancient seed of royalty, the powerful king, the sun of Babylon, who causes light to go forth over the lands of Sumer and Akkad.'[54] The phrase 'who causes light to go forth over the lands of Sumer and Akkad' indicates a parallel of role between Hammurapi and the Sungod in the three key aspects of revelation, justice and beneficence, motifs which appear in the Prologue and Epilogue to the laws. An Assyrian courtier could likewise laud Esarhaddon to the skies:

> The father of the king, my lord, was the very image of Bel, and the king, my lord, is likewise the very image of Bel . . . The king, the lord of the world, is the very image of the Sungod . . .[55]

When the sun is personified as a deity and when the king is likened to the sun, that association produce the mixed metaphor of the king's face shining on someone in favour. This idiom combines the turning of the face towards someone in favour—as the opposite of turning away from them in anger. It implies a comparison between majesty and the sun. The face-sun idiom is illustrated in the Ugaritic letter in which the writer tells his mother of his successful audience with the king:

> (4) May it be well with you.
> May the gods of (5) Ugarit guard you,
> may (6) they keep you well.
> My mother, (7) you must know that
> I have entered (8) before the Sun
> (9) and the face of the Sun shone (10) upon me greatly.
> So may my mother (11) cause Ma'abu to rejoice
> (12) and may she not be discouraged,

---

[54] *ANET*, p. 165 from the Prologue to the Code of Hammurabi, v:1f. The Sumerian logogram ^{dingir}. *Utu^{ši}* does not equate Hammurapi with god Shamash so as to deify the king as such, but fits into the pattern of address whereby subjects addressed the king as 'your majesty' which we could render literalistically as 'my sun', *šamšī*. See *AHw*, 1158f *šamšu* and Dalley's article above, p.98f. Outside Egypt, the ideologies of kingship which made the king a deity during his lifetime were the exception. On self-legitimation and Hammurapi's other phrase 'the ancient seed of royalty', see WG Lambert, 'The Seed of Kingship', pp. 424–440 in P Garelli (ed), *Le Palais et la Royauté*, RAI 19, Paul Geuthner, 1974 and 'Enmeduranki and related matters', *JCS* 21 (1967) 126–138.

[55] Letter from the court astrologer Adad-shum-usur. The Assyrian word for 'image'(*salmu*) is the Akkadian cognate of Hebrew *selem* in Gen 1: 26f. In another letter, the parallel phrase is used—'The king is the perfect likeness of the god' (*šu kal muššuli ša ili*). See S Parpola, *AOAT* 5/1, 1970, p. 113, No. 143 & No. 145.

(13) (for) the guardian of the army am I.
(14–15) With me everything is well.[56]

The reason that the words of this Ugaritic letter may sound familiar is that they call to mind the words of the priestly blessing of Num 6:24–26:

> The LORD bless you and keep you
> the LORD make his face to shine upon you and be gracious to you;
> the LORD lift up his countenance upon you, and give you peace.[57]

The final word *šālōm* 'peace, well-being' in the Hebrew corresponds to *šlm* 'be well', 'keep you well', 'is well' in lines 4, 6 and 14 of the letter. 'Keep you' corresponds with 'guard you' in line 5. 'Make his face shine on you' and 'lift up his face upon you' correspond with 'the face of the Sun shone upon me greatly' of line 9f. Yahwistic blessing uses the language of royal favour.[58] It is linked with sun language in Psalm 84 as well:

> For a day in your courts is better
> than a thousand elsewhere.
> I would rather be a doorkeeper in the house of my God
> than live in the tents of wickedness.
> For the LORD God is a sun and shield;
> he bestows favour and honour.
> No good thing does the LORD withhold
> from those who walk uprightly.
>
> (Psa 84:10–11)

In the light of this psalm and of the priestly blessing, we might say that the sense of blessing within covenant relationship was as reassuring to a devout Yahwist as the tangible human favour of the king, or as the visible sunrise after nightime. The priestly

---

56 *KTU* 2.16 lines 4–15 transcribed and translated in D Pardee, 'Further Studies in Ugaritic Epistolography' *AfO* 31 (1984), p. 220.

57 Recently, variants of this blessing, dated by script to the 7th century BC and inscribed on small silver plates, were found in Jerusalem. These may represent orthodox prayers, but equally they could mark a step towards a talisman mentality in which the words take on the power and function of a protective amulet, as Weinfeld assumes (*Deuteronomy 1–11*, AB 5, New York: Doubleday, 1991, p.342). For a study of these variants and a later prayer from Qumran, see MCA Korpel, 'The Poetic Structure of the Priestly Blessing' *JSOT* 45 (1989) 3–13.

58 Prov 16:15 offers an example of the royal idiom: 'In the light of a king's face there is life, and his favour is like the clouds that bring the spring rain.' For a review of light–life imagery see S Aalen's entry on אוֹר *'ōr* in GJ Botterweck (ed) *Theological Dictionary of the Old Testament, Vol. 1* (Grand Rapids: Eerdmans) 1977 revised edition, pp. 147ff.

blessing acknowledges Yahweh as the source of all life and well-being.[59] If it is Yahweh who is the source of well-being, the king is secondary.[60]

To transpose this from ancient Israel to modern life is not difficult if its core is understood as a fundamental orientation. The Old Testament does not despise or neglect material blessing as the book of Deuteronomy or the attitude of Qohelet demonstrate. Yet relationship with Yahweh is the heart of the matter. That relationality does justice to Deuteronomy's injunctions, to the preaching of the Prophets and to the theology of the poor. It contrasts starkly with ingratiating oneself with the human monarch.

C. THRESHOLDS AND AMULETS

'And it was morning and it was evening, day one . . . ' In Gen 1, the role of God as Creator is modelled on the pattern of the Israelite working week and working day. The religion of Deut 6, of Psa 104, of Qohelet and indeed the religion of *The Great Hymn to the Aten* and *The Shamash Hymn* continues this intermingling of divine and human life in a daily cycle because the individual experiences his or her faith in the flow of diurnal rhythm. One might object, what other way is there to experience Yahwistic faith, other than in those ways described in the morning, working and evening pattern? This would be to overlook the obvious in the Torah or the Psalms. So much of Israel's Yahwistic faith expresses itself in corporate experience in communal or national dimension, and in cultic and ritual activities on a longer cycle. There is, for instance, the Passover festival. This is a national and family ritual once a year in the month of Nisan. In the texts that we have considered in this chapter, Temple and cultic activities may be acknowledged—as they are tangentially in Qohelet—but the

---

[59] Writing in the 1970s and reflecting on C Westermann's analysis of blessing-providence and salvation-deliverance, PD Miller made the point that the priestly blessing redresses an unbalanced emphasis on 'a too heavy kerygmatic theology or emphasis on the mighty acts of God . . . in extraordinary events rather than at the centre of ongoing life'—'The Blessing of God: an interpretation of Numbers 6:22–27' *Interpretation* 29 (1975) 240–251, p. 251.

[60] Israel did develop a concept of blessing mediated through the king, and court language crept into her speech—'you are the most handsome of men' (Psa 45:2); 'May he be like rain that falls on the mown grass, like showers that water the earth' (Psa 72:6, cf. vv. 5 and 7); 'The LORD's anointed, the breath of our life . . . the one of whom we said, "Under his shadow we shall live among the nations." ' (Lam 4:20). This said, Israel's faith formed without a monarchy and survived the permanent demise of the monarchy at the Exile.

spirituality is the spirituality of the individual about his or her daily routine.[61]

Psa 121 as well as Deut 6 and Psa 104 speak of the crossing of the threshold at the beginning and end of the day. This contrast between the corporate national and cultic events and a daily routine means that the kind of diurnal spirituality that emerges from our texts may find more obvious dynamic equivalents in modern society than do Tabernacle or Temple rituals and the centralized worship and national renewal ceremonies depicted in Deuteronomy. There is the direct equivalence of marking the beginning and ending of the working day on leaving home and returning home with a conscious recollection of God. In the cities this consciousness of God might be synchronized with turning the key in the door or in the ignition, or stepping off and on to the platform at the station or bus terminal.

There are other thresholds and other time scales to the rhythm of our lives. These do involve the literal crossing of architectural thresholds. There are many more thresholds and doors to modern life than the two sets of *meᶻūzot* and *šeᶜārīm* mentioned by Deut 6:9. Life is more complicated than village life in Canaan, where going to work might have meant emerging from your house and going through the city gates into the surrounding fields. In cities today getting to work involves pneumatic doors, revolving doors, sliding doors, elevator doors, automatic doors, fire doors and corridors, not to mention check-in and check-out points, barriers and tickets of all sorts, uniforms, badges and identity tags. The fact that commuters can get to and fro from work on auto-pilot with little need to ponder each set of doors en route does indicate that familiarity reduces complexity to manageable proportions. Does familiarity leave any room for a depth dimension?

There is another sense to crossing thresholds, a symbolic one. This symbolism is interwoven into the goings-out and comings-in that mark phases of our working lives by the architectural thresholds that change with age or marriage or job or hospitalis-ation. These thresholds may impinge upon our awareness when we cross them for the first time. Those are moments of daily life to open to deity, the departures from routine, the beginnings and endings, doors opening and closing before us both factually and metaphorically. The question, then, is not so much whether an

---

[61] In Qohelet, for instance, there is a nod in the direction of the Jerusalem Temple in 5:1ff which admonishes against ill-considered vows—'Guard your steps when you go to the house of God; to draw near to listen is better than the sacrifice offered by fools.' In 8:10 reference is made to the hypocrisy of the wicked who 'used to go in and out of the holy place, and were praised in the city'.

awareness of God can accompany a city commuter on her or his route to work and back, but whether there is any depth dimension to daily life. Does a new threshold that interrupts the routine produce an effect that fosters spirituality?

The husband carrying his bride across the threshold for the first time marks the moment with a symbolic gesture. It is a magical moment, a threshold to a life shared in a new way. The same couple coming home or leaving for work a few weeks later settle into a less romantic expression of their affection for one another. They part with a kiss, a hug or a calling out to one another. These daily rituals of parting and returning play their part in preventing the love relationship from declining into taking each other for granted. On the other hand, these nurturing greeting rituals can become perfunctory. Is there a spiritual analogy?

Two features of concern to a spirituality for the rhythm of daily work are routine and magic, or, in combination, magical routines. Dynamic equivalence between ancient and modern magical routines can be suggested. The Arslan Tash plaque was hung at the doorpost to forbid entry to nocturnal demons:

> The house I enter, you shall not enter.
> and the residence I step into, you shall not step into.[62]

It prohibits Sasam from crossing the threshold, on the grounds of a covenant of protection invoking major Syro–Palestinian deities. Deut 6:9 and the Arslan Tash plaque share the concepts of covenant and doorpost,[63] and biblical theology shares the world view of a daily life that is open to supernatural powers, demonic and divine. The danger of this awareness of the supernatural degenerating into a magical and amuletic approach to life is very real, no less in a Christian spirituality than in a pagan superstition. Prayer may rapidly degenerate into the repetitive muttering of magical incantations, whether in liturgical or charismatic settings, or in the private world of anxiety and stress. The mind's door between earth and heaven may be ever open, but there is a deep human tendency to turn the crossing of this threshold into touching wood.

The commuter crossing the threshold of home or public transport to work in the mega–city cannot invoke God as a formula for success. The threats of redundancy, polluted air,

---

[62] JC de Moor, 'Demons in Canaan' *Ex Oriente Lux* 27 (1981–2) 106–119, p. 108.
[63] *mzzt*, the cognate to Deut 6:9's $m^e z \bar{u} z o t$ 'doorpost', and *'lt 'lm* 'eternal oath' appear in the plaque. On the semantic parallels, see the discussion by Z Zevit, 'A Phoenician Inscription and Biblical Covenant Theology' *IEJ* 27 (1977) 110–118.

assault or stress disorder are not warded off by remembering God at the beginning or ending of the day. As Qohelet observed,

> the race is not to the swift, nor the battle to the strong, nor bread to the wise, nor riches to the intelligent, nor favour to the skilful; but time and chance happen to them all. For no one can anticipate the time of disaster.
>
> (Ecc 9:11f)

Morning, noon and night, Christians participate in the statistics of redundancy, road accidents, debt, illnesses and the lesser set-backs that make up daily life. No plaque or promise of material well-being can be plucked from the Old Testament and pinned on the lapel, dangled from the driving mirror, attached to the key chain, or worn as a wrist bracelet. There is no magical protection in a diurnal awareness of God. Nor are the assurances offered in Psalm 121 of round-the-clock protection renewed in the New Covenant, unless they be in the form of a preservation unto eternal life, as the prayer of Jesus in John 17 suggests and Rom 8 envisages.[64]

Yet Qohelet and Deuteronomy still speak to us about the pattern of daily life. Qohelet speaks in its own characteristic denunciation of serving God and mammon (Ecc 4:6f; 5:10). It speaks in its concept of doing with your might whatever your hand finds to do, because making the most of things is to make the most of life while it lasts (9:7–10), and enjoying the enjoyable things in life is a form of thankfulness for them as a gift of God while they are there (Ecc 2:24; 5:19). Deuteronomy speaks to us about the implications of monotheism and covenanted relationship in its Shema. This is not a contentless awareness of God. It is behavioural and focused on the implications of a covenant relationship at home and at work (Deut 6:4–9). Pleasure and obedience to God's commandments are drawn together by joining Qohelet and Deuteronomy's perspectives on daily life lived in awareness of God. The lyrical hymnody of Psalm 104 and the celebration of the Creator of the natural world may form part of rising and lying down as well. If so, praise and delight with the way that the natural world operates will not drift apart from ethics, behaviour and realism about the state of society. Spirituality will be a part of the day in the life and not apart from it.

SUMMARY AND CONCLUSION

We began by considering the deep human instinct of turning to God in worship or plea as daylight dawns and consciousness

---

[64]   I am not asking you to take them out of the world, but I ask you to protect them from the evil one. (John 17:15)

returns after sleep. There was a natural optimism detectable in linking daylight with life and hope. It is echoed in the aphorism—'the darkest hour comes just before the dawn.' We also found that praise of the sun in Egypt and Mesopotamia was illuminated by a natural theology—if one is so bold as to use that term—whereby the deity is understood as a universal Creator or sustainer. In Atenism, the deity who is manifested in the solar disc brings everything to life day by day and receives the joyful response of human beings, birds, fish and animals. Shamash of Babylon brings justice to bear on human affairs and is ever vigilant and receptive to human cries for help. No special paraphernalia or intermediaries are needed to reach him.

Yet it must be said that Amarna monotheism celebrating creation and the *Shamash Hymn* with its ethical thrust are exceptional poems within Near Eastern polytheism and politics. Polytheism is more broadly represented in the incantational approach to life of *Maqlû* and *Shurpû*, or by letters courting the king's favours. The *Aten* and *Shamash* hymns share truths and imagery about the majesty of God and his accessibility in the rhythm of daily life with biblical psalms which express worship, thankfulness and a sense of justice.[65] Psalm 104, *The Great Hymn to the Aten* and *The Shamash Hymn* also cluster together because they represent the genre of hymnody with its optimistic view of life. Perhaps the sunny Egyptian climate with its unfailing food source linked with the inundation of the Nile and the deposit of fertile silt explains the optimism of Amarna monotheism. Biblical monotheism, as one glance at the books of Psalms bears out, could not live by hymns alone but by every word of lament that proceeded from the Israelite's mouth as well.

We turned to Qohelet for a reflection on life 'under the sun', and found one intended as a universal perspective like Akhenaten's and that of *The Shamash Hymn*. Qohelet was not one for a false optimism, nor for a magical or ritual approach to life. He is rather thin on praise. He focuses instead on the incessant rhythm of life as a constant round in which 'the sun rises and the sun goes down', 'all things are wearisome' and 'it is an unhappy business that God has given human beings to be busy with' (Ecc 1:5, 8 & 12). Nevertheless, Qohelet's perspective on 'toil' turns out to be both realistic and tinged with positive features.

---

[65] There are those who believe that Akhenaten inspired Israel's monotheism or that Psa 104 borrows from Aten poetry. The case is far from demonstrable and not really convincing. On Psa 104 and its relation to the Aten hymns, Genesis 1 and Ugaritic material, see the literature cited and the judicious evaluation of it in LC Allen, *Psalms 101–150*, WBC 21 (Waco: Word) 1983, p. 29ff.

Daniel stopped work three times a day and faced Jerusalem to pray. The morning and evening sacrifice of Yahwistic worship mark the beginnings and endings of a daily communion with God. No specific pattern of worship, prayer or communion with God is presented in the New Covenant for structuring life's ordinary rhythm. There is no record of Jesus' life during the years of practising his daily trade. His ministry is exceptional and marked by exceptions—Jesus rose early to pray on occasion, but also prayed through the night on occasion and withdrew to remote places on occasion.[66]

According to Torah, which was normative for Jesus and for Daniel, the daily round must be permeated with thoughts of God. Whether Deut 6:8f ever envisaged a physical fastening of commandments on hand and forehead, doorpost and gate, it is alien to Deuteronomy to reduce the revelation which guides daily life in the covenant into a talisman, an amulet, an appendage to success or safety. The words are to be kept in mind and conversation, rather than treasured as trinkets, according to Deut 6:6.[67] Nor can we turn Deuteronomy's words into a prescription for a content-less form of God-consciousness. Neither the Psalms nor Deuteronomy propounds a consciousness that consists of an exotic mode of alpha rhythms, however helpful these meditative techniques may prove to be to harried executives and stressed commuters in need of relaxation. The Torah's God-consciousness is linked with covenant requirements as exemplified by the Ten Commandments.[68] What is spoken of is a life-involved behaviour, not a detached state of mind.

---

[66] Mk 1:35f (Lk 4:42), Lk 5:16, Lk 6:12, Matt 14:23.

[67] The metaphorical sense of binding on the commandments is suggested by the parallel language used about parental instruction in Prov 6:20–22. This urges the son to 'bind them upon your heart always' in parallel with 'tie them around your neck'. The passage goes on, like Deut 6, to speak about them accompanying the subject when he is out and about, asleep in bed or awake. They are a way of life, or, as Hebrew idiom expresses it, a *derek ḥayyīm* 'a route to life' (v. 23b). The 2nd millennium simile referring to treaty stipulations and the Amarna letter metaphor from an Egyptian vassal, cited by Weinfeld, further illustrate these Near Eastern figures of speech: 'as you wear a dress, so shall you carry with you these oaths' and 'I carry upon my belly and upon my back the words of the king' (Weinfeld, *Deut 1–11*, p. 341; EA 147:39 is from Abi-milku's 'Hymn to the Pharaoh' referred to earlier in this chapter).

[68] The Ten Commandments are referred to in Exod 20:1 and Deut 5:22 as 'these words' (*hadd^ebārīm hā'ēleh*). Deut 6:6, as well as Deut 11:18–20 which parallels Deut 6:6–9, uses 'these words' as a general summary of all the exhortation and covenant stipulations. Weinfeld (*Deut 1–11*, p. 455) notes that Deut 6:4–9 and 11:13–21 form an inclusio bracketing all the commandments in between and draws attention to their use in the daily liturgy according to Mishna Tamid ('The Daily Whole Offering', 5.1 in H Danby, *The Mishnah* London: OUP,

How exactly our biorhythm may be interwoven with the relationship with God amidst the pace and congestion of city life or in other contexts without the deadening effect of routine setting in is for us to ponder. Between morning and evening there are many thresholds to cross. The threshold of our consciousness is a subtle one. It is prone to the various quirks of our biology, culture, psychology and occupation. If God-thoughts are to slip across the threshold of our consciousness in the course of the daily rhythm of our life, they may need some assistance of the kind that we deploy to prevent other matters slipping from our attention. They may need to be linked into the daily rhythm and routines in the same way that the multiplicity of other doings such as dressing, undressing and gathering our things together is part of this rhythm. Those activities almost run on auto-pilot, but not quite. We check ourselves in the mirror, we pat our pockets or look in bags for tickets and keys. We take our faith with us into the day and return with it at night. Our spirituality too is our key, our ticket, our mirror.

BIBLIOGRAPHY

S Aalen, אור 'ōr, in GJ Botterweck (ed) *Theological Dictionary of the Old Testament, Vol. 1*, (Grand Rapids: Eerdmans) 1977 rev. ed.

T Abusch, 'Mesopotamian Anti-Witchcraft Literature: Texts and Studies, Part I: the nature of, *Maqlû*: its character, divisions, and calendrical setting', *JNES* 33 (1974) 257–262.

CH Aldred, *Akhenaten: king of Egypt* (London: Thames & Hudson) 1988.

LC Allen, *Psalms 101–150*, Word 21 (Waco: Word) 1983.

FE Bloom & A Lazerson, *Brain, Mind and Behaviour*, 2nd edition (New York: Freeman & Co) 1988.

JR Cochrane & GO West (eds), *The Three-Fold Cord: theology, work & labour* (Pietermaritzburg: Cluster Publications) 1993.

D Collon, *First Impressions; cylinder seals in the Ancient Near East*, (London: British Museum Publications) 1987.

S Dalley, 'The God Salmu and the Winged Disk', *Iraq* 48 (1986) 85–101.

DC Dennett, 'Consciousness' , in RL Gregory (ed), *The Oxford Companion to the Mind* (Oxford: OUP) 1987.

———, *Consciousness Explained*, Penguin 1993.

MA Eaton, *Ecclesiastes*, TOTC (Leicester: IVP) 1983.

Th Jacobsen, 'The Graven Image', pp. 20–23 in PD Miller *et al, Ancient Israelite Religion* (Philadelphia: Fortress) 1987.

D Kidner, *A Time to Mourn and a Time to Dance* (Leicester: IVP) 1976.

R Johnston, ' "Confessions of a Workaholic": a reappraisal of Qoheleth', *CBQ* 38 (1976) 14–28.

MCA Korpel, 'The Poetic Structure of the Priestly Blessing' *JSOT* 45 (1989) 3–13.

1933, p. 586), although we cannot tell how far back this Second Temple liturgy goes.

M Lichtheim, *Ancient Egyptian Literature: Vol 2, the New Kingdom,* (Berkeley: Univ of California) 1976.

PD Miller, 'The Blessing of God: an interpretation of Numbers 6:22–27', *Interpretation* 29 (1975) 240–251.

JC de Moor, 'Demons in Canaan', *Ex Oriente Lux* 27 (1981–82) 106–119.

WL Moran, *The Amarna Letters* (London: Johns Hopkins) 1992.

RE Murphy, *Ecclesiastes*, Word 23a (Dallas: Word) 1992.

DB Redford, *Akhenaten the heretic king* (New Jersey: Princeton Univ Press) 1984.

E Reiner, *Shurpû, AfO* Bei. 11, Graz 1958.

——, *Your thwarts in pieces, Your mooring rope cut: poetry from Babylonia and Assyria,* Michigan Studies in the Humanities 5, Univ of Michigan, 1985.

HC Shank, 'Qoheleth's World and Life View as seen in his Recurrent Phrases', *WThJ* 37 (1974) 57–73.

MS Smith, 'The Near Eastern Background of Solar Language for Yahweh', *JBL* 109/1 (1990) 29–39.

ER Valentine, *Conceptual Issues in Psychology,* 2nd ed (London/New York: Routledge) 1992.

M Weinfeld, *Deuteronomy 1–11,* AB 5 (New York: Doubleday) 1991.

RN Whybray, 'Qohelet, Preacher of Joy' *JSOT* 23 (1982) 87–98.

——, *Ecclesiastes* NCB (Eerdmans/Marshall, Morgan & Scott) 1989.

Z Zevit, 'A Phoenician Inscription and Biblical Covenant Theology' *IEJ* 27 (1977) 110–118.

[11]

A Spirituality Of Times and Season

INTRODUCTION

In the previous chapter, we looked at the daily rhythm of life. We shall now explore its wider context—the flow of time and the way this flow is divided, characterized and commemorated in calendar and cult. We shall review the links and the contrasts between Yahwistic concepts of time and cult and those of the wider Semitic world.

Our solar system generates local time and the seasons that in turn relate to food supply. The experience of time and dependence on food link all human beings to the elliptical orbits of the earth and the moon around the sun. But what else is there to this passage of time besides elliptical orbits, the agricultural cycle, calendars, diaries, digital watches and time-checks? Day and night, moon and ocean tides are physics and mathematics, astronomy and biology. In the end, we might describe accumulated time and human records as history, and try to give that some meaning. But is there a spirituality to the human experience of time?

The short answer is 'No, not necessarily', because time in and of itself is a neutral phenomenon, whether measured in hours or in heartbeats. We make of time what we will. In post-Christian Europe, and in other urban cultures, time is secularized, for practical purposes. Our year date relates to business and taxes and school terms. When we write a cheque it scarcely penetrates our consciousness that the year date itself is a Christian phenomenon. The longer answer to the question of a spirituality of time might be 'Yes', because we are creaturely and we express both our creaturely dependence and our creative independence in the dimension of time, task and life on earth. In this chapter, we shall explore some of the divisions of time and the way Israel marked them as expressions of her life with Yahweh, and then go on to ask in what ways Israel's perspective on time might contribute to a Christian spirituality.

We shall look at different time scales, first the lunar month common to the Near East, then the calendar year and especially its inception, New Year. After that, we shall cosider the week and the Sabbath. We want to determine what symbolism survives from ancient to modern times, or what new myths and ideologies compete with an authentic spirituality of times and seasons. Because we are working from the Old Testament rather than from the New, our main concern will not be with an exposition of the Christian year, of Advent, Christmas, Lent and Easter, or other festivals of the Christian calendar in current practice. Our focus will be on the contribution of the Old Testament to a spiritual paradigm of times and seasons.

A.1 TIME BY THE MOON

Awareness of the passage of time is a universal human experience. Looking at the moon must also rank as a universal cross-cultural experience because the moon outshines weather, oceans and ecology as a common environmental feature. The way that a culture perceives the moon will be a significant item for cross-cultural comparison.[1] In the Near East, the moon was a deity worshipped along with the sun and stars by all Semitic peoples, as well as by non-Semitic peoples such as the Sumerians, Hittites, Hurrians and Egyptians with whose cultures the Semitic peoples interacted.[2]

To us, the moon is where the Apollo astronauts left their boot prints. With bounding gait across the grey dusty moonscape, they demonstrated the reduced gravity on the moon's surface. The 1969 view of earth from moon literally brought home via TV what Galileo, Newton and Einstein had been talking about with the aid of their telescopes and equations. Seeing was believing and more emotional. The Apollo film and posters enhanced our appreciation of the moon and earth's aesthetic beauty hanging in

---

[1] Theories and superstitions about the influence of the moon (e.g. in 'lunacy') or solar and lunar eclipses are two fields in which cultures exhibit a variety of colourful ideas, ritual activities and symbolism.

[2] Compare the statement in Deuteronomy: 'And when you look up to the heavens and see the sun, the moon, and the stars, all the host of heaven, do not be led astray and bow down to them and serve them, things that the LORD has allotted to all the peoples everywhere under heaven. '(Deut 4:19)

the blackness of space. The Moon was demythologized, but poetry did not suffer a geologic extinction.

The Psalmist wonders at the splendour and immensity of the night sky—

> When I look at your heavens, the work of your fingers,
> the moon and the stars that you have established;
> what are human beings that you are mindful of them,
> mortals that you care for them?
>
> (Psa 8:3f)

But the moon had a utilitarian role in Israel as well as providing aesthetic delight. The moon marked the passage of time and supplied a twelve–month calendar.[3] 'You have made the moon to mark the seasons', remarks the psalmist in his review of life on earth.[4] The day/night sequence of sun and moon sets the clock for patterns of work and sleep, but there was a longer unit of time than daylight and darkness which was also set by sunset and moonrise—the month. The moon began this unit by the appearance of its first visible crescent after sunset. This new moon was the month's beginning.[5] To full moon there were fourteen days and its waning came after another two weeks.[6] Besides the

---

[3] For the moon as a symbol of a fixed order, see Jer 31:35. The duration of the monarchy is compared with the constant existence of the moon in Psa 72:5—'as long as the moon, throughout all generations', and Psa 89:37 speaking of the dynasty—'it shall be established for ever like the moon, an enduring witness in the skies'.

[4] Psa 104:19 *ʿāśāh yārēaḥ lᵉmôʿadīm*, or perhaps reading the vowels of the Participle (*ʿōśēh*) with BHS and Allen, which adds a polemic nuance—'You are the one who made the moon to show the seasons' (LC Allen, *Psalms 101–150*, WBC 21 (Waco: Word) 1983, p.27 note 19a. The moon is given the A-line, and the Sun the B-line probably for two reasons: the calendar was lunar, and the poem moves through sunset in v.19b to the darkness of night in v.20.

[5] Word studies support the long history and importance of lunar concepts in Mesopotamia. The Sumerian term *u₄-sakar* meaning 'house/chapel/station of the crescent' is known from around 2300 BC and was borrowed into Semitic as *uskaru* or *askaru* with the meaning 'crescent'—see WW Hallo, 'New Moons and Sabbaths: a case-study in the contrastive approach' *HUCA* 48 (1977) 1–18, p.4 and *AHw*, p.1438 *usk/qāru, ask/qāru*— „(Mond-)Sichel". In lexical lists, the scribes equated Sumerian *u₄-sakar* with Akkadian *arḫu, ūm arḫu*—'moon, day of the moon' that is 'new moon'. In Akkadian *arḫu* also means 'month' (*AHw* p.1466f *(w)arḫu* „Mond;Monat"). In Hebrew the same close association of 'month' and 'new moon' is observed. The noun *ḥōdeš*—'new moon/month' is probably based on the idea of the moon renewing itself: *ḥiddēš*—'to renew, make new', the Piel of the root *ḥdš*. For the moon in the Old Testament, see the useful overview by Clements in GJ Botterweck & H Ringgren (eds), *Theological Dictionary of the Old Testament*, Vol VI (Grand Rapids: Eerdmans) 1990, pp.355–362 under *yārēaḥ*.

[6] The synodic lunar month, from new moon to new moon, which is the basis for calendar reckoning, lasts 29 days, 12 hours, 44 minutes, 3 seconds, making a 12 month lunar year of roughly 354 days, that is 11 days short of the solar

seasonal pattern governed by the sun and the monthly pattern
governed by the moon, there was a point when sun and moon
shared equal parts of light and darkness, the days of the spring and
autumn equinox. These equinoxes divided the year into two
sections of six months each. Cohen points to the parallel rituals in
the first and seventh months in Mesopotamia and speaks of a six-
month equinox year that 'appears to have been a major factor in
the establishment of the cultic calendar throughout the Near
East'.[7]

Whether or not Cohen is right about the equinox, the cult and a
six-month cycle, we move to sure ground when we inquire about
counting time in months. Over four thousand years ago the lunar
months, grouped into a calendar, went by various names according to language, region and era. From 2600 BC an early Semitic
version spread as widely as from Syria to northern Iraq using
month names such as 'Sheep' and 'Ploughing', based on farming
activities.[8] Political and administrative unification eventually com-
pressed the variants from city-state cults into what is now called
the Standard Mesopotamian calendar whose month names we can

---

year. The month begins with first visibility after sunset of the new crescent
moon. Babylonians called months 'full' or 'hollow', meaning they were
reckoned at 30 days or 29. The sequence of 12 months had fixed names, so the
lunar year was re-aligned with the 365 day solar year by adding in a repeat of a
month name from time to time. Inter-calation, as this is called, is better
documented in Babylonia than in the Old Testament. By inter-calation,
Judaism managed to keep key religious festivals in their place in the solar-
agricultural year. Thus Passover night is prescribed for Nisan 14 which is the
full moon of the 'first month ' (Exod 12:2). But Nisan as the first month (mid
March–April in our calendar) needs to keep in step with spring and the vernal
equinox, so a second Adar (the month before Nisan) was added when
necessary.

[7] ME Cohen, *The Cultic Calendars of the Ancient Near East* (Bethesda: CDL
Press) 1993, p. 6. He finds references to the autumn and spring equinoxes as
turning points in the Hebrew year in Exod 34:22 (the Feast of Ingathering in
autumn at the 'turn of the year' *t̊qūfat haššānā*) and 2 Sam 11:1 ('at the turn of
the year, the season when kings go out [to battle]', ie. spring). See F.
Rochberg-Halton and JC Vanderkam, 'Calendars' *Anchor Bible Dictionary I*
(New York: Doubleday) 1992, p. 810ff for a recent and accessible discussion.

[8] It is said that two forms of 12-month calendar can be reconstructed from the
economic tablets of 3rd millennium Ebla. Seven of the 12 month names from
the 'Old Calendar' at Ebla are known from Mari texts which predate Sargon
the Great. This overlap between Ebla and Mari suggests that the 12-month
pattern is older than the local variants and predates 2500 BC. See now Cohen,
Cultic Calendars, pp. 23ff with reference to the earlier discussions of Ebla
material by G. Pettinato and I. Gelb, and of Mari material by D. Charpin.

recognize in their Hebrew forms.[9] The connection between month and moon—not as obvious in English—is evident in the Hebrew words *yārēaḥ*—'moon' and *yeraḥ* —'month', as well as in the cognate Semitic languages.[10]

A.2 DEMYTHOLOGIZING TIME

The Creation account, like Psalm 104, demotes the sun and moon. No longer are they deities. They are timekeepers for humankind:

> And God said, 'Let there be lights in the dome of the sky to separate the day from the night, and let them be for signs and for seasons and for days and years, and let them be lights in the dome of the sky to give light upon earth.' And it was so. God made the two great lights—the greater light to rule the day and the lesser light to rule the night—and the stars. God set them in the dome of the sky to give light upon the earth, to rule over the day and over the night, and to separate the light from the darkness.
>
> (Gen 1:14–18)[11]

This radical demythologization is easily overlooked by contemporary readers, but it stands out against the background of Near Eastern polytheism where personal roles are ascribed to the sun,

---

[9] See Cohen, *Cultic Calendars*, pp. 297ff for a full discussion of when the Standard Mesopotamian Calendar emerges—somewhere between 1750 and 1000 BC, probably beginning in the reign of the Amorite dynasty king of Babylon, Samsuiluna in the 18th century BC. The Babylonian names are *nisānu, ayāru, simānu, du'ūzu, abu, elūlu, tešrītu, araḫ-samna, kislīmu, ṭebītu, šabāṭu, addaru* which appear in Judaism as *niysān, 'iyyar, siywān, tammuz, ab, elul, tišriy, mar, ḥeswān, kislēw, ṭebet, šᵉbāṭ, ᵃdār*, seven of which are mentioned in the Old Testament. The Old Testament also reflects Canaanite names of the month such as *'ābīb, ziw,'ētānīm* and *būl*. When it comes to interpreting the chronological data of the Old Testament and converting them to our Julian dates, there is ample room for disagreement and much ingenuity exercised- —for a recent hypothesis invoking computer technology, see G Larsson, 'Ancient Calendars Indicated in the Old Testament' *JSOT* 54 (1992) 61–76.

[10] Compare Akkadian cognate *warḫu* or *arḫu*—'month, moon' (*AHw*, 1466). The moon god at Ugarit is *Yāriḫ*, who is male, and appears at Mari and Hazor as the variant *Eraḫ*—W Horowitz & A Shaffer 'An Administrative Tablet from Hazor: a preliminary edition' *IEJ* 42:1–2 (1992) 21–33, p.30f. The Moon god is male in Sumer, Babylon and Assyria as well.

[11] Some commentators think the use of 'greater light' and 'lesser light' marks a deliberate choice to omit 'sun' and 'moon' and so add insult to injury against polytheism. That aside, the detail devoted to the Fourth Day is quantitatively significant and weights it theologically.

moon and stars.[12] The names by which godMoon was known and worshipped in the Fertile Crescent varied from group to group, but it would be a startling event to discover an ethnic group without moon worship, given its documentation in the regions which have left written material and religious images.

The Babylonian Creation story *Enūma eliš* illustrates this religion of moon and calendar. The myth is really a propaganda piece promoting Marduk of Babylon. It was likely composed in the seven-tablet form in which we know it in the Middle Babylonian period towards the end of the 2nd millennium in the time of Nebuchadnezzar I, though it incorporates elements from earlier mythologies.[13] It was recited to Marduk's cult-statue as a New Year hymn. In this Creation epic, Marduk is credited with fixing the calendar. At New Year the destinies for the next year were determined by the Divine Council, but the calendar was more basic than the Council decisions in the sense that the calendar regulated the cult and hence the festivals in which all the gods had their prayers and offerings. It advances Marduk's claim to supremacy among the gods for him to fix the calendar at the Creation of the world.

We quote from the epic at the point where the warrior Marduk has killed Tiamat, goddess Sea, who threatened a take-over of the Divine Assembly. He slices her corpse in half and forms the sky

---

[12] For instance, in Mesopotamia the Moon god Nanna visited the Underworld where he acted as a judge. He also played a role in fertility, participating in a sacred marriage ritual at Ur where the high-priestess enacted the role of goddess Ningal, the Moon god's wife—see *Treasures of Darkness*, p.122ff.

[13] Nebuchadnezzar's dates are 1125–1104 BC. Babylon rose to prominence politically under Hammurabi (1848–1806) in the Old Babylonian period, but no tablet copy or other hard evidence for the myth has come to light from that period. WG Lambert's arguments for dating *Enūma eliš* to Nebuchadnezzar I are set out again in 'Studies in Marduk' *BSOAS* 47 (1984) 1–9, reviewing W Sommerfeld's *Die Aufstieg Marduks*, 1982. On Marduk's take-over of Ninurta's role, see Lambert's paper to the Rencontre assyriologique internationale 32 on 'Ninurta Mythology in the Babylonian Epic of Creation', pp.55–60 in K Hecker & W Sommerfeld (eds), *Keilschriftliche Literaturen*, Berlin Bei. zum Vorderen Orient 6, (Berlin: Dietrich Reimer) 1986. S Dalley argues for Amorite and West Semitic components in *Enūma eliš* and an earlier dating for Tablets 1–5 on the basis of titles for Marduk in the *An–Anum* text and a god-list from the Hittite capital, as well as Marduk's equation with the West Semitic storm deity Addu, more familiar from the Old Testament as Hadad, as in the name Ben-Hadad. She points out that the battle with Sea is a West Semitic motif, best known to us from the Ugaritic texts in the form of Baal's struggle with Yam. (*Myths from Mesopotamia* OUP, 1991, p.228ff). In any case, *Enūma eliš* in the form that we know it is a charter myth for Babylon linked to the spring New Year festival celebrated in the 2nd millennium.

out of one piece. Next he organizes cult shrines for Anu, Enlil and
Ea and then he fixes the calendar.[14]

> He fashioned stands for the great gods.
> As for the stars, he set up constellations corresponding to them.
> He designated the year and marked out its divisions,
> Apportioned three stars to each of the twelve months.
> When he had made plans of the days of the year,
> He founded the stand of Neberu[15] to mark out their courses,
> So that none of them could go wrong or stray.
> He fixed the stand of Ellil and Ea together with it,
> Opened up gates in both ribs,
> Made strong bolts to left and right.
> With her liver he located the Zenith;
> He made the crescent moon appear, entrusted night (to it)
> And designated it the jewel of night to mark out the days.[16]

---

[14] In other Mesopotamian traditions, the calendar was fixed by senior deities of
the Sumerian pantheon:

> When Anu, Enlil and Ea, the great gods,
> Had created heaven and earth, had made manifest the token
> Had established the 'stand', had fixed 'the station',
> Had appointed the gods of the night, had distributed the courses,
> Had [installed] stars as (astral) counterparts, had designed the 'images',
> Had [measured] the length of day and night, had created month and year,
> Had [ordered] the path for Sin and Shamash (and) had made the decrees concerning
> heaven and earth

Sin and Shamash are Moon and Sun god. The passage is translated and
discussed by B Landsberger and JV Kinnier-Wilson, 'The Fifth Tablet of
Enuma elish' *JNES* 20 (1961) 154–179, p.172.

[15] *nēberu* is the planet Jupiter, known as the 'star of Marduk' (*AHw*, 774). In
Tablet VII, the name *Nēberu* is conferred on Marduk with the wish 'May he
establish the paths of the heavenly stars, And may he shepherd all the gods like
sheep' (VII:130f, Dalley, p.272f). The stars are the deities under their astral
symbols led across the sky in regular order by Marduk's planet Jupiter—though other scholars think Mercury fits the astronomical picture better here
(Foster, *Muses*, p. 378 note 4 referring to a recent article by J Koch). Contrast
Yahweh's claim to this role of marshalling the stars as Commander-in-chief of
the heavenly armies (Isa 40:26).

[16] Line 12 opens : DINGIR SES.KI-ru which in normalized Akkadian reads
dNannaru, the name of the male moon deity (WG Lambert & SB Parker,
Enūma eliš the Babylonian Epic of Creation. The Cuneiform Text [Oxford: OUP]
1966, p.27). Lines 12–13 are aptly translated by Livingstone:

> He (Marduk) made Nannaru appear and entrusted to him the night.
> He designated him as the night's adornment, to define the days.

(A Livingstone, *Mystical and Mythological Explanatory Works of Assyrian and
Babylonian Scholars* [Oxford: Clarendon Press] 1986, p. 39). The Akkadian for
'night's adornment ' is *šuknat mūši* in which *šuknat* is the construct of
šukuttu—*AHw*, 1266, '„Ausstattung, Schmuck", 1(wertvolle) Ausstattung.'
In these lines, then, we have both mythology and metaphor. The moon is

'Go forth every month without fail in a corona,
At the beginning of the month, to glow over the land.
You shine with horns to mark out six days;
On the seventh day the crown is half.
The fifteenth day shall always be the mid-point, the half of each
    month.
When Shamash looks at you from the horizon,
Gradually shed your visibility and begin to wane.
Always bring the day of disappearance close to the path of Shamash,
And on the thirtieth day, the [year] is always equalized, for Shamash is
    (responsible for) the year . . .'[17]

What strikes one immediately about this passage is that 'the jewel
of night', the moon, fills an identical calendrical function in
Babylon as in Jerusalem but its mythological context propagates a
radically different ideology and theology. The same human
experience of time passing, of lunar months and solar cycles does
not lead to a common religious perspective on life.

We inherit planet Earth, the sun and the moon, and we inherit
from the ancient world some of the mathematics and mythology,
albeit in dead letter. The 'seasons', 'days' and 'years' of Gen 1: 14
and the 'twelve months' of *Enūma eliš* are still with us in our
calendar which links us with time and with times past. The
Christian week of seven days we seem to have inherited from
Judaism with Greek astronomical components.[18] Our days and
months, discounting their names, we owe indirectly to Greeks,

---

mythologized as god Nannaru, and described poetically as the 'adornment' or
'jewel' of the night.

[17] *Enūma eliš*, Tablet 5, line 1ff in the translation of Stephanie Dalley, *Myths from
Mesopotamia*, p.255f.; For another recent translation, see Foster, *Muses*, p. 378.
The Sun god 'is responsible for the year', but the Moon god for the month.
The twelve month calendar is thus a lunar-solar combination, or hybrid as we
might see it. On the relation between *šapattu* the day of full moon and
šabbāt—'the sabbath', see the later discussion.

[18] Astronomy and religion were a confused mixture in Babylon because stars
were equated with deities and hence mathematical astronomy emerged only
slowly out of religious astrology. The Greeks used seven planets in the
sequence Sun, Venus, Mercury, Moon, Saturn, Jupiter, Mars. When each is
allotted an hour of the day in this sequence starting with hour 1 on Day 1, the
planet which falls on hour 1 Day 1, hour 1 Day 2, etc gives us a run of 7 days
with the planet in hour 1 position giving its name to our day of the
week—thus Sun-day, Moon-day, Mars-day, Mercury-day, Jupiter-day,
Venus-day and Saturn-day (some names are closer in French). See Hallo 'New
Moons', p.17 fig.1.

Egyptians and Babylonians.[19] What about the twelve month cycle? What significance did Babylonians and Israelites attach to its inception, and why do we celebrate New Year?

B.1 NEW YEAR IN THE CULTIC CYCLE

Babylonian New Year was celebrated by reciting the Creation poem *Enūma eliš* to the statue of Marduk during the Akitu festival.[20] Babylonians believed that the destinies for the coming year were determined at this juncture by their gods meeting in Assembly. There is a longstanding academic debate about the influence that Babylonian New Year concepts had on the Israelite cult, or whether there are analogies with Babylonian practice in the way that New Year was celebrated in Israel rather than direct influence.[21] Old Testament scholars have postulated several

---

[19] Hellenistic astronomy divided the day into 24 hour parts of equal length by doubling the 12 parts inherited from late Babylonian astronomy. Because daylight hours vary with latitude and season, the concept of units of equal duration is not obvious, but a mathematical abstraction, enabling calculation and prediction to be done. Babylonian astronomers had divided their time of field activity between sunset to sunrise into 3 equal night watches of 2 *bēru*. The day was then added, allocated 6 equal parts, giving a total for day and night of 12 *bēru*. The Greeks chose to work with 24 units as a refinement. The Akkadian *bēru* is conventionally translated as 'double hour'. Details on the Babylonian contribution to the calendar via lunar observations and later astronomy are given in HWF Saggs, *The Greatness that was Babylon*[2nd rev.ed]. (Sidgwick & Jackson) 1988, p. 412–414 and *CAH III.2*, p.282f.

[20] Discussions by Assyriologists illustrate that different interpretations are still placed on the Babylonian material as well as on its comparability with the Yahwistic cult. WG Lambert thinks a cultic representation of Marduk's battle with Tiamat is likely, while van der Toorn does not. See Lambert, 'The Great Battle of the Mesopotamian Religious Year: the Conflict in the Akitu House' *Iraq* 25 (1963) 189–190; K van der Toorn 'The Babylonian New Year Festival: new insights from the cuneiform texts and their bearing on Old Testament study' pp.331–344 in JA Emerton (ed), *The Congress Volume Leuven 1989*, VTS 43, (Leiden: Brill) 1991; JA Black 'New Year Ceremonies in Ancient Babylon: "Taking Bel by the Hand" and a Cultic Picnic' *Religion* 11 (1981) 39–59. With translations of the relevant texts, Mark Cohen devotes a chapter to the history of the *Akītu* festival, identifying its 3rd millennium origins as a biannual equinox festival of the moon in Ur, adapted by various cities to celebrate the taking up of residence by their city-god, and in its late Babylonian version honouring Marduk and Nabu (*Cultic Calendars*, pp. 400–453).

[21] For judicious overviews of New Year and the Psalms, see DJA Clines 'New Year', *IDBSupp. Vol 5*, 1976, pp. 625–629 and 'Psalm Research since 1955: I. The Psalms and the Cult' *TB* 18 (1967) 103–126.

versions of an Israelite autumnal festival, not all of which are New Year festivals. Most of these link the renewal of dynastic kingship with renewal of God's enthronement as King, epitomized by the phrase in the psalms *Yhwh mālak*, meaning 'Yahweh reigns!', or 'Yahweh has become king!'. Some believe that this Hebrew phrase echoes the acclamation of Marduk— 'Marduk is king'—in *Enūma eliš*.[22]

Commentaries on the Psalms usually locate whole clusters of psalms in this New Year festival or else allocate them to an alternative festival such as a covenant renewal festival or a Zion festival.[23] Despite broad agreement with Mowinckel's dictum that to understand a psalm is to see it in its correct cultic setting,[24] scholars do not agree on the dynamic of the cult in Israel, whether there was cult drama or whether there was a concept of a cultic determining of fortunes for the year to come. Mowinckel represents one theory of cultic enactment with his statement—

> In the cult, the creative and saving events took place again and again, in regular recurrence. Life is a constant struggle between good and evil powers, between 'blessing' and 'curse', between 'life' and 'death'. In this struggle the powers of good must be renewed and strengthened,

---

[22] The phrase *Yhwh mālak* is characteristic of the so-called Enthronement Psalms which are identified as Pss 47, 93, 95–100. For a recent discussion of *Yhwh mālak* and the Enthronement psalms, see BC Ollenburger, *Zion, the City of the Great King: a theological symbol of the Jerusalem cult*, JSOTS 41 (Sheffield: JSOT) 1987, p. 24ff. The Babylonian enthronement of Marduk includes the whole proclamation of his 50 names in Tablet VII as well as acclaim of his kingship before and after the battle with Tiamat.

> When the gods his fathers saw how effective his utterance was,
> They rejoiced, they proclaimed: 'Marduk is king!',
> They invested him with sceptre, throne, and staff-of-office.
> S Dalley, *Myths from Mesopotamia*, p.250.
>
> (Tablet IV:27ff; *ANET*, 66; *Muses*, p. 372)

Compare too the post-battle sequence of acclamation with oath of allegiance in Tablet VI:95ff (Dalley, p.264; *ANET*, 503; *Muses*, p. 387).

[23] A 'moderate' approach to autumn Tabernacles as New Year is exemplified by AA Anderson, *The Book of Psalms Vol 1 & 2*, NCB, (London: Oliphants, Marshall, Morgan & Scott) 1972. He subsumes Weiser's postulated Covenant Festival and Kraus' Royal Zion festival within a New Year model—'These three festivals do not represent contradictory views, but rather various stages in the history of the great Autumn Festival and/or different aspects of it' (p.31). JH Eaton, *Kingship and the Psalms* (London: SCM) 1976 presses analogies with the humiliation ordeal of the Babylonian king and his reinstatement and speaks of the Davidic king's atoning role in the cult, which goes beyond what many scholars are willing to find in phrases which seem metaphorical but which Eaton takes as actual blows or humiliating effects.

[24] 'To understand a psalm means to see it in the right cultic connexion'—S Mowinckel, *The Psalms in Israel's Worship* (Oxford) 1962, p.34.

otherwise the world would perish. This renewal takes place in the cult.[25]

Mowinckel assumes rather than explains why an Israelite should have thought that 'the world would perish' if Yahweh's New Year enthronement was not celebrated. When Judah went into Babylonian Exile, the world as such very obviously did not perish. Mowinckel's statement, and others like it, tend to line up Israel's Yahweh cult with the cyclical and mythic qualities of the cult in Mesopotamia. This is unjustified, at least for orthodox Yahwism, though what happened in the Jerusalem Temple was seldom orthodox Yahwism in the view of Yahwism's canonical prophets and historians.

In Mesopotamia of the Neo-Babylonian period, though not necessarily before this era, the spring Akitu festival in Nisan is very definitely linked to Marduk's kingship, his regulation of the calendar and the determination of destinies at the New Year Assembly. The connection between the festival and the calendar is explicit in the ritual texts. On the 5th of Nisan in the middle of the festival, the king and šešgallu priest pray to astral manifestations of Marduk-Bel and his spouse.[26] In the late Babylonian era, the heliacal rising of stars, the spring equinox, the agricultural season of barley, Marduk's kingship and the year to come are linked together by a conglomeration of rituals and mythic traditions.[27] We gain the impression that the political dimensions of the New Year ritual have come to dominate their agricultural antecedents. The later Akitu festival legitimates Babylon and the king.[28]

The Nisan Akitu festival marked the beginning of the civil year. Marduk sitting on the 'Dais of Destinies' and the fixing of

---

[25] *The Psalms in Israel's Worship*, p. 113

[26] The main ritual texts are translated in *ANET*, 331–334. Others are needed to fill gaps—see the references (van der Toorn, p.332 note 4) to some available in G Cagirgan's Ph.D dissertation *Babylonian Festivals*, presented to Birmingham, 1976. The prayers to Bel and Beltiya on Nisan 5 are said appropriately during the night when the stars are out. Marduk is hailed as 'God of heaven and earth who decrees the fates'.

[27] JA Black makes a good case for the later Babylonian cultic events being composed by processes of accretion from previous Akitu rites and cultic traditions from different eras, cities and shrines. For instance, the god Nabu from the Ezida shrine of city Borsippa plays an important role in the Neo-Babylonian rites, making a special cult journey to Babylon.

[28] K van der Toorn sees it as a rite of passage involving transition through a temporary and marginal phase (liminality) that is symbolised by the siting of the Akitu chapel outside the urban centre. 'This renewal takes the form of a ritual process in which the old order is momentarily jeopardized, emerges intact, and is reaffirmed . . . The Akitu-festival is not concerned with the rebirth of nature . . . but to consolidation of some of the central values of Babylonian civilisation' (*Congress Volume*, p.339).

destinies for the year ahead in the Akitu ritual corresponds with the Tablet of Destiny motif in the Creation myth. In the myth, Marduk retrieved the Tablet of Destiny from the rebel commander-in-chief, Qingu, and hung it around his own neck after he had killed Tiamat and captured her forces.[29] The Nisan Akitu rites and the Creation myth do conjoin myth and ritual, but enthusiasts of the myth and ritual school have pressed beyond the evidence warranted by both the Babylonian and the biblical material.[30] To sum up positively, we can underline that in Babylonia the calendar, and hence the whole concept of time that went with it, was cultic, ritual, and mythicized for political legitimation.[31] In Israel, hard evidence is lacking for a cultic determination of destiny at New Year. Indeed, the whole content of a postulated Autumn New Year festival in Israel remains a matter of inference and analogy, though some analogies seem to have a high degree of plausibility.[32]

Accompanying this debate about festival, kingship and cultic dynamics tied in to a 12–month cycle has been the debate about Israel's perception of time as linear rather than cyclical. At the time of the Biblical Theology movement of the 1950s onwards, when Old Testament scholars were seeking to restate the distinctiveness of Israel's Yahwistic faith against its polytheistic environment, a catch–phrase was 'the God who acts'.[33] This emphasized that

---

[29] Tablet III, Dalley, p.248.

> He (Marduk) defeated him (Qingu) and counted him among the dead gods,
> Wrested from him the Tablet of Destinies, wrongfully his,
> Sealed it with (his own) seal and pressed it to his breast.
> (Tablet IV, Dalley, p.254; Muses, p. 376, line 119ff)

[30] Compare the cautious and accurate studies by WG Lambert 'Myth and Ritual as Conceived by the Babylonians' *JCS* 13 (1968) 104–112 and 'Old Testament Mythology in its Ancient Near Eastern Context', pp. 124–143 in JA Emerton (ed), *Congress Volume Jerusalem, 1986* SVT 40 (Leiden: Brill) 1988.

[31] I discussed theology and self-legitimation from a Babylonian starting point in 'Nebuchadnezzar's Theology and Ours', pp. 12–30 in A Billington, T Lane and M Turner (eds), *Mission and Meaning* (Carlisle: Paternoster) 1995.

[32] JH Eaton's words illustrates how a leap from motif and analogy is made to cult and liturgical content: 'Nothing from the foreign worship should be read into the Israelite, but the Bit Akitu ritual does help us to see how a god's kingship and epiphany, his triumph over water and other foes, his creating, judging, saving and providing could form a pattern and supply content to the principal annual festival of a kingdom.' (*Kingship and the Psalms*, SCM, 1976, p.105)

[33] Two books from GE Wright typify the reaction of the Biblical Theology movement—*The God who Acts: biblical theology as recital*, SBT 8 (London: SCM) 1952 and *The Old Testament against its Environment*, SBT 1 (London: SCM) 1950. The deficits of exaggerating Israelite distinctives was pointed out by B Albrektson, collecting texts showing polytheistic examples of the gods acting in historical events—*History and the Gods: an essay on the idea of historical events as divine manifestations in the Ancient Near East and in Israel*, Coniectanea

Yahweh disclosed himself in unique historical events such as the Exodus, not in the seasonal cycle of the fertility cult. This polarized nature and history, cult and revelation, myth and truth. It tied Yahweh to linear time and history, and thought of Israel's cult as recital of the historical deeds of Yahweh.[34] As with many reactionary movements, the shortcomings of the debate lay more with what was omitted or denied than with what Biblical Theology affirmed.

In retrospect, it seems that Israel's experience of time was both linear and cyclical. Ours is today. Of course, 'cyclical' cannot be equated with mythical or with cult-dramatic or with liturgical. Any discussion of cyclical and linear needs to spell out what the theological or ideological nuances are of recurrent events and one-off events. All human experience will include both the linearity of time involved in the ageing process, and the cyclical quality of time in the biology of sleep and work, hunger and eating and the menstrual cycle.

When we turn back to Israel's distinctive expression of the ritual cycle and the experience of Salvation History, we are confronted with the Passover rite. This stamps the calendar with a cultic festival that commemorates a one-off, non-recurrent, linear time event. The Passover festival of Exodus is in essence historical, whatever its agricultural antecedents may have been.[35] This comes through forcefully in the text:

This month shall mark for you the beginning of months (*rō'š ḥᵒdāšîm*); it shall be the first (*rī'šōn*) month of the year for you.

(Exod 12:2)

Biblica OT series 1 (Lund: CWK Gleerup) 1967. Wright wanted to rescue Israel's faith from existentialism, mysticism, fundamentalism and systematic theology at the same time.

[34] The tussle over time and its distinctives in Biblical Theology was played out in the Greek versus New Testament domain more than in Old Testament studies, and ten years after Wright's book James Barr entered the hermeneutical debate over word studies and semantics with *Biblical Words for Time*, SBT 33 (London: SCM) 1962. SJ de Vries offered *Yesterday, Today and Tomorrow: time and history in the Old Testament* (London: SPCK) 1975 to the Old Testament debate, but the density of reference and attempt at comprehensiveness compared with yield in clarity and conclusion weighed against this contribution.

[35] It is commonly thought that Passover/Unleavened Bread/Firstborn displaces a pagan agricultural or flock festival of the spring period. The arguments are plausible but not compelling. Along the lines of Christmas displacing a winter solstice festival and Easter a spring fertility festival, Passover–Unleavened Bread–Firstborn may have displaced indigenous cult rites by using some of the same physical elements but investing them with a new symbolism based on associations with the Exodus liberation.

The force of the wording appears to be that Nisan is not simply the beginning of the calendar year, but that it will mark the most important month—principal month as well as initial month.[36] The lunar month which is cyclical is set in the lunar year which is cyclical, yet the cultic event celebrated annually is not cyclical but linear. It is punctiliar in terms of what it commemorates—a one-off historical event. It is also punctiliar theologically in the sense that it fits into a promise-fulfilment series as one element, one step in taking Israel from Egypt to Promised Land.[37]

B.2 ELLIPTICAL ORBITS AND THE FOOD CYCLE

The year of twelve lunar months fell short by about 11 days of the earth's 365–day orbital period around the sun. The solar year with its regular pattern of equinox and solstice came to dominate because it regulates agriculture better. Sunlight, not moonlight, correlates the seasons of planting, rain and growth-time relevant to agriculture. This link between the passage of time and the agricultural cycle is made explicit in the Genesis Flood story. In the phase of re-creation after the Flood, Yahweh's promise takes this form:

> As long as the earth endures,
> seedtime and harvest, cold and heat,
> summer and winter, day and night
> shall not cease.
>
> (Gen 8:22)

---

[36] A point made by JI Durham, *Exodus*, WBC 3 (Waco: Word) 1987, p.153—'connected to the annual calendar, but . . . surely an affirmation of the theological importance of Yahweh's Passover . . . The Passover month is the "head" of the months not primarily as the first month of the year in a calendar, either a "civil" calendar or a "religious" calendar, but because it is the month during which the Israelites remembered and so actualized their redemption.' On most reckonings 14th Nisan, Passover night, is full moon and near to spring equinox.

[37] Exod 19:1 likewise sets a one-off historical event—the arrival in the Sinai wilderness—in relation to the previous lunar cycles: 'On the third new moon after the Israelites had gone forth out of the land of Egypt, on that very day, they entered the wilderness of Sinai'—BS Childs, *Exodus* (London: SCM), 1974, p.340 and 342. If *ḥōdeš* in the prepositional phrase *baḥōdeš* means 'new moon', as it often does, then this verse specifies the day and month of time elapsed since leaving Egypt. It could alternatively simply specify three lunar months of elapsed time not calculated to the day of the New Moon's first crescent appearance. In either event, lunar and linear time are conjoined.

This pronouncement invites two comments. Firstly, this is a thoroughly demythologized concept of agriculture and fertility. By way of contrast, Near Eastern polytheism thought in terms of numerous deities manifest in the rains, crops, sunlight and the night. Secondly, our understanding of, though not our control over, weather systems and agriculture has advanced. For us, this verse points to the mathematical regularity of planetary orbits, and to solar solstice and equinox which fix seasons exactly. Yet human life on earth depends on more than elliptical orbits, as famine in Africa and flooding in Asia bear witness. Human experience will remain one that combines experience of the regular with experience of the unpredictable, and this holds true whether we are talking motorways, mutations, market forces or metereology.

Orthodox Yahwism waged a perennial battle with Baal worship and the fertility cult. Whether the sadly fragmented texts of the Baal myth from Ugarit have been restored to their original order and correctly interpreted as a mythologizing of the seasonal cycle is disputed,[38] but this in no way detracts from the radical struggle that took place between monotheistic Yahwism and the polytheistic fertility cult in Palestine. Elijah's contest with the prophets of Baal on Mount Carmel dramatized it. Hosea's denunciation of Baal religion as prostitution verbalized it. Rain and crops were not the gift of Baal. When the wilderness manna stopped, the crops of Canaan sufficed Israel (Josh 5). There is no suggestion in the Hebrew scriptures that the regularity of the seasons precluded the hard work of ploughing, sowing, reaping and threshing the grain, precluded dependence on Yahweh for the rain, or precluded acknowledgment of food as Yahweh's gift in

---

[38] The seasonal interpretation of the Baal material is strongly advocated by JC de Moor, *The Seasonal Pattern in the Ugaritic Myth of Ba'lu*, AOAT 16, Neukirchen 1971, and *New Year with Canaanites and Israelites*, Kamper Cahiers 21–22, Kampen, 1972 updated by *An Anthology of Religious Texts from Ugarit*, Nisaba texts (Leiden: Brill) 1987, pp.101–108 'Table of Seasonal Pattern in Baal'. Other scholars plausibly deny that there is an annual cycle of fertility and summer drought reflected in the mythic texts. They argue for a balance of the forces of life and death in nature, symbolized by Baal's struggles with Mot (Death) and Sea (Chaos). See, for instance, LE Toombs, 'Baal, Lord of the Earth: the Ugaritic Baal Epic', pp. 613–623 in CL Myers & M O'Connor (eds), *The Word of the Lord shall go forth* (Winona Lake: Eisenbrauns) 1983 and MS Smith, 'Interpreting the Baal Cycle', *Ugarit Forschungen* 18 (1986) 313–319.

the ceremonies of the first-fruits.[39] Spirituality and food production were interwoven.

C.1 SABBATH

Turning from the annual cycle and the seasons back to the shorter cycle of the week, we must focus on the symbolism involved in this time span of six days plus one. The week uses a 7 base. This is not obvious mathematically. The lunar month, for instance, is not divisible by 7 so the Hebrew month was not made up of four weeks of equal length. Most likely the week as such is Semitic, that is, the product of some number symbolism in which 7 occupies a privileged place, associated as it is with completeness.[40] This 7 symbolism appears to predate our written records of Semitic culture.

The attempts to derive the Sabbath, the seventh day of Judaism, from Semitic culture or a lunar calendar are not realistic, despite the tempting etymology. In Babylonian, *šapattu* means 'full moon' or as a numeral in a lunar calendar, 'day 15'.[41] It may share a

---

[39] This is forcefully stated by Deuteronomy, e.g. Deut 8 on the regular water supply of Palestine and Deut 26 with its firstfruits ceremony.

[40] Five and ten correspond to fingers, four to directions at right angles, but the background for seven is not obvious from outside Semitic culture. In Mesopotamia, many things came in sevens. The tendency to relate 7 to primal events is evident in *Atraḥasīs*. There are 14 pieces of clay are divided into 7 on the left and 7 on the right for making mankind. Twice seven birth-goddesses assemble. Seven produced males, seven produced females. The birth brick is to be left in place for seven days during confinement rites. The Flood arrives on the 7th night after Enki's tip-off, determined by clock, and the Flood storm lasts 7 days and 7 nights (*Atraḥasīs* I:255–258; S iii:5–15, III i:36f, iv:24f—Lambert & Millard, p.60–63, 90f, 96f; Dalley, p. 16f,30, 33). In *Enūma eliš*, Marduk uses the 7 Winds he creates to overwhelm Tiamat (Tablet IV: 47, Dalley, p. 251) and after the building of Babylon and Marduk's shrine Esagila 'The fifty great gods were present, and/ The gods fixed the seven destinies for the cult' (VI:8of, Dalley, p.263). The Seven (*dSebetti*) are sometimes wind demons (*AHw*, 1033 *sebe*) who may be identified with the 7 Evil Spirits of the Incantation texts known as *Utukkū lemnūti* (published by RC Thompson, *The Devils and Evil Spirits of Babylonia*, 2 vols., Luzac:London, 1903). The *dSebetti* are later identified with the Pleiades. In cylinder seals dating back to the 3rd millennium, there are 7 astral dots, thought to represent divination lots but later equated with the Pleiades—ED van Buren 'The Seven Dots in Mesopotamian Art and their Meaning' *AfO* 13 (1939–41) 277–289. There were 7 antediluvian Sages (*apkallu*). This is a sample of Mesopotamian 7 symbolism.

[41] *AHw*, 1172 „15.Monatstag,Vollmond". In *Atraḥasīs*, the fifteenth day of the month is one specified by Enki for a ritual bath, along with the first and seventh day: 'On the first, seventh, and fifteenth day of the month/ I will make a purifying bath' (*ina arḥi sebūti u šapatti*—Tablet I: 206f and .221f; Lambert & Millard, 56f & 58f; Dalley, 15). In the phrase *ina arḥi sebūti u šapatti, sebūtu* is a numeral (7), but *arḥu* is 'month,moon' doing duty for a numeral ('the 1st of the month', ie. new moon), while *šapattu* is 'full moon' or in number

common etymological derivation with Hebrew *šabbāt* 'sabbath', but that is all. There is no shared meaning between Hebrew *šabbāt* and Babylonian *šapattu*. It is obvious that there are not four full moons per month, nor is there one sabbath in the middle of the month.[42] We must look for the religious significance of the Hebrew sabbath in a different direction than an origin in appeasement of the Moon god.

What the Old Testament does share with Babylonia is the writing up of Creation and Flood in ways that relate them to contemporary experience. Where *Atraḥasīs* connects purification rites and birth rituals to the creation of humankind, the Old Testament relates Creation to its sabbath observance. The word is 'relates' because the author does not explicitly equate the seventh day of creation with the sabbath. From the author's viewpoint, this would have been an anachronism because the sabbath day was officially inaugurated as a cultic event after the Exodus by the 4th Commandment.

By avoiding the explicit use of the word *haššabbāt*—'the sabbath' in Gen 1, the author connects the later sign of the Sinai covenant with the Creation of the world implicitly. In Genesis, we read:

> Thus the heavens and the earth were finished, and all their multitude.
> And on the seventh day God finished the work that he had done, and
> he *sabbathed* on the seventh day from all the work that he had done. So
> God blessed the seventh day and hallowed it, because on it God
> *sabbathed* from all the work that he had done in creation.
>
> (Gen 2:1–3)

Three times 'the seventh day' is mentioned. God's activity on this 'seventh day' is cultic, or as we might say, 'spiritual', that is confined to blessing and consecrating.[43] Apart from this spiritual activity, God 'sabbaths'. In English, there is no word-play

---

terminology, day 15 of the month. It is a good illustration of how closely counting days by numeral (calendar) and lunar phases correlate in Mesopotamian culture, and how calendar and cult tie in together. The myth is etiological, that is, it explains the origin of a contemporary ritual practice—
—purifying lustrations—in terms of primeval decree of the gods.

[42] The article by WW Hallo is a very careful review of this controversial debate by a competent cuneiformist—'New Moons and Sabbaths: a case-study in the contrastive approach' *HUCA* 48 (1977) 1–18.

[43] Cultic in the sense that *qdš*, Piel 'to sanctify, consecrate, make holy, dedicate' is an activity associated with priestly acts and cultic procedures. Blessing is a wider term, but also associated with Aaron's high-priestly blessing in Num 6 where 'bless' is both God's action and Aaron's—v.23, 24, 27.

between 'stopping' and 'sabbath'—but no Israelite could have missed the word-play in Gen 2:2–3.[44]

The first association of the 'seventh day' in Genesis is stopping from work, which is explicit.[45] There is more to it than that. God 'sabbaths' as a primal response to the success of a 'very good' week. The quality control phrase ('God saw that it was good') has been a recurrent motif in the chapter, matching the phases of creation.[46] This is capped with the superlative at the end of the Day Six inspection—'very good' (Gen 1:31). This sevenfold satisfaction with the goodness of creation is augmented by the blessing and hallowing of Day Seven. So the blessing of Day Seven does not stand alone in the account. It recalls the previous pronouncements of blessing—on Day Five of creatures, and on Day Six of Man and Woman (1:21,28). Thus what happens on Day Seven gathers up the effects of the whole week. It is not the consecration of a numeral. It is not punctiliar, a focus on a full stop, but a reflection on the meaning of the whole sentence.

Genesis 1 is primal in another sense, a theological sense. Creation is the work of one God who is the universal God, not a tribal God or a national deity. If the seventh day of Genesis 1 sets a precedent for the sabbath and the national covenant, does it also carry a trans-Israelite, cross-cultural message? Does this perception of time, of the working week, relate to humankind and always so? Is Genesis 1 a product of Hebrew culture or a model for

---

[44] The author of Exod 16:29f explicitly links the verb *šābat* with the noun *šabbāt* and in the Genesis 1 Creation account there is no controverting the sound-play, which is all that is needed to establish author's intention. The sabbath is *šabbāt, yōm haššabbāt*—'the sabbath', 'the sabbath day'. The verb is *šābat*—'to cease, stop'. A good example of the verbal meaning is provided by Gen 8:22 where '. . . day and night shall not cease' (*lōʾ yišbōtū*). Some dispute lingers over the philology of *šabbāt*. The attempt to link it with *šebaʿ*—'seven' is unconvincing. On the philology and the failure of many pan-Babylonian hypotheses on the origin of the Sabbath, including those which start from *šapattu*, or festivals in clusters of 7 days, see N-EA Andreasen, *The Old Testament Sabbath*, SBLDS 7 (Missoula: Univ of Montana Press) 1972, p. 94ff on etymology and p.1ff on the history of *šapattu/šabbāt*.

[45] Gen 2:2–3 has *min*—'from' twice with the verb *šabat*. This supports a basic sense of 'stopping' rather than resting, as G Robinson argues ('The Idea of Rest in the Old Testament and the Search for the Basic Character of Sabbath' *ZAW* 92 (1980) 32–42). But because dictionary meanings and etymological roots do not supply discourse meaning, the word comes to mean what it means by processes of development and association. There is a natural association between stopping activity and relaxation or taking a holiday. The Creation account exploits this association. REB sticks to the narrower meaning in its translation—'he ceased from all the work', whereas NRSV renders it 'rested from'.

[46] Gen 1:4,10,12,18,21,25—that is, 6 occurrences up to and including the creation of the beasts of the earth on Day 6.

a universal spirituality? This type of hermeneutical debate is preliminary to a model of spirituality based on the Old Testament.

If Judaism retains the sabbath and Christianity departs from it, does New Covenant spirituality also dispense completely with sacred time? After all, it dispenses with sacred place—the Temple, so why not with all the features of the cult, including all festivals and calendars and markers of the passage of time? The fact that 'sacred time' still divides Christians shows that this debate is a lively and practical one with implications for lifestyle.[47]

C.2 SABBATH AS TIME MARKER, GIFT, COMMAND AND SYMBOL

We have noticed that Genesis sets the Seventh Day apart from Days 1–6 in a way that associates it with Israel's working week and covenant sabbath. The difference, of course, is that God stops on the seventh day in Genesis, whereas Israelites stop on the seventh, fourteenth, twenty-first and twenty-eighth, that is, on the sabbath. The Creation account is composed within an existing Semitic culture which supplied the seven as a symbol of completeness, but not, as far as we know, the blueprint for a seven-day week. Working from within an Israel already in covenant with God and familiar with the sabbath as a sign of covenant, the Genesis author modelled his Creation account on the Israelite experience of time and work.[48] To apply this model to the Creator was a bold anthropomorphism. It was bold because it locked God into a diurnal work pattern, stopping overnight and resuming the next day. It was also bold because it drew such a clear line after Day Six that God might have seemed detached from any concept of continuous creation.[49]

---

[47] Ecclesiastical politicking centred on calendar and cult is very old. It is in evidence in the Dead Sea Scrolls in the disputes between the Qumran community and those running the Jerusalem temple, and in the Book of Jubilees with its maverick solar calendar. The bitter controversies in the early church over the mode and date of Easter celebration continue the story into the Christian era.

[48] One could argue that cult legitimation is the motive for associating the last day in the week of Creation with the nation's weekly routine and marker of covenant. There is, no doubt, some truth in this perspective, but it is not a sufficient and adequate account of the theology of Gen 1 nor of the author's intention related to the whole Creation story which is not that easily reduced to sacerdotal nationalism. As we see it, the author of Gen 1 deliberately avoided using *haššabbāt* or *yōm haššabbāt*, or appending the kind of editorial footnote of the kind we meet with in Gen 2:24, which explains contemporary marriage custom etiologically.

[49] In fact, Mesopotamia and Israel thought of each human gestation and birth as God's act of creating as well as his making of the first humans by a special creative act.

For Israel, the seventh day was a gift, a sign, a symbol and a commandment. The manna experience before Sinai offers a preview. Israelites are commanded to collect double manna on day Six and suspend food-gathering and cooking on the seventh day. The motivation is to keep the seventh day holy to Yahweh (Exod 16:23–30).[50] When some Israelites ignore the instructions, go looking for manna on the sabbath and find none, Moses admonishes them and emphasizes the gift aspect of the sabbath:

> See! The LORD has *given you* the sabbath, therefore on the sixth day he *gives you* food for two days.
>
> (Exod 16:29)[51]

The command to stop work and consecrate the seventh day to Yahweh is linked with God's generosity.

In the Ten Commandments of Exod 20, cessation of work is emphasized, using Creation as the motive clause.[52] There is no detail given of how the sabbath is to be consecrated —other than by stopping work. The effect is to construct a tight typology between God's primeval sabbath and its weekly recollection by Israelites. After all, God did not banquet, play music, dance, process, or receive praise, sacrifice and worship in the Heavenly

---

[50] Durham's translation of Exod 16:23 reflects the re-iteration of the *šbt* root: 'The sabbath-keeping of the sabbath holy to Yahweh is tomorrow' *šabbātōn šabbat-qōdeš lyhwh māḥār* (JI Durham, *Exodus*, WBC 3 (Waco: Word) 1987, p.22). *šabbātōn* is a noun derived from the verb and used to intensify so 'sabbathing' or 'sabbath institution' seems indicated: 'tomorrow is the sabbath-institution sabbath-of-holiness to Yhwh'. Less accurately, the NRSV introduces 'rest' into its translation—'Tomorrow is a day of solemn rest, a holy sabbath to the LORD'. Stopping work and being provided with a double portion on day six which lasts through day seven amounts to a rest day, but does not supply the whole content of what it means to consecrate the day as Yahweh's.

[51] The verb *nātan* is used twice which underlines the giving factor by putting the gift of a double-portion in parallel with the gift of the sabbath. The verb *nātan* can mean 'to appoint, set' but the parallelism here turns away from the bureaucratic nuance of 'appoint' to the gift nuance emphasising generosity

[52] In Exod 20:8–11 there are 55 words in Hebrew. Verses 8 and 10a, using 10 words, enunciate the general principle of consecrating the sabbath by acknowledging God's ownership of it . Verses 9 and 10b use 19 words to specify details about work. Verse 11 is the motive clause describing creation using 26 words. That 26 out of 55 words are devoted to the Creation model as motivation is an indication of theological weighting. There are also motive clauses appended to the 2nd Commandment (vv. 5b–6), the 3rd Commandment (v. 7b) and the 5th Commandment (v.12b), but none of these use God as a model. Subsequently, Exod 23:12 provides a humanitarian motive clause while Exod 34:21 and 35:2f reiterate the prohibition of work and add a death penalty as motivation.

Court on the seventh day of Creation.[53] So none of these elements of keeping a day holy to Yahweh appear in the sabbath commandments—only stopping work. Other festivals did include processions, meals and psalms.

Compared with the Exodus version, Deut 5 both omits material and augments the Fourth Commandment. It omits the creation model altogether and substitutes the Exodus liberation as its model for conduct. If God freed Israelites from slavery, they should compel no human being, Israelite or alien, and no animal, to slave seven days a week.[54]

Sabbath as sign of covenant is also enunciated in terms of creation and enforced with death penalty and 'cutting off'.

> You shall keep my sabbaths, for this is a *sign* between me and you throughout your generations, given in order that you may know that I, the LORD, sanctify you . . . therefore the Israelites shall keep the sabbath, observing the sabbath throughout their generations, *as a perpetual covenant*. It is a *sign* for ever between me and the people of Israel, for in six days the LORD made heaven and earth, and on the seventh day he sabbathed and was refreshed.
>
> (Exod 31:13,16f)[55]

The sabbath joins the rainbow and circumcision as a sign of covenant.[56] As a sign it functions as a symbol, something that

---

[53] Perhaps this contrast with *Enūma eliš* is part of the polemic, or simply an effect of the pared–down style of the Genesis 1 Creation account. The Heavenly Court is probably implicit in Genesis 1, and certainly is in Gen 2–3 where cherubim appear and 'lest he become like one of us' is spoken. See Wenham, *Genesis 1–15*, WBC 1 (Waco: Word) 1987, p.28 favouring the Heavenly Court concept in Gen 1, though commentators such as Clines and Westermann disagree with this and with each other.

[54] There is no conflict between Creation and Exodus models of Exod 20:8–11 and Deut 5:12–15. The motive clauses supplement each other. The tradition history of these versions of the 4th Commandment, and of the other references to the sabbath within Exodus and Deuteronomy is a special subject of its own and is reflected in the tradition-history approach of Andreasen's monograph and discussed by the major commentaries. For our purposes, the canonical form and order is sufficient guide for theological discussion.

[55] The NRSV translation is emended here. In v.17a NRSV makes the sabbath a sign 'that in six days . . .'. Instead, this is a motive clause introduced, as normal, by 'because' (*kīy*)—drawing the analogy between God and Israelite practice. NRSV renders v.17b as 'he rested, and was refreshed' (*šābat wayinnāpaš*). More accurately, 'sabbathed' here means 'stopped' while the relaxation element belongs to the second verb *npš*—Niph. 'to draw breath, refresh oneself'. God stopped in order to draw breath. So REB—'he ceased work and refreshed himself'. Nevertheless, this verse demonstrates the close association of ideas between sabbathing and renewal.

[56] The same Hebrew word *'ōt* is used in Gen 9:13 and Gen 17:11 in covenant-making contexts in which the rainbow and male circumcision function *lᵉ'ōt*—'for a sign' of the covenant relationship. Sabbath as a sign is also referred to in Ezek 20:12,20.

points beyond itself to another reality in which it participates. The sabbath is not the covenant. The covenant is the relationship. Yet without the sabbath, the covenant is broken and lacks this key external observable testimony.[57]

C.3 SABBATH AS PARADIGM, NOT BLUEPRINT

When the Israelite week of six days + 1 is enunciated as a commandment, it re-enacts the pattern of the primal week. Yet the sabbath is more than the marking of the passage of time according to the primal blueprint. It introduces into the passage of time the qualities of divine–human relationship in a way that the phases of the lunar month did not. In the end it is not the 6+1 week that claims our attention, original and distinctive of Israel as this appear to be,[58] but the resonance of the God–mankind link. The highly original *imitatio dei* whereby Israelites model themselves on Yahweh's stopping of work has a long trajectory in biblical theology and is exploited typologically as a divine rest conferred on the New Covenant community by the letter to the Hebrews.[59] Within Israel, other elements of the blessing and spiritualizing of time associated with the sabbath come to the fore as well. Re-enactment of creation is one dimension, divine gift is another, but sabbath as covenant-sign becomes fundamental.[60]

The fundamental meaning of Sabbath for Israel was stopping to acknowledge Yahweh as Lord. By interrupting the flow of work, this recognition of Yahweh's covenant partnership acknowledged his lordship over the Israelite's time as well. The Jewish scholar Matitiahu Tsevat has brought 'The Basic Meaning of the Biblical

---

[57] Since Moses' rod, the Pillar of Cloud and Fire, the Ark of the Covenant, the Tabernacle and the High Priest's paraphernalia all contribute visual symbols of the covenant relationship, we should perhaps talk of the covenant relationship as trans-visible rather than invisible. In Exile with the cult destroyed and when stopping work was at the captor's whim, the rite of male circumcision may have been the only visible token of covenant.

[58] The rainbow covenant included humanity and animals. Circumcision was distinct in its symbolism in Israel, but not in its practice because other Near Eastern peoples practised male circumcision—the Egyptians at puberty, for instance. Sabbath, as far as we can tell, is both original with Israel and as distinctive as her national covenant with God.

[59] 'So then a sabbath rest still remains for the people of God', Heb 4:9.

[60] The sabbath law expresses God's humanitarian concerns—as attested by the Deuteronomy version of the 4th Commandment, but also by God's provision of sufficient to allow for stopping work and trade. The humanitarian dimension of the sabbath is invoked by Jesus when he says 'The sabbath is made for man, not man for the sabbath' (Mark 2:27). The sabbath as a wider principle applicable to letting fields lie fallow and to Jubilee legislation involving liberation of slaves and return of ancestral land continues this motif of divine provision. Work, land and food are linked in Yahwism through divine gift and sabbath keeping.

Sabbath' into clear focus. Creation and Exodus demonstrate the lordship of Yahweh. Stopping work relieves servants and live-stock. Yet Sabbath is more than desisting from work or recalling creation.

> Man normally is master of his time. He is free to dispose of it as he sees fit or as necessity bids him. The Israelite is duty-bound, however, every seven days to assert by word and deed that God is master of time. God's dominion over time parallels and complements that over the land.[61]

As Tsevat points out, other cultic events were linked to the rhythm of nature by lunar calendar and agricultural seasons, whereas Sabbath 'represents a neutral structuring of empty time', that is filling time 'with a content that is uncontaminated by, and distinct from, anything related to natural time, ie. time as agricultural season or astronomical phase.'[62] The seventh day and the rhythm of the lunar-solar calendar were bound to undergo changes when Jesus enacted a New Covenant independent of land, crops, sacrifice, national festivals and ethnicity.

As the Christian community spread beyond Palestine and parted company with Jewish practices, observation of the seventh day disappeared.[63] With the sabbath went the whole Old Testament calendar by which time and worship were linked—new moons and their sacrifices, morning and evening sacrifice; Passover, Sheaves and Tabernacles from spring, summer and autumn; the day of Atonement and autumn New Year; Purim and Hanukkah from the winter months.[64] What remains in Christian-ized cultures is counting days in a seven cluster without the seventh day acting as a sign for Sinai covenant.

---

[61] M Tsevat, 'The Basic Meaning of the Biblical Sabbath', *ZAW* 84 (1972) 447–459, reprinted in *The Meaning of the Book of Job and other biblical studies* (New York: Ktav) 1980, pp. 39–52, p. 48.

[62] 'Basic Meaning', p. 50f.

[63] See DA Carson (ed), *From Sabbath to Lord's Day: a biblical, historical and theological investigation* (Grand Rapids: Zondervan) 1982, for a collection of essays by New Testament scholars documenting the relationship between Sabbath and Sunday.

[64] The agricultural and cultic cycles are more easily grasped diagrammatically —see, for example, *The Illustrated Bible Dictionary*, p.223. Still helpful is the overview of the Old Testament calendar and festivals given by R de Vaux, *Ancient Israel: its life and institutions* 2nd. ed. (London: Darton, Longman & Todd) 1965, Chapter 12 'Divisions of Time' under the heading 'Civil Institutions', supplemented by Chapter 15 'The Liturgical Calendar', Chap 16 'The Sabbath Day', Chap 17 'The Ancient Feasts' and Chap 18 'The Later Feasts'. Anyone confronted with Israel's calendar and cult has a problem organizing the material, a problem created by the lack of systematic layout in the canonical books themselves and by our own theological categories such as 'civil' and 'liturgical'.

The New Covenant enactment itself, as well as this long history of the parting of the ways between Judaism and Christianity, excludes the Old Testament from providing an exact blueprint for a Christian spirituality of times and seasons. Yet this is not the last word. If there is no transference akin to the implementing of the design specifications of a blueprint, there may be continuities of another kind. While the Old Testament legislation is culture and covenant specific, it may provide a paradigm. This word needs a little explanation. It is a metaphor borrowed from grammar books which use a particular verbal root as an example which illustrates the way that all other verbs in that class inflect. Generations of school children raised on Latin and French primers of the old style will picture these tables at the back of their books. Theology students will visualize them in Hebrew and Greek. Along the lines of this analogy, the laws of the Pentateuch are specific verbs—but they embody general principles of wider applicability.[65] Extending the grammatical metaphor a little, we might say that we could choose other verbs to express ourselves than those used in Israel's tables. This means that we might express our spirituality of times and seasons in ways that owe much to Israel's life with Yahweh without reproducing Israel's time system or cultic events.

D.1 SECULARITY

The first step for a spirituality in continuity with Israel's perspective on time is to clear time of myth. We saw how the sun, moon and stars were demoted from the rank of deity with influence over people's lives. At one stroke, this eradicated lucky days and astrology—quite the opposite of Babylonia where compendia were compiled of days and months in which things were propitious or must be avoided.[66]

In the West, superstitions linger about dates such as Friday the 13th, while horoscopes based on birth-dates have spread from Babylonia to Europe. Lines from a clay tablet more than a couple of thousand years old sound somewhat contemporary:

---

[65] This approach to Old Testament laws is exemplified in CJH Wright, *Living as the People of God: the relevance of Old Testament ethics* (Leicester: IVP) 1983 who uses 'paradigm' interchangeably with 'model' and 'example'. See pp.40ff for 'Israel as God's Paradigm', pp. 88ff and 100ff for the relation between typological, eschatological and paradigmatic and pp.166ff for discussion of criminal laws as paradigmatic.

[66] These texts are called Hemerologies and Menologies. One from 9th century Assyria, written by the high-priest of Ashurnasirpal, gives advice on things to avoid for the first seven days of the seventh month Tashritu. It advocates abstinence from foodstuffs such as garlic, dates, onions and from activities such as sex, journeys, river crossings, going on the rooftop, gardening and swearing oaths, among other things. On the eighth day is a day of rejoicing

The child was born (in) year 48 [of the Seleucid era], (the month of)
Adar, night of the twenty-third. At that time
  the sun was in 13½° Aries,
  the moon was in 10° Aquarius,
  Jupiter was at the beginning of Leo,
  Venus was with the Sun,
  Mercury was with the Sun,
  Saturn was in Cancer,
  Mars was at the end of Cancer . . .
He will be lacking in wealth . . . His food will not satisfy his hunger.
The wealth which he has in his youth will not remain, (although) for
thirty-six years he will have wealth. His days will be long. . . .[67]

Birth signs and astrology occupy space in newspapers and magazines on sale in every local newsagent.[68] Signs of the zodiac dangle
from ears, wrists and neck rather like the star and fertility
jewellery excavated in the Near East.[69]

Confronted with this ill-starred spirituality, we must conclude
that the radical secularization of the Old Testament that demoted
mythology has not carried the day in contemporary culture
despite assistance from education in science and the supposed
popularity of secularism. In truth, many Israelites failed to
embrace this extraordinary Yahwistic counter-culture.[70] The prohibitions of the Pentateuch and the records of syncretism disclose
that sun, moon and stars had their devotees in Israel, including
kings of Judah, while the vigorous polemic against Babylonian

---

and on this day when a man has intercourse with his wife he will conceive a
son—P Hulin, 'A Hemerological Text from Nimrud' *Iraq* 21 (1959), 42ff.

[67] Quoted in Saggs, *Greatness*, p.445. In considerably more depth, F Rochberg-
Halton, 'Babylonian Horoscopes and their Sources' *Orientalia* 58 (1989) 102–
123 and *Aspects of Babylonian Celestial Divination: The Lunar Eclipse Tablets of
Enuma Anu Enlil*, AfO Bei 22, (Horn: Ferdinand Berger)1988.

[68] A variation on the astral mythologizing of time is the commemoration of
Chairman Mao's birthday. The centenary of his birth is 1992 in the Julian
calendar. This Chinese event combines the number symbolism of 100 with
political mythologisation. It forms a retrospective complement to a birth
horoscope and proves to be as selective of the facts for authentication.

[69] The 2nd millennium gold and silver pendants from Ugarit and earrings from
sites like Tell el-Ajjul in Palestine are the best known illustrations, including
star shapes, crescent shapes and fertility icons. e.g. *IllBD*, 1124 Tell el-Ajjul
samples.

[70] See J McKay, *Religion in Judah under the Assyrians*, 732–609 BC, SBT 26
(London: SCM) 1973 Chap. VI 'Astral Beliefs in Judah and the Ancient
World', pp. 45–58. His general thesis is that sun, moon and star worship was
more indigenous to Palestine and adopted syncretistically by Judeans than
imposed by the Assyrians as part of their vassaldom policy.

astrology underlines its seductiveness.[71] Given this deep human propensity, ancient and modern, to invest time with mythical significance, a biblical spirituality will do well to scrutinize the ways in which the calendar is mythicized in contemporary cultures.

D.2 SACRALIZING THE CALENDAR

Countries that pride themselves on being civilized, educated or secular mark the passage of time in many ways that invest the calendar with a symbolic or emotional or ideological dimension. At the simplest level, an individual invests certain days with emotional symbolism when commemorating birthdays. These and wedding anniversaries illustrate a numeric symbolism fused with emotional recollection. Thus the birthdate is commemorated, but even more so the 21st birthday or the decade.[72] Likewise, the 25th or 50th wedding anniversary. The card industry has been glad to add Mother's Day and Father's Day to its repertoire. Therapists and clients are acutely aware of the recurrent emotional effects of bereavement dates. Nationally in Britain, Poppy Day links the colour red, the battle-fields of war in Europe and commemoration of the dead with accompanying public rituals involving among other things the laying of wreaths, carrying of flags, sounding of trumpets and observing of silence.

Some ways of marking time are numeric-economic rather than emotional in nuance. There are five–year plans or decades of development or periods devoted to geo-physical exploration and advance of knowledge through international cooperation. Years are designated for a good cause such as global ecology or the conservation of a species or an aspect of world health. More prosaically, certain days are invested with significance because of their place in the calendar—New Year's Day, marked at midnight

---

[71] Deut 17:3 forbids worship of sun, moon or host of heaven ($\d{s}^e\bar{b}\bar{a}^{\circ}$ $ha\check{s}\check{s}\bar{a}mayim$) on pain of death, while Jer 8:2 prophesies the spreading out of the bones of apostates under the sun, moon and stars which they worshipped. In the reform of Josiah, the vessels made for the Canaanite deities Baal and Asherah were cleaned out from the Temple, and apostate priests were dismissed who had 'made offerings to Baal, the sun, the moon, the constellations, and all the host of the heavens' (2 Kgs 23:5). This astral worship is linked with Canaanite deities and is therefore itself likely to be the indigenous form of Moon worship, already attested by the cult stele from Hazor with hands uplifted to crescent moon (Y Yadin, *Hazor*, London: Weidenfeld & Nicholson, 1975, pp. 43–47 and *ANEP*, No. 871). On Isa 40–55 as anti-Babylonian polemic, see DCT Sheriffs, ' "A Tale of Two Cities": Nationalism in Zion and Babylon' *TB* 39 (1988) 19–57.

[72] Gail Sheehy's popular paperback, *Passages*, (London: Bantam Books) 1977, reprinted, explores lifestories, lifestages and the psychological and emotional

by ringing bells, blowing car horns or getting drunk enough to plunge into public fountains. The turn of the millennium was marked in AD1000 with apocalyptic superstitions. The year AD2000, ahead at this date of writing, looks likely to be a special New Year with celebrations and aspirations for human progress planned.

Shops link days in the calendar with seasons and sales. May Day parades link spring with social and industrial ideologies. Many countries mark their calendar by political commemorations—of the revolution, or national independence, or past victories, or remembering the dead. Very often the form these commemorations take is cessation of normal work and the holding of public rituals, especially processions through the streets or military parades. These markers of time may be community-bonding events. They are, in any case, ideologically charged and serve to legitimate particular social structures and institutions. Obviously where there is ideology, it may conflict with the values of the Kingdom of God and the ideology may succeed in co-opting theology into a legitimating role, creating a civil religion. In some countries, public commemoration of calendar dates by a majority or by an empowered minority may underline the marginalization of the rest of the nation.

An example from South African history illustrates this within the context of Christian religion. The Day of the Vow commemorated the Battle of Blood River as a national holiday. Its name was based on the solemn vow made to God to build a chapel and remember God on that date in perpetuity if the participants, a small group of Afrikaner trekboers, survived an impending Zulu attack. Dec 16th commemorates the survival of the ox wagon laager and the death of thousands of Zulus. This event had the usual complex historical background of tribal migrations, colonial expansion and conflicting bids for dominance and independence. In narrower compass, the event demonstrated the superiority of guns over assegais, or an answer to prayer, depending on perspective. As an ongoing event, Dec 16th in South Africa was the occasion for political speeches perpetuating the claim to land made by white Afrikaners, invoking divine legitimation for this and for the apartheid policy which secured 87 per cent of the land against the majority population. Inaugurating Dec 16th as a national holiday was part of a mythicizing and politicizing process. Putting it another way, a Christian spirituality of prayer and promise practised by Dutch ancestors evolved into a full-

---

connotations of decades in American culture, e.g. Chap 13 'Catch-30', Chap. 20 'The Age 40 Crucible'.

blown civil religion imposed on the nation and sacralized in the calendar.[73]

For others, time and season are marked by festivals that are not so overtly political. These are the festivals devoted to music, art or flowers, or the latest in design.[74] For many millions of people in the contemporary world, the actual experience of time and seasons is linked to events publicised by television, particularly sporting events such as the annual opening game of the season or the cup final, or events on longer cycles such as a World Cup or the Olympics.[75] For some devotees, these events might pass Tillich's test of religion as 'ultimate concern'. At mundane level, the week is experienced in terms of distinct days marked by favourite TV programmes. For some, it is in these that we live and move and have our being—the soap operas qualifying as a virtual reality in which the passage of time in the characters' lives is by segmented episode.

None of this is necessarily the subject for moralizing comment, but it does reflect the structure hunger, symbolizing and ideologizing approaches to calendar and time which actually operate in our contemporary societies. Days and seasons are not neutral, colourless quantities of time.

D.3 LITURGY AND DAILY OFFICE

Christianity has its own long history of sacralizing time, or investing it with symbolic significance. In terms of spirituality, two examples suffice—the liturgical year and the daily office. In some Catholic countries, the liturgical year is still marked by festivals involving public parades and national holidays. Cult objects and decorative regalia might take the form of statues of

---

[73] Examples of Christian theology becoming the tool of political ideologies litter history. For South Africa, see the documentation in such studies as JA Templin, *Ideology on a Frontier: the theological foundations of Afrikaner Nationalism, 1652–1910*; L Thompson, *The Political Mythology of Apartheid* (New Haven/London: Yale Univ Press) 1985; DJ Bosch, 'The Root and Fruits of Afrikaner Civil Religion', pp. 14–35 in JW Hofmyer (ed), *New Faces of Africa: essays in honour of Ben Marais* (Pretoria: UNISA) 1984 and 'Afrikaner Civil Religion and the Current South African Crisis' *Transformation* 3.2 (1986) 23–30.

[74] London has succeeded in establishing displays such as the Chelsea Flower Show, Crufts Dog Show, the Earls Court Boat Show and Wimbledon tennis as familiar names within English language culture and internationally.

[75] There is a commercial basis to these televised events, even if this is tourism rather than the immediate promoting of brand names and there are usually cultural ideological values attached as well and those promoted by the host country. In London, colourful cultural festivals are televised such as the Trooping of the Colour, Royal Weddings, the Lord Mayor's show or the

saints or the Virgin Mary or relics of the saints. In places like Latin America, there appear to be secularizing forces at work turning ecclesiastical festivals into tourist carnivals. Revived indigenous religious expressions syncretize with Christian ones, creating new 'polytheisms'. The advantages of enculturation and the hazards of syncretism need evaluation by those who are within the culture and conversant with an ecumenical spirituality.

Where Christianity is a vigorous minority of non-established outlook, churches have introduced alternative liturgical years. For instance, in the UK the year is marked by Sundays, weekends or weeks with a particular focus—Women's World Day of Prayer, Harvest Festival, Christian Aid Sunday, Lent Bible studies, Sunday School anniversaries, Beach Missions in summer, Bible Week, Overseas Missions week, the church camp. Then there are collective national events such as Keswick, Spring Harvest, New Wine, Greenbelt, or Festival of Light marches.[76] Along management and priority lines, the Decade of Evangelism set targets for faith sharing and church planting. The participants form a high percentage of those who take their faith seriously and the majority would testify to the significance of some of these events in their spiritual formation.

The 'Daily Office' is associated with churches with a priesthood or sacred orders obliged by canon law or founding charter to hold services with a particular content. Prescribed passages may be read from the Bible, a liturgical order of service followed using written prayers such as collects for the day, and the sacrament of communion is observed. The daily routine would normally be part of a wider approach to the liturgical division of time. For instance, the Benedictine Rule was widely adopted in the monastic

---

closing night of the Proms concerts. These project an image of Britain as much for export as local consumption.

[76] Some of these gatherings number in the thousands, but are overshadowed numerically by a Southern hemisphere event in which 2–3 million of the Zion Christian Church gather at Pietersburg in the Northern Transvaal, South Africa for their annual Easter conference. This gathering achieved televised newstime in recent years because it was addressed by the Afrikaner heads of state, PW Botha and FW de Klerk, and by Nelson Mandela of the ANC and Chief Gatsha Buthelezi of Inkatha. It is interesting to note that Josephus calculates the total number gathered in Jerusalem for Passover in the 1st century AD at 3 million in round figures. Scholars such as Joachim Jeremias tend to regard the data from Josephus as 'such fantastic figures that we cannot accept them as historically accurate'. Jeremias calculated the figure by surface area for slaughter and came up with a figure of 125,000 pilgrims plus 55,000 Jerusalem residents, subsequently revised downwards to 180,000 participants—J Jeremias, *Jerusalem in the Time of Jesus* (London: SCM) 1969, pp. 77ff.

period. It organized time into communal patterns of prayer, study and work around the clock.[77]

Protestantism has tended towards a less communal, more individual pattern of daily routine, though often Protestant individualism is exaggerated and the reality is of a spirituality centred around the nuclear family with grace sung at meals, a family prayer time, or a daily children's bed-time routine with prayers and Bible reading. Today many children and adults use a system of daily Bible reading which is very different from early lectionaries and yet serves a similar function.[78] At congregational level, the weekly routine augments the daily one and many church members gather in home groups or prayer groups for worship, Bible study, intercession and encouragement during the week. Likewise, contemporary Christian fellowships feature early morning prayer meetings or twenty-four hour prayer chains or all-night prayer vigils rather than regarding them as extraordinary or culturally alien. In some ways these are modern adaptations of monastic spirituality.

Though not all theological colleges would want to be seen as continuing the monastic tradition of spirituality, they are places where the timetable rules and built into the day and into the week there are expected and voluntary slots for prayer and worship and study. If a theological college did not see its timetable as a

---

[77] The Rule of St.Benedict dates to the 6th century and consists of seventy-three chapters regulating communal life under an abbot. Thirteen chapters are devoted to the order of divine service which was thought of as the *Opus Dei*, the Work of God. The Hebrew Psalter was repeated every week. The daily round was marked by eight offices. Lauds at first light, Prime at sunrise and Compline at sundown are three of the eight offices which link prayer with the seasons, varying as they do throughout summer and winter. Clock-watching through the night became essential to wake the community on cue by bell-ringing to observe the nocturnal offices. The Benedictine Rule was not the only monastic model, but its influence on Western liturgy is widely recognized. See CH Lawrence, *Medieval Monasticism: forms of religious life in Western Europe in the Middle Ages* (London: Longman) 1984, chap. 2, pp. 17ff. Continuing interest in it is represented by C Clary-Elwes and C Wybourne, *Work and Prayer: the rule of St.Benedict for Lay people* (Tunbridge Wells: Burns & Oates) 1993.

[78] Scripture Union Bible reading notes geared to different age levels are widely used, but there are other systems which aim to take readers through the Bible or through a representative selection of passages on an annual or tri-annual cycle. Specific examples are *Daily Light* and Cliff Richard, *Through the Year with Jesus*. Some systems are based on memorizing verses, others on collecting verses or passages under rubrics. Many people play Scripture choruses or Psalms set to modern music on tape in their cars or around the home. Others listen daily to devotional slots on the radio before work or as epilogues, and in some countries a Bible reading and prayer are part of the daily output of the television network.

contribution to spirituality, it would need to ask itself some searching questions about its ideology and motivations.[79] In many theological colleges, personal devotions are expected to fit into a daily routine in addition to communal sessions in chapel or in small groups. Likewise, the average week of a seminary or Bible college is dotted with prayer times with a prayer-partner or with regional focus prayer groups.

The question raised by this division of time into timetables, routines or programmes covering a day, a week, a term or a year is whether these serve their purpose. Is there quality as well as quantity? Is there an optimum mix of the spontaneous and the timetabled, the individual and the group activity? Is boredom or fatigue or burn-out built into a particular pattern? Certainly different cultures tolerate different mixtures, whether these are measured by time duration or level of organisation or degree of repetition. This makes it impossible to specify what a Christian spirituality of time will involve in detail rather than in broad outline or distinctive features. A Bible college, theological college or seminary is a very different institution from a local church or family unit, despite existing in the same culture. Sociologically such Christian tertiary education institutions are better regarded as sub-cultures. Likewise the Sunday service of particular local churches demonstrates that each forms a sub-culture with its own dynamics. The week is common to the secular culture, the seminary, the local church and the family or household but the spirituality of time will differ markedly in each.

D.4 THE SPIRITUALITY OF STOPPING

There is, however, one feature which might transfer between cultures, sub-cultures and sociological clusters and that is the need to stop activities periodically. In this way, we come back to Israel's Sabbath as a paradigm of stopping, as cessation. Perhaps stopping is the major issue for activists. The literature on spirituality is filled with panegyrics on the benefits of quietness and solitude but the experience of students and faculty on a Quiet Day in the middle of a busy term at a theological college is testimony to the difficulty of living this out. To spend time stopping normal activity and to remain quietly in one place without a structured programme is extremely difficult for people who live by the timetable and the clock and deadlines. Adults wanting to change their lifestyle to include stopping are confronted with many

---

[79] There are certainly signs that serious questions are being asked about syllabus—but that is another matter. See, for instance, S Amirtham & R Pryor (eds), *Invitation to the Feast of Life: resources for spiritual formation in theological*

external pressures to get things done—and this in a culture where Maslow's hierarchy of needs has many items ticked off as achievable.[80]

We are also trapped by habits developed from adolescence, including for instance filling the unfilled moments with passive viewing, or retreating into 'solitude' by putting on earphones. Literacy and the magazine culture makes its own contribution to time-filling, as opposed to stopping. The airlines cosset Airport Man against really stopping when the rush to the airport is over and when seatbelts symbolize staying put, relatively speaking, for some hours. Travel agents promote holidays, but not stopping. Educational systems and urbanisation are geared to productivity. Stopping is not taught or built in. Besides this, three kinds of enforced stopping hover at the periphery of our consciousness with threatening effect—hospitalization, redundancy and death.

Less existentially and more mundanely, it would be unrealistic to urban life, which embraces the world's millions, to think in any other terms than a daily pattern governed by getting to work and back. The rich, by their own choice, as well as the poor, without choice, spend many hours in travel time. Given the density of urban populations and the pressures of commuting, the need to stop, the need for space and the need for solitude seem greater than ever. One might think that church services would reflect this need to stop, to sit quietly and let time pass in silence with God. Apparently not. Few services, if any, have three minutes without speaking, singing or listening to someone talking. So stopping and especially stopping before the Lord is not fostered or modelled in the routine communal worship of the church.

At the individual level, and within evangelicalism, there has been a strong tradition called 'the Quiet Time'. On closer scrutiny, this is somewhat of a misnomer since the traditional Quiet Time is a very structured event of personal devotions patterned around a Bible reading, often with notes or a commentary, a prayer list, and possibly some jottings in a prayer diary or personal journal.[81] It is a stopping of other daily activity, and a

---

education, WCC Programme on Theological Education, Conference in Indonesia, 1989.

[80] Abraham Maslow proposed a scheme of motivation and personality development whereby basic needs such as thirst and hunger demand attention before those higher up the ladder can be given attention. Self-actualization was at the apex of this hierarchy. See AH Maslow, *Motivation and Personality,* 3rd rev.ed. (London: Harper & Row), 1970.

[81] Compare the comment from within a USA context by LO Richards:

It is important not to mistake prayer of the heart, which is intent simply on being with God, for what many have called "quiet time". In general, Protestant quiet time has been viewed as a time for studying the Bible, making requests, expressing needs

conscious desire to orientate mundane life Godwards. It is reflective in the sense that listening for God to speak through Scripture is central and many who have abandoned this daily routine have not settled on a better alternative for nurturing their spiritual life. Yet the 'Quiet Time' still involves more of input and output —working at one's faith—than stopping and being. For this reason alone, the 'Quiet Time' seems not to give God as much space as the 'quiet' and the 'time' of its sobriquet might suggest.[82] To judge by best-selling paperbacks, there are now indications that Western evangelical sub-culture is acknowledging stopping, solitude and silence as part of its spiritual heritage, without abandoning its activism.[83]

Given the pace of life and the pace of change in the post-war era, it is not a surprise that modes of stopping for individuals or groups have been staging a come-back. The retreat, solitary or communal, guided or self-directed, has been explored by ministers and lay people, singly and in groups. Many are rediscovering a spirituality that became isolated in the realm of the specialist and that within a very few Christian denominations, mainly Roman Catholic and Anglican. A contemporary example of rediscovery from the Continent is Taizé whose monastic community and music have drawn secularized young people wandering around Europe on

---

and problems, etc. Such a time is surely valuable. But it is not the same as prayer of the heart, in which the focus is on intimacy—on simply being with God, sensing his presence, and responding to him with praise. *A Practical Theology of Spirituality* (Grand Rapids: acy—Academie, Zondervan) 1987, p.107f from Chap. 8 'Prayer of the Heart'.

[82] Though writings from the charismatic era on personal devotions cannot be categorized as activist or as advocating glossolalia without silence—note, for instance, D Watson, *Discipleship* (London: Hodder) 1983 rp—"To begin with, we must learn *silence*—to be still, until we consciously know that God is God and he is with us at this moment as a loving Father and as a mighty God . . . Posture can often help in cultivating this inner silence.', p.119f. from the chapter on Prayer.

[83] Note, for instance, writers from after the charismatic renewal wave such as R Foster, *Celebration of Discipline: the path to spiritual growth* (London: Hodder) 1978 rp, which devotes a chapter to 'The Discipline of Solitude' opening with a quotation from Teresa of Avila—'Settle yourself in solitude and you will come upon Him in yourself', pp. 84ff. Or Joyce Hugget, *Open to God* (London: Hodder & Stoughton) 1989 or Anne Long, *Listening* (London: Daybreak, Darton, Longman & Todd) 1990, pp. 149ff 'Listening in the Desert'. Quotations from Thomas Merton, Morton Kelsey and Henri Nouwen indicate that streams of the reflective tradition have flowed across denominational and traditional boundaries into circles which are normally characterized or caricatured as activist, enthusiast, charismatic or fundamentalist.

summer 'pilgrimage'. Taizé has provided a place to stop and be, if not exactly providing solitude, given its popularity.

SUMMARY AND CONCLUSION

We started from the universal experience of time, moved into the orbit of Semitic culture with its lunar calendar and 'seven' symbolism and explored the sabbath as witness to a distinctive spirituality of creation and of covenant relationship. We saw that Israel's annual cycle was invested with theological symbolism, combining the blessings of nature and the recital of Salvation History. This cycle of cultic events was 'secular' by contrast with Babylonian myths of Divine Assembly, fixing destiny and New Year rituals. For Israel, passage of time and the first of months was linked with the worship of Yahweh in family ritual and national recollection at Passover. Linear time and cyclical time intersected in spiritual experience and in worship. Time was governed by moon and sun, not by god Moon, god Sun and by Marduk of Babylon.

We noted that Christians share in the cultures of their environment. This involves more than sharing a common calendar system and pattern of national holidays because the calendar is invested with symbolism. At national level, calendar symbolism is ideologically charged whether this symbolism legitimates state institutions or serves market and consumer interests. The drive of Yahwism to break with the Near Eastern environment by demythologizing time and fertility and instead to invest time and season with Yahwistic symbols challenges Christians immersed in national cultures or sub-cultures to scrutinize the values embodied in the way their culture marks the passage of time and season. If need be, this involves unmasking and demythologizing the gods of national 'salvation history' and prosperity.

Knowing that Christian spirituality begins with a meal in the Upper Room around Passover in Jerusalem, with a day called Good Friday and a celebration called Easter Sunday, we asked whether a New Covenant spirituality could look back to the sabbath for inspiration. The links suggested were along the lines of the Genesis model and the Sinai stipulations providing a paradigm rather than a blueprint.

The roots of all the spiritual traditions of time structuring —Quiet Time, Scripture lectionary, daily office, Christian week, liturgical calendar—reach back further than medieval monasticism and further than Christianity. The sabbath, the Psalms and the cultic calendar of the Old Testament have indeed provided the paradigm. Western Christendom replicated segments from this fundamental DNA of time and season when introducing its own culture-specific and culture–bound mutations. It is inherent in a paradigm that new replications will evolve, adapted to their changing environment. The passage of time is a universal and a constant. The experience of time is not. Individuals and groups of believers make of time what they will before the Lord, and this depth dimension to the flow of time and seasons is a fundamental expression of human spirituality. Christian spirituality needs to evolve its own culture-specific ways and means of investing time with a depth dimension. The hallmarks of authenticity will be the cultural naturalness, the quality as opposed to the quantity, and the sense of God's reality experienced through these means.[84]

BIBLIOGRAPHY

S Amirtham & R Pryor (eds) *Invitation to the Feast of Life: resources for spiritual formation in theological education*, WCC Programme on Theological Education (Consultation, Indonesia, 1989).

AA Anderson, *The Book of Psalms Vol 1 & 2*, NCB, (London: Oliphants, Marshal, Morgan & Scott) 1972.

N-EA Andreasen, *The Old Testament Sabbath*, SBLDS 7 (Missoula: University of Montana Press) 1972.

Peter Berger & T Luckmann, *The Social Construction of Reality*, Penguin 1967 reprinted.

JA Black, 'New Year Ceremonies in Ancient Babylon: "Taking Bel by the Hand" and a Cultic Picnic', *Religion* 11 (1981) 39–59.

DJ Bosch, 'The Root and Fruits of Afrikaner Civil Religion', pp. 14–35 in JW Hofmyer (ed), *New Faces of Africa: essays in honour of Ben Marais* (Pretoria: UNISA) 1984.

———, 'Afrikaner Civil Religion and the Current South African Crisis', *Transformation* 3.2 (1986) 23–30.

DA Carson (ed), *From Sabbath to Lord's Day: a biblical, historical and theological investigation* (Grand Rapids: Zondervan) 1982.

C Clary-Elwes & C Wybourne, *Work and Prayer: the rule of St. Benedict for Lay people* (Tunbridge Wells: Burns & Oates) 1993.

R Clements, *yārēaḥ* יָרֵחַ pp. 355–362 in GJ Botterweick & H Ringgren (eds), *Theological Dictionary of the Old Testament* Vol VI (Grand Rapids: Eerdmans) 1990.

DJA Clines, 'New Year' pp. 625–629 in *IDB Supp. Vol 5*, 1976.

———, 'Psalm Research since 1955: I. The Psalms and the Cult', *TB* 18 (1967) 103–126.

---

[84] Peter Berger & T Luckmann, *The Social Construction of Reality*, Penguin 1967 rp, have a chapter on 'Legitimation' (pp. 110–147) and they discuss mythology, politics and theology in terms of 'symbolic universes' which structure social life and function as legitimating forces. Modern states and institutions do not use the Babylonian Creation poem *Enūma eliš*, but the point is that time is not left secular, neutral, symbol-free or without ideology. Christian theology invests time with symbolism and faces similar questions about the

ME Cohen, *The Cultic Calendars of the Ancient Near East* (Bethesda: CDL Press) 1994.

JH Eaton, *Kingship and the Psalms* (London: SCM) 1976.

R Foster, *Celebration of Discipline: the path to spiritual growth* (London: Hodder) 1978.

WW Hallo, 'New Moons and Sabbaths: a case-study in the contrastive approach', *HUCA* 48 (1977) 1–18.

J Huggett, *Open to God* (London: Hodder & Stoughton) 1989.

P Hulin, 'A Hemerological Text from Nimrud', *Iraq* 21 (1959), 42ff.

T Jacobesen, *The Treasures of Darkness: a history of Mesopotamian religion* (New Haven/London: Yale) 1976.

WG Lambert, 'Studies in Marduk *BSOAS* 47 (1984) 1–9.

———, 'The Great Battle of the Mesopotamian Religious Year: the Conflict in the Akitu House', *Iraq* 25 (1963) 189–190.

———, 'Myth and Ritual as Conceived by the Babylonians', *JCS* 13 (1968) 104–112.

———, 'Old Testament Mythology in its Ancient Near Eastern Context', pp. 124–143 in JA Emerton (ed), *Congress Volume Jerusalem, 1986*, SVT 40 (Leiden: Brill) 1988.

CH Lawrence, *Medieval Monasticism: forms of religious life in Western Europe in the Middle Ages* (London: Longman) 1984.

A Livingstone, *Mystical and Mythological Explanatory Works of Assyrian and Babylonian Scholars* (Oxford: Clarendon Press) 1986.

A Long, *Listening* (London: Daybreak, Darton, Longman & Todd) 1990.

AH Maslow, *Motivation and Personality*,[3rd rev.ed.] (London: Harper & Row), 1970.

J McKay, *Religion in Judah under the Assyrians, 732–609 bc*, SBT 26 (London: SCM) 1973.

JC deMoor, *The Seasonal Pattern in the Ugaritic Myth of Ba'lu*, AOAT 16, Neukirchen 1971.

———, *New Year with Canaanites and Israelites*, Kamper Cahiers 21–22, Kampen, 1972.

———, *An Anthology of Religious Texts from Ugarit*, Nisaba texts (Leiden: Brill) 1987.

BC Ollenburger, *Zion, the City of the Great King: a theological symbol of the Jerusalem cult*, JSOTS 41 (Sheffield: JSOT) 1987.

LO Richards, *A Practical Theology of Spirituality* (Grand Rapids: Academie, Zondervan) 1987.

G Robinsdon, 'The Idea of Rest in the Old Testament and the Search for the Basic Character of Sabbath', *ZAW* 92 (1980) 32–42.

F Rochberg-Halton, 'Babylonian Horoscopes and their Sources' *Orientalia* 58 (1989) 102–123.

———, *Aspects of Babylonian Celestial Divination: The Lunar Eclipse Tablets of Eunuma Anu Enlil*, AfO Bei 22, (Horn: Ferdinand Berger) 1988.

---

kind of social reality which this symbolism legitimates—monastic, individualistic, communal, denominational sub-cultural, nuclear family, hierarchical, job-related and so on.

HWF Saggs, *The Greatness that was Babylon*[2nd.rev.ed.] (London: Sidgwick & Jackson) 1988.

G Sheehy, *Passages* (London: Bantam Books) 1977, reprinted.

MS Smith, 'Interpreting the Baal Cycle', *UF* 18 (1986) 313–319.

L Thompson, *The Political Mythology of Apartheid* (New Haven/London: YUP) 1985.

LE Toombs, 'Baal, Lord of the Earth: the Ugaritic Baal Epic', pp. 613–623 in CL Myers & M O'Conner (eds), *The Word of the Lord shall go forth* (Winona Lake: Eisenbrauns) 1983.

M. Tsevat, 'The Basic Meaning of the Biblical Sabbath', *ZAW* 84 (1972) 447–459 reprinted in *The Meaning of the Book of Job and other biblical studies* (New York: Ktav) 1980.

K van der Toorn, 'The Babylonian New Year Festival: new insights from the cuneiform texts and their bearing on Old Testament study', pp. 331–344 in JA Emerton (ed), *The Congress Volume Leuven 1989*, VTS 43, (Leiden: Brill) 1991.

Affogato

Affogato is an Italian coffee-flavored beverage or dessert, usually gelato, drowned in espresso. This is a light version of the traditional treat. No espresso? Strong brewed or instant coffee works fine. In Italian, affogato means "drowned."

SERVES 4

2 cups (9 oz/280 g) nonfat vanilla ice cream

2 cups (16 fl oz/500 ml) espresso, chilled

¼ cup (10 g) frozen nonfat whipped topping, thawed

1 teaspoon unsweetened cocoa

Scoop ½ cup ice cream into each of 4 tall glasses. Pour ½ cup espresso into each glass. Top each with 1 tablespoon whipped topping and sprinkle each with ¼ teaspoon cocoa. Serve immediately.

Pyramid Servings

VEGETABLES	◀○○○○○
FRUITS	◀○○○○○
CARBOHYDRATES	○○○○○○○○
PROTEIN & DAIRY	○○○○○○●
FATS	○○○○○

PER SERVING	
calories	100
kilojoules	419
protein	3 g
carbohydrate	22 g
total fat	2 g
saturated fat	1 g
monounsaturated fat	0 g
cholesterol	6 mg
sodium	68 mg
fiber	4 g

Blueberry-Walnut Oatmeal Cookies

MAKES **45** COOKIES

Crunchy and sweet, these cookies contain blueberries and walnuts. Both are great sources of antioxidants.

Pyramid Servings

VEGETABLES	◀○○○○○
FRUITS	◀○○○○○
CARBOHYDRATES	○○○○○○●
PROTEIN & DAIRY	○○○○○○○
FATS	○○○○●

PER COOKIE	
calories	99
kilojoules	414
protein	2 g
carbohydrate	15 g
total fat	4 g
saturated fat	1 g
monounsaturated fat	1 g
cholesterol	10 mg
sodium	63 mg
fiber	1 g

Preheat oven to 350°F (180°C).

In a bowl, combine flour, baking soda, and salt.

In a medium bowl, using a mixer at medium speed, beat cream cheese and butter until fluffy. Add sugars, beating until blended. Add egg and vanilla, beating just until blended. Gradually add flour mixture to butter mixture, stirring just until combined. Fold in oats, blueberries, and walnuts. Drop by tablespoonfuls 2 inches (5 cm) apart onto baking sheets.

Bake until lightly browned, for 10 minutes or until lightly browned. Remove from pans, and cool completely on wire racks.

1½ cups (6 oz/190 g) all-purpose flour

1 teaspoon baking soda

½ teaspoon salt

½ cup (4 oz/120 g) reduced-fat cream cheese, softened

6 tablespoons unsalted butter, softened

¾ cup (5.25 oz/165 g) packed light brown sugar

½ cup (3 oz/100 g) granulated sugar

1 large egg

2 teaspoons vanilla extract

2½ cups (6.5 oz/200 g) regular oats

1 cup (5 oz/160 g) dried blueberries

1 cup (3.75 oz/120 g) chopped walnuts

Ginger-Berry Granita

Juicy, plump blueberries, convenient frozen strawberries, and fresh ginger make this icy treat satisfying, healthful, and delicious. The make-ahead frozen concoction is a cool ending to a summer meal.

SERVES 3

2 teaspoons grated peeled fresh ginger

1 (10 oz/300 g) package frozen strawberry halves in light syrup, thawed

1 cup (5 oz/145 g) blueberries

2 cups (16 fluid oz/500 ml) sugar-free ginger ale

Mint leaves (optional) for garnish

Place first 3 ingredients in a blender; process 30 seconds or until pureed, stopping as necessary to scrape sides. Stir in ginger ale; pour mixture into an 8-inch (20-cm) square pan. Cover and freeze 8 hours or until firm.

Remove mixture from freezer; scrape entire mixture with a fork until fluffy. Garnish with mint leaves, if desired.

Pyramid Servings

VEGETABLES	◀ ○○○○○
FRUITS	◀ ○○○○●
CARBOHYDRATES	○○○○○○○○
PROTEIN & DAIRY	○○○○○○
FATS	○○○○○

PER SERVING	
calories	62
kilojoules	260
protein	1 g
carbohydrate	16 g
total fat	0 g
saturated fat	0 g
monounsaturated fat	0 g
cholesterol	0 mg
sodium	56 mg
fiber	3 g

Strawberry Balsamic Sorbet

SERVES 4

Good-quality balsamic vinegar is the key to this frozen version of a classic Italian dish. Perfect served as dessert or as a between-course intermezzo, it's loaded with vitamin C.

Pyramid Servings

VEGETABLES	◀○○○○○
FRUITS	◀○○○●●
CARBOHYDRATES	○○○○○○○○
PROTEIN & DAIRY	○○○○○○○
FATS	○○○○○

PER SERVING	
calories	98
kilojoules	410
protein	1 g
carbohydrate	24 g
total fat	<1 g
saturated fat	0 g
monounsaturated fat	0 g
cholesterol	0 mg
sodium	17 mg
fiber	1 g

In a small nonaluminum saucepan, bring the vinegar to a simmer over medium-low heat. Cook until reduced by half, about 5 minutes. Remove from the heat and let cool.

Place the halved strawberries in a blender or food processor. Process until very smooth. Pass the purée through a fine-mesh sieve placed over a bowl, pressing firmly on the solids with a rubber spatula or the back of a wooden spoon to extract all the juice. Discard the solids. Add the balsamic reduction and the honey to the purée and stir to combine. Cover and refrigerate until cold.

Freeze the strawberry mixture in an ice-cream maker according to the manufacturer's instructions. Store in the freezer until ready to serve or for up to 2 days. Spoon into individual bowls and garnish with the chopped strawberries.

¾ cup (6 fl oz/180 ml) balsamic vinegar

4 cups (1 lb/500 g) strawberries, hulled and halved, plus 4 berries, coarsely chopped

1 tablespoon dark honey

Balsamic Vinegar

At its best, balsamic vinegar is a costly condiment, made from wine grapes and aged in barrels, to be enjoyed drop by drop on vegetables, fruits, or ice cream. At its worst, it is an overly sweet, caramel-colored vinegar that can overwhelm a dish. Between the extremes are many midpriced Italian balsamics with subtle flavors. As a rule, the more expensive the better, but try a few brands to find one you like.

Morning Mojito

The mojito is the national drink of Cuba. It is based on a sweet syrup flavored with fresh lime juice and crushed fresh mint. This super-citrusy nonalcoholic version also includes orange and grapefruit juices.

SERVES 6

½ cup (6 oz/185 g) dark honey

½ cup (4 fl oz/125 ml) fresh lime juice

½ cup (½ oz/15 g) firmly packed fresh mint leaves

2 cups (16 fl oz/500 ml) fresh grapefruit juice, chilled

2 cups (16 fl oz/500 ml) fresh orange juice, chilled

2 teaspoons grated lime zest

1 lime, cut into 6 slices

In a small saucepan, combine the honey and lime juice. Bring to a boil over medium heat. Add the mint leaves and remove from the heat. Steep the honey mixture for 5 minutes, then pass the mixture through a fine-mesh sieve placed over a bowl, pressing down lightly on the leaves with the back of a wooden spoon. Refrigerate the syrup until cold.

In a large pitcher, combine the mint syrup, grapefruit and orange juices, and lime zest. Stir until the syrup is dissolved.

Pour into tall, chilled glasses and garnish each glass with a lime slice.

Pyramid Servings

VEGETABLES	◄○○○○○
FRUITS	◄○○●●●
CARBOHYDRATES	○○○○○○○○
PROTEIN & DAIRY	○○○○○○○
FATS	○○○○○

PER SERVING	
calories	163
kilojoules	682
protein	1 g
carbohydrate	42 g
total fat	0 g
saturated fat	0 g
monounsaturated fat	0 g
cholesterol	0 mg
sodium	4 mg
fiber	1 g

Citrus Zest

All citrus fruits are rich in vitamin C, but, surprisingly, the peel and spongy white layer beneath, called the albedo, contain about 75 percent of the fruits' healthful antioxidants. That's no reason to eat oranges like apples, peel and all. But it does add to the pleasure of using the tangy, aromatic zest in muffins, salad dressings, marinades for meats and fish, garnishes, and drinks.

Orange Dream

SERVES 4

Whip up this frothy cooler in seconds—it tastes like an old-fashioned Creamsicle. For best results, start with ice-cold soy milk, and use freshly squeezed orange juice. Creamy, custardlike silken tofu adds extra body.

Pyramid Servings

VEGETABLES	◄○○○○○
FRUITS	◄○○○○●
CARBOHYDRATES	○○○○○○○○
PROTEIN & DAIRY	○○○○○○●
FATS	○○○○○

PER SERVING	
calories	105
kilojoules	439
protein	4 g
carbohydrate	20 g
total fat	1 g
saturated fat	<1 g
monounsaturated fat	<1 g
cholesterol	0 mg
sodium	56 mg
fiber	0 g

In a blender, combine the orange juice, soy milk, tofu, honey, orange zest, vanilla, and ice cubes. Blend until smooth and frothy, about 30 seconds.

Pour into tall, chilled glasses and garnish each glass with an orange segment.

1½ cups (12 fl oz/375 ml) fresh orange juice, chilled

1 cup (8 fl oz/250 ml) vanilla soy milk (soya milk), chilled

⅓ cup (3 oz/90 g) silken or soft tofu

1 tablespoon dark honey

1 teaspoon grated orange zest

½ teaspoon vanilla extract (essence)

5 ice cubes

4 peeled orange segments

Frosty Almond Date Shake

SERVES 4

This thick, creamy shake—great for a snack—is a breeze to make. Just be certain that the almond milk and yogurt are truly ice cold, and the banana is frozen. Peel and halve the banana before freezing.

Pyramid Servings

VEGETABLES	◀○○○○○
FRUITS	◀○○○○●
CARBOHYDRATES	○○○○○○○○
PROTEIN & DAIRY	○○○○○○●
FATS	○○○○○

PER SERVING	
calories	141
kilojoules	590
protein	3 g
carbohydrate	31 g
total fat	2 g
saturated fat	<1 g
monounsaturated fat	1 g
cholesterol	0 mg
sodium	97 mg
fiber	2 g

Put the dates in a small bowl and sprinkle with the warm water. Let soak for 5 minutes to soften, then drain.

In a blender, combine the dates, almond milk, yogurt, banana, ice cubes, and the ⅛ teaspoon nutmeg. Blend until smooth and frothy, about 30 seconds.

Pour into tall, chilled glasses and garnish each with a dusting of nutmeg.

⅓ cup (2 oz/60 g) chopped pitted dates

2 tablespoons warm water

2 cups (16 fl oz/500 ml) vanilla almond milk, chilled

½ cup (4 oz/125 g) nonfat vanilla soy or dairy yogurt

1 very ripe banana, frozen

4 ice cubes

⅛ teaspoon ground nutmeg, plus extra for garnish

Almond Milk

Made from raw almonds that have been ground, soaked, and pressed, almond milk is a sweet, faintly nut-flavored alternative to low-fat or non-fat milk. Although it sounds new, it has been made since medieval times. It is usually richer than 1-percent low-fat milk, but its fat is largely the heart-healthy monounsaturated kind. It can replace milk or soy milk in most recipes.

Sweet Ginger Tisane

A tisane is a soothing drink made by steeping herbs, spices, fruits, or flowers in hot water. Here, ginger gives this welcome alternative to coffee or tea a pleasant spiciness.

SERVES 6

6 cups (48 fl oz/1.5 l) water

¼ cup (1 oz/30 g) peeled and chopped fresh ginger

⅓ cup (3 fl oz/80 ml) fresh lemon juice

½ cup (½ oz/15 g) firmly packed fresh mint leaves

6 tablespoons (4½ oz/140 g) dark honey

1 lemon, cut into 6 slices

In a large saucepan over high heat, combine the water, ginger, and lemon juice. Bring to a boil, then reduce the heat to low and simmer for 5 minutes. Remove from the heat, add the mint, and let steep for 5 minutes.

Pass the mixture through a fine-mesh sieve, placed over a pitcher, pressing down lightly on the ginger and mint. Discard the mint and ginger.

Stir the honey into the tisane. Serve hot or iced, garnished with a lemon slice.

Pyramid Servings

VEGETABLES	◀○○○○○
FRUITS	◀○○○○●
CARBOHYDRATES	○○○○○○○
PROTEIN & DAIRY	○○○○○○○
FATS	○○○○○

PER SERVING	
calories	77
kilojoules	322
protein	<1 g
carbohydrate	20 g
total fat	0 g
saturated fat	0 g
monounsaturated fat	0 g
cholesterol	0 mg
sodium	8 mg
fiber	0 g

Fresh Ginger

Found year-round in supermarkets, fresh ginger, or gingerroot, has a sweet, multilayered spiciness that surpasses the simple flavor of ground dried ginger. Its smooth skin must be peeled away, but peel gently—the flesh beneath is especially pungent, with a hotness unlike that of red or black pepper. Store unpeeled ginger in plastic in the refrigerator for up to 3 weeks or the freezer for up to a year.

Watermelon-Cranberry Agua Fresca

Aguas frescas are popular fresh-fruit drinks in Mexico. Although water is a standard ingredient, this undiluted version is a thirst-quenching refresher whether accompanying spicy foods or sipped in the sun.

SERVES 6

2½ lb (1.25 kg) seedless watermelon, without rind and diced (about 7 cups)

1 cup (8 fl oz/250 ml) fruit-sweetened cranberry juice (sometimes called cranberry nectar)

¼ cup (2 fl oz/60 ml) fresh lime juice

1 lime, cut into 6 slices

Place the melon in a blender or food processor. Process until smooth. Pass the purée through a fine-mesh sieve placed over a bowl to eliminate the pulp and clarify the juice. Pour the juice into a large pitcher. Add the cranberry and lime juices and stir to combine. Refrigerate until very cold.

Pour into tall, chilled glasses and garnish each with a fresh lime slice.

Pyramid Servings

VEGETABLES	◀○○○○○
FRUITS	◀○○○●●
CARBOHYDRATES	○○○○○○○
PROTEIN & DAIRY	○○○○○○○
FATS	○○○○○

PER SERVING	
calories	94
kilojoules	393
protein	1 g
carbohydrate	22 g
total fat	0 g
saturated fat	0 g
monounsaturated fat	0 g
cholesterol	0 mg
sodium	1 mg
fiber	0 g

GLOSSARY

The ingredients used in this cookbook, many of which are described in this glossary, can be found in most well-stocked supermarkets or natural-foods stores. However, several items, especially exotic spices and condiments such as sumac and chipotle chiles, are easiest to find in Asian, Latin, Middle Eastern, or other specialty markets. Farmers' markets are a great source of uncommon fruits and vegetables.

ANCHOVIES These tiny fillets of sardinelike fish, preserved in salt and most often sold packed in oil, can add richness to a range of dishes from pastas to vinaigrettes. When used in small quantities, they have little impact on fat or sodium levels. Anchovy paste, sold in squeeze tubes, can be substituted in recipes in which the anchovies are minced, crushed, or blended.

ARTICHOKES The unopened flower heads of a thistle originally cultivated in the Mediterranean region, artichokes rank among the high-fiber vegetables. The edible part of a medium artichoke has almost 7 grams of fiber, about one-fourth of the suggested daily minimum.

ARUGULA Also known as rocket, arugula has small to mid-sized leaves and tender stems with a mild pungent flavor. It is common in gourmet salad mixes but is also delicious in pastas and sandwiches. Once a rarity, it's now sold widely (and easy to grow at home). Shop for arugula that's dark green, with no sign of wilting. Remove any thick stem ends. Store in a sealed plastic bag in the refrigerator; use within a day or two.

AVOCADOS Hass avocados have a pebbly skin that ripens from green to purple-black and firm, buttery flesh. Fuertes avocados remain green and have a lighter flavor. Choose hard avocados and let them ripen at room temperature. A ripe avocado dents easily when pressed at the stem end. Although avocados are high in fat, it's mostly the monounsaturated kind that helps lower cholesterol. They also contain beta-sitosterol, glutathione, and vitamin E, all of which have health benefits.

BARLEY Like wheat, oats, and rice, barley is a true grain—that is, the seed of a cultivated grass—eaten for at least 8,000 years. Barley contains small amounts gluten, a protein in wheat that when wet becomes elastic, permitting dough to rise. Barley breads are therefore more dense and dry. However, the grain abounds in soluble fiber, in particular a kind called beta-glucan that helps lower cholesterol. Pearl barley has had its tan bran removed and has been steamed and polished.

BLOOD ORANGES Native to Sicily, blood oranges have a peel and flesh that ranges in color from bright orange to deep red. Their juice is as sweet as that of navel and Valencia oranges, with a more intense flavor. Blood orange segments add spectacular color to salads and desserts. Once an exotic rarity, blood oranges are now becoming widely available during their winter harvest season.

BOK CHOY A cabbage-family, or cruciferous, green, bok choy has tender white stems and dark green leaves that are mild when cooked, commonly in stir-fries or soups. Baby bok choy is sweeter and more delicate and is often steamed or braised whole. Like other cruciferous vegetables, bok choy is rich in compounds that appear to help the body defend itself against cancerous cells.

BRAISING Meats and vegetables browned in a bit of oil, then simmered slowly with minimal liquid, develop superb flavor and texture. A braising pot should be heavy, to prevent scorching, with a tight lid, to retain moisture. Long, slow cooking tenderizes the connective tissue (collagen) in lean meats and the cellulose in fibrous vegetables.

BULGUR Whole wheat berries that have been parboiled, dried, and then crushed or ground into grains of various sizes, bulgur can be cooked briefly or simply soaked before being incorporated into a variety of dishes, from tabbouleh, the classic parsley salad, to baked goods and casseroles.

BUTTERMILK Cow's milk to which a yogurt-like culture has been added, buttermilk is a tangy, slightly thick dairy product that is especially good as a mildly acidic ingredient in baked goods such as waffles and pancakes. Most buttermilk available now is made from low-fat or nonfat milk, but check to verify that the product has 2 percent or less butterfat. "Old-fashioned" versions are typically made with whole milk.

CAPERS These young, olive-green flower buds of the Mediterranean caper bush are unpleasantly bitter when raw, and so are always pickled in salty vinegar or packed in salt for eating. They have a peppery flavor that comes from mustard oils in the buds. Rinse and blot dry brined capers before use. Soak salt-packed ones for several minutes, then rinse and dry. Both preparations are excellent in pasta sauces and with fish and meats. Caper berries, similar in appearance to green olives, are immature fruits of the same plant, pickled and served as a condiment.

CELLOPHANE NOODLES Also known as bean threads, these light noodles, made from the starch of green mung beans, are nearly transparent when cooked. Store them in airtight containers in a cool, dry place for up to 6 months. To prepare cellophane noodles for use, soak them in hot water or broth for 30 seconds, then drain thoroughly.

CHIFFONADE The culinary term for leafy fresh herbs or vegetables, such as basil, spinach, or lettuce, that have been cut into slender ribbons. To make a chiffonade, assemble the leaves to be cut into a neat stack, then fold or roll them lengthwise into a tight bundle. With a sharp kitchen knife, slice the stack crosswise into strips—thin for basil and other herbs, wider for large greens. Separate the ribbons before adding them to a dish. *See also* julienne.

CHILE PASTE A long-lived condiment easy to keep on hand, chile paste—made from hot red peppers mashed with salt and vinegar—can put a spicy Asian spin on basic dishes. It keeps indefinitely in the refrigerator.

CHILES Many markets now stock several kinds of fresh and dried chiles. Some, such as Anaheim, New Mexico, and poblano (called ancho when dried), are usually only mildly hot. Others, such as serranos and jalapeños, have been bred for hotness. Jalapeños smoked and then canned in a tomato sauce are sold as "chipotle chiles in adobo," used to give Mexican-style dishes a smoky hotness. They are best chopped finely or puréed. Freeze unused chipotles in an airtight container. With all chiles, the secret is to add them slowly and taste as you cook. For safety, wear rubber gloves or avoid touching your face until you've washed your hands and kitchen tools in hot, soapy water.

COCONUT, DRIED Sweetened varieties of dried coconut, available in supermarkets, are slightly moist and extremely sugary. Unsweetened versions, found in natural-foods stores and Asian markets, are drier and have a more pure coconut flavor. Both come shredded or flaked.

COCONUT MILK An indispensable ingredient in many Southeast Asian dishes, unsweetened coconut milk can be purchased in both full-fat and low-fat versions. The low-fat kind, usually labeled "lite coconut milk," contains one-third of the fat and fewer than half the calories of an equal amount of the regular. It's worth looking for; the fat in coconuts is even more highly saturated than butterfat.

COLLARD AND TURNIP GREENS Close relatives of cabbage and kale, with a hearty flavor, these greens are endowed with vitamin C, folate, beta-carotene, and especially calcium. Cooked collards and turnip greens have about 200 milligrams of calcium per cup; milk, 300.

COOKING SPRAYS Simply oils of various kinds mixed with a small amount of alcohol and lecithin (an emulsifier) in a pressurized can, cooking sprays are convenient for applying a thin coating of oil to pans and utensils. Canola oil spray is nearly flavorless, while olive oil versions have a mild olive taste. Use them lightly and always spray away from open flames or burners.

COUSCOUS Although it looks like a tiny grain, couscous is made from roughly milled kernels of durum wheat, or semolina. It is a staple in North African nations. Whole-wheat couscous, made from whole wheat berries, retains the brown bran and germ, making it more nutritious than the refined version. It cooks just as quickly.

CRYSTALLIZED GINGER Also known as candied ginger, crystallized ginger is sliced, peeled gingerroot that has been simmered in a sugar syrup and coated with coarse sugar. Sold in jars, it's handy for adding a note of sweet spiciness to both savory dishes and desserts.

DRIED CHERRIES Unlike raisins, which are simply grapes allowed to dry, dried cherries—typically made from a naturally tart variety—are sweetened with sugar, although they retain many of the fruit's nutrients.

EGGS Although they've been treated as a virtual emblem of cholesterol-rich foods, eggs can fit into a healthy eating plan. Because the main causes of high blood cholesterol are animal fats and hydrogenated oils, some recommendations allow up to four eggs a week, unless your cholesterol is high, in which case it's advisable to eat just two a week.

EGG WHITES, FOLDING Beaten egg whites lose volume if simply stirred in common fashion into a batter. To keep the final dish light and airy, incorporate the whites by a method called folding. Using a rubber spatula, gently scrape stiff, just-beaten egg whites into the bowl holding the batter or other mixture. Gently plunge the spatula into the mixture and, with a scooping motion, fold the bottom of the batter up and over the top. Repeat, rotating the bowl after each fold, until just a few pale streaks remain. If the mixture is thick, stir in one-fourth of the egg whites to lighten it, then gently fold in the rest.

ESCAROLE A member of the large family of edible greens that includes lettuce, radicchio, Belgian endive, and others, escarole grows in loose, pale heads of broad, somewhat frilly leaves. Its sweet but mildly bitter flavor is similar to endive's and can be served raw in a salad with other greens, or lightly cooked in soups or side dishes. Store in plastic in the refrigerator for up to 3 days.

FENNEL A fennel bulb is actually the white base of a tall, feathery-leaved plant in the carrot family. Its subtle licorice flavor makes it a pleasing addition to salads, stews, and other dishes. Shop for crisp, white bulbs with bright green tops; strip away outer layers that are tough or browned.

FIGS Look for Mission figs, which are purple when fresh and almost black when dried, or Calimyrna figs, which are golden in color and make fine snacks. Serve fresh figs promptly. Figs are higher in fiber than most fruits and are a tasty nondairy source of calcium.

FISH If you're a woman who is pregnant or nursing a baby or considering pregnancy, research suggests that you should eat no more than 12 ounces of fish a week, since many varieties contain small amounts of mercury. When the metal is consumed in a mother's meals, it poses a risk to unborn children and breast-feeding infants. Pregnant women and very young children should not eat shark, swordfish, king mackerel, or tilefish, four kinds of fish that naturally contain high amounts of this metal.

FISH SAUCE A dark, thin, salty liquid with a complex flavor, fish sauce, also known as *nam pla* (in Thailand) or *shottsuru* (in Japan), is an essential seasoning in many Thai and other Southeast Asian dishes and sauces. Left in its bottle, it keeps indefinitely in the refrigerator.

FLAXSEED The tiny reddish-brown seed of the flax plant, flaxseed—also known as linseed—is rich in omega-3 fatty acids, which appear to help lower heart disease risk. Flaxseed has a mild, nutty flavor that's good in baked goods and breakfast cereals. Because its oil spoils quickly, flaxseed should be stored airtight in the refrigerator or freezer and ground, if desired, just before use.

HARICOTS VERTS Also known as French green beans, *haricots verts* (pronounced AR-ee-coh vare) are a special variety of slender string beans harvested while very young so that they are stringless, seedless, and exceptionally tender. Small green beans are a fine substitute.

HOISIN SAUCE A common ingredient in Chinese dishes, hoisin sauce is a sweet and spicy, thick brown condiment made from soybeans, garlic, chiles, and spices. Refrigerated in a sealed jar or plastic container, it will keep indefinitely.

JULIENNE The culinary term for vegetables cut evenly into matchstick-shaped strips. Raw or lightly cooked vegetables are first thinly sliced lengthwise (about the thickness of a coin), then stacked and again thinly sliced in neat parallel rows, producing slender strips that are square in cross section. These can be lined up and cut to any length desired. *See also* chiffonade.

LEAN MEATS To cut back on fat, look for "select" grade red meats, which are less fatty than those labeled "prime" or "choice." The leanest cuts have fewer than 5 grams of fat per 3½ ounces (100 g). For comparison, 3½ ounces of skinless chicken breast meat has 1.2 grams of fat; chicken thigh meat, 3.9 grams. The leanest beef cuts (select grade, trimmed of visible fat) include top round (2.5 g), tip round (3.2 g), eye of round (3.6 g), sirloin, (3.7 g), and top loin (4.5 g). For extra-lean ground beef, ask to have one of these cuts specially ground by a butcher. The leanest pork cuts include the tenderloin (3.4 g), top loin chop (5.3 g), and ham (5.4 g). The leanest lamb cut is the leg (4.5 g).

LEMONGRASS A citrus-scented herb essential in the cuisine of Thailand, fresh lemongrass has a rigid, papery, pale green stalk about the shape of a green (spring) onion. Only the bulbous base is used, typically thinly sliced or chopped and added as a seasoning to soups, stir-fries, and teas. Lemongrass can also be purchased dried.

LENTILS Small legumes about the size and shape of split peas, lentils come in several varieties other than the common brown one. Relatively small varieties, such as French green lentils, or *lentilles du Puy*; black belugas, named for a type of caviar; and brown Spanish *pardinas* all hold their shape during cooking and are excellent in salads. Red and yellow lentils, typically used in Indian and Middle Eastern cooking, are usually sold skinned; they cook faster and break apart more readily than other varieties and are best in purées and thick soups.

MASA HARINA Spanish for "dough flour," *masa harina* is a fine flour ground from corn kernels that have been boiled in water with a small amount of powdered lime, or calcium hydroxide (called *cal* in Spanish). The flour is used mainly to make Mexican specialties such as corn tortillas and tamales. Some Latin groceries carry refrigerated *masa* dough prepared specially for tamales.

MASCARPONE CHEESE A product of the Lombardy region in northern Italy, mascarpone cheese is a very soft, mild-flavored cow's-milk cheese with a smooth texture like that of sour cream or yogurt. Look for it in small tubs in the cheese or dairy case of well-stocked supermarkets, or in specialty-food shops. Sealed and refrigerated, it will last up to a week.

MUSHROOMS Beyond the common white and brown, or cremini, many varieties of mushroom are now under cultivation. Portobello mushrooms—hearty enough to stand in for beef—have exploded in popularity. Despite their Italianate name, portobellos are simply fully developed white or brown mushrooms, best used soon after purchase. Fresh enoki, oyster, shiitake, and straw mushrooms are also now widely available. Porcini, most often sold dried, have a strong, earthy flavor that adds depth and sophistication to pastas, gratins, risottos, and other dishes. (Milder fresh porcini are also available but are harder to find.) To rehydrate dried porcini, place the mushroom pieces in a bowl and add boiling water to cover. Let stand for 5 minutes, then pour the soaking liquid through a fine-mesh sieve into another bowl. In a colander, rinse the softened mushrooms. Use both the mushrooms and liquid to taste. While treasured mainly for their woodsy flavors, mushrooms are also an excellent source of niacin and a good source of riboflavin.

NAPA CABBAGE Also known as Chinese cabbage, napa cabbage has white ribs and pale yellow to pale green crinkly leaves formed in loose, oblong heads about the size of romaine (cos) lettuce heads. It is crisp and sweet, with a flavor that is milder than that of green and red cabbages. Use shredded napa cabbage in salads, soups, or side dishes.

NUTMEG Because the singular aroma and flavor of this spice come from volatile compounds that dissipate quickly, nutmeg that is freshly grated adds more to a dish than does the ground nutmeg sold in jars. Whole nutmeg is readily available in supermarket spice racks, and small, inexpensive graters designed specifically for nutmeg help produce the fine grains that look and taste best.

OLIVES Where supermarkets once offered only jumbo black and pimiento-stuffed green olives, they now shelve a widening array of domestic and imported olives. Commonly available are brine-cured Niçoise, Kalamata, and Greek black olives, as well as heavily seasoned Sicilian and other Italian-style green olives. Find more exotic varieties, such as French picholines and Spanish arbequinas, at specialty-food stores.

OYSTER SAUCE An essential seasoning in many Asian dishes, especially stir-fries, oyster sauce is a cooked and concentrated blend of oysters, brine, and soy sauce. Although salty, it adds a great deal of rich flavor in small quantities.

PARMESAN CHEESE Supermarkets now typically carry a variety of foreign and domestic Parmesan cheeses, but the version widely considered to have the most complex and appealing flavor is Parmigiano-Reggiano, an aged cow's-milk cheese named for the Italian provinces of Parma and Reggio Emilia. Although all Parmesans are quite salty, a small amount can add great depth of flavor to a dish, especially when the cheese is top quality, purchased in block form, and grated just before serving.

PARSLEY Mild curly-leaf parsley is the traditional favorite, but flavorful flat-leaf, or Italian, parsley is gaining in popularity. Renowned as a decorative garnish, parsley also deserves respect as a nutritious vegetable. One-fourth of a cup of chopped parsley has as much vitamin C as a whole cup of romaine lettuce. Parsley also contains calcium, potassium, and folate.

PEANUT BUTTER To avoid a quantity of unwanted sodium and artery-clogging fat, shop for "old-fashioned" or "natural" peanut butter made without added sugar, salt, or hydrogenated vegetable oil. Jars of these pure versions are often topped with a layer of separated peanut oil. Simply stir it in, then refrigerate.

PEARL ONIONS About the size of a grape or an olive, tiny white pearl onions are mild and sweet when cooked. Boiling onions, also mild and white skinned, are somewhat larger, typically around 1 inch (2.5 cm) across. To peel pearl or boiling onions, bring a saucepan half full of water to a boil, add the onions, and cook for 1–2 minutes, depending on their size. With a slotted spoon, transfer the onions to a large bowl partially filled with ice water. When the onions are cool, remove and squeeze each at its root end; the skin should slide off in one piece.

PINE NUTS Excellent raw or toasted, these small, ivory-colored nuts are the shelled seeds of several varieties of pine tree, treasured for their subtle flavor. Ground finely and blended with basil, olive oil, and garlic, they are a crucial ingredient in traditional Italian pesto. They are also delicious toasted and sprinkled whole or chopped on salads and side dishes, or baked into tarts and cookies.

PITA Also known as pocket bread, pita is a round Middle Eastern flat bread made from both white and whole-wheat (wholemeal) flours. Sliced crosswise, the rounds can be split open from the cut edge to form a pocket for salad greens, beans and meats, or other ingredients. Sliced into wedges and toasted in the oven, the bread makes an excellent appetizer or snack.

PLAINTAINS Like bananas, their softer and less starchy relatives, plantains sweeten and turn from green to yellow with dark spots as they ripen. To speed the process, place green plantains in a loosely closed paper bag at room temperature for up to several days.

PLUM TOMATOES With their dense flesh and scant juice, egg-shaped plum tomatoes, also known as Italian or Roma tomatoes, are ideal for pasta sauces and cooked dishes. For smooth sauces, peel and seed plum tomatoes before use (page 155); for best flavor, store all varieties at room temperature.

POSOLE The Spanish word for the large, specially treated corn kernels called hominy in English, *posole* can refer to both the grain and the Mexican and Southwestern stew in which it's key. Kernels of dried *posole* are soaked in water and powdered lime (calcium hydroxide) until their tough skins soften and slip off. The starchy white or yellow kernels are then rinsed and canned or used fresh. Cans of *posole* and hominy are sometimes labeled in both Spanish and English.

POTATOES Waxy round red and white potatoes (called new potatoes or creamers when small) are moist and firm and are the best choice for salads and soups. Starchy russet, long white, and purple- and yellow-fleshed potatoes turn crumbly during cooking and are best mashed or baked. Potatoes contain potassium, vitamin C, and iron.

PRESERVED LEMONS An essential ingredient in many North African dishes, preserved lemons are prepared by submerging whole or quartered lemons in lemon juice and salt, often with spices added. After curing for weeks, the lemons soften and develop a distinctive flavor. Both the rind and pulp can be used; as with other strongly flavored ingredients, such as olives or anchovies, a little goes a long way. Look for preserved lemons in specialty-food shops.

QUESO ASADERO A commonly available Mexican-style melting cheese, *queso asadero* is slightly lower in fat than similar cheeses, such as Monterey jack.

RACK OF LAMB, FRENCHED The cut of lamb called a rack typically yields six to eight tiny but flavorful rib chops. For ease of serving and elegance of presentation after roasting, the rack should be frenched beforehand. This preparation, done by the butcher, involves trimming any meat and fat from between the ribs, leaving the rib-eye meat intact, then scraping the rib bones clean. Once roasted, the rack is cut into individual bone-in chops and served.

RICE PAPER ROUNDS Also known as spring roll wrappers or *banh trang,* these thin white sheets made of rice flour are a standard ingredient in Southeast Asian cooking. Soaked briefly, the dry rounds become flexible, translucent wrappers that can be topped with vegetables, noodles, and fish or meat, then rolled up to create fresh spring rolls.

SESAME OIL Plain sesame oil, pressed from untoasted seeds, is mild and nearly colorless. It is an excellent cooking oil, widely used in Asia and the Middle East. More widely available is roasted, or Asian, sesame oil. Made from toasted sesame seeds, it is pale to medium brown with a strong flavor and is best used with a light hand as a seasoning, not as a salad or cooking oil. Store roasted sesame oil in the refrigerator; use within 6 months.

SESAME SEEDS Raw sesame seeds are mild and faintly sweet, but when toasted they turn a golden color with a rich, nutty, and slightly bitter flavor. Black sesame seeds, with their dark hulls, or outer coverings, are widely used as a garnish in Japanese and Chinese cooking. (The seeds inside are a pale ivory color, with the usual crunch and mild flavor.) To toast sesame seeds, heat a small frying pan over medium-high heat, then add the seeds and toast, stirring, until the seeds are light brown and starting to crackle, 3–5 minutes. Always toast seeds just before using. Sesame seeds are rich in polyunsaturated oil, which can spoil over time; store untoasted seeds in an airtight container in the refrigerator for up to 6 months.

SHALLOTS Their tan, papery skins and pungent, layered flesh show that shallots are related to onions. They grow in loose clusters of small cloves, however, and have a distinctive flavor that some describe as midway between onion and garlic. Shallots are often used chopped or minced as a seasoning in sauces and vinaigrettes, but can be sliced and sautéed like yellow onions.

SHRIMP For years, seafood lovers were counseled to reduce their cholesterol intake by cutting back on shrimp (or prawns, as some sizes and varieties are known). Although shellfish vary, shrimp on average have twice as much cholesterol as dark-meat chicken. However, the chief cause of clogged arteries is the saturated fat in food, not the cholesterol. Eight large shrimp contain just 85 milligrams of cholesterol and less than 1 gram of fat, only a fraction of which is saturated. In other words, shrimp don't have to be banned from the kitchens of health-minded cooks.

SOBA NOODLES Delicious in soups or as a side dish, these tan-to-purplish Japanese noodles are made from wheat and buckwheat flours kneaded into a dough that is rolled thin and sliced or extruded into ribbons about the thickness of spaghetti. Soba noodles are widely available dried, but are sometimes available fresh in Asian groceries.

SOY MILK Made from cooked, mashed, and strained soybeans, soy milk has a flavor and texture much like ordinary milk but with a nutrition profile like that of the bean itself: respectable amounts of protein and unsaturated fat, along with compounds that appear to fight cardiovascular disease and cancer. It can be used cup for cup in place of milk in most recipes.

SOY SAUCE Known as shoyu in Japan, soy sauce is made from steamed soybeans and roasted wheat mixed with water, salt, and a yeastlike culture. After several months, the fermented mash is pressed and the sauce pasteurized. Some soy sauces, including wheat-free tamari, are thick, with a dark-chocolate color and intense flavor, while light soy sauces are thinner, paler, and often saltier. Standard soy sauces have as much as 920 milligrams of sodium per tablespoon. Reduced-sodium versions have 75 percent less sodium. Low-sodium varieties have no more than 140 milligrams of sodium per tablespoon.

SQUASH, SUMMER Prized for their mild flesh, thin skin, and edible seeds, summer squash are most tender and sweet when small. Crookneck, pattypan, and zucchini (courgettes) are popular examples, but more exotic varieties such as chayote (mirliton), ronde de Nice, and others have begun to appear in markets. Refrigerate in plastic for up to 5 days.

SQUASH, WINTER The sweet flavors, rich colors, and long shelf life of winter squash make them a welcome arrival in autumn. Acorn, butternut, delicata, kabocha, and sugar pumpkin squash all contain beta-carotene and vitamin C, as well as potassium and fiber.

SUN-DRIED TOMATOES Once an exotic Italian specialty, sun-dried tomatoes are now sold widely in a variety of forms. To avoid the extra helping of fat in oil-packed versions, shop for dry-packed tomatoes, available leather-dry in plastic bags or tubs, or slightly moist in antiseptic vacuum packs. To reconstitute sun-dried tomatoes before use, place them in a bowl and add boiling water to cover. Let stand until softened, about 5 minutes, then drain.

TAHINI Simply toasted and hulled sesame seeds ground to a smooth paste, tahini is a traditional seasoning in Middle Eastern dishes such as hummus and baba ghanoush. Like nut butters, it is flavorful but fatty and is best used in small amounts.

TAPENADE The southern French condiment called tapenade (tah-pen-AHD) is always made with chopped or crushed black or green olives. A classic version also includes garlic, capers, anchovies, lemon juice, and olive oil blended in a mortar and pestle or food processor.

TOMATILLOS Sometimes called Mexican green tomatoes, tomatillos are firmer and less juicy than tomatoes and grow to ripeness inside a pale-green papery sheath. Used both raw and cooked, they are an essential sweet-sour ingredient in many Mexican green sauces. Look for fresh or canned tomatillos in well-stocked supermarkets or Latin groceries.

TORTILLAS Corn tortillas are full of the flavor of yellow corn kernels and are more healthful than those made with white flour. Flour tortillas are typically made with hydrogenated shortening, which can raise blood cholesterol; corn tortillas have half the calories and no fat beyond what's naturally in the corn.

TURBINADO SUGAR Pale brown or blond with coarse, dry crystals, turbinado sugar is a partially purified form of raw sugar, manufactured from the residue left when sugar cane is processed into granulated white sugar and molasses. Preferred for some recipes for its mild molasses flavor, it can be used interchangeably with granulated sugar in most dishes.

VANILLA Many cooks keep two kinds of vanilla on hand: whole vanilla beans, the aromatic, coffee-colored seed pods of a tropical orchid, and pure vanilla extract (essence), a dark liquid made by steeping the beans in alcohol. The beans, mainly from Madagascar, are expensive but more flavorful than the extract. To use vanilla beans, slit them lengthwise with a small, sharp knife and scrape out the tiny dark seeds. Add the seeds to desserts, cookie and pastry doughs, and sauces.

WALNUT OIL Pressed from walnuts that have been lightly toasted, walnut oil has a pleasing flavor like that of the nuts themselves. It is best used as a flavor enhancer, not a principal ingredient, in salads and side dishes, especially those containing toasted walnuts. Because walnut oil spoils readily, it should be purchased in small quantities and stored in the refrigerator.

WATERCRESS A peppery-flavored, small-leaved green in the cabbage family, watercress is a native of Europe that thrives in soil flooded with flowing water. It is sold in bunches that include many thick, tough stems that should be trimmed off and discarded. The thin stems and leaves are delicious in salads and soups and as a garnish. To store, fill a large jar partway with water, immerse the watercress stems in the jar, and cover the tops with a plastic bag. The greens will stay fresh for up to 5 days. Like all the other cruciferous vegetables, watercress contains compounds that may help prevent cancer.

WHEAT GERM Renowned as a healthy food, wheat germ is the grain's unsprouted green bud, or embryo, which is lost, along with the fiber-rich bran, during processing. It contains a big portion of the wheat seed's proteins, minerals, and vitamins, including vitamin E. Raw or toasted (both kinds are available), the germ has a crunchy texture and nutty flavor that's delicious in breads and cereals. Because of its oil, which can spoil, wheat germ should be bought in small quantities and stored in an airtight container in the refrigerator.

WHIPPED CREAM CHEESE Available in most supermarkets alongside regular cream cheese, this lighter version has the same ingredients but approximately two-thirds of the fat, cholesterol, and sodium per tablespoon.

WILD RICE Not a true rice variety, this flavorful grain is the seed of a type of native American grass harvested by hand in shallow lakes near the central border of the United States and Canada. Its grains are longer than those of long-grain rice and are darker, chewier, and more strongly flavored than brown rice. Wild rice is best when blended with milder grains.

YOGURT CHEESE Simply yogurt drained of its liquid whey, thick and creamy yogurt cheese is a handy homemade ingredient that can replace whipped cream, crème fraîche, and sour cream in many recipes. A few hours in cheesecloth (muslin) or a coffee filter renders this cheese from yogurt; use nonfat or low-fat versions, and be sure to start with yogurt made without gelatin, gums, or other thickeners, or it will not drain.

INDEX